Sudan has been at war with itself for the last forty years, except for a ten-year period of peace from 1972 to 1983. This book traces the root causes of the Sudanese conflict: the remnants of slave culture and the rift between North and South, exacerbated by a conflict of culture and religion. Despite past divisions, the author identifies new points of departure in the conflict, particularly after

the agreement reached by John Garang de Marbos in the South and the leadership of the Northern parties. The main tenets of this agreement are: recognition of the country´s religious and cultural diversity, separation between religion and the state, recognition of citizenship as the sole determinant of political rights and duties, and radical restructuring of the state as a quasi-confederal state. The author avers that these measures hold the last chance for Sudan to be united.

WAR AND PEACE IN SUDAN

WAR AND PEACE IN SUDAN

A Tale of Two Countries

MANSOUR KHALID

KEGAN PAUL
London • New York • Bahrain

First published in 2003 by
Kegan Paul Limited
UK: P.O. Box 256, London WC1B 3SW, England
Tel: 020 7580 5511 Fax: 020 7436 0899
E-Mail: books@keganpaul.com
Internet: http://www.keganpaul.com
USA: 61 West 62nd Street, New York, NY 10023
Tel: (212) 459 0600 Fax: (212) 459 3678
Internet: http://www.columbia.edu/cu/cup
BAHRAIN: bahrain@keganpaul.com

Distributed by:
Turpin Distribution
Blackhorse Road
Letchworth, Herts. SG6 1HN
England
Tel: (01462) 672555 Fax: (01462) 480947
Email: books@turpinltd.com

Columbia University Press
61 West 62nd Street, New York, NY 10023
Tel: (212) 459 0600 Fax: (212) 459 3678
Internet: http://www.columbia.edu/cu/cup

ISBN: 0-7103-0663-6

British Library Cataloguing in Publication Data

A catalogue record for this book is available from the British Library.

Library of Congress Cataloging-in-Publication Data

Applied for.

CONTENTS

ABBREVIATIONS

AACC	=	All Africa Conference of Churches Movement
ACNS	=	Advisory Council for Northern Sudan
AF/AFP	=	Agence France Press
ALC	=	Army Legitimate Command (NDA)
AP	=	Associated Press
ASPCO	=	Sudan African Peoples Congress
DOP	=	Declaration of Principles, IGAD Peace Initiative
DUP	=	Democratic Unionist Party
FO	=	Foreign Office
GGC	=	Governor-General's Council
HEC	=	High Executive Council, Regional Government, South Sudan
ICF	=	Islamic Charter Front
IGAD	=	Intergovernmental Authority on Development
IGADD	=	Intergovernmental Authority on Drought and Desertification
IHT	=	International Herald Tribune
IISS	=	International Institute for Strategic Studies
IMF	=	International Monetary Fund
INN	=	The International Negotiating Network, Carter Center at Emory University
JMC	=	Joint Military Command (NDA)
KDD	=	Koka Dam Declaration
LC	=	Leadership Council (NDA)
MDC	=	National Dialogue Conference
NC	=	National Congress
NDA	=	National Democratic Alliance, Sudan
NDC	=	National Defense Council, Sudan
NIF	=	National Islamic Front
NSRCC	=	National Salvation Revolution Command Council
NSCC	=	New Sudan Council of Churches
NUP	=	National Unionist Party
OAU	=	Organization of Africa Unity
PDF	=	Popular Defence Force
PDP	=	People's Democratic Party
PNC	=	Popular National Congress
PPP	=	People's Progressive Party
PRO	=	Public Records Office, London
RTC	=	Round Table Conference on South Sudan Conflict,1965
SAC	=	Sudan African Congress
SAF	=	Sudanese Alliance Forces
SANU	=	Sudan African National Union

SAPCO	=	Sudan African Peoples' Congress
SC	=	Supreme Council
SCP	=	Sudan Communist Party
SEC	=	US, Securities and Exchange Commission
SUNA	=	Sudan News Agency
SPFP	=	Sudan Peoples and Federal Party
SPLM/A	=	Sudan Peoples Liberation Movement/Army
SRCC	=	Salvation Revolution Command Council
SSIM/A	=	South Sudan Independence Movement/Army
SSLM	=	Southern Sudan Liberation Movement
SSPA	=	South Sudan Political Association
SSU	=	Sudan Socialist Union
TG	=	Transitional Government
TMC	=	Transitional Military Council
UDSF	=	United Democratic Salvation Front
UMC	=	United Military Command (NDA)
UNDP	=	United Nations Development Programme
UNESCO	=	United Nations Education, Science and Culture Organization
USAP	=	Union of African Parties
WCC	=	World Council of Churches
WFP	=	World Food Programme
XINHUA	=	National News Agency, China

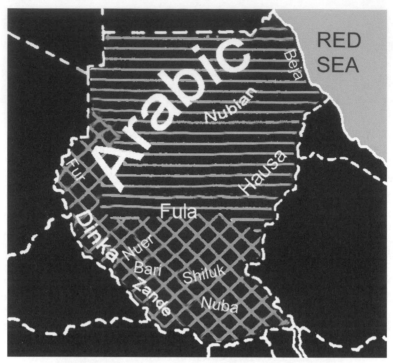

Simplified Linguistic Map of Sudan

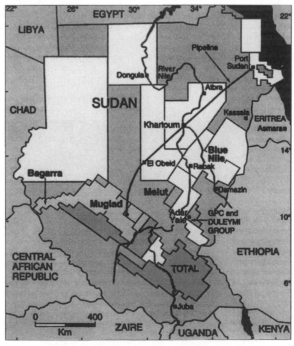

Oil Concessions in Sudan

PREFACE

I have fought against white domination
and I have fought against black domination.
I have cherished the ideal of a democratic society
in which all persons will live together
in harmony and with equal opportunities.
Nelson Mandela,
Statement in the Dock, 1964

Nearly half a century ago the first flares of Sudan's civil war were enkindled. Today, as the world enters a new century and a new millennium, Sudan's civil war has degenerated into an inferno of carnage and destruction. Despite the trumped-up romanticization of the era of independence, no Sudanese can look back to the last century with pride. If only for the underachievement of their leaders to bring peace and stability to their country, the Sudanese have more to grieve than to sing paeans for. This underachievement is the more deplorable as the last half-century held out numerous routes to peace. That Sudanese leaders have taken an alternative route that woefully induced more carnage and self-destruction, should be a matter for serious reflection. The dawn of a new century, therefore, offers us an opportunity to pause, reflect and introspect.

Sudan's war, however, is no different from wars elsewhere; it is an entangled political, cultural and social weave with equally intricate international ramifications. Long before Leo Tolstoy wrote War and Peace in 1869, the subject of war was a cause of bewilderment to scholars. Over time, they have developed it into a discipline of great scope. To military theorists like Carl von Clausewitz, war was rationalized as an instrument of diplomacy. On the other side of the globe, Sun Tzu also rationalized war as a tool of policy. He laid down that the art of war and martial prowess was 'a matter of life and death, a road either to safety or ruin'. But nothing in what has been said on the subject of war subtracts from the truth of what Tolstoy wrote about it when he addressed himself to the numerous conflicts of his time in Europe. Tolstoy observed: 'If the aim of the European wars at the beginning of the nineteenth century had been the aggrandizement of Russia, that aim might have been accomplished without all the preceding wars, and without invasion. If the aim was the aggrandizement of France, that might have been attained without either the Revolution or the Empire. If the aim was the dissemination of ideas, the printing press could have accomplished it far better than soldiers. If the aim was the progress of civilization, it was extremely easy to see that there were more expedient ways of propagating civilization than destroying men and their wealth. Why did it happen this way instead of some other way? Because that was how it happened, chance created the situation; genius utilized it.'

Leo Tolstoy saw war as an irrational phenomenon, its causes purely opportunistic. In effect, wars had been fought for the ostensible causes of defending national interest or spreading whatever political or religious gospel. But underlying every gracious reason offered, wars were time and again fomented either by the self-centered ambitions of errant politicians or by dogmatic crusaders who have no doubts in their pre-ordained missions. Wars were also lashed into fury by self-absorbed groups to sustain a complex array of vested interests, even when those interests were demonstrably ill-begotten. Thus, while one generally agrees with Tolstoy's judgment that wars are a result of chance utilized by genius, one also contends that, for the most part, wars have their root cause in the desire of one leader, group or country to maximize self-interest with no regard to, if not to the exclusion of, the interests of others.

Nevertheless, as World War II ended in 1945, no one would have imagined that a time would ever come when any man again picked up a gun against a fellow human being in an attempt to resolve a political conflict, nor that a group of people would seek to eradicate another because of ethnic unrelatedness, religious differences or political disparities. The world thought and hoped then, that the monstrosity of the war and genocide it had just endured would be a living lesson against reversion to armed conflict as a solution to political problems. Woe, war between and within states had since then raged on with venom all over the globe.

In the case of Sudan, the mainspring of war has been iniquitous attempts by one group to gain immoderate advantage over a presumed rival under the pretence of enhancing 'national' acquirements narrowly perceived. In this light, Sudan's war may fairly be traced to a sense of perverted nationalism that never cared to keep the mean between two extremes. Invariably, perverted nationalisms are driven by a winner-take-all inclination. On no account do they put up with relinquishing a little; they always hunger for taking all. This acquisitiveness invites, as a matter of course, retortion by those who suffer most from its consequences either to reparate injuries or end injustices (real or perceived). Those root causes of conflict, if not identified, recognized and dealt with, inescapably fester and burst.

I have been involved in the national politics of the Sudan for a large part of my adult life. And though it is said that those engaged in politics approach every issue with an open mouth and a closed mind, I had always wrestled – as far as that was humanly possible – to have my mind open wide enough to observe the causes and atrocities of war in my own country from both sides of the divide. This is the only way to see both the forest and the trees. Those atrocities were generally accepted in the North, from where I hail, with apparent equanimity. Their spectators seldom disapproved them. Oftentimes they exhibited a remarkable capacity for not even noticing them.

In reality, the responsibility for Sudan's bedlam falls squarely on the shoulders of its elite in the North or South, not on its people. In the preface *to The Government They Deserve*, a study by the author on the role of Sudanese elite on their country's political evolution, it was stated: 'In this book I shall deal with governments which the Sudanese elite, of whom I am one, have brought upon the Sudanese people as a whole, and why those governments reflected the intellectual, if not moral failures which characterized that elite both in the days prior to and after the declaration of independence in 1956.' That work, in part, was an auto-critique. So was another work in Arabic on the same subject and to which I gave a title that was sparing of praise: *Al Nukhba al Sudaniyya wa Idman al Fashal* (The Sudanese Elite and Addiction to Failure). In this work I would endeavour to expose further the inadequacies in the approach of those governments as well as that of public opinion formulators to the issue of war and peace in Sudan. Disagreeably, that approach evinces an unrestrained and almost pathological delight in beating the same track that had always led to failure. And when an attitudinal temperament does not lend itself to rational explanation, one is often forced to resort to psychoanalysis to discover the hidden impulses that drive people to destructive ways. The author is evidently not an alumnus of the Carl Jung school, nonetheless he is persuaded by the sheer irrationality of the behaviour of the Northern elite to venture into the diagnosis of this confusing behavioural disorder in order to identify the endorphins that stimulate it. One stimulant may be the reluctance by Northern elite and political class to look their faces straight in the mirror so as to confront reality about themselves. Instead, they repeatedly rejoice their hearts by looking at themselves in concave mirrors.

Sudan's civil war began in earnest in the 1960s, though its antecedents went back to the eve of Sudan's independence: August 1955. As early as that date, the conflagration could have been arrested. Its prolongation had everything to do with the astigmatic vision of successive governments in Khartoum of what Sudan was about. They assumed, for good or ill, that the Northern trans-tribal sub-nationalism, should be the ultimate badge of national identification to be affixed on all people of Sudan, including Southerners. The non-inclusive nature of that assumed identity led to the emergence of ethnic based and biased politics, even within the geographic North itself. Accordingly, the issue of identity – rather than being an add-on to the political debate – became a matter of considerable bearing on Sudan's conflict. Sudan, a country that comprises a range of fluid nationalities each with its own history and cultural proclivities is thus reduced to an exclusive ethnocentric country. It was not allowed to mature into an inclusive civic state comprising different peoples who could only be united in diversity. That would have been the only befitting approach to curtailing the atavistic tendencies of ethnicity.

This, combined with the ruling elite's refusal to accept a situation in which all regional components of the country had equal say in its governance, led to simmering unrest in the regions and hostilities in the South. Those hostilities have now entered into their fifth decade save for a 10-year respite between 1973–83 (the period which followed the Addis Ababa Accord of 1972). That was the only period of relative peace in Sudan's tumultuous post-independence history.

The ten-year hiatus was terminated by a Northern ruler (Nimeiri) who, in connivance with a Southern one (Joseph Lagu), abrogated the agreement that produced it. Contrary to the terms of the agreement, they divided the South into three regions with reduced constitutional powers. Subsequently, in another collusionary enterprise – with Sudan's Muslim Brothers this time – Nimeiri imposed on a multi-religious country, religion-based laws. Those laws were later euphemistically referred to as the September laws. For such a monumental folly to come from the only Northern leader who was assumed to have understood the multifaceted and multi-stranded nature of Sudan's national composition and thus came closest to recognizing the country for what it was, that was the height of lunacy. From then on, Southerners could not be blamed by any fair-minded person for their reactive resentment and distrust of Northern politicians of all stripes.

One may wish to single out the Addis Ababa Accord though, for objective and subjective reasons. The foremost objective reason is that the Addis Ababa Accord is the first peace initiative that has been actualized by the Sudanese themselves. Its success and failure reflect what is wrong with Sudan's body politic. For instance, that agreement was based, almost to the letter, on a document prepared during the regime of the parties prior to Nimeiri's assumption of power; but the sordid cleavages among the parties hindered its implementation. I, among others, have had opportunity to play a role in the conclusion of the Addis Ababa agreement, so my reproach of Nimeiri for dismantling that agreement is no less intense than my censure of the ill-fated politicians whom he had dislodged, if only because they had missed a great opening for the pacific settlement of Sudan's crisis. Wrath against Nimeiri, nonetheless, never made me deny the man his due. President Nimeiri, in effect, could have achieved for himself a place in the ramparts of history had he not gratuitously undone an agreement whose implication and significance were probably beyond his comprehension. All the same, Nimeiri's institution of religious laws (*shari'a*) afterwards, changed the political landscape beyond recognition. His second thoughts on the peace deal were in a peculiar way egged on by his nemeses, Sadiq al Mahdi and Hassan Turabi, when they virtually goaded him towards an allegedly Islamist path. That was an adventure they lived to regret. Paradoxically, it was the revulsion of this same religionization of politics and its impact on the country's political unity that catapulted Nimeiri to power in 1969.

Withal, on leaving Nimeiri's regime in the summer of 1979, I intimated to everybody – including the President – that the Sudan would not be the same again. They scoffed at that judgment and brazenly said: 'How dare you say that, if the two Southerners who signed the agreement, Joseph Lagu on behalf of the South Sudan Liberation Movement (SSLM) and Abel Alier on behalf of the Government, were unperturbed by its abrogation?' Lagu was then well ensconced in his position as the country's Vice President and Alier soldiered on, accepting shortly after Nimeiri's *coup* against the agreement the insignificant post of Minister of Public Works. Of the two, Lagu's position was not a cause of surprise. Like Nimeiri, he obviously had not comprehended the full import of the agreement he had signed. Alier belongs to a different variety; he is a man of character and probity. But unlike those of his class who had either chosen to leave the government and the country after Nimeiri's abrogation of the agreement, or made their views known and ended behind bars, Alier – reputed for his *sang-froid* – took his decision in the fullness of time.

For years, after the abrogation of Addis Ababa agreement, the war deflagrated with vengeance; only with this new phase of the war came a great paradigm shift. Under the leadership of John Garang de Mabior, the Sudan People's Liberation Movement/Army (SPLM/A) was launched as a politico-military organization. One 'S' of Lagu's organization had been dropped. The newly formed Southern-based movement dedicated itself to remedying the mistakes of the past through the creation of a New Sudan to put an end to all historical hegemonies: political, economic and cultural. This is to be achieved through going back to the drawing board: convening a national constitutional conference that brings together all political, social, military and regional forces of the country to redraw the political map. The SPLM/A, therefore, did not seek to recreate Sudan through the barrel of a gun. On the contrary, it left it to the Sudanese people to decide for themselves whether they wanted to have a stable, peaceful, just and united Sudan, or wanted their country dismembered. Also, by presenting those broad lines for a new political dispensation, the old Southern calls for justice, which were in the past ill-defined and sometimes inchoate, would find their articulation in a united Sudan writ-large. Besides, by giving a socio-economic dimension to the political aspirations of Southerners, and a cultural dimension to their cultural sensitivity, the proposed political dispensation had virtually decoded the mute anguish as well as the monosyllabic aspirations of the people of the South.

Garang's first fight was with his own dissidents who called for instant separation. Why was it so? Over the years I was increasingly persuaded that what impelled the SPLM leader to fighting separatists was an ardent belief in African unity and, one may say, a sense of history. Sudan, to him, is a product of historical and contemporary realties that are interlinked. Any attempt to de-link those consequential constituents would inescapably unweave the whole fabric of the nascent country. Also, as a quintessential African – which I am convinced he is – Garang is ever cognizant of the fact that the continent's unity can hardly be achieved by encouraging centrifugal forces that shall lead to dismembering its existing parts, unless one is forced to. The concept of the New Sudan, therefore, is not only an aspiration; it is also an inspiration.

It is this inspiration that brought me close to Garang and to the ranks of the SPLM/A. This stance, by someone who came from the inner sanctum of the Northern elite, was not agreeable to some colleagues, indeed very close friends. Their reaction was innately racist. Such a latent racist frame of mind is both pitiable and disgraceful, particularly when it is displayed by those who belonged to a supposedly liberated elite. But understandably, people are so often victims of their own history. There is a host of historical causes behind this racist disposition which remains opaque even to those who are cursed by it. Those causes shall be identified and analysed.

Regardless, in the course of the years that followed the emergence of the SPLM, Garang proved to all and sundry that he is not only a master strategist and consummate tactician in war, but also a venturesome thinker in politics. What he has achieved through parleying with Northern politicians was no less significant than what he realized through the gun. However, those who did not want to give him his due persisted in thinking that he could not be but the creature of others around him. To his deprecators in the North, Garang belongs to a class destined to be on the receiving end and thus is disentitled to chart the way forward for the Sudan. Among those are politicians who deliberately misread his every action or pronouncement because they know deep in their hearts their real consequence and magnitude: challenging myths deemed inviolable in the Northern mind. Surprisingly, even within the Northern elite who were intellectually captivated by Garang's vision and excelled in rehashing his themes on the New Sudan, some segments were loathe to accept his pioneering contribution to Sudan's political thinking, or conceding his vital role in realizing a New Sudan. This did neither good to their political credibility nor intellectual creativity. His Southern detractors, on the other side, might have thought that Garang's Sudanism was too good to be true. Manifestly, they were more comfortable with the old stereotypes of Muslim versus non-Muslim and Arab versus non-Arab.

Two things, however, stand out since Nimeiri's demise and the rekindling of war in 1983. The first was the emergence of the National Islamic Front (NIF) following the fall of Nimeiri, and their usurpation of power through a military *coup* led by General Omar Hassan Ahmed al Bashir in June 1989. The *coup* was unguilelfully masqueraded as a patriotically inspired act to save the nation from the mayhem caused by the parties. Ten years later, General Bashir unabashedly acknowledged publicly what everybody knew all along: that he was a pawn of the NIF. The second, which is a corollary of the first, is how the idea of a New Sudan caught on and culminated in the Asmara Resolutions of June 1995. Probably what Northern politicians and elites have suffered under the

NIF made them more sensitive to the historical sufferings of others. The Asmara Resolutions, however, were adopted by all political and social forces of Sudan under the umbrella of the National Democratic Alliance (NDA). The only political group that was conspicuous by its absence from the Asmara gathering was the NIF. Obviously, the Northern parties at Asmara sought to shape up collectively what they had messed up severally. Still, the Asmara Resolutions represent a watershed in Sudan's political history. But by themselves, they would not produce workable peace.

At the personal level, the author participated, on the SPLM side, in the earlier negotiations with the NIF and was later honoured by the SPLM to be its representative within the higher organs of the NDA. In those capacities he was privy to negotiations with the NIF as well as to the deliberations of the Alliance, particularly the agonizing exercises it had gone through to reach the Asmara compact. In the Asmara deliberations, two issues had the pride of place: peace and democracy. Though some may think otherwise, the two issues are interconnected. Those who take issue with this postulatum may only be driven by a desire to absolve former civilian governments from culpability in destabilizing democracy, either through the willful escalation of war, or failure – by omission or commission – to put and end to it. The upshot in the Asmara Resolutions on the issue of war and peace is the determination by all parties from the North and South to foreclose force as a means to achieve unity. All Sudan's parties now concede that the only viable formula to consecrate peace and unity is through the exercise by the South of the right of self-determination. Even the NIF later pretended to have come around to that conclusion. But evidence abounds as to its duplicity on this issue.

The political weather in Sudan has radically changed as a result of the Asmara Resolutions. Those resolutions represent a package deal that includes, *inter alia*, separation of religion from governance, administrative decentralization, voluntary unity through the exercise of the right of self-determination for all people of Sudan and the restructuring of the state and the economy. Hence, they are not *a menu* from which any party can choose *a la carte*. Consequently, to give coherence to their commitment to the resolutions, all parties (including the SPLM), have to build a stock of political credibility. The regurgitation of the double-talk of the past is not only counter productive, it shall also open the door to Sudan's disintegration. Only when every party is ready to take risks, can we hope to foresee a brilliant future for peace in Sudan. The idle hypothesis that things cannot continue the way they were before 30 June 1989, simply because an agreement on fundamental issues was reached in Asmara, may be refuted by the proposition that they probably will, if Asmara is construed only as a cryptic verbal commitment. The essence of the resolutions cannot and should not be befuddled by inconsequent loquacity, as some Northern leaders endeavoured to do. They have to be implemented in letter and spirit. That needs moral courage, magnanimity and a leap of imagination. Sudan is now at the end of a race between self-awareness and disintegration. The choice lies in the laps of its leaders. Forty years is time long enough for Sudanese leaders and elite to realize that they were too smart for their own good. Only when fantasy is isolated from fact, and moth-eaten mythologies about the self are unraveled, can we know whether Garang's New Sudan is a feasible project or a *Hop of Tantalus*.

M. K.

INTRODUCTION

Study the past if you
would divine the future.
Confucius

Everything to one extent or the next, is a product of history, which in itself is a product of our shared subjection to the laws of cause and effect. The problems that have beset Sudan, therefore, cannot be abstracted from events stretching back many centuries. They have linkages in a very comprehensive manner to geographic location, geophysical and climatic conditions, foreign influences and historical intercourse between diverse cultures and civilisations. Moreover, the train of tribulations through which the country has gone is to a large measure, a direct result of multiple political dualities. Those dualities had lastingly stained Sudan's post-independence politics. Hence, Sudan's malady is not just a nettlerash; it is endemic. The virus is deep in the blood stream. Failure to reconcile differences between the North and South has nothing to do with an intrinsically dysfunctional nature of diversity, or because Southerners from their very genes are lawless. It has everything to do with entrenched fissures within Sudan's body politic deriving from the country's ingrown fissiparities and antagonistic dualities.

At the outset, there was the colonial duality, which created gross cleavages among the Sudanese, even in the pursuit of their country's independence in a manner unknown to other national liberation movements. Secondly, there was the politico-sectarian duality, leading to indecorous adversarial politics that were often irrelevant to the priorities of the nation. Thirdly, there was the North–South duality which is a natural outgrowth of geographical, historical, demographic and cultural factors. None of those factors is peculiarly Sudanese. So the failure of Sudanese leaders to turn the country's multiplicities to good account for the benefit of its people – as some other countries have done – makes Sudan stand out as a textbook example of how a country can translate fortuity into affliction and prospects into mischances. Many countries of the size of, or larger than, Sudan had similar national characteristics. But with the vision and high-mindedness of their leaders, they were able to turn challenges into opportunities. For example, India, a subcontinent with the second largest population in the world, was able to transcend much more complex diversities (ethnic, religious and linguistic) than the Sudan could ever dream of. Without the foresight of its leaders, India could not have surpassed those cleavages and produced the most robust democracy in the developing countries – indeed the world – given the size of its electorate. Amazingly, the Indian national struggle was hailed by the fathers of Sudan's independence and embraced by them as a model to be emulated. But only in form were Sudan's fathers of independence inspired by that model, ever and anon by the vision that gave birth to it, or the policies on nation building it had articulated. Accordingly, references shall be made over and over, to the experiences of post-independence India, especially those relating to issues such as cultural and religious diversity, economic disempowerment and religion and politics.

As if this multitude of dualities was not enough, another politico-ideological polarization was lately loaded on an already stacked heap. Since the early 1960s Sudanese politics became haunted by the polarization of the 'traditional' versus 'modern' forces, 'right' versus 'left' and 'secular' versus 'theocratic'. This made of Sudan's political history an analyst's nightmare. Unmistakably the classification of Sudanese political forces into right and left reflects an ideological parochialism dating to the revolutionist eras of the 1950s up to the 1970s when the right was deemed to comprise conservative religious-based or inclined parties, while the left encompassed liberal secular groups. Those diffrentiations, subjectively defined on the basis of ideological proclivities, became meaningless since the late 1970s, more so after the collapse of Soviet Union when the differentiation of right and left lost its assumed legitimacy.

On the other hand, the term 'modern forces' has no meaning in the literature; political groups are generally defined on the basis of rigorous social differentiations. Even so, the term applies within the broader Sudanese context to metropolitan elitist groups active in university students and professional trades union movements,[1] notwithstanding that trades unions are principally brought together by a desire to articulate, promote and defend professional rights, irrespective of the partisan and sectarian affiliations of their members. Nevertheless, it is true that the Sudan's renewal shall hang for a long time on the vibrancy of the middle class of which this elite forms part. However, the paradox ensuing from that plastic compartmentalization into modern and traditional is that the most ideologically insular party in the history of modern Sudan (the Muslim Brothers) was propagated in the same fertile soil of student politics and trades union movement in which the 'modern forces' had grown. So both the term and its political import, as far as they relate to Sudan, need to be revisited by scholars.

'Traditional' parties, on the other hand, are not as 'traditional' as the term connotes. They have progressively incorporated within their ranks many elements who belonged to the same self-styled 'modern forces', and espoused some of their slogans. Some of them became political home to the majority of the lower and upper middle classes to which the modernists belong. All the same, the term 'traditional' may aptly apply to social forces or groups determined to conserve time-honoured values and received wisdom, even when contemporary experiences had proven their inappositeness to present-day realities. Thus, in using the term 'traditional parties' in this book, we only refer to those parties whose membership is historically based on sectarian and tribal allegiances. The term traditional, thus defined, includes the majority of Southern parties whose agenda is, *au fond*, parochial and region-based, and accordingly malapropos to the wider concerns of the Sudan. Conversely, 'modern forces' include all other political formations with a non-traditional base.

This pattern of group categorization, however, is less purposeful in relation to the issues at hand: war, peace and national identity. For behind the facade of innovativeness which the term 'modern' implies, Sudanese 'modern forces' include elements who often exhibit appurtenances of irredentism, not different from those expressed by the so-called 'right' such as the deterministic persuasion to culturally dominate the South. One such case is the dogmatists among Pan-Arabists, who up to the early 1990s categorically rejected the existence of a peculiar Sudanese cultural identity. That obduracy was based on an ardent belief by that group in the existence of only one Arab Nation *(qaumiya)* that was deemed superior to its component parts defined as *wataniyyas* (sub-nationalities). Both Arabic terms are synonyms for the English word 'nationalism' which adds to the confusion. This fictitious differentiation between *qaumiya* and *wattaniya* was, time and again, exploded by recurrent conflicts among Arab nation states that were assumed to be part and parcel of one nation. Those conflicts were not triggered by ideological cleavages or clashing social systems (which would have been understandable), but broached by claims of sovereignty over resources and borders. So, undeterred by the spurious right–left and modern–traditional categorizations, we shall touch in this work on the intellectual genealogy as well as the contribution of the Arabist political school to the debate on Sudanese multiple identities and the evolution of its thought since the 1990s.

Within the organized forces of the 'left', the Sudanese Communist Party (SCP) stood apart on the twin issues of nation building and cultural identity. Firstly, by building from scratch a labour trades union movement, it has created a modern nucleus beyond tribe, region or ethnic origin, around which Sudanese working forces coalesced. Secondly, it was one of the first parties to recognize the peculiarities of the South and call for granting autonomy to that region, though it did not go at full tilt to support the unanimous Southern call for federalism as the Republican's had done. Thirdly, it was a pioneer in elevating political officers within its higher structures without discrimination on the basis of gender or racial origin. And lastly, it was the only Northern-based political party that expressed a degree of wariness about cultural hegemonization. But again, on some of the issues at hand, the SCP's Achilles heel, like all ideologically based parties, was its religious belief in the inconvertible verities of Marxist ideology. Those shall be referred to with a view to exposing their inconvenience in analysing Sudan's *sui generis* situation.

As it were, the failed experiences of Sudanese politics in the last forty years eroded the legitimacy of the ideological truisms that had held sway, at least in so far as the issues of unity and national identity were concerned. Moreover, the correlation and interplay of power among socio-political forces in Sudan since the mid-1980s proved that there was another alternative to pull Sudan out of its present predicament. In this respect the prevailing ideological verities that had dominated the scene up to that date were proven wanting, sometimes irrelevant, to Sudan's burning issues: peace, unity and development. This applies equally to ideologies that were caught up in a time warp of Marxist or pseudo-Marxist definitions of right and left, as to Arabists who remained hostages to the phantasm of an exclusively Arabic Sudanese identity. It is also more true of the Islamists' desideratum to determine Sudanese nationhood – if a nation we may call it – on the basis of one parameter: religion. Obviously the Islamists' subjectively conceptualized identification could have made sense if Sudan was limited to its Northern riverain part; but not to the wider Sudan, which is an unwieldy behemoth plagued by multiple diversities. All those ideologically conceived constructs did not spare a thought to the deeply entrenched roots of conflict in Sudan and their complex ramifications. A conflict with such complexity neither lends itself to quick fixes nor shall it be resolved by the contentment of elitist aspirations (be they of modern or traditional persuasion or of marginalized provenance). And surely, it should also not be prey to the satisfaction of elitist intellectual vanities.

As alluded to in the preface, important segments within the Northern elite assumed that Southerners were intrinsically inferior, and Northerners congenitally superior. This was reflected in the symbolic categorization of groups on a racial basis, leading to the emplacement of some of them at the bottom of the human scale. That process of self-appraisal issued from a culture that can be traced back to the discredited slave trade. It also produced enduring master–slave images in the Northern mind as well as an equally enduring psychic trauma among Southerners. Nonetheless, the Northern elite had sealed their minds shut of the history and phenomenology of slavery. This is penetratingly redolent in the air of nonchalance by which the Northern elite treats the issue. Not only was the elite reluctant to muse over the marginalization and deracination of others as a result of slavery, but also they consistently sought to deform historical realities in order to deny the relevance of slavery to Sudan's present crisis. In general, were the North to make a clear breast of that unedifying page of its history, a process of national healing could have been spawned. To the contrary, the reaction to slavery and slave culture by the majority of Northern historians and politicians had invariably been the laundering of history. If only because of this wilful disregard by Northern political and social historians of the role (direct or indirect) of slavery in Sudan's crisis, the issue needs to be historicized and merits special focus. For this reason the history of slavery in Sudan shall be part of this dissertation.

Indubitably, the colonialists have gone to extremes to foster and retain the worst memories of the slave trade in the minds of Southerners so as to enrage them against the North as a whole. As a result, even the present-day generation of Northerners is held responsible by some Southerners for the mistakes of their forefathers. Indeed, the North is collectively perceived by misinformed Southerners as the enemy. But blanket condemnation of a whole people for the mistakes of their ancestors is not only unfair, it is unscientific too. However, that does not absolve us in the North from moral responsibility, because it was only the North that benefited from chattel slavery. The Southern psychic trauma would have been long-expired had Sudanese post-independence ruling and intellectual elites faced the problem without prevarication, and in a way that would have erased from the minds of both parties derogatory mental images inspired by the slave culture. If they had, the trauma would have tapered off. It would also have been the case, if the post-independence ruling elite created a level ground for political competition by all Sudanese irrespective of race or religion. Thus, critical as the role of colonialism is, an even greater responsibility for the perpetuation of the conflict lies with national governments.

Consequent to this perverse vision, Southern claims for their rightful place in Sudan were never viewed as calls for the reparation of historical errors, but as an infringement on the North's exclusivity. Concomitantly, since the late 1930s when a Sudanese proto-nationalism began to emerge in the riverain North, Arabo-Islamism was assumed by the Northern intelligentsia to be the only centralizing force of Sudanism. Those who rejected that notion of an imposed identity – even among the Northernized descendants of slaves – were treated as undutiful knaves; one notch above the Southern *indigene* who were deemed to be as good as lesser sons of God. As for the *indigene*, they refused to live with their wounds or bear their pain in mute silence. Instead, they challenged being effectually condemned to a status of innate inferiority. At best, they considered the paternalism of the 'North' tantamount to infantalization. Does all this make Sudan a nation? This question we venture to ask and shall strive to answer in this book. The reality, however, is that Sudanese politics since independence had virtually made of Sudan two countries, hence the subtitle of this book. But in no way would this contention pre-empt our conclusion that the country has also the potential to produce a united viable nation.

To add insult to injury, some Northern politicians took a turn for the worse when they became engrossed in a meaningless chest thumbing about the benefits bestowed by Arab culture, not only on the South, but also on 'black' Africa as a whole. Excluding the maladroit nature of this patronization, the deportment itself conveyed blissful ignorance of the nature of Sudan's conflict. What was, and still remains, at issue is political and economic empowerment, not cultural excellence. It is also not axiomatic that the 'culturally advanced' have a moral right to enthrall the 'culturally backward'. In all likelihood, it is this gloating about their innate excellence that made Northern leadership suspect in the eyes of the South.

Furthermore, by postulating a cultural relativism in such a tawdry manner, champions of cultural superiority were not only curtailing the historical process of cultural symbiosis that created the multiplex cultural identity of the geographic North itself, but also made Arabic culture suspect in the eyes of non-Arabs. Those began to see it as yet another tool of domination, not a rich and commodious culture in its own right. In addition, this rough-hewn approach to culture divested Sudan, which is *par excellence* the epitome of Afro-Arabism, of any claim to play a role in unifying the peoples of Africa. Africans, after all, are a conglomerate of diverse peoples with different cultures, religions and ethnic groups. By virtually appearing to be distancing themselves from Africanity within the borders of their own country, the Arabicized Northern Sudanese were effectively denigrating a component that had contributed to the shaping of their own 'national' identity. By the same token, Southerners who claim for themselves an Africanity that is racially defined in order to contradistinguish themselves from their Northern 'Arab' brothers are no less in error since Africa embraces different races, ethnic groups and cultures.

As for the religious dichotomy that became more acute in the 1960s, not only was it false, but was also contrived. Since the mid-1960s, the Islamists were engaged in a fictitious and impertinent anti-secular war in which religion was used as a Damoclean sword. It was used by the Muslim Brothers in 1967 against the Communist Party. It was used by them in 1986 against the parties who called for the abolition of Nimeiri's religion-based laws. And it was used in 1989 by the same group to intimidate those who showed no enthusiasm for the NIF's religious radicalism. In reality, neither were the parties who called for the secularization of Sudan's constitution anti-religious, nor did they ever advocate banishing religion from society in the light of Diderot's dictum: 'Humanity would be free when the last king is strangled with the entrails of the last priest.' Instead, the 'secularists' argued that if Sudan was to remain united and stable, *shari'a* should be dissociated from politics and religion should remain a matter of individual conscience. This formulation would have provided a social and political space in which all religions were treated equally. Nonetheless, the Islamists remained interminably absorbed in fighting 'secular' windmills. The unrelentant characterization of Sudan's 'secularists' as anti-religious had obviously served the Islamists well. It was a handy whip to stir up religious sentiments against their 'political' opponents.

Regardless, the demeaning Northern attitudes towards the South could not have been made easy without the collaboration of a string of Southern political nomads. Those kept migrating from the laps of one Northern party or government to another. Some of them did it with astounding alacrity, in the course of exacting their price at the cost of subsidizing the humiliation of their own brothers and sisters. Even today, under Sudan's Islamic fundamentalist regime, there are willing Southern accomplices, including unembarassable priests and former warriors, who chose to be an icing on an unpalatable cake that no person with a *bonne bouche* would like to taste. This dimension of the tragedy is generally ignored by Southern scholars and political analysts in their persistent critique of Northern politics.

There is no denying that the antecedents of the South–North cleavages go as far back as the *Turkiyya* and the *Mahdiyya*. A brief reference to that shall be made. So shall reference be made to the colonial era and the role of the colonial administration in sowing the seeds of the present fissures between the two parts of the country. However, we shall also demonstrate that attempts by Sudanese scholars and politicians to write off Sudan's current political problems as merely an outgrowth of colonial policies is a sham. The Northern political discourse bristles with examples of this flimsy alibi. Within the years of independence, there has been enough time and opportunities to heal the wounds, redress the mistakes of colonial policies and embark on the path of constructive co-existence and prosperity. That there is war today in Sudan cannot be seen as anything but the result of a complete dereliction by Sudan's ruling class – and a large section of its elite – of their duty in governance and public awareness. It also reflects a recalcitrance to come to terms with the realities of the Sudanese situation, especially when there is no dearth of alternative viable solutions that were before them. As a consequence, we shall not only trace in this book sources of war, but also inspired efforts by unhymned Northern and Southern Sudanese heros to bring peace, unity and stability to post-independence Sudan.

In addressing those and other issues we shall analyse five historical landmarks: the declaration of independence and the acquiescence of the South to that declaration contingent on the acceptance of a federal status for the South (December 1955); the Round Table Conference (1965); the Addis Ababa Agreement (1972); the Koka Dam Declaration (KDD) (1986); and the Asmara Resolutions (1995). This historically- based analysis shall prove that the tired references by Northern politicians to the singular role of the colonialists in creating the Southern problem is a cover-up for their mismanagement of the crisis. The colonialists created a problem; the national governments perpetuated it.

In all conscience, how long can we continue ascribing our failure to love our country to external forces? For forty years after independence, the Northern ruling class was myopic enough not to see that something was basically wrong with a house divided upon itself. Instead, they ceaselessly went on torturing their country and people by pursuing policies of divide and rule, sometimes divide and destroy. Only when the chickens came home to roost, thirty years after independence, did the same parties come to accept the idea of a federated Sudan. And as if they were experiencing an epiphany, none of those parties had the courage to accept part of the responsibility for the carnage and destruction that had stalked the land for those four decades because of their procrastination on that issue. Even Nimeiri, who came closest to laying down the foundation of Sudan's national unity, turned the clock back ten years after the success of his own regime in bringing peace to Sudan. He, too, had mistakenly thought that having 'subdued the South'; the field was wide open for him to engage in a policy of forced acculturation. Little did he and others know, that cohesion of any nation can only be predicated on shared values and universal membership with no inclusions or exclusions subjectively determined.

Nimeiri's reversion was a direct cause for the emergence of the SPLM/SPLA as a political movement of Southern provenance with a pan-Sudanese vocation. His reincarnation as an Imam in 1983, which bordered on farce, aggravated the situation. The emanation of the SPLM/A has virtually trapped both the ethnocentric politicians of the North and the opportunistic politicians of the South in their own perfidious ingenuity. The SPLM/SPLA, obviously had not resorted to arms to recycle past regimes or to reinforce unity a *'l' ancienne*. Its declared intention was to create a New Sudan free from all the inequities of the past and embracing all the country's historical cultural mosaic: the Cushite, Nubian Christian, Arabo-Islamic and Nilo-Hamitic. John Garang also liberated himself from the SPLM as conceived by Southern secessionsts who suffered a syndrome of denial. In substitute, he chose to be an exemplar of national rejuvenation and a new brand of unity.

This call for rejuvenation was welcomed by the disempowered in other parts of Sudan (Nuba, Fur, and Funj) who joined the SPLM/A with their daunting array of grievances. That constituency happened to comprise through geographic accident non-Arab groups, but this *de facto* congruity of marginalization and ethnicity gave rise to surmises that the SPLM wished to create a New Sudan in which non-Arabs predominated. Remarks emanating from some SPLM middle-level cadres lumping together all Northerners and categorizing them as the 'Arab' exploiter did not help either. In defiance of the Movement's manifesto and discourses of its leader, such enunciations, time and again were exploited to the hilt by axe grinders in the North. This evidently added to Northern fears. In time, the SPLM/A cadres had the opportunity to rub shoulders with other fighters from the West, the Centre, the far North and the East, including the Beja and the Rashaida Arabs. The latter represent the only pure Arab group left in Sudan. Without doubt, the undifferentiated classification of the marginalized in the peripheries and marginalizers in the central riverain North by the misinformed in the South generally, and elements within the SPLM in particular, led to fallacious conclusions. All things considered, the dominance by the centre over the peripheries is more of a social than an ethnic group sway. A substratum of that social group is amazingly made of elements within the very metropolitan 'modern forces' (army officers, civil servants). Despite its disapprobation of the traditional parties' hegemony over politics and the economy, that substratum continued to be beneficiary of those hegemonistic policies. In reality this elitist group is engrossed in a myth characteristic of a split personality. For while they continue to benefit from injustice to others and justify that injustice using the feudalistic arguments, they nonetheless persist in spewing pseudo-liberal ideas that they are not obviously ready to carry to their logical extreme. The feudalistic intellectual baggage continues to weigh heavily on their thinking. This adds another dimension to the complexity of the Sudanese crisis.

Equally amazing is the ambivalence of the 'modern forces' to the SPLM. Though the majority of them identified themselves with the New Sudan concept and saw in the SPLM/A a political organ with the vision and the wherewithal to bring it about, some still failed to transcend instinctive beliefs. One of those is the perusasion that a Southern-based political movement, led by a non-Muslim and non-Arab, is inherently unqualified to have a say at the national level. In the New Sudan there should be no place for the debilitating and insular views of yore. The New Sudan agenda is not only a comprehensive *projet de socie'te'* that cannot be compartmentalized, but it also represents the last chance for Sudan's unity. If it fails, no one should, in all fairness deny Southerners the right to abandon a so-called nation state that neither offers them recognizable gains nor discernible shared values. Besides, if unity collapses, then a domino effect may be inescapable. Those are the realities of today's Sudan, without varnish.

The effect of Sudan's war on the country and its neighbours has been devastating. It is estimated that the Sudan government spends 1.5 to 2 million US dollars every day to finance the war. Together with the amounts spent by the other warring party (SPLA fighting both the government army and its own mini-wars against splinter groups), the cost becomes incalculable. This does not include the toll taken on natural resources and lost opportunities for development. The statistics of death, on the other hand, are numbing; but the magnitude of death figures obscures the cruelty with which the war has been, and still is, prosecuted. Awareness of this calamitous situation was behind two landmark agreements: the KDD signed by the SPLM and Northern political and social forces in the spring of 1986, one year after the fall of Nimeiri, and the Sudan Peace Initiative signed in November 1988 by Mohamed Osman al Mirghani and John Garang. That serious and genuine attempts to actualize the KDD took three years, was to a large extent due to the NIF's blackmail of the traditional parties and the meekness of those parties to face up to that *chantage.* And so was the reluctance of Prime Minister Sadiq al Mahdi in 1988 to put into effect the Sudan Peace Initiative. Consequently, when everybody was at long last ready to proceed with the implementation of the conditions triggered by the two agreements, disaster struck.

The Sudanese conflict took a new turn since the middle of 1989 when the country was taken over by the NIF and darkness descended over it. The NIF's declared purpose was to Islamize Sudan in its image and carry the faith beyond the country's border. Their interventionism in neighboring countries, including Egypt, was sufficiently catalogued by international media and human rights organizations. Within Sudan, the

NIF endeavoured, in light of its own interpretation of Islam, to control man's body and soul. This orthodoxy rendered the neo-Islamists intellectually indurate and when they later relaxed the fetters, it was only because of internal and external pressures on them. However, in its first decade in office the NIF's government was not, like all governments, only involved in managing or mismanaging the country's politics and economics; it had also possessed itself with the right to take charge of people's social behavior, practice of the faith and even the way men and women were attired. The state had thus become the sanctimonious keeper of people's morality. Such attitude by any state not only represents an overstepping of due limits, but also amounts to an assault on people's humanity, since it kills all that makes men and women humanly different. The whimsicality with which that killjoy regime carried those policies was astounding. No question, were it not for the infernal nature of its policies, the NIF could have been dismissed as an infinitely boring lot.

The NIF failed to understand that people in the famished Sudan expected their government to fill their hungry stomachs rather than saturate their metaphysical vacuity. And even though its vision of Islam is not shared by the majority of Sudanese Muslims, the NIF still behaves as if it owns the absolute truth and has Allah on its side. Obviously, its political reference map is one of a different country. All the same, by invoking the name of the Lord, the Islamists have strained every nerve to acquire legitimacy. Their words were transmogrified into those of God and *shari'a* was presented as a code of absolutes, though *shari'a* as an interpretation of God's word by humans is not arithmetic. Fortunately, true Muslims know that Allah, the Most Merciful and Most Beneficent, does not ordain despots. It is vile men who do. Following upon that, the NIF had both defiled humanity and blasphemed the name of the Lord.

Under the NIF rule, the ruination of the country became comprehensive. A major reason of the economic ruination was the NIF's attitude to war. The NIF ceased to see Sudan's historic fratricidal conflict as a civil war; it recreated it into a *jihad* (holy war). The Southern warriors had thus become infidels who should be subjugated by the sword, and their Northern adversaries were elevated to the rank of *mujahideen* (fighters for Allah's cause). Those who met their deaths among them were decreed as *Shuhada* (martyrs) who would reside in heaven and be instantly rewarded. Far from heaven, those 'martyrs' are now entombed with their bones in the wilderness of South Sudan. One day they shall be commemorated the way the Greeks commemorated their youth who died in vain in the wars with Sparta.[2] For all that, the degree of the NIF's self-deception was appalling. Heedless of the raging war, the precipitous deterioration in all walks of life, the deepening poverty and the total breakdown that stared everybody on the face, the NIF continued to apotheosize 'their' Sudan as Allah's heaven on earth and light unto nations. With such maximalist agenda, absolutist vision and the total misanthropy of Sudan's current leaders, the country's farce had lurched to its finale. Absolutists as a rule are politically undiscerning. They exclusively see primary colours. Inescapably, such vision distorts Sudan's multicoloured political panorama.

The survival of the NIF's regime for nearly eleven years, despite the universal hatred it has generated, engendered a sense of pervasive despondency within Sudan, based on the feeling that the regime was invincible. This seeming invincibility was neither justified by the realities on the ground nor by similar historical experiences. After all, notwithstanding its ten years of absolute power and the unprecedented reign of terror it had unleashed, the regime had since December 1999 met its waterloo. The NIF committed the same mistake all fascisit regimes were prone to commit: pushing people to the point beyond which they could bear suffering no more. Indeed, the frustration of those who were sunk in despair within Sudan was a result of their own crisis of expectation. Day in, day out, they kept going to bed every night in the last ten years, with the hope that the morning would bring good tidings, only to be faced in the crack of dawn by yet another dreary day under the NIF. Outside Sudan, some governments – especially European and North American (Canada) – fell victim to the optical illusions of the NIF's charm offensive. Charitably, their perverse compliments to the regime were based on the assumption that destructive regimes like the NIF's should be offered a carrot in order to engage them constructively. Not to be discounted, also, were economic interests generated by the exploitation of oil and activities associated with that. Politics is both heartless and mean spirited. However, the wishful thinkers who believed that the NIF regime could be reformed obviously failed to see the political beast for what it was: a fascist regime with a perverted sense of destiny and a strong belief in its invincibility. The Sudanese people who have gone through forty years of cold and hot wars and over a decade of abomination under this fascism cannot afford – nor do they deserve – a Munich.

For the more discriminative, though, the political and ideological cracks within the NIF monolith, especially since December 1999 when Turabi and Bashir parted ways, revealed both organizational deficiencies and intellectual vacuity. As a result of its internal wrangling the NIF regime is now imploding. Radical movements (the worthy as well as the unworthy) invariably devour their own. On the other hand, the regimes dissimulative beseeching of the opposition in the name of peace and reconciliation demonstrated not only the NIF's weakness, but also the hollowness of its defiant postures in the early years of its rule. With such frailties and vulnerabilities, the regime's demise, like similar fascist regimes in other parts of the world, becomes a matter of time. Truly, if the pervading economic failure, political *bouleversements*, military setbacks and ideological bankruptcy of the regime, are not enough to persuade believers and make-believers in the regime's perpetuity, then the mathematics of probability will. In this connection, the charm offensives of the NIF and its sham political and economic liberalization measures are nothing but the last kicks of a dying mule that deserves neither to be saved nor commiserated with.

This surely does not mean that opposition to the regime should close all avenues for a pacific settlement of Sudan's conflict and spurn dialogue with both components of the NIF. It would be remiss if it did. Fortunately, the NDA continued to affirm that the resolution of Sudan's conflict through a negotiated peace remained to be its preferred option. Yet, certain benchmarks must be observed; it took the Sudanese forty years to define those at Asmara in 1995. The Sudan, naturally, remains ever indebted to its friends all over the world; those who came to its help in the time of crisis, as well as those who tried and tried again to rescue it's leaders from themselves through various mediation efforts. Even then, one hopes that those friends realize how important those benchmarks are for the interest of peace, regional stability and the welfare of the people of Sudan. That, of course, if what they wish for Sudan is unity, permanent peace and stability, and not only dousing the flames of a bothersome bush fire in the African wilderness, or creating a lull so that 'oily' business goes on as usual with an obnoxious and tottering regime. Such an approach, to be sure, shall neither realize peace, nor mirror an enlightened self-interest.

The book falls into four parts. Part One provides a background to Sudan's multiple crises and traces their genesis to the evolution of modern Sudan as we have known it since the Turkish colonial rule and the *Mahdiyya*. It also identifies the disruptions caused by the two regimes to the historical processes of unity and indigenous nation building dating back to the Funj Kingdom. That happened in a way that had sown the seeds of the ongoing conflict. This phase of Sudan's political history had been ably covered in numerous academic writings to which reference would be made. Repeating this history, however, may weary readers who are versed in Sudan studies. But there is also a large number of newcomers who are increasingly interested in, or concerned with, what is happening in Sudan today. For those to comprehend the whys and wherefores of Sudan's present mayhem, an overview of the historical factors and undercurrents that have induced or contributed to the mayhem, may be helpful. References to the Turkish, Mahdist and later British colonial periods should be seen in this light.

Part Two deals with the most crucial period in the history of war and peace in Sudan: the period immediately prior to and following independence. It was the period of betrayal of the Sudanese expectations from independence; charitably one may call it the era of the tragedy of good intentions. And, since betrayal begins with trust, this part also reflects various schemes of unity offered by trusting Southerners so that the Sudan remains united, and demonstrates how those schemes were aborted by Khartoum rulers. This includes, *inter alia*, the calls for federalism propounded by the South and scuttled by the fathers of independence as well as the collapse of the hopes generated by the October uprising.

Part Three tracks back the emergence of contemporary political Islam since the mid-1960s and the political rumpus that ensued from it, leading to the seizure of power by the NIF. The radical religionization of politics in the decade of the 1990s is not an isolated episode, its roots go back to the mid-1960s when Sudan's Islamists emerged as a viable political force. Finally, Part Four of the book dissertates on three related issues. The first is national identity which became central to, and a blistering issue in, the debate. The second relates to the escalation of war to unprecedented dimensions including the humanitarian catastrophes that stemmed from the intensification of violence and the international concern this has generated. That heightened international concern resulted in numerous diplomatic interventions and mediation efforts. This part concludes with a chapter on the overdue realization by the Sudanese themselves of the inappositness of the old political paradigm that typified the Old Sudan. All Sudanese agree today that Sudan is better united. However, unlike in the 1960s and 1970s, there is almost a consensus that unity can neither be achieved against people's will nor when the society is permanently stratified along rigid cultural, religious and ethnic lines.

In the preface we referred to the role of Sadiq al Mahdi and Hassan Turabi in giving an impetus to Nimeiri's abrogation of the Addis Ababa agreement. The thoughts and motivations of the three political leaders shall, therefore, be scrupulously analysed, first, to catalogue the damage wrought on Sudan severally and jointly by this trio, second, to underline the conceptions or misconceptions that drove them to the sliproad they had taken. Surely, other leaders have had their fair share of responsibility for the state in which the country is today, but their failure has often been a result of myopicness deriving from the cultural proclivities of their time, not from ideological biases. Unlike those leaders, al Mahdi and Turabi are political ideologues with justifiable intellectual claims. Nimeiri, on the other side, neither had an intellectual pretence, nor did people expect much from him. So, when he went into a well-deserved obscurity and resurfaced in Sudan a decade and a half later, it was only to make a fool of himself. Ostensibly, he continued to behave as if he still had a role to play. To be sure, no man is a fool to his own mirror. As for the two ideologue modernizers, they failed to see how otiose and irrelevant to contemporary Sudan their politics was, even after it had been tested to destruction. And though their political models for Sudan were consistently proven wrong in almost every possible detail, the two leaders refused to retrace their steps or accept the unpalatable truth that their time was up. To the contrary, they persisted in the belief that the nation's salvation lay in their hands.

Moreover, the two leaders – like all ideologues – endured in giving the impression that if their ideological models did not tally with Sudan's realities, then the realities should be contorted to fit the model. That, in a way, explains their intellectual meanderings and political twists and turns. To give fillip to their murky political models the two went on uttering palpable contradictions. But dissimulation and half-truths are hardly the way to approach serious political situations. For example, in the face of the recurrent failure of the political models they espoused, the two politicians, time and again, found an easy escape in describing every failed model as an aberration. To Turabi, Nimeiri's Islamic Republic was a bizarrerie. To Sadiq, Turabi's Islamic state was obliquely disoriented. But in sober earnest, how long shall Sudan continue to suffer in the hands of ideologues, before those are convinced that all that the good old Sudanese want is peace and pursuit of happiness?

Contrary to all reasonable expectations, of the two, Turabi was the first to question the myths he had built for nearly four decades when he signed with the SPLM a Memorandum of Understanding in February 2001. The purport and reasons for Turabi's change of heart shall be analysed in the relevant chapter of this work. Nevertheless, Turabi's model shall be intensively scrutinized, given its avowed moral overtones. People with moral claims should always be held to high moral standards. The regime created by Turabi admittedly is not the first despotic regime in post-independence Sudan. But with no reservations, it is by far the most tyrannical and infinitely more bloodstained than any of its infamous predecessors. Turabi also took Islamic radicalism to a record height by assuming that whatever he described as Allah's word was *ipso facto* so. As the years wore on, the capacity of the regime he has built to behave monstrously became as clear as day. Those monstrosities shall be detailed in this work.

As for al Mahdi, who is a leader with recognizable democratic credentials, his problem is that he proffers a political project based on a theosophical reference point: the *Mahdiyya*. For all ends and purposes, it is an anti-democratic model that is tangential to Sudan's – indeed the world's – contemporary realities. Thus, in addition to exposing al Mahdi's role in aggravating Sudan's conflict in the last thirty years, we shall endeavour to demythologize the ideological underpinnings of his political project: the Mahdist tradition. However, it would not do justice to sober analysis if one left the reader to run away with the notion that all Sudan's problems shall be resolved if the two left the centre stage. Sudan's problems are much too intricate to be resolved by the abdication of this or that leader. They are profusely contaminated with prejudices, obliquity of judgement, cultural insularity and endless *parti pris*.

Sudan today is at a crossroads and one hopes that the new self-persuasion reflected in the Asmara Resolutions is a beginning of a new vision that would foster a change of direction from the perilous way to which Sudan was driven by visionless powerseekers. Sudan's elite, both in North and South, will have to face with courage and magnanimity not only the portent of their undertakings in Asmara but also the realities of the country's present situation. This is the elite's historical responsibility. Whatever choices they make, the country shall forever live with their consequences.

ENDNOTES

1. The term modern forces denotes a social category 'distinguished by their organization into trades unions through which they have been able to gain considerable political influence, primarily their position in the modern economic sector'. E. Kameir, in John Garang, *The Vision of the New Sudan*.
2. The epitaph on the graves of the young Greek martyrs who died in the wars of Sparta reads:
    'Go tell those men, safe in bed,
    We took their orders and are now dead.'

PART ONE

Genesis of Sudan's Multiple Crises

CHAPTER ONE

Fractious Dualities and Colonial Muddle
1898–1945

> *On no account had a greater amount of
> ingenuity to be exercised in effecting
> an apparent reconciliation by a
> pardonable fiction between the facts as
> they existed and the facts as they were
> supposed to exist.*[1]
> **Lord Cromer**

Introduction

Perhaps the curse of the Sudan or the blessing thereof, depending on the persuasion of the observer, is its location. Being across the Red Sea from Saudi Arabia and the Middle East and bordering Egypt to the north meant that it was exposed to religious and cultural Middle Eastern influences. It also meant that all the successive regimes that had ruled Egypt, from the Turks to the British, never did so without the irresistible desire to stretch their influence down into the Sudan; invariably in search of riches in the form of slaves, mineral wealth or and control of natural resources. On the other hand, bordering East and Central Africa to the east and south – including countries coveted by France in the Great Lakes region – signified that Sudan would inevitably be dragged into the squabbles occasioned by the acquisitiveness of European powers during the scramble for the continent. Britain, in particular, did not hide its avid desire to control the country.[2]

Sudan, as we know it today, is a modern creation (nineteenth century). Over five hundred tribal groups and sub-groups speaking nearly 150 languages were in 1821 brought together by the Turkish colonialists under one administration. The basic aim of the Turks was not territorial aggrandizement but hunting for military slaves to man the Khedive's army, and mining gold to fund his war chest. The twin process of unification of present day North and South Sudan, and the Turkish colonialist's lust for slave hunting, ushered in the worst era of slave trade in Sudan. Up till the Turkish invasion, intruders from the North into the South were, by and large, attracted to that region by gold, ivory and ostrich feather for export to Egypt and Turkey. Demands for export slaves were mainly satisfied through Dar Fur. Nevertheless, credit should be given to the Turks for laying the foundation of a modern state and economy in Sudan. Ironically, even with the benefits accruing to the community from the modernization of the economy, Northerners were touched in the raw by the harsh way in which that economy was managed. In the South, the brutality with which slave hunting was carried out, and the coarse treatment to which military slaves were subjected, turned the Turkish colonial regime into an object of hate. Eventually, the abomination of that regime by the two parts of the country whipped up against it a national rebellion that was to have a profound effect on future political developments in Sudan. And though the regime born of that rebellion, the *Mahdiyya* sustained the process of national unification started by the Turks, it also became a source of disunity in the country as a result of its radical and strait-laced approach to religion. In the meantime, it turned out to be no less brutal than the Turks in the way it ruled Sudan, leading to disaffection by large groups of Sudanese who ultimately turned against it. Moreover, the disastrous foreign exploits of the *Mahdiyya,* coupled with its internal brutality, arrayed against it both internal and international forces in a manner that led to its demise.

Great Britain stepped in after the demise of the Mahdist state in the guise of a fictitious colonial partnership between her and Egypt known as the Condominium, an ingenious term unknown before to colonial jurisprudence. Lord Cromer, the architect of this fiction, was the first to call it so. The manoeuvring of the two new colonial powers was to have a weighty effect on the political and economic development of the country and enduring consequences on North–South relations.

Creation of Modern Sudan

In 1821, Muhammed Ali Pasha of Egypt, then a dominion of the Ottomans, invaded, and established colonial authority over the Sudan. Interestingly, the Pasha wasn't acquiring the new territory for the benefit of his liege in Constantinople. The invasion was part of devious ambitions of the Pasha to create an Egyptian empire of his own, quite probably funded by the riches he expected to extract from the Sudan. Mohammed Ali achieved through that occupation something else; he created and delineated the boundaries of the Sudan as we know them today. His armies, under the command of Samuel Baker, penetrated the South up to Gondokoro (modern Juba rebaptized then Ismailia, after Ismael Pasha), and southward to the Great Lakes in Central Africa. South Sudan nominally included, at that time, areas up to Albert Nyanza comprising portions of the Kabarega kingdom of Bunyoro. To the west, with the help of Zubeir Pasha Rahama, his rule was extended up to Dar Fur. So did Mohammed Ali expand the borders of Egypt eastwards to the Horn of Africa. However, one important consequence of Mohamed Ali's invasion was the disruption of the process of indigenous nation building that was started by the Fur Kingdom in the west and the Funj in the centre. The Funj, in particular, brought together disparate Islamized and non-Muslim tribes using Arabic as a common language. By founding their kingdom much further south than Soba, the citadel of power at the time, they were able to communicate easily with the South given the fluidity of frontiers between North and South, if any such distinction existed then.

Wary of potential intrusion into the Nile Valley by other Europeans, and ever conscious of threats to their then extended global interests – particularly India – the British were haunted by the possibility of control by other powers of an uncharted land sitting astride vital routes to their Eastern dominions. They were determined to defeat whatever designs other powers may have had on these lands. Hence, the British prevailed upon Constantinople to tame the Pasha and force him to abandon his ambitions. As the carrot of the deal, he was made the hereditary ruler of Egypt and governor of the provinces of Nubia, Darfur, Kordofan, Sinnar, and all their dependencies outside the limits of Egypt.[3] However, according to Holt, the designation of the conqueror and conquest as Egyptian is misleading. No Egyptian nation state existed then and Egypt itself was a province of the Ottoman empire administered by Turkish-speaking Ottoman subjects.[4] Equally misleading was the designation of the conquest as Ottoman, since it was the Pasha's own private venture though 'the provinces were governed by the same Turkish-speaking elite that ruled Egypt'.[5]

Thus, 'Egyptian' dominion over the Sudan that was to have such a profound effect over the political development of the nascent country was in this rogue manner established. The military successes of 'Egypt', perhaps in keeping with the character of the larger Ottoman Empire at the time, were neither matched by administrative competence nor financial prudence. Also, the increasing harshness with which the Turks treated Sudanese won them few friends, despite their successes in establishing a semblance of a modern state: formal education, monetary system, post and telegraph services, law courts etc. Those developments helped uplift the country and brought its disparate parts together. In this regard, one of the most significant contributions of the *Turkiyya* to the unification of Sudan was the development of road transportation (Sawakin–Kassala, Swakin–Berber) as well as river transportation up to the South. In the broader economic field, the *Turkiyya* created 'political conditions under which widespread accumulation of private landed property in Northern Sudan became possible', and the value of land and fruits of its exploitation were incorporated into a network of commercial and financial institutions.[6] That was not a mean contribution to Sudan's pre-capitalist economy. Among the new economic measures was a new tax system in which 'coins, slaves and other commodities', were used for the payment of levies and dues.[7] As a result, the old system of land tenure was gradually destroyed, and a new landownership system created. That system resulted in extending rights to landowners beyond the confines of the geographic area in which they lived.[8] Large agricultural schemes were also introduced by the *Turkiyya*, e.g. the Taka agricultural scheme on the Gash River which enhanced both the value and *usufruct* of land. Thus, the impact of trade was no less great in the unification of the country than that of transportation.

At the beginning, the Turkish regime enjoyed the support of many Sudanese notables and *ule'ma* because of the advantages it had bestowed on them, while non-Muslims were heartened by the accomodative attitude of the regime towards religion. Even though it was ruling Sudan in the name of the Muslim Caliph, the *Turkiyya* never imposed *shari'a* on its people and reserved Islamic laws solely to family and personal causes of action. Unlike the regime that succeeded it, the *Turkiyya* was also open-minded about other religions; Christians of all denominations were allowed to practise their faith freely and build their worship centres. Coptic and Catholic churches existed in many towns of northern Sudan from Dongola to El Obeid, thus maintaining a tradition that started in the sixth century.[9] Interestingly, it was also during the Turkish rule that the first Catholic missions to South Sudan were dispatched (1848) comprising the Mazza Brothers at first, then followed by the Verona Fathers. It is equally remarkable that both Khartoum and Gezira were administered, at one point during the *Turkiyya*, by a Christian, the Armenian Arakel Bey.

Notwithstanding, the Muslim colonial rulers sought to modernize the prevailing Islamic legal system. An Egyptian *Kadi* (supreme judge) was appointed and a number of Sudanese *ule'ma* were enrolled in the service of the system. On the other hand, traditional *fuqaha* were shunned and their Qur'anic *Khalwas* (literally a hermitage, but in common parlance the term refers to a Qur'anic school, sing. *Khalwa,*) were discouraged, allegedly because of the impertinence of their tuition system to the needs of modern society. As a result, in its drive to 'modernize' Sudan's traditional Islam, the *Turkiyya* alienated Sudan's *fuqaha*, and made of them a fertile ground for incitement against the regime. At the end, the *Turkiyya's* increasing harshness gave people a pause. The Sudanese in both North and South were agonized by its pitiless brutality. In the North that was manifested in the back-breaking taxes levied on, and abrasively collected from, the well and not so well-to-do,[10] while in the South the yoke of slavery became unbearable. Not to be discounted also was the abolition of slave trading that had galvanized the Northern notables against the Turks. Probably that was more determinant than any other factor.

Slavery during the Turkiyya: Myths and Realities

Allied to this expansion in, and modernization of, the agrarian economy there was a remarkable growth in slave farmers. In the pre-colonial state, slave owning remained a 'privilege bestowed by feudal noblemen on their favoured supporters'.[11] Those slaves mainly carried out domestic chores, or were used by Sinnar rulers as an instrument of power, e.g. as guardians of outer regions in an increasingly centralized government. During the *Turkiyya* demand for domestic or agricultural slaves was not as important as that for military purposes. In this regard, Mohammed Ali Pasha never concealed his intentions. In a letter to his Viceroy in Sudan, the Pasha wrote: 'Our only purpose in sending you ... to undertake such a difficult mission, in sending so many troops, and in spending so much money, is to gather the greatest possible number of negroes. Show me your zeal ... have no fears, go everywhere, attack, strike and grab.'[12] The recruitment by the Turks of Sudanese military slaves was in keeping with the military tradition in earlier Islamic caliphates.[13] It is worthy of note, however, that slavery under those caliphates was colour-blind; slaves were drawn from different 'enslavable' nationalities according to their aptitude for the jobs entrusted to them. For example, military slaves were broadly hauled from amongst Turkish and Circassians at the Black Sea, while sex slaves (concubines) were drawn from the *rūmiat* (women from southern and central Europe), Persians and *gundahariat* (Afghan women). As for agricultural slaves, they were mainly drawn from Abyssinia, though, unlike in the old Roman empire, agricultural slaves were not the principal factor of production.[14] Segal appropriately remarks that 'slaves in Islam were directed mainly at the service sector – concubines and cooks, porters and soldiers – with slavery primarily a form of consumption rather than a factor of production'. The more telling evidence of this, according to Segal, is that while in the Atlantic slave trade there were two males for every female, in the Islamic black slave trade there were two females for every male.[15] Recruitment of black slaves in Islamic armies only started in the ninth century when the Aghlabids in Tunisia brought them into the army to neutralize soldiers of Berber origin, especially after the conflict between the ruler of Qairawan, Abdel Rahman ibn Habib, and his brother and army commander, Elias ibn Habib. That tradition was followed later in that century by the Tulunids.[16] In effect, on the death of Ahmad b. Turlun there were 24,000 white soldiers counterbalanced by 45,000 black soldiers in his army.[17] The majority of those came from Nubia, Dar Fur and the Horn of Africa. The practice continued in the eras of the Ayyibids and the Mameluks.[18] Amazingly, one of the Nubian military slaves, Kafur (Musky Camphor), became the regent of the son of the Akhsidid Mohamed b. Tughj and later ruled Egypt.[19]

Up to that point, Sudanese slaves were mainly drawn from Nubia in the form of a tribute exacted by the Islamic ruler Àbdullahi ibn Ali al Sarh. That agreement remained in force for six hundred years. Nubians, to whom slavery was not known, embarked, in their turn, on hunting slaves from the weaker tribes around them so as to meet that obligation. Beside Nubian or Nubian-hunted slaves, Dar Fur was by then the only region in Sudan that engaged in slave hunting for export purposes; their main catchment area was the peripheral regions occupied by weaker African tribes. In effect, both Nubians and Fur were defining their own freedom by dominating weaker tribes.[20] As O'Fahey argued, the Fur slavers were 'acting out of triumph of political and military organization of the Sudanic state over the acephalous societies that were their victim'.[21] However, the Fur-hunted slaves exported to Egypt were highly prized, and those of them who were integrated in the army were accredited with courage and military prowess. That was the reason why Napoleon, during his campaigns in Egypt and Syria, was so impressed by their performance as part of the 'enemy' army, that he wrote to Sultan Abdel Rahman of Dar Fur to provide him with two thousands of them. Only during the *Turkiyya*, did the Turks turn to recruitment of military slaves from South and Central Sudan. In this regard slave hunting was mainly conducted within three martial 'tribes': Nuba, Shilluk and Dinka.

The unification of the two parts of the country by Mohamed Ali, though beneficial to the country at large, had thus accentuated slave raids into the South and encouraged traders to engage in slave hunting. At the height of the enlistment, Sudanese military slaves in the Turkish army reached 10,000 (soldiers and officers) who played an important role in the Turkish as well as other wars.[22] But due to their abusive exploitation and ill-treatment by the Turks, military slaves from those 'tribes' were never at ease with their colonial masters. Several mutinies were reported in different parts of the country between 1844 and 1865, e.g. in Kassala and Wad Medani. Being armed and trained in the arts of war, they were surely able to fend for themselves. Johnson had appropriately described the term 'military slaves' as a contradiction in terms,[23] for if power lay in the barrel of a gun – as Mao Tse Tung believed – then enslaving an armed person would be a untenable proposition. However, the treatment meted out to the mutineers was extremely harsh. For instance, in a survey compiled by Ja'far Mazhar Pasha after the Kassala mutiny, out of a total regiment of over 10,000, only half reached Egypt. Of the other half, 1,408 were reported dead, 267 shot by firing squad, 531 sent to penal colonies in the Taka and the rest were divided among garrisons around the country.[24] According to Prunier there was also a high rate of attrition among those military slaves who 'were poorly fed, poorly housed, poorly paid and poorly equipped. The *Jihadiyya* (infantry) were often sick and could fall prey to massive epidemics'.[25]

Moreover, slave raids were not only limited to government troops. Concessionaries of all nationalities were often used by the Turks to hunt on their behalf. That was the period when Zubeir Rahama Mansour embarked on his heinous avocation. Zubeir was undoubtedly the greatest Northern slave hunter, but more than a trader in slaves, he was also a whimsical conquistador. One of his objectives of slave hunting was to raise his own army. Indeed, using that army, he was able to conquer Dar Fur, an action that provoked the Turks against him and drove them to arrest him and take over dominion over his newly acquired 'property'. Zubeir's bravura, however, would not make him less of a slave hunter, but certainly Zubeir was not in the same league of Northern Sudanese and foreign concessionaries[26] who solely traded in humans as chattel, and whose malfeasance still casts a heavy shadow on the North/South relations.

All the same, to understand properly the slavery institution, it has first to be contextualized, both in the historical and substantive senses. Second it has to be demythologized and rid of the emotive political overtones in which it has become increasingly shrouded. Failure to do so would neither do justice to scientific analysis nor facilitate a proper understanding of the inveterate sequels of that disgraceful phase of Sudan's history. Slavery was indisputably a notable institution of the Northern Muslim society whose demands were satisfied from the non-Muslim populations of the South, Nuba Mountains and the lower reaches of the Blue Nile on the Ethiopian borders. Ethiopia itself was not given a wide berth by Sudanese slave hunters; its people – known as *Makada* after the region bearing that name – were repeatedly subjected to slave hunting. Albeit, slavery was neither a peculiarly Sudanese institution, nor was it alien to other African countries in the north, east and west. For example in West Africa, the Ashanti and Dahomeyans – both warrior tribes – were notorious for enslaving weaker tribes surrounding them. To the east, slavery was a recognized institution in Ethiopia till the 1920s.[27] Its ready target were the Gallas and the inhabitants of the lower reaches of the Blue Nile, known as the Shankalla. The Shankalla were also looked down up on by the Funj in Sudan who disdainfully called them *Hamaj* (riff-raff).[28] Ironically, the misprized *Hamaj* revolted in 1762 under the leadership of Mohamed Abu Likaylik against Sinnar rulers and established ascendancy over them. Slavery was also common among the Arabs of the East African coast, particularly in Zanzibar as well as among the Buganda. Though in the case of the latter, internal social mobility facilitated the assimilation of slaves into that society. On the coast, the hunting of slaves by Arab raiders was aided by indigenous agents, chief among whom was Tippu Tip, the Zubeir of Zanzibar.[29]

Besides, slavery was by no means a distinctive institution of Sudan's riverain North, nor was it always North–South based. Indeed, before the unification of Sudan, raids were common among Northern Arab tribes, mainly for purposes of concubinage, paramilitary activities or domestic chores. In addition, as alluded to earlier, a large part of the transnational Sudanese slave trade was carried out by the Muslim Keira kings of Dar Fur. Their victims were primarily Bantu tribes known as Fertit.[30] Three to four thousand slaves were transported annually from that region to Egypt and onward to Turkey and Europe.[31] Even during the Funj era, slave hunters did not target the South, the frontiers of slave hunting in that period extended from Fazughli to Jabal Al Dayer in central Sudan. To the east, the Funj preyed on the Hamaj and Gumuz, and to the west on the Nuba. The latter were captured through the intermediation of the Muslim kings of Tegeli. Furthermore, the Sultanate of Massalit which was infamous for its rigid social stratification, placed the *Majir*[32] (male slaves) at the bottom rank of society after the rulers *(hukam)* and commoners *(masakin)*.[33] Their catch were largely from the weaker Daju tribe. Within the South itself, the Zande were notorious for raids on the Fertit of Bahr el Ghazal,[34] though trade in slaves was not known to them till the arrival of the *jellaba* (slave catchers and traders). Nonetheless, male and female slaves were known to have been kept by the Zande in the households of their chieftains. In due course, and as a trade-off for acquiring commodities – particularly fire arms – the Zande joined voluntarily the *bazinqer* (paramilitary formations created by slave traders for both defensive and offensive missions) and engaged in slave hunting. However, as we shall have occasion to explain later, what continued to pollute North–South relations was not so much the memories of the old institution of slavery itself, as it was the unconscionable and abiding remnants of slave culture in the North.

By August 1877 when the Anglo-Egyptian Convention of Abolition was signed, the Khedive was prevailed upon by the British to prohibit slavery in the provinces that he then ruled. That mission was assigned in 1869 to Samuel Baker and Charles Gordon after him. Gordon reported that between eighty and one hundred thousand slaves were exported from Sudan in the period 1875–1879. Given the fact that one of Mohamed Ali's main objectives from conquering Sudan was hunting military slaves, it was ironic that the termination of that heinous profession came at the hands of one of his successors. But that was only in theory; the Turks resorted to indirect means to gather military slaves. For example, while freeing slaves from their captors allegedly in pursuance to the terms of the convention, the 'freed' slaves were soon thereafter conscripted into the army. This action was justified under the pretext that if slaves were let loose, they would be recaptured by their old 'masters'. Thus, instructions continued to be given by the Khedive on the military recruitment of so-called Negroes in army.[35] Equally ironic was that the abolition decision – sham as it was– served to align against the Turks erstwhile allies: the slave hunters in the South whose human chattel was confiscated, and the notables who benefited from slavery in Northern Sudan. The abolition, therefore, had a direct bearing on the attitude of the Northern notables towards the Turkish government, as it had on the policies of the regime that succeeded the *Turkiyya*. So, while the South detested both Northern slavers and Turkish colonialists for slave practices that had decimated whole communities and torn the communal fabric of others, Northerners who had their own reasons to abhor the Turks, were also given an added reason to do so: the freeing of slaves.

Advent of the *Mahdiyya*

The degeneration[36] of the *Turkiyya* paved the way for the success of the Mahdi, fulfilling hopes prevalent among many Muslims that the End of Time would witness the arrival of the saviour. The idea is neither alien to Christianity or Judaism.[37] However, within Islamic tradition the belief in the emergence of an expected saviour descending from prophet Mohamed's family has more to do with *Shi'a* than *Suni* tradition. Substantially, that belief is one of the main separating lines between the two sects. Neither the Qur'an nor fully authenticated traditions of the prophet predicted the emergence of such a redeemer. Remarkably, the only reference in the Qur'an to the emergence of a redeemer at the End of Time related to Jesus. His return to Earth was predicted as follows: 'He shall be the sign of the Final Hour, so doubt not the event you people and follow him who shall guide you to my path of rectitude'[38] As to be expected, therefore, nearly all Mahdist pretenders emerged from within the *Shi'a* community.[39] Nonetheless, the idea of a Mahdi 'whose advent foreshadowed the end of the age' was sneaked into the popular belief of *Suni* communities beyond the Middle East where the majority of Muslim saints claimed descendence from the Prophet's family, obviously to legitimize their sanctity.[40] Within Africa there were earlier manifestations of 'saviours' that were not met with success e.g. in 1790 at Futa Jalon (modern Guinea) and later in Haussa land (Nigeria). In Nigeria, Usuman Dan Fodio, who carried the title of Commander of the Faithful, was hailed by his followers as the Mahdi. The man, however, knew his limits and had the modesty to decline the honour. He was reported to have told his followers: 'How can I be the awaited one when I was born in *Bilad al Sudan* (Land of the Blacks) in a place called Maratha. Surely the Mahdi will be born in Medina'[41]. That was probably the reason why the Emirs of Kastina, when approached by the Sudanese Mahdi, described him as a *dajjal* (anti-Christ).

In Sudan, Muhammad Ahmed 'Abdalla, a *Sammaniyya* sheikh declared himself the Mahdi in March 1881 and called on the faithful to rise against the Turkish intruders. Rather than emerging as a national liberator or religious reformer, the Mahdi declared himself the successor of Prophet Mohammed and the Expected Mahdi whose message transcended Sudan to the whole Muslim world. Although Muhammad Ahmed did not claim any thaumaturgies, his enunciations were expressed all along as auto-revelations, directly communicated to him by the Prophet.[42] His appeal to Sudanese Muslims and *fuqaha* was immediate; all efforts by the Turks to dissuade the general populace from being 'ensnared' by the Mahdi failed. So did religious appeals by the *ule'ma* to the Muslims of Sudan, including the *fatwa* issued by al Azhar at the behests of the Sultan of Constantinople which villified the Mahdi's claim.

The success of the Mahdi was total; through charisma, political dexterity and manipulation of religious symbols, he was able to change his dreams into possibilities. Wingate adeptly described the Mahdi's success as follows: 'with rapid earnest word, he stirred their hearts, and bowed their heads like corn beneath the storm'.[43] It was, therefore, not long before the Mahdi turned against the *fuqaha* and notables who either denied his Mahdist claims or had doubts about them. In his zeal to revive Islam, al Mahdi banned all *mazahib* (Islamic doctrines sing. *mazhab*) save for the Qur'an and *Sunna* (precepts enunciated by the prophet), and ordered burned all Islamic source books which were heretofore the intellectual mainstay of Islamic *fiqh* in Sudan. In their place, he developed his own politico-religious manifesto known as the *ratib* (anthology of daily readings). As far as theological exegesis was concerned, the Mahdi believed that he had reached a degree of mystical perfection that made him the only explicator of the Qur'an and the prophet's tradition. This monopoly of religious authority and wisdom, more than anything else, had inconvertibly turned the sheikhs of traditional Islam against him.

By 1885, the Sudan was under the Mahdi and was to remain so until a British-led invading force triumphed over the *Ansar* (followers of the Madhi) at the battle of Omdurman in 1898. The Mahdi was indubitably an inspired and inspiring leader; he was far above his peers in the way he developed Islamic-based social policies. In war, he was a masterly tactician and a daring combattant. None of those attributes was bequeathed on his successor, the Khalifa. Nevertheless, al Mahdi's monopolization of religion and politics went against the grain. Traditionally, especially during the Funj and Fur Kingdoms, the relationship between the kings and the *fuqaha* was of a very special nature; neither did the kings assume a religious role, nor the *fuqaha* claim a temporal one. Being drawn to piety and shying away from the vanities of life, the *fuquha* eschewed direct involvement in the worldly affairs of men, though they were steadfast in calling the rulers and the ruled to order on all matters that impinge on property, justice and rightfulness. Their advice – sometimes admonitions – was tolerated by the rulers, presumably because the *fuqaha* never represented a direct threat to their authority.

Of direct relevance to our thesis, three things are worthy of note in this chapter of Sudan's history. First, the perpetuation by the Mahdi of the unity of Sudan instituted by Muhammad Ali; second, his imposition, for the first time in the history of Muslim Sudan, of a strict religious rule, and third, the far-reaching impact of his regime's professed anti-sectarianism that brought it in direct conflict with other religious sheikhs who were either wary or jealous of his claims. The Mahdi proceeded to ban all religious sects, though he himself was originally a disciple of one. Foremost among those was the *Khattmiyya*; its leaders were hounded into exile only to come back after the Anglo-Egyptian invasion. Thus, the animosity between the *Khattmiyya* (the religious sect established by Mohamed Uthman al Mirghani, Senior) and the *Ansar* (sectarian and political successors of the Mahdi), had its roots this far back. Failure of those two religious groups to convert their historical dissonance into purposeful consonance was, by far, the most important factor in the future failures to create a viable Sudanese state.

Despite its religious radicalism and universalist call, the *Mahdiyya* is still recognized by Sudanese historians as a national liberation movement that delivered Sudan from the yoke of Turkish rule. But, given the universalist nature of his call, the Mahdi never intended to consolidate a nation or engage in building one along the lines of the Funj and Fur Sultanates, the two indigenous kingdoms which exemplified the tolerance, permissiveness and absorptive capacity of Sudanese popular Islam. As observed earlier, the lines of demarcation between the political dominion and the religious domain were clearly laid down in those two kingdoms, even though the rulers used Islam and Arabism as tools of legitimization.[44] Mahdism, therefore, was a deflection from the natural trajectory of indigenous Muslim kingdoms in the North, and a radical departure from the nativist bearing of Sudanese Islam. Furthermore, the

Mahdi's motives were manifestly extra-national, saving the whole Muslim commonwealth from corruption as defined by himself. But regardless of the moralistic overtones and universalist persuasion, Mahdism had effectively created 'a past around which a mass nationalist movement might form'.[45] This nation-building vocation that academic writings and scholars attribute to the Mahdi 'is an interpretation of the consequence of his revolt, rather than an appreciation of his motives';[46] his motives were to carry the message beyond Sudan.

This discursive exposition of the genesis, objectives and guiding principles of Mahdism, however, has a contemporary relevance in view of the indefatigable efforts of his grand grandson (Sadiq al Mahdi) to consolidate the Sudanese nation, with all the diversities that are already tearing it apart, on the moralistic model established by his great grandfather.[47] Albeit, by reducing Mahdism to a morality play, the great grandson of the Mahdi missed the point about the socio-economic factors that triggered the Mahdist revolt, and paradoxically led to its fall.

The Mahdi did not live long enough to carry his universalist message into lands beyond the Sudan (which incidentely included Egypt and West Africa); that mission he left to his successor, the Khalifa. The Mahdi's attempts after the fall of El Obeid to extend his influence to the west (Sokoto and Borno in modern Nigeria) were resisted by the rulers of those sultanates. The Khalifa, on his part, continued with the crusade; he appointed the grandson of Dan Fodio (Hayatou Ibn Said) as his representative and went ahead to throw down the gauntlet at both Egypt's Khedive Tewfik in the north, and Emperors John and Menelik of Ethiopia in the east enjoining the Abyssinian potentates to submit to the will of the 'successor of the Apostle of God'. Amazingly the same appeal was made to Queen Victoria with an offer of marriage, the Khalifa promising the Queen of England to be his wife once she converted to Islam. The Khalifa's missive to King John was staggering in its intrepidity, as was John's reply staid and well advised. Khalifa wrote to John: 'If you choose disobedience and prefer blindness you will undoubtedly fall into our hands as we are promised the possession of the earth of which you possess only a small part'.[48] To that vainglorious message John replied: 'Let us not kill the poor and harmless for no purpose, but let us both unite against our common enemies, the Europeans. If those conquer me they will not spare you, but will destroy your country.'[49] Markedly, the no-less-fanatic Christian monarch had put national interest and probably regional solidarity above injudicious religious zealotry. The Khalifa's adventurism of the nineteenth century, as we shall see, had considerable bearing on Sudan's experiences in the late twentieth century. It was not only during the present-day NIF regime that the ethos of Sudanese religious tolerance and humility were destroyed and regional peace destabilized. Indeed, in their discourses, the NIF time and again described their wrong-headed crusades in neighbouring countries as a continuation of the *Mahdiyya's*, though they had precious little to show for the Mahdi's forte, prodigious moral courage and uncanny sense of timing.

Mahdism and the South

While its ascendancy in the North was total, Mahdism did not succeed in establishing complete control over the South, save for few pockets in Bahr el Ghazal and Upper Nile, including garrisons like *Rajaf* which became an outlandish district for exiling dissidents. In effect, the *Mahdiyya* was most remembered in the South for the reaction it had engendered by forcing a *pur et dur* Islam onto Southerners, and the wide-spread abhorrence of the free rein it gave for the slave trade. This happened after a short honeymoon during which the Mahdi was hailed by Dinka Southerners as a liberator from the hated Turkish exploiters and perceived as a manifestation of one of their deities who emerged to deliver them from that rule.[50]

Surely, Mahdism had prohibited private slave trading, but that was not because of its abominable nature, but for the fear that slave masters might form private armies of slaves (*bazinger*) which would eventually challenge the state's authority.[51] Also, heedful that slaves might be used by the Turks to reconquer Sudan, the Khalifa wisely prohibited the export of slaves to Egypt.[52] Alongside those expedient measures, the Mahdist edicts on slavery were clear: to enslave by the sword (allegedly in the name of the faith) all those who did not yield to Islam or acknowledge the Mahdi as the awaited saviour. For example, the Mahdist commander, Mahmoud Ahmed, brought back to Omdurman 650 Jàliyeen women and children as booty of war after the battle of Metema. Those were later released by the British.[53] Indubitably, enslaving Muslims (including taking women as concubines) for no reason other than spurning Mahdism, contravened the basic tenets of historical Islam on war slaves. On the strict basis of *shari'a*, the Mahdists had manifestly erred when they enslaved co-religionists and equated non-recognition of the Mahdi's claims with lapse of faith. Unquestionably, slavery was sanctioned by Islam as it was by Judaism and Christianity, but according to Islam it was only permissible under explicit terms.[54] It is to be noted, though, that while Christianity equalized servitude with an act of obedience to God (The epistle of Paul to the Ephesians 6:5), Islam encouraged Muslims to manumit slaves as an act of piety. Nevertheless, historical Islam permitted the taking as slaves in war of all those who refused to submit to the word of Allah. This made slavery a consequence of *jihad*, not a reason for it. Equally, Muslims were circumscribed by strict religious fiats that i) no Muslim should enslave a co-religionist and, ii) a slave should not be treated as chattel, but as a person who enjoyed prescriptive rights. None of those two edicts were observed by the Mahdist state.[55] Verily, the Khalifa had ruled that all captured slaves should be treated as common (not private) property. This banning of private slave trade was not an abolitionist decision, as it was, strictly speaking, a politically motivated decision to 'nationalize' slave trade.

Some historians[56] asserted that the Turks abolition of slavery was the determinant factor that drove Northern notables to align themselves with the Mahdi. To those notables, slavery was an institution cardinal to the

14

country's economic stability. The Mahdi's favourable attitude towards abolition was exhibited in a circular addressed to his agent in Berber, Mohammed Kheir Abdalla Khojali. The agent was admonished by al Mahdi for not reinstating to 'their rightful owners' all slaves who were freed by the Turks.[57] In point of fact, the *Mahdiyya* had reignited in the South the dreaded slave trade, which was greatly extinguished by Gordon and Baker. Thus, in the light of the Mahdi's stance towards slavery, it was not surprising that the Mahdist's *ghazwas* (slave raids) into the South intensified. The success of those raids was limited to Bahr el Ghazal and Upper Nile, particularly that of the Mahdi's agent in Bahr el Ghazal, Karam Allah Kurqusawi who 'owed his military training and combat experience to his pre-Mahdist slave trading activities'.[58] Equatoria, which remained under Turkish rule under the German Governor, Edward Schnitzer (known as Amin Pasha), was saved from that onslaught. Nevertheless, the Mahdist agents never ceased to capture slaves from that province, despite the very insightful message dispatched to the Khalifa by his commander in Equatoria, Omar Salih.[59] One should also not discount the fact that by pursuing the attack on Equatoria, the Khalifa might have been driven by a desire to remove the last vestiges of Turkish rule in the South. However, his foremost objective was to recruit former *Jihadiyya* (infantries) who served under the Turks and who were given credit as fighters and riflemen. Those of them who were enrolled in the Mahdist army were immediately integrated into the Mahdist elite forces of *Jihadiyya* and *Mulazmeen* (orderlies). But even those prized soldiers cherished a grievance under the Mahdists. Unease amongst them was recorded since the early days of the *Mahdiyya*. For example, in 1885–87 some contingents of the *Jihadiyya* rebelled against the Mahdi in El Obeid and, as a sign of their cold comfort, they raised the Turkish flag and appointed one of their number as a 'Pasha' to lead them. The revolt was eventually extinguished by Hamdan Abu Anja.

Consequently, while in the North Muslims were enraged by the Mahdist's unconventional practices, particularly taking dissenters as war slaves, aggressive policies of compulsory conscription turned 'admirers' into foes in the South. That was aggravated by the policy of enforcing on the South a strict Islam, notwithstanding advice to the contrary by Khalifa's own commanders. At the end, the Mahdist were perceived by Southerners as another brand of 'Arab aggressors'.[60] At all events, whatever way the Mahdists conceived the Islamic laws of war to be, niceties of classical Islamic jurisprudence were neither relevant to non-Muslims who were enthralled by the *Mahdiyya* in the South, nor to their Northern Muslim counterparts who suffered the same fate for slighting the Mahdi's pretensions.

Both in the North and South, therefore, the *Mahdiyya* had a discrepant effect on society. On the one hand, it had created a sense of national worth around which Sudanese later united; on the other, it destroyed the ethos of political and religious tolerance in the North which distinguished earlier Muslim kingdoms. Ultimately, the Mahdist excesses generated abiding divisions within the North from which Sudan took time to recover. In the South, it had undermined tribal societies and, by its radical approach to religion, created an image of Islam unattractive to Southerners. With this history fresh in peoples minds, one would expect the heirs of the Mahdi to be the first to realize the dangers immanent in predicating the future of Sudan on a political paradigm that many Sudanese, both in the North and South, wished to forget.

But it is not only the heirs of the Mahdi who mythologize the *Mahdiyya*. Sudan's contemporary politico-Islamists often revert to that era as a reference point for their radical Islamization policies. One Islamist author recently claimed that the 'ultimate destruction of the Mahdist Community was the work of foreign powers that physically liquidated the Mahdist project.'[61] The same author, in another work maintained that 'Mahdism had abolished barriers dividing Sudan's regions and tribes and activated their energies to turn the country into an influential regional power, not an abandoned quantum'.[62] According to this thesis, the collapse of the 'project' was not due to the regime's inherent frailties and adventures, but to malign external factors. This is the same argument often advanced by Sudan's neo-Islamists to explain away their self-inflicted woes. However, the Mahdist project they continued to laud entailed nearly sixteen years of misrule during which the sole function of governance was internal wars,[63] suppression of the other[64] and ill-advised foreign exploits to Islamize the world. In the process, all Sudan's *ule'ma* who did not vouchsafe the *Khalifa's* obscurantism were submitted to the sword, tribe was pitted against tribe, enslavement (even of co-religionists) was justified in the name of Islam and as a result of internecine wars, Sudan's population was cut by half (from 8 to 3.5 millions). Half a million was swept away by famine and disease, notably small pox, while the rest died in tribal wars, foreign exploits and resistance against the invading army. Ultimately, the country was reduced to a shell of itself, 'rank with blood'.[65]

Entry of Great Britain

Britain's attitude to Sudan was ambivalent, she was reluctant to put her money on it, and it was also not ready to let it fall into the hands of another power. On the other hand, she was not indisposed to having access to the country by proxy, i.e. through Egypt. However, the state of the Egyptian treasury was so indigent at the time that it provided a pretext for Britain to put the country under receivership. In 1882, the British assumed 'temporary' control over Egypt which was to last until independence in 1922. Britain's involvement in Egypt brought it closer to the Sudan as a matter of course. At first, the British advised Egypt that the Sudan was an unnecessary expense to the Egyptian treasury and intimated to the Khedive that they would not allow themselves to be involved in the reconquest; nor would they permit use of Turkish troops that Egypt, as a dominion of the Ottomans, could have resorted to. Ultimately, the 'Egyptians' appeared to concede the loss of Sudan and the maverick General Charles Gordon was sent to Khartoum to supervise the withdrawal of their forces in the face of the Madhi's successes. Gordon himself was equally unenthusiastic about Sudan; to him Sudan was 'a useless possession, ever was so'.

Gordon was first recruited by Khedive Ismael as Governor of Equatoria whose paramount mission was to complete Baker's work in putting an end to the slave trade. Despite his successes, Baker's excesses steamed up against him, not only slave hunters but also their victims and local leaders. With 'messianic' zeal, Gordon gave much time to the abolition of slavery. Flaunting his aversion to slavery, Gordon wrote: 'I am quite averse to slavery, and even more so than most people. I show it by sacrificing myself in these lands which are no paradise ... I do what I think is pleasing to my God; and, as far as man goes, I need nothing from anyone.'[66] Gordon's anti-slavery zeal, however, did not tie in with his expedient pragmatism. His attitude towards the slave hunter, Zubeir Pasha was,[67] to say the least, freakish. While the 'Black Pasha' was in exile, Gordon appealed to Sir Evelyn Baring, the British Consul-General in Cairo, to recruit him to lead the fight against the Mahdi. In his message to Baring, Gordon said that 'Zubier without doubt was the greatest slave hunter who ever existed', but he was also 'the most able man in Sudan'. He called Zubeir a 'capital general' who had the 'capacity for government far beyond any man in Sudan'.[68] Gordon believed that 'all followers of the Mahdi would leave him on the approach of Zubeir', though he wondered whether the 'Black Pasha' would ever forgive him for the death of his son.[69] Ironically, the wheel of fate pushed Gordon himself to face the Mahdi and be killed in the process.

Even the killing of Gordon by the Madhists did not seem to have changed British opinion regarding Sudan; they ostensibly didn't attach much value to the country and were most reluctant to encourage reconquest. This disinterest may explain the ambivalence of the British towards the development of the Sudan in subsequent years. But, in 1886 the whole ball game changed; Belgian and French presence in Central Africa was becoming more notable and their expansion into the Sudan was just a matter of time. At the urgings of her allies, and more importantly due to her determination to keep the French off the Nile Valley, Britain reluctantly acquiesced to intercede, allegedly on behalf of Egypt, and it might be added, against the wishes of the Ottoman Sultan.

On 4 September 1898, Lord Kitchener hoisted the Egyptian and British flags over the Mahdist capital, Omdurman. And no sooner had Kitchener established his authority in Khartoum, than he proceeded on 19 September to take on the French at Fashoda, thus completing the reconquest of the Sudan. This presented a new set of problems; Britain couldn't very well annex Sudan to her properties as this would have antagonized the French, Egyptians and the Ottomans. It would also add to the burden on her treasury. On the other hand, she wasn't about to hand the country on a silver platter to the Egyptians and the Ottomans, no matter how useless she held it to be. The British came up with a clever ruse by which Egypt would entirely pay the costs of governing Sudan,[70] while Britain ruled on its behalf. This was formalized in what was known as the Condominium Agreement of 1899. Thus the Sudan became the first and only colony in Africa with divided sovereignty. From the start, there was no doubt as to who was calling the shots; in an address to assembling sheikhs in Omdurman, Lord Cromer alerted his audience: 'You shall, from now on, be governed by the Queen of England and the Khedive of Egypt in a partnership of two; of which England is the predominant member'.[71]

Colonial Policy of Two Sudans

The British were crassly irresolute in their approach to the South at the beginning; on the one hand, for their abolitionist Christian eyes, Southerners must have appeared particularly woeful in the face of the Northern Islamic theocracy. On the other, as old-fogey colonialists, they never concealed their belief in the inferiority of black Africans. As a consequence, they treated Southerners with no less derision than the Northerners did. In their estimation, Southerners were backward people with an almost Hobbsian propensity to violence.[72] This view of Southern peoples was not new. Even colonialists who were purportedly driven in the nineteenth century by humanitarian considerations to 'save' the South from the 'cruelty' of Northern slave traders were unsparing in their contempt for the people they sought to save.[73]

Notwithstanding this disdain to Southerners and their later ambivalence towards immediate release of slaves in the North,[74] the British should still be credited for abolishing slavery. On their part, Christian missionaries made a lot of mileage out of the phenomenon of slavery. So, without absolving them from ulterior motives (and there were many), slavery and its sequels might well explain why some of the well-meaning Christian missionaries adopted the South and sought to protect it from the 'slaver' to the north. Their anti-slavery zeal, however, went to the extreme. As some Northern scholars rightly argued,[75] Christian missionaries had indiscriminately inculcated into the hearts of Southerners, bitterness against the whole North based on the humiliating slave experiences. On its part, the British administration did nothing to fend off the intense missionary interest in the South, while it was very circumspect about missionary activities in the North, principally because it did not want to excite the ire of Northeren Muslims and Egyptian nationalists. Cromer, for example, was very guarded on allowing missionary activity in the North, but not so in the South.[76] But since they shared with missionaries the desire to minimize Arabo-Islamic influence in the South, the British eventually succumbed to pressures and allowed unfettered missionary activity in that region. Naturally, by viture of their profession, Christian missionaries wanted to contain the spread of Islam in Africa and, to that end, they worked to eliminate Arabic and supplant it with English. Islam and Arabic, they thought, were different sides of the same coin. They also saw in the South a large population that could be won for Christ and form a buffer between 'Christian' Africa and the

Muslim north. In this they may have been encouraged by views expressed by Lord Kitchener himself before the conquest.[77] As a result of these missionary endeavours, English, by 1918, became the official language of the South and Sunday, rather than Friday, the official day of rest. In this respect one readily accepts Ranger's thesis on the role of missionaries in Africa.[78] According to him missionaries were 'organic intellectuals for the volk. They operated out of schools, churches and clinics' to give an ideological character to primordial institutions'.

Nonetheless, the attitude of the British administration, as far as the spread of Christianity was concerned, other than for the partiality of a shared faith with missionaries, can best be described as murky and clumsy. The British saw the danger in becoming entangled in religious wrangles with Northern Muslims, which inspired the banning of missionary activities north of the tenth parallel. On the other hand, being Christians and with the missionary societies wielding substantial influence back home, they weren't about to encourage the spread of Islam in the South either. In effect their position towards religion was more expedient than ideological; they did not energetically promote Christianity in the South, but made little effort to hinder its spread. This was understandable from a people who, despite their imperial militancy, were not known for religious passion. But before such enlightened contemplation became policy, the views espoused by missionaries and close-minded administrators held sway.

The European-Christian influence in the South was further enhanced by the so-called Lugardian[79] policy of indirect rule by which the administration of the region was left in the hands of traditional institutions, cutting it off, as it were, from the rest of the country. Indirect rule became the order of the day in the whole Sudan, especially after the 1924 mutiny by Sudanese officers and intelligentsia against the British. That mutiny was amazingly led by an officer of Dinka origin.[80] Perceiving a betrayal by the intelligentsia, the British decided to give back the reins of authority in the North to tribal and traditional leaders who shared the colonialists distrust of that intelligentsia. The colonialists, however, rationalized the institution of native administration as it was reflected in the Powers of Nomad Sheikhs Ordinance 1922, by introducing modifications allegedly to remove 'native' practices 'which may seem repugnant to humanity',[81] whatever that term meant. As for the South, direct rule continued; the British could not see in the traditional institutions any attributes of organization and orderliness. That was perhaps the reason why they destroyed the most advanced kingdom in the region, the Azande, which was endowed with fairly developed legal, military and administrative systems.

As it were, in pursuance of their policy of de-Arabization in the South, the Equatoria Corps was formed in 1917, following recommendations by R.C.R. Owen, Governor of Mongala. Its recruits were exclusively from amongst the Southern tribes. The rationale behind the decision was that 'all Sudanese *askaris* (soldiers) from the North made a point of seeing that every recruit was converted to Islam'.[82] The battalion's language of command became English, the religion Christian. The withdrawal of all Northern troops from the South commenced in December of the same year and the Equatoria Corps was to remain the only military presence in the Southern region until the 1955 mutiny.

Two things are worthy of note in this murky policy. First, it failed to see that Arabic, rather than being the other face of Islam, was developing as the main medium of cultural integration among Arabs and non-Arabs even in the geographical North, e.g. among Beja, Nubians, Nuba, Fur etc. This process of peaceful cultural interaction had allowed for a natural mutation of Sudanese cultures that drew from, and were enriched by, Arabic language. There is abundant evidence of how non-Arabic vocables and grammer influenced Arabic parole in Sudan.

Second, the view held by missionaries and some old colonial administrators that the South be truncated and turned into a buffer between Christian and Muslim Africa, was not necessarily shared by a new breed of colonial administrators.[83] That view also paid no mind to the fact that Islam had been adopted and indigenized all over Africa; to the west (the Sahel and the Gulf of Guinea) and to the east (the Horn of Africa and the East African coast).

For all this, the British southern policy was not a policy at all, but a series of isolated decisions taken by senior administrators in Khartoum on the basis of advice from their subordinates in the South. Nevertheless, despite their intensive activity in the South, the missionaries could neither supplant English for Arabic nor eradicate indigenous cultures. Paradoxically, their attitude towards those cultures, was no less derisory than that of Northern intelligentsia of the day. According to a Southern commentator, missionaries 'disdained Southerners as unconscious and uncivilized ... people who do not know what is good for them'.[84]

The First World War crucially changed the way the British perceived their obligations in Sudan. First, Britain had fought on opposite sides with the Ottomans and, therefore, was technically at war with the partner with whom it ruled Sudan. Second, the Ottoman Sultan had attempted during the war to foment religious trouble for the British by calling for *jihad* against the 'infidel' English; a *fatwa* to that effect was issued on 11 February 1914. Those calls found a fecund ground among Egyptian nationalists in particular, and Muslims in general.   The period after the war was thus marked by concerted efforts on the part of the British to degrade Egyptian influence in the Sudan on the one hand, and Northern influence in the South on the other. A 1930 memorandum by Sir Harold MacMichael, the Civil Secretary, was an apt summary of the direction that British policy on the Sudan took, and was expressive of the desire to create, in effect, two Sudans, containing the North within its geographical definition while, at the same time, nurturing a Christian South that would have a non-Islamic, non-Arabic and non-Northern identity.[85]

In order to fulfil MacMichael's objectives, the British administration promulgated and enforced a series of draconian laws and policies:

a) The South was to be administered as a separate entity; for example in 1921 the governors of the three Southern provinces were freed of the obligation to attend the annual provincial governors meetings which, up to that time, brought together governors from both North and South. Instead, governors of Southern provinces were encouraged to build bridges to other British interests further south, particularly British East Africa and Uganda.

b) In 1922, the Passports and Permits Ordinance was promulgated to empower governors to limit the access of any Northern Sudanese or non-Sudanese into the 'Closed Districts'.

c) In 1925, yet another restrictive law, The Permits to Trade Order, came into effect. Targeted at Northern Muslim traders, then forming a dominant and influential merchant class, the order made it illegal to trade in the South without a permit.

The policy of separation reached bizarre proportions, for example when local colonial administrators urged Dinka pastoralists living in South Kordofan to go back to the South and ruled that contacts between Northerners and Southerners in borderline grazing areas be reduced to the minimum.[86] But the height of absurdity of that policy was exhibited in decisions to restrain Southerners from the use of Arab names or attire.[87]

Concomitant with those laws and policies was another, even more powerful process: education. Education policy in the South was geared towards a simple end, producing enough clerks and junior administrators to replace the departing Northerners. Mainly conducted by missionaries, the programmed instruction met this need and was therefore looked upon with a degree of favour. A grants-in-aid system was instituted for missionary schools, the consequence of which was an appreciable expansion in missionary-led education and educational facilities in the South. Whereas that was beneficial for the people of the region, the uncritical belief that informed it did not bode well for the future of Sudan. The attitudes of both missionaries and colonial administrators towards language were fostered by the so-called Rejaf Language Conference of 1928 which brought together delegates from missions in Uganda, the Congo and the International Institute of African languages. The meeting resolved to encourage the development of Southern vernacular languages as well as English in order to impede the use of Arabic because Arabic 'would open the door to the spread of Islam, Arabize the South and introduce the Northern Sudanese outlook'.[88] Education from three to six years, therefore, was to be imparted in nine indigenous languages: *Bari, Dinka, Kresh, Lotuko, Moru, Ndogo, Nuer, Shilluk and Zande.*

Undoubtedly, upholding Southern cultural and communal ethos and, to that end, nurturing indigenous languages and restoring a sense of worth to them, was a deserving exercise. However, resorting to such policy only to control the spread of the singular Sudanese *lingua franca* that united all Sudanese, was foolhardy. This is much more so when it is realized that none of the Southern languages, including *Dinka*, which is spoken by almost half of the population of the South, managed to transcend tribal boundaries. In a sense, the situation was richly paradoxical, for while the British policies consolidated the unity of Sudan through a controlling central administration in Khartoum in a manner that had never been achieved before (under the *Mahdiyya* or *Turkiyya*), their cultural policies disrupted an ongoing process of cultural interaction. Besides the colonial administrators were aware of the spread of Arabic in the South and, therefore, wary of the viability of their policy to curb it arbitrarily. For example, apprehensive of the application of the vulpine colonial policy to 'weed out' Arabs from Bahr el Ghazal, MacMichael wrote to the Governor of that province suggesting that the 'weeding out must be gradual, and in each case adequate cause must be shown so that, should the necessity arise, we may be in a position to supply a complete answer to any complaints or inquiries from interested quarters here'. [89] Thus, while taking all care not to aggravate the North, the aim of the British was clear. MacMichael put it unreservedly as follows: 'In short, whereas at present Arabic is considered by many natives of the South as the official and, as it were, the fashionable language, the object of all should be to counteract this idea by every practical means.'[90] The ambivalence of the colonial attitude to language could not have been more succinctly expressed than in the report of the Governor-General himself. Said Governor General Sir John Maffey: 'Wherever I penetrated, whether to the top of the Imatong or to the Belgian Congo border, I found Arabic in ready use by the local spokesman of the people. In the face of this *fait accompli* we shall have to consider very carefully how far it is worth effort and money to aim at the complete suppression of Arabic. Indeed, we shall have to consider, whether Arabic, in spite of its risks, must not be our instrument.'[91]

To all intents and purposes, there was a profusion of arguments adduced and evidence unfurled about the adversative impact of both missionary activities and colonial policy on the future relations of North and South Sudan. It would be enough to note that the policy of enforced separation did little to eliminate the Southerners' suspicions towards the North; in effect the suspicions became mutual. Northerners began to look at all educated Southerners as 'stooges' of colonialism and 'pawns' of the church. On the other hand, to all appearances, commitment by the colonial administrators to protect the South from the North with a view to safeguarding its cultural identity was implausible, since it was not complemented by any economic development of the region or advancement of its people. It was, therefore, surprising to see the British representative to the UN Security Council,[92] Sir Alexander Cadogan, defending the Closed Districts Ordinance in the Security Council when Egypt presented her claim over Sudan to that body. Safeguarding the South was seemingly the most trenchant weapon the British could have used against Egyptian claims, even when they had nothing to boast of in so far as development was concerned Puzzlingly, the British were more concerned about developing the North than the South they were supposedly set to protect. According to Cromer, 'it would be morally quite indefensible to leave the large Moslem population of the Sudan in their present condition without making every effort to assist them'. On the South, he said, 'no service could be provided … beyond what was necessary for the maintenance of government personnel and hence law and order'.[93] Cromer was not even convinced that the South was worthy of a 'civilized' legal system.[94] Cromer's harsh words might have also been a result of his choler against the tough Southern anti-colonial resistance up till the 1930s.[95] To their discredit, Northern – and more so Southern – historians hardly delved on the analysis of this page of the history of the South as part and parcel of the national anti-colonial struggle. But while Northern political historians might have considered the Southern anti-colonial struggle as resistance by primitives to civilization (the way the British saw it), Southern historians had absolutely no reason for that remissness.

Clearly, the colonialists main concern in the South was stability at the lowest cost possible, not development. It was only four decades after the pacification of the South that the colonial administration began a semblance of development under the Equatoria Projects Board conceived by Dr. J. D. Tothil[96] in a racially biased and condescending memorandum entitled 'An Experiment in the Social Emergence of Indigenous Races in Remote Areas'. Tothill's original plan recommended the introduction of four cash crops: sugar, oil palm, coffee and cotton, but the local administration chose only coffee because 'they knew nothing of the other crops to recommend them to local cultivators'.[97] It is therefore, appropriate to question whether the cultural and political insulation of the South wasn't also accompanied by economic losses occasioned by curtailing trade between the North and South which may have contributed to economic development even through a trickle-down effect. As an incisive scholar wrote: 'had the colonial regime made or guaranteed massive European investment in the South, the British government in the 1950s might have taken greater care over the fate of the region … South Sudan was treated like some wilderness of the first British Empire; to be traded off like New Foundland or the *asiento* rather than as a creation and responsibility of paternalistic imperialism.' Instead, it was 'sealed into a museum case of suspended animation'.[98]

Conclusion

Though, during their sixty-four years rule, the Turks never succeeded in completely pacifying the tribes of the North and less so of the South, they should still be credited with the creation of a centrally controlled Sudan that brought together the North, the South and the West. The Turks extremely centralizing process of governance impeded the natural evolution of indigenous kingdoms, but it had also developed social and physical infrastructures that could have in time consolidated unity of Sudan. But although that administrative centralization brought the South closer to the North, it also brought in its wake the escalation of slave trade, particularly in the first three decades of the regime.

The *Mahdiyya* that followed was welcomed by the Sudanese who were exasperated by the imperiousness of the *Turkiyya;* nonetheless, it had aborted the modernizing and unifying processes initiated by its predecessors as a result of its abstruseness and regressive approach to governance, especially during the Khalifa's stewardship. The Khalifa, despite his highly developed native wit and grit, clearly lacked statesmanlike wisdom and circumspection; his misguided external adventures alone proved that beyond any reasonable doubt. He was also merciless; not even his most trusted commanders were saved from his wrath.[99] The *Mahdiyya*, in its own way, succeeded in creating an indigenous core around which a nation could have been formed, but its religious excesses against Muslims and non-Muslims alike worked against it. Accordingly, it failed to give birth to a pan-tribal nation, let alone a multi-religious one. Besides, its policies of divide and rule, exhibited in setting tribe against tribe, was certainly not the way to unify a nation. Over and above, the preoccupation of the Mahdist regime with foreign exploits did not leave much time for it to attend to domestic issues. The foreign exploits, however, lined up regional and international powers against it, and eventually led to its demise. Within Sudan, the Mahdists' religious fanaticism galvanized major tribes in the North against them, including some of those who suffered immensely under the *Turkiyya* and should have, therefore, been heartened by its collapse. However, the disenchantment of those tribes with the Mahdist regime was such that they wholeheartedly embraced the British conquest.[100]

Colonialism is often regarded as the watershed of civil discord in the Sudan. The Closed Districts Ordinance of 1922 created a system of administration that essentially divided the country into two: North and South. At the same time, the British colonialists left the day-to-day administration of the South in the hands of eccentric administrators, while turning over authority for education and health to Christian missionaries. In the North, the economic development they initiated was concentrated in the riverain areas where relatively large sums were spent on infrastructure: railways, river transport, port facilities etc. The South, and indeed other non-riverain areas of Sudan, were neglected and left mired in squalor. This was not the result of a premeditated policy to impoverish the South and other regions, inasmuch as it was an outgrowth of a colonial economic design. The South had a forbidding terrain which made it difficult to exploit and obtain the immediate imperial returns the British were interested in; while the riverain North was strategic in respect to colonial economic interests. The colonial administration thus concentrated development in that region and effectively marginalised all other regions including the South, the Centre (Nuba Mountains), the West (Dar Fur), the East (Beja land), and the South East (Funj). The recognition of the economic neglect by the colonial administration of regions other than the South had largely been ignored in most discussions of the Sudanese crisis, maintaining the focus on the North–South dichotomy. Obviously, the North–South conflict was compounded by other aspects of diversity: race, religion and culture.

The role of colonial policies in setting the stage for conflict in the Sudan was undoubtedly significant. Nevertheless the Northern ruling establishment could not be absolved from blame for perpetuating the root cause of conflict. In effect, they found it convenient to drum up the colonial factor as the sole explanation for the crisis, thereby obscuring their own insufficiencies in rectifying policies instituted by colonialists for their own ends. Had the Northern regimes that inherited the mantle of power from the British risen above their myopia after assuming the reins of power, the colonial legacy could have been reversed and war averted. The valid argument can therefore be made that the post-colonial governments bear greater, not less, responsibility for causing the war in the Sudan.

ENDNOTES

1. The statement reflects Cromer's cynical view on the notion of condominium rule, the name given to the joint Anglo-Egyptian partnership for the administration of Sudan.
2. In a note to Rosebury (12 April 1895) Cromer wrote about Sudan: 'If the Egyptians do not take it, the French and Italians will some day walk in. I greatly doubt the possibility of keeping them out by arrangements on paper. ... What I now fear is that the activity of the French will force on us a premature consideration of the issue. Remember that, though the French might object to English reconquest, as to which I conceive there can be no serious question, they could make no objection to reconquest by Egypt'. PRO. Fo/633/7.
3. Ferman of Sultan Abd al Majid 13 February 1841 op. cit Holt and Daly, *A History of the Sudan*, p. 39. The Sultan commanded the Pasha 'to administer and organize these provinces according to my (Sultan's) equitable views and to provide for the welfare of the inhabitants'.
4. Ibid., p. 42.
5. Ibid.
6. Spaulding, Jay, *Slavery, Land Tenure*, p. 3
7. Ibid. In fact, slaves were used as a 'legal tender' by the Sultans of Dar Fur, long before the coming of the Turks; goods in Egyptian markets were exchanged for slaves.
8. Ibid. According to private documents perused by Spaulding, some of dating to the Funj era, there was evidence of notables in Swakin owning land in Berber, and prosperous families in Metema extending their commercial activities up to Fasher, Rahad and Kassala, a matter that was unheard of before the *Turkiyya*.
9. Christianity was consecrated in Sudan since 566 during the Kingdom of '*Alwa* by Bishop Longinus of Nobatia and remained the religion of the court till the fifteenth century.
10. According to Mekki Shibeika, the main reason that compelled farmers in Dangola to migrate to Khartoum, Blue Nile and Kordofan was the back-breaking taxes imposed on them by the Turks; out of 5,900 farms in Dongola Province, 2,011 were deserted. Shibeika, *Sudan abr al Quroon*, p. 144.
11. 6 supra, pp. 3–5. The scholar revealed, on the basis of the aforementioned private family papers, that slaves were not commonly employed in agriculture all over Sudan. For example, while near the capital city a great number of cultivators were slaves, in the Shaigiyya country there were almost none.
12. Sudan Archives (1821-2), Khartoum. See also Holt and Daly, *A History of Sudan*, p. 39.

13. Military slaves swelled the armies of earlier Islamic Caliphates from the Abbasids up to the Ottoman era.
14. Lewis, Bernard, *The Arabs in History*, p. 112.
15. Segal, R., *Islam and Black Slaves*, p .4.
16. Ibid.
17. Ibid.
18. *Mameluk* was the name given by the Turks to white martial slaves to distinguish them from 'humble' slaves undertaking domestic functions. The *Mameluks* eventually took over Egypt and ruled Syria in the sixteenth century. Lewis, Bernard, *The Arabs in History*, p. 159.
19. This is a case without parallel among the counterparts of Islamic slaves in the West. Segal p. 9. Another son of a Nubian ex-slave mother, Al Mustansir became the longest reigning ruler in the era of the Fatimides.
20. Wendy James maintains that societies always sought victim societies of outsiders to be dominated. By this they define their own freedoms, political coherence, ethnicity and Kinship links'. *Perceptions from an African Slaving Frontier*, p. 133.
21. O'Fahey, Sean, Slavery and Slave Trade in Dar Fur, *Journal of African History*, p. 33.
22. Some of the enlisted Sudanese soldiers and officers fought alongside the Turks in Greece; a small contingent was 'loaned' to Napoleon III to fight in Mexico as part of Maximilian's army. Johnson, D.H., *The Legacy of Sudanese Slavery in Modern Africa*, lecture at Durham University, 6 May 1987.
23. Johnson, Douglas H., *Sudanese Military Slavery from the 18th to the 20th centuries*, p. 142.
24. Prunier, Gerard, op. cit., *Military Slavery in the Sudan during the Turkiyya (1820-1885)*, p. 132.
25. Ibid.
26. Notorious slave hunters included Al Nour' Anqara, Karam Allah Kurkusawi (Sudanese); Ahmed al Aggad, Ali Abu Amouri, Abu al Sa'aud, Mahjoub al Bisaili, Ghattas (Egyptians); Khalil Al Shami (Syrian); and Balzac, a French man who controlled the slave camps at Rumbek.
27. Slavery, which reached its zenith during Meneliks new empire, was not officially abolished in Ethiopia till 1942. The term *galla* was a pejorative expression describing the Oromo nationality. As in other African societies, slaves were being used in military activities, domestic labour or for debt bondage.
28. Slave hunting continued within the Funj region till 1929 when the disreputable slave trader sheikh Khogali al Hassan was arrested and convicted. Beshir, M.O., *South Sudan*, p. 21.
29. Hamid Bin Mohamed bin Juna al Marjebi, commonly known as Tippu Tip, was an Arab but in name. Like Zubeir of Sudan, he was a buccaneer who wanted to build his own empire.

30. In the Fur language the term *firtingu* (i.e. of the Fertit) became synonymous with slave.
31. Sikainga, A.A., *Slaves into Workers*, p. 9. Sikainga is a pioneer, among Sudanese scholars in addressing the issue of slavery critically and boldly. Northern scholars generally deal gingerly, sometimes speciously, with this unattractive page of Sudan's history. See also Spaulding, *Kingdoms of Sinnar and Dar Fur*, pp. 56–80.
32. Johnson, 23 supra.
33. Kaptejins, Ltdwien, *Massalit Sultanate*, pp. 138–9 and 152–3. See also Tully, Dennis, *The Process of Market*, p. 23. Tully maintains that slaves were captured in raids and freely sold and bought in the Massalit kingdom. But, in his judgement, slavery within the Massalit was also a way of incorporating other ethnic groups in the society, comparable to the Nuer interaction with the Dinka reflected in Evans-Pritchard's works.
34. Collins, Robert O., *Land Beyond the Rivers*, p. 219.
35. Prunier, 24 supra. Instructions issuing from Abdin Palace (the Khedive's Palace) to his military representatives in Sudan called for the integration of the physically able men in the army, the not so able were to be employed as farmers and women should be married off. P. 135.
36. According to Holt the fact that the first open universal revolt against the *Turkiyya* took place twenty years after the inception of the regime, demonstrated that it was probably because of the regime's increasing weaknesses rather than its oppression *per se*, that the Sudanese were emboldened to take it on. It was that weakness that vitalized Orabi Pasha in Egypt and Al Mahdi in Sudan, to challenge the *Turkiyya*. The regime, according to Holt, had obviously regressed into a toothless and vulnerable administration easy to confront. Holt and Daly, p. 72.
37. The second coming of Christ in the New Testament and the emergence of Prophet Elijah in the Old Testament (Malach). The imminent expectation of Christ is part of preparing the way for the Lord (Matthew 3:3).
38. *Al Zukhruf*, The Adornment 43/61.
39. The first Mahdist pretender was Mohammed *al Nafs al Zakiyya*, the grandson of Caliph Ali (Prophet Mohammed's cousin and his fourth Caliph). Other pretenders included Mohamed Ibn Obeid Ullahi, the founder of the Fatimid dynasty, Al Mahdi, Mohamed b. `Abd Allah ibn Tumart, the founder of Almohad dynasty in the Maghreb, Ghulam Allah al Qadiani in the Punjab etc. The *Shiítes*, however, dogmatically believe in the emergence of the awaited one in the person of a descendant of Ali, namely his great grandson Mohamed ibn al Hassan Al `Askri. `Askri who was born in the tenth century is presumed to be still alive, hence the *Shiá* describe him as *sahib al ghaiba al kubra* (the man of the long-

drawn absenteeism).

40. According to Ibn Khaldoun, 'It is a universal belief amongst the Muslim masses through the ages that at the End of Time a man of the family of the Prophet shall manifest himself to confirm the faith and proclaim justice. The Muslims will follow him and he will establish his rule over the Islamic Kingdom', Ibn Khaldoun, *Al Muqaddima* p. 218. However, Ibn Khaldoun himself contested the authenticity of the various *hadiths* attributed to the Prophet in this regard. On the other hand, a number of classical *fuqaha* affirmed the idea of the emergence of the Mahdi, not on the basis of the *Qur'an,* but on sayings of dubious origin ascribed to the Prophet. Among those are Jalal al Din al Sioutty in *Al Hawi 'ala al Fatawi*, Imam al Qurtubi in *Al Tazkira* as abridged by Imam Abdel Wahab al Sh'arani, al Barazanji in *Al Isha'a fi Asharat al Sa'a and Ibn 'Arabi in Al Futuhat al Makiya*.
41. Al Haj, M.A, op. cit., *Sudan in Africa*, p. 130.
42. In his *Manshur* (circular) in 1881, al Mahdi claimed that he was called upon by Prophet Mohamed to go on a *hijra* (religious-ordained flight) to Qadeer in western Sudan. Many of his other *manshurs* were enounced as direct revelations from the Prophet.
43. Wingate, *Mahdism and the Egyptian Sudan*, p. 13.
44. In their origin legend, the Kings of Sinnar, starting with Sultan Muhammad Bade Ajib, promulgated an Ummayyad pedigree, a matter that many historians challenge. Holt, P.M., *The Funj Chronicles*.
45. Daly, M.W., Carter Center.
46. Holt and Daly, 27 supra.
47. Sadiq often predicated his political philosophy, even in this day and age, on the Mahdist moralistic agenda. He attributed the Mahdi's success to three factors, all of which had to do with religion. First, he said, Islam needed revival as a result of the moral inadequacy of Muslim leaders. Second, Islam in Africa was in an even worse shape than in Sudan and thus it called for a redeemer. Third, the prevalence of corruption in both religious and civil lives was such that it made the success of Mahdism a foregone conclusion. Inherent in this thesis are three things: first, Sadiq's assumption that public policy in Sudan can still be postulated on religion as it was in the nineteenth century. Second, the supposition that Sudan has a role in the redemption of Africa suggests that Sudan's 'new Mahdi' believes that he has a God-given mission in Africa. Third, by setting himself out to morally purify people, Sadiq the 'modern democrat' is making of the state a guardian of people's private lives. Sadiq al Mahdi, *Yas'alunaka*, p. 142.
48. Sanderson, G.S., op.cit., *Sudan in Africa*, p. 173.
49. Ibid.
50. Hymns of praise composed by the Dinka elevated the Mahdi to a

deity and called him the 'Son of Deng', according to Francis
Deng. *Dynamics of Identification*, p. 28.

51. Collins, R.O., *The South Sudan 1883–97*, p. 57.
52. In a letter to Kurkuawi, his agent in Bahr el Ghazal, the Khalifa
wrote: 'we have banned the selling of slaves without
authorisation of, and training by, *Bait al mal* (Treasury). This is in
accordance with religious edicts. If free trade in slaves is allowed
uncontrolled, slaves may eventually end in the hands of the
infidels'. Nugud, M. Ibrahim, *Ilaqat al Riq*, p. 232.
53. Shugair, N., *Tarikh al Sudan* p. 887.
54. Exodus 21: 2-10 sets rules for treatment of slaves, Leviticus 25:39
prohibited Jews to enslave their own even when one of them
offered himself for that purpose. See also 2 Chronicles 28:9.
55. Nugud (52 supra) listed numerous records of sale of slaves by *bait
al mal* in which slaves were classified according to sex and age,
alongside other war spoils like goats, donkeys and sheep. This
was a flagrant departure from Islamic edicts on war slaves; in
actuality, Prophet Mohamed's sermon on his last pilgrimage to
Mecca was instructive in this respect: 'as to your slaves feed them
with what you eat yourself; clothe them with what you wear. If
you cannot keep them or they commit any fault; discharge them.
They are God's people like unto you and be kind unto them.'
56. Shuqair, Naum, *Tarikh al Sudan*; Shibeika, Mekki, *Al Sudan Abr al
Qurun*.
57. Warburg, Gabriel, op.cit., *Ideological and Practical Considerations*, p.
250.
58. 51 supra, p.247.
59. Ibid., p. 77. Salih wrote to the Khalifa: 'there is no possibility of
any recruitment or increase of the army … those negroids whom
we conquer cannot stand our customs, nor can they practise our
rules, for they find our life very strange. This religion of ours is
very difficult for them to understand and follow, so they desert
us.'
60. Deng, F.M., *War of Visions*, p. 72. Curiously, in a recent exchange
of letters between John Garang and Sadiq al Mahdi (See Ch.10)
the former recalled the Mahdists' role in kindling slavery in the
South after its abolition in the mid-nineteenth century. To that
charge, al Mahdi retorted by quoting Francis Deng's exposé on
the Dinka espousal of the Mahdist call. Sadiq al Mahdi was
manifestly selective in his recitation; for Deng added that conflicts
soon erupted between the Dinka and the Mahdists who
'fanatically inspired by, and sure of, their divine mission to rid
the world of infidels, carried the holy war into the South and,
with it, full-scale slavery returned'.
61. Affendi, Abdel Wahab al, *Turabi's Revolution*, p. 6.
62. Affendi, Abdel Wahab al, *Al Thawra wa al Islah al Siyyasi*, p. 211.
63. The sixteen years of Mahdism witnessed mutinies against the

Mahdiyya by major tribes such as the *Shukriyya* (whose leader was banished to Omdurman and humiliatingly turned into a fuel-wood vendor), the Kababish and the Fur who began clamouring for the restoration of their throne.

64. In consequence to the monopolization of religion by the Mahdists, prominent Sufi sheikhs launched a campaign against Mahdism throughout the North. Leading among those were the *Khattmiyya* chiefs (Mohamed Osman the second in Kassala; Mohamed Sir al Khatim in Swakin; Bakri al Mirghani in the Taka).

65. G.W. Steevens, an English journalist who accompanied Kitchener wrote on the Sudan he saw then: 'For three years ... the Egyptian army has been marching past broken mud hovels by the river side. Dust has blown over their foundations, Dead Sea fruits grow rankly within their walls. Sometimes, as in old Berber, you come on a city with streets and shops quite ruined and empty. Here lived the Sudanese whom the Khalifa has killed out. And in the more fertile parts of the Sudan it is the same ... the very fertility woke up the cupidity of the Baggara, and the owner was driven out, sold in the slave market, shipped up the Nile to die in Fashoda fever, cut to pieces, crucified and impaled – anything you like as long as the Khalifa's fellow tribesman got his land. *With Kitchener to Khartoum*, p. 32.

66. Op.cit from Hill. In Warburg, G., *Ideological and Practical considerations Regarding slavery*, pp. 248–9.

67. Zubeir Rahama was made a Pasha by the Khedive of Egypt in recompense for his services to Egypt, particularly the subduing of Dar Fur, which extended the areas of Sudan under Turkish rule to present-day Chad. Zubeir was dubbed the Black Pasha. However, on the urgings of European powers, Zubeir was exiled to Gibraltar as a punishment for the very deeds for which he was rewarded by the Khedive.

68. Crabites, Pierre, *Gordon, the Sudan and Slavery*, p. 21.

69. Suleiman, the son of Zubier was killed in 1879, on Gordon's orders, by the Italian Governor of Bahr el Ghazal, Romolo Gessi Pasha. Gordon's remark on receiving the news of Suleiman's death was effulgent with righteous symbols: 'Thus does God make gaps in his enemies.' Wingate, *Mahdism and the Egyptian Sudan*, p. 11. Zubeir never forgave Gordon for that act, especially that his son was reported to have been willing to hand himself over to Gordon.

70. In a statement reverberating with sarcasm, Wingate told a member of Balfour's government who was inquiring about England's financial contribution to the administration of Sudan: 'By the Condominium Agreement, the British and Egyptian flags must always be flown together, but for several years past I have had the greatest difficulty in getting the Admirality to supply the bunting for the British flag. I hope you can help us.' Abdel Rahim,

M, op. cit, *Imperialism and Nationalism*, p. 56.

71. Cromer, *Modern Egypt*, p. 116.
72. In a letter to the Foreign Secretary, Cromer justified the onslaught by British forces on the South as a lesson to 'teach these savages the elements of common sense, good behaviour and obedience to government'. Governor General's Annual Report, 1905, Sudan Government archives.
73. For example, Gessi Pasha, Governor of Bahr el Ghazal, took issue with the proposition by some historians that the Funj kings who claimed an Arab pedigree were indeed descendants of the Shilluk. 'Such a sophisticated state as Sinnar could not be attributed to savage people like the Shilluk,' he said. Gessi, R., *Seven years in Sudan*, p. 152.
74. In its first two decades in office, the colonial administration prevaricated on the issue of freeing slaves. There were abundant colonial statements on the need to tolerate slavery for some time. For example, Lieutenant Colonel Stewart who was sent in 1883 to evaluate the abolition situation in Sudan, reported that: 'Slavery is woven into the habits and customs of the country; that to eradicate it will be both difficult and tedious ... of the two trades, the export and the home, the former might, if active measures are taken, be almost entirely put a stop to. The latter is more difficult to deal with.' This view was embraced by Cromer; slavery he claimed, 'should be tolerated, based on recognition of its pervasiveness, its essential contribution to the economy and the possible effects on Sudanese opinion of enforcing its abolition'. Memorandum from Cromer to Salisbury F/078/4957 memo No. 10. Daly, M.W., op.cit, *Empire on the Nile*. Daly also quoted Kitchener's memo to *mudirs* (governors) requesting them to leave the institution alone as long as servants were willing to serve their masters.
75. Beshir, M.O., *The Southern Sudan: Background to Conflict*, p. 22.
76. In a letter to Lansdown, Cromer wrote: 'I have no objection to giving missionaries a fair field amongst the black pagan population in the equatorial regions, but to let them loose at present amongst the fanatic Muslims of Sudan would, in my opinion, be little short of insane.' PRO / FO / 633, 9 March 1900.
77. Kitchener, who was to conquer Sudan afterwards, maintained in a speech he made in Uganda before Sudan's conquest (September 1892) that 'unless the Christian powers held their own in Africa, the Mohammedan Arabs will, I believe, step in and in the centre of the continent form a base from which they will be able to drive back all civilizing influences to the coast and the country will then be given up to slavery and misrule as is the case in the Sudan at present'. Collins, *Land Beyond the Rivers*, op. cit., p.17.
78. Ranger, Terence, *Rhodes Professor of Race Relations at oxford in*

People, Nation and State: The Meaning of Ethnicity and Nationalism, p. 22.

79. Lord Lugard introduced the policy of indirect rule and separate development in Nigeria in 1914. That policy, which was replicated in other British colonies in Africa, was one of the causes of Nigeria's simmering conflicts up to this day. The policy was fine tuned by Luggard, in a book published in 1922 entitled *The Dual Mandate in British Tropical Africa*.

80. The mutiny had a wide support among the intelligentsia and was led by Ali Abdel Latif, a Dinka officer. Abdel Latif was an accomplished officer who was decorated by the British as the most efficient cadet. Through sheer daring, he was able to muster the support and recognition of the Norther intelligentsia, though notables in the North were not comfortable with him as a result of what they deemed to be his 'lowly' origin. The Khartoum daily, *Hadarat al Sudan*, the mouthpiece of the notables, lamented the fate of Sudan in a heavily racist tone: 'What a lowly nation is this that is now being led by people of Abdel Latif's ilk: who is he and to what tribe does he bolong?' 25 June 1924. Far from Abdel Latif's origin, the notables, with good reason, saw in Abdel Latif's movement a challenge to their authority. The British were no less scathing; Abdel Latif was denounced as an Egyptian puppet because of his call for the exercise by the Sudanese of the right of self-determination and for unity with Egypt. The call for unity was probably impelled by Abdel Lalif's desire to strengthen the hand of the budding nationalist movement against the British. He was ultimately imprisoned for sedition and described by his colonial prosecutors as a 'half-civilized dupe of Egyptian politicians'. Holt and Daly, *A History of the Sudan*, p. 113.

81. MacMichael, Harold, *The Anglo-Egyptian Sudan*, p. 234.

82. M.O, Beshir, *The Southern Sudan*, p. 38.

83. Henderson, one of the more enlightened British administrators stated 'from North to South the Sudan presents a cross-section of North Africa with the Nile as the base', Henderson, K.D.D., *Sudan Republic*, Ernest Benn, London, 1965. Henderson's view was shared by his mentor, Sir Douglas Newbold. In a lecture at the Arab Centre in Jerusalem (October 1947), Newbold concluded that the 'language, religion and national consciousness of the greater part of the Northern Sudan attach them undoubtedly to the Arab group of nations and no other'. 'Though Arabicized', he added, 'signs of older African culture remain embedded in their "Arabism", their Islam and in their Arabic dialects – notably certain Hamitic, Nubian and African influences on customs connected with marriage, child birth and death'. Henderson, K.D.D., *The Making of Modern Sudan, The Life and Letters of Sir Douglas Newbold*, p. 476.

84. Ruay, *The People of Two Sudans*, p. 101.

85. What came to be known as the Southern Policy sought to achieve the following:
    a . Build tribal cocoons based on traditional institutions and into which no other outside (than perhaps British) influence was to be allowed.
    b . Remove all Northern administrators (and ultimately all Northerners) from the South and subsequently replace them with Southerners in the effort to achieve (a) above.
    c . Impose English as the official language of the South.
86. MacMichael, Sir Harold, Policy Memorandum, January 25, 1930, Sudan Government Archives.
87. The District Commissioner in Raja, Bahr el Ghazal, ordered local tailors that 'shirts should be made short with a collar and opening down the front in the European fashion and NOT with an open neck as worn by the Beggara of Dar Fur. Also *taqias* (skullcaps) worn by Arabs should not be sold in the future'. op. cit. Abdel Rahim, Imperialism and Nationalism P 78.
88. Beshir, *South Sudan*, p. 51, op. cit., policy statement issued by Governor, Bahr el Ghazal on 13 February 1930.
89. Ibid., op. cit., p. 44.
90. MacMichael to Governor, Bahr el Ghazal, op. cit. Abdel Rahim, p. 76.
91. Note by the Governor-General, 12 June 1927, Sudan Archives.
92. Security Council Records, No. 70, 1947. The Closed Districts Ordinance, claimed Cadogan, was a necessary tool for safeguarding the interests of the South.
93. Rahim, Abdel, op cit., p. 71.
94. In his Annual Report (1904) Cromer wrote: 'I do not suppose that the most ardent advocate, whether of internationalism or of equality of freedom to all creeds and races, would have been possible in practice to have worked a system under which Kwat Wad Awaiting, a Shilluk who murdered Ajok wad Deng because the latter bewitched his son and caused him to be eaten by a crocodile, would have been tried by a procedure closely resembling that followed at Paris or Lyons.' Ibid., op.cit., p. 71.
95. In 1901 the Agar Dinka attacked Rumbek in 1905, the Azande revolted against the British and their leader, Gbudwe, was killed, between 1907 and 1921, the Atuot Dinka fought intermittingly against the colonial administration, in 1912 the Anwak defeated a British force of 354 soldiers in Odonga and for eight years remained independent of the Anglo-Egyptian Sudan, while in 1919 'Aliab Dinka sacked a colonial outpost at Minghamman, killing the commander of the force and the govenor of Mongala. Mawut, Lazarus Leek, *The Role of South Sudanese People in Building Modern Sudan*, Juba University Conference, 1985.

96. Voll, John O. and Sarah P., *The Sudan Unity and Diversity in a Multicultural State*, p. 107.
97. Ibid.
98. Daly, M.W., Carter Center, Workshop on Sudan, 1990.
99. Al Zaki Tammal, one of the most valiant commanders in the Mahdist army, was imprisoned by the Khalifa and left to die of starvation.
100. No Northern Sudanese group has suffered under the Turks as much as the *Ja'alyeen;* the punitive reprisal of the Turks against them, following the murder of Ismail Pasha, was humiliating and almost genocidal. Hundreds of their women were reduced to servitude and sent to Cairo as domestic slaves or concubines. However, the brutality of the Turks towards that group was almost matched by the Mahdist attack on their citadel, Metema. The *Ja'aliyeen* were chastised by the Mahdists for no reason other than brushing off the Mahdi's religious claim. According to historical records, only 1,300 persons, the majority of whom were women, remained alive after the battle of Metema. Consequently, like their neighbours the *Shaikiyya*, they *ja'aliyeen* received the Anglo-Egyptian forces with open arms.

PART TWO

Betrayal of the Nation's Expectations

CHAPTER TWO

Sudanese Nationalism:
The Special Preserve of the North
1946–1956

Beware the man who does not return your blow; he neither forgives you, nor allows you to forgive yourself.
G.B. Shaw:
Man and Superman

Introduction

The politics of Sudan, even in the non-Islamic fundamentalist sense, has developed as a religious affair. Antagonism to the pseudo-religious influences on politics became a main feature of Northern Sudan politics and added an infectious dimension to the country's crisis. It also provided in the post-independence era an added impetus for political agitation in the South. But the influence of religion over politics until the mid-1960s was of a very special character in view of the unique nature of Sudan's popular Islam. Sudan's brand of Islam evolved as a blend of Islamic normative ideals tempered by the cultural essence of tribal Africa. It has often been said that the Sudanese have taken Islam and adapted it to their own circumstances. This owes a great deal to the way the indigenous tribes were Islamized in the North, i.e. Nubia and Beja land. Over centuries Muslim nomads, traders and holy men, migrated from Arabia into Sudan either for preaching purposes or seeking greener pastures. Through those migrants the Islamic empire was able to achieve peacefully what it failed to achieve militarily when its attempt to conquer Dongola was foiled. The migrants – particularly traders and nomads – moved further south into the more verdant and water-rich riverain Sudan where they implanted their language and culture, leaving behind them areas closer to home across the Red Sea (Beja land) and Egypt (Nubia). This explains why the Nubians and Beja managed to keep intact their indigenous cultures and languages. It also accounts for the spilling back of Arabo-Islamism from the centre to its points of entry, rather than flooding out from the north and east to the centre. In the riverain North, however, migrant Arabs did not overthrow the socio-cultural structure, as they had indeed 'turned it inside out'.[1] Arabic language became the *lingua franca* that enabled disparate ethnic groups to communicate with each other and trade with the outside world (which was at that time mainly limited to Egypt and Arabia). It also put them in the way of reading and understanding the Qur'an, the holy book of the new faith. Inescapably, with language came value systems and cultural patterns. Moreover, Arab migrants married into, and lived among, Nubian communities and embedded Islamic values and rites into the culture of those communities, though they left the core communal values intact. In the process, Islam supplanted traditional cultures, but by no means did it efface them. Soupçons of those cultures that are easily traceable in enduring practices of Muslim Sudanese, clearly indicate that Islam was cast in a mould other than that of the Middle East. In a manner, Sudanese popular Islam was virtually paganized by Hamitic and Negro-Hamitic traditions to the extent of claiming that there was a lot in it that was decidedly non-Arabic, sometimes non-Islamic.[2]

The most durable institution of Sudanese Islam, is the Sufi [3] orders or *'turuq'* (religious sects, sing. *tariqa*). The sufists (otherwise known as *fuqara*, i.e. ascetics)[4] played a much more significant role in the spread of Islam than the *fuqaha* (learned men) whose dry casuistic and scholastic approach to religion was less appealing to the average Sudanese. In effect, popular mysticism became more of a binding force of Muslim unity than the teachings of the *fuqaha*. The *turuq,* however, developed into something more than a religious phenomenon; they became institutions of social organization to the point of replacing tribal allegiance in terms of personal identification. Whereas in other African countries the tribe provided the nucleus around which political consciousness was consolidated, in Sudan the Sufi orders had served the same function, and to a large measure, in a pan-tribal manner. No such process of integration existed in the South, even though Christianity could have expectedly produced a pan-tribal affiliation among its Southern adherents. However, in view of its own denominational cleavages and the restriction of Christianization to elitist groups within the community, tribal affiliations persisted. The *turuq* were also personalized religious fiefs that coalesced around a founder and carried his name. The loyalty of the faithful was thus transmitted to his heirs from generation to generation in such a way as to preserve the integrity and sanctity of the founder's family. This had been the case even with religious fraternities that adjured the sufist *turuq* like Mahdism. Actually, the Mahdi himself did not establish a dynastic order,[5] but his posthumous son and successor, Abdel Rahman, initiated this process that was persevered after his death.

Of interest to this study are the two dominant sects, the *Khattmiyya*, founded by Sayyid Muhammed Uthman al Mirghani (Senior) in the sixteenth century, and the *Ansar*, the successors of the Mahdi who developed into a *quasi tariqa,* despite their professed anti-Sufi origin. During the Turco-Egyptian rule, the *Khattmiyya* fraternized with the new Muslim rulers, a matter that did not endear them to the Mahdists. As a result, they were maligned and run down by the *Mahdiyya*. With the triumphant Anglo-Egyptian forces, the *Khattmiyya* mandarins returned to Sudan. That did not mean that the new colonial power was enthused with them. In reality it set sheikhs of other *turuq* to keep an eye on them.[6] But, given their anti-Mahdist stance, the *Khattmiyya* enjoyed some favour and recognition by the authorities. Besides, the sympathies of the *Khattmiyy*a with Egypt did not abate at a time when the Madhists were apprehensive of that country's claims of sovereignty over Sudan.

As a result of the differences in outlook, and the persecution of the *Khattmiyya* during the Mahdist State in the 1880s, intense rivalry has characterized the discourse between the two groups and bedeviled Sudan with futile adversarial politics. One notable difference between the two sects, though, was the way they had approached politics. While, on the one hand, the Mahdists endorsed and sustained political groups that supported Sudan's independence, they continued to predicate their politics on the glory of the *Mahdiyya*. The *Khattmiyya,* on the other, 'left the sphere of central political organization separate', and only gave the order's political sustenance to the party of their choice.[7] Another observation that needs to be made is that the bulk of the agitation against colonialism and most of the processes of political organization took place in the North within the confines of this Northern politico-religious agenda; the South, till 1956, was in a state of political insomnolence.

Pseudo-intellectual Origins of Sudanese Nationalism

The First World War was a waymark in the political development of Sudan. First, it signalled the beginnings of nationalist awakening amongst the intelligentsia. Second, it ushered a turning point in the fortunes of the sects; a change in fortunes that was to greatly give them economic, and therefore, more political clout. As indicated earlier, Britain fought on opposite sides with Turkey and as a strategy of war, the Turks tried to incite an Islamic rebellion against it. Given that the *Ansar* were the more mobilizable and, in the eyes of the colonial administration, the more dangerous of the sects, the colonial administration was apprehensive of Sayyid Abdel Rahman, though at the time, he was lying low in view of the odds stacked against him. Nonetheless, in the words of a Sudan political historian, the British were not very sure, given the fanaticism of al Mahdi's supporters and their understandable animosity towards the new regime, whether his son was 'a respected and valued leader of Sudanese opposition or an interloper, a charlatan, a secret revolutionary'[8] On the other side, since the *Ansar* were traditional foes of 'Egyptian' occupation, the British had no alternative but to court their leader. So ultimately he was allowed back to Gezira Aba, the cradle of Mahdism and encouraged to engage in cotton growing.

As the *Ansar's* leader prospered, so did his influence, leading the British to resort to their famed divide and rule tactics in order to contain him. The *Khattmiyya* and their leader Sayyid Ali al Mirghani, were thus reinvigorated and his supporters, within the merchant class, were kept in good humour so as to neutralize the growing influence of al Madhi. In consequence, the *Ansar* prospered in agriculture, the *Khattmiyya* in trade and commerce. Al Mirghani himself was awarded one of the highest decorations of the Empire, the CMG. According to Cromer, he was 'highly gratified at the distinction' and expressed 'appreciation for what Britain has done for the welfare of Sudan.'[9] Al Mahdi, too, was later to be knighted by the British Crown as a sign of esteem. That was a far cry from the bestial vindictiveness with which Kitchener treated his father's remains, probably in revenge for Gordon's killing.[10] In return, al Mahdi donated his father's sword of victory to the British sovereign as an expression of fealty to the British throne.[11] In this process of enticing old foes, the son of Khalifa Abdullahi (heir of the Mahdi) was also drawn to the Governor-General's court as an *aide de camp* (ADC). This backhanded appraisal of old foes prompted Winston Churchill's caustic remark: 'Wonderful are the ways of England, the son of the Mahdi is knighted for his services to the Empire, and the son of the Khalifa is made the *aide de camp* of the Governor General.' In reality, Britain's policy of divide and rule was more exemplified by such sordid wiles in the North, than in manoeuvres to create fissures between the North and South as Northern political commentators often assume. Notwithstanding, the power that was acquired by the traditional elite (sectarian leaders and tribal chiefs orbiting around them) firmly consolidated their influence. The principal tool of that influence – in addition to religious dominance – was control of the means of production (land and cattle) as well as proximity to the colonial authority.

By the 1940s, the North, through its wealthy and unifying *tariqas*, was able to express itself politically with considerable homogeneity and impact. In an aberrant way, the divisive *turuq* were the midwife of this budding homogeneity that transcended tribal allegiances. The *turuq* in the beginning did not form political parties; instead they offered patronage (and the brawn) to sections of the intelligentsia who were the brains behind the nationalist movement. Still, parties became sectarianized political outfits and pawns of the two adversarial sects. The intelligentsia had thus deprived itself from what other national liberation movements gave to their nations: national consolidation around a common cause, shared common national symbols and a common nationalist outlook. Within the intelligentsia, the graduates of the Gordon Memorial College provided the intellectual drive for the burgeoning nationalism. That was to have an enduring effect on Sudan's political development.

In keeping with the traditionally divided (both in sectarian and colonial allegiance) nature of Sudanese politics, there were expectedly two embryos of nationalism since the 1920s. Those took the form of study groups in Omdurman, one the *Abu Rouf* (with its satellite in Medani), the other the *al-Murada-Hashmab*.[12] The *Abu Rouf* group shared a common *Khattmiyya* background, were anti-British and pro-Egyptian. Their nationalism was Arabo-Islamic and completely oblivious to other strands of Sudanese culture, including those that gave to Sudan's Arabo-Islamism its peculiarly home-grown character. *Al-Murada-Hashmab* group, on the other hand, was more racially diversified, had anti-sectarian leanings and advocated a Sudanese nationhood, separate from Egypt. But despite its multi-racial composition, that school had manifestly failed to transcend the racist prejudice of Northern intellectuals towards their 'non-Arab' comrades.[13]

It is from this manner of groups that Sudan's traditional political parties sprang. The group that favoured a Sudanese nation separate from Egypt gravitated towards the *Ansar* and together formed the Umma party; the pro-Egyptian group sought the patronage of al Mirghani and formed the *Ashiqqa* party and its coalition partners. However, the sectarian alignments of the intelligentsia were not as cut and dried as it appeared. For example, the migration of the *Ashigga* from one Sayyid to the other revealed a different story. It was not only political persuasion that inspired the alignments of the intelligentsia with this or that sect, political expediency also had a role and an important role for that matter.[14] Albeit with a little pushing from Egypt, all pro-unity groups coalesced prior to independence to form the National Unionist Party (NUP), while the independentists tilted basically towards the Umma.

In spite of the improbity inherent in their meanderings between the two sects, the intense desire of some of the Northern intelligentsia to infuse an intellectual content unto the hitherto inane Northern politics should not be minimized. Whether they succeeded in that or not is a different matter. It has also been assumed that due to their shallow formal education, the intelligentsia of that era were unable to formulate a cogent political agenda that could have gone beyond sectarian rivalry and age-old prejudices, particularly that clashes among them were broadly around personalities more than ideas. Undeniably, the formal education system at that period was geared towards satisfying colonial penetration by providing low- and middle-level cadres. Still, it would be unfair to condemn totally the product of that education; for in spite of the limited formal education of the intelligentsia, that groups also included high-minded self-educated intellectuals and service-oriented government functionaries whose integrity in governance was a byword in all Sudanese quarters. Regrettably, that moral integrity was not matched by political vision or managerial elan.

In addition, almost all of the leaders of that era were not sufficiently exposed to the wider world, and certainly not at all to African cultures and realities. Hence, regardless of their intellectual savvy, a large number of them entertained basically racist views on Africa. Those views either emanated from distorted and confining European images of Africa or from condescending Arab perceptions of the black man reflected in classical Arabic works. To the Europeans, 'the ill-digested Darwinian theories were assumed to confirm that Africans were backward people who had a lot of evolving to do before they approached European standards of civilization'.[15] Apparently, the intelligentsia of the day held this to be a god-given truth. As for the manner in which the 'Sudan' (blacks) were mentally mapped by earlier Arab geographers, this was invariably based on conjectural judgements by Arab geographers and historian, never empirical knowledge. The 'Sudan' described by Arab geographers was not a disaggregated quantum;[16] it included the *Zang* (Negroes) – the name given by Arabs and Persians to the natives of East Africa and generally to Bantu-speaking peoples of the continent – the *Habbasha* (Ethiopians) and Nubians. This perception was not limited to Arab geographers; also renowned scholars like Ibn Khaldoun shared the same vision.[17] Moreover, major works of Arabic literature – including the classical Arabic corpus poeticum – abound with demeaning descriptions of blacks.[18] That some Northern Sudanese intellectuals of the pre-independence era brooked such vision of the black man was ludicrous beyond measure. Dark pigmentation and Negroid features are not limited to purely African Sudanese; many Arabicized Northerners share those 'demeaning' attributes.[19]

According to this obtuse vision, non-Arabicized 'African' Sudanese were generally not viewed as other human beings endowed with their own cultural traits and social mores, but assumed to be untamed primitives with a prelogical mentality. This perception applied to the majority of the racially non-Arabicized blacks, though it was not as acrid and unsavoury when it related to those among them who became Islamized. In all likelihood, Southern non-Arabs and non-Muslims were presumed to be positively lacking in the cognitive skills of other humans. Accordingly, their 'big brother' in the North believed that it was incumbent on him to save them. This patronizing attitude might have been guided (indeed misguided) by a desire to uplift the 'primitive' brothers. But what the patronizers missed was that people generally take pride in their culture, irrespective of the worth given to it by others. Surprisingly, this patronizing attitude is typical to that fostered by colonialists towards Africa; for nowhere in the world did colonialists so affirmatively rationalize colonialism on account of the cultural inferiority of the colonized, than in Africa; not in India, the Middle East, China or Latin America.

From those derogatory assumptions about African culture, even otherwise forward-looking elements within the Northern intelligentsia were not free. Some of them had the temerity to reflect this racist disposition in print with an unfeigned sense of pride. One of those was Khidir Hamad, a veteran independence fighter, the bard of the national struggle and a luminary of the 'progressive' *Abu Rouf* School. In his memoirs, published ten years after his death, Hamad recounted an unblushing story that took place during his visit to Mecca in 1954 as *amir alhaj* (leader of pilgrims).[20] Hamad remarked that his main concern during that visit was to explain to the Saudis the difference among the pilgrims he was escorting, between the Sudanese Arabs and the *takarna*[21] (the name given in Sudan to Nigerian Muslims who settled in Sudan). Obviously, the Saudi's could not see a visible difference between the two and Hamad, as he conveyed in his memoirs, was very much aggravated by their lack of discrimination. He also claimed that such confusion would not have happened were it not for the 'imperialists' who granted the *takarna* Sudanese pilgrimage passports.

The *takarna* were not only Africans, they were also Muslims and, therefore, shared the same religion with their Sudanese deprecator. Islam, therefore, should have brought them closer to Northern Sudanese Arabo-Muslims because it did not distinguish between its adherents on the basis of ethnic origin. Besides, since the *takarna* assumedly shared with the North elements of the mainstream Islamic culture, their subculture should not have been an impediment to their integration in a Muslim community or to their recognition by Sudanese Muslim intellectuals as equals. But as one scholar maintained, 'in Sudan it may be difficult to justify the notion of a West African subculture as an existing entity distinct from the mainstream culture which is the contrasting pole by which other subcultures are defined'.[22] The scholar aptly stated that in Sudan there was a different perspective of culture apart from Islam which excluded Nubas, Nubians, Equatorians, Nilotics; 'its context is inescapably racist'.[23] As a result of this bias even new generations of the *takarna* who were eventually integrated in the Sudanese society through upward social mobility and occupied high places in society, including membership of parliament, had to assume a counterfeit Arab lineage so as to hide their original identity.[24]

Evidently, this level of asinine racism could have been tolerated if it came from the average unlettered Northerner, not when it issued from those who were held to be the *crème de la crème* or what the British called *la jeunesse dor'ee* (the gilded youth). Furthermore, Hamad was not only a minister in a number of post-independence cabinets, he was also a member of the Supreme Council (Head of State) of Sudan. In that capacity he should have participated in the meetings of the OAU Summit, the highest instance of the African organization. Sadly, his views were no less contemptuous of African people than those of any European supremacist. Such a level of racism betrayed a crassness preposterous in its proportions, for how could any right-thinking person pass a wholesale judgement on any people, solely on account of their ethnic origin, let alone when those people belonged to a country that had produced to Africa some its best men of letters, economists, musicians and soldiers. Even Lord Lugard was much kinder to that country. As we shall have occasion to illustrate later, many North Sudanese intellectuals were hard put to reconcile their disdainful attitude towards their non-Arab co-citizens, with their ardent desire to play a leadership role in Africa's renaissance. The Sudan thus gained her place in the family of nations weighed down by a heavy sectarian baggage, useless political rivalry and a culturally insular political elite.

Precipitate and Ill-fated Unification: 1945 – 1953

At the end of the Second World War, the Sudan had thus been administered as two separate countries. It wasn't a situation much to the liking of the Northern political elite. Indeed, the Graduates' Congress, in its famous memorandum of 1942,[25] called for the repeal of the Closed Districts Ordinance, the opening up of the South to the North, the standardization of the education system in the country and finally granting the Sudanese the right of self-determination. In view of the above, the Graduates' Congress was by some commentators accused of flirting with the idea of 'ruling the South as part of the North and expanding Islam and Arab influence into Central Africa'.[26] Why was it so? And why did the Congress, which was modeled on the Indian Congress,[27] fail to take a leaf from Nehru's book on national cohesion? The failure of the Congressists was all the more surprising when we know that the issue of national identity or 'Sudanism', as they called it, was high on their agenda.

The Congress was born on the 12 February 1938, when one thousand one hundred and eight high school 'graduates'[28] (a high number of educated Northern Sudanese by the tally of those days) met in Omdurman to launch that association as a vehicle for national struggle, as well as an engine for industrial action. Unerringly, one of the first things the Congressists called for was the abdication of tribal allegiances and the espousal of only one loyalty; that to Sudan. In a message to the Congress one of its adherents wrote: 'is it not time to assert ourselves as Sudanese and be proud of our Sudanism? The countries of the world are divided into an India, a China and an Egypt. Citizens of those countries are called Indians, Chinese and Egyptians. You and I are Sudanese and this is our Sudan. If we are not Sudanese, what are we then?'[29] In a more pointed remark another Congressist said: 'You son of Halfa, you descendant of the *Ja'aliyeen*, you son of the South, you all have the right to be proud of your ancestral homes, but do not forget that you live in the land of Sudan. Declare it now that you belong to one nationality and are but one thing, Sudanese.'[30] Though John Garang may not have had access to the records of that era of Sudan's history, it strikes one's notice that he has repeated the same argument at Koka Dam in support for his call for Sudanism. Thus, the issue of 'Sudanism' as an identity surpassing tribal, ethnic, cultural and religious divides was very much in the minds of Congressists. In effect even the question of slavery as a 'black spot in the history of Sudanese nationalism that must be erased' was out in the debate.[31]

It would appear that the Congressists as thinkers had got it right, but not so as political practitioners. In reality, they got it wrong all the way. To the mind of the Northern intellectuals of that era, Sudanism was what they assumed it to be: Northern subnationalism imposing its will on other Sudanese nationalities including those who were neither Arab nor Muslim. In this fashion, the multi-ethnic, multicultural and multi-religious Sudan was reduced to a geographical state without a nation. The process of nation building (indeed the concept of a nation itself) is problematic. Nations are not natural organic institutions but, to a great extent, are imagined ones. At the same time, there is no nation in the world that is a totally homogenous mass. But whatever way one may look at it, the creation of a nation presupposes awareness by people within a defined territory of the existence of a national bond, put otherwise, of a national consciousness. Professor Kellas defines a nation as a 'group of people who feel themselves to be a community bound together by ties of history, culture and common ancestry'.[32] Kellas also classifies nations as ethnic nations (which presumably qualify for his above-mentioned definition of a nation) and social nations, i.e. nations that comprise more than one ethnic group.[33] But Kellas's view on ethnic nations, which seems plausible enough, may be a recipe for disaster in supposedly ethnic nations, if ethnicity is only limited to that of the dominating majority group. This may be true of countries like Sudan where the dominant ethnic group is interspersed with a medley of other ethnic groups, or where ethnic groups have divergent views about the historical processes that had produced the country's assumed ethnic identity. For, unlike race which is based on inborn physical characteristics, ethnicity is culturally determined through historical processes. That is probably why Kellas's definition was challenged by other scholars like Parekh who argued that neither collectively agreed upon national goals nor a uniform view of history were necessary for building a nation. The first, he said, was subject to dispute and constant redefinition; the second was necessarily open to divergent narratives and interpretations and likely to prove divisive.[34] Moreover, there is always an element of choice and voluntarism in nation formation. For unity to be viable, it has to be predicated on free will and choice. In effect, even scholars who strenuously pleaded for nation building through a strategy of modernization and social mobilization (as the Northern intelligentsia sought to do in the pre-independence era), had their misgivings about the success of this strategy. Karl Deutsch, the foremost advocate of this strategy,[35] qualified his opinions about modernization and communication as tools of national cohesiveness. He maintained that while the process of social mobilization might promote the consolidation of states whose people already share the same language, culture and major social institutions, the same process would 'strain or destroy the unity of states whose population was already divided into several groups with different languages or cultures and basic ways of life'.[36]

Clearly, the intelligentsia's mental image of the socially less-developed ethnic groups of Sudan was that of backward tribes who do not qualify for being treated as nationalities. Tribalism is, of course, the appellation frequently given by Western scholars and colonial administrators to African ethnic conglomerations and invariably accompanied by regressive connotations. Within the parameters of this categorization, those conglomerations are not assumed to represent separate nations or even potential nations. Credibly, self-contained and highly structured ethnic groups like the Hausa in Nigeria, the Dinka in Sudan and the Zulu in South Africa may be considered embryonic nations or, as Connor maintains, symbolize potential nations in and by themselves.[37] However, in all Africa, whenever such ethnic groups

47

encountered a more powerful culture, e.g. Christianity or Islam, they either accepted a selective assimilation into that culture (espousing some features of the powerful culture and merging them with their own), or reacted, in the face of attempts to impose forcibly the powerful culture, by asserting their weaker culture. Also, as many experiences in Africa had proven, attempts to encompass diverse tribes/nationalities in a powerful culture without a mechanism to tone down primordial allegiances in favour of a wider allegiance, or to address legitimate concerns of those nationalities, proved counterproductive.

Even so, the unity of the diverse people of Sudan would not have been a problem were those clamouring for it – indeed going to war to achieve it – were heedful to, or aware of, those intricacies. Admittedly, Arabo-Islamism was a nucleus around which socio-cultural cohesion in the North was achieved. But the grand Sudan that Northern leaders spoke boastfully of was not only made of Arabs and Muslims. *Al Fajr*, the mouthpiece of one of two intellectual study groups, had no doubt as to what Sudanese nationalism was. A Sudanese researcher quoted the following revelatory statement from that journal describing the conditions for consolidating national unity: 'Belonging to the country, *rewriting* [emphasis by the author] Sudan's history so as to cleanse it from flawed notions, upholding the pillars of religion, shunning tribalism and parochialism and attending to Arab language with a view to ensuring its supremacy over all other languages'.[38] The researcher pertinently maintained that postulating a national identity on the unity of religious faith and racial pre-eminence was faulty to the extreme. In effect, such theses, according to the researcher, betrayed a desire to rationalize the politico-economic hegemony of a certain group over the rest of the community.[39]

Because of this intellectual and political inadequacy we are still left uncertain as to who the Sudanese are. 'Who are the Sudanese then?' The issue, in effect, is not what shall the answer to the question be, but that the question is at all asked after forty years of independence. However, this question was recently posed by a scholar steeped in the study of Sudan's history.[40] The nonplussed scholar was searching for the identity of this 'new man', the Sudanese, who was neither Arab nor African. Evidently, he was Sudanese but that truism was less obvious to many Northern Sudanese elitists. As for the 'son of the South' who should have been proud to assert his Sudanism within the lines defined by the Congressists in 1939, he might still have no other response to the question whether he was Sudanese, than saying: 'Maybe one day.'

At the level of practical politics, the insensitivity of the emerging political class, even towards non-Arab Sudanese who have culturally identified themselves with that class, was unconscionably perverse. From 1938 to 1944) the Congress was run by a committee of sixty drawn from amongst the educated elite who served in government offices, liberal professions or trade. Throughout the six years of the life of the Congress, not a single member was chosen to the high instances of that body from the South, the West, the Nuba Mountains or, more importantly, from among the sons of assimilated ex-slaves.[41] The absence of Southerners within the Congress power structures was of course comprehensible in view of the colonial education and administration policies which made of Sudan two countries for all practical purposes, but this was not the case with the descendents of former slaves, of whom many were active participants in the national struggle and literary debate circles. In the language of that day (and probably of some today) leadership in this titular nation was reserved to *awlad al balad*[42] (sons of the homeland), a term laden with a myriad of racial overtones. As likely as not, the descendants of ex-slaves must have belonged to another homeland.

Sequels of Military Slavery

The evolution of the institution of military slavery to which reference was made in the previous chapter is of great significance for three reasons: first, to better understand the phenomenon of slavery. Second, to disambiguate Northern attitudes towards the assimilated descendants of slaves. And third, to illustrate the tortuous process of socialization through which that group had to go in the North. The presence of large contingents of demilitarized ex-slaves within the North brought both groups closer in greater numbers, often in conflictual situations. Why was it so? According to a discerning Northern scholar, military slavery created a Southern Sudanese diaspora with far reaching implications on North–South relations involving issues of class, ethnicity and culture.[43] But despite its significance to North–South relations, the subject of military slavery and its sequels (especially as exhibited in the morphology of human settlements in Northern cities and the attitudes of Northern communities to those settlements) received little attention in earlier academic discourses. Johnson, who immensely contributed to lifting the veil of mystery from this subject, stated that both the 'geographical spread of Sudanese military slavery and the sensitivity of the subject in the Sudan, and in other African countries, have inhibited a comprehensive study and an appreciation of the importance of this institution in the formation of colonial states'.[44]

The first signs of conflict appeared during the colonial period when the military slaves (renamed 'enlisted blacks' by Slatin Pasha) were disbanded after the conquest. The released soldiers and officers were allocated (for ease of control) special residential precincts outside major towns. Those 'ghettos' became known as *radifs* (appendages or adjuncts) or *malakiyya* (civilian) quarters and provided the nucleus for urban centres in the South. In the North, those ghettos were soon to become sanctuaries for runaway slaves and sources for cheap domestic and agricultural labour. By 1923, according to Daly, there were 35 colonies of ex-slaves retired from the army in Kordofan, Nuba Mountains, White Nile and the Funj.[45] But in view of prevailing poverty and the squalid conditions under which the ex-slaves lived, the ghettos degenerated into hotbeds for crime. In segregating the two communities, apparently, the British sought to achieve two things: first to hinder assimilation of the so-called enlisted blacks into the Northern society, and second, to protect that society from a subculture which they, as much as the Northern Sudanese, did not hold in great esteem.[46] Because of their distinctness from the society around them and the disdain with which both the society and the colonial rulers treated this group, the ex-slaves became doubly vulnerable. But in spite of this vulnerability, they were able to leave their mark on Northern society in different spheres. Apart from their contribution to the economy of the North, they also left an unmistakable mark on the Northern town culture. This was particularly reflected in the field of music, both through military-based melodies (*Kingi* and *Birinji* music) and traditional African *tam tam* known in Northern Sudan as *tum tum*.[47] They, too, were influenced by the Northern culture (religion, language and attire), and some of them settled for the patriarchal protection of their masters and adopted their names. This patriarchal adoption, however, did not carry with it any rights, e.g. right of the inheritance, while the adopted sons continued to do menial duties within the families that had adopted them. That was of course a choice of last resort by people who were affrighted of being lost in a strange environment.

Public feelings towards ex-slaves in Northern towns, however, were never convivial; they ranged from disdain (the master–slave syndrome) to fear and phobic unease. This unease increasingly diminished as a result of the integration of the descendants of former salves in Northern society and their increasing social upward mobility within that society. In time, the slave soldiers and their descendants became fully northernized: they adopted Islam and Arabic culture and completely abandoned their ancestral beliefs, cultures and behaviour patterns. Some of them contributed immensely to the political and cultural lives of the country and could have been role models for others, if Arabism was solely considered to be a tag for cultural identification and not an issue of pedigree. In all probability that was why the descendants of slaves at that time were never fully recognized in the Northern Sudanese political establishment despite their cultural assimilation. Their curse was evidently their ethnic origin.

Decidedly, the policy of cantonment of people according to their ethnic origin spoke volumes of the way the British treated the two Sudans. But, on their side, Northerners also perpetuated that fictions differentiation based on racial origin for their own utilitarian ends. That was mentally to relegate groups defined by their ethnic origin to a position of enslavability. Those mental image, as we shall elaborate, were sustained by the mythologization of pedigree as a medium of domination and by ideologies that defined who was free and who was enslaveable. The 'enslavable' ineluctably retreated into ethnic-based political organizations, not only in the South but also within the North itself. Anomalously, the descendants of slaves who lived in the North were not only subject to Northern condescendence, they were equally looked at with suspicion by their own kith and kin in the South.

As a result, the descendants of ex-slaves, in the run-up to self-government, chose to create their own political party, portentously called, *al Kutla al Sawda 'a* (the black bloc). Their mouthpiece was a weekly named *Afriqia* (Africa). The *Kutla* was led by a group of retired officers and professionals of non-Arab stock whose forefathers originated from the South, the Nuba Mountains and Dar Fur.[48] The first meeting of the group took place in 1942 and was attended by 3,000 participants (more than twice those who launched the Graduates' Congress). That meeting resolved to create the Sudanese Unity Cooperative Society within the Cooperative Societies Ordinance, since the colonial administration refused to recognize them as a political party. The *Kutla* was thus registered as a voluntary social organization engaged in the promotion of the welfare of its members. Even so, the group was condemned by *awlad al balad* as a 'racist' conspiracy hatched by colonialists, notwithstanding the fact that the colonial administration withheld recognition from that group as a political party just like similar groups from the North. Eventually the *Kutla* emerged, six years later (1948), as an organization dedicating itself to strengthening national unity, eliminating distinctions among Sudanese and ensuring social justice for its supporters.

One of the social issues that tormented this group was the humiliating activities which its members were called upon to undertake. Admittedly, the allocation of menial tasks to endogamous casts is not limited to the North. For instance, iron mongery is a job that the Dinkas disdain and relegate to 'inferior' bantu tribes. But this, by any stretch of imagination, cannot be compared to dehumanizing *metiers* like the scavenging of human faeces from public and private latrines. Like the *Dalits* (untouchables) in India, this job was accorded in Sudan to the Nuba since the colonial days. The practice continued throughout the post-independence era up to June 1969 when it was stopped by Nimeiri's government as a dehumanizing activity. There was thus a crying need for social organizations to attend to the concerns of those 'wretched' groups. The Northern elite, however, only saw in the emergence in their midst of such organizations a conspiracy to derail the 'democratic' process. Verily, the attitude of the Northern political class towards the *Kutla* was induced by two factors, both discreditable. The first was their belief that the nationalities the *Kutla* claimed to represent comprised the very people the parties took for granted as a strategic reserve for party support in the impending elections. Any attempt to stir the political senses of that quiescent human mass was not looked at favourably by those who benefited most from their passivity. Second, there was a total ignorance by that class – professedly committed to 'democracy' – of the real meaning of democracy. Democracy is not about repeating a smattering of constitutional democracy speeches, nor does it stop at institutions and procedures. Above all, the kernel of democracy is respect for the dignity of man. So, the imperviousness of the political class to the social woes and dehumanization of ill-used groups living in Northern ghettos, revealed a gross ignorance of the inner meaning of democracy.

The attitude of the Indian Congress towards the downtrodden could, once again, have been instructive to those who claimed to have taken the political experience of that country for a gospel. One of the first decisions taken by the Indian fathers of independence was to abolish the caste system which originated three centuries before independence and was enshrined in Hindu scriptures. To be sure, the institution persists up till today in India, particularly in so far as the *dalits* are concerned. However, the Indian fathers of independence could take pride in having officially abolished the system and promulgated laws and devised policies to uplift those who suffered under it. That India, 50 years after independence, had elevated a *dalit* to be President of the Republic told its own tale about the high-mindedness of India's fathers of the nation. Addressing the Indian nation at the fiftieth anniversary of independence, President Narayan (a *dalit* himself) said that without improving the conditions of that group, democracy in India would be 'like a palace built on a dung heap'. Collectors of human excrements in Sudan were certainly not in the same predicament of the *dalits* in India where the higher castes went into rites of purification as a result of touching any of them. Nevertheless, that would not make the moral insensibility by Khartoum governments to this phenomenon up to 1969 pardonable. And positively not when Revd Phillip Abbas Ghabboush, the elderly Nuba leader, relished in calling his people in election rallies *Ya bitaeen al alta* (Ye, scavengers of excrements). By such demeaning description, Ghabboush was evidently trying to work his constituency into a passion. For all this, it is not unfair to say that, from its inception, Sudan's democracy was built on a 'dung heap' which that the ruling elite either refused or failed to see.

Appeasement of the North

Howbeit, the Sudan government moved to appease the Congressists by creating an Advisory Council for Northern Sudan (ACNS) to counsel Sudanese on the running of the state. From that council the South was excluded. Instead of assuaging the fears of the Northern intelligentsia, this decision convinced them further that the Colonial government was determined to split Sudan. The creation of the ACNS came at a time when colonialism was beginning to be perceived as an outdated institution and when calls for self-determination and freedoms of peoples were on the ascendancy. Britain, broke and exhausted after the war, was preparing her colonies for independence. Clearly, the moment had come when Britain had to reach a final determination on the fate of the Sudan.

In 1945, Sir Douglas Newbold, the Civil Secretary presented the Governor General's Council with a set of options:

i.   Unification of the South and North,
ii. Annexation of the South to East Africa, and
iii. A compromise of the two above options involving a division of the South between the North Sudan and East Africa.

The feeling was that the first would be the better option owing to the reluctance of East African administrators to take on the problems of the South, as well as opposition to such a plan within the Sudan and by Egypt. Things would of course have been different were it not for the Egyptian factor.[49] The British administrators were also aware that the South was too poor to stand alone as a separate nation, a matter they well knew since they did nothing to develop it socially and economically. This turn of events was unequivocally expressed by Sir James Robertson in response to a question raised at the Sudan Administration Conference (SAC) as to Britain's attitude towards the South. 'The policy of the Sudan Government,' said Robertson, 'is that Southern Sudanese are distinctly African and negroid but that geography and the economy combine (so far as can be seen at the present time) to render them inextricably bound for future development to the Middle Eastern and Arabicized North Sudan.'[50] The British equally believed that the North, left to itself, would dominate the South. They therefore entertained very strong feeling that only federalism or regional autonomy of a manner, would safeguard the interests of Southerners.

SAC held its first meeting on 12 June 1946 under the chairmanship of the Civil Secretary, Sir James Robertson, to obtain the views of Sudanese. The British administration interpreted the feelings of this conference to be that the Sudanese favoured a union, and had no desire to see any part of their country annexed into other parts of Africa. The only problem was that the conference brought together colonial administrators and Northern politicians without a single Southerner to represent the feelings of the South. In effect, the decision to unify the Sudan had already been taken and all that the authorities wanted was to have it rubber stamped.[51]

The Juba Conference which succeeded SAC was an important milestone; it brought together for the first time both Northerners and Southerners to deliberate on the unification of the two parts of the country.[52] The Southern representatives aired all Southern known fears (mainly those caused by the traumas of slave trade) and expounded their disquietude about Northern domination, were the British to leave them in the hands of their Northern brothers. Shingetti[53] did more than anybody else to subdue those fears without suggesting specific guarantees to be entrenched in any future Sudanese constitution. But the Southern fears were real; if the doom-laden words of the Southern member, Chief Lado, did not persuade the Northern members of the conference, nothing else would. 'The ancestors of the Northern Sudanese were not peace-loving and domesticated like cows,' said Chief Lolik Lado, and 'the younger generation claims that they mean no harm, but time will show what they will do in fact.'[54] To those qualms only Ibrahim Bedri, among the Northern members, was the most perceptive; he missed nothing. Said he, 'his is a psychological situation, which no verbal appeasement, however solemn, would change'.[55] Bedri was all feeling for Southern susceptibilities and accordingly agreed with the idea of guarantees for the South. Unlike other Sudanese politicians of his time, Bedri was also the most forthright and self-critical of slavery and its impact on the psyche of Southerners. His views on the South were later presented to the Constitutional Amendment Commission and were refreshing in their farsightedness and candour.[56]

Out of the Juba Conference emerged some decisions that had far-reaching impact on the turn of events. The South did not want incorporation in Uganda. In fact it would have been the other way round as South Sudan, whose size was many times larger than that of Uganda, would have swallowed up that country. It also agreed to remain united with the North because that was deemed more advantageous, provided that the terms of unity were not dictated by the North. To that end, the South demanded a guarantee that their wishes would be catered for in any future political arrangement. To enable Southerners to catch up with their brothers in the North, Buth Diu called for the enhancement of the teaching of Arabic.[57]

Regardless, colonial administrators in the South were disturbed by the hasty course of events, believing that Southern interests were being subordinated to Northern pressure. Furthermore, they felt that their views as well as the feelings of the South had not been sufficiently represented at the conference. It has also been argued by some colonial administrators in the South, that the Southern representation at the Juba conference was flawed; the handpicked representatives were accused of being inexperienced and, therefore, susceptible to blackmail and intimidation. Those accusations were not borne out by the records of the meeting. However, we will merely record here that out of the Juba Conference emerged some basic home truths: that the South favoured 'qualified' unity and was afraid of Northern domination and adamant in its demands for safeguards in the form of veto power to be vested in the Governor-General over laws that would be passed by the envisaged Legislative Assembly and which might impinge on the South. The North, on the other hand, was united in its condemnation of such safeguards and it won; no such safeguards were incorporated in the Legislative Assembly Ordinance (1948). The Assembly, which held its first sitting on 15 December 1948, had 76 members of whom 13 were from the South. No sooner had the Assembly met, than the 13 members moved a draft resolution demanding safeguards for the South and arguing for continued British presence until the South was strong enough to stand on its own. The Northern representatives, being in the majority, defeated the motion overwhelmingly.

The Legislative Assembly itself was far from a reflection of the will of the nation; instead it was an expression of its tragic flaws. On the one hand was the North, represented by tribal chieftains and the Umma Party which was calling for independence; the unionists boycotted the Assembly. Even then, the Northern members of the Assembly, like those who boycotted it, were confident of their wit and impatient with the

South's assumed intractability. They manifested a highly developed consciousness and sense of purpose to rid themselves of the British and reclaim virtual dominion over the South. On the other side, was the South, unsure, resentful and frustrated by its inability to influence even its own destiny. Moreover, the processes of independence proceeded along similar lines, the South playing little or no part. Firstly, it was excluded from the handover of power and from the independence negotiations with Egypt. Secondly, the Legislative Assembly, the only forum within which they were represented and had opportunity to express their views and anxieties, was disbanded in October 1952 before completing its mandatory term. Weak as it was, the Assembly was the only political forum available to Southerners in the North. For whatever reason they had to dissolve the Assembly, the British were the first to recognize the problems created by that decision.[58]

However, the exclusion of Southerners from the Cairo negotiations was perhaps the most disastrous decision taken by Egypt and the Northern parties. As a Southern commentator wrote, that decision was the height of irresponsibility; 'What wisdom', said the writer, 'was there in ignoring the wishes and aspirations of people who constituted more than one-third of the whole population and who inhabit approximately one-third of the land?'[59] Consequently, Southerners felt that independence held nothing in store for them, and some thought that they were merely swapping a European colonial master with what they called an 'Arab' one. Today's Southern misapprehensions, real or perceived, have an old pedigree of which the Northern ruling class is comfortably amnesiac.

Towards the close of the 1940s, the rivalry between the British and the Egyptians was at a fever pitch. Britain rushed through with the preparations for independence, no doubt with the intention of circumventing Egyptian claims over the Sudan. In 1947, Egypt took on Britain in the UN and when that bid failed, it abrogated unilaterally the Condominium Agreement of 1889 and the Anglo-Egyptian Treaty of 1936 and declared a constitution for its 'province', the Sudan. The decisions were taken by Prime Minister Mustafa al-Nahas Pasha who, on tabling the constitutional bills before the Egyptian Parliament, said, 'I'd rather have my hand amputated than allow Sudan to be truncated.' The pro-Egyptian elements in Sudan were also actively agitating for 'Unity of the Nile Valley', but Northern politicians, as they were to demonstrate many times later, were a utilitarian breed. They would work together against a common enemy and, given their sectarian-based discordance, work against each other when the enemy was vanquished. As it were, unlike national liberation movements in other countries which emerged as vehicles for the promotion of national integration and the creation of shared values, the Sudanese nationalist movement turned out to be another tool of division in Sudan. In 1951, the Constitution Amendment Committee (CAC)[60] took advantage of the wrangling between Britain and Egypt to demand the resignation of the Governor-General. Its report, which was published on 17 January 1952, became the draft constitution of self-government which the British approved in the same year, but only after removal of the clause on Southern guarantees. That action prompted Buth Diu, the only Southern member of the Commission to withdraw. Obviously, the levity with which Northern politicians took the South for granted reflected their most flagrant lack of vision.

To the North, things took a more favourable turn; King Farouk was deposed and replaced by General Neguib, a half-Sudanese soldier. Neguib had a different way of dealing with the Sudan question. He supported the course of Sudanese independence, no doubt seeing better opportunities for bringing Sudan into Egyptian embrace after the exit of the British. In 1952, he held a meeting with Sudanese political parties in which he formally recognized the Sudanese right to self-determination. The South, we observed, was not represented at that meeting. In February 1953, the Anglo-Egyptian agreement was signed, putting the seal of approval by both colonial partners to Sudanese self-government. The only loser was the South; Article 100 of the Self-government Statute that was intended to provide safeguards for the South was already struck out from the draft agreement. So, not only was the South unrepresented in the Cairo talks that were to determine, among other things, its future, but also the only safeguard it had requested in order for it to join their Northern brothers in the march towards self-determination was removed by the very parties they sought protection from. Understandably, both Egypt and the Northern parties were worried of granting the Governor-General special powers to safeguard Southern interests, lest he would use them to frustrate the self-governance process itself.[61] But other arrangements could have been worked out by the Northern politicians, were they more perceptive of the apprehensions of their Southern 'wards'. Even the modest request proposed by Buth Diu for the creation of a post of Minister for Southern Affairs to be held by a Southerner, was rejected by CAC and the Legislative Assembly. Buth Diu was supported in the Assembly by two Southern members (Zakaria Jambu and Stanislaus Payasama) who toured their constituencies in the South in order to galvanize support for the proposal with a view to briefing the Assembly on the sense of the South[62] regarding the issues under review by that body.

The Northern political class, therefore, not only foundered in laying down firm foundations for the unity of the Sudan for which they had struggled since 1945, but also failed to understand the meaning of consensus politics. The Northern politicians' self-enhancing political rhetoric about majority rule, displayed a sad ignorance of constitutional architecture in countries like Sudan. Constitutions in countries riddled with multiple diversities are not meant to regulate society as it exists, but to define consensus on fundamental issues as a prerequisite for regulating that society. Majoritarian politics, mechanically conceived, is hardly the way to build a nation, since it perpetually puts the minority at the mercy of the majority.

The failure of CAC and the Legislative Assembly was the more disturbing since they had before them Ibrahim Bedri's memorandum, which could have been an excellent point of departure. Bedri had served extensively as an administrator in the South and made his case succinctly at the Juba Conference. But the major Northern parties would not listen. Probably Bedri was deemed a colonialist minion, as the Southern politicians were dismissed as hirelings of the church. Two points were highlighted by Bedri in his memorandum: the first was the traumatizing effect of slavery on Southerners and the obligation on the North to sanitize its past from those odious experiences before it could even think of winning the South. The second was his discerning conclusion that it was not only the South that was disempowered; there were other regions too that need special attention, e.g. the Nuba Mountains, Southern Blue Nile etc. That prescient remark was made over three decades ago, before Garang ventured to articulate the afflictions of the marginalized.

The Northern-dominated institutions of self-government moved quickly to erase the remnants of the Southern Policy; the Executive Council declared its intention to make Arabic the official language of Sudan. Schools were asked to take on Arabic teachers and missionaries were advised to teach that language. The policy was initiated by Abdel Rahman Ali Taha and there was nothing threatening about it since it accorded with the wishes of the Southerners themselves as expounded by Buth Diu at the Juba conference. But, as sure as anything, Buth and those of his mindset believed that teaching Arabic to Southerners was a necessary step to level the ground for Southerners and build their capacity to competitive levels with Northerners, not as a tool of domination. As a scholar aptly said, the use of Arabic as a *lingua franca* is not problematic in daily social life, but it becomes a salient factor in segregational cleavages within the context of the formal national education system in situations where its imposition on the South carries tones of racial supremacy'.[63] The imposition of Arabic, therefore, alongside policies that perpetuated political and economic disempowerment, acquired a life of its own. Regardless, as the cocoon the British had built around it was being cracked, the South began to organize politically. In 1953, the Southern Party was formed, and in 1954, it changed its name to the Liberal Party to give it a less parochial ring. No Northerners joined it, nor were they expected to.

Behind the Scenes
Even on the issue of independence, the British colonial policy was incoherent and muddled to the point that the colonial administration was castigated by both sides. The misapprehensions of the South were angrily expressed by a Southern commentator who submitted that 'the South was crucified by Northern Arabs, and the British played the part of Judas'.[64] The Northerners, on their side, were persuaded completely that the endgame of the colonial administration was to separate the South and frustrate unity with Egypt. This, at best, was a half-truth because, at that

time, Whitehall was ready to abandon the whole of Sudan as part of a grand strategy to appease Nasser, while British administrators in Sudan were dead bent on granting Sudan independence and assuring Southerners of guarantees. The US was the main driving force behind the strategy of appeasement. In one incident Jefferson Caffrey, the US Ambassador to Cairo, was reported to have told his UK opposite number, Sir Ralph Richardson, 'I do not understand why anybody should be bothered about the fate of a ten million niggers;'[65] Caffrey was referring to the totality of the Sudanese population according to that times count, including Northern 'Arabs'. In fact, it was not only the British who were muddled in their Sudan policy; so were the Americans. Quite contrary to Caffrey's racist construct, the State Department maintained after Sudan's declaration of independence, that the 'ten million niggers' had a regional role to play. On the morrow of Sudan's independence, the US Department of State announced that, as a new nation, 'Sudan will be deeply involved in the future cause of Africa and as a Middle East nation too, it will also be a bridge to Africa, importing to it ideas, philosophies and forces which may have great influence on Africa's decisions on its future.'[66] Describing Sudan as a Middle Eastern country was a proposition which could not be readily validated by geography, but the State Department's observation made sense within a geopolitical context.

Hence, whether based on Caffrey's assumption that Sudan was only made of a bunch of expendable 'niggers' who could be sacrificed for the sake of appeasing Nasser and attaining US wider strategic interests in the Middle East, or that of the State Department's strategic vision for the Sudan as a 'Middle Eastern country', that was scarcely the way to oppose unity with Egypt or sever Sudan's umbilical cord with the Arab world. If anything, the US diplomacy had placed Sudan within a broader regional context and imbued it with a mission that it had hitherto failed to fulfil. Notwithstanding, Northern Sudanese and Arab commentators continued to cultivate the myth that colonialists and 'neocolonialists' invariably harboured designs to dismember the Sudan along ethnic and religious fault lines and to bar its unity with Egypt. This is yet another example of the almost congenital delusion of Sudanese Arabists and Arab political commentators about foreign conspiracies; an easy escape route from disciplined political analysis and wholesome self-searching.

In reality, there was no uniform British policy towards unity between Egypt and Sudan. A tearful personal correspondence from Sir James Robertson, the Colonial Civil Secretary who saw Sudan into self-government, tells a curious story.[67] Robertson was obviously bitter that Sudanese politicians whom he considered his proteges or allies against the 'wiles' of Egypt, were now ensnared by Cairo and London. For whatever reasons, London was then ready to 'hand over' Sudan to Egypt. On the other hand, the patronizing colonial administrators in Khartoum, ever protective of their 'wards' against Egypt's 'wooing', were not only struggling against that country; they were also engaged in a rearguard battle against their own bosses at Whitehall. Their motives were more romantic than political, otherwise they would not have fought against their masters in London. The British colonial administrator thought of their Sudanese friends as partners in a common enterprise. In the words of Donald Hawley, a former colonial administrator, 'The stuff of history lay in the human relationships between individual Sudanese and the British.'[68] It is ironical, though, that the very colonial administrators who laboured very hard in the 1930s to create cleavages among sects and tribes in Northern Sudan, ended in the 1950s sponsoring Sudanism; *al Sudan lil Sudanieen* (Sudan for the Sudanese).

Conclusion

The system of dual administration planted the seeds of discord among the two regions that were later to become components of one state. The North and the South had grown separately and unequally during the era of colonization. The riverain North grew as the favoured and domineering segment, while the South was kept subservient, and other non-riverain regions marginalized. Come 1956, and colonialism had gone. The Sudanese were now masters of their fate. To the ruling class in the North who assumed power from the British, as well as to the majority of Sudan's intellectual elite, the Islamization and Arabicization of the South passed as an unquestionable article of faith. In view of other cleavages and historical injustices, that was taken by the Southerners to be equivalent to changing one master with another.

On the other hand, the historical inequalities were also taken for granted by Northern rulers. For many countries in the world, inequality of regions had always been a central issue in the agenda for transformation. For example, in post-colonial India attention to the development of downtrodden castes and marginalized areas was at the top of the priorities of government. Deliberate policies, based on the recognition of cultural, linguistic and social differentiations, were formulated. The extent of attendance to regional inequalities at the time of the creation of a state determines the life span of that state. Also, the adoption of federal systems or the creation of separate sovereign states was generally based on the realization that unequally developed regions made weak components of unitary states and perpetuated the domineering attitudes of colonial masters through the prevalence of dominant tenements over subservient ones.

Failure to attend to these regional inequalities in Sudan marked the second step towards war. Firstly, by virtue of the lack of political development of the South, the heart of the nationalistic drive towards independence rested with the North. That gave Northern politicians an inordinate role in determining the fate of the whole country. Secondly, arising from Anglo-Egyptian rivalry marked principally by an anti-British uprising in 1924 and the subsequent expulsion of Egyptian military personnel and civilian officials from Sudan, Egypt began to demand a renegotiation of its relations with Britain over its condominium authority in, and sovereignty over, the Sudan. This assumption by Egypt of the position of patron for Sudanese independence gave the Northern parties closer to it more clout in the negotiation for independence.

For all that, it was by crafty manipulation of the Anglo-Egyptian rivalry that the Northern elite secured an independent Sudan and dominated the decision-making process during the transitional period before independence. Ismail al-Azhari cultivated Egyptian support to eliminate the British influence in the region and indeed, his transitional government also saw the removal of British administrators from the South. No sooner had the British left Sudan than Azhari showed his real colours as the patron of Sudan's independence from both Britain and Egypt.

ENDNOTES

1. Hassan, Yousif F., *Sudan Notes and Records*, Vol. XLIV, No.44, 1962.

2. Wad Deif Allah, the great chronicler of Sudanese Islam reported numerous incidents where the *fuqaha* permitted custom-based practices that were strictly prohibited by *shari'a*. He also related incidents that revealed that Sudanese Islam of the time was, in his words, 'nominal'. *Tabaqat Wad Deif Allah*

3. *Sufism* is the process of mastering the mind and body to achieve development of man's total being and, in the process, discover God.

4. In Persia and Turkey those spiritual atheletes are denominated as *dervishes*, a term that has a derogatory ring to it to the in Sudanese ears.

5. The first chosen successor of al Mahdi was not one of his kith and kin (Khalifa Abdullahi). Al Mahdi was also reported to have publicly lambasted his relatives *(Ashraf)* for their pervasive corruption.

6. The colonial administration was generally suspicious of all sects, lest a new fundamentalist movement emerged from their belly. Accordingly, the British set the *Khattmiyya* against the independent-minded *Majaz_b* and the *Idrisiyya* sect against the *Khattmiyya*. Referring to the former, Wingate instructed Mr Jackson, the Governor of Dongola, to 'keep them in good humour'. Warburg, G., *Sudan Under Wingate*, p. 107.

7. Shahi, Ahmed al, *Themes from Northern Sudan*, p. 40.

8. Daly, M., *Empire on the Nile (1898-1934)*, p. 18.

9. Letter from Cromer to Queen Victoria, 29 December 1900, FO/633/8 p. 304.

10. In a letter dated 12 March 1899 to Lord Salisbury (P.R.O. Fo/78/5022). Cromer wrote with indignation that Kitchener, before leaving for Fashoda, ordered the destruction of the Mahdi's tomb as a politically adviseable act. 'In Kitchener's absence,' Cromer said, 'the body of the Mahdi was disinterred, the bones thrown into the Nile and the skull handed over to Kitchener for disposal.'

11. Rahim, Adbel, *Imperialism and Nationalism*, p. 97. That act of submission to the colonial sovereign was resoundingly expressed by the two sectrarian leaders alongside a number of religious and tribal dignitaries in a declaration entitled, *sifr al wala'a* (manuscript or *bouquin* of fealty). The dignitaries included Sheikhs El Tayeb Hashim, Mufti of Sudan; Abul Gassim Ahmed Hashim, President of the Board of 'Ulema; Ismail al Azhari, Grand Kadi of Dar Fur and grandfather of former Prime Minister Ismail al Azhari and Mirgahani El Sayed El Mekki, head of *Ismailyya* tariqa. In their message, the dignitaries distanced themselves from the Egyptian uprising against the British and assured the British sovereign of their utmost loyalty to the crown. Ibid., p. 99.

12. See Rahim, Abdel, *Imperialism and Nationalism*, p. 112.

13. For instance, among the most active members of that group were two prominent Arabic-speaking literati (the brothers Mohamed and Abdalla Ashri al Siddiq), who were descendants of ex-slaves that settled in the North. Though both were renowned for their erudition and intellectual profundity, neither of them was deemed worthy for political elevation by the group to the higher structures of the Graduates' Congress.

14. Initially the *Ashigga* sought the support of al Mahdi before changing to their subsequent benefactors, Egypt and al Mirghani. Ahmed Khair, one of the most incisive political historians of the era, accused the *Ashigga* of opportunism. According to him, the *Ashigga* were endowed with two traits: demogogy that enabled them to mobilize the masses, and dictatorship that was reflected in the concentration of absolute power in the hands of the leadership. Khair, A., *Kifah Jeel*, p. 93.

15. African Art, Black Magic, the *Economist*, 24 December 1994.

16. Al Masudi (*Muruj al Zahab;*), Al Idrissi (*Kitab Nuzhat al Mushtag)* and Ibn Batouta (T*uhfat al amsar)* are replete with demeaning descriptions of the Sudan ie. blacks. Abul Fida, the renowned Arab geographer, defined *Bilad al Sudan* as the area that encompassed the 'Nuba (Nubians) on the east of the Nile, Tekrur in the west (actually it referred to Senegal of which Tekrur was only part), Beja lands, Zaghawa (a community that lives in Western Dar Fur and Chad) and Abyssinia. *Taquim al Bildan.*

17. Ibn Khaldoun, the leading classical Arab social historian, maintained in his magnum opus *Diwan al'Ibar* that 'the only people who accept slavery are the *Sudan* (negroes) owing to their low degree of humanity and their proximity to the animal stage'. His views, in essence, were not different from those of classical Greek philosophers who stratified people into masters and those who were inherently enslavable. For example, Aristotle in his Politics justified slavery because 'just as some are by nature free, so others are by nature slaves and for them the condition of slavery is both beneficial and just'. Nonetheless, for the Islamic social historian to approximate human beings to animals, that was astounding since it overstepped the mark established by the *Quran* on equality of men irrespective of their race. Indeed, some to those 'blacks' approximated by Ibn Khaldoun to animals were close disciples of the Prophet.

18. The predominant view of the black man in classical Arabic literature is that of barbarism, crudity and benightedness. This picture proliferates in classical creative prose such as *One thousand and One Nights* and major works of verse. For instance, in one of his most celebrated poems *al Mutanabi* described the Nubian ruler of Egypt, Musky Camphor as follows:

> There the eunuch has become a chieftain of the runaway slaves,
> the free man is enslaved, and the slave obeyed.
> Or his ear bleeding in the hands of the slave broker?
> Or, his worth, seeing that for two farthings he would be rejected.
> Translated by Lewis, B., *Race and Color in Islam*, pp. 78–9.

19. Gregory Kane, an Afro-American journalist who was investigating cases of enslavement of Dinkas by Arab militias in South Sudan, recounted the following revealing anecdote: 'In Sudan all Arabs I saw looked like African-Americans, ranging in complexion from dark brown to light skinned … my colour inspired much merriment among the Dinkas of the South.' The *Baltimore Sun*, 16 June 1996. In all probability the Dinkas mistook Kane for an 'Arab' from the North.

20. Hamad, Khidir, *Al Haraka al Wataniyya lil Sudaniyyn*, op.cit., Warburg, Gabriel, *Discord*, p. 170.

21. The term is derived from *Bilad Tekrur*, the name given by early Arab geographers to a location on River Senegal inhabited by the Fulanis. The *takarna* began settling in Sudan since the days of the Fur Sultanate (the era of Sultan Terab) as the *fuqaha* of the court. Their migration towards central Sudan increased in the begining of the twentieth century. Some chose to settle in Sudan on their way back from pilgrimage to Mecca, seeking job opportunities either as smallholding farmers or landless farm labourers in the Gezira. Others gravitated to Sudan on a *hijra* (religiously ordained flight) following the conquest of their land by the 'infidel' British. Foremost among those was Bello Mai Wurno, the son of Mohamed Attahiru, the Caliph of Sukoto, who fled to Sudan after the defeat of his father by the British. Bello established residence on the Blue Nile near Sennar in a settlement bearing his name and currently known as Mairnu. Duffield, Mark, *Capitalism and Rural Life in Sudan*, p. 1.

22. Yamba, Bawa, *Permanant Pilgrims*, p. 137.

23. Ibid., p. 140; the author made an interesting comparison between the Haussas in Sudan and those in Ibadan, Nigeria. In Sudan, he remarked, they are made to use their Haussaness, not Islam, as a source of cultural identity, unlike in Ibadan where they would say 'we are Muslims and thus Arabs but the Arabs wont accept us, so we must be Haussa'.

24. Of late, Sudanese *takarna* scholars became more open about their identity as well as about the contribution of their community to Sudanese politics and Islam. See Al Tayeb Abdel Rahim al Falatti, *Al Falatta fi Afriqia* and Mohamed Ahmed Badeen, *Al Flatta al Fulaniwoon*

25. Memorandum dated 3 April 1942 and signed by the Congress Chairman, Ibrahim Ahmed.

26. Asseffa, Hizkias, *Mediation and Civil Wars*, p.

27. Both M..A. Mahjoub, *Democracy on Trial*, p. 40 and Ahmed Khair, *Kifah Jeel* affirmed that Sudan's Congressists were illuminated by the Indian

experience. In fact, the Sudanese intelligentsia were greatly stimulated by the Indian struggle against colonialism, particularly Ghandi's peaceful resistance. In structuring the Graduates' Congress, they evidently sought to model the Sudanese national struggle along the lines charted by the Indian Congress. The writings of Nehru (especially his prison letters to his daughter) were frequently read in intellectual study groups. Alas, nothing of Nehru's political pedagogy on national reconciliation, nation formation and respect of cultural diversity, registered in the minds of the father's of Sudan independence.

28. The term graduate is a misnomer since the so-called graduates were all high school leavers.
29. Taha, Faisal A. A., *Al Haraka al Siyassia al Sudaniyya*. Op cit. p. 124
30. Ibid.
31. Khartoum daily, *Al Nil*, 29 April 1939, op cit., in Taha, *Al Haraka al Siyassia*, p. 124.
32. Kellas, James G., Professor of Politics, University of Glasgow, *The Politics of Nationalism and Ethnicity*, p. 8.
33. Ibid., p. 4.
34. Parekh, Bhikhu, Professor of Political Theory, Hull University, *Defining National Identity in a Multicultural society*, in *People, Nation and State: The Meaning of Ethnicity and Nationalism*, p. 66.
35. Deutsch, Karl, *Nationalism and Social Communication*.
36. Deutsch, Karl, *Social Mobilization and Political Development*, p. 501.
37. Connor, Walker, Professor of Political Science, Trinity college, Hartford, Connecticut, *Ethnocentralism: The Quest for Understanding*, pp. 107–8.
38. Haj, Mu'atasim Ahmed el, op. cit., in Qadal, M.S. al, *Al Islam wa'l Siyyasa*, p. 122.
39. Ibid.
40. Collins, *In Search of the Sudanese*, Sudan Studies Association of the US. Collins, who was clearly chagrined by the inability of the Sudanese to discern the obvious, recalled St John de Curvecoeur's question over two centuries ago: 'What is this American? This new man! He is neither European, nor descendant of a European. He is American.'
41. For the composition of the successive congress committees of sixty see Hassabou, Abu, *Factional Conflic*, Annexes.
42. The term was originally used by sedentrized riverain Arabs to distinguish themselves from the Baqqara (relatives and follows of the Khalifa) who were condemned by riverain Sudanese as lawless marauders. Truly, the Baggara fighters exhibited considerable lawlessness during military action in the North; however to condemn a whole group for the mistakes of some of them, bespoke of the racist mindset of their detractors. In fact, the term was coined by some of the Mahdi's relatives (Khalifa Sharif and his associates) who were

loath to see the mantle of power passing from them to an 'unworthy' Baggara, the Khalifa.

43. Sikainga, A.A., Military Slavery and Emergence of a Southern Sudanese Diaspora in North Sudan 1884-1954, in *White Nile, Black Blood*, pp. 23–4.

44. Johnson, Sudanese D. H., *Military Slavery*, p. 144. Thanks to Johnson's pioneering work, the issue of military slavery is now gaining increasing prominence in the literature. Johnson served in the Southern Region, as Deputy Director of Archives in the Ministry of Information and Culture, a position that availed to him records that were hitherto inaccessible to scholars.

45. Daly, *Empire on the Nile*, p. 443.

46. For example, H.C. Jackson, a senior administrator in the early days of the conquest wrote that by giving free rein to ex-slaves, the government would be 'letting loose upon society thousands of men and women with no sense of social responsibility, who would have been a menace to public security and morals'. Jackson, *Behind the Modern Sudan*, pp. 93–4.

47. Sikainga, 42 supra.

48. The *Kutla* was chaired by retired army officer Osman Mutwali, a Dar Furian from the Daju tribe; Zein El Abdin Abdel Tam (of a Dinka father and a Northern mother) was Vice Chairman. Abdel Tam was a retired officer who had close association with Ali Abdel Latif. Others included Dr Mohamed Adam Adham, a medical doctor and son of a retired army officer from Dar Fur and Abdel Nabi Abdel Gadir Mursal, a former army officer descending from a Shilluk father and an Egyptian mother. Mursal was an Arabic-speaking poet of renown. Yoshiko Koreta, Ali Abdel Latif, p. 55.

49. One colonial administrator believed that 'had the Sudan been a colony and not an Anglo-Egyptian Condominium, the splitting of the South in the early years might have been possible'. Bell, Sir Gawain, *Shadows on the Sand*, p. 207.

50. Op.cit., Alier, Abel, *South Sudan*, p. 19.

51. As evidence of this, the British authorities took four measures: posting Northern administrators to the South; restrictions on trade and movement were lifted; use of Arabic as a medium of instruction in the South was allowed; and restrictions on Islam were eased.

52. The South was represented by Buth Diu, Clement Mboro, Cyr Rehan, Hassan Fartak, James Tumbura, Laulik Lado and Phelemon Majok; the North by Hassan Ahmed Osman, Habib Abdalla, Ibrahim Bedri, Mohammed Saleh Shingitti and Surur Ramli.

53. Mohamed Salih Shingetti, an Umma veteran, was a highly respected Northern judge; he later became the first speaker of the Legislative Assembly during the self-government period.

54. Proceedings of the Juba Conference, June 1946, Sudan Archives.

55. Ibid.
56. For the text of Bedri's memo, see Khalid, M, *The Government They Deserve*, Annexes.
57. 53 supra.
58. Sir James Robertson, who was instrumental in taking that decision, described the decision as the greatest mistake he made as Civil Secretary. 'From October 1952 until January 1954,' said Robertson, 'there was no representative body in existence which could speak for the Sudanese as a people, and because of this lacunae the Southerners and country people generally lost any opportunity of influencing events.' Robertson, James, *Transition in Africa*, pp. 147–8.
59. Ruay, *The Politics of Two Sudans*, p. 67.
60. Under the chairmanship of British High Court Judge, R.C. Stanley Baker, the Commission was formally convened on 29 March 1951; its mandate was to recommend to the colonial government 'the next step to be taken in the constitutional advance to full self-government'. For genesis and activities of the Commission see Abdel Rahim, M, *Imperialism and Nationalism*, pp.190–2.
61. Article 5 of the Anglo-Egyptian Agreement provided that ' the two contracting parties agree that, it being a fundamental principle of their comman policy to maintain the unity of the Sudan as a single territory, the special powers which are vested in the Governor-General by Article 100 of the Self-Government Statute shall not be exercised in any manner which is in conflict with that policy'.
62. *Legislative Assembly Weekly Digest*, 9 February 1952.
63. Tredt, Terje, *Short-cut to Decay*, p. 20.
64. Yangu, A.M., *The Nile Turns Red*, op. cit., in Ruay, *The Politics of Two Sudans*, p. 56.
65. Mavrogordato, Jack, *Behind the Scenes*, p. 106. The author was the Advocate General of Sudan and the Legal Advisor to the British negotiating team in Cairo.
66. Op.cit., in Deng, Francis, *Dynamics of Identification*, p. 9.
67. Robertson wrote to Graham Thomas, 'Mr Eden and co. and the Cairo Embassy – in spite of all we said – thought they could buy a settlement on the Canal [Suez Canal] at the price of Sudan. That was why Eden told SAR [Sayyid Abdel Rahman al Mahdi] in October 1952 to go to Cairo and make agreement with Neguib: SAR did so and *hic illae lacrimae* I did my best with SAR, Abdel Rahman Ali Taha, Shawgi [both were ministers in the Executive Council during the period of self-Government] and others, but they thought Eden and Neguib were better guides to follow than the British officials in Sudan.' Thomas, Graham ,*The Last of the Proconsuls*, p. 46.
68. Hawley, Donald, *Sandtracks in the Sudan*, Michael Russel Publishing, Wilby, Norwich, 1995. Hawley served in Sudan as a District

Commissioner, Police Magistrate and finally as Chief Registrar of the Judiciary.

CHAPTER THREE

Betrayal of the Nation's Expectations
1956–1965

> *O, What tangled web we weave,*
> *when first we practice to deceive.*
> **Sir Walter Scott: Mamion**

Introduction

Sudan, in the period under review, has had a rainbow of governments ranging from military dictatorship to divisive and irresolute civilian governments. During 1953–58 and 1965–69, the Sudan experimented with Westminster style democracy, while between 1958–1964 the country was ruled by a naked military dictatorship. It is to the examination of these experiments and their role in war and peace that the present chapter turns. Far much more abiding than ideology and other aspects that distinguish political parties in other geographical planes, Sudanese parliamentary democracy was indelibly marked by personal, factional and sectarian rivalries of a mind-boggling insensitivity and magnitude. It was these senseless rivalries, probably more than any other factor that had played a leading role in perpetuating conflict and destroying democracy.

In their euphoric hurry to declare independence on 1 January 1956, the ruling class in the North had no time to confect a constitution responding to Sudan's political and socio-cultural peculiarities; instead they adopted with a little face-lifting the constitution drawn by Justice Stanley Baker for the purposes of the self-government interim period. Thus, independent Sudan adopted the Westminster mantra and uncritically espoused its self-evident truths. Neither was Sudan's socio-cultural infrastructure fit for the new political superstructures, nor were the parties ready to reinvent themselves to face up to the challenges posed by the ethos and conventions of democracy. Chief among those were the principles of full equality among citizens without discrimination on the basis of religion, ethnic origin or gender, and the overriding principle of accountability of leaders to their constituencies. The traditional parties were at that period a conglomerate of sectarian and tribal fiefs that willingly accepted the pontifical omnipresence of a virtually sanctified leadership. However, things would not have been as bad were the two traditional parties in concord on major national issues. Instead, they pendulated from one sordid infighting to the other. Times without number, the infighting was on matters that had no relevance to the nation's interests, supreme or otherwise.

By their sheer political insufficiency in addressing boldly and conclusively the nation's most crying problem, war, the parties thrust the army into the fray and inexorably militarized politics. It is, therefore, unsurprising that whenever the army wrested power from civilians, their first declarations had always set, as a primary goal, putting an end to war in the South. Being the Northern group most directly affected by war, the army presented its role as that of a vehicle for crisis management and damage limitation. Thus, the intervention of the army in politics would not have been possible, or at least as easy, were it not for the failure of civilian regimes to bring war to an end. Little surprise, military *coups* were often received with open arms by disgruntled, and tolerated by apathetic, citizens. The military do not need people's approval to overthrow governments, they only need their apathy. That should have been a cause for contemplation by the leaders, but the cycle went on. Governance in Sudan remained a transit camp alternatingly occupied by inept soldiers and wobbly politicians whose only function in government was to destabilize their own regimes. The tenure of the military, as numerous experiences had shown, was no less disastrous. Consequently, keeping the soldiers in the barracks is not a function of political exhortations, but of mending bad old ways.

Independence: A Prelude to Worse Things to Come

The rivalry between the Co-Domini led to internal political developments that pushed the Sudan ever closer to independence. But it was an uncertain independence since the new political elite was hurtfully divided, firstly, between the two colonial powers, and secondly, against each other. On the other hand, whilst pretending to have no ambitions as regards Sudan, Egypt was eager to have Sudan united with it. Its encouragement of Sudanese self-government was, above all, a stratagem to see the British off in the hope of using the political process to achieve eventual union of the two countries under the Egyptian flag. This explains the great lengths to which the Egyptians went to influence the 1953 elections in such a way that the Unionists won the elections.[1] Hence, the Unionists triumphed in the cold-blooded sense of the word, and former *Ashiqqa* leader Ismail al Azhari became the country's first prime minister. Prior to, and during the elections, Azhari gave the appearance of playing his role very well in accordance with Egypt's script. But in his inmost thoughts he entertained his own aspiration for Sudan's independence. In effect, the standard bearer of unity with Egypt soon abandoned the banner he had raised for almost two decades. The change came in fragments. Initially, Azhari made a cryptic statement in which he said: 'those who govern you today will not surrender you either to the Egyptians or to the British'. However, the first inkling of Azhari's change of heart came in a declaration he made in London during an official visit to the Court of St James.[2] Both the statement and the venue in which it was made, bothered Egypt immensely.

To achieve his new objective (independence of Sudan), Azhari decided to circumvent the stipulation in the 1953 Anglo-Egyptian agreement, which offered the Sudanese the exercise of the right of self-determination to decide whether they wanted to be independent or united with Egypt. According to the agreement the 'Sudanese Parliament shall pass a resolution expressing their desire that arrangements for Self-Determination shall be put in motion and the Governor-General shall notify the two Contracting Governments of this resolution' (Article 9). 'When the two Contracting Governments were notified of the resolution, the Government of Sudan (then existing) shall draw up a draft law for the election of the Constituent Assembly that shall decide on Sudan's future' not later than 31 December 1955 (Article 10). Notwithstanding this clear stipulation, the Sudanese Parliament unanimously resolved on 29 August 1955 that the wishes of the Sudanese people would best be ascertained through referendum and not via a Constituent Assembly. In a surprising *volte face*, the same Parliament revoked in mid-December 1955 (less than four months later) that unanimously passed resolution and decided instead that self-determination could be exercised by the sitting parliament. Those incongruous manoeuvres not only reflected lack of a credible strategic vision, but they were also signs of reckless tactics regarding a matter of gravity and consequence to the whole people of Sudan. This heedless attitude, as demonstrated in endless future experiences, became the stock-in-trade of parliamentary politics in Sudan.

In strictly legalistic terms, the Parliament's resolution in December 1955 was an act of betrayal of majestic proportions. First, it went against the terms of the Anglo-Egyptian agreement and made nonsense of the sanctity of international agreements. Second, it evinced lack of the seriousness and serenity with which parliaments in other parts of the world would have addressed national issues of moment. Third, it frustrated the will of the people to determine their own future. Sudan's Parliament, according to the basic law that created it, was not elected to exercise the right of self-determination on behalf of the people of Sudan, but only to legislate for the interim government and oversee governance during the period of self-rule. Yet Azhari's action, in political terms, was a shrewd move by a masterful player of *real politik*. He capitalized on Egypt's support to get rid of the British, and then moved on to show to Egypt his real colours. Those who genuinely believed in unity with Egypt, or had put their trust in Azhari as the spearhead of that cause, might have other descriptions of this about turn. In the world of wily politics, however, guile and indifference to favours are the tricks of the trade. Asked whether he felt indebted to Russia for helping him crush the Hungarian uprising of 1848, Prince Schwarzenberg of Austria answered: 'Austria will astound the world with its ingratitude'. And so did Azhari, with respect to both Egypt and confirmed unionists with in Sudan.

Egypt was understandably enraged by the turn of events, prompting serious manoeuvres by Major Salah Salem[3] to destabilize Azhari. More discomfiting to Egypt was the fact that Azhari's first open declaration of intent on independence was made in London. Some surmised that he was duped by the British, a conjecture that could not be validated by verifiable or even observed evidence. Amazingly, General Neguib, who was deposed by Nasser shortly after his return from an aborted visit to Sudan, claimed in his memoirs that his removal from the presidency was 'exactly the same as signing a decision to split Sudan from Egypt'.[4] The Sudanese unreservedly adored Neguib for his avuncular attitude, humility and love for the country and its people. But it was most unlikely that his removal from office had any impact on Azhari's decision to opt for independence.

In reality, many believed that the commitment to unity with Egypt by a large number of professed unionists was bogus from the start. The call for unity was believed to be a ploy to pre-empt the perceived designs by the *Ansar* to impose al Mahdi as king of Sudan. That does not mean that the Sudanese political class was not mindful of the significance of a close and special relationship with Egypt; to the contrary Northern Sudanese of all political stripes shared the belief in desirability of that special relationship and the indispensability of an *entente cordial* with Egypt. The issue loomed large in the debates of the Graduates' Congress. One point of the famed Congress Memorandum of 1942 referred to the 'natural right' of the Sudanese to conclude a 'special agreement' between the two countries. At the same time, the Sudanese were ever conscious of the importance of preserving their own identity in relation to that of Egypt. But this keen awareness by Northern Sudanese politicians of their specific national identity *vis-à-vis* that of their 'brothers' in the North (Egyptians) paradoxically never accorded with their denial of the special nature of the identity of their other brothers to the South (Southern Sudanese).

The fears of Mahdist monarchical aspirations were pervasive and even shared by some of al Mahdi's British friends.[5] Those fears were probably evoked by al Mahdi's persona, not his political enunciations; the Imam glaringly exuded the aplomb of a king. As a result, not only unionist but also independentist groups like the Republicans and the Socialist Republicans partook of those fears. The worries of those groups were not sufficiently allayed by al Mahdi's categorical declaration in August 1953 in which he expressed his support for a democratic republican system. All the same, the Umma party was not all too happy with Azhari's opting for independence. That a government with a 'dubious' commitment to Sudan's independence should preside over the dismantling of the last vestiges of the condominium rule was extremely unnerving to the Umma and the *Ansar*, the independence standard bearers. The Umma misgivings about Azhari, according to British sources, were not entertained by colonial British officers.[6]

Azhari did not have an easy ride at first; his change of position came on the eve of violent demonstrations by the *Ansar* on 1 March 1954, which delayed the opening of Sudan's first parliament. From then on the British, to the dismay of the Umma, reversed gear and warmed up to Azhari whom they had earlier dismissed as 'unscrupulous and opportunistic'.[7] The 1 March incidents were a watershed in the Umma–British relations. The British read in the Umma's defeat in the election, irrespective of Egypt's blatant intervention, an expression of fears by the Sudanese of the return of Mahdism whose memories were still alive in the minds of many of them.[8] Sir William Luce, advisor to Governor-General, Robert Howe, was in all likelihood the main force behind this change of policy. This did not endear him to al Mahdi.[9] The Governor-General upheld Luce's views as reflected in his memorandum to Eden in which he contended that: 'If independence came through the Khatmia and NUP so much the better, for then the Umma would have no valid political reason to contest the decision and would be forced back on the far less plausible sectarian division to justify violent opposition.'[10]

Prior to Azhari's independence announcement, the unionist government was far from a competent exercise. First, the component parties were deeply divided, and the façade of unity that they presented was deceptive. Within the NUP there were several factions intriguing for power. These manoeuvres culminated in the dismissal of three *Khattmiyya* ministers subsequent to their attempt to overthrow al Azhari in 1955 through a vote of non-confidence in Parliament. The reason given by the three ministers for their action was Azhari's prevarication on the issue of independence.[11] Besides, with the exception of a few hands-on former bureaucrats, there was a genuine lack of experience in government within the new leadership. Good intentions alone – and there were none – would not have overcome the inadequacies of untried hands at a time that required clarity and delicate diplomacy, particularly as regards the South. In addition, with the leadership immersed in the Anglo-Egyptian rivalries and their own power schemes, none had the presence of mind to focus on devising economic strategies and policies for the future.

During the Sudanization process, the NUP put party political considerations ahead of national ones by influencing the distribution of jobs to the benefit of its supporters or those close to it. Not even the highest organ of state, the Supreme Council, was saved from impetuous party manoeuvrings. For example, in the wake of the March violence, the NUP decided, as a punitive measure against the Umma, to reconstruct the Governor-General's Council (GGC) and remove from it the Umma representative (Ibrahim Ahmed).[12] To succeed in reconstructing the GGC, the NUP needed the numbers in Parliament, and those could only be acquired from the Southern bloc. That the NUP did, and an eminent Southern politician (Siricio Iro) was brought into the Council. Doubtlessly having a Southerner in the GGC was an adroit political act, if only to assuage the concerns of the South. But doing so as an after-thought, and only to undermine opponents, revealed both want of seriousness and lack of schematic approach to politics. Moreover, it was certainly not the way to establish a supreme council that was deemed to be the revered symbol of national unity.

The 1 March violence and Ahmed's removal from the GGC could have precipitated a constitutional collapse under Section 102 of the Self-Government Statute. That view was taken by Foreign Secretary, Selwyn Lloyd, on the strength of the advice of Sudan's British Chief Justice, John O'Brien Lindsay. Nevertheless the Governor-General held a different view, again as a result of the persuasion of Sir William Luce and his team.[13] In due course, when the GGC was reconstructed after the declaration of independence, into a Supreme Council (SC) of five to take over the functions of head of state from the Governor-General, it ended by having two members of the ruling party[14] and none of the Northern opposition party. That was certainly not the type of presidency that represented the national will or reflected the nation's political diversity.

The Sudanization process also embittered the South. Despite wild promises made during the elections, the South got a paltry six posts out of the eight hundred that were up for grabs. Among the wild promises made, according to the Cotran Commission report,[15] was Azhari's pre-elections undertaking to give priority to Southerners, not only in the Sudanization of the administration in the South, but also in the higher ranks of the central government. The wildest of promises, according to the report, was the one given by Major Salah Salem. Addressing a group of Southern junior officials, Salem persuaded the officials that they – and nobody else – would inherit from the British when they left. When asked by a dresser in Juba hospital whether he (the dresser) would replace the departing PMOH (Province Medical Officer of Health), Salem (probably without caring to understand the meaning of the term) answered in the affirmative. Charitably, one may assume that the Sudanization Commission, in its decisions to apportion the jobs vacated by the departing British officials, bypassed Southerners because it was guided by considerations of competence. Still, this does not explain the wild and irresponsible promises made to Southerners, nor the devil-may-care attitude that had accompanied those wanton promises.

In summary, the actions of the first democratic government had three main effects on the South:

i. Widespread resentment against the administration in the region, then almost entirely Northern.
ii. Southern politicians felt excluded from government and the political process and, therefore, turned against the government.
iii. Inattention to these simmering undercurrents finally led to the outbreak of violence and hence ushered the beginning of rebellion in the South.

The Southern political leadership did try to get the attention of the new rulers in Khartoum. The Liberal Party, then under Stanislaus Payasama, united all Southern MPs to work as a group. In April 1955 they met in Juba and demanded federalism, but their demand neither slowed the Sudanization process nor attracted the attention of the government. In fact, it was within the means of Khartoum rulers to prepare the ground for a united stable Sudan on the morrow of independence, but they chose differently. The veteran Southern politician, Stanislaus Payasama, recounted in his autobiography published in 1990 the stunning story of his meeting with Sayyid Abdel Rahman al Mahdi, Azhari and Abdalla Khalil. Azhari was by then presiding over an all-party coaltition government and Khalil was his minister of defence. Al Mahdi asked Payasama in the presence of the two politicians and other dignitaries: 'What does the South want?' In response, Payasama said: 'We don't seek separation but autonomy to run our region.' Al Mahdi, according to Payasama, turned to the politicians in attendance and said: 'Go and give them what they want. The Turks could not conquer them. My father, the Mahdi, could not. The British did it with difficulty.'[16] The writing on the wall was therefore clear to the meanest capacity. Distressingly, high-handedness rather than high-mindedness got the better of the political class.

Nowhere was this high-handedness more exposed than in the way newly appointed Northern administrators approached their duties in the South. According to the Cotran Commission report, the Assistant District Commissioner at Yambio cajoled thirteen Zande chiefs following the Juba meeting of Southern parliamentarians to denounce that meeting and coerced them to telegraph Khartoum accordingly. A similar act by a civil servant in the North would have been condemned as meddling in politics and its perpetrator would have been brought to task. But this was not the case with the Northern administrator in the South. As if this was not churlish enough, the same administrator instructed the chiefs to put on trial the parliamentary representative of Yambio (Elia Kuzi) for organizing a political rally for members of his constituency to brief them about the conclusions of the Juba gathering. He also reprobated the chiefs for meeting with their parliamentary representative. Kuzi was condemned under Section 441 of the Sudan Penal Code to twenty years in prison, five times the maximum penalty that the offence carried. Besides, as an MP, Kuzi was covered by parliamentary immunity. He could not have been arrested without clearance by the Speaker of Parliament. That matter was ostensibly of no concern to the Northern administrator. Cotran's report described the Assistant District Commissioner's ill-considered action as 'deplorable in a moral and an administrative sense'. It was this type of provocative action that heightened fears, bred discontent and provoked anger.

Of the Southern institutions that felt the direct impact of Northernization, none did so more keenly than the Police and the Equatoria Corps. Of the 33 officers' posts in the Corps, 24 of the most senior were allocated to Northern officers. Only nine junior officers were recruited from the South. At the Zande Development Scheme, the only one of its kind in the South, 300 Southern workers were fired to make way for Northerners, or so it was perceived by the dismissed workers. Demonstrations broke out and police opened fire, killing eight demonstrators. Insecurity persisted and the Khartoum authorities felt that they could not entirely depend on Southern security forces in the region who were all presumed to be sympathetic to 'trouble makers'. Detachments of Northern troops were thus sent to the region to replace them. This further exacerbated the tension, so when an attempt was made to disband the Equatoria Corps by ordering it North, mutiny broke out at Torit, Yei, Juba, Yambio and Maridi. By the time the mutiny was put down, 261 Northerners were dead and the main body of mutineers took to the forests with their weapons. The government executed those apprehended despite promises of clemency by the British.[17] The Southern leadership seemed to have invested considerable diligence to ward off violent confrontation. In this respect, it is to be noted that acts of violence were averted in other parts of the South due to efforts by senior Southern administrators where those existed. For example, the Cotran Commission credited Inspector of Police Gordon Mourtat with success in sealing off Bahr el Ghazal from the fallout of the Equatoria mutiny. Were there senior Sourthen officers or administrators in Equatoria, they might have been able to stop the spiral of violence.

Cotran summed up the Southern problem succinctly. The problem, he said, 'was political not religious since there was abundant evidence that Christian, Muslim and animist Southerners participated in the mutiny'. He also stated that some of the propagandists against the North were Muslim Southerners.[18] Incredibly, Egypt, which went to great lengths in the Anglo-Egyptian Agreement to curtail the use by the Governor-General of his exceptional powers in the Self-Government Statute, emerged, after the Southern disturbances, to favour such intervention. Major Salah Salem, probably in a spoiling act against Azhari, wrote to the British Ambassador in Cairo proposing the dispatch of an Anglo-Egyptian force to the South to restore law and order. Strikingly, Salem's appeal was made about one year after the evacuation of the Anglo-Egyptian forces from Sudan through Egypt's propulsion. According to Sir Humphrey Trevelyan, the British Ambassador in Cairo, neither the British government, nor the Governor-General took the appeal seriously.[19]

At the political level, Southern parliamentarians persevered up to the time of the declaration of independence in presenting their demand for federalism as the only means to quell fears and subdue resentment in the South. Azhari's government was implacable; it saw the Southern demand as an attempt to dismember the Sudan. It also threatened to use the 'force of iron', should Southerners persist in their 'conspiracies'. Consequently, Southern MPs of the ruling NUP, including cabinet ministers Dak Dei and Bullen Alier (the only Southerners in Azhari's cabinet) quit the government and party. The Umma party saw in these developments an opportunity to further discredit the NUP among Southerners and accordingly cooperated with the Liberal Party in campaigns against the government in the South. In its turn, the NUP launched an equally vehement Southern crusade, reminding the South that the Umma was made up of the descendants of slave traders and that slavery awaited them should they pitch their tent with that party.[20]

To placate the South and smooth the way for the declaration of independence which was then imminent, the Northern political class told another lie. On 22 December 1955, Parliament resolved that the Southern demand for a federal status for the region would be given 'full consideration by the Constituent Assembly'. That formulation was presented by the Northern parties in response to Benjamin Lowki's explicit proposition to an all-party caucus on 12 December 1955 that the declaration of independence should be accompanied by a statement announcing the creation of two federated states within a united Sudan. The Southern members of parliament took the proposed dispensation at face value, but not before Stanislaus Payasama, leader of the opposition in the Senate, told the Northern political class that the South would settle for nothing less than a federal system. Only the future would tell if that was the case, he said. The two leading Northern parties (Umma and NUP)[21] paid no heed and might have thought that they had won the day through guile. Such was the height of shamelessness.

On that note, and with the South reasonably placated – albeit temporarily – the Sudan passed to independence on the first day of 1956. That was not to last for long. A few weeks after that commitment was made, the organ of one of the two parties who incurred a duty to 'give due consideration' to the issue of federalism, launched a virulent attack against federalism, describing it as a colonial plot hatched by Sir William Luce.[22] This statement not only demonstrated bad faith, but also shameless ignorance. That jaundiced view on federalism was also subscribed to by the SCP, notwithstanding their support for autonomy to the Southern region. Federalism, it seems, was thought by the communists to be a colonial brainchild and, were it not for their anti-imperialist phobia, they could have learned something from Lenin's decentralization of the Soviet Union. Here again, the fathers of independence failed to be informed by India's experience. India could not have survived without decentralizing the subcontinent into autonomous states and territories of the union endowed with far-reaching powers, very much more than the Southerners had aspired for. Indeed, whether it was in India, Canada or the United States, federalism was adopted, primarily to manage unwieldy countries and reconcile political variations within the polity. Justice Oliver Wendell Holmes, in Lochner v New York (1905), opined that a federal state encompasses fundamentally different entities and the role of federalism is to 'allow local political variations within broad national limits'. Those legal niceties should not have escaped the minds of post-independence politicians and lawyers, if they were at all less chauvinistic in their approach to the issue.

Khartoum had a distinctly short memory. Neither the mutiny in the South, the thoughtful Cotran recommendations nor the foreseeing advice of the Imam of the *Ansar* to the coalition government persuaded the new rulers that something was the matter with the way they were approaching the administration of the South. Also, the dire consequencies of inaction or prevarications on Cotran's recommendations, should have been obvious to the rulers. Just one year before the declaration of independence, Prime Minister Azhari had on his desk a letter from Benjamin Lwoki, Chairman of the Southern Conference a t Juba. That letter was copied to the Governor-General, British Foreign Secretary and Egypt's Foreign Minister. In that letter Lwoki said, in no uncertain terms, that the Sudan could either be united on the basis of two autonomous regions under a federal status, or divided the way Pakistan was separated from India. 'We are no religious fanatics,' said Lwoki, 'but we are unwilling to have Northern colonialism in the South.'[23]

Independence Governments: 1956–1958

When the Egyptian and British flags came down, and the new blue, green and yellow standard of the independent Sudan was hoisted, there were tears of jubilation in the whole of Sudan. Such was the joy of the moment that Sayyid Abdel Rahman al Mahdi fainted from emotion. The people's joy was in large part based on their unfounded hope, as i t turned out, that with government passing into their own hands, their leaders would work for the improvement of their standard of life and healing the wounds of their divided country. That those trusting and optimistic aspirations were sacrificed at the altar of personal ambitions, opportunism, factionalism, sectarianism and greed for power, was indeed a grave indictment of post-independence regimes. Rivalry and jostling for power commenced immediately after independence. Prime Minister Azhari, with a wise eye to strengthening his hold on power, invited the *Khattmiyya* ministers he had earlier fired back to the government, but this did not even postpone the inevitable for long. In July 1956, the *Khattmiyya* faction defected to form the People's Democratic Party (PDP). In alliance with Umma, the PDP defeated Azhari in a confidence vote and a coalition of the Umma and PDP ascended to power with Umma leader Abdalla Khalil as Prime Minister. The perceived secularization of politics by Azhari and his team in government was evocative of the challenge posed by Ali Abdel Latif to the traditional sectarian and tribal leadership in the 1920s. That challenge brought the two sectarian leaders, tribal leaders and urban dignitaries together to smash the budding detribalized and anti-sectarian movement.

Azhari's main failing, it would appear, was his attempt to try to govern without sectarian support, although for the two sectarian 'enemies' to act in concert would appear unusual given the historical animus between them. But it should be recalled that much as the two sects were implacable rivals, they were shrewd enough to join forces when that was required for the good of both. They had done so against the British and they were prepared to do it once more against this new enemy: Azhari's pseudo-secularism. That alliance was a defining moment in Sudan's post-independence history since it marked the beginning of the coalition of the two brother enemies, the two sectarian parties. This coalition enabled them to control politics and through it economic power. In Sudan, government's authority had always been pervasive in the economic sphere. For better or worse, government then controlled the allocation of land and water resources, trade permits, licences for industries and services, bank loans and access to foreign capital and expertise. Amazingly, the most caustic critique against that sectarian alliance came from a politician who had risen on its crest, Mohamed Ahmed Mahjoub. Writing with the benefit of hindsight, Mahjoub used very strong words to describe the concordat between the two sectarian leaders as 'the most catastrophic event in the history of Sudanese politics'.[24]

According to British sources Mahjoub's views on sectarian politics were shared by Mirghani Hamza, another political luminary of that era.[25] However, Azhari lost in that fight both politically and ideologically. He was the last Northern civilian political leader to ever try to govern without sectarian backing. His government was the last ever to enjoy an outright majority in parliament. Azhari never harnessed that power to reinvent his party for the good of the country. He only held the record for the longest serving prime minister in a parliamentary regime by playing into the hands of sectarianism.

Following the pattern that was to bedevil democracy in later years, the PDP–Umma alliance focused most of its energy on electoral politics rather than on the national agenda. They changed electoral laws and gerrymandered constituency boundaries to favour the new axis. The graduates' constituencies, which were seen to favour the NUP, were scrapped. Inevitably, the sectarian parties had a very strong showing in the 1958 elections; Umma returned 63 seats and the PDP 26. As to whether the results were a true representation of the will of the people was a matter for some considerable debate. It has been argued, for example, that the NUP, with 44 seats, had a larger share of the popular vote than any of the other two parties. This showed that the ground was set for desensitizing politics, were Azhari ready to stand his ground and accept the role of a political stimulator, even if that meant his remaining in the opposition for as long as it took to reform Sudanese politics.

Now that electoral victory was achieved, the sectarian parties got down to what they did best: rivalry. There were two bones of contention: the first was the issue of relations with Egypt. Nasser, who had replaced Neguib, and the PDP felt that the Sudan should not accept an American aid package which was then on the table. In the pandemonium of connivance and double-dealing, each coalition partner fished for another coalition partner. Azhari was courted by both, and the running of the country was all but neglected altogether. Amidst this confusion, Premier Khalil quietly handed power over to the military on 17 November 1958.

The second was the South. The first experiment with democracy had left the nation even more deeply divided, floundering like a rudderless ship in rough seas. In parliament, the South occupied one quarter of the seats, but this numerical position did not matter a thing in terms of influence on government and material development of the region. It became customary for each of the Southern provinces to be given a minor ministerial post and it was assumed that this would satisfy them. Power-sharing was thus reduced to elite accommodation and satisfaction. Indeed, it satisfied some Southern self-seeking politicians who were ready to substitute their personal interests for those of their electorate. Ethnic and personal differences also divided the Southern political elite and degraded their ability to articulate more convincingly that the problems of the South were deeper than that of a few ministerial posts. Accordingly, Southern members of parliament became an easy prey for Sudan's political predators. The Khartoum Arabic press called this sordid process *al nikhassa al barlamaniyya* (parliamentary slave hunting). True to the scripts of Wingate and Cromer, the new 'nationalist' rulers resorted to divide and rule tactics to break the ranks of Southern representatives in Parliament. As for the Northern parties' ability to stay in power, that became the fortune of the highest bidder.

The promise of federalism, on the other hand, was bogged down in the Constitution Committee in which the South was represented by 3 members.[26] Finally (May 1958) the voice of the South was muffled as their demand for a federal status was rejected out of hand because 'its disadvantages outweigh its benefits'.[27] To that act of betrayal Fr Saturnino Lahure made a historic statement on behalf of his Southern colleagues. The echo of that statement should have remained to torment all Northern political parties who thought to rule through chicanery and self-delusion, if they had any level of sensitivity or knew how to yield an apology. Said Saturnino: 'The South has no ill intention whatsoever towards the North. The South simply claims to run its local affairs in a United Sudan. The South has no intention of separating from the North, for had that been the case nothing on earth would have prevented the demand of separation. The South claims to federate with the North, a right that the South undoubtedly possesses as a consequence of the principle of free self-determination.'[28]He also added, 'the South will at any moment separate from the North if and when the North decides directly or indirectly through political, social or economic [means] to subjugate the South.' Saturnino eventually emerged as the virtual leader of the Southern movement and was killed during the second regime of the parties (1967) in circumstances in which the hands of the government, in complicity with Ugandan security services, were immersed.[29]

While the political claims of the South were being frustrated in the Constitution Committee, the economic circumstances and deprivation of the South relative to the North was not getting any better. In the North, a windfall profit had been made with proceeds from the cotton boom in the ten years preceding independence. Most of those profits had benefited the riverain North. Besides, the move to shut down the only major development scheme in the South (Nzara project) generated considerable bitterness that was further deepened by the knowledge that federalism had been subjected to the ruthlessness of political expediency. Premier Khalil, on this issue, gave in to his coalition partners (the PDP), who were dead set against federalism. Fedaralism, we recall, was dismissed by that party's daily organ as a colonialist plot. Given the other problems that Khalil was having with his partners, defaulting on the 1956 federal promise was the cheaper option.

Resultantly, Khalil lost the support of Southern representatives and had to keep postponing parliament to avoid losing power in a no confidence vote. To make things worse, Stanislaus Abdalla Payasama was dismissed from Khalil's government, prosecuted and sentenced for 18 months imprisonment. The charge against him ironically was campaigning for federalism that was deemed a seditious act. Both judge and prosecutor were comfortably oblivious to the fact that federalism was one of the pillars on which the declaration of independence was raised aloft. In the circumstances, if anybody believed that intellectual deficit and substandard performance was limited to the political class of that day, he would have to revisit that conclusion. Naturally, feelings in the South hardened. As an example, Izbone Mundiri Gwanza, a Southern MP formed the Southern Federal Party with a decidedly hard-line agenda.[30] To Gwanza's taste, Payasama and company were too soft with the North.

In the face of all those ominous tremors, the government responded half-heartedly to the recommendations of the Cotran Commission. The measures it had taken did not go beyond window dressing and placatory gestures designed to bribe the South into acquiescence, while the policy of assimilation was vigorously prosecuted. The recommendations made by the Cotran Commission were specific and feasible. Rather than implementing those well-thought recommendations, the government shuffled administrators in the South and promoted a handful of Southerners to middle-level positions. The decision against elevating Southerners to senior administration posts was taken by the government after consulting *itihad al-idarieen* (the Sudanese Administrator's Association) which mainly comprised Northern administrators. The *itihad* ruled that Southerners were not sufficiently trained to occupy high posts. Insentience towards Southern aspirations, we repeat, was not limited to the political class. Like the Sudanization Commission, the *itihad* as well as the government lost sight of the political underpinnings of Cotran's recommendations. The question at issue was basically equality of opportunity, political empowerment and removal of historic injustices, real or perceived. It was not meritocracy. Truly, was merit not to be viewed through an ethnically distorting prism, many Northern civil servants would not have been elevated to the positions they were made to occupy after the British left. Sudanization was a political, not a managerial process. Its objective was to ensure political neutrality of civil servants during the transitional period. The scandalous and professionally unethical behaviour of the assistant district commissioner at Yambio clearly pointed out that this neutrality was lacking in the South. Sadly, the government failed to grasp the essence of the Commission's report that was trenchantly expressed in the following words: 'the Northern administration in South Sudan is not colonial, but the great majority of Southerners unhappily regards it as such'.

Those episodes can fairly be summarized in one sentence: the first two civilian governments lost a golden opportunity to unite the Sudan and ward off the inevitable war. By failing to do this, they betrayed both the nation's trust and expectations. The judgement of history on the first two post-independence governments is harsh. The politics of factionalism and senseless manoeuvring rendered both governments useless in leading the nation on a path of unity and prosperity.

The Abboud Regime: 1958–1964

According to some authors, Prime Minister Khalil confessed to a group of Southern MPs the following: 'My experience has shown me that this country is not yet ready for democracy. I have therefore decided at the suggestion of my advisers, to hand over power to the army. Though political parties have now been banned I still believe that the Umma party and the people of the South will work in close cooperation.'[31] From the authors recollection, [32] those advisors included Zein el Abdin Salih and Dardiri Nugud who were Khalil's confidants; Ziyada Arbab, the Minister of Education and Justice in his government who retained the Education portfolio under the military; Ahmed Abdel Wahab, the Second-in-Command in the army, and Yousif al Tinay, Sudan's Ambassador to Egypt. El Tinay was highly regarded by Khalil and his advice was the most decisive. He reported to the Prime Minister that a military *coup*, sustained by Egypt, was impending. At that time, Khalil in his capacity as Secretary General of the Umma Party, was negotiating with al Mirghani to reform the coalition of the two secretarian parties, while Siddiq al Mahdi, Chairman of Khalil's party, was parleying with Azhari (behind Khalil's back) for yet another coalition between the Umma and NUP.[33] The ambassador, more importantly, intimated to the Prime Minister that Egyptian activities were afoot behind the scenes to reintegrate the NUP and DUP. That report raised Khalil's temperature. He was clearly riled by the tawdry manoeuvres within his party and among his allies. As a born and bred soldier he knew what to do, democracy notwithstanding. The Government was handed over to the military in the vain hope that the military would hand it back once the politicians got their act together. But the military men who were let in the door were not merely figures of fun; they were bungling figures of fun.

The military may not have been invited in 1958, or later intervened in 1969; but the conditions created by the politicians were an invitation that the army could not decline. One of those conditions was the inability or unwillingness to make peace with the South. That necessarily led to the exposure of the army to a war that it could never win. There was therefore little justification in laying all the blame on the shoulders of the officers for meddling in politics. That is not to say that the army would have done any better in solving the country's problems. The experience with military governments taught us otherwise. The Sudanese army, notwithstanding its belief that it could do better than the divided civilian governments, suffered from the same fissures that afflicted the parties. It is not a cohesive interest group; rather it 'tends, in political terms, to be a microcosm of the Sudanese society with all its diversity and its potential unity on specific issues'.[34] Both the army and parties, in effect, synthesize common historical experiences.

Furthermore, chiding Khalil alone for handing over the reins of power to the military while turning a blind eye to the blessing of the military *coup* by the parties did no justice to objective analysis. Those who propound such a view are implicitly arguing in a circle.[35] Subsequent developments proved that commitment by the political class to democracy was skin deep. For no sooner had Abboud and his *junta* entrenched themselves in office, than they were publicly blessed by the two sectarian leaders, the guarding angels of democracy. The statement of Sayyid Ali al Mirghani was read over Sudan Radio by his son Mohammed Osman; that of al Mahdi was delivered by an illustrious minister in Khalil's government, Abdel Rahman Ali Taha. More discomforting was the declaration of support to the military a few years later by Sheikh Ali Abdel Rahman, the Minister of Interior in the government overthrown by Abboud. At the head of a delegation of unionist politicians, euphemistically calling themselves *Kiram al Muwatineen*, (notable citizens), the Sheikh made a declaration of allegiance to Abboud evocative in its crypticness of *sifr al wala'a* made by Sudanese notables during the colonial era to Queen Victoria. Ali Abdel Rahman, who sought to bring down the 'democratic' government in which he was a key member because of its 'treacherous' acceptance of US aid, had no qualms in endorsing a non-democratic military government whose first foreign policy initiative was to undersign the very same US aid agreement. The reason for that awkward contradiction was simple: Abdel Rahman and his colleagues were heartened by Abboud's success in concluding an agreement with Egypt over the Nile waters for which he received Nasser's accolades. Democracy was signally sacrificed by its supposed upholders for considerations that had nothing to do with good governance or the supreme interests of the nation. To make bad worse, Abdel Rahman dedicated his book (written after the collapse of the second civilian regime) to the 'valiant free officers who overthrew the Abboud regime.[36] In Sudan's theatre of the absurd that should take nobody aback.

Abboud, however, came to power with a staccato volley of despotic edicts including the declaration of a state of emergency, suspension of the 1956 constitution and imposing a ban on political parties. Executive power was vested in the Supreme Council of the Armed Forces who, in turn, delegated its powers *in toto* to Abboud. The regime also issued a Sudan Defense Ordinance, stating that 'whoever acted for the formation of parties or called for a strike or acted to overthrow the government or spread hatred against it, is to be either sentenced to death or life imprisonment'. The Sudan Defence Regulation, 1958, gave the interior minister exhaustive powers befitting a police state.

The regime seemed to do quite well in managing the economy a t first. Accumulated cotton stocks were disposed of and there was accelerated capital inflow. A 10-year development plan (1961/62–1970/71) was launched with the professed intention of improving the welfare and living conditions of the people. That led to an economic boom and some improvement in growth in the riverain North. But it was not long before things changed; the big spending, big borrowing, ambitious economic development plans of the regime soon caught up with it. More importantly was the cost of war. Abboud was implacably determined to fight the South and war expenditure began to weigh down on the economy.

In its relations with the South, the Abboud regime assumed, indeed developed, the attitudes of the civilian regime that had preceded it. The military believed in a rather buffoonish manner that the South could only be tackled through brutal Islamization and Arabicization. In so doing, the regime adopted four specific steps:

i. Qur'anic schools and intermediate Islamic institutes were established in the South.
ii. A decree issued in 1960 abolished Sunday as the day of worship in South, replacing it with Friday.
iii. The Missionary Societies' Act, which came into being in 1962, compelled missionaries to obtain licences and banned preaching, as if missionaries came to the South on a Safari.

In the period between 1960 and 1964 all missionaries in Southern Sudan were expelled.

The Abboud regime was also typical of despotism: it brooked no opposition, no protest, and its indefatigable prescription for the Southern struggle was repression and yet more repression. A catastrophe therefore ensued. South Sudanese politicians got up and left the country in increasing numbers. Military resistance, in the shape of the *Anya Nya*,[37] resurged and the position of Southern political organizations hardened further and leaned towards secession. The expelled missionaries took the gospel abroad and mobilized world opinion against the regime. At the same time, the South's loathing for the regime and, by extension for the North, became almost total.

In the North, particularly to the political class, the regime presented a very interesting scenario. The military had come into power with the connivance or acquiescence of part of that class. It also received the benediction of the two sectarian guardians of party politics. But once they were established in power, it became abundantly clear that the military had little intention of ceding power to civilians. Duly, opposition grew and an opposition front was formed under the leadership of Umma leader, Siddiq al Mahdi. The front immediately demanded an end to military rule, the lifting of the state of emergency and the formation of a government of national unity to write a constitution and organize fresh elections. Abboud reacted by putting in jail the leaders of the opposition political parties. Yet opposition was not only restricted to political parties. Towards the end of the regime ordinary people felt the pinch of the mismanaged economy, an unpopular war and a dictatorship that didn't seem to have an end in sight. Resentment grew, strikes broke out and Abboud was ultimately deposed in 1964. But, unlike his military successors, Abboud had the wisdom and humility to step down once he perceived that people had had enough with his rule.

That was the period when Hassan Turabi emerged on Sudan's political scene as a popular leader. Till then, Turabi was known among the Islamists as a distinguished academic with barely little contribution to the political thinking of the movement to which he belonged, the Muslim Brothers. Turabi's first emanation as a public orator was during a debate organized at the University of Khartoum on the problem of the South. In that debate, which triggered the first open revolt against the regime in Khartoum, Turabi maintained that the problem of the South was the problem of the North, in the sense that the issue was one of denial of human liberties by the 'military oppressors' in Khartoum.[38] What a paradox! A little over three decades later, the South was still saying that its problem was the denial of basic liberties by Khartoum oppressors. The only difference this time over was that Turabi had become a reincarnation of Abboud.

The damage that the Abboud's regime had done to relations between the South and the North had never been repaired. It was during his regime that the Sudanese refugees' situation developed from a calamity to catastrophe. As repression and massacres continued, hundreds of thousands of Southern Sudanese fled to neighbouring Ethiopia, Kenya, Uganda, the Central African Republic and the Congo.[39] In addition, the Southern political establishment relocated its activities to neighbouring countries. At the organizational level, the Southern Africa Closed Districts National Union (SACDU) was formed by, among others, Joseph Oduho, William Deng Nhial, Marko Rume, Saturnino Lohure and Ferdinand Adyang. In 1963, SADCU petitioned the UN seeking autonomy for the South. In the same year, it changed its name to Sudan African National Union (SANU). Furthermore, the South virtually became a colony of the North; the merchant class, army and police officers, senior administrators, school headmasters, were all Northerners. Though there was a fair need for Northern expertise in the South, the perception of a Northern occupation created in the minds of Southerners by this Northern ubiquity was inexorable.

Now that the conditions in the South were so adverse to Southern politicians, and that exile was the preferable option, many began to feel that their only salvation lay in the force of arms. In 1963, armed resistance achieved a more strident note with the consolidation of the *Anya Nya*. The Southern political forces were at first wary of the violence with which the *Anya Nya* responded to army atrocity, sabotaging infrastructure and attacking the army and government installations. Retaliatory attacks by the government only served to win the *Anya Nya* more sympathizers and adherents.[40] Among Northern civilians, the atrocities and outrages by the army in the South were a matter of some concern. But it would appear that to the political elite, the only agenda was to end the military rule and recover government from the *junta*. A curious quality of the Abboud regime and a section of Northern opinion was their pretence that there was no serious problem in the South at all, that the only situation that they confronted was a matter of a few mutineers that could be handled by the use of force, and foreign missionaries to be expelled. As the armed struggle intensified, the stark reality finally got home. Abboud and his generals had either to persist in their expensive and extremely unpopular war with no sign of victory in sight, or come up with an appropriate and peaceful accommodation.

In September 1964, the military bowed to popular pressure but came with a galling response: appointing a commission of inquiry to look into the causes of the problems in the South, as if there was something new to discover. Abboud would have done his regime some good, if he only took note of the extent to which government officials in the South had gone to destroy the identity and culture of the South. For example, in those days a district commissioner called a Southern chief to his office and addressed him by a 'Muslim' name, congratulated him for being a live part of the government whose religion was Islam, raised his salary as a token of the step he has taken in embracing Islam and told him finally that his new name and conversion would be announced on Radio Omdurman. Into the hands of the new convert were thrust ten pounds for the purpose of purchasing the required 'religious' outfits.[41] This was as farcical an attitude as that of the British District Commissioner in Raja who banned 'Arab' dress, to which reference was made in Chapter One. As for conversion to Islam the Sudanese District Commissioner has out-Heroded Herod; the foreheads of Christian children were rubbed with sand and washed with soap. The children were told that the sign of the cross having been erased, they should now embrace Islam.[42] Southern petty traders, on the other hand, were told by their Northern counterparts *(Jallaba)* and administrators alike, that unless they became Muslims, they would never make good in business.[43] As for the Southern political rallying cry, federalism, it was as good as dead according to the Governor of Equatoria, Ali Baldo. The Governor told a gathering of Southern elders, 'during the days of parliament, Southern members advocated a federal government. Those ideas are gone with the politicians.'[44]

Southern resistance to this outrage took two distinct paths. The politicians in exile heckled, feuded and drafted memoranda; inside South Sudan, a formidable guerrilla army was slowly coming into being. It was clear to all by now that the chances for a peaceful settlement were well nigh non-existent. In September 1963, the various armed pockets merged to form the Land and Freedom Army, subsequently called the *Anya Nya*. Southern politicians encouraged *Anya Nya* only to attract the attention of the world to the situation in the South, not as a tool for the implementation of a well-articulated politico-military strategy. When this seemed not to work, the political leadership left the military struggle to its own designs and concentrated almost entirely on seeking a political settlement.

The October Uprising (1964–1965): A Government of the People

By 1964 the economic malaise, the intensification of war in the South and Abboud's denial that there was anything like a Southern problem, all conspired to a level of discontent that the people of the Sudan could take no more. On 21 October 1964, a popular rebellion overthrew the military and a transitional government was formed to oversee the transfer of power back to an elected government. Thus began the second parliamentary era. At hand was a task of a more urgent nature. Upon assuming power, the military suspended the 1956 constitution and in its place adopted an eggshell constitution that was only intended to consecrate their power. Their exit therefore resulted not merely in a power vacuum, but a constitutional one as well. The 1956 quasi-secularist constitution was refurbished to pave the way for a constituent assembly charged with the dual task of legislation and promulgation of a fresh constitution. So, Sudan was back to the face-lifted constitution drafted for the country by the British, with very minor amendments. Sir James Robertson, who superintended the birth of that constitution, should have been chortling with gratification in his grave over what was happening in the good old Sudan.

The October government – as the transitional government was called – was a government like no other the Sudan had ever seen. First, it put the problem of war and peace as its topmost priority. Second, it was created with the awareness that the style of governance by sectarian parties was inimical to the interests of the nation. The composition of the cabinet reflected this, with professional groups having eight representatives, the political parties five and the South two; that of course was only a formal change. Third, its leader, Sir al Khatim al Khalifa, was a man with no past association with sectarian politics and had some experience in the South. Fourth, it put an end to the historical marginalization of women in the political process by granting women the right to vote and stand for elections. The October government, therefore, had a holistic approach to the nation's problems and courageously confronted its ills with determination. It also shunned the tokenism of the past and appointed Southerners to the crucial ministries of the Interior and Transport and Communication. In addition, it reached out to Southern politicians and won their trust, a consequence of which SANU, the premier Southern political force at the time, recognized it and signaled a willingness to return from exile. It was on the basis of this trust that the idea of holding a roundtable conference between the South and North to determine their constitutional powers was mooted.

The October government had also a radical reform package whose aim was not merely to placate the South but also to repair the very institutions of government and put the nation on the path of peace, reconciliation and development.[45] Some of the measures that the nation desperately needed horrified the sectarian parties who regarded them as a threat to their electoral prospects. Tampering with the native administration, for example, was seen as undermining the tribal power base of the parties while the Unlawful Enrichment Act and the cleansing of the civil service were seen by rapacious politicians as adverse to their interests. The idea of civil service cleansing was also dreaded by senior civil servants and not unjustifiably so. The amateurishness with which the process was conducted as well as its over-politicization and the vindictiveness that accompanied it, proved the worst fears of some civil servants. Ergo, the sectarian parties ganged up against Sir al Khatim's government arguing that the policies of the transitional government were illegal since its mandate did not extend beyond preparing the nation for elections.

Effectively, the transitional government had committed itself to holding elections within the time frame prescribed by the Charter (not later than March 1965), but the trades union elements within it, under the umbrella of the Professionals Front (PF) considered the implementation of its programme more important. Hence, they wanted the elections delayed until national reconciliation had been attained. On account of that, the parties presented Sir al Khatim with an outright ultimatum: organize elections as arranged or resign. To give credence to that threat, the Umma party brought out tens of thousands of *Ansar* militias in the streets of Khartoum, subsequent to which (in February 1965) the Prime Minister had little choice but to resign. A new caretaker government was formed, one in which the sectarian parties had the clout they desired, though still presided over by Sir al Khatim. With the exit of the first October government, the reformist zeal of the uprising died, and so did the prospects for genuine reconciliation and hopes for ensuing stability and prosperity.

The Round Table Conference, 1965

Between 16 and 29 March, under the auspices of the Round Table Conference, (RTC), 18 representatives of the Northern political parties, 24 from the South and observers from Ghana, Kenya, Uganda, Nigeria, Algeria and others sat down under the chairmanship of the Vice-Chancellor of the University of Khartoum, al Nazeer Dafalla. The RTC was one of the major milestones in the search for peace in Sudan. Sir al Khatim's government succeeded in getting a fractious Southern leadership to the negotiating table basically by convincing those in exile that there was a genuine desire by the new leadership in Khartoum for a permanent and peaceful solution to the war in the South. The disunity of the South may have worked against it; within SANU a power struggle pitted two factions against each other. One faction headed by Aggrey Jaden was the more hard line of the two; it demanded negotiations outside the Sudan and eventual secession. The moderates, led by William Deng Nihal, weren't particular where the negotiations were held. Accordingly, they went to Khartoum to prepare the ground for the conference, after successful intermediation by Dawood Abdel Latif, one of the ablest Northern administrators. Abdel Latif was accompanied by two up-coming Southern politicians.[46] The other faction, fearing being left out followed suit.

At the negotiation table SANU called for the exercise of self-determination by the South. In that decision it was influeneed, according to Abel Alier, by the newly formed Southern Front (SF) initiated by Southerners living in the country.[47] To be sure, the first scheme of proposals to the conference presented by SANU and the Southern Front called for a plebiscite to ascertain what the majority of the people in Southern Sudan wanted. The conference was therefore conducted along three fronts, rather than two, as one would have expected. The North, on its side, was united in its purpose. The South, on the other, was divided between moderates and hardliners. Not content with this division within the Southern ranks, the North strove to introduce a third Southern group into the arena. For instance, part of the Northern delegation, determined to frustrate the Southern drive for self-determination, promoted a group of Southern politicians under the dubious name of 'Other Shades of Opinion' (OSO). The group included a non-existent party that argued for the unity of the South with the North. Santino Deng Teng had entertained the idea of forming a unity party, but at the time of the conference, that party had not yet been formed. The Sudan Unity Party, which had no place at the table, rejected what it called Northern 'concessions' to the South as well as the Southern demand for federation. Instead, it called for a 'decentralized system of government' for the whole of the Sudan, a concept it didn't go very deep in defining. Santino, together with another member of the OSO group (Ambrose Wol Dhal) were very close to the Abboud regime. He was the only Southerner to serve as minister in that regime, while Ambrose served the regime as a senior official in the Ministry of Information. Nonetheless, both were embraced by the Northern political establishment, notwithstanding its pompous call for the banishment from politics of Abboud's 'collaborators'.

Consequently, the seeming hardening of positions among Southerners was but a natural response, not only to the North's reneging on the promise of federalism at independence, but also to the deviousness with which the ruling class and a significant number of the Northern elite addressed the Southern question. For despite all the history of broken promises, Northerners unrelentingly continued to pose the question: 'What do Southerners want?' Abel Alier appropriately maintained that the call for self-determination had put within historical context the long-standing Southern demands expressed at the Juba conference and the pre-independence discussions on a federal status for the South.[48] By March 1965 that long history should have been known, or presumed to be known, by Northern politicians and elite.

Nonetheless, some Southern politicians came to the table with a singular inability to recognize that the purpose of the meeting was not to offer an occasion to restate old positions, but to explore new opportunities and how best to take advantage of them. There is such a thing as ripe moment for reconciliation and a need to make the best use of it. SANU's Aggrey Jaden was categorical in his statements that the South and the North were incompatible because of ethnic and religious factors: 'There are in fact two Sudans and the most important thing is that there can never be a basis of unity between the two. There is nothing in common between the various sections of the community, no body of shared beliefs, no identity of interests, no local signs of unity and, above all the Sudan has failed to compose a single community,' he said.[49] The Northern political parties, on their part, blamed the British and the Abboud regime for the breakdown of relations between the North and South. But after all the history we have narrated, heaping all the blame on Abboud and colonialism was not a good starting point. Indeed, that stance was a pointer to failure, for in the words of the Duke of Wellington, 'a person who is good in making excuses, is seldom good in anything else'.

Notwithstanding Jaden's extreme position, the gist of the Southern demands was to grant the people of the South the right to determine their destiny. For the most part, Northern delegates responded by virtually accusing die-hard Southerners of being stooges of imperialism and claiming that the 'Arabs' have brought civilization to the country as opposed to the plunder that 'Westerners' brought in their train. Northerners also chest-thumped about their Arabic origins and Islamic faith. This could not have been more vexatiously expressed than in the opening speech before the RTC by the independence veteran and first Prime Minister of Sudan, Ismail el Azhari. Azhari saw little to write home about on Africa or African cultures. Africa, he said, had to be civilized by the Arabs because the Europeans, at the time, were culturally too low to do that. His praise of the Arabo-Islamic culture was epic: 'The Arabs came to this continent as pioneers, to disseminate a genuine culture and promote principles which have shed enlightenment and civilization throughout Africa at a time when Europe was plunged in an abyss of darkness, ignorance and doctrinal and scholarly backwardness.'[50]

The Round Table, need we recall, was not about African or Arab cultures; nor was it about Europe and the 'Arabs'. It was about the resolution of a conflict that pitted brother against brother, about a house divided and a nation torn apart. By condensing the debate on what 'our ancestors' the 'Arabs' have done to uplift 'your ancestors' the 'Africans,' the Northern interlocutors proved the worst fears of their Southern counterparts. Azhari's opening speech summed up both the myopicness of Northern leaders towards Sudan's cultural diversity, as well as their blindness to Africa's indigenous cultures. Blindness of this nature often brings out man's worst iniquities. Paradoxically, Azhari's statement proved the veracity of Jaden's contention. Equally, the calumnious insinuations by Azhari about Africa's cultural patrimony, in the presence of African observers, were impolitic in the extreme. Clearly, Azhari's mental vision of Africa did not differ in the least from that of Britains's arch-colonialist, Sir Harold MacMichael.[51]

Nonetheless, all parties agreed on tabling three choices before the conference: federation, unconditional unity with the North or separation. The South wanted those choices to be made through a referendum. This should neither have been a cause of dismay for Northerners who were keen to know 'what the South wanted', nor a matter of surprise for democrats to whom the will of the people should be supreme. The South also maintained that for the referendum to take place, certain measures were necessary; those included appointment of an autonomous supervision corps, lifting of the state of emergency and transferring security powers from the army to civil authorities. Parallel to those conditions for conducting a referendum, there was also an undertaking from Southern leaders to persuade the *Anya Nya* to lay down its arms.

The Northern parties, par contra, were opposed to the idea of a plebiscite and, in all appearances, disinclined to allow Southerners to run their own affairs entirely. Their version for Southern autonomy, as it transpired from the deliberations of the Constituent Assembly, later comprised a regional assembly whose powers to legislate would be 'subject to national legislative approval' and an executive branch, whose head was to be chosen by Khartoum.[52] Oblivious to all the debate that was going on since January 1956, the draft constitution of 1968, which was presented after the RTC was adjourned, called for the decentralization of administration in the whole Sudan by dividing the country into nine regions. The authority of the Southern regions would be limited to local administration and education up to the secondary level without forstalling the right of the central authority to establish its own secondary schools in the region. It also covered environmental protection and school health, local industries, tourism and the development of indigenous languages and cultures. As for the regional president, he was to be appointed by the President of the Republic from amongst three names he proposed to the regional assembly to choose a nominee from.[53] The role of the regional assembly in selecting the regional president was thus reduced to that of a rubber stamp. It was given the authority neither to propose, nor to nominate the region's president.

In the face of this Northern obduracy, Southerners raised the ante a few notches; they immediately counter-proposed to be allowed to assume control of finance and economic planning, foreign affairs, armed forces and the internal security of the region. What the Southerners ended calling for was virtually a confederal arrangement. According to Clement Mboro, a settlement could have been reached were the Northern parties ready to accept the original Southern demand. 'If the Northern parties accepted our view that the regional assembly should elect the president of the regional government, we could have solved the Southern problem a long time ago,' he said. 'The mere fact that the North was to select a leader for us was to give the South a government without powers. ... Democracy advocates that the governed should elect their governors,' added Mboro.[54]

It has been argued that the South failed to grasp the hand of reconciliation genuinely extended by the North; that the negotiators chose to pander to the extremist demands of the *Anya Nya;* and that they lacked the political will to stand up to the extremist demands of their constituency.[55] Southern politicians were also castigated by the same author for their lack of unity for the common good and for allowing personal, political and tribal differences to overshadow the imperatives of peace and prosperity. The truth of the matter is that the hearts of Northern politicians were not really in the conference, which was held in the shadow of a general election. Each party was hesitant to make concessions to the South, lest it provided its opponents with a weapon to use against it in the forthcoming elections. This was reflected in two things: the fickleness with which the genuine demands of the South were treated, and the divide-and-rule tactics to which the Northern parties resorted in dealing with Southern politicians. With the old bribes readily given and eagerly accepted, the RTC failed completely to come to terms with the central issues of the conflict: relationship between the centre and the margins and political and economic empowerment.

In retrospect, an examination of the conference reveals dialogue in its most unstructured form. It also reveals a curious situation where cultural bigotry rather than diplomacy was brought to bear on an environment where almost every party had a different agenda and a different approach. Utmost delicateness in addressing the intricate issues at hand was needed, but was sorely lacking. Ultimately highfaluting statements, bad faith and unyielding stances sealed the fate of the conference. The Northern political establishment would not condescend to descend from its high horse, and the extreme fringe of Southern politicians was close-set against any reconciliation with the North. And much as this group of Southern politicians was traumatized by the string of betrayals since the early 1950s, the Northern political class failed to see the cause of their bitterness. That was why as far as the Southern eye could see, Northern parties were perceived to be at the conference not to negotiate away privileges or grant the South its rightful share in the political and economic management of the Sudan. Sure enough, Northern politicians wanted Sudan to remain united, but only in the manner of the unity between the horse and the horse rider.

To nobody's surprise, therefore, the conference wound up in failure on 22 March 1965. It was only able to salvage a few resolutions, none of which could form the basis for a permanent peace. It was resolved, for example, that regional administration, police, prisons and information services in the South should be manned by local personnel. Pursuant to that decision, all Southern administrators, police and prison officers and information personnel were to be transferred to the South. As well, i t was agreed that where there were no Southerners to take up the new appointments, available personnel would be promoted and trained to meet the new challenges in the region. Easier said than done, particularly when the implementation of the project was solely dependent on the goodwill of those who had most to gain from the status quo, the same Northern administrators who advised the government against going along with Judge Cortan's recommendations. In effect, senior local government administrators in Khartoum threatened to resign *en bloc* were the new recommendations for the southernization of the administration to be implemented forthwith. Besides, even if such recommendations were to be carried out, the question remained as to whether it served any useful purpose in integrating the South as an equal partner in the development of the Sudan.

Another recommendation called for the creation of a National Economic Council with a subsidiary agency for the South, the reopening of the Nzara cotton scheme and the establishment of an agricultural college. Clearly, neither the proponents of those recommendations, nor those who acquiesced to them in the South, had gone deep enough into the root causes of the economic underdevelopment of the South or that of other marginalized peripheries. For instance, from the time of independence, Sudan's economic development plans had religiously replicated the colonialist development paradigm which favoured the riverain North, and hence perpetuated the underdevelopment of the peripheries. The total investment on development between 1946 and 1961 amounted to 14.6 million Sudanese pounds of which only 1.3 million was allocated to the South, mainly covering the Equatoria region (Zande scheme).[56] During the period 1956–1960 – which is more relevant to the purposes of this chapter – national development allocations amounted to 69.5 million pounds of which 66.9 was actually spent. The bulk of that expenditure went into large irrigation projects in the North such as Managil cotton plantation, extension of the Sennar hydroelectric power, Jineid sugar etc. In the meantime, the post-independence period witnessed an unprecedented expansion in mechanized rain-fed farming in historically marginalized regions, e.g. Habila in the Nuba Mountains, Renk in South Sudan and Agady in Southern Blue Nile, as part of a grandeous plan to encourage export-oriented production of cash crops.

Important as they were for the country's development, the pattern of mechanized farming introduced wrought havoc on the environment, e.g. deforestation, destruction of the vegetation and increasing soil erosion. Worse still, the new developments were of no direct benefit to the inhabitants of the regions. Large parcels of land were allocated to retired Northern army officers, civil servants and Northern notables and politicians. Instead, traditional farmers in those areas were transformed into agricultural workers. Besides, in not one single case did those absentee landlords replough the profits they had reaped in the regions where the profits accrued. Invariably, the earnings were repatriated to the capital city (Khartoum) to be invested in real estate, manufacturing and trade. Even the *Zakat* (almsgiving) which is an act of charity ordained by Allah on well-to-do Muslims did not find its way to the needy in those areas, but went instead to the needy in the ancestral homes of the givers.

To keep the spirit of the RTC alive, a twelve-man committee (six representing Northern, and the six Southern parties) was constituted to pursue the work of the conference. The committee commenced work on 27 May and struggled hard to save what it could of the conference's essence. It was also to make recommendations for another session of the RTC that was to resume in three months. The committee was chaired by a Northern administrator, Abdel Rahman Abdalla, who was later replaced by a Northern lawyer, Yousif Mohammed Ali. Both were highly regarded by the parties to the conflict for their integrity and professional approach to the issues. Apart from the habitual Southern demands for a fully fledged regional administration and greater control of the affairs of the region, the agenda placed before the committee included only token gestures reflected in programmes for economic and social development for the South together with the establishment of a Southern University at Juba. Even so, whatever partial success the committee was able to achieve would not have been possible without the judiciousness and perseverance of its chairman, despite the unwholesome political pressures on him.

Within the committee, one issue was high on the minds of Northern parties: to prevail on Southern parties to condemn the violence fostered by *Anya Nya*. To that request Southerners retorted that violence from all quarters should be condemned. Even the SCP joined the chorus calling for this uneven-handed condemnation. The SCP later withdrew from the committee and requested other Northern parties to freeze their membership. The most improbable ally of the SCP in the committee was Hassan Turabi who argued that a denunciation of the army's violence was inadvisable since it would affect the fighters' morale. Surprisingly, that position by the SCP was taken at a time that had witnessed an unprecedented escalation of violence by the army, which was condemned by the independent media. An independent and level-headed newspaper in Khartoum openly denounced the 'blind oppression' and called it 'unjustifiable and harmful to the cause of unity'.[57] As a result of this public cry the committee invited the Prime Minister on 22 July to brief its members on the unraveling security situation.

The failure of the RTC was attributed by some Northern scholars to the intransigence of the South. Beshir, the secretary general of the conference and one of the few Northern intellectuals known for their sensitivity to the South wrote: 'The majority of the Southern delegates proved to be uncompromising and bad negotiators. They lacked experience and tended to suspect the motives of the Northern leaders, seeing pitfalls in any move by the North.'[58] Southerners, on the other hand, saw nothing but traditional bigotry in such an assessment. Writes Ruay, 'this (Beshir's) accusation is neither borne out by the minutes of the RTC nor by any of the reports and comments supplied by disinterested journalists and observers who attended the conference. In franker terms, that accusation not only lacked cogent evidence, on the contrary, the opposite was true. Never before in the history of the South–North conflict, had the majority of Southern parties been able to approach and negotiate the Southern problem with remarkable maturity and foresight than in the Round Table Conference Hall.'[59]

One tends to agree with that conclusion. For if blame is to be apportioned, the larger share of it shall go to Northern paties. Not only did they fail to grasp the essence of the conflict, they also went all out to divide the ranks of Southerners. Some self-seeking Southerners, as they had done many times before and after, played right into the hands of those disuniters. The creation of the unity party and the exceptional treatment of Santino and his colleagues was in piece with the North's politics of divide and rule. This view is shared by Southerners who saw how delighted the North was to see Southerners divided. Writes Ruay: 'it has been suggested that the idea was to bring the Southerners into a squabble during which time the Northern side would stand up and say they would not do anything in the way of solving the Southern problem since the Southerners were divided over a solution'.[60] At any rate ,whether Beshir's conclusion was right so or not is a matter of considerable debate. The inescapable fact is that neither the tentative gestures nor the recriminations that went with it formed a useful basis upon which to build a lasting order.

With the virtual collapse of the work of the RTC and the Twelve-man Committee, the peace initiative died. Mahjoub, who replaced Khalifa as Prime Minister, pretended like Abboud before him that there was no genuine problem in the South, only a case of few mutineers that the army had in its power to disarm. This was ridiculous, for at that time the *Anya Nya* was well organized as a guerrilla force and was beating the army bloody. As we shall argue elsewhere, the greatest failure of the peace initiative was that it sought to treat the symptoms rather than their cause, that it was targeted at a Southern problem rather than a national one. On this both Northern and Southern politicians got it wrong. The problems of Sudan are not to do with inborn antagonisms downstream; they were more to do with foul squabbles and visionless politics upstream.

Conclusion

The Northern intelligentsia and political class had promoted the view of a united Sudan by lobbying the British to renege on their promise to protect the special character of the South. To calm the fears of the South, they promised to give due consideration to Southern demands for federation once a constitution for the independent united Sudan was promulgated. With Britain out of the picture, the Northern leaders went back on that engagement and proceeded to administer the South almost as a dominion of the North. Within two years of the transitional government, the idea of a federal structure had been abandoned and the Northern rulers virtually designated themselves as the sole administrators of the South. Even calling for federal status became tantamount to high treason. That was the original sin. Unity and independence were achieved through a ruse. That was not a very good start.

In addition, in the run-up to independence, the parties commenced their march to independence on the wrong foot. The first elections in 1953 were in many ways a debacle. First, they were held under the cloud of Southern resentment. The Northern political parties, busy with their own ambitions, ignored the South and excluded it from all the vital decisions. Second, while the independence political parties – the Umma Party, the Republicans and Liberal Party – were all united in their call for independence, the Unionists were assumedly all-out for a union with Egypt. That facilitated meddling by Major Salah Salem, in what was essentially a Sudanese affair. Major Salem should be damned for the introduction into Sudan's political culture of corrupt practices. Finally, the Northern parties, rather than honestly addressing the real issues underlying Southern resentment, chose to 'plunder the South' for votes. The electioneering was direfully irresponsible. Parties began to poke old wounds to win support and make ridiculous promises that they had neither the will nor the capacity to deliver. As we have seen, the South was promised by Azhari a quarter of all the jobs in the Sudan and all the senior posts in the South. That was really a most cruel joke, for when the Sudanization Committee published the list of appointments the following year, the South had been given only six minor posts. As it were, Northerners moved into the South, as the new overlords replacing the British. From that date on, colonialism ceased to be an alibi. The Sudanese were now masters of their own destiny and architects of their own disasters.

The history of modern Sudan is a history of conflict and self-imposed pain. In trying to ascribe a cause to that conflict, there is always the temptation to trace its genesis to the racial and religio-cultural dichotomy of the country. This is only part of the problem, probably not an insurmountable part. But, for all practical purposes, the inadequacy of the governing class in applying itself seriously and honestly to come to grips with the root causes of the country's problem had a far-ranging effect on the protraction of the crisis. This failure left the structures of state open to prejudices of race, religion and sect. In spite of claims to the contrary, this remissness applied to both civilian and military regimes. The thesis repeatedly trotted out by civilian politicians that it was only the army's intervention in politics that scuttled democracy and sabotaged chances for peace is misleading. For, as we have argued and shall have occasion to argue again, whenever the military intervened, it had always done so either at the invitation and blessing of elected leaders (1958) or because the civilian administrations were hamstrung and leading the country towards inevitable tragedy. This was often the result of inaction over, or inattention to, national crises, or (as in 1969) because their warmongering left the military to fight a political war that it never could win. In those cases the army, perforce, became the arbiter of the nation's fate.

The October transitional government had many good ideas, but it was so nebulous and lacking in a powerful central control that its disintegration was inevitable. Each of its components had its own priorities, which it refused to compromise in favour of the other. The PF wanted to secure a majority representation in the intended new parliament in order to retain its role as the guiding authority in government. But having surrendered its power to the coalition, it found itself voiceless in the clamour for top positions that was underway. Each of the factions lacking power by itself to push any of its preferred policies to the fore, some factions began to coalesce into political fronts. Besieged by those squabbling factions, Prime Minister al Khalifa had largely become a lame duck. With that the October gains frittered away.

In reality, the PF misread the political map. First, for any political party to survive, it has to be anchored on a social base. Social bases, in Sudan are either religious (Umma, DUP) or ethnic (Beja, Nuba and Southern parties). As observed earlier, the SCP was an exception, since it was able to carve a niche for itself among the unionized working force, given its leading role in nurturing trade unionism. However, it too continued to be dominated by urban elites. Truly, since the days of the Graduates' Congress Sudan's intelligentsia assumed for itself a role in the country's politics incommensurate with its numerical weight. On the other hand, sectarian parties, notwithstanding their innumerable failings, were tied to bedrock institutions and would continue to be so till further notice. Those institutions can neither be wished away or jettisoned at will; they can only be forced through the democratic process itself to reinvent themselves. If they don't, they shall eventually elect themselves out of existence by the sheer weight of political and social change. If the six years of Abboud's rule, the sixteen years of Nimeiri's and the eleven years of Bashir's afterwards, were not enough to unhinge secretarian loyalties, socio-economic development and a patient policy of political stimulation would be.

Perhaps the most enduring and misleading myth that emerged from the October uprising, despite all the accolades we pinned on it, was calling it a revolution. A revolution is not a spasm. Revolutions are focused exercises committed to well-articulated and defined objectives. They also have a discernible leadership and are anchored on an identifiable powerbase. Leon Trotsky was not off the mark when he opined that 'insurrection is an art, and like all arts it has its laws'.[61] This is not an issue of nomenclature; it is a mistake in perception that has bedevilled Sudanese politics of the right and left since October 1964. That false construction was no more than a pie in the sky. Indeed, if the 'modern forces' retreated from the political salient they had occupied during the October uprising, it was because of the nature of the multi-party popular democracy for which they were clamoring, and not because they were pushed away by the traditional forces. The 'modern forces' sincerely call for multi-party democracy, but they also wish, by subjective determination, to apportion a secondary role for traditional parties. This is an eventuality that these parties would battle against to the last. It also makes no sense of multipartism.

ENDNOTES

1. Abdel Fatah Hassan, the Egyptian member in the Sudanization Commission, made a revealing statement to Graham Thomas, a British official who had close links with all Sudanese parties. In response to Grahams' question about Egypt's role in the elections, Hassan said: 'I really don't understand you British, you spend millions of pounds conquering a country by force – that is valour and patriotism – our distribution [disbursement of funds] did not create any widows or orphans and three million [Egyptian pounds] is a relatively cheap way of conquering a country'. Thomas, G., *Death of a Dream*, pp. 53–4. The Egyptian funding of the 1953 elections was surprisingly admitted in court, under oath, by two leading ministers in Azhari's government; Mirghani Hamza and Khalaf Alla Khalid, the latter being the treasurer of the NUP. The revelations were made in the course of the trial of the editor of *Al Nas* weekly under the charge of sedition. Taha, Faisal A.A., *Al Haraka al Siyyassia*, p. 654.

2. In an interview by Bashir Mohamed Said, Azhari declared in London that 'Sudan would not give up its identity nor would it exchange one colonial ruler with another'. *Al Ayam*, 2 September 1954. Azhari eventually, made his long-awaited about face regarding his, and his party's, intentions on unity with Egypt, in March 1955. *Sawt al Sudan*, 16 March 1955.

3. Major Salim, a member of Nasser's Revolutionary Command Council, was detailed by that Council to oversee and manage the situation in Sudan.

4. Neguib, M., *Kalimati* (My Words), p. 240 op. cit., Warburg, Gabriel, *Discord*, p. 78.

5. Graham Thomas, a close friend of the Mahdi, recalls a meeting with Imam Abdel Rahman al Mahdi in which he advised him against the nomination of his son, Siddiq, for Parliament. Apart from being the son of the Mahdi, Siddiq was overly qualified for nominations to parliament on his own merits. The Imam was, therefore, understandably vexed by the question and asked his British friend about the reasons for his advice, Thomas told the Imam that Siddiq's nomination would send wrong signals and confirm perceptions that the Mahdi cherished a political role; the monarchy. Thomas, G., *Death of a Dream*, op. cit., Warburg, *Discord*, p. 89.

6. J.W. Kennrick, a colonial officer attached to the Governor-General, discussed the issue with Sayyid Abd al Rahman al Mahdi and his

son Siddiq. Kennrick, according to his report to the Foreign Office, was brutal in his judgment. 'Their (Umma) defeat in the elections,' he said, 'was primarily due to the fact that against all [British] advice they had insisted on fighting the elections on sectarian lines. Instead of pressing the contrast between Sudanese independence and Egyptian control ... they had chosen to presume that the idea of independence was the monopoly of the *Ansar*.' FO 371/102760, 2 December 1953.

7. Sir Gawain Bell, the acting Civil Secretary, drew an interesting profile of Azhari: 'his comfortable figure, benevolent appearance and gold-rimmed glasses masked a character of single-minded ambition, political astuteness and shrewd opportunism ... However much I disliked and distrusted his policies, however often he seemed to me and to others unscrupulous and irresponsible, my only course was to try and win his confidence and if possible a measure of his friendship and in so doing attempt to exercise some influence', Bell, *Shadows on the Sand*, p. 211.

8. Note from Kennrick to Bromley 25/5/1954 FO/371/108323. The same view was held by the acting civil secretary, Gawain Bell, who wrote in his memoirs that ' the Umma had been unwisely blatant in their pre-election propaganda. Memories of the Mahdia were still alive and there still existed a genuine fear over much of the country of what might happen if the Mahdists came to power. Britain was leaving, and Egypt provided a lifeline to be used if necessary and discarded if no longer required', *Shadows on the Sand*, pp. 210–11.

9. Al Mahdi told Luce that he should not abandon the 'real Sudanese' (*Ansar*) to the *Khattmiyya* who were 'not Sudanese but people who were brought by the Egyptians', op. cit., Warburg, *Discord*, p. 93.

10. Top Secret Memorandum FO 371/108381, 8 December 1954.

11. The there ministers, Mirghani Hamza, Khalaf Alla Khalid and Ahmed Jali, founded and launched in January 1955 the Republican Indepedence Party; they were thus the first Khattmiyya-backed politicians to opt openly for independence.

12. Alongside Ahmed, the GGC comprised a pro-*Khattmiyya* Sudanese member, (Dardiri Mohamed Osman); a Pakistani Chairman (Mian Ziaul Din), a British member (Sir Lawrence Graffty Smith) and an Egyptian one (Hussein Zulfigar Sabri). Ahmed, an academic turned politician, was known for rectitude as well as slide-rule precision in his acts and utterances. He was also the least partisan of the Umma leaders and was highly regarded among the intelligentsia for his role in the Graduates' Congress. His removal was therefore a matter of consternation to many of his students and admirers across the political divide.

13. Luce was supported by two colonial officers, J.W. Kenrick and J. Ducan, as well as Jack Mavrogordato as legal advisor. The constitutional collapse was averted as a result of the dexterity of Sir William Luce in cooling tempers. Luce used to good measure the excellent working relations he has established with Azhari's foreign minister, Mubarak Zaroug. Unlike many of his *Ashigga* colleagues, Zaroug was known for his professionalism and managerial approach to politics. Luce was also armed in his argument against constitutional collapse by the advice of the Legal Counsel to the Governor General, Jack Mavrogordato. See Mavrogordato, J., *Behind the Scenes*, p. 109.

14. The two members were Dardiri Mohamed Osman and Ahmed Mohamed Yassin. The Council included two other non-partisan members who were regarded as national achievers, Abdel Fatah al Maghrabi and Ahmed Mohamed Salih.

15. Cotran, Tawfik, *Report of the Commission of Inquiry into the Disturbances in South Sudan during August 1955*, Khartoum. The commission was chaired by Judge Cotran, an able British jurist of Palestinian extraction who served as Police Magistrate in Khartoum. The two other Commissioners were Khalifa Mahjoub, a Northern police officer with a distinguished record of service and who was at the time Chairman of the Equatoria Projects Board, and paramount Chief Lolik Lado of Equatoria.

16. Payasama, Stanislaus Abdalla, *Autobiography*, pp. 69–70.

17. Cotran Commission Report,.

18. Ibid.

19. Trevelyan, Sir Humphrey, *Middle East in Revolution*, p. 18.

20. 15 supra.

21. The motion on federalism was presented to Parliament by a leading Umma tribal chief, Mirghani Hussein Zaki el Din.

22. *Sawt al Sudan*, 15 February 1956. *Sawt al Sudan* was the daily organ of the *Kattmiyya* sect.

23. FO371/108326, 16 November 1954.

24. Mahjoub wrote in 1974 that the 'alliance between al Mahdi and al Mirghani was the most catastrophic event in the history of Sudanese politics. The two life-long foes prompted by their greed for power, their vanity and personal vested interests, sought to dominate the political field.' Mahgoub, M.A., *Democracy on Trial*, p. 176.

25. British reports revealed that some of the leading lights of sectarian politics were not happy with the sectarianization of politics. In a memorandum to the Foreign office a colonial officer quoted Mohamed Ahmed Mahjoub and Mirghani Hamza as saying that

sectarianism would vanish as soon as the two sectarian leaders died. Message from Kennrick to Foreign office. FO 371/108336, November 1953, op.cit., in Warburg, *Discord*, p. 88.

26. The South was represented by Stanislaus Payasama, Bullen Alier and Father Saturnino Lohure.

27. The Constitution Committee was divided into subcommittees, with one dealing with the issue of federalism. That subcommittee comprised seven members of whom three were from the South. The Committee of the whole dragged on for almost one year, before coming out with a report shorn of federalism. When the report came for discussion in the Constituent Assembly in May 1958, Southern parliamentarians boycotted all sessions in which it was discussed. Minutes of the Constitution Committee, Parliamentary Records, 1958.

28. Ibid.

29. Alier, Abel, *Southern Sudan*, p. 69.

30. The agenda of Mundiri's party comprised recognition of English and Christianity as having an equal status with Arabic and Islam; an autonomous Southern Army and an economic development package for the three provinces of the South.

31. Ruay, op.cit., p. 93.

32. The author has served with Khalil as a voluntary worker in the field of media communications and as such he was sufficiently close to Khalil to observe what was going on without being part of the inner decision-making circle.

33. Khalil was never at ease with Azhari's ways of managing politics. His intention was therefore to extend the ongoing coalition between the Umma and PDP.

34. Voll, John O. and Sarah, *The Sudan, Unity in Diversity in a Multicultural State*, p. 79.

35. In an intervention to a human rights' seminar, Sadiq al Mahdi referred to Abboud's so-called *coup* as follows: 'The Prime Minister, in the absence of the President of the Party abroad, clinched a deal with the Armed Forces High Command to take over power.' The Second Birth in Sudan, Contribution by the Umma Party to the Conference on Human Rights in Transition, Kampala 8–12 February 1999. Sadiq obviously missed the point, for the question at issue was neither to incriminate the Prime Minister for an action he undeniably had done without consulting the party, nor to vindicate the President of the party (Sadiq's father) who was positively against the *coup*. The issue is about the commitment of the political class in both parties to democracy. The decision by Khalil (who was Secretary General of the Umma), the messages of support to the

army emanating from the two Sayyids (of which one was read by an illustrous Umma Minister) and the fealty towards Abboud by the PDP ministers, did not leave any place for that political class to hide.

36. Rahman, Ali Abdel, *Al Dimoqratia wa al Ishtirakiya fil Sudan*.
37. The term in the Madi language means 'snake venom'.
38. Affendi, A. al, *Turabi's Revolution*, p. 71.
39. Holt and Daly, *A History of the Sudan*, pp. 154.
40. For developments within the *Anya Nya* see Wakson, Elias Nyamlell, *The Origin and Development of the Anya-Nya Movement 1955-1972 in Southern Sudan, Regionalism and Religion*, Khartoum University, Press, 1984.
41. Oduho Joseph, and Deng, William, *The Problem of South Sudan*, p. 56.
42. Ibid.
43. Ruay, op.cit., p. 102.
44. The *Morning News*, Khartoum, 29 March 1961.
45. The October agenda included: declaring a general amnesty for all Southerners who had borne arms, holding a peace conference with the South, enacting laws to cleanse public life, specifically the Unlawful Enrichment Act that would arrest the rampant rot and corruption within the government and the military, restoration of the freedom of the press, a purge of corrupt elements in the army and the civil service, granting the vote to all Sudanese women, scrapping the native administration which the sectarian parties particularly had honed the skills to exploit in the electoral process.
46. Abdel Latif served as governor in Bahr el Ghazal and Kassala during Abbound's regime but fell into disfavour with that regime as a result of his opposition to its policies relating to the dislocation of Nubians from Wadi Halfa following the construction of the Aswan dam.
47. The SF included young Southern professionals (Darius Beshir, Lubari Ramba, Bona Malwal and later Abel Alier who resigned his post in the judiciary to join the group). Alier, Abel, *South Sudan*, p.30.
48. Ibid.
49. The *Vigilant*, 23 March 1965.
50. Minutes of the Round Table Conference, 1965, Sudan Archives, Khartoum.
51. MacMichael, the archetypical overweening colonialist, wrote:
    'Of the history of the Southern spheres, the home of Negroes, nothing is known and little can be
    guessed, save that from the beginning of time,
    Tatooed cannibals danced in files,

And "Blood" screamed the whistles and the fifes,
"Blood" screamed of the warriors, the skull-faced lean witch
doctor.'
MacMichael, *The Anglo-Egyptian Sudan*, p. 21.

52. Minutes of the Constitutional Committee of the Constituent
Assembly, 1968.

53. Ibid.

54. Khartoum News Service, 25 June 1965.

55. Beshir, M.O., *Background to Conflict*, p. 96.

56. Bore, Yongo, *South Sudan in Sudanese Development Policy
(1946–1971)*, Juba University, First Conference, 1985.

57. Editiorial, *Al Ayam*, 13 July 1965.

58. Beshir, M.O., *Background to Conflict*, p. 99.

59. Ruay, *The Politics of Two Sudan*, p. 115.

60. Ibid.

61. Trotsky, Leon, *History of the Russian Revolution*, p. 1020. Trotsky
also opined that mass movements, even if they were united by a
common hostility against the old regime, were condemned if they
had no clear aim, deliberated methods of struggle and a leadership
consciously showing the way to victory. Ibid., p. 1019.

PART THREE

Religion, Politics and the
State

CHAPTER FOUR

Conversion on the Road to Damascus
1966–1969

It is no accident that the symbol of a bishop is a crook and the sign of the archbishop is a double cross.
George Dix:
Letter to the Times, 1977

Introduction

For all their ostensible commitment to democracy and justice, the Northern ruling establishment turned out, in the period between the demise of the first October government and the rise of Nimeiri, to be inadequate in several counts. To begin with, their unrelenting struggle for power had only one principal objective; to remain perpetually chained to that power. Those who struggle for power generally have an inkling as to what they want to do with power once they obtain it. In the case of Sudan, one would suppose that as a first priority, the attention of political leaders would inescapably be riveted on the actualization of national goals on which nobody disagreed: peace, national unity, political stability, justice for all citizens and sustained development. None of those goals appeared to be a priority for the leadership of this period. Worse and worse, in every step of the way they erected hurdles for themselves that made the attainment of those goals beyond the bounds of possibility. Curiously, the leaders seemed to believe that by the very dint of their being entrenched in office, all would be milk and honey in Sudan. To the supposedly high-minded among them, the failure was compounded; not only did they surpass the bestiality of the Abboud regime in their approach to the Southern war, but they also demolished all the groundwork established by the October government as a foundation for a just peace and national reconciliation.

In addition, they aborted democracy itself by countermining, on the one hand, the will of the people when they dismissed from Parliament duly elected members, and, on the other, by frustrating the rule of law when they refused to abide by the decisions of the courts. It goes without saying that respect of popular will and the sanctity of the rule of law are the *sui qua non* of democracy. Above all, this period also witnessed the formal religionization of politics in Sudan. For their own mortal ends, the prime movers of that cause sought to transform politics into a theology. Over and above, they sparked off religion-based conflicts through fraudulent appeals to deep religious sentiments, thus igniting religious antagonisms which destroyed the ethos of traditional Islam. This religious bullying may have sustained its perpetrators' appetency for wishful thinking and satisfied their intellectual peacockery, but it had also done an immeasurable damage to the cause of peace and unity. As things went, the political climate was changed beyond recognition.

Spurious Elections and Shaky Coalitions

The October transitional government, as we have seen earlier, was divided over the issue of elections. The SCP and the PDP wanted elections put off, citing as a reason the security situation in the South. Whether that was the real reason or just a pretext, it would have been the most prudent thing to do. Umma and the NUP countered that if the elections couldn't be held in the South, they ought to go ahead in the North as planned, and in the South when conditions allowed. The SCP and the PDP maintained that such a formula would legitimize the notion that the Sudan was divided. On their part, the Southern parties were afraid that an election that excluded them would lead to a constituent assembly that would write a new constitution without their input.

The matter was put to the Supreme Council which ruled that elections should be delayed. Notwithstanding, elections were held on 21 April 1965 and boycotted by the PDP. Umma took 75 seats, the NUP 52 and the Muslim Brothers – in their new guise as the Islamic Charter Front (ICF) – 15. Equally important were the results of the Graduates' Constituencies where the SCP captured more than half the seats (eleven out of twenty). Of the rest, five seats went to the Muslim Brothers, of whom one was Hassan Turabi who scored the highest vote among the twenty. This was certainly due to his courageous position on the issue of the South during Abboud's regime, not because of support to him by graduates within the Islamists.[1] Besides, a most curious occurrence took place; a group of 21 candidates who stood unopposed in Southern constituencies declared themselves elected without opposition to represent the South. The Southern parties were frantic with frustration since, in keeping with the ruling of the Supreme Council, they had refrained from fielding candidates. The matter was taken to the courts which ruled that the 21– the majority of them Northerners – had been legally elected and were duly sworn in. Southerners retorted that the issue was not simply legal, it was political and might have serious ramifications. The government would not listen, so in the end, the South was dubiously represented by Northerners on the basis of legal formalities. Manifestly, the Northern parties to whom those elected members belonged were more concerned with augmenting their numbers in parliament than with genuinely addressing the problem of the South. That could not have been done in the absence of *bona fide* representatives of the people of the South. But the two parties were in a hurry to rule irrespective of the harm this would cause to peace in the country or to its unity. They evidently didn't mind in the least the resentment of

Southerners to this specious election. Despite their bitter experiences, the parties' formalistic approach to democracy betrayed a misreading of its real meaning, in the manner of T.S. Elliot, they 'had the experience but missed the meaning'.[2]

Umma and the NUP struck a coalition deal by which the NUP got the presidency of the Supreme Council, while the Umma got the Premiership. Thus Ismail al Azhari was back, this time as permanent President of the Supreme Council. The Council, a symbolic body representing the whole nation, had a rotational presidency in the Swiss style, which gave all its members (including the one from the South), opportunity to head the state's supreme organ when his turn came. But Azhari would not accept being subordinate to anyone, so the constitution was amended to meet that voracity for primacy. Apart from undoing the symbolism inherent in the rotational chairmanship, that decision proved to be most disastrous when it came to managing politics; the head of state, who was meant to reign but not rule within Sudan's Westminister-like constitution, assumed for himself an executive role in governance which resulted in clashes between himself and the Prime Minister.

On the other hand, by an internal Umma arrangement, Mohammed Ahmed Mahjoub became premier in place of Sadiq al Mahdi, the heir presumptive to the *Ansar's* political mantle; Sadiq believed that the chairmanship of the party and government should be his by right of birth. But since he was not by then qualified for membership of Parliament, there was little that he could do about the latter. Albeit, it soon became clear that the new government had policies distinct from those of October's, it reverted to the old denial of any legitimate problem in the South and went back to the old cliches about 'mutineers', 'imperialist stooges' and 'enemies of Arab civilization and Islam'.[4] Mahjoub declared that his government would face the Southern problem 'which was inherited from the imperialists by adopting a clear and firm policy which will affirm unity of the country and the prosperity of the people without discrimination'.[5] He also added that he would 'not permit any foreign intervention while liquidating terrorist organizations'.[6] On top of the escalation of violence, war rehetoric and xenophobia reached their acme. Wild accusations were levelled against 'foreign' traders in the South, especially Greeks and Syrian Christians, even though the majority of those traders were Sudanese by birth and many of them had married into Southern tribes. The daily organ of the PDP went to the extent of accusing those hapless citizens of collusion with 'mutineers'and called for their expulsion and the confiscation of their property.[7] There was no explanation to this gung-ho xenophobia other than race hatred; xenophobia, by its very nature, is racially biased. Obligingly the government took steps to expel 'foreigners' from South, imposed press censorship to mask what was going on in the region, and purged South-based security forces of Southerners suspected of collusion with 'mutineers'.

On the other hand, military operations intensified, and soon degenerated into open atrocity that went beyond any justifiable use of force to supress rebellion. A Southern commentator talked of 'the hour of terror' having arrived. 'Mahjoub's method of destroying Southern lives and property,' he said, 'were similar to those applied by Malzac, a European slave raider on the White Nile in 1856, but given modern weapons, modern means of transport and a highly disciplined army, the degree of suffering faced by the Southern people under the Mahjoub era was unprecedented in the history of the South.'[8] Knowing what used to happen in the South during the slave raids, statements like this were probably exaggerations to make the point. All the same, under Mahjoub, a Southerner became synonymous with 'rebel'. In those actions Mahjoub was armed by a unanimous resolution of the Northern-controlled parliament that granted the army battalions operating in the South a *carte blanche* to deal with 'law and order' in all areas within the purview of their control. The Muslim Brothers and surprisingly the SCP voted for that resolution,[9] on the strength of which the army maximized its offensives. No amount of atrocity and reprisal was to be questioned by the government. In June 1965, Mahjoub issued an ultimatum giving the South 15 days to surrender. When they did not, he unleashed a reign of terror beginning with the massacre of 1,400 civilians in one night in Juba and 76 government officials in Wau, as reported in the media.[10]

With that *carte blanche*, the army eliminated any Southerner who was thought to pose a potential threat to the government. Educated Southerners lost their lives as a matter of course. All organized associations in the South were forcefully broken up. Muslim Southern intellectuals were not spared this fate; for example, Abdel Rahman Suli and Ahmed Morjan were driven by the army excess into the laps of the 'mutineers'. This provided further proof to the conclusion of the Cotran Commission that the Southern problem was not about religion. The prominent Southern leader and foremost advocate of federation, William Deng Nihal, was assassinated during the second Mahjoub government. On that occasion the whole Northern establishment looked the other way it was a tragedy they wished to pass. Seemingly, the harrowing memory of Deng's assassination continued to torment his close parliamentary ally, Sadiq al Mahdi.[11] In due course those wanton killings envenomed the situation and fanned the embers of conflict to hellfire.

While Mahjoub was treated as the monster of iniquity in the South, in his power-base all was not well; power struggles in the sectarian parties knew no end. This one pitted the youthful Sadiq al Mahdi against his uncle, al Hadi al Mahdi, the Imam of the *Ansar*, and by extension against Mahjoub. When Sadiq's father, Siddiq al Mahdi, died, the imamate of the *Ansar* passed to al Hadi. Seeing the leadership of the sect slipping from his fingers and going to his uncle, Sadiq wanted to take over the political leadership of the party (Umma). Nevertheless, he chose to lie in waiting till the opportune time came. Once he attained the statutory age to be an MP, the Umma Party persuaded one of its supporters (Bushra Hamid representative of a Kosti constituency) to vacate his seat for Sadiq. In essence that was a contumelious act against both the incumbent and the electorate. No matter what, Sadiq took the oath as a member of Parliament on 23 June 1966 and about one month later (27 July 1966) he challenged Mahjoub. On the strength of the support he was able to muster from his followers within his party as well as from Turabi's IFC and William Deng's Southern group, he became Prime Minister.

Evidently, Sadiq al Mahdi neither had the patience to waite for his turn, nor the courtesy to allow the aging prime minister to continue his term in office till the next elections. Having become an MP, he wanted to go immediately into the fray, not as a junior MP who had something to learn from his seniors, but as an instantaneous Prime Minister. Certes, it would have been unthinkable for any other Umma stalwart at the age of Sadiq, no matter how word-perfect and well-groomed he was, to aspire to that position without the magical name, al Mahdi; his elevation lay less in his academic achievements than in his name. Mahjoub naturally allied himself with al Hadi against the young Sadiq. Still, he lost power through a no-confidence motion on 26 July 1996. But Mahjoub did not leave before he gave Sadiq a drubbing. He described his successor as green and inexperienced and lamented that government has become a 'family property bequethed from father to son'.[12] Surprisingly, al Mahdi's rationale for the *coup* against Mahjoub was that the party and government needed new blood, an argument that he scarcely remembered thirty years later, when he continued to hang on to the command of both religion and politics within the Umma party and *Ansar* sect and to rev up plans for a third coming.

Sadiq soon took on his uncle, pleading for the separation of the party from the sect, the spiritual from the political. That division of labour would have represented a departure from the Umma tradition. Accordingly the new Imam stuck to his guns as his predecessor (Sadiq's father) headed both the party and the sect, though not the government. As a consequence Sadiq unleashed a scathing offensive against his uncle, which impelled the uncle to teach his nephew his place. In the following elections that took place in the height of the family feud, Sadiq was humiliatingly defeated in his bid to recapture his constituency which incorporated Aba Island, the citadel of mahdism. As a result of that crushing defeat, one thought, Sadiq would have been chastened. Far from it, he went on to form a coalitian christened the Congress of New Forces which encompassed Turabi's supporters and SANU.

Sadiq al Mahdi's first term in office was disappointing; in his maiden speech to Parliament, his views on Sudan's identity caused shivers among Southerners and other Sudanese non-Muslims. In that speech he declared that 'the dominant feature of our nation is an Islamic one and its overpowering expression is Arab ... this nation will not have its cultural identity defined and its prestige and pride upheld except under an Islamic revival'.[13] Coming from a man who advocated separation of the spiritual from the temporal and was engaged in a vituperative quarrel with his uncle on that matter,[14] those words were decidedly off course. Al Mahdi, beyond doubt, was as undisguisedly mindless of other strands in Sudan's cultural identity as he was inattentive to the impact of his perception of Sudanism on the current conflict. The statement was not a fleeting remark by a zealous leader, it apparently represented a general trend among Sadiq's supporters. For example, the main organ of the *Ansar* confirmed this impression in one of its editorials when it said: 'the restoration of the Arab Islamic civilization in the South does not mean Arab colonization but the sharing of one culture which is the natural access for Southerners to civilization'.[15] Apart from the inveracity of the term 'restoration', this postulation summed up a view prevalent among Northern intellectuals to the effect that they knew better what was good for the South. The protagonists of this philosophy may have been well-meaning in their belief in the beneficence of Arab culture to Southerners, but what made such belief dubious was the political motivation behind it and the divisive tactics that accompanied it.

For instance, following al Mahdi's statement, a Khartoum English daily reported him saying that there was an 'African conspiracy to dispossess Sudan Arabism.[16] Also, in a discourse entitled 'Future Prospects of Arabism and Islam in Sudan',[17] al Mahdi declared a plan to change the cultural landscape in the South through, *inter alia,* exploiting differences among Southern leaders, particularly those who hail from pastoral tribes, and dispatching Islamic scholars and Northern merchants to the South 'in a friendly way'. Whether out of genuine belief in the merits of Arabicizing the South, or a desire to pander to Northern public prejudices and Arabist xenophobia against assumed African enemies, al Mahdi's call for the conversion of a group of citizens to one religion in a multireligious country was seriously ill-advised, especially when the methods of this conversion were grossly devious. As we shall see, al Mahdi's religious certainties never abated, and the circuitous manner in which they were expounded clearly hid behind it earthly designs.

After all, al Mahdi's emergence as political leader in the mid-1960s was marked by two important departures from the traditional Umma stance under the patronage of his father (Siddiq al Mahdi) and grandfather (Abdel Rahman al Mahdi). Both leaders recognized the multiple diversities of Sudan and thus eschewed calls for the Islamization of politics. Consequently, they left the running of the state to worldly politicians who were not bothered about the religion of others; some of them were not even followers of the *Ansar* sect or known for their piety. Par contra, Sadiq viewed himself as the heir of the grand Mahdi, his thinly veiled aim had always been to reincarnate Mahdism to his own image, as if he knew better than his two predecessors. Sadiq's father and grand-father obviously had stronger nostrils to sniff the political air around them, but he lacked that olfactory sense.

Sadiq's mini-revolution didn't go down very well with the Imam's backers; nine months after he was ousted, Mahjoub was voted back into power. In reaction, Sadiq's faction of the Umma Party constituted itself into an opposition in parliament and frustrated all government efforts at legislation. That the leader of government's business, and the leader of the opposition in the House, belonged to one party showed how farcical parliamentary democracy was in Sudan. The battle cry of Sadiq's spoiling opposition was separation of religion from politics and distinguishing the sacred from the secular. Many young Sudanese, including some who did not belong to the *Ansar*, hailed Sadiq as the 'hope of the nation', *(Al Sadiq amal al Umma)*. They saw in his daredevil challenges to the sectarian establishment signs of a break with the past and of good things to come. He was also young, articulate and perceived as ready to espouse progressive causes. Regrettably for Sadiq, his dilemma was that his past dictated his present and continued to be his Achilles heel, a matter he never cared to realize or admit. From that point he went sliding down a political helter skelter, and his future performance agonized and tested the core belief of those non-*Ansar* who pinned their hopes on him.

Sadiq's views on the role of the Mahdist tradition in the Islamic revival in, and governance of, Sudan were made clear in a major work he wrote a few years later;[18] the work was an extremely defective and self-serving milestone in the treatment of the Mahdist era. Though assuming to write as a political historian, Sadiq's selective approach to historical events made of him a propagandist for Mahdism, not a disinterested analyst. To begin with, he claimed that any socio-political change in Sudan should, by necessity, be anchored on the country's tradition and historical background, a statement with which nobody would disagree. But, to the mind of the Umma Leader, Sudan's historical background was only confined to Mahdism. The antipathy towards Mahdism by large groups in the North as well as by almost the entire population of the South, was of no consquence to the political historian. His thesis also contained two revealing statements. In the first he opined that 'the surrounding circumstances informs that Sudan shall witness an Islamic revival predicated on Mahdism[19] since Mahdism has charted the way to Islamic revival in its time and future times'. His second contention was that such revival would only be carried by inspired leaders; those 'giants,' he said, 'must be buttressed by solid popular support, understand the logic of their time, communicate with others in the language of the age and be endowed with contemporary enlightenment'. In addition, 'they must be self-aware that they are inspired.'[20] Aware of his own 'inspirational' capacities, Sadiq never relented in propagating the idea of inspired leadership. For example, in an academic seminar organized by the University of Khartoum in 1980 to commemorate the *Mahdiyya*'s centenary, he addressed the seminar on the ideology of Mahdism and its bearing on Islamic revival in Sudan. 'Mahdism,' he said, 'was the most successful enterprise to revive the glories of earlier Islam, satisfy the aspirations of Muslims and challenge European dominance.' He went on to state that Mahdism had also 'proved beyond doubt the efficacy of popular energy when that energy was armed with faith and mobilized by an inspired leadership'.[21] With those definitions, Sadiq al Mahdi the Islamic revivalist left nobody in doubt that he was confecting a job description that fit only him. Provenly, there was no shadow of doubt in the grand Mahdi's inspired and inspiring qualities, but the thought to revivify Mahdism in this day and age, borders on lunacy, especially in a country where nearly all the people living in its Southern part do not share Sadiq's religion, and a large number of those who share his religion in the North are not partial to his idolism of the *Mahdiyya*. Evidently, humility is not a strong suite for 'divinely-inspired' leaders. Sadiq may well be sincere in his belief that he can clone Mahdism in the twenty-first century and stir up its embers, and here lies his vulnerability as a national leader. Were Sadiq to use that language to generate support for his party among the *Ansar*, that could have been tolerated as a tool of mobilization. Not so when he was defining a political dispensation for ruling the whole country in the twenty-first centurty.

One doubts, however, whether Sadiq al Mahdi knew where he wanted to go and take the country along with him, as his utterances and performance were often a riot of incongruity. His failure began within his own household when, as a tactic of survival, he planned to isolate his political constituency from the control of his uncle by preaching that the Umma party had to be separated from its *Ansar* sectarian roots. It was indeed surprising, therefore, that as a Prime Minister, Sadiq al Mahdi sought to justify his religion-based politics on the claim that religion and politics were inseparable in Islam. That sure enough was the *raison d'être* of the Mahdism he wanted to reincarnate, but it did not congeal with his desire to deny the *Ansar* leadership any say in politics. Sadiq was at his contradictory best when he told the House in one of his speeches to Parliament that he belonged to the left politically, and to the Islamic right ideologically. This was the type of muddled slogans Sadiq became so adept in coining and purring with pleasure about. But having built all his political philosophy on the restoration of what he considered to be a pristine indigenous religious heritage, Sadiq also wished, in one of his ever so many political phases, to separate the embodiment of that heritage from politics. How could those contradictions live within one body without destroying it?

Back to the endemic fissiparity of the parties and their congenital inability to work together for any reasonable measure of time. Azhari with the connivance of Mahjoub dissolved parliament, an action al Mahdi refused to accept. In a buffoonish way he went on transacting parliamentary government business under a tree outside the parliament building from which he was locked out. Al Mahdi also appealed to the High Court seeking an injunction against Azhari's decision which he claimed was unconstitutional. But alongside his justifiable resort to legal redress, Sadiq committed a grievously seditious act; he wrote to General Khawad, the Commander-in-Chief of the army, protesting against

Azhari's 'undermining of the constitution'. That did no justice to al Mahdi's democratic credentials, nor to his purported revulsion of the meddling by the military in politics. The only way General Khawad could have 'protected' the constitution was to stage a military *coup* against a duly elected government. Sadiq's appeal to the army was, therefore, nothing but a spoiler's act. Mahjoub, on the other hand, prevailed and elections were held in April 1968, the elections in which al Mahdi was humiliatingly defeated. The al Hadi faction of the Umma and the DUP carried the day and Mahjoub was back in power. He was not destined to stay there for long, as the military took over power in May of the following year. How much time could such self-absorbed governments have had to attend to the real concerns of the nation?

Birth of the Islamic Constitution

When Sudan's constitution was first being debated, the sectarian parties were opposed to proposals by Islamic groups to make it a religious document. The first National Constitution Committee (NCC) received a memorandum from the Islamic forces, led by the Muslim Brothers, urging it to adopt an Islamic constitution. They argued that in an Islamic country like Sudan, where the 'social organization has been built upon Arab customs and Islamic ways and where the majority was Muslim, the general principles of the constitution must be derived from Islam'. In addition, laws governing the country should also be enacted in accordance with Islamic tenets and injunctions. The Islamists argued, moreover that Islam is both a 'religion and a state' and that it cannot be practised to the full save under an Islamic constitution.[22] Sure enough, Islam has historically developed to be an important feature of the identity of Muslims, but certainly not the principal or exclusive feature. Within the Muslim world, people continued to identify themselves according to linguistic, racial and ethnic markings and lineaments of which they remained proud. Halliday observed that adopting Islam as a badge of identification is 'either a stereotypical projection employed by those who have sought and still seek to dominate or exclude people of Islamic origin, or it is an equally spurious claim made by people within an Islamic community who seek to exercise authority over a social group by advancing their particular interpretation as the sole legitimate and authoritative Islam'.[23] There is abundant evidence to substantiate Halliday's contention. In the West, for example, there is an increasing tendency to lump together Muslims of all races, languages and indegenous cultures and treat them, by virture of their Islamism, as terrorists, barbaric, gender insensitive or generally not at home with Western civilization. On the other hand, the secession of Bangaladesh from Pakistan, and the clamouring by the Kurds in Iraq for an independent state, prove that Islam is not the only glue that keeps Muslims together. Befittingly, Halliday's description as spurious of the claim to adopt Islam as the principal badge of identification applies to claims by Sudanese Islamists to make of Islam the only defining mark of identification in Sudan.

Islam has also permeated the body politic of Muslim states from the days of Prophet Muhamad up to the Ottoman era. This permeating influence of Islam on politics was attributed by Bernard Lewis to the fact that 'Islam rose amid the birth of an empire, and became the creed of a vast, triumphant and flourishing realm created under the aegis of a new faith'. Christianity, on the other side, arose amid the fall of an empire and, therefore, created its own structures independent of the state which it did not look favourabvly upon any way, according to Lewis.[24] He further added that 'while for St Augustine and early Christian thinkers, the state was a lesser evil, for Muslims, the state – that is of course the Islamic state – was a divine good'.[25] But, in as much as this reasoning was tenable in the old Islamic Empire where the Muslim community was cohesive and non-Muslims knew their place within that society as second-class citizens, so to speak, it became increasingly implausible to maintain in an evolving new world where basic human rights and duties were not determined by religious affiliation but inherent in citizenship. Muslim states which incorporate non-Muslims as citizens are thus expected to guarantee them political rights, no less than those guaranteed to Muslims. Also, secular international and regional covenants are generally assumed to govern the behaviour of all states towards their citizens. And since Muslim states cannot say: 'stop the world, I want to get off' they have no way but to adapt themselves to the imperatives of this evolving world.

To aggravate an already problematic situation, the approach by Sudan's traditional and modern Islamists to the islamization of politics was postulated on the application of *shari'a*. That approach is both frayed and impertinent, and in some cases hypocritical. For one, by postulating that Islam and *shari'a* are synonymous, the Islamists are indeed striving to drive a square peg in a round hole. *Shari'a*, as we shall elaborate later, represents the corpus of jurisprudence that was developed by Islamic scholars over the years to meet the needs of their time. But times have changed and new social concerns and values emerged. By necessity, that calls for the formulation of a new *shari'a* that responds to the emergent conditions. But as long as the Islamists insisit that *shari'a* has the same sanctity as the *Qur'an*, they cannot by any manner of means address meaningfully those emergent conditions. This problematique is further compounded by the fact that *shari'a* was never applied in Sudan except during the *Mahdiyya* which represented an aberration in country's history.[26] From the Turkish era when the country was ruled in the name of the Islamic Caliphate and through the colonial rule and the post-independence era, *shari'a* was only the basis of legislation in personal matters concerning Muslims. No two ways about it, policymakers in all those periods must have come to the conclusion that *shari'a* – as it had developed and was historically applied – could in no way be a basis for legislating for a modern state.

Nonetheless, Sudan's Muslim Brothers proceeded with their plans to establish a *shari'a*-based constitution and legal system. Their views presented to the National Constitution Committee which, incidentally, was also to define the coutnry's constitutional status taking 'due consideration of the legitimate demands of the South'. The Islamists propositions were presented to the NCC by Mirghani al Nasri, but were so isolated within the committee, that they lost the vote at the NCC not once, but twice. That happened despite the Islamists brandishing of the support of the two religious leaders, al Mahdi and al Mirghani, as well as that of the Grand Kadi.[27] Other than the NUP, the mainstream sectarian-based parties (the PDP and Umma) voted against an Islamist's proposal and rightly said that people may differ in their religious beliefs but agree on other matters.[28] They also proffered that Sudan was composed of various beliefs and religions, a matter that necessitated a search for broader identities transcending religious denominations. Citizens' loyalty, it was maintained, should be to the state as such, and not to a state with a particular religion. In this sense the phrase 'Islamic' Republic did not add anything beyond identification of the state's official religion, a matter which may be specified in a particular section of the constitution, if need be.

As well, equality before the law imposes the necessity for constituting a non-religious state, because in an Islamic state a non-Muslim could never aspire to become head of state, no matter how talented he or she may be. Furthermore, since all civilizations have contributed to the democratic ideas and systems, Sudan need not necessarily refer only to Islam to define democracy. Finally, there were the fears that may be engendered among Southerners by the promulgation of a religion-based constitution; religion is for God but the nation is for everybody.[29] Behind those bold enunciations were Mohammed Salih al Shingetti and Ahmed Khair.[30] Shingetti, a wordly Umma politician and an erudite lawyer, had served during his forensic career as a *shari'a* judge, and since the days of the Juba Conference had been ever conscious of the complexities of Sudan's situation. Shingetti also had the courage of his conviction to face up to the agitation of the rabble-rousers in the Committee, he described their call for a religion-based constitution in a multireligious country as 'demagogic'. Khair, on his part, rejected outright the message of support to the Islamic Constitution attributed to the two sectarian leaders; the two Saiyyds, said Khair, were neither members of the committee nor should the committee be influenced by external pressures.[31] People of Shingetti's and Khair's metal served as role models to leaders, especially purported 'modernizers,' who every so often opted to lead from behind.

Equally of note was the alignment of forces within the committee against the so-called Islamic Constitution. While the two sectarian-based parties (Umma and PDP) rejected the idea despite the support of the two Sayyids, the supposedly secular NUP went along with the call for an Islamic Constitution. That party, we recall, was ostensibly dedicated to the dissociation of religion from politics, but it turned out to be the party of anything goes. In Sudan's political theatre of the absurd that was hardly a cause for surprise. The issue to the NUP was neither religion, good governance, political stability nor the country's unity, it was scoring a point against its political adversaries, albeit at the cost of abdicating principles which it vociferously defended in the 1950s.

After the failure of the first constitutional committee to reach agreement on a permanent constitution for Sudan, another committee was formed in 1967 following Abboud's demise. Sadiq al Mahdi, working in unison with Turabi, became the intellectual powerhouse behind the new committee.[32] Both he and Turabi believed that the function of the committee was to Islamize the constitution. There was every evidence to show that the al Mahdi's position, though ideologically inspired, was not free from ulterior motives, just like that of the NUP in the first constitutional committee. On account of the growing influence of the radicals and communists, especially within the trades union's movement and among the intelligentsia at large, a very serious challenge was presented to the traditional establishment inducing it to seek to contain and ultimately destroy the communists. This, too, was the foremost objective of the Muslim Brothers.[33]   Islam, being a sensitive bond, presented itself as the handy sword with which this perfidious political ploy was to be achieved. The soft underbelly of communism in Sudan was its supposed atheism; and it was at that spot that the sword was directed. On 24 November 1965 duly elected communist parliamentarians were expelled from parliament and in December the SCP was banned.[34] The High Court ruled the ban unconstitutional, but the government dismissed the ruling of the court as declaratory order, not an enforceable enjoinment. Sadiq al Mahdi, contrary to the stance he took later to seek redress from the same court against Azhari's alleged violation of the constitution, went along with the government in discounting the court's decision. In a statement broadcast over Sudan Television (13 January 1967) he declared that the Assembly was not obligated to abide by the court's ruling. So, in cohort with Azhari, Turabi and Mahjoub, he went on to rewrite the constitution in a way that illegalized the SCP. A witchhunt, mainly driven by the Muslim Brothers, ensued.

Of the four, Mahjoub's position was the most surprising; he was for all ends and purposes, a 'secular' politician who had resolutely stood with his other colleagues in the Umma Party against the Islamization of the constitution during the first parliament. He was also a liberal thinker and a lawyer's lawyer. Mahjoub ostensibly became hostage of the contradictions that brought him to, and maintained him in, power. However, by his approach to the Islamization of the constitution, he gave short shrift to the democracy that was supposedly his pride. In retrospect Mahjoub had second thoughts of his position on the Islamization of politics. Writing after the fact, Mahjoub averred that there should have been no quarrel on whether the constitution should have been Islamic or secular. 'The Sudan could have had a constitution without calling it

Islamic, thereby practicing Islam and using the tolerance embodied in its tenets.'[35] That apologia was too little too late.

Though clad in a pseudo-Islamic garb, the parties' real intention was to obliterate completely the left as a political alternative in the Sudan. Writ large on the script, therefore, was the dissolution of the SCP. True to design, other than expressly prohibiting communism, renewing commitment to the spread Islam and, stating that *shari'a* was the primary source of law; the Islamic content[36] of the so-called Islamic Constitution was at best symbolic and fell short of what could be expected from a constitution based on the 'spirit and guidance of Islam' as aptly remarked by a Sudanese scholar.[37] That was yet another proof of both the inadaptability of *shari'a* to the running of a modern state as well as to the insufficiency of the Islamists to induct from the main sources of Islam rules that were pertinent to the exigencies of modern societies and states. Indubitably, there was also an element of hypocrisy in the attitude of both traditional and modern Islamists towards *shari'a:* paying lip service to it through symbolic gestures, while maintaining Western institutions and procedures of governance, let alone non-Islamic laws.[38] For example, the *shura* (consultation) which the Islamists claim to be the Islamic equivalent of democracy was never exercised in deliberative assemblies encompassing non-Muslims, women and so-called heathens like the one that was meeting in Khartoum, to legislate *shari'a*-based laws. A scholar has aptly described this false piety as follows: 'To a Muslim it has always been a more heinous sin to deny or question the divine revelation than to fail to obey it. So it seemed preferable to continue to pay lip service to an inviolate *shari'a*, as the only law of fundamental authority, and to excuse departure from much of it in practice by appealing to the doctrine of necessity *(darura)* rather than to make any attempt to adapt that law to the circumstances and needs of contemporary life.'[39] However, future experiences revealed that even innocuous symbols like declaring *shari'a* as a source of legislation, contained more than met the eye. A similar article in Nimeiri's otherwise secular constitution of 1973 was the basis of Turabi's draft constitution that consecrated Nimeiri's imamate. Consequently, Fr Phillip Abbas Ghabboush (Nuba) was on target when he denounced the seemingly inocuous clause, arguing that Sudan was a multi-religious country that could only be governed by a constitution neutral on the issue of religion. Despite Ghabboush's portentous statement, the levity with which Parliament took the matter was astounding; the disproportionately composed Constitutional Committee,[40] gave the public only one week to express their views on the two controversial issues: religion and state and banning communism, otherwise called aethiesm.

The draft constitution also included an indeterminate and threatening stipulation that obligates the state to purify society from corruption and moral degeneration. Imbuing any government – let alone one run by self-righteous politicians – with powers to watch over people's morality was frightening and not in keeping with the tenets of democracy.

Accordingly, the espousal of the 1968 draft constitution by the sectarian-based parties became a defining moment in the history of Sudan; it has put Sudanese progress towards a permanent constitution out of gear. That also was the first time Southern opposition used the term secularism in its political discourse.[41] So, it was thanks to the traditional parties, that secularism was enacted into Sudan's political literature.

The debate on the Islamic constitution was revealing in another sense, exposing the Islamists' circuity and lack of intellectual honesty. For example, when Turabi was called upon by the Constitution Committee, in his professional capacity as member of the technical advisory group to that Committee, to respond to a question regarding the right of non-Muslims to assume the presidency in an Islamic republic, he evaded the issue not once, but twice. His questioner, Revererand Phillip Abbas Ghabboush (Nuba Mountains) would not relent; he wanted a yes or no answer. In the face of Ghabboush's adamance, Turabi answered in the negative.[42] A Sudanese scholar appropriately described this episode as follows: 'It is remarkable and very significant that a trained modern lawyer, who has successfully led his movement for 25 years into national and regional prominence and political power, has avoided expressing the objective of his movement in concrete constitutional and legal terms.'[43]

Turabi also quibbled on the issue of *álamaniyya* (secularism) which was raised by Southern members of the committee: 'I do not know from where the Arabic term is derived,' he said. 'In France they coined the term *laique* which distinguishes between an ordinary citizen and the clergy; in English they talk of secular to destinguish between spiritual and temporal authority,' Turabi opined.[44] However, he went on to add that the term did not accord with Islamic precepts and therefore was unacceptable to Muslims. Islam, Turabi said, never places religion and public life in a conflictual position. Another member of the technical committee, Natalie Alwak, took Turabi to task; he explained that the term *álamaniyya* simply connotes that laws and public policy should not issue from any religion; it did not necessarily mean that the state was opposed to religion.[45]

Whatever way you look at it, those developments proved that Southern apprehensions were plentuously justified. The Constitution Committee that was formed to write Sudan's constitution and encompass some of the ideas reflected in the report of the Twelve-man Committee closed all avenues for reconciliation after the adoption by the Northern parties of an Islamic constitution. Abel Alier, the spokesman for the Southern group within the Constitution Committee, announced the withdrawal of the group from that Committee stating, that: 'the South only saw in the Islamic constitution, the supreme expression of a way of life, of a culture, or a mystique known as the Arab Nation. Because of the overriding religio-racial components of the constitution, Christian, Muslim and pagan African Negroes of the South appeared unanimous in their rejection of such a document.'

In their 'sacred' war to write a constitution that would consolidate their influence and eliminate the opposition, al Mahdi and the so-called

Islamic wing within the traditional political establishment conveniently forgot Sudan's non-Muslims, pretending that what would serve the interests of the Muslim majority should serve the interests of the non-Muslim minority as well. Equally, they cared less about the impact of their wheeler-dealing on peace and unity. When they did, it was in such a way as to destroy whatever was left over from the RTC resolutions.

As we have seen earlier, Prime Minister al Mahdi received the report of Twelve-Man Committee in June 1966, but in place of calling the RTC who created the Committee and resolved that it should report to it, al Mahdi claimed that the situation had changed and arbitrarily created, in place of the RTC, a so-called All-Party Conference.[46] That 'All-Party' conference was boycotted by SCP who initially participated in the Twelve-man Committee then withdrew, the PDP who never participated in the Twelve-Man's Committee and the Southern Sudanese in exile who were locked out by al Mahdi. The Prime Minister was not alone in this arbitrariness, being supported by the NUP. Sadiq's action, as future practices confirmed, was prompted by his desire to put his personal distinctive mark on any political development in the country, even on issues on which there was a prior consensus. On the basis of this self-centered approach to politics, Sadiq opted for creating his own peacemaking forum since the RTC was not his creation.

Surely, whatever came out from the All-Party Conference could not have been a basis for consensus, even a limited one like that achieved in the Twelve-Man Committee. According to Alier, there were three reasons for this. The first was the exclusion of Southern politicians in exile who were not going to be bound by any decision taken by the conference in their absence. Secondly, fears that *Anya Nya* would not abide by decisions of the conference in the absence of agreement on security arrangements to which it was party. Thirdly, the presentation of the draft Islamic Constitution after the Committee of Twelve concluded its work, drove the last nail on the coffin of reconciliation, a matter to which Sadiq was utterly oblivious.[47]

Sadiq al Mahdi never reconciled himself with the realities which Alier had ably exposed. He continued to believe that he deserved a standing ovation for his 'successes' in laying the foundations for peace during his ten months in government through the All-Party Conference, the RTC and the Twelve-Man Committee. Those, he said, were landmarks that were erected by civilian democratic governments, including his.[48] He went further in the same statement to claim that, within the context of those meetings, 'the political and cultural nature of the North–South civil war was recongnized', obviously by those civilian governments. This is an unbearable statement. Al Mahdi might not have recalled Azhari's injudicious opening statement at the RTC: the statement about 'your ancestors the Africans and our ancestors the Arabs'. But he could not be incognizant of his own maiden speech in Parliament in which the maintained that Sudan's cultural identity could only be expressed in Arabo-Islamic terms. Nor could he be clueless about his marshalling, together with other Northern party leaders, of the Islamic constitution which drove the last nail on the coffin of reconciliation, as Alier said. Evidently, leaders make mistakes. The discerning among them become wiser in the process. But Sadiq's consistent mutilation of facts, economy of truth and astounding inadequacy in contrition, rattle his ability to make a meaningful contribution to the resolution of Sudan's multiple crises.

The irony of the political parties' squabbles was such that they could not unite long enough to pass a constitution that was written specifically to secure their hold on the reins of power. The NUP had supported al Mahdi's claim to power with two ulterior motives: first, to deepen the rift between him on the one side, and his uncle the Imam and Mahjoub on the other, and second, they wanted to humble and, therefore, blunt the burning ambitions of the young Mahdi. Once those objectives were achieved, the NUP deviously switched sides, merging with the PDP to form the Democratic Unionist Party (DUP) which went on to garner more than half the votes in the elections that followed. The refurbished DUP, fresh from its victory, entered a ruling coalition with the al Hadi faction of the Umma and settled down to enjoy the fruits of power; its aims achieved to its liveliest satisfaction. Once again the parties went into another spell of congenital misreckoning; they reduced governance to two things, electioneering and coalition-forming, and believed that they could get away with it. To their dismay, the army intervened; this time uninvited. And when the army returned to power at the end of May 1969, the second parliamentary regime was to have as few defenders as the first.

Conclusion

The way Northern political parties carried themselves in addressing the cardinal issue of war and peace, as well that of governance in general, is a scorching indictment of party politics. Rather than learning from Abboud's misadventures in the South, they pursued his policies to a nicety. In reality, all the way from the pre-independence process in the early 1950s to the mid-1960s, civilian governments in Sudan behaved in the South more like neo-colonialists than democratic nationalists. Examples ranged from bare-faced lying to their citizens and economic neglect to outright invasion and physical, human assault. In addition, during Abboud's regime, as in Mahjoub's, the Sudanese army acted in the South the way an invading army would have done in a foreign land. As for the Islamists (sectarian and otherwise), they set in motion for their own sublunary interests a politico-religious maelstrom which eventually led to the ruination of all that was amiable and humane in the psyche of the average Muslim and non-Muslim Sudanese. Moreover, by enshrining in the constitution of a multi-religious country they wished to see united, one religion as the only determinant of governance and legislation, they displayed a warpped appreciation of what was fact and what was fancy.

Once again, Sudan's Northern political establishment (of the neo-Islamist stripe this time) could have drawn yet another lesson from the Indian experience, in this particular instance from that of Hindu fundamentalists. Like Sudan's fundamentalists, the Hindu version vociferated against the principle of secularism enshrined by Nehru in India's constitution; their argument was kindred to that of their Sudanese counterparts. Secularism, they said, was an alien Western concept and, accordingly, India should be governed by laws that were aligned to the culture and religion of the majority. If that was to happen, the hearts of Sudanese Islamists would have bled profusely for the fate of India's Muslims who only represent ten per cent of the population. Indeed, the Sudanese Islamists often lamented abuses to which Indian Muslims were subjected by Hindu fundamentalist groups in contravention to India's secular laws and constitution. For instance, they made a *cause celebre* of the desecration of the Babiri mosque in Ajodhya by Hindu fundamentalists. However, those bleeding hearts never called to mind, in the course of their lamentaions, the fate to which thirty per cent of their own non-Muslim brothers and sisters would have been reduced by the sheer logic of majortarian religion-based politics. Those are the sombre realities with which Northern leaders have to come to terms with in order to understand Southern skepticism, anger and violence, before they ever think of finding a solution for the Sudanese crisis. Ironically, in spite of all the agony created by their myopic Southern policy, Northerner politicians still persist in asking the tired question: 'what do Southerners want?' The answer is not far away, it lies in Sudan's museum of broken promises, frustrated hopes and cretinous political manoeuvres. And as long as that hypocrisy and political sottishness endure, so long will the search for a lasting solution for Sudan's crisis evade searchers.

Some Southern politicians must also bear their portion of responsibility for prolonging the war in the Sudan by their wavering at critical moments. The vulnerability of those politicians to corruption and bribery by equally unscrupulous Northern politicians, was unpardonable and so were the senseless splits that had blighted Southern politics since independence. Had the Southern leaders been more united and less garrulous, an acceptable settlement might have been reached, or forced by events, at some crucial moment. The country would have been spared the agony of a prolonged armed conflict. The wavering, corruption and divisiveness among Southern politicians paved the way for the success of the mischievous policies of divide and rule which became a leitmotiv in Sudan's inharmonious politics, all the way from Azahari to al Bashir.

Recognition has to be made to the first generation of Southern leaders who did stand their ground and shunned graft, such as Stanislaus Payasama, Buth Diu, Saturnino Lahure, William Deng, Gordon Mourtat, Benjamin Lowki, Clement Mboro and many others whose names we have and shall come across in this book. Ironically, it was precisely because of their fortitude that those leaders were intimidated by successive Northern governments and steered clear of by corrupt Southerners who colluded with those governments. For all those actions and inactions by the powers that ruled Sudan, the country became a seedbed for the germination and propagation of conflict.

Given all those political obscenities, one needs to look nowhere else for reasons why the second parliamentry democracy collapsed under the jackboots of the army in May 1969. In actuality, even simple rules of workshop management – known to any shop steward – informs that when a machine outlives its usefulness and the curve of utility goes down while that of cost and maintenance goes up, one should get rid of the damned plant. Nimeiri, or any other soldier for that matter, had his job cut for him.

ENDNOTES

1. None of the other ICF members elected in the Graduates' Constituencies came close to Turabi in the number of votes he scored. That proved that support to Turabi did not only come from the ICF cadre.
2. Elliot, T.S., *Dry Salvages*.
3. Sadiq al Mahdi was yearning for the two positions, but at the time he had not attained the statutory age for membership of parliament, or for the office of Prime minister. His attitude was a far cry from that of his father who, though President of the party, opted to take a back seat throughtout the post-independence governments; the premiership in Umma-led governments was entrusted to a politician from outside the Mahdi's family, Abdalla Khalil.
4. Malwal, Bona, *People and Power*, p. 42.
5. *The Vigilant*, 27 June 1965.
6. Ibid.
7. *Al'Alam*, editorial 15 July 1965.
8. Ruay, p. 133.
9. Abel Alier saw in the resolution a declaration of war against the *Anya Nya* as well as Southern intellegentsia living in the South. He also traced in it a sign of the prevalent feeling among the Northern elite of the left and right alike that the Southern educated class were the source of trouble. Alier, Abel, *Southern Sudan*, p. 38.
10. An investigation conducted by a Judge of the Court of Appeal concluded that the number of civilian Southern intellectual slaughtered in cold blood by the army in the Juba massacre was 430 and not 1,400 as reported by the press. Abel Alier stated the numbers as 473, which is much closer to the Judge's. Ibid., p. 33.
11. In a letter to Bona Malwal in August 1992, al Mahdi revisited the issue with a view to absolving himself of responsibility for massacres in the South that took place during his party's rule in the mid- 1960s. Malwal saw through that tardy apology, and reminded the former Prime Minister that while the perpetrators of Deng's murder were known, none of them was brought to justice. 'The idea of the investigation,' said Malwal, 'is not to punish but to serve to bolster a political culture.' He added that the 'perpetrators could even be granted immunity from prosecution if it would help clear up these atrocities and prevent repetition in the future'. The letters were made available to the author by Malwal.
12. Mahjoub, M.A., *Democracy*, p. 200.
13. Constituent Assembly Records Records, October 1966.
14. In the fend with his uncle, Sadiq described his uncle as a Pope who should have nothing to do with politics.
15. *Al N_l*, 14 July 1965.
16. *The Vigilant*, 6 November 1966.

17. *Mustaqbal al Islam wa al 'Uruba fil Sudan* (Future of Islam and Arabism in Sudan), pp. 14–115, op. cit., Garang, *Garang Speaks*, p. 134.
18. Mahdi, Sadiq al, *Yasal_nka 'an al Mahdiyy.*
19. Ibid., pp. 35 and 248.
20. Ibid., p. 35.
21. Ibid., p. 19.
22. Qadal, M.S. al, *Al Islam wa'l Siyyassa*, op.cit., p. 75.
23. Halliday, Fred, *Islam and The Myth of Confrontation*, p. 115.
24. Lewis, Bernard, The Multiple Identity of the Middle East, p. 29.
25. Ibid.
26. Professor An-N'aim rightly stated that 'to the extent that any aspect of *shari'a* was applied at all, it was implemented as part of the customary law of the community and heavily modified by local practice. But it was never the official legal system of a centralized political authority except for some fourteen years at the end of the last century'. *Reforming Islam: Sudan and the Paradox of Self-Determination*, Harvard International Review, Spring 1997, p. 25. That of course does not include Nimeiri's masquerade of the 1980s.
27. The Muslim Brothers engineered an Islamic Front for the Constitution (IFC) whose limited objective was to ensure that Sudan's constitution be derived from Islam. Through blackmail and intimidation they succeeded in persuading Hassan Mudathir, the Grand Kadi (most senior *shari'a* judge) to address a memorandum to Parliament entitled: 'Memorandum for the Enactment of a Sudan Constitution Derived from the Principles for Islam'. They also inveigled the two setarian leaders, al Mirghani and al Mahdi, to release a joint pubic statement in which they favoured the promulgation of a constitution based on the principles of Islam. Affend, A, el, *Turabi's Revolution*, p. 57–8.
28. Sid Ahmed, A., *Politics and Islam*, op. cit., p. 63.
29. Ibid.
30. Al Qadal, 22 supra.
31. Ibid.
32. Turabi, in addition to his membership in the Constituent Assembly, was also an influential member in the technical committee on the constitution. In that capacity he provided almost all the inputs on how to islamize Sudan's constitution.
33. According to el Affendi the Brothers were troubled by the ascendancy of the SCP because of its massive victory in the Graduates' Constituencies and their control of the political landscape through the trades unions. The writer reported that the Brothers decided to take the fight to the mosques and schools. El Affendi, *Turabi's Revolution*, p. 81.
34. The parties were in such a hurry to dismiss the communists from Parliament that Prime Minister Mahjoub asked Parliament to suspend Article 25 (8) of the internal statutes to in order to deliberate on an 'urgent matter'. The statutes stipulated cumbersome procedures for the introduction of bills or questions on adjournment. Mahjoub's

motion was seconded by the Minister of Justice, Mohamed Ibrahim Khalil (Umma) and supported by Hassan Turabi and Nasr el Din Al Sayed (DUP). When put to the vote, the motion was carried by 151 votes with 6 abstentions and 12 against.

35. Mahjoub, M.A., *Democracy*, p. 181.
36. The draft constitution provided that Sudan is a Muslim republic guided by Islam (Article 1); that Islam is the religion of the state; (Article 3) that *shari'a* is the main source of legislation (Article 113) and any law that is contrary to it shall be null and void, and that the state shall gradually review all laws with a view to abrogating those that are not in accordance with *shari'a* (Article 115). The resolution on the religion of the state was presented by Sheikh Mahjoub Osman Ishaq and supported by Mohamed Salih Omar; both were members of the Islamic Charter Front (ICF), the name by which the Muslim Brothers were to be known during the second regime of the parties.
37. 28 supra.
38. A technical committee comprising Sudanese lawyers and Islamic scholars was formed by Nimeiri in 1977 under the Chairmanship of Dr Turabi. The committee was to review all laws of Sudan with a view to aligning them with *shari'a*. The committee concluded that out of 286 acts and ordinances only 38 were not in consonance with *shari'a*.
39. Anderson, J.N.D., Law Reform in the Muslim World, op.cit., in An-N'aim, *Civil Rights in the Islamic Constitutional Tradition*, p. 283.
40. The committee comprised 13 members (NUP and DUP), 12 (Umma with six for each wing of the party), 2 (ICF), 1 (SCP), 5 for Sourthern parties and one each for Nuba and Beja.
41. Henry Paulo Lugali, a Southern member of parliament told a Khartoum daily that Southerners shall cooperate with any political force that wishes to work with them for the promulgation of a secular constitutuion. *Al Ayam*, 27 March 1969.
42. Minutes of the Constituent Assembly, 1968, p. 168.
43. An-N'aim, *Constitutional Discourse*, p. 102.
44. 42 supra, p. 171.
45. Ibid.
46. The All-Party Conference was chaired by Mohamed Salih Shingetti; that veneer did not change the reality; the decision to bypass the RTC was frayed because it went against the spirit of that conference and against the will of its parties. The term All Party was also misleading, since the parties in question were not limited to parliamentary parties but, above all, all parties to the conflict including those excluded by al Mahdi from his so-called All-Party Conference, e.g. Aggrey Jaden's Sanu.
47. Alier, Abel, *Southern Sudan*, p. 40.
48. Mahdi, Sadiq al, *The Second Birth*

CHAPTER FIVE

Nimeiri Era: From Euphoria to Dementia
1969–1985

Nothing is ended with
honour which does not
conclude better than it begun.
Samuel Johnson

Introduction

The Nimeiri regime (1969–85) was the most outstanding era in the history of post-independence Sudan. Firstly, on account of its contradictions, it depicted both the narcosis and dementia that symptomized the political psychology of the Sudanese body politic. Secondly, the Nimeiri era would forever stand out as the most wasted opportunity to establish a lasting peace in the South.[1] Rarely had a Sudanese leader since independence had a chance to be a national hero without borders, and thoroughly bungled it.

As observed earlier, political parties were given to blaming the failure of democracy on armies that intervene in politics. They continued to argue that Sudan had 32 years of military and transitional, and only ten years of democratic, rule. According to this arithmetic, the army should bear the brunt for all Sudan's political ailments. This argument is fallacious, and the arithmetic wrong. Truly, Sudan has had over 30 years of military rule and nearly 10 years of democratic rule. But it is equally true that Sudan has gone through 42 of years of hot or cold wars. Besides, the only period during which South Sudan enjoyed relative peace for about 10 years was during one of the military spells (1972–83). The deformity of the argument rests on the fact that it was the politicians who, in the first place, brought the army into the fray. By so doing, they dragged it into a civil war that was political in nature and for which a political solution was conceivable, as future experience has shown.

There were two other factors at play in the military takeover on 25 May 1969. The first was the distemper of the SCP and its allies against the traditional parties. Against all universally accepted principles of liberal democracy and Sudan's own history of political tolerance (at least within the North), the parties banished the SCP and its adherents to a Sudanese political Siberia. Whether the SCP was an accomplice in the engineering of the 1969 military coup or simply an accessory to the act, is immaterial. It would have indeed been against the nature of things if the SCP shed any tears for the demise of a democracy that sought to obliterate it.

The second was the pervasiveness of military culture in the region, frequently represented in ideological guises and revolutionary terms. The guises came galore: Arab nationalism, Arab socialism, national regeneration etc. Those slogans had been totally discredited after a battery of disastrous experiments. But in the decade of the 1960s, it was considered bad manners in the Arab region not to identify with the hue and cry of Nasserism, Ba'athism and Arab nationalism. To the south, the one-party mania held sway in all Africa with very few exceptions. Those ideologically centered one-party systems – whether in Africa or the Arab world – were modelled on the only prototype that existed then: the totalitarian Leninist model. Within that model the state swallowed up society, and the party engorged the state. The party thus became the motivator, manipulator and prime mover. The Leninist model, however, had the saving grace of grass roots support and a time-honoured ideology whatever one thought of it. In the Arab world all one-party regimes issued from military *coups*. Military takeover was taken for granted as the legitimate tool of political change. Ironically, a very influential school of political thought, which emerged in the United States in the 1960s, argued strongly for the intervention of the military in politics. Those pedants came from both sides of the ideological divide.[2] The ascension of Nimeiri to power was one of a piece with this perverse and pervasive politico-military culture.

However, in Sudan we did not follow the caricature of the original Leninist model as Egypt had formalistically done. Instead, we had the dubious distinction of making a parody of the frayed Egyptian model: the Arab Socialist Union. Ours was christened the Sudanese Socialist Union (SSU). But prior to Nimeiri's *coup* the radical and not-so-radical members of the Sudanese Northern elite (both civilian and military) joined, like their homologues in the Arab world, Nasser's revolutionary bandwagon, and flirted with power through the military. In effect, what we had aspired for was to govern by proxy in order to realize our dreams for radical regeneration. With the benefit of hindsight, those dreams became the nation's nightmares.

To a large section of the community, Nimeiri's *coup* was, nonetheless, a relief from the political malaise in the country. The military takeover was received with discernible satisfaction. But from the start, the traditional parties viewed it with suspicion. And rather than blessing it, the way the two Sayyids blessed Abboud, some of them immediately took up arms against it. This was the case of Imam al Hadi of the *Ansar* and Sharif Hussein al Hindi of the NUP. The Muslim Brothers aligned themselves with this duo because they saw in the *coup* a triumph by their nemesis, the communists.[3] Although I had been, at that time, on Nimeiri's side of the fence, wisdom after the event led me to conclude that the challenge of the regime by those from whom power was unsurped was the most honourable thing to do. Any democrat worth his salt would rather die on his sword – the way Allende did in Chile – than succumb to usurpers. Even so, past and future experiences in the Sudan told their own story about alignments by Northern and Southern 'democrats' with military usurpers of power, as well as about leaders from whom power was usurped, yet they became the first to extend an olive branch to the usurpers.

As for the 'modern forces', they came out in droves on 2 June 1969 to embrace with open arms the military regime, which was then dubbed *thawrat Mayo* (the May Revolution). That page of the 'revolutionary' era's history was benignly forgotten by many of the erstwhile confederates and comforters of the 'revolution', when it collapsed in April 1985. At that date they came out, in flocks again, to lambaste the crimes of the May regime against humanity, as if the May 'revolution' they hailed on 2 June was there to venerate the Universal Declaration of Human Rights. This venal distortion of facts would have deserved no more than a footnote in this book, were it not for the self-serving misconstruction of history by some politicians of the left, and the mendacious obfuscation of verifiable accounts by guileful scholars. If anything, the self-enhancing misconstruction of events during that period by the one-time Nimeiri supporters points to a dearth of moral courage to concede past mistakes. It also mirrors lack of analytical rigour in the anatomization of that period. By necessity, selective reading of history by critics of that regime debilitates their capacity to dissect correctly the past and, therefore, curtails their ability to chart the way forward.

At all events, from the very beginning Nimeiri endeavored to break clean with the past in order to install a new political order. He denounced the traditional parties and former rulers of the country and had many arrested. He sacked civil servants claimed to be unscrupulous and confiscated the properties of some of the former ruling class, particularly those who declared war against the regime. To endear himself to the rank and file, he adopted a populist style in politics that earned him admiration by the people and acquiescence by those who remained reluctant among the elite. By taking on the traditional parties and addressing, across sectarian divides, the yearnings for development and economic rehabilitation by their constituencies, Nimeiri won the hearts of millions. Indubitably, he was very adept in touching the political nerves of the crowds. Also, by giving priority to the solution of the 'Southern Problem', he appeared to have gotten his priorities right; political stability, national unity and development were inextricably tied to putting an end to the blood-letting that had sapped the nation's vitality.

The general public had admired Nimeiri for all those reasons as well as for the macho and brio with which he carried himself. But rather than being inspired by high-minded political wisdom, Nimeiri was in reality a tyrant in the ancient Greek sense of the word, a peasant ruffian who espoused the causes of the downtrodden against the nobles and humiliated the nobles in the process. As for the high-mindedness, Nimeiri had left that to his aides of all political hue from the far left to the extreme right. That was why Nimeiri kept gravitating from left, to centre, to extreme right. For a kickoff, Nimeiri emerged in June 1969 as a firebrand leftist and ardent Arabist; in September 1983 he ended almost to the right of Attila the Hun. That was the time when he reached the end of his journey, from Nasserism to fetishism. In that month Nimeiri metamorphozed into an Islamic Imam and thereby lost both the South and North. For the Southerners, the imamate that came in the wake of the abrogation of the Addis Ababa peace agreement evoked memories of the so-called Islamic Constitution of the 1960s and led to renewed armed resistance. The Northerners, on their part, rejected Nimeiri's imamate; they would rather suffer under two benign imams (the leaders of the two main religious sects) than agonize under a dubious imamate with unfettered powers and authority. At the end, on 6 April 1985, Nimeiri was ousted through a popular uprising, with no less enthusiasm than the one he was received with on 25 May 1969. By deliberately driving his regime in a trajectory of rack and ruin, Nimeiri has only himself to thank for his demise. He also thought that he had become Sudan's unchallenged taskmaster but, unmistakably, tyrants may subdue men for some time, but they can never defeat the power of humanity.

Nimeiri and the South

After declaring his intention to sue for a peaceful solution to the Southern question, Nimeiri appointed two Southerners (Abel Alier and Joseph Garang) to the cabinet, one of whom was nominated minister in charge of Southern Affairs. Read out of historical context, this appointment would appear to be a common-sense decision, the reality in the obtuse Sudanese politics was different. In the run-up to independence, we recall, the Northern political parties turned down the proposition made by Buth Diu to CAC for the appointment of a Minister for Southern Affairs who should be a Southerner supported by an Advisory Board on the South whose members were to be selected by that minister. Both the Umma and NUP rejected the proposition. It therefore took Northern Sudanese politics fifteen years to come to that simple and well-grounded decision.

On 9 June 1969, Nimeiri made the famous 9th of June declaration in which he recognized the historical and cultural differences between the North and South, asserted that unity should be based on the recognition of those differences and promised to grant the South regional autonomy on its local affairs. He later appointed Joseph Garang as the Minister of State for Southern Affairs. The declaration was greatly influenced by the SCP and probably Joseph Garang, who was himself a leading communist. It represented a welcome departure from past political statements on the South, though it did not escape the mesmerizing influence of Marxist ideology and communist shibboleths when it called for the formation of a 'socialist-oriented democratic movement' in the region in order for the South *beau ideal* to take root.

The year 1971 closed with the most important event in the history of Sudanese civic relations; with little mediation by the All Africa Council of Churches (AACC), a meeting was held in Addis Ababa between representatives of the government and those of the newly formed Southern Sudan Liberation Movement (SSLM). The meeting took place against the background of developments that instilled optimism about the resolution of the problem. After being elected President on the 12 October 1971, Nimeiri elevated Abel Alier to the position of Vice-President, a position Alier shared with a Northerner, Babiker Awadalla. No Southerner had occupied a similar post in the past. A proposition to that effect, made during the RTC, was eschewed by the Northern parties. Alier was also appointed as the Minister for Southern Affairs in place of Joseph Garang after the latter was executed following an abortive *coup* attempt on 19 July that year.

Moreover, Nimeiri appointed three Southerners as governors to the three Southern provinces of Equatoria, Upper Nile and Bahr el Ghazal. To boot, the governors were made members of the cabinet. None of the three was a professional administrator but all of them were competent professional Sudanese in their own right: Hilary Paulo Logali (Equatoria), Toby Madut (Bahr el Ghazal) and Luigi Adwok (Upper Nile). That was far afield from what the first democratic government did on the advice of the 'Northern' Sudanese Administrators' Association; denying Southerners higher administration posts because they were purportedly not sufficiently trained to come up the ladder of the civil service. The second democratic government did not do better; they succumbed to the threats by the Northern local government officers to resign *en bloc* if 'underqualified' Southerners were promoted to replace them. Even those reluctant to give Nimeiri credit for anything might find it a little easier to admit that the Addis Ababa agreement might have been the last hope for a negotiated settlement in the Sudan without external intervention. That the Agreement finally collapsed had more to do with Nimeiri's approach to peace than the inherent mechanics of the deal.

Several factors were at play in expediting Nimeiri's pursuit of peace in 1971, and he was battered and buffeted in every direction. On 19 July 1971 there was the *coup* attempt allegedly instigated by the SCP and supported by the Iraqi Baath party. In the South, Joseph Lagu's *Anya Nya* was increasing in strength. A year before the 1971 *countercoup*, Nimeiri faced a revolt of the Mahdists led by Imam al Hadi. Increasingly, he was finding himself in a tight spot that was getting tighter. On the other hand, his main adversary, Joseph Lagu, wasn't having an easy time either. The Ugandan buffoon, Idi Amin, was growing restless about the use of his territory by the Israelis to arm the *Anya Nya*.[4] He wanted to squeeze out the Southern fighters in an attempt to curry favour with Nimeiri and talk him into expelling the man he had overthrown (Milton Obote) who was then holed up in the Sudan. The Israeli intervention in the Sudan conflict, as recently reported by an African daily in a serialized feature article, was provoked by other motives, Israel offering to help the *Anya Nya* following Nimeiri's declared 'pro-Egyptian' stance.[5] In these circumstances, the two parties had every motivation to sit down and seek a negotiated bolt-hole. Neither must it be forgotten that by 1971 the war casualties were becoming more and more alarming. Therefore, whereas there was a genuine desire for peace, there were also dictates of political necessity which could not be ignored.

Consequently, on 9 November 1971, delegates from the AACC, World Council of Churches (WCC), Sudan government and the Southern Sudan Liberation Movement, (SSLM), sat down in Addis Ababa for preliminary negotiations. Their conclusions were that a genuine sincerity was evoked in the preliminary negotiations and a mutual desire for peace observed, despite initial signs of lack of confidence in each other. Both sides agreed to start negotiations on 20 January 1972 in Addis Ababa. SSLM also agreed to the principle of one Sudan and on modalities and conditions that would ensure that the legitimate interests of the South were achieved through a negotiated settlement. On 12 February 1972 negotiations commenced and ultimately produced what was later referred to as the Addis Ababa Accord. Whereas lots of nit-picking had taken place, especially after the collapse of the agreement, it remained an important landmark in the history of peace in Sudan. It had demonstrated that a negotiated settlement was feasible.

The crux of the agreement were the articles of autonomy under which the three Southern provinces of Bahr el-Ghazal, Equatoria and Upper Nile were constituted into a regional sphere to be administered by an Executive Council overseen by a Regional Assembly. That special measure of administrative empowerment for the South was denied by the parties in the draft constitution of 1968. In its place, a caricature of regional antonomy was proposed. The Assembly, however, had jurisdiction over all regional matters, while mineral and natural resources, defence, foreign trade and foreign affairs were reserved for the central government. Juba was declared the capital of the region. The SSLM proposed, at the start of the negotiations, the division of Sudan into four regions (North, South, East and West), but that proposition was uncritically rejected by the government negotiators. In retrospect, that might have been the right thing to do, as it would have ended the North–South adversarial politics and created other regional centers of power that may have helped attenuate Khartoum's extensive powers over the regions. The Southern negotiators benefited immensely from the advice of an eminent British lawyer, former Solicitor General Sir Dingle Foot.[6]

The issue of language was bothersome during the Addis Ababa negotiations, some members of the SSLM, led by Mading de Garang, calling for the adoption of English as the official language of the South. Arabic he said was a foreign language. The government side resisted the proposition. I recall asking Mading: 'Foreign to whom? Certainly not to Africa since Arabic, whatever its provenance, is recognized now as an African language by the OAU and UNESCO.' It was clear in my mind then, as it is clear now, that Arabic was guilty by association. Being the language of the Northern 'hegemonists', Southerners had come to see in it only a tool of cultural hegemony. Gaafer Bakheit also retorted:[7] 'It is bad enough that you reject a language which is admittedly the *lingua franca* among all Sudanese including Southerners, but to suggest in its place a decidedly foreign European language that is spoken only by a minority of the educated class is inappropriate. We may appreciate your thesis if you propose Dinka or Zande in place of Arabic,' said Bakheit. Eventually agreement was reached on an arrangement that was reflected in Article 6 of the Agreement: 'Arabic shall be the official language for the Sudan and English the principal language for the Southern Region without prejudice to the use of any other language or languages which may serve a practical necessity or the efficient and expeditious discharge of executive and administrative functions of the region.' This is contrary to what one Sudanese scholar claimed when he argued that the Addis Ababa agreement was not mindful of Sudan's linguistic diversity.[8] In addition to this constitutional stipulation, Article 10 of the Powers of Regional Assembly Act authorized the Assembly to legislate on matters relating to customs, traditions and development of local cultures and languages. Surprisingly, religion was not an issue in the negotiations at Addis Ababa, though it was not absent from the minds of both parties.

The Addis Ababa meetings were concluded on 27 February with the signing of the Accord in the presence of Emperor Haile Selassie of Ethiopia. Six thousand former *Anya Nya* soldiers were to be absorbed in the national army. On 12 March 1972, the war between the South and the North was called off. Peace had, at long last, arrived in Sudan, or so we thought. The re-establishment of tranquillity and security was certainly the most immediate and significant achievement of the Accord. It was a difficult task, especially in the prevailing atmosphere of uncertainty. With a few tumbles here and there, stability was virtually realized. This made it possible for the government, with the help of the international community, to embark on the repatriation of refugees back to the Sudan which proceeded speedily and satisfactorily. The superstructure of the state in the South that had shrunk during the hostilities was rebuilt. Southern Sudanese civil servants in the North returned to the South. Those were augmented by the cadres that returned from exile. Abel Alier himself was appointed to head the Southern regional administration and the Commander of the *Anya Nya*, Joseph Lagu, was reinstated in the army with the rank of Major-General and appointed as Inspector General of the Army. Subsequently, he was entrusted with the command of the Southern Division, the first time a Southern soldier was elevated to that post. Reconciliation, it appeared, was taking root. By 1974, the regional government was able to conduct democratic elections for the regional and national assemblies.

The rehabilitation of civil society and the infrastructure was the more difficult part, but here too, significant strides were made in the first years of the new dispensation. The international community was of great help. Development programmes in the agricultural sector and road reconstruction were funded by diverse bilateral and multilateral donors. The UNDP despatched a task force headed by Paul-Marc Henry, a leading development expert with deep knowledge of the Sudanese scene. A World Bank initiative was launched by its President, Robert McNamara, after a visit to Khartoum and Juba. Following that visit, Sudan became the second largest (after India) per capita recipient of World Bank assistance. Due to all those efforts, the South became self-sufficient in food by 1977. The number of secondary schools had more than quadrupled. Vocational institutions for teachers, artisans, veterinarians, cooperative officers and agricultural extension workers were established and there was a university to boot. By all accounts, Southern Sudan had begun to look like a normal, important and functioning part within the Sudanese body politic. That was not to last for long.

The success of the experiment depended partly on the ability of the Southern government to deliver, and deliver fast, on development. This was not only contingent on the quality of leadership and the efficiency of the Southern bureaucracy, but also on the availability of funds. Article 25 of the Southern Sudan Provinces Regional Self-Government Act, 1972, specified that funding for the regional government would be sourced from 'direct and indirect taxation from the region, contributions from local government councils; receipts from commercial, industrial and agricultural projects in the region; revenue from the national treasury and a special development budget for the Southern region'. Interestingly, one delegate of the SSLM to the Addis Ababa negotiations proposed that a tax be imposed on all Southerners, irrespective of their place of residence. But who were the Southerners residing outside the South? Abel Alier wisely objected to that suggestion fearing the Pandora's box this proposition would open. It was obvious that Alier had in mind the millions of descendents of Southern ex-slaves who lived in the North and who, to all intents and purposes, became Northernized. Consequently, it was decided that taxes should only be imposed on all residents in the South including Northerners. The South, however, was a war-shattered region, traditionally poor and completely underdeveloped. No meaningful tax revenue could be obtained there, not in the short term and not until reconstruction and considerable investment had taken place. The bulk of the money, therefore, would have to come from the national treasury.

But in Khartoum a battle raged behind the scenes, even before the conclusion of the agreement. Within the regime itself self-styled Arabists were blatantly unhappy with the Accord; they were only subdued because of Nimeiri's seeming espousal of reconciliation. Nonetheless, every attempt was made by this group to frustrate the agreement since the initial stages of the negotiations. For starters, the 'Arabists' were angered by the recognition of the 'rebels' as a 'liberation' movement.[9] To that objection we said that nomenclature should not divert us from essence. Another bone of contention, before the commencement of the talks, was a ceasefire as a prerequisite for the creation of a conducive atmosphere for the talks. Such a measure was deemed demoralizing to the army by high powered Arabists within the government, despite the willingness of Nimeiri and the army high command to go along with it.[10] Amazingly, this was the same position taken by Northern parties in the Committee of Twelve.

Attemps to undermine the Accord, even before it took root, were also observed in the attitude of Treasury officials. The creation of a Special Fund (SF) to finance the rehabilitation of the South was, in effect, a device to avoid the penny-pinching of the Treasury, at that time under a Minister of Finance (the late Musa al Mubarak) who belonged to the pro-Arabist group within the government. Unlike their minister, civil servants in the Treasury were not motivated by ideological considerations, as they were indeed exhibiting parsimonious tendencies characteristic of men who superintend the public purse, especially when they did not have a say on the way funds were to be used. Initial funding to the SF, however, came from a donation by Sultan Qabus of Oman and was entrusted to the Minister of Trade, Ibrahim Mansour, and not to the Treasury. Eventually, the donation was transferred to the Special Fund, under the stewardship of Mamoun Beheiri. Afterwards, the floodgates opened for contributions to the Fund by international organizations and Western and Arab donors. Important donations came from Africa too: Emperor Haile Selassie of Ethiopia, King Hassan of Morocco and President Nyerere of Tanzania.

The situation got worse as the years went by, and this frustrated not only the civil service and political leaders, but also business contractors who were owed money by the government of the region. It became virtually impossible to tender for procurements, services or construction in the South. Doubts began to deepen among Southerners about the wisdom of accepting the Addis Ababa terms in the first place. Both Abel Alier and Joseph Lagu began to take a beating for having 'sold out' the South at Addis Ababa. This may partly explain why the SPLM did not go into transports of delight as a result of the offers made to it by the interim government that succeeded Nimeiri to reinstate the Addis Ababa Agreement. Indeed, that offer was repeatedly scoffed at by the SPLM.

The myopia was not limited to elements within the political class and civil servants. The academic class was not fervent about the Addis Ababa agreement, and their attitude towards creating a university in Juba was revealing. The creation of a university in the South was provided for in the conclusions of the Committee of Twelve, but no government saw the urgency of honouring that undertaking. When the issue was raised after the Accord, the University of Khartoum authorities took a negative stand and argued that whatever funds were available should be used for strengthening the existing university. The author, as Minister of Education (1977), fought a rear-guard battle against those academics and the bureaucracy of the Ministry who were loath to the creation of Juba and Gezira universities and the elevation of Khartoum Technical Institute (KTI) to university status. That bias was also clear in the refusal of the Khartoum University authorities to admit Southern returnees into that university, then the only Sudanese university. The returnee pupils did not meet the entrance requirements set by the Khartoum University and determined by a so-called boxing system. Though one was happy with the university's concern with the integrity of the academic process, one also saw in the university's attitude imperviousness to a historic development. Probably some of the decision makers in the University, who were unqualifiedly against the regime, thought that nothing good would come from that regime and therefore underestimated the meaning of the Addis Ababa Accord. But the university authorities also should have known better; Southerners were perhaps the most afflicted Sudanese group, in relative terms, when it came to access to higher education. A World Bank report indicated that in 1978/9 there were less than ten out of 1,000 students from the South undertaking studies in agriculture in Khartoum University, though 90 per cent of the population of that region were farmers and pastoralists.[11] Howbeit, hundreds of those returnees were eventually incorporated in Egyptian universities.[12]

In the broader Sudanese social sphere, the Addis Ababa Accord had several social, economic and political gains for the country as a whole. Mobility within the country was opened up, Southern Sudanese youth were able to compete for admission into national institutions of higher learning including, ultimately Khartoum University, the Police College and Military Colleges. This need not be overly exaggerated since, for example, Southerners admitted to the Military College in the 10 years that followed the Addis Ababa agreement, did not exceed 5 per cent of the total college intake. Southerners and Northerners, nonetheless, were able to seek employment opportunities in any part of the country, though Southern extremists wanted all the *jelaba* (originally the term meant slave hunters but in current Southern parlance it refers to Northern traders and by extension all Northerners) wanted all Northern traders removed from the South. That was also one of the misconceptions prevalent among many Southerners. Rather than treating the *jelaba* as an exploitive group that extended its tentacles to all marginalized areas (South, West and Centre), they looked at them through an ethnic prism. Abel Alier and his colleagues, however, prevailed on the extremists and decided that all Northerners who settled in the South were free to remain there and conduct their business unhindered.[13] Moreover, religious freedoms were unimpeded by the state. Nimeiri himself made the symbolic gesture, which no other Northern Muslim leader before him ever made, of attending a mass for peace at the Juba Cathedral.

In general, the Sudanese economy began to earn a peace dividend. Foreign capital flows improved considerably to take advantage of the conducive atmosphere ushered in by the ending of the armed conflict. Large projects like the Jonglei Canal and oil exploration gave the country hope and dignity. A 'permanent' constitution was written and passed by the National Assembly in 1973 but, carried in the womb of a one-party regime, it was far from democratic. Regarding the South, the constitution incorporated the Addis Ababa agreement as an organic law that could only be amended according to its terms (three-quarter majority vote in the Regional Assembly and two-thirds popular support by registered Southern voters through a referendum).

The constitution also adopted secularism (without using the term) by removing all references to a state religion and recognizing all Sudanese creeds – Islam, Christianity and African belief systems. The latter were described by the constitution as 'noble spiritual beliefs' (Article 16). The Article also prohibited misuse of religion for political purposes, criminalized actions that foment hatred against religions and noble spiritual beliefs and deemed such actions unconstitutional. That did not materialize without a sustained political and intellectual fight against the Islamists within the regime who endeavoured to incorporate two articles in the draft constitution that would have made nonsense of the purport of the Addis Ababa agreement. The first was that Islam should be declared the religion of the state; the second that the president of the republic should be a male Muslim. The Islamists were not only nonchalant towards the rights of non-Muslim citizens, they were also lacking in gender sensitivity. Small wonder that Turabi, who was then held in preventive detention, addressed a memorandum to leaders of Northern parties, following the promulgation of the constitution, in which he appealed to them for the creation of an anti-South front. The memorandum, which was intercepted by security agencies, maintained that, 'the challenge of the South dictates that Northerners should come together in self-defence against threats to their interests and cultural identity from the missionary octopus and ethnic extortion'. Turabi also wanted the proposed front 'to work for the conversion to Islam of individuals and groups in the South who do not profess that religion'.[14] Turabi was thus back to his unmistakable bias which was demonstrated beyond doubt during the debate of the so-called Islamic constitution in 1968.

Internationally, the Sudan became an example of how Africa can resolve its own problems without external involvement. A keen Sudan observer maintained that 'with the exception of the Zimbabwe settlement in 1979 – in which there was significantly greater external involvement – it is difficult to think of another twentieth-century internal war that was ended through a negotiated agreement'.[15] Nimeiri himself was hailed at home and abroad as a visionary and a possible role model for the rest of the developing world, particularly where newly independent states were embroiled in civil wars. Future developments showed that this was an undeserved praise. Nevertheless, the Sudan rightly became the melting pot of the African and Arab worlds. The period between 1972 and 1977 was a time when Sudanese diplomats and emissaries were proud of their country and leadership. In sum, tranquillity and a positive image of the Sudan in the early and mid-1970s were largely attributable to the Addis Ababa Accord. Without it, Nimeiri could have neither survived in power nor received the acclamation he had received in Africa and beyond. Thus, his unmaking of the agreement became his own unmaking.

One would have thought that this reality would be known to Nimeiri himself more than to anybody else in the country. Alas, no sooner had the ink dried on the agreement than Nimeiri began to undermine it.

While he was being praised by the world for statesmanship, Nimeiri inwardly regarded the achievement of his own regime as a shrewd tactic for ending the Southern rebellion. His first false step was the ill-advised decision to nominate Abel Alier for the position of President of the Regional Government without sufficiently undertaking the consultations stipulated in the Protocol for Interim Administrative Arrangements. According to that Protocol, the President was empowered, in consultation with the SSLM and Southern chapters of the Sudan Socialist Union (SSU), to appoint the President and members of the first High Executive Council (HEC). The agreement itself provided that the President of HEC be nominated by the President of the Republic on the recommendations of the Regional Assembly, but since the newly elected Regional Assembly was only convened in March 1974, an interim government had to be in place.

Alier was not in a rush for the job; his nominee was Hilary Logali, a judicious and winsome person who was by then Governor of Equatoria. Besides, Alier had enough support within the South to win the presidency without a helping hand from Nimeiri. The impression that consultations with the SSLM, before Alier's appointment, were not sufficiently exhaustive was reflected in the murmurings of two leaders of that organization who were vying for the post: Joseph Oduhu and Ezboni Mundiri. To them, as well as to some of their colleagues, Nimeiri's action was an attempt to sideline the 'outsiders' in favour of 'insiders'. Still, the intervention informed Southerners that Nimeiri, and by association the North, had no intention of letting them run their own affairs, after all.

The doubts were not entirely unjustified; in his own convoluted way of thinking, Nimeiri did not want anyone who worked under him to feel that he had his own autogenous power base, or feel independent of the leash of the *Rais* (President). Furthermore, the idea that the President of the region was to be selected by the Regional Assembly and only formally appointed by the President was evidently not to his liking. Within the SSU's scheme of things, election laws envisaged only one candidate for the presidency of the Sudan to be nominated by the SSU. The regional autonomy laws did not impose such a limitation. Southerners, particularly the 'outsiders', did not resort to violence in this instance, but the outrage was translated into a feeling of suspicion and mistrust within their ranks. Had the incident of 1973 been an inadvertent enthusiasm by Nimeiri in support of a trusted political ally, Abel Alier, the Southern murmurs could have served him well as an early warning about Southern sensitivity.

The way to peace was not without hiccups; a young officer within the ranks of *Any Nya* by the name of John Garang de Mabior told General Lagu that he had no trust in the Addis Ababa negotiations. Garang was then Lagu's information officer. Asked by Lagu for his reasons, Garang said, 'any agreement that ensued from the negotiations would not last unless it was based on a fundamental change in Sudan's body-politic'. He underlined a number of issues: separation of religion from politics, the nationalities question, full responsibility for security in the South during an interim period by the forces of the SSLM and popular ratification of the agreement through a referendum. A five-year interim trial period, Garang said, should be envisaged. That should be followed by a referendum to endorse the new arrangements. Lagu asked Garang to put his ideas in writing, which he did on 24 January 1972. To Garang's surprise, the response to his recommendations was brusque. Lagu removed his name from the list of delegates to the negotiations and transferred him from the SSLM's HQ to Upper Nile. The young Garang was wary of the problems that may ensue from hasty integration in the army and keen to have such a landmark agreement publicly endorsed. Garang, after the signing of the agreement and his absorption in the Sudanese army, repeated to Lagu his view that the agreement would not last. In the euphoria of the Addis Ababa accomplishment, our reaction to Garang's premonitions would have been that they were ill-advisedly disputatious. Ten years on, they became a self-fulfilling prophecy, as the agreement was dismantled by no other than Nimeiri and Lagu.

Other hiccups, very serious this time, were associated with major development plans in the South, such as the Jonglei Canal and oil exploration. The Jonglei Canal project has been mentioned as one of the icons of economic development attributable to the realization of peace. However, in view of the way it was introduced, it turned into a source of conflict between the government and certain political formations in the South. The canal project was on the drawing board for decades, indeed since the 1920s,[16] and its construction was envisaged in the 1959 Nile Waters Agreement. But when agreement was reached by Egypt and Sudan to implement it on the request of Sudan, the Southern population was neither educated by the government (at the Centre and in the Region) about its benefits, nor were fears of its perceived nefarious effects on the livelihood of the people addressed. The first time people heard of the project was when it was announced by Abel Alier who was himself a member of the Jonglei Board. Juba erupted in violent demonstrations, which led to the death and injury of several school children. The technical merits of the canal project were not the subject of the discussion; its impact on the people's livelihood was. Indeed, the issue of the environmental impact of the drainage schemes on the Sudd had been raised in the early 1930s by British administrators.[17]

For inexplicable reasons, the government and its political party (SSU) found no necessity to educate the citizenry about such a major scheme that would have irreversible consequences on the environment and people's livelihood. As would be expected, pessimists and the opponents of the regime in the South took advantage of the issue and capitalized on it. Abel Alier later paid politically for his assumed inattention to the interests of his own constituency. In addition to fair concerns such as the impact of the canal on the life cycle of the nomadic pastoral Dinka and the climatology and the natural habitat of the flora and fauna of the Sudd, scary tales were added that millions of Egyptian farmers would settle along the canal, that the South would become a desert like the Sahara, etc. Official explanations and assurances carried no credibility because they were not proactive. We in government had shown no leadership or attention to the people's concern. It was no surprise then that when open military hostilities resumed ten years later, the Jonglei project was the first economic casualty. A little ironical too, since the leader of the insurrection, John Garang, wrote his doctoral thesis at Iowa State University on the Jonglei Canal, arguing its importance to the socio-economic development of the region while decrying the insensitivity of politicians to the people's concerns. The Jonglei Canal scheme has another dimension that cannot be discounted as later developments have demonstrated: its importance to Egypt, particularly in view of the impending water deficit in that country. Consequently, for any future settlement of Sudan's conflict, it will have to be sensitive to Egypt's legitimate concerns about water.

Also, a Fabian Society paper on Sudan published in 1947, as if reading the future through a crystal ball, prognosticated that the loss of the South 'would be a matter of prestige and, to some extent, a matter of anxiety; but there is also the fear that in the South might subsequently be discovered the wealth which could guarantee Sudan's independence'. In 1978, Chevron Oil Company of Sudan, a subsidiary of Standard Oil of California, struck oil at Bentiu, a Nuer area in the north-western fringe of Upper Nile. The oil deal was characterized from the beginning by avoidable blunders and venality of awesome proportions. First, the government sponsored a contentious plan to build a refinery in Kosti further north, rather than in the area of production. Building the refinery in the area of production would have made a sea-change in that area by creating job opportunities, improving physical infrastructure and enhancing social services. Nimeiri was not even ready to accept suggestions for establishing a small cracking unit at Bentiu to satisfy the immediate needs of the South. Second, there were serious accusations on the way tenders were made for the construction of the refinery and a pipeline to Port Sudan; this process was shrouded in secrecy and handled by ministers in the central government, of whom one was the President's Chief of Cabinet. Third, neither the Regional Council nor the Vice-President from the South were involved in that limited circle of decision-makers. Sharif al Tuhami, the minister in charge of energy, was not only insensitive to the anxieties of Southerners, he was disdainful of all things Southern.

Unsurprisingly, after the Chevron discoveries, Nimeiri decided to carve the oil-producing area from the South and gave it an Arabic name (*Hejlij*) in place of its traditional name *Pan Thau* (acacia village). The district was incorporated in a newly created Unity Province whose governor was Nimeiri himself. That added fire to an already combustible situation. There were two reasons behind Nimeiri's decision, both devious. First, by appointing himself governor of the 'oil province' he wanted to ensure the exclusion of Southern politicians and administrators from overseeing the oil industry; it had now become the special preserve of the President. Second, he wanted to protect the oil mafia within the central government from interventions by Southern administrators into the lucrative field. Corruption had never been alien to Sudan and no former regime was free from it, and while corruption in the early days of Nimeiri's rule was, as in previous regimes, a fact of life, since the late 1970s it became a way of life.

The gerrymandering of borders between the North and South and within the North itself was not new in Sudan. For example, Kurmuk district, which is now part of the Blue Nile Province, was administered up to 1953 as part of Upper Nile, a Southern Province. By 1956 the boundaries between the North and South were definitively demarcated. Nonetheless, on the discovery of copper ore in Hufrat al Nihas in Western Sudan, Abboud's regime decided to incorporate that district in the Province of Dar Fur. The situation should have reverted to the original position of 1956 following the Addis Ababa agreement that defined the borders of the South as they stood on 1 January 1956 (date of the declaration of independence). However, by 1980 Nimeiri's Minister of Interior, Ahmed Abdel Rahman (Muslim brother), asserted that Hufrat al Nihas was part of Southern Dar Fur, despite the definition of borders in January 1956. Bentiu (the oil district) too, was deemed by Abdel Rahman to be part of South Kordofan. The decision caused an uproar in the South, and a judicial committee headed by Chief Justice Khalaf Allah al Rasheed was asked to adjudicate on the matter. On the strength of evidence (particularly the delineation of borders at independence and the Addis Ababa agreement) both districts were ruled by the Chief Justice to be part of the South. Nimeiri, as mentioned earlier, went deviously around the Chief Justice's advice by carving out a new Southern province with himself as its governor. This situation lasted till the advent of the NIF regime, when both districts were firmly incorporated in the North; the NIF had no time for legalities. The decision was taken by Dr Ali al Haj, the NIF minister for Regional Government.

Fears by the Fabians twenty years ago, therefore, were proven right. Leases to foreign companies for the exploration of oil in the South were made without informing, let alone consulting with, the Southern government. And when the South asked for a fair share of the new wealth in order to develop itself, the central government, especially the Minister of Energy, did not want to hear anything about that. Imperviousness to Southern calls for having a share in a wealth discovered in their region led to sustained demonstrations in the South and clashes between Northern and Southern forces based in the region.[18] In Khartoum, apprehensions deepened, leading to the replacement of all Southern soldiers manning the garrison in Bentiu by a contingent from Western Sudan. The Bentiu garrison was then commanded by Captain Salva Kiir who later became the second-in-command of the SPLA.

The most serious crisis in the implementation of the agreement related to the integration of the *Anya Nya* into the army. Several incidents of mutiny were reported and were quickly contained without addressing their underlying cause. Instead, they were allowed to rankle. All clashes that erupted during the integration phase ensued from fears by former warriors for their lives, especially when they were ordered to move North. The absorbed soldiers, as Alier puts it, were 'reacting to the outside world as they perceived it, a world of Northern Sudanese (labelled as Arabs)'.[19] The Addis Ababa agreement provided for two technical military commissions, one to supervise the integration of forces, the other to monitor ceasefire. The latter was to be assisted by external observers, but given the spirit of *commeraderie* that developed between the two sides, both agreed to do without the foreign element.[20]

One casualty on the road to the reintegration of the forces was the little-remembered peace veteran, Brigadier Emmanuel Abur. Abur was the second-in-command after Lagu was shot dead in 1976 when he was trying to persuade and restrain a unit of former *Anya Nya* soldiers who had mutinied in Wau and moved into the bush under the command of Captain Alfred Agwet Awan. Abur had a vision for Sudan larger than that of his immediate bosses both in the North and South. In an interview with Elias Nyamlel Wakson at Aweil on 27 June 1975 he had this to say: 'the geographical position of Sudan is unique in Africa in the sense that the Negroid South is geographically and politically bound with the Islamized, Arab North. For a proponent of African unity, who aims at the solidarity of the whole continent, to divide Sudan is to divide Africa.'[21]

The implementation of the military protocol, particularly as far as the integration of the forces was concerned, proved to be the most bothersome of all aspects of agreement. The letter of the agreement provided that the units should be separate for a specified number of years, but the army command was anxious to neutralize the *Anya Nya* through absorption. Naturally, the rank and file of the *Anya Nya* were suspicious and afraid. Lagu and the senior officers were evidently less apprehensive and this won the day for a while. It also emboldened Nimeiri to try more daring moves like retiring the very officers on whose faith the integration programme depended. In addition, the government pretended to have forgotten the quantitative ratio of military deployments in the South by violating the one-to-one ratio of Southerners to Northerners in the South provided for in Article 26 of the agreement. Moreover, the provision that the composition of the entire armed forces of the country should reflect the North-South population ratio at all levels of service was similarly ignored. The *Anya Nya* adopted a wait and see attitude. They waited and Nimeiri saw the consequences not too many years down the road of history.

The Rise and Fall of the Addis Ababa Accord

The process of the unmaking of the Addis Ababa agreement was not only Nimeiri's independent design. On the one hand, the political forces he displaced in 1969 were ultra-hostile to a peace formula that in any way empowered Southerners to the level provided for in the Addis Ababa agreement. We have seen in previous chapters how reticent were those political forces to grant the South even lesser powers. Intense pressure was brought to bear on Nimeiri to undo the Addis Ababa agreement because it had allegedly diluted the Arabo-Islamic component of the Sudanese identity and compromised national sovereignty. Turabi, who by then had become Nimeiri's Attorney General and afterwards Senior Presidential Aide, has always thought that the South was a major obstacle to the creation of an Islamic state in Sudan. This feeling was shared by some Arabs outside Sudan; for example, when the whole of Africa was hailing the Addis Ababa achievement, Libya's delegate to the OAU summit in 1972 was vociferous in his condemnation of the Accord as a sell-out to the WCC. Besides, Nimeiri's opponents operating from Tripoli disseminated false information about the agreement, ranging from betrayal of Arabism to collusion with the WCC, Ethiopia and the AACC. The conspiracy theory had out-of-the-way ramifications; for instance, the Muslim Brothers thought that the agreement had secret clauses against Islam.[22] An accusation was also making the rounds that Nimeiri's government had ceded parts of the country to Ethiopia as a price for her role in facilitating the agreement. That accusation was not only vaporous, it was blatantly mischievous.[23] Whether the party's attitude was motivated by heart-burning because the agreement was based on the conclusions of the Twelve-Man Committee which they failed to implement, or by sheer grudge against a regime they most loved to hate, their attitude towards the Addis Ababa agreement was not civically minded, not to say unpatriotic. Even after Nimeiri's demise, party leaders like Sadiq al Mahdi persevered in misprising Nimeiri's achievement.[24]

Undoubtedly, Nimeiri's political experience informed him that reconciliation pays. What he did not realize was the difference between an honourable compromise that rectified a wrong and a perfidious artifice to cool tempers though it would inexorably perpetuate injustice. Thus, in trying to appease the Northern opposition, he simultaneously isolated himself from his single largest and most reliable support base, the South. But Nimeiri, being the survivalist he was, wanted to bring his old foes into his embrace, especially those forces that were organizing themselves into a National Front with the support of Libya and Iraq. An attempt to dislodge Nimeiri's regime was made on 5 September 1975 in which the broadcasting station at Omdurman was seized. That mutiny was quickly broken and those directly involved in it summarily executed. Ten months later, on 2 July 1976, a group of armed dissidents made yet another attempt to topple the government. The attempted *coup* was a close call. The plotters controlled Khartoum airport, the national broadcasting station and laid siege to a number of army garrisons in Khartoum. Sadiq al Mahdi, at the head of a heavily armed contingent, was reported to have been 300 kilometres north of Khartoum after a strenuous journey from Libya across the desert.[25] When the forces loyal to the regime rebounded, al Mahdi received a distress signal from his supporters after which he reversed gear quoting the *Qurānic* verse *'wa la tarmu bi aidiyakum lil tahluqa'* (and cast not yourselves with your own hands into ruin) (The Cow, 2 195). That was the message of the commander-in-chief to his beleaguered supporters in Khartoum, before he made a U-turn, leaving his invading army to face alone that *tahluqa* (ruin). Although that daring bid for power was put down decisively, Nimeiri still felt the need to reach out to the National Front and bring it to the fold. Of all the mistakes he made, this one proved to be the most fatal. Unlike the Southerners who worked to strengthen his regime after the Addis Ababa agreement, the National Front leaders hoped to use their return to the country to organize themselves against him.

Sadiq al Mahdi, one thought, would never forgive Nimeiri for the humiliation of having been made to support publicly the 1969 *coup* and denounce the democracy he presided over.[26] Nor would he pardon him for the slaughter of his supporters following the failure of his bid for power in July 1976. But to the surprise of his comrades in arms, al Mahdi met Nimeiri for a second time in 1977 at Port Sudan.[27] The meeting was hurriedly and secretly arranged by an amiable businessman, Fatah al Rahman al Bashir. According to the minutes of the meeting (to which the author had access) al Mahdi congratulated Nimeiri on his rebirth as an Islamic leader. Probably he was looking for a justification for his reconciliation with Nimeiri that would appease his constituency (*Ansar*) to whom war against the regime was presented as *jihad*. To confirm his fealty to Nimeiri, however, al Mahdi made three important concessions. He endorsed Nimeiri's nomination for another term in office, approved the one-party system represented by the SSU and sanctioned the SSU's socialist option, whatever the term socialism meant to both interlocutors. With all those concessions, Nimeiri would have been remiss if he did not incorporate his one-time enemy into the system. Sadiq appropriately became a member of the SSU Political Bureau.

About a year after his return, al Mahdi abandoned his position in the SSU and decided to return to exile to rejoin an unwelcoming National Front that had refused to sign on in 1977; apparently Sadiq got from Nimeiri less than he bargained for. In one of his most revealing statements, Sadiq equated the transition from dictatorship to democracy in Sudan with the experience of Franco's Spain where Franco voluntarily handed over power to King Juan Carlos. What Sadiq did not realize was that neither was Nimeiri a clinically dead Franco, nor did Sudan have a Juan Carlos, hard as Sadiq may had wished to think.

On leaving Sudan, however, Sadiq told Nimeiri that his mission outside was to reinforce international mediation efforts with Iran to release the American Embassy officials held hostage in Teheran. He also requested Nimeiri to assist him in that endeavour. And if you think that al Mahdi was only trying to pull the wool over Nimeiri's eyes, you are wrong. As sure as eggs is eggs, Sadiq al Mahdi arrived in Teheran and was received by Sudan Ambassador, Ali Nimeiri, (not a relative of the President). Meetings were arranged with the Iranian authorities, but the mission, as any right-thinking person would have expected, was a fiasco. There was no reason why Sadiq al Mahdi should have anticipated to succeed in achieving what the UN, UNESCO and the Algerian government had failed to do. But, obviously, al Mahdi never took a break from delusions of grandeur.

The Port Sudan meeting came shortly after rapprochement between Nimeiri and Hassan al Turabi, who was unflinchingly committed to transforming Sudan into an Islamic state. Characteristically, he was ready to stoop as low as it took him to conquer. Regardless, by hailing Nimeiri's Islamism, the two leaders were in effect goading him towards the nullification of the Addis Ababa agreement which could not have survived outside the politico-cultural context within which it was sculpted: separation between religion and politics, recognition of diversity etc. Turabi's strategy, unlike Sadiq's, was more durable, subtle and effective. He ingratiated himself with the system and, like al Mahdi, paid an oath of allegiance to its 'secularist' constitution. Consequently, he ascended to the position of Attorney General. Using the debate on constitutional reform that he had raised during the reconciliation talks, Turabi gingerly introduced the issue of revising the laws of Sudan to bring them into consonance with *shari'a*. He also used an indeterminate clause in the 1973 constitution to the effect that *shari'a* and custom were the primary sources of legislation, to reconstruct the whole constitution and turn it into an Islamic one. In effect, Dafa'a Allah al Haj Yousif, Nimeiri's Chief Justice, declared that 15 per cent of the clauses of the 1973 Constitution were not in conformity with *shari'a*.[28] Surprisingly, the Chief Justice had been a member of the parliament that adopted that constitution. The only objection he had made then to that constitution was on Parliament's resolution not to ascribe a religion (Islam) to the state. Manifestly that would not comprise 15 per cent of the constitution. Nevertheless, Nimeiri overstepped the mark set by his Chief Justice when he ordered 100 articles of the constitution to be amended because they did not conform to the edicts of Islam.

Be that as it may, the constitutional arrangement engendered in the Addis Ababa Accord was, to begin with, anomalous. The regional government was fashioned as a parliamentary democracy with a chief executive answerable to a regional parliament. On the other hand, the central government was a one-party presidential system that eventually turned into a one-man-no-system. Hence, right from the beginning, the structure of the relationship between the region and the central government was bound to be a complex one, necessarily creating a good deal of friction. So, while the SSU was increasingly becoming a rubber stamp for a one-man dictatorship in the country, the South laboured to assert democratic principles on the regional administration. This was demonstrated by the parliamentary elections of 1978 in which some of the SSU's most prominent leaders lost their seats in the Regional Assembly. Vice-President Abel Alier himself was defeated in the regional presidential race by General Joseph Lagu. Nimeiri did not repeat his meddling of 1973 and Lagu was allowed to assume office, but he was displeased by those developments, since he had little patience with the existence of another centre of power. He also might have thought that Juba was setting a bad example for other Sudanese by ensuring the people's power and right to change leadership.

On the other hand, Turabi and al Mahdi saw the relative independence of the South as an impediment to the creation of a religious state in a unified Sudan. Turabi's position was logical, since it accorded with his views on the Addis Ababa Accord that he expressed during his incarceration as referred to earlier. In consequence, he wouldn't have cared less if religious politics ultimately led to the mutation of the autonomous South into an independent state. That would not apply to al Mahdi who was presumably standing on the platform of an inclusive democratic governance. With characteristic self-delusion, al Mahdi might have thought that he could have it both ways: dismantle the constitutional underpinnings of the Addis Ababa agreement and still keep the South in the loop. In effect, in a sermon on the occasion of *al'id al kabīr* (September 1983), Sadiq al Mahdi welcomed the application of *shari'a*. And though he criticized the application of *hudud* (Islamic penal law) and described their version in Nimeiri's laws as a distortion of Islam, he went on to say: 'The application of *shari'a* presupposes the creation of an Islamic political and economic system. *Hudud* can then be applied to protect that system.' Frankly, Sadiq was doing his own bidding for introducing a better *shari'a* which Nimeiri was presumed to have been incapable of introducing. The irony, however, was that Nimeiri was right. He applied historical *shari'a* as it has been developed by the *fuqaha* since the days of the early caliphates. The endless mission statements by al Mahdi and Islamists of his mindset about appropriate and inappropriate *shari'a*, either masked an ignorance of what historical *shari'a* was all about or reflected intellectual deficiency, if not a craven spirit. Islamists who sincerely believe in the universality and timelessness of Islam must first declare that historical *shari'a* is irrelevant to the needs of modern society and proceed to devise a new *shari'a* that responds to the needs of contemporary society, the way historical *shari'a* was devised by scholars to meet the evolving needs of their societies. If they don't, then whatever they describe as an Islamic state shall be no less than pious fraud. Effectively, Sadiq begged the question by going into scholastic polemics about what was good and what was distorted political Islam. Democrat Sadiq should have first analysed how would a religion-based state, impact on a multireligious country like Sudan. As for Nimeiri, his decision to reconcile with al Mahdi and Turabi on the terms above was most injurious to the confidence of the South. By extending an olive branch to the Islamist leaders and inviting them back into government with their time-worn intellectual baggage, he invited back old attitudes, prejudices and animosities.

While this double-think was going on, things were not moving well in the South. In the face of the high expectations of the people of that region, the Southern bureaucracy – except for a few tried hands –had neither the skills, experience nor the leadership to rise satisfactorily to the occasion. Cases of egregious corruption were reported, though not of the size reported in Khartoum. Equally, there was considerable opposition to power-sharing within the civil service at the level of the central government; bureaucrats were not ready to cede the powers allocated to the Southern bureaucracy even in areas where power-sharing was clearly delineated by the agreement. In this, they had the support of elements within the Ministry of Finance who, as mentioned earlier, demonstrated singular reluctance to disburse budgetary allocations for the South despite explicit provisions in the law that 80 per cent of the South's budget was to be met through those disbursements. Neither was the government beyond playing politics by proposing and approving projects for the South and then quietly shelving them.[29] In the early 1970s, projects such as the Kenaf Factory in Tonj, White Nile Brewery in Wau and sugar factories in Mongalla and Melut were proposed and approved. Decades later not a single one of them was commissioned. Failure to implement some of those projects may be attributed to the top-down approach to development planning that paid attention neither to the views of the beneficiaries nor to the sociocultural environment within which the projects were to be implemented. A further grievance was what the South perceived as a deliberate policy to starve the South of donor-funded development. In what has been described as the 'Breadbasket Policy', the oil-rich Arab countries, as a measure to achieve food security, resolved to fund agricultural development in the Arab region with the aim of securing food supplies for the Arab world. This dream was particularly centred on Sudan, which had abundant land and water resources. The Arab Authority for Agricultural Development was created for that end and based in Khartoum. In the mid-1970s, it was estimated that in 10 years hundreds of millions of dollars would be spent and Sudan would be in a position to supply Arab countries with 50 per cent of food crops and about 20 per cent of sugar. About the only project the South got was the Jonglei Canal – and even that was meant to supply additional water for irrigation to Northern Sudan and Egypt.

Despite the above, questions will always abide as to why Nimeiri took the path of conflict and self-destruction he had taken. On this, events tend to show that political expediency, together with Nimeiri's make-believe that the accommodation with the South could be treated merely as a question of political tactics and not a strategic political decision, may be an answer. This cleverness by half did not stop at the South. By bringing to the fold the Imam of the *Ansar* (Sadiq al Mahdi) and the proclaimed principal Islamic theoretician in Sudan (Hassan al Turabi), Nimeiri wanted to pull a fast one on both. Surely, Nimeiri is no Brahmin, but he is an astute tactician in the art of political survival. So, in an attempt to out do his two rivals/allies, he declared himself Imam of the whole Sudan and not only of one sect or political conglomeration. That was Nimeiri at his best, a man suffering from the pathological desire of always being at the top. That the imamate was a calling for which one should have perspicacity, training and ethics was immaterial to Sudan's new Imam. Nimeiri must have said to himself that as Sudan from the time of the declaration of independence had been a construction site for amateur political masons, why shouldn't he too engage in that exercise? But whatever he had said to himself, that turned out to be Nimeiri's ride before the fall.

Other than bringing peace to the South, the Addis Ababa Accord also served to create a ruling clique that monopolized the regional government to the exclusion of the emergent educated younger elite. Besides, even in peace, the South became substantially restive as a result of the manipulative nature of Sudanese politics, including wranglings in the Regional Government and constant meddling from Khartoum. So, as in 1955, renewed civil war broke out with a mutiny. In May 1983, Battalion 105 refused transfer to the North leading the government to order an invasion. As a consequence of that invasion, the battalion fled to Ethiopia with its arms. Out of that mutiny, and fed by the difficult conditions that Nimeiri had created in the South, sprang the Sudan Peoples Liberation Movement and its military wing Sudan Peoples Liberation Army (SPLM/A). The invasion was ordered by the National Defence Council (NDC) headed by Vice-President General Omar el Tayeb. The mutiny could have been delayed, if not averted, were it not for the arrogance and belligerence of the commander of the Southern region, Major-General Siddiq al Bana. Initially, the mutiny was instigated by the government's failure to pay soldiers outstanding emoluments. To ease the situation a delegation led by the Vice-Chairman of HEC, Dhol Acuil Aleu, and comprising members of the Regional Assembly from Bor as well a Northern trader from the area, Abdalla Elias, appealed to the General to be more circumspect. The trader was more weatherwise and predictive than the bigoted General. To him the trader said: 'If the resolution of this conflict costs now some thousand pounds which I am ready to pay from my own pocket, it shall soon cost the Sudan a price that it shall not be able to pay.' The General would not listen. On the contrary he instigated the NDC to order an assault. Brigadier James Loro Siricio was subsequently despatched to calm nerves at Bor, but that was too late. The conclusions of the NDC meeting left an indelible mark on future developments and haunted, for years to come, those who took part in them.[30]

Emergence of SPLM/SPLA

Unlike any other 'rebel' movement in the South, the SPLM/A sought not to liberate the South from 'Northern tyranny' but to create a new Sudan, one in which justice and liberty would strengthen the whole nation. The agenda of the SPLM/A was not the resurrection of the Addis Ababa Accord that became of historical interest, but the liberation of the whole country from what it saw as defective political infrastructures. It is this new vision that Nimeiri and, indeed, the whole Northern political establishment were either incapable or unwilling to accept. At the centre of the SPLM's new thinking was the salvation of all the marginalized areas of Sudan. Those areas, in comparison to the riverain North, had been for decades eking out a life without hope and mired in squalour. The SPLM/A was launched by the very young officer, John Garang, who had derided the Addis Ababa agreement. Like Worcester, 'Rebellion lay in his way, and he found it'.[31]

Though it was the pattern of historical injustices and neglect that created widespread and restive resentment among Southerners, Garang maintained that it was to Nimeiri that the 'honour' of precipitating outright armed rebellion went. In one of the inaugural speeches of the SPLM/A,[32] Garang listed an array of charges against Nimeiri:

1. Assailing the inviolability of the Addis Ababa Accord and finally abrogating it. This, Garang said, was done by stages and in various instances of unconstitutional actions, notably dissolving Southern Regional Assembly and government.
2. Threatening the territorial integrity of the South by annexing agriculturally rich parts of it and transferring them to the North. In doing so, he was sending the loud and clear message that he did not see the future of the South as an integral part of the Sudan and, therefore, grabbing as much of it as possible while he still could. He also gerrymandered the borders upon the discovery of oil at Bentiu, transferred the oil fields to the North and then went to great lengths to mask the fact by pretending to create a new province with himself as governor.
3. Unilateral and unconstitutional segmentation of the South, contrary to the expectations of the South and to the law.
4. 'Dishonesly' attempting to transfer Southern forces to the North.

Even in the face of clear betrayal of the Southern people by the government in Khartoum, the SPLM did not see itself as a Southern force but as an armed struggle that would 'engulf the whole of the Sudan' as a 'vanguard of the Sudanese people' fighting for the integrity and unity of the whole nation. The SPLM correctly perceived that Nimeiri had not betrayed the South alone, but Sudan as a whole. It pledged itself to the solution of the Sudan crisis 'within the context of a united Sudan under a socialist system', a solution that would necessarily take the path of a 'protracted armed struggle'. The term 'socialist' was one of the ideological watchwords of the 1960s and 1970s before political ideologies were eroded to the point of being irrelevant to on-the-ground realities. Like other idelogically biased political movements, the SPLM had grown up. One, however, is inclined to believe that, except for few intellectual Marxists and pseudo-Marxists within the Movement, the leadership and the hard core of the SPLM had never been hostage to any ideological shibboleths. This may be gleaned in a statement outlining the Movement's philosophy in which Garang addressed an accusation levelled at him by Sadiq al Mahdi. The Umma leader claimed that Garang planned to introduce into Sudan 'scientific socialism of Negroid non-Arab origin'. To that accusation the SPLM leader said: 'as for socialism, communism and all these *isms*, one cannot be socialist or capitalist without one's presence. We have to be, to be Sudanese, to form a New Sudan. Therefore, our starting point would be and is Sudanism, not capitalism or socialism or whatever.'[33] Equally, though it was at Nimeiri that the nascent movement directed its anger, it also underlined that it was not Nimeiri the man who had single-handedly created the Sudanese malaise. This was a recognition that the crisis had a much older genesis and could not be attributed to the present dictator, however vile he was. Consequently, the overthrow of dictator was not necessarily the panacea.

In its rejection of the South–North cleavage as the only explanation of Sudan's dilemma, the SPLM/A pointed to the fact that within its ranks were people who do not belong to the geographic South, and in this it read a confluence of aims and a desire by a cross-section of Sudanese of whatever race or religion, to liberate and unite their country. Thus, the movement presented its agenda as the follows:

1. Liberation, unity and defence of the territorial integrity of the Sudan. This was an unequivocal rejection of secessionism and separatism.
2. Democracy, equality, freedom, social and economic justice; a pointer to the Movement's determination to redress regional and sectoral inequities.
3. Secularism as the only viable alternative for a religiously heterogeneous society.
4. Genuine regionalism in which power was devolved to the *masses* rather than regional elite. Despite the populist tone of this statement, the SPLM was evidently calling for a people-based, rather than an elitist, development.
5. Radical reform of the central government to render it safe from the manipulation and intrigue by 'political processes, family dynasties, religious sects and army officers'.
6. Ending the uneven and unequal development of parts of the country.
7. Fighting racism and tribalism.
8. Transformation of the Sudan from 'the sickly degenerate dwarf of the Arab world' and the 'starving bastard of Africa' to a proud and economically vibrant modern nation.

Collapse of the Regime

After the fall of the Addis Ababa Accord, Nimeiri's political position became increasingly untenable. The fall of the Accord had itself totally alienated the South and gave cause for the rebirth of the *Anya Nya* as *Anya Nya II*. This was just one of the failures faced by Nimeiri towards the end of his rule. Economically, Sudan was experiencing a backlash of spiraling expenditure. Whereas quantitatively the economy had grown at a tremendous rate for over a decade, the socio-economic impact of this economic growth had dire political consequences: inflation rose, the balance of payments tripled and the budget fell into grave deficit. Moreover, the so-called Islamization of the economy dealt a heavy blow to the institutions of economic management in the country. This brought in the IMF and its ruthless Structural Adjustment Programme. High-level corruption, not so far from the President's office and the villainous business class surrounding it, contaminated politics and aggravated the economic mismanagement. Surprisingly, corruption continued, indeed intensified, during Nimeiri's religious phase; religion, apparently, was not only an act of faith, but also became an act of self-enrichment.

Unfortunately for Nimeiri, the economic 'growth' of the Sudan had created a 'Paris Mob' in Khartoum. By 1983, the population of the capital city had increased to over 1,343,000 from 784,000 in 1973. Unemployment figures grew higher, desperation escalated and the city population became increasingly ruralized. Attempts to send the displaced forcibly back to their villages failed miserably. Even the middle class was afflicted by a proletariat mentality and as the economic deterioration began to bite, doctors, lawyers, judges, bankers and other professional groups took to labour strikes against the regime. Nimeri resorted to the supernatural to explain away those social and natural phenomena. All Sudan's economic misfortunes, he said before his last official visit to Washington, were heavenly afflictions because people abandoned Islam. He also surrounded himself with a group superstitious dabblers and fortune tellers who continued to calm him down, promising that the storm would soon be over. Obviously, the crystal ball of those charlatans was excessively cloudy. Nimeiri's powerbase, therefore, was becoming increasingly eroded by the discontent with the country's economic fortunes. Even those who used to hold him dearly ceased to do so.

At the political front, Nimeiri failed to get the support he had counted on from Islamic constituencies. The promulgation of the September laws which, among other things, was meant to cultivate support to him by those constituencies, backfired. Sadiq al Mahdi and Hassan al Turabi, who were the chief patrons of an Islamic mode of government, felt upstaged by Nimeiri's sudden imposition of *shari'a*. They fought to impose it in the future; Nimeiri offered it immediately. For their own political survival, they began their fight to remove Nimeiri from power, each in his own way. In those circumstances, it was not surprising that many, including some who had for decades been concerned with the revitalization of Islamic values in Sudanese society, were driven to express openly their dissent and opposition, both within and outside the People's Assembly.

The ruthlessness of the reprisals that Nimeiri took against his 'Islamic' opponents was unreasonably demonstrated in the case of Mahmoud Muhammad Taha, the respected leader of a small elitist group, the Republican Brothers. Taha, aged 76, was charged with the distribution of seditious literature. Rather than challenging Nimeiri's temporal role, Taha only berated his religious dabbling. He was subsequently condemned to death for apostasy and publicly executed in January 1985. The Taha case provoked international protest and reinforced the growing opposition to Nimeiri within the country. Like the execution of Thomas More, that was a crucial moment in Nimeiri's chequered history. It revealed the extent to which imperious tyranny would go. Taha died the way More did, smiling. He almost said to his hangman: 'no temporal man may be head of spirituality'. Also, for his opposition of Nimeiri's policies as a gross distortion of Islamic principles, Sadiq al Mahdi was imprisoned for over a year. Sadiq described the September laws as not worth the paper on which they were written. Their place, he said, was 'the dustbin of history'. Meanwhile, relations between Nimeiri and al Turabi's Muslim Brotherhood (the only substantial political force which continued to cooperate with the regime) steadily deteriorated, not only because it was ignored by Nimeiri and his aides in the formulation of the Islamization policies, also because the Brotherhood appeared increasingly as potential contenders for state power. In a surprising reversal, Nimeiri began lambasting the group publicly and calling its members *akhwan al Shaitan* (brothers of satan).

By the end of February 1985, disillusionment and exasperation with the regime and its policies, whether internal or external, economic or otherwise, was rapidly crystallizing. At this late juncture, Nimeiri moved to deal with the Brotherhood by incarcerating its leaders on the charge of sedition. By so doing, he alienated the last vestige of popular support. Additionally, public sentiment was agitated against the government for its failure to deal with the effects of prolonged drought and the problems created by the continuing influx of refugees from neighbouring countries. To this situation, Nimeiri reacted by adopting a conciliatory stance. The state of emergency which he had declared in April 1984 was lifted, and the operation of the special Islamic courts was suspended, while an offer was made to revoke the division of the South, if a majority of Southerners so desired.

In the South, where war intensified, the monkey was running out of tricks. Nimeiri tried his last trick in March 1985 when he formed a national committee to advise him on how to address the Southern problem. Abboud did the same thing in his last months in power. Sir al Khatim al Khalifa, the popular Prime Minister of the October government, was to chair the committee. Nimeiri also dispatched his chief of cabinet, Baha'a al Din Idris, in the company of the British tycoon, the late Tiny Rowland, to meet Garang and explore his readiness to reconcile with

Nimeiri. His offer to Garang included the Presidency of the Southern Region, the Vice-Presidency of the Republic, together with seven ministerial posts in the central government. The offer was too stale to the taste of the man who went through all the betrayals of Addis Ababa agreement and was, therefore, rejected forthwith. Nimeiri, who had by now been given to dealing with Northern and Southern politicians who were only out for what they could get, was surprised by Garang's reaction. In his response to Nimeiri's offer, the SPLM leader told the President's emissaries: 'You had few Southerners as vice-presidents; that did not solve the problem. As for your offer to give the South seven ministerial posts at the centre, what shall then be left in your cabinet for those from the Nuba mountains, Dar Fur and other marginalized groups?'

Public discontent with Nimeiri's regime reached its vertex in April when Khartoum was immobilized by a general strike as part of a campaign of civil disobedience planned by professional organizations, including doctors, lawyers and engineers. On the 6 April, while Nimeiri was visiting the USA, those professional organizations negotiated with the military for the removal of Nimeiri, following upon which Lt-Gen Abd al-Rahman Swar al-Dhahab, the recently appointed Minister of Defence and Commander-in-Chief of the Armed Forces, overthrew Nimeiri's government, his own government, in a bloodless coup.

Conclusion

Nimeiri came to power under the pretence that the 'May Revolution' was a continuation of the October Revolution. With the passage of time, the May 'revolution' gravitated inexorably towards the religious right. By 1983 Nimeiri declared himself the Imam of the whole of Sudan. Thus the Sudan woke up one morning in September of that year to find that Nimeiri had decreed *shari'a* over it and made himself *Amir al mu'munin* (prince of the believers). There were reasons for this uproarious trajectory; his 1977 reconciliation with the Islamists had a lot to do with it. Other reasons had to do with Nimeiri's personality, especially his roguish approach to gorvernance (often conceived by him and viewed by his admirers as machismo). Second was his lack of appreciation of the impact and ramifications of his own decisions. That was amply demonstrated in the way he made light of his decision to abrogate the Addis Ababa agreement. With Joseph Lagu to his side, Nimeiri declared: 'This agreement was made by Lagu and myself. Both of us agreed to annual it; so what is the fuss.' Furthermore, political power is addictive, moreso to leaders who lack a sense of history and a measure of proportion. It is all those factors put together that led to Nimeiri's contradictions and meanderings. Evidently, on the issue of reconciliation with the South he also lacked goodwill. To him the settlement of the Southern problem was purely a means of cooling the political temperature in the South, not an end in itself.

Driven by such self-serving circuitous reasoning, Nimeiri persuaded himself that he could create institutions and promulgate laws and then contravene them at will. Manifestly, he was not a stickler for rules, including those he himself promulgated. That was why in 1972 he interfered to appoint Abel Alier against his will, as regional president. His interference didn't stop there. If anything, it became more brazen. He twice dissolved the Regional Assembly, the first time in 1980 followed by the dismissal of Abel Alier and his government, and the second time in October 1981, when, alongside the discharge of Lagu's government, he appointed General Gasm Allah Rassas as Southern President. Rassas was neither nominated by the Assembly (as the Addis Ababa Accord stipulated), nor was he even a member of that Assembly. Above all, Nimeiri had no constitutional power, according to the agreement, to dissolve the Regional Assembly.

His greatest blunder, however, was the division of the South into three regions, in contravention of the Addis Ababa Accord. Even by the standards of his own political acrobatics, that was a mighty somersault. Inherent in that clumsy mistake were three serious political blunders. First, he went against the constitution which stipulated that any modification in the agreement should be adopted by a three-fourths majority of the national parliament and confirmed in a referendum by two-thirds of the registered voters in the South. Second, by creating of the South three independent administrative units, each with its own governor, government and parliament, he was clearly angling for enticing Southern politicians to power and privilege. He never counted the economic cost of that thoughtless project. Third, in 1983 as a born-again Arabist he issued a republican order, contrary to Article 5 of the Regional Government Act in which he removed all references in that Act to the use of English as a working language or to that of indigenous languages.

From the beginning it was clear to Nimeiri that the South was against those disastrous decision, and so were the Northern negotiators in Addis Ababa. Nevertheless, he thought that with a few self-seeking Southern politicians he could rewrite history and, with impunity, trample on a solemnly concluded agreement. To shore up his plan for the division of the South Nimeiri was persuaded by a gang of four Southern politicians who failed to garner any support in the 1980 regional parliamentary elections.[34] With that shady support he moved to act. The majority of Southern politicians, both in the Regional Assembly and the Southern chapter of the SSU, took a different position. Nonetheless, Nimeiri went ahead with his plan to abrogate the agreement.

Emboldened by what he thought to be a meek reaction by Southerners, Nimeiri moved in 1984 to repeal unilaterally the constitution and retreat on the question of Southern autonomy. In effect, by 1983 it was clear that the Addis Ababa Accord was dead and buried. Nimeiri had done everything that the Accord said he could not. The South, naturally, took up arms again. Peace and reconciliation with the South, however tentative, was thus made to fail by yet another Northern leader. That leader was aided if not abetted by a Southern leader, Lagu. The gang of four who supported Nimeiri were purportedly swayed by what they called 'Dinka domination' of the regional government. The Dinka, the largest tribe in the whole of Sudan, accounted for about 40 per cent of the population of the South. By sheer force of numbers they were apt to be the most formidable force in any Southern parliament and the majority in any government. This is a reality that other Southerners have to live with, if the South has to remain united and democratic. However, despite their undisguised pride,[35] Dinka politicians have never worked in unison in a manner that would justify the accusation of a Dinka conspiracy. They belonged to different political parties, some of them working under the command of Lagu and others voting him to power. Interestingly, many Northerners who must have taken the cue from Lagu, much too often refer to Dinka domination when they discuss the SPLM. Those aching hearts who are tormented by the Dinka's assumed domination of other Southern tribes are not in the least pained by the Northern domination of the whole South. However, the charge of Dinka domination over other Southern tribes impelled Garang to tell a London-based Arabic publication the following: 'I'm not responsible for being a Dinka. It was not a matter of choice. I'm also not responsible for the Dinka tribe being larger in size than other tribes and consequently the greater number of its members are in the movement. This does not, however, give its members any advantage over members from other groups.'[36] Lagu's claim, therefore, was a cloak to hide his frustration as a result of lack of support at the Regional Assembly. It was also an expedient ploy to garner support among the Equatorians and smaller Nilotic tribes. Lagu's opportunism, however, knew no bounds. Not only did he collude with Nimeiri to unmake the Addis Ababa agreement which he signed, he also twice gave publicly the *bai'aa* (Islamic oath of allegiance) to Nimeiri when *shari'a* was declared. And that he did without going through the transitional stage of becoming a Muslim. Hence there is no running away from the SPLM's worry about the contextual framework within which the agreement was concluded. The agreement may have worked if it was concluded within a democratic ambience, but that is an if too many.

ENDNOTES

1. For an overview of the May regime see the author's works, *The Government They Deserve* and *Nimeiri and the Revolution of Dis-May*, and Abel Alier's, *Southern Sudan*.

2. Huntington, Samuel, *Political Order in Changing Societies*, Cowan, Gray L., *The Dilemma of Africa* and Woodis, Jack, *Armies and Politics*. Huntington's theory was that armies were more equipped to achieve nation building and modernize society. Cowan, in the same light, defended the *coup* against Nkrumah, arguing that officers, as modern professionals, were to be trusted with getting Ghana out of the political morass allegedly left by Nkrumah's ideologically based policies. In turn, Woodis justified *coups* but classified them as progressive and reactionary. To the Marxist author, Nasser's *coup* belonged to the former category, while that of General Abboud belonged to the latter.

3. A number of Muslim Brother activists joined Imam al Hadi, e.g. Mahdi Ibrahim, Ahmed Saad Omer, Mohamed Sadiq al Karouri and Mohamed Salih Omar; the latter died in the course of skirmishes with the army. According to an Islamist writer, the Brothers concluded that the military *coup* had virtually curtailed their movement's freedom of action and 'took Sudan towards scientific socialism'. Mekki, Hassan, *Al Haraka al Islamiyya*, p. 31.

4. On Israeli involvement in the training of Southern guerillas in the seventies, see Alier, Abel, *Southern Sudan*, pp. 111–18.

5. The feature, entitled 'Spy in the Cabinet', appeared on the Kenya Daily Nation, on 31 March 2000. It recounted the story of cabinet Minister Bruce Mackenzi, the only white man in that cabinet. The article alleged that Mackenzi served three foreign security agencies including the Mossad. He was reported to have been the conduit through which the Israelis transacted business with the *Anya Nya*. However, the Nation reported that the operation was suspended by President Kenyatta when he came to know about it.

6. Foot was retained for the SSLM by the Barrow and Geraldine Cadbury Trust in conjunction with the British Council of Churches. Assefa, Hezkias, *Mediation and Civil Wars*, p. 121.

7. Gaafer Bakheit, the Minister of Local Government, was one of the most inventive negotiators in Addis Ababa. With his wide experience in local government in Sudan (including the South) and his scholarly approach to issues (he taught public administration in the University of Khartoum), Bakheit was able to make inspiring suggestions that won the support of both sides.

8. 'Abdullahi 'Ali Ibrahim in *al Marxia wa masalat al Lugha* maintained that the 1973 constitution was silent on the issue of indigenous languages. There was not even a hint about them, he claimed. Indeed the Addis Ababa agreement, as an organic law, became part and

parcel of the 1973 constitution.

9. Those views were mainly expressed by the so-called Arabists within the government, led by Mahdi Mustafa and the late Musa al Mubarak.

10. It is worthy of note that it was not Nimeiri and his top army brass who were concerned with the army's morale, but civilian politicians with a decidedly Arabist outlook, e.g. Babiker Awad Allah and Abu el Gassim Hashim. Their position on the issue was in marked contrast with that of Generals Mohamed al Baghir Ahmed, Yousif Ahmed Yousif and Mirghani Suleiman Khalil. Alier, Abel, *Southern Sudan*, p. 78.

11. Op. cit., *Short-cut to Decay*, (Sharif Harir and Terje Tredt (ed.), p. 77.

12. This could not have been achieved without the support and direct interventions by Egypt's Foreign Minister Murad Ghalib, Education Minister Mustafa Kamal Hilmi and Rector of the University of Zagazig, Tolba Oweda.

13. Alier, Abel, *Southern Sudan*, p. 132.

14. Mekki, Hassan, 2 supra.

15. Nelson Kasfir, Sudan's Addis Ababa Agreement, Statement to the Seminar on Post-independence Sudan held by the Center of African Studies, University of Edinburgh, November 1989.

16. Howell, P. *et al.* (eds.) *The Jongeli Canal and The Nile, a Scarce Resource.* For a short summary see Alier, A., *Southern Sudan*, pp. 195–214.

17. In a letter to the Financial Secretary, C.A. Willis, Governor of Upper Nile wrote: 'the imposition on their habits (people of the region) of a project of irrigation involving the most modern machinery and a complicated organization must create disturbances not merely to their material conditions, but their moral and mental outlook'. Willis, C.A., *The Upper Nile Province Handbook, Southern Sudan*, 1931, p. 377.

18. Clashes were reported in Juba 1974, Akobo 1975 and Wau 1976. In 1982 forces in Aweil were compelled to go to Dar Fur. For details see Alier, *Southern Sudan*, Ch. 12.

19. Alier, Abel, *Southern Sudan*, p. 162.

20. Ibid., p. 173. Alier gave in detail incidents of mutiny and the reasons that gave rise to them. According to him, all the incidents were either instigated by fears and mistrust on the part of *Any Nya*, or the close-mindedness of some Northern officers who failed to absorb the spirit of Addis Ababa. Some of those officers were unwilling to accept the ratios determined by the agreement for the composition of the forces in the South. Alier, pp. 150–63.

21. ....

22. Affendi; A. el, op. cit., in Deng, *War of Visions*, p. 167.

23. In effect, Nimeiri's government has achieved with Ethiopia on the of the borders issue between the two countries, what no other government had done before since independence: delineating the borders and settling for good a dispute that had irked the two governments following Sudan's independence. The border's agreement was signed in Addis Ababa on 18 July 1972 and, based on

that agreement, Ethiopia ceded territory to Sudan, (*Fashaga*), and not the opposite.

24. Sadiq al Mahdi, on more than one occasion, claimed plaudits for the Addis Ababa Accord, simply because the Accord was based on proposals mooted in the negotiations between the North and South when he – or his party – were in power. By this he was referring to the resolutions of the Twelve-Man Committee which authored the document. That his government and party failed to implement those proposals in the course of four years was, to him, a non-issue, nor was the open opposition in parliament by a number of luminaries of the parties in power (including the Umma) to the issue of regionalization in the manner proposed by the Committee. Worse still, the pretensions of the former Prime Minister hardly took note of the consequences of his promotion, and subsequent adoption, of an Islamic constitution. That act alone dealt a death-blow to the then ongoing peacemaking process as clearly expounded in the statements of Abel Alier and Hilary Logali in Parliament.

25. Mekki, Hassan, 2 supra.

26. In the beginning, Sadiq did not join his uncle who was holed in Aba Island. In favour of that, he sought a meeting with Nimeiri to tell him, first, that he was not surprised by the *coup*, and second, that he personally knew of an impending *coup*. That, Sadiq said, was amply justified by the dire situation to which the party's type of democracy had led the country. In the previous chapter we saw how Sadiq was enraged by Azhari's action, in collusion with Mahjoub, to dissolve Parliament and had no regret to appeal to the Army. In his meeting with Nimeiri, Sadiq also disparaged sectarianism and recalled his own fight with his uncle, the Imam of the *Ansar*. Manifestly, Sadiq al Mahdi's *hypocrisma* was meant to endear himself to the *coup* leader who 'destroyed' democracy. The meeting was organized by Al Fatih Abdoun, a Sudan Air Force Officer and the son of one of the Umma Party bigwigs. For details see Khalid, M., *The Government They Deserve*, p. 250.

27. When al Mahdi made up his mind to see Nimeiri for the second time, he chose to evade his allies in the National Front and engage them in a dialogue to win them to his cause. Instead, he left them a tape-recorded message in which he gave reasons for his initiative. Sharif al Hindi (DUP), his deputy in the Front circulated a two hour video-recorded message in which he lambasted al Mahdi, using unprintable words.

28. *Al Raya*, Qatar, 8 December 1983.

29. Kok, Peter Nyot, *Ties that will not Bind*, pp. 52–3.

30. Other members present at the NDC included Attorney General Turabi, Energy Minister Sharif al Tuhami (both known for their militancy against the South), Chief-of-Staff; General Swar al Dhahab and General Yousif Ahmed Yousif. All to a man, excepting General Yousif, supported the attack, though Yousif was the only conferee who was

directly involved in the process of integrating the forces from the start. Ironically, the attack was carried out by a Southern officer, Dominic Kassiano, who later emerged as member of Bashir's NS RCC.

31. Shakespear, William, *Henry IV*, 1, VI.
32. Garang, John, *Call for Democracy*, pp. 37–48.
33. Ibid., p. 134.
34. Joseph Lagu, Othwon Dak, Phillip Obang and Oliver Albino. Division of the South into three regions was a blatant contravention of Articles 3 and 4 of the Regional self-Government Act.
35. The Dinka call themselves *monyang* (men of men) to distinguish their ethnic group from other tribes surrounding them, particularly the non-Nilotes.
36. Interview with *Afaq Jadida*, London, July 1993. Op. cit., in Sawi, Abdel Aziz Hussein el, *Dialogue on Identity and National Unity*, p. 106.

CHAPTER SIX

Civilian Regimes after Nimeiri,
Business as Usual
1986–1989

*Politics is supposed to be the
second oldest profession. I
have come to understand that
it bears a very close
resemblance to the firs.*
Ronald Regan

Introduction

Any rational human being would have expected that the lessons of many
years of war, economic collapse and dabbling by the military in politics
would have been learnt by the political class in Sudan, and that they
would realize the need to mend their destructive ways. Lamentably,
study of the post-Nimeiri Sudan demonstrated that the ruling class was
simply impervious to such learning.

By 1985, the whole of Sudan, in one manner or another, suffered
under Nimeiri. But the political parties, in particular, had borne the brunt
of attrition and incarceration or exile of their leaders. These afflictions did
not change fundamentally the way the parties, especially those of the
traditional *mien*, conducted business. In many ways, *plus ca change, plus
c'est la meme chose.* Sudan in 1986 was more or less where it had been in
1964. An *intifada* (popular uprising) had just overthrown a dictator, and
the nation was under a Transitional Government (TG) charged with much
the same task as that of the October government. But the *intifada* in 1985
differed from that of October 1964 in two crucial aspects. First, it was the
military who removed the statue from the pedestal, and as it were,
through the Transitional Military Council (TMC), stole the victory of the
people. Second, in the South things had changed beyond detection. Those
who carried arms against Nimeiri, unlike the *Anya Nya*, were not fighting
for *qadiat al janub* (problem of the South), but for restructuring politics in
the whole Sudan so that problems like that of the South would be
banished for good from Sudan's political landscape.

The key players in the *intifada* were the political parties and the
trades unions under the banner of the Alliance for National Salvation
(ANS), on the one hand, and the military that pretended to have executed
a *coup* against Nimeiri, on the other. The Muslim Brotherhood, then
renamed the National Islamic Front (NIF), were left out of the new
process and were not signatories to the *Intifada* Charter, the transitional

document under which the country was to be ruled. The Brothers had exploited the Nimeiri years more adroitly than other political parties to spread their influence, albeit in an underhanded manner. This was significant in two ways; first, there was fear from the traditional parties of the extent to which the NIF had made inroads into the political space in a way that affected the prevailing balance of power and portended new challenges to the parties. Second, the NIF had a completely different power game, one in which a just and mutually agreed peace did not feature very prominently. Their objective was to sustain Nimeiri's *sharia*, believing that they were better placed to implement it. It was only because of the equivocation of the TMC and its executive arm, the TG, on the issue of *shari'a*, and later the windings and turnings by the Prime Minister Sadiq al Mahdi in his efforts to appease the NIF, that the agenda of the *intifada* was contaminated and eventually undermined. Garang called the new regime May II and was castigated for it. Four years later his prescience was validated, the April *coup* was more or less a palace *coup*,[1] in which the choice between Tweedledum and Tweedledee was no choice.

Subverting the Nation's Wider Concerns

The *Intifada* Charter isolated four priorities: the economy, Nimeiri's September laws, war in the South and elections. True to traditional politics, the first three were almost ignored and bickering and grandstanding over elections became the main agenda. By concentrating on the elections while the war was raging and the economy in shambles, the nation's wider concerns were subverted. The situation in 1985 was formally similar to that in 1964, but the conduct of the *intifada* was significantly different to that of October in a number of key ways.

First, the ANS opened its arms to the military, accepting the TMC's offer to act as overlord with a tame civilian cabinet functioning as the executive wing of government. What the Alliance seemed not to have realized was that there had been no *coup*; General Swar al Dhahab, the new ruler, had been Nimeiri's Commander-in-Chief, and the TMC was made up of Nimeiri's senior officers. Further, the Alliance conceded the key ministry of defense to a TMC member, Brigadier Uthman Abdullah Muhammed, an ambitious and duplicitous soldier, who shortly before the *intifada* was calling security agents at a meeting of Nimeiri's National Security Council to shoot point blank at demonstrators; his ominous order was:'shoot to kill'. In fact, the Alliance left it for the military and the police to select, respectively, the ministers of defence and interior. In a democratic system, even without Sudan's unhappy experience with the meddling of men on horseback in politics, the first thing to do would have been to ensure the exercise of civilian control over agencies of state terror and deterrence.

Garang did not go astray when he perceived the TMC for what it was: Nimeiri regime without Nimeiri. As a consequence, the SPLM/A, which had played an important role in the fall of Nimeiri, was alienated or indeed alienated itself from the transitional process in Khartoum. Its view was that on the issue of war, neither was Nimeiri the only enemy, nor was the army as such the real enemy. The real enemy, it maintained, was the prevailing political, economic and cultural superstructures occupied by Nimeiri's toadies who either acquiesced to, or helped in, the dismantling of the Addis Ababa agreement and thus reignited war. They also stood accused by the SPLM of encouraging Nimeiri's recondite decision to turn Sudan into an Imamate.

Secondly, unlike the October Government, the new Transitional Government was not a radical government with a well-articulated agenda for reform to which all parties were priorly committed. The fact that the government was supported by a well-meaning and genuinely progressive constituency was immaterial. Truly, those who held the reins of power to carry out the change – as future events had shown – were not well disposed to carry out the most cardinal of the *intifada's* objectives: repealing September laws. Hence, it shocked nobody that the leading members of the TMC were rewarded by the NIF with positions within the hierarchy of NIF front organizations, only a few years later.[2] It was also a matter of common knowledge that General Swar al Dhahab had telegraphed Nimeiri, on the morrow of the promulgation of the September laws, pledging his suppport and that of the Armed Forces to the discredited laws.[3] By arrogating to himself the right to speak for all the Armed Forces (of whom none was consulted), the General in point of fact ignored the views of thousands of non-Muslims within the army, as well as of many Muslims who did not share Nimeiri's vision of Islam. Additionally, the two generals at the apex of the TMC were among the first to give an oath of allegiance to the *Prince of the Faithful*. Furthermore, the king-makers who put the government in the saddle had also no reason to be unaware of the background of the men they had nominated to, or acquiesced to their nomination for, the cabinet including the ANS's favoured choice for prime minister, Dr Jizouli Dafa'a Allah. Dafa'a Allah had, on record, telegraphed Nimeiri congratulating him on the initiation of *shari'a*. His warm message of support was broadcast over Radio Omdurman and published in the regime's press.[4] Like the General, Dr Dafa'a Allah hailed the regressive laws not only on his own behalf, but also on behalf of Sudan's Medical Association. He alleged that the Association's support and approval of Nimeiri's laws was spurred 'by their obligation to God and the Nation'. In his message of support, the Prime Minister also singled out for special praise, the *shari'a* penal laws (*hudud*). That was both fraudulent and scary. Fraudulent because it did not reflect the true position of the majority of doctors. It was a matter of common knowledge that almost the totality of Sudanese medical doctors refused to be associated with the implementation of the harsher aspects of *hudud*, e.g. amputations for theft, and cross amputations (amputating the right hand and left leg) for highway robbery.[5] The statement was also scary because the penal laws in particular were a cause of consternation among the Sudanese Muslims including those who believed in the existence of viable Islamic models for good governance.

With this combination of civilian and military leaders, the fate of the September laws was sealed. They were to remain on the books for as long as that heartless and artless group was in power. As it turned out, even those who genuinely believed in the necessity of abrogating the discredited laws took their time, counting the costs. In fact, they became so watchful to the point of lacking the temerity to call the discredited laws by their name *shari'a*. They were repeatedly referred to by a euphemism: 'September laws'. No law in the annals of Sudan's legal history had ever been identified in the official gazettes by the month it was promulgated. Laws were always classified under the rubric of their subject matter.

Thus, the government for the one year that it was in power did absolutely nothing on the burning issues at hand, except in one area. They all knew that without the SPLM at the table,[6] the cost of war to the economy and the continuing humiliation of the army would undermine what they hoped to be an easy stay at the top. At the start, the TMC delegated retired general Yousif Ahmed Yousif[7] to test the waters. Yousif was both close to, and respected by, Garang. The general met with the SPLM leader in Addis Ababa and, instead of being won to the calls of the TMC, Garang sought to win the general to his side. 'I have no trust in the TMC, they stole the people's revolution and they do not have the guts to make the structural changes needed,' Garang told Yousif. He also added; 'I know also that many people in the North may not believe that a Southern-based and led movement would work for unity. To allay their fears I am ready to step down for you to take charge of the Movement. I know you and trust you'. Yousif did not take the offer seriously.

The SPLM held out to the last against the TMC and demanded the immediate resignation of the government of Swar al Dhahab. In its place, the SPLM called for the transfer of power to a broad-based government in which the SPLM would participate. As a gesture of goodwill, it declared a seven-day ceasefire to facilitate that eventuality. The TMC ignored both the ceasefire and the demands of the SPLM. What was the reason for Garang's seeming obduracy? At the heart of Garang's call for the removal of the TMC was his conclusion that that group's vision of the crisis was not basically different from the older regime's, most settlements since independence were little more than bribes – the South would be promised autonomy, a few Southerners would get peripheral jobs – without any real commitment to genuine healing and veritable justice. As a consequence, the SPLM refused to negotiate with the TMC arguing that (i) the TMC had neither the constitutional mandate to govern nor to negotiate and (ii) that the SPLM could not enter into negotiations confined to the solution of a Southern problem, since it was a national movement committed to the solution of national problems.

Garang was also nettled by the decision of the TMC to reinstitute the Addis Ababa agreement without realizing the seismic changes that had taken place since its abrogation by Nimeiri.[8] On this issue the position of the Movement was clearly spelt out by its leader and read on radio SPLM over two consecutive days.[9] Besides, Garang was riled by the irony, if not pious fraud, in the whole episode. It was the same officers who aided and abetted Nimeiri's abrogation of the agreement who had now emerged as the ones pressing for its reinstatement. In the same address, Garang stated that the SPLM wished to participate directly in the shaping of a New Sudan with other democratic and patriotic forces in the country. 'It is not a matter of a group of 15 generals seizing power in Khartoum, forming a military council and their civilian cabinet and then calling on the SPLM to come in to take some reserved posts. No, we shall not take from anybody, we shall make the New Sudan together with other democratic forces in the country.'[10] Garang also said: 'We are not cardinals to bless whatever those at the helm in Khartoum dictate, we are politicians who are entitled, as of right, to work together and on equal terms with the decision-makers in Khartoum to map out the way ahead.'

This was a clear break with established pattern of changes of government, which would normally be followed by the co-option of Southern opposition nabobs to give the new regime a patina of representativity. The SPLM refused to be used in window dressing the TMC government, arguing that if the military could not correctly diagnose the problem of the nation – that there was a national crisis and not a Southern problem – then that meant it could not prescribe, let alone administer, the appropriate cure. 'A bad peace based on lies, deception and insincerity like the one we had in 1972 is in reality worse than war,' said Garang.[11] The SPLM also argued that the only viable solution to Sudan's problems would come through a broad-based national democratic consensus. In order to bring that about, it appealed for mass action against the TMC. It also signalled its willingness to commence negotiations with other 'democratic forces' for the eventual overthrow of what it called the May II regime.

The suspicions of the SPLM were further augmented by the facetious perception of the Transitional Government of Sudan's crisis. That was reflected in a letter by the Prime Minister to Garang in which he described war in the South as Sudan's 'bleeding sore'[12] In that letter Prime Minister Dafa'a Allah enumerated what he saw as a suitable compromise for Garang to join the government:

    i.   The resolution of the 'Southern problem' within a regional framework according to the National Charter agreed upon by trades unions, political parties and army.

    ii. The revival of the Addis Ababa Accord.

    iii. Recognition of the cultural and ethnic characteristics of the South.

    iv. Owning up to the fact that the South was underdeveloped and pledging to redress the imbalance.

On the issue of the religious laws the Prime Minister waffled around the issue; he did not commit himself either way. This, he said, should better be left for a constitutional conference.[13]

Nevertheless, the Prime Minister came down like a ton of bricks on Nimeiri, whom he described as the 'hateful degenerate oppressor'. Of all Nimeiri's sins against humanity, his crimes during the phase of the imamate would remain indelibly inscribed in Sudan's history. Little did the Prime Minister remember that the 'degenerate oppressor' had ready comforters and supporters at the zenith of his degeneration.

At all events, Garang's message on the national vocation of the SPLM or the irrelevance of the Addis Ababa agreement did not resonate well with the government. Like rulers of the past, they could not bring themselves around to the fact that Southern-based politics had anything to do with national issues, even when all of them implacably contended that the South was part and parcel of the 'nation'. They also could not see Garang's puzzlement at the call for the reinstatement of the Addis Ababa agreement as a viable solution for the 'problem of the South', all the more that the call came from the very men who, in the first place, connived with Nimeiri to abrogate it and later to destroy the constitutional infrastructure on which it was anchored: removing the 1973 quasi-secular constitution and replacing it with a religion-based one. The SPLM, therefore, had every reason to doubt the sincerity of the invitation to dialogue with this group. The reinstatement of the Addis Ababa agreement had another downside to it, the perception that the business of the day was a North–South one. Southerners, said Garang, should not be 'fossilized into sub-citizens of regions'.[14] This appreciation was evidently necessary before the SPLM could be constructively engaged in any dialogue. The SPLM, therefore, rejected its relegation to a movement of a minority people and warned against false solutions within the confines of such a frayed perception. 'Nobody is anybody's minority. We are all Sudanese, full stop', wrote Garang to Prime Minister Dafa'a Allah.[15]

Nevertheless, the SPLM reaffirmed its commitment to engage in dialogue with the ANS and set out conditions that had to be met before the commencement of any talks.

Those included:

i. Discarding the self-delusive notion of considering the crisis as the 'problem of Southern Sudan' and instead seriously addressing the germane issue: namely, the problem of the Sudan. That would call for convening a national constitutional conference to discuss fundamental issues such as the system of government in Khartoum and the regions.
ii. Lifting the state of emergency.
iii. Dissolving the TMC and replacing it by an interim government in which the SPLM would be represented.
iv. Repealing these *shari'a* laws.
v. Abrogating the defence pacts with Libya and Egypt as well as the cancellation of the Economic and Political Integration Agreement with Egypt.

On the issue of the defence pacts, the SPLM suspected that the joint defence pact concluded by Nimeiri with Sadat was designed to shore up Nimeiri's war in the South, particularly that joint defence arrangements were never envisaged in the talks between Egypt and Sudan in the mid-1970s which culminated in the Sudanese–Eyptian Charter on Economic integration in 1974. That, however, should not have caused tremors in Khartoum since the agreement with Egypt was one of *athar mayo* (remnants of the May regime) which the TG vowed to wipe out. The defence arrangement with Libya, signed by the TMC Minister of Defence, was a different matter; its main purpose was to enhance the war effort against the SPLM. As a result of that pact Libya supplied the Sudan's armed forces with considerable weaponry including four MiG fighters with their pilots.[16] Amazingly, Libya was the first country to come to the help of the SPLM during its fight against Nimeiri. The reaction of Khartoum to the SPLM's call for the abrogation of the two agreements was typical: 'How dare Garang challenge the right of a sovereign state to conclude agreements with whoever she deems fit?' The new Khartoum rulers clearly failed to bring themselves around to see the real or perceived nexus between the two agreements and the war in the South. Paradoxically, the TMC had no compunctions in creating bad blood with Egypt for a less important issue; Nimeiri's refuge in that country.

At any rate, while the TG accepted the idea of a national constitutional conference, it stood by the TMC and rejected the SPLM's preconditions arguing that it was not 'for any party at all to impose preconditions prior to the convening of the conference'.[17] It did however concede that the fate of *shari'a* and the defence pacts would be decided in the anticipated national constitutional conference, not before. There was manifestly a wide gap between the vision of the two as to what the Sudan was about as well as about the questions at issue. The Prime Minister's prescription for curing Sudan's 'bleeding sore' and claims of sovereignty may have been good enough for the Sudan as it has been traditionally conceived by Northern politicians. The SPLM, on the other hand, did not share that conception, and was pleading for a national consensus on how to consummate an unfinished product, building the nation.

Subsequent peace efforts resulted in the Koka Dam Declaration (KDD) of March 1986 mainly at the behest of the trades unions. Of the two major Northern parties, only the Umma participated at the meeting, but soon after the announcement of the KDD, Sadiq al Mahdi announced that his representatives at Koka Dam were not authorized to sign to the declaration. Evidently, Sadiq al Mahdi was jarred by the agreement at Koka Dam to abrogate the September laws, notwithstanding his claim that those laws were fit only for the dustbin of history. The NIF's blusters and blackmail had a lot to do with Sadiq's reversion. This contradiction was characteristic; al Mahdi had oftentimes adapted himself to the political circumstances obtaining at any given time, but soon changed his position to fit new circumstances.

Regardless of Sadiq's position, the KDD made an important breakthrough. The parties agreed on holding a national constitutional conference, tentatively slated for June 1986, i.e. within three months. The SPLM maintained that the envisaged conference should be held under the auspices of a government of genuine national unity in which all political parties, the SPLM, the army and other social forces were represented. The only issue on which the SPLM refused to mellow was *shari'a*. It contended that the conference could not be held under the cloud of the infamous September laws. Truly, if the decision on *shari'a* was taken at that time, and not three years later, things would have drastically changed.

Back to the Bad Old Ways

Sudan had always been ruled by restrained coalitions of Northern political parties, divided more by personalities than by ideas. Those coalitions were studded with pro-forma Southern ministers who always played second fiddle and relished it. What was required, according to the SPLM, was a wider coalition encompassing the North, South, West and East together with other recognized social forces and the army. Yet, the major political parties, lacking the will to transcend the old thinking on the South and other marginalized regions, went behind the scenes against the letter and spirit of what they had assented to at Koka Dam. Scenting the impending election, they left it to the TMC and the transitional government to repeal the September laws alone, each party afraid to enter the campaign with the tag of the party that had a hand in the repeal of 'God's laws'.

On its part, the TMC and the TG were determined to have nothing to do with having to make any difficult decisions, they preferred to reserve this 'arduous' task for the impending civilian administration. With the TMC in power and *shari'a* in the statute books, there was no way for the SPLM to be involved in the political process in Khartoum. Probably Nimeiri was right when he said to a gathering of Sudanese in Abu Dhabi, a few years after his demise, that *shari'a* was a *khazoug*,[18] and he alone had the power to remove it. The war, consequently, went on. On top of the cost of war, the economy, already weighed down by an onerous external debt, continued to sink until the IMF declared the Sudan uncreditworthy.

The elections in March 1986 were business as usual. An agreement on a wide-based government of national unity, even at the cost of delaying the elections for a few months, could have overseen a national constitutional conference and the participation of the SPLM in government. That, in turn, would have instituted the badly needed reform of the state. But by all appearances the chief interest of the political parties wasn't necessarily permanent peace, wresting power hastily. They were only too happy to go back to where they had been in 1969 before they were interrupted by Nimeiri. Using old allegiances, the Umma won the elections, returning 100 seats with votes from its traditional support base in Kordofan, Dar Fur and the Central region, while the DUP garnered 60 seats from its captive constituencies in the North and East. As for the NIF's new brand of religious politics, after many years of organizing and fundraising under the umbrella of Nimeiri's government, they made important inroads amongst the intelligentsia and some territorial constituencies, returning a surprising 51 seats. It is to be noted that of the 51 seats, 23 were raked up from the Graduates' Constituencies. This accentuated the fact that the NIF's popular base was not necessarily reflected by the number of seats they had won. Besides, the way the Graduates' Constituencies were drawn weighed heavily in favour of the NIF. Graduates, from wherever they hailed in Sudan, were allowed to register as voters in a province of their choice. The efficient NIF political machine went into top gear to register electors for every possible constituency where the Front had the remotest chance for success. In this way three Graduates' Constituencies in Southern Sudan were captured by NIF voters, the majority of whom were absentee voters from Saudi Arabia and the Gulf.[19] Notwithstanding this political swindling, one should put in a good word for the NIF's ability to organize its ranks and use the prevailing conditions for its own good. This could not be said of the collectivity of the 'modern forces' who were defeated in their own home front: the Graduates' Constituencies. On the other hand, the NIF's limited electoral victory within the territorial constituencies had been largely at the expense of the DUP, due to the multiplicity of their competing aspirants in a number of constituencies.

As for the South, no elections were held in areas that were under SPLM/SPLA control. This was a repeat performance of the disastrous elections of the 1960s, and probably worse. Out of 2,780,000 eligible voters in the South, according to Sudan's Electoral Commission, only 560,698 (less than one-fifth) registered their names. Instead of drawing the appropriate lesson from this dismal disinterestedness in the elections, the government decided to proceed with the process in any constituency that reported 6,000 registered voters. That was less than what was required for elections in the North for a precinct in local government elections. Elections were thus conducted in the South in 26 out of 68 geographical constituencies (9 in Equatoria, 5 in Upper Nile and 7 in Bahr el Ghazal). As a result, nearly two-thirds of the South remained unrepresented in Sudan's third democracy. The parties, in their hurry to rule, were not ready to envisage even a six-month delay of the elections so as to allow for the consummation of the agreement arrived at in Koka Dam. The blame for this serious blunder was also shared by the 'modern forces' who were in a hurry to get rid of the TMC. They argued that any elected government was better than the military. That was a miscalculation for which the Sudan paid dearly only three years later.

After the elections, the Umma and the DUP were in a quandary. They wanted the NIF in government because they felt that it would make political capital of the unpopular decisions they might have to make, particularly in the economic sphere. On its part, the NIF was implacably opposed to the repeal of *shari'a* laws, favouring instead, their full implementation. The DUP, having already suffered from the NIF's successes, felt that outright support of the repeal, however important that was to the peace of the nation, would be to further surrender political advantage to the NIF. It therefore shifted gear and advocated the amendment, rather than outright repeal, of the laws. That was also the Prime Minister's position as expressed in an interview with an Egyptian weekly. While describing the September laws as barbaric, he went on to tell that weekly that they could not be changed with a stroke of a pen.[20] Both positions (the Prime Minister's and the DUP's) towards the 'September laws' were contrary to the *Intifada* Charter which called for the repeal of the laws.

Substantively, none of the sectarian-based parties was really committed to the repeal of *shari'a* at that point, not with an election looming. The parties surely misread the sentiment of the people as the experience of al Mirghani–Garang agreement later proved. The situation in 1986 required moral courage, which was not present at that time. In fact, the two sectarian parties were competing in a race to appease the NIF, or rather forestall its political extortion. It was perhaps this apprehension that led to shady political manoeuvrings that resulted in the most thoughtless and gutless document concluded by the two parties (Umma and DUP) with the NIF. The document entitled 'Charter for National Unity', called for the promulgation of a constitution based on the 1968 draft (draft Islamic Constitution). It also advocated the repeal of all laws passed by the May regime, particularly the September laws which were described by the three signatories of the charter as a 'falsification of Islam'. In their place, the charter proposed 'the promulgation of laws resting on God's book'.[21]

The document was defective in many ways. First, by anchoring the new constitution on the 1968 draft, the authors obviously paid no heed to the divisiveness that draft had brought in its wake in 1968 in a manner that almost tore the country asunder. Second, by calling for alternative 'good' religious laws, the authors of the document failed to appreciate the magnitude of the fears engendered among non-Muslims and a large section of Muslims by the religionization of politics since the promulgation of *shari*a laws by Nimeiri in 1983. Those fears could not be removed easily. Third, the reference to the repeal of 'all laws' passed by the May regime reflected palpable lack of moral courage. What the authors really wanted – but failed to say – was the abrogation of specific laws passed by Nimeiri in September 1983. No government, whatever the degree of its hatred for the May regime, could have repealed all laws passed by that regime. It was, therefore, quizzical when the Sudan Bar Association adopted, as an alternative to Nimeiri's 'Islamic' penal laws, the 1974 Penal Code which was promulgated during the Nimeiri era and remained in force till it was repealed in 1983. With such level of unheroic dissembling the two parties served neither Islam nor the nation.

Before assuming power, al Mahdi, decided to sue personally for peace and resolve Sudan's intricate problems in a one-off meeting. The

Koka Dam arrangement that his party signed, reneged on and ultimately recognized, was a combined effort; a matter that the Prime Minister-elect was not aflamed with. He would rather have his own initiative. Time and time again, al Mahdi, appeared not to be comfortable with arrangements that were not ascribed to him personally. That, we recall, was why he did not abide by the consensual decision to reconvene the RTC to receive the Twelve-Man Committee's report. As an alternative, he came up with the idea of the All-Party Conference. To beat his own drum, therefore, Sadiq met for nine hours with Garang at Addis Ababa on 31 July 1986. The meeting was attended by three representatives of the unions, Taiseer Ali, Mamoun Mohamed Hussein and Mukhtar Osman. In that meeting the Prime Minister-elect made bold statements as well as revealing declarations. He began by defending the TMC. Theirs, he said, was not a classical military *coup* but a people-inspired one. He enumerated six points of contention that needed to be addressed in order to achieve peace: *sharia'a*, Sudan's Arab and African identity, balanced development, exploitation of natural resources, participation in public life by all citizens without discrimination on the basis of race or religion and removal of all historical injustices.[22] That was a tall agenda and an impressive diagonosis of the country's ailment. Those who did not know Sadiq would have said that Sudan at last had a leader who was up to the task. But those who were in attendance knew that they were dealing with a man who was so adept in espousing any vogue word, only to twist its meaning if need arose. For example, the first two items on al Mahdi's list were revelatory because; first, it was him – and nobody else – who had declared when he was first installed as Prime Minister that Sudan's identity was Arabo-Islamic. In the face such declaration one would be plunged in doubt as to his new characterization of Sudanese identity as Afro-Arab. Second, considering *shari'a* as a debatable issue put one in a maze. After all, the first time that a basic law precluding non-Muslims from aspiring to the presidency in Sudan was proposed, was when the Turabi/al Mahdi-led draft constitution was approved in 1968. Sadiq's reference, therefore, to 'participation in public life by all Sudanese without discrimination on the basis of race or religion' was staggering. Unbearably, al Mahdi's assertions were neither accompanied with a preface or prologue in which he unburdened his conscience of his old political sins. Clearly, al Mahdi should have underestimated the political savvy of his interlocutors.

But more importantly, all the issues al Mahdi brought up in his long laundery list were not relevant to the questions at hand. After the KDD, only two issues remained to be resolved before the parties could sit down to deliberate on how to resolve Sudan's crisis: the abrogation of September laws and annulment of foreign pacts. All the other issues on al Mahdi's list were amply covered in the KDD and he had nothing more to improve on them. The best contribution he could have made in order to hasten the peace process was to adumbrate feasible suggestions on the two outstanding issues. Manifestly, what al Mahdi was possessed with was not the expedition of the peace process but the creation of his own peace framework as an alternative to Koka Dam and dictating the parameters of the discussions, even if that meant reinventing the wheel.

As regards *shari'a*, al Mahdi blamed the TMC for not repealing it (as if he wanted them to save him the embarrassment to do so). Now, he said, 'give us forty days to do so through parliament'. He also lamented that the SPLM did not join the *intifada* forces immediately. Its 'recalcitrance' gave rise to 'all types of jingoism; Arab and Islamic', he claimed. He comfortably forgot that the SPLM was ready and willing to join the *intifada* forces in three months after the adoption of the KDD, on terms agreed upon by the parties who participated at the Koka Dam meeting, including his own party. Al Mahdi also referred to alleged attacks on the White Nile Arabs by a so-called Melut Liberation Movement. 'Actions like this may derail peace efforts' to which 'we are firmly committed', he said. In display of his abhorrence for violence, Sadiq al Mahdi denounced the excesses in the South by the government of Prime Minister Mahjoub (Umma Prime Minister in the mid-1960s), particularly the Juba and Wau incidents.[23] Mahjoub was also accused by al Mahdi for his 'cynicism' towards the Twelve-man Committee, a cynicism that was more than matched by Mahdi's initiation and sustained support to the draft Islamic Constitution in 1968. Al Mahdi, however, concluded his marathon pleading by saying: 'Today I became Minister of Defence not to become a Marshal of the Sudan Army but because this is the post which can easily be abused.'

By the end of the meeting Garang told al Mahdi: 'Sudan is a unique country, nowhere in the world would the chief "rebel" meet the Prime Minister he is rebelling against in such a cordial manner. If you go back to Khartoum and initiate the process for the abrogation of the September laws, I shall unilaterally declare a comprehensive cease-fire. From then on we shall be set for a government of national unity.' Al Mahdi replied: '*in sha'a Allah*' (God willing), but added that he had a parliament which had to decide on this matter. Garang riposted: 'I know the Muslim Brothers shall attempt to frustrate your efforts. I equally know that the Sudanese people want peace and they shall be out in droves in the streets of Khartoum backing you.'

Shooting the Peace

The shooting of a Sudan airways plane on 16 August near Malakal was the pretext used by al Mahdi to stall the talks, especially in view of the callous statement by some elements in the SPLA in which they assumed responsibility for the incident. No clear-headed person would have bragged about killing civilians, nor consider such an incident a cause for elation. That incident exasperated the situation beyond endurance. The Prime Minister, understandably, suspended the talks because of that 'act of terrorism'. The suspension of the talks was admittedly a necessary measure to calm nerves, but it should not have been turned into an occurrence to build up hatred and disaffection that would derail the process of reconciliation. Only when peace was achieved could acts of wanton violence, from whatever side they came, be arrested. Garang, therefore, responded to Sadiq al Mahdi's statement by saying: 'Sadiq did not shoot one plane, he shot the whole peace process.'[24] The Prime Minister, following the incident, was so unhinged that he planned to call a constitutional conference without the participation of the SPLM.[25] If that was to happen, it would have been a repeat performance of al Mahdi's All-Party Conference from which he excluded those who carried arms in the South, but still made believe that he was laying down the foundations of peace.

Eight months later, al Mahdi decided to resume negotiations with the SPLM. As if constrained to do so, his initiative was expressed in an unsigned and undated letter delivered anonymously to the SPLM.[26] Probably the letter was meant as a sounding board. In that letter, the Prime Minister once more skirted the issue of repealing *shari'a* and suggested a new alternative: modify the KDD to the effect that the parties concede to the 'majority' the right to apply *shari'a*, if they so wished. To that dubious proposition, the SPLM answered on 20 April through Radio SPLM: 'the proposition is unacceptable, first because it seeks to bypass the KDD and, second because it defines the Sudan on the basis of religion.'

Al Mahdi's move came after a spell in which he denounced the SPLA for wilful violence and dismissed Garang as a 'puppet of Mengistu'. His perception of Garang's 'clientelism' to Mengistu was reflected earlier in one of his discourse less than a year before he assumed power. In a lecture delivered in Riyadh, Saudi Arabia, he declared that Garang should be isolated both inside and outside Sudan because 'he only acts on the blessings of the Addis Ababa regime'. That regime, according to al Mahdi, would settle for no less than establishing a scientific-socialist Sudan of Negroid non-Arab people.[27] Mendacity apart, the accusation was ludicrous; scientific socialism – for whatever it is worth – is a tool of analysis, not a social system to be imposed. As for the concept of a Negroid non-Arab socialism, that was simply an inanity. That perception of Garang's 'subservience' to Mengistu was also conveyed to the American Ambassador in Khartoum, probably to curry favour with the US administration who was known for its resentment of the Ethiopian regime. The American Ambassador, however, told the Prime Minister that 'Ethiopia would not prevent any peace achieved between the SPLM and Khartoum'; and 'If Khartoum had offered acceptable terms, neither Mengistu nor other outsiders could have kept Sudanese civil war going'.[28] Nonetheless, al Mahdi was so assured of Ethiopia's influence over Garang that he once envisaged a punitive attack on the 'minority Amharic tribe regime [who] have feet of clay'. His American interlocutors, (both the Ambassador in Khartoum and Assistant Secretary of State for Africa, Chester Crocker – who was no less disinclined towards Mengistu – cautioned al Mahdi against that move.[29]

Al Mahdi's outburst at Garang's 'Ethiopian Connection' was the more bewildering since Mengistu's Ethiopia had been the staging post for the *Ansar* forces who were mobilized by al Mahdi in the 1970s to destabilize Nimeiri, long before Garang's rebellion against Nimeiri was launched. Those fears about Garang's independence of judgment lingered on. In a letter to Bona Malwal dated August 1992, al Mahdi accused Garang of subservience to Mengistu. To that accusation, Malwal answered back in a letter dated 18 October 1992 said that 'subsequent events have demonstrated that the alignment did not impair SPLM/A's ability to act independently and take its own decisions'. He also asked al Mahdi, 'was your National Front [the opposition front against Nimeiri] severely compromised through alignment with Libya'. Ironically it was in the Ethiopian bosom (under Mengistu) that the NDA was launched by no person other than Mubarak al Mahdi, representative of the Umma Party and coordinating Secretary of the NDA at the time. Those were not only contradictions of a confused mind there was something more sinister to them. Southerners, unlike their brothers up North, are not trusted by some Northerners such as al Mahdi, to be masters of themselves. They are always deemed to be wards of somebody.

Back to the Political Stadium

In Khartoum, a coalition government was formed and from which the NIF was excluded. The positions of government were shared out to the utmost satisfaction of both parties. Ahmed al Mirghani, the younger brother of the *Khattmiyya* leader became Head of the Council of State, and the DUP Secretary General Zein al Abdin al Hindi, a convivial local politician who would care for neither Belgium nor Bulgaria, became foreign minister. Sadiq al Mahdi, of course, became the new Prime Minister. That could have been an occasion for the parties to show a minimum of recognition to the South or to the marginalized regions in the apportionment of portfolios, the way the October government did. Balefully, no degree of sensitivity to those groups was shown in the allocation of significant executive posts or in the election of officers to parliament. Not only the heads of the three branches of the state (executive legislative and judicature) came from the North, but also the second tier. For instance, Father Phillip Abbas Ghabboush (Nuba) was denied the position of the first deputy speaker of Parliament (a position for which he vied). His position, he was told, could be the second and not first deputy, if at all. Both the speaker and his first deputy came from the North. When refused the right to speak up and challenge the arrangement reached by the three parties (Umma, DUP and NIF), Ghabboush and Eliaba Surur (South) walked out of the meeting in protest against what they considered a dictatorship of numbers. Eliaba was harsh in his words: 'We tolerated the Arabs for all these years and called this an Afro-Arab country, but from now on it is an African country only'.[30] Extremism, undoubtedly begets extremism. The Prime Minister could not see the underlying cause of Surur's resentment, only its apparent manifestations. He disparagingly described the angry walk-out by the Southern and National Party (Nuba) representative in the following words: 'those people hate democracy'.[31] Rarely has a politician been so impervious to the failings of the system he superintended.

In his own way, the Prime Minister moved to placate the South. In the fissiparous tradition of Sudanes politics [32] there were five Southern parties [33] to choose his ministers from. Some of those parties, however, had no popular base, not even as much as the electors of one single constituency. On the 1 January 1987, al Mahdi recreated the High Executive Council (HEC) but under the new name of Council for the South. He appointed at its head, to the chagrin of the majority of Southerners, Mathew Abur who was one of the few Southern politicians who stood fast behind Nimeiri on the issue of the division of the South. The Prime Minister promised Southern politicians that he would take their views in forming that Council, but in March 1987 he went ahead and appointed it without consulting them. At that instance, even Southerners with shorter memories did not fail to recall how the ruling Northern parties reneged on their promise to give 'due consideration' to the South's demand for federation, once those parties assumed power after independence. In consequence, SAC and SSPA withdrew from the cabinet and their withdrawal precipitated a split within the latter.

As history has proven time and again, even within the North itself, a coalition of sectarian-based governments was never without backstabbing and petty rivalry. That rivalry was not episodic, but chronic. A year of dithering thus followed during which the coalition cracked, was reformed, then cracked again. Since political honeymoons in Sudan are short-lived, the country between 1987 and 1988 went for long periods without government due to the lack of agreement between the two parties on how to share the spoils. Effectively, in the course of the three years of his tenure, al Mahdi reshuffled his cabinet five times, a sign of a deep self-inflicted crisis. The Prime Minister was not short of explanations. In a statement to the American Ambassador in Khartoum, rather than admitting that the cause of Sudan's political ferment were serious domestic problems that his government failed to attend to or sufficiently prioritize, al Mahdi chose to philosophize. 'Sudan's transition from dictatorship to democracy,' he said, was 'like horses confined too long in their stables ... when let loose they run about wildly without purpose before they settle down'.[34] Truly, Sudan's problem then was not the loose horses, but one loose cannon.

One stunning development during this political whirl was the resignation in May 1987 of the DUP Minister of Commerce, Mohammed Abu Harira. On submitting his resignation, Abu Harira made serious charges against senior Umma Party ministers for unsavoury practices. Instead of ordering an investigation on the serious charges, the Prime Minister sacked all his cabinet on 13 May. Nothing was heard of the charges subsequently. Coming from a leadership that made a lot of mileage of corruption in the Nimeiri era, that indifference to corruption was scandalous. More scandalous were the arguments made by some elements within the Umma Party to justify graft and nepotism. It has often been said that having been barred by Nimeiri from office for 16 years, the party in power had a right to make up for lost opportunity in order to sustain itself. Sustenance of the regime and its political organization through extra-budgetary resources collected from commissions was the argument hushedly proffered by the 'Chief Pilferer of the Republic', Dr Baha'a al Din Idris, during Nimeiri's government. Idris, who was the chief minister at the Presidency was prosecuted and condemned to prison for his misdeeds by the TG and remained in prison during Sadiq's government. Those accused by Abu Harira of being mired in corruption were never haunted by their alleged obliquity. Clearly, a regime that condones corruption and takes it for granted cannot be counted upon to fight it. It lacks the moral platform to do so. Sadiq's government, therefore, was not only politically inadequate, it was also morally uninspiring.

When dismissing his ministers, however, the Prime Minister did not make the whole cabinet (including himself) resign according to established parliamentary traditions in democracies. Those traditions hallow the principle of collective responsibility. In a confusing statement, the Prime Minister claimed that he was a victim of the lack of cohesion in government and the machinations of his coalition partner.[35] That was Sadiq al Mahdi in the raw. Despite his intellectual edge on many of his peers, his intellectual attributes were never matched by the moral courage to own up to mistakes. His compulsive desire to demonstrate that he never committed a mistake often drove him to straining living truths to no end. Even after his demise in the most humiliating of circumstances, al Mahdi persisted in complacent exonerations of himself.[36] As the US Ambassador to Sudan put it, al Mahdi 'learned little from the errors committed while in power and remained wedded to high-blown strategic thinking far removed from reality.'[37] Sadiq's self-satisfaction with the triumph of rehetoric over reality inescapably evokes Disraeli's damnatory remark on Gladstone: 'a sophisticated rhetorician, inebriated by the exuberance of his own verbosity'. Indeed, the problem with Sudan's former Prime Minister was that he had miserably failed to come to terms with one basic reality: that after all the rhetoric, governments are only judged by one thing. Results.

At all events, in May 1988, the red carpet was finally turned out for the NIF and Hassan al Turabi breezed into the government as Attorney General and Minister of Justice. Turabi was priorly accused by the Prime Minister of committing *tajawzat khatira* (gross excesses) when he served as Attorney General under Nimeiri. But in his wisdom the Prime Minister found no other place in his government for Turabi, than the department in which he had committed those *tajawzat*. However, by bringing the NIF into his government, al Mahdi had effectively tied his own hands. The agenda of the NIF was the implementation, rather than the repeal, of the September laws. Patently, the Prime Minister was afraid that the NIF would gain political advantage, were he to champion their repeal. But without repealing the hated laws, he had nothing to offer the SPLM. The army, therefore, went on receiving a battering in war, a war, al Mahdi's government had the power to stop. Seemingly, other political considerations were so important to the parties that each was happily willing to trade peace for illusory political gains. The new coalition, therefore, proceeded to put its own version of *shari'a* on the books. Al Mahdi, two years earlier, told an Egyptian paper that *'shari'a* should be applied if the majority wanted it'.[38] That was an unconcealed digression from his declarations about *shari'a* and 'the dustbin of history' as well as from the KDD. The Prime Minister had now turned into a cosmetician whose duty was to glamorize the September laws with a little plastic surgery. Evidently the cosmetician did not care a hoot about the implications of such legislation on the unity of the country. His views on this matter were made behind closed doors to an American diplomat. Sadiq told the US Ambassador to Sudan: 'If the choice was between alienating the South or the North, I would have to choose against the South.'[39] He did not elaborate what North he was referring to. Interestingly, before that statement, the Prime Minister received propositions from a host of 'Northern' organizations and individuals on the September laws.[40] All those parties (excepting the NIF) favoured their repeal. Subsequently (6 November 1987) he invited to his house a wide-based working group made up of Sudanese lawyers and politicians to debate the issue. The prevailing view of that group was in support of repeal leading to the eventual withdrawal of the NIF representatives. Clearly, all those deliberations were not enough to make Sadiq make up his mind. He continued struggling to square the circle. However, future events, as we shall see, proved that the Prime Minister was only playing politics. When push came to shove, he did exactly what he told the US Ambassador that he would not do: 'alienating' the North.

On their part, Southern members walked out of Parliament when Turabi's laws were debated so as not to legitimize the debate. Even al Mahdi's newly hand-picked Chairman of the Council of the South stated that time was 'not ripe' for *shari'a*, even though Turabi's laws gave 'temporary' exemption for the South.[41] The leader of the opposition, Eliaba Surur, was forthright in his denunciation of the laws and of the insensate politics of the ruling parties. Surur deplored the government for resorting to its mechanical majority to decide on such an important issue. He also accused the Prime Minister of divide-and-rule tactics and of being uncomfortable with the African component of Sudanism. 'I am an African who wants to be a Sudanese,' said Surur.[42] The Prime Minister was also blamed by the DUP of being anti-South and by fracturing the country.[43]

The General of Peace versus the Professors of War
Turabi was not the only Nimeiri minister who joined al Mahdi's government; Nimeiri's former ministers populated the new government, with almost two-thirds of the cabinet portfolios being in their hands.[44] Outside cabinet offices, street shouts (often initiated by the leaders inside) continued: 'Down, down butcher Nimeiri'. In Sudan the real oftentimes merges with the surreal. One of the former Nimeiri ministers who joined

the government was General Abdel Majid Hamid Khalil, a no-nonsense soldier. Khalil was brought in to tidy up the army and prosecute the war more efficiently, but he surprised his colleagues by his stance. The General advocated an honourable end for the war through peaceful means. His nemesis in the cabinet was a civilian professor of jurisprudence, Hassan Turabi. The professor wanted the war to continue and promised all manner of support to that end.

Khalil was also one of the few generals held in high regard by Garang[45] who earlier had worked under him. He was profusely praised by Garang on his appointment as a courageous soldier who stood against Nimeiri, while condemning 'the ruling trio' (the three coalition parties) as 'an unholy trinity of war-mongering sectarian bigots masquerading as national leaders'.[46] When Khalil resigned in protest against Sadiq's war policy, his replacement was also a stalwart of Nimeiri's government.[47] An American ambassador who had the opportunity to talk to both the Prime Minister and his Minister of Defence, made an interesting comparison between the two: 'Abdel Majid [Khalil] had a practical intelligence distinct from Sadiq's abstract erudition ... while Sadiq was never at a loss to analyze and verbalize any situation, he more often than not found himself at odds with reality. Abdel Majid, on the other hand, understood an important truth that Sadiq failed to grasp it was in Sudan's interest to refurbish its image by working energetically and visibly in favour of peace.'[48] One incident glaringly reflected Khalil's resolve and unwavering commitment to peace. Two days after the signing of the peace agreement between al Mirghani and Garang, an airforce transport plane (a C-130) carrying Khalil together with the Army Commander-in-Chief, General Fathi Ahmed Ali, from Wau to Khartoum, was hit by a missile, knocking out one of its engines. The Prime Minister immediately grasped the incident to play up emotions the way he had done on the occasion of the downing of a civilian plan near Malakal, though the SPLA did not claim credit for this later incident, nor was it really involved in it. Khalil, unlike the Prime Minister, downplayed the incident and refused to allow it dent his faith in a peaceful settlement.

Conflict intensified, but this time it was accompanied by a disquieting development in the conduct of war. For the first time in the history of Sudan's civil war, Northern border tribes were armed to fight against Southern 'rebels'. This new development agitated tribal animosities and revived irredentist immoderation and sentiments, both in the North and South. Among the tribes mobilized by the government were the Misseiriya, Rizeiygat and Ma'aliya Arabs bordering Bahr el Ghazal. Tribal feuds were not uncommon among those tribesmen and their co-citizens in Dinkaland as a result of competition over natural resources, mainly pastures and water. Some incidents of cattle raiding were sometimes reported between Northern and Southern tribes, on the one side, and within the Northern tribes themselves, on the other, e.g. Rizeiygat and Ma'aliya. Those feuds were again and again contained through the efforts of tribal elders, and amends were made to the satisfaction of conflicting parties. The reconciliation meetings also provided a forum for resolving myriad problems.[49]

Sadiq al Mahdi had not initiated the militias. It was to General Fadl Allah Burma of the TMC that the *success de scandale* went, even though the TMC was heralded as a crusader for peace.[50] But not only did al Mahdi maintain the discredited forces; he also enlarged them despite criticism in Parliament and opposition by the army. The ferocity with which the tribal wars were, and continue to be, fought, shall leave a permanent blot in the history of those who had initiated or sustained them. For example, in 1987 the Missiriya unleashed a tribal pogrom against the Dinka, leaving in its trail about 1,500 dead. Similar attacks were launched by the Sabha against the Shilluk at Jabalein in Upper Nile, South Sudan. Also, the Baggara raided the Nuba in the mid-1980s within the context of counter-insurgency efforts spearheaded by the army. One astute Sudanese scholar (who himself is a Baggara)[51] asked why a movement in the South that advocated equal rights for citizens should be met with such hardened attitudes by Northern leadership. 'Could it be,' the scholar, asked, 'that the ruling class would rather maintain the old power structures in which it has the upper hand, than equitably share power for the sake of a peaceful, united Sudan.'[52] The scholar, in a private correspondence to Francis Deng, was more outspoken when he described tribal 'Arab' attitudes towards the Dinka as representative of 'a mindset that has dominated Sudanese politics for centuries, basing its justification of their holding of power on an apparition of a superrace'. 'A mindset,' he added, 'that is largely immersed in an abstract notion of historical realities misinformed by an imagery constructed on the need for the reproduction of ideological fad'.[53] Apart from envenoming intertribal relations and disturbing social tranquility, the introduction of tribal militias revived bygone practices based on notions of superiority and inferiority of racial origins, e.g. slave raids. Evidently, the tribesmen had their own agenda: to maximize gains in land, pastures and slaves in a way reminiscent of olden days. Wingate, referring to the old slave trade era, described those border tribes as the Red Indians of Sudan and depicted them as 'the fiercest of all tribes who owned the soil' and to whom "'lave trade was at once the religion, occupation and the principal source of income'.[54] Fortunately, the old slave trade had gone, but not the arrogance with which it had been practiced. Also, it shall be unjust to condemn whole tribes for the misdeeds of some of their members. In effect, were it not for political mischief-makers and merchants of violence, chauvinistic sentiments among the errant tribesmen would have remained dormant.

The government's attitude towards those practices had shamefully been one of indifference. For example, when cases of enslavement resulting from tribal raids were reported by two university lecturers,[55] the government chose to prosecute the lecturers, instead of investigating the alleged heinous crimes. Obviously, apart from considerations of justice and the rule of law, it would have also been in the interest of democracy itself that facts be exposed to citizens; nobody would have been the better for it than a government that had repeatedly vaunted its democratic credentials. But in Sadiq's democracy, cover-up triumphed over transparency, though transparency is one of the hallmarks of democratic governance. Moreover, effective popular participation in politics under democratic governance presupposes the existence of an informed citizenry. Sadly, some of Sudan's democrats wish to keep citizens in the dark. Of all Sadiq al Mahdi's blunders in the arena of war and peace, the tribalization of war obscured all the others. Mahjoub's 'excesses' in the South, which al Mahdi denounced in his meeting with Garang in 1986, were just a picnic compared to the damage wrought by the tribal militias, sustained by government, even against the objections by the Army.

Al Mirghani's Peace Coup

When the DUP entered into talks with the SPLM,[56] the Umma saw this as an attempt to score political points. The DUP, who were not party to the Koka Dam discussions, decided to have their own initiative. The leader of the party, Mohammed Osman al Mirghani, was fighting a rearguard battle against dogmatists within his party who were adamant against the repeal of the September laws. To those al Mirghani said: 'If the present situation persists, there shall neither be a Sudan nor Islam'. Those were indeed strong words, coming from a religious leader. Al Mirghani's approach to religion in politics, like that of his father, has always been non-ideological. As a religious leader, he could not but defend *shari'a*, and that he did in terms that were more accommodating and less strident. Asked by a Cairo weekly about the role of *shari'a* in Sudan, he answered, 'Islam in Sudan is based on *shura* (consultation) and the spirit of forgiveness, human kindness and mercy. But the main concern of Islam is human dignity wherein the individual's fate, honour and property are fully guaranteed.'[57] In a very down-to-earth manner, al Mirghani was markedly endeavouring to chime with the political tune of the time, without engaging himself in any philosophical hair-splitting.

The NIF saw in the DUP's new position a threat to *shari'a* laws and called it an abnegation of the words of Allah. Both NIF and Umma therefore hung back on the DUP peace initiative. Turabi told the American ambassador in Khartoum that if the government endorsed the agreement, his party would go to the opposition[58] He was also not very sure of al Mahdi's position at the time, hence he intimated to the ambassador that, 'Sadiq would dither on the issue [and make] ambiguous and contradictory statements designed to please everybody.'[59] One observer agreed with that judgement but went on to tell the ambassador; 'If Sadiq is faced with a decision, he will procrastinate. If he cannot avoid a choice, he will make the wrong one.'[60] To the cold comfort of the Prime Minister, al Mirghani was rapturously received on his return from Addis Ababa after concluding with Garang an agreement on the settlement of Sudan's conflict, called on 16 November 1988; the 'Sudan Peace Initiative'. The people of the North were not 'alienated' by the agreement which abrogated *shari'a*. Equally, al Mirghani's reception proved Garang's hunch that the Sudanese people wanted peace and were ready to face up to the NIF's agitation. The new Addis Ababa agreement, however, confirmed the DUP's adherence to the KDD and proposed a new date for the formation of a national unity government in which the SPLM would participate once the September laws were frozen.

Al Mirghani's jubilant reception must have irritated the Prime Minister and raised his bile, but the Sudan TV decided to overlook the episode as a non-event. Some Umma leaders minimized al Mirghani's success, recalling the failure of his party to participate at Koka Dam. The Prime Minister could have espoused the initiative and made capital of it, since he was the one to implement it. But instead of throwing himself full throttle into the peace effort, his pique got the best of him. He went into some word-fencing and tautological contrivances to change the terms of the agreement so as to put his personal mark on it, the way he tried to do with the resolutions of the RTC and the KDD. That took six months, leading to the fated 30 June *coup d'état*, indeed ten months after the date he promised Garang in their Addis Ababa meeting that the September laws would be repealed by parliament in 40 days.

The army, on the other hand, could take no more humiliating losses. In the spring of 1989, fed up, it gave al Mahdi's government an ultimatum: put your act together and empower us to stop the humiliation resulting from a string of defeats, or else. The twenty-one-point memorandum was delivered to the Prime Minister on 21February, one day after Khalil's resignation.[61] In the face of what he thought to be an impending *coup*, the Prime Minister yielded. Interestingly, General Norman Shwarzkopf, who was by then heading the Central Command in the US Army, advised a visiting Sudanese army officer, General Abdel Rahman Said, that whatever disagreements the Army had with al Mahdi's governments, they should not lead to a *coup d'état*. Democracy, the American general told his Sudanese visitor, should be upheld at all costs. Howbeit, the Prime Minister promised to accept al Mirghani–Garang deal, strengthen the army and abolish tribal militias. In return, he requested that the army should respect the constitution (probably not to stage a *coup*), and that trades unions stop strikes (a matter of no relevance to the issues raised by the army). He also threatened to resign within a week (on 5 March). The army conceded and gave the Prime Minister a twenty-day period of grace to carry out his promises. But on the appointed day, the Prime Minister retracted his promise to resign in a characteristic manner of indecision and double-dealing. One thought that after Khalil's resignation, al Mahdi would have captured the mood of the army; it was obvious that the army, given the position of the outgoing minister of defence, would rather have a negotiated settlement than continue with a war which was unwinable by either side. According to the American Ambassador in Khartoum, 'This differing perception contributed to making Sadiq's peace efforts often desultory.'[62]

Even after accepting the DUP peace initiative, al Mahdi proved ambivalent in his support for the Sudan Peace Initiative. Mainly out of his political fears, pride and prejudice he did not push for peace as hard and as fast as he ought to have done. The Prime Minister first asked parliament for a mandate to declare a ceasefire (as if war had been launched, in the first place, on the strength of a parliamentary resolution). He also called for a constitutional conference with neither reference to Koka Dam nor to the al Mirghani–Garang accord. Those dilatory tactics only eroded the Prime Minister's credibility, since he knew fairly well what the prerequisites for holding such a conference were. He was also aware that his government had not yet met any of them. Once again, the issue to the Prime Minister was not pursuing peace *per se* but seeking to sculpture his own initiative for peace. In the course of those meanderings he told the US Ambassador; 'If he [Garang] can shake off his Ethiopian masters, I [al Mahdi] can solve the problem with him in *one hour*.'[63] The Prime Minister's faith in his capabilities to do wonders was limitless. Much as his nine-hours meeting with Garang in Addis Ababa in 1986 came to naught he still believed that Sudan's unwieldy problems could be resolved in one hour by a stroke of genius.

Having exhausted all options, al Mahdi ultimately succumbed to pressures and ordered the alternative *sharia* laws presented by Turabi withdrawn which opened the way for the DUP to join government once more.[64] So out went the NIF and in came the DUP. Hassan al Turabi contented himself with calling in vain for a *jihad*, after which he must have settled down to some serious scheming. The SPLM, in response to this development, declared a ceasefire on 1 May in order to enable the new government to carry out al Mirghani–Garang accord. However, the time al Mahdi wasted in trying to keep one step ahead of the game gave the NIF the time they needed to plot against his government and deepened the angst of the army. Thus, on 30 June 1989, a group of officers, allegedly on behalf of the army, overthrew the government and General Omar Hassan al Bashir became the new ruler. The military takeover happened the same day the cabinet was scheduled to meet and adopt the draft legislation repealing the September laws. Knowing well enough that this decision meant the end to their politico-religious agenda, the NIF had no alternative but to subvert the government. The atmosphere of pervasive anxiety within the army, and the general expectation of a *coup* following the army's ultimatum, helped the plotters immensely. An NIF clique of officers pretended to execute the *coup* in the name of the Army High Command. Their success, nonetheless, would not have been as easy were it not for the sloppiness, if not utter helplessness, of the government in facing up to the usurpers. Instead of challenging the *coup* plotters, the government ran for cover. The government's collapse did not surprise observers, for, as succinctly put by Ambassador Anderson, al Mahdi's 'ineffective government has been living on borrowed time, with most analysts giving it little prospect for long-term survival.'[65]

Conclusion

The third multiparty democracy was not an era, but a sad interlude. The transitional period witnessed hopeful signs for peace after the conclusion of the KDD. The failure to realize that dream had contextual, conceptual and political dimensions. First, the interim period was too short to allow for practical changes in Sudan's political infrastructure. Second, by entirely abdicating their responsibility for erasing the discredited 'September laws' to the TMC and the TG, the 'modern forces' committed a grave error. They should have known where the leadership of the two organs stood on the issue. And although General Swar al Dhahab, among all the men in uniform, was a safer pair of hands – given his humility and disdain for power – he was simply not to be trusted with repealing laws in whose validity and desirability he genuinely believed. Third, the forces of change, rather than working at the political level as a united front to articulate a new vision for Sudan with a view to rationalize politics cumulatively, they allowed themselves to be pulled down the sluices of conventional politics. Since October 1964, the 'modern forces' assumed that they were Sudan's government-in-waiting and thus invariably engaged themselves in power struggles with the parties. That proved to be suicidal. Manifestly, democracy is not about soldiers handing over power to men in civilian attire with a view to taking back the country to the *status quo ante*. But in Sudan, multiparty democracy inexorably leads to that. Consequently, were the 'modern forces' to consider their main political role as one of political stimulation and not of snatching the mantle of power from the 'traditional forces' through guile, things might have turned out to be different. Fourth, the preoccupation with the struggle for power and the ideologically based schisms amongst them, left little time for the 'modern forces' to organize their ranks so as to make a better showing. In reality, they underachieved even in the political constituency they claimed to represent, the Graduate's Constituencies.

Fifth, comes al Mahdi. For the second time, he failed to navigate the ship of state to safer shores. Twice he had the opportunity to burnish for himself a niche in history, and twice he bungled it. Under Sadiq's stewardship hopes of the Sudanese to delight on a bed of roses after the demise of Nimeiri evaporated. Instead they found themselves on a bed of nails. Al Mahdi, therefore, left historians with no opportunity to remember him for what he had done, only for what he failed to do. Those who had tears of sympathy for him might have concluded that he harboured good intentions. They might have also argued that the wrong-headed ideological project he pursued was a function of the history that had shaped him. But first, good intentions are not necessarily good policies, nor do they translate automatically into that. Second, Sadiq had to make a choice between being first and foremost the Imam of the *Ansar* (with all that entailed politically and ideologically), or the leader of the whole of Sudan. Unlike his nemesis al Mirghani, Sadiq presented himself as the embodiment of an ideological Islamist model and never hid his desire to recreate that model. His father and grandfather made a different choice and lived with it. Excepting using religion as a tool of mobilization, the line of demarcation between the secular and the temporal was very clear in their minds. By deciding to take a different route than that taken by his father and grandfather, Sadiq made an ideological choice. In making that choice, Sudan's urbane Prime Minister failed to capture the mood of the time or, possibly misconstrued it. His contention that the abolition of the 'September laws' would alienate the North was demonstrated to be false by the multidudinous crowds that came out to receive al Mirghani after his agreement with Garang on freezing those laws. Al Mirghani's reception proved conclusively the fallaciousness of al Mahdi's assertion about what the majority wanted.

To all appearances, the Prime Minister either adduced the argument as a justification for his own ideological preference, or he was not ready to out-dare the Islamist blackmailers. In that case he should be presumed to have chosen to lead from behind. As a result of those ditherings and misconstructions of reality, al Mahdi made himself redundant, if not superfluous, to the ongoing peace efforts. Leaders who quiver at historic moments can never call the shots or turn the scale. Resultantly, on issues of both war and peace, Sadiq al Mahdi's self-acclaimed achievements in government added up to nothing in real terms. The tragedy of the Prime Minister is that he had all the intellectual attributes that could have made him emerge as a Northern Sudanese De Klerk, someone who lived within the system and was willing to review critically what he had taken for granted throughout his life. Unfortunately, he was captive of the historical framework that both constituted and circumscribed him. Those who are obsessed with the past shall ever fail to grasp the present, let alone pry into the future.

One other enduring weakness of al Mahdi is his aversion to self-criticism. In his prolific writings, particularly after his ouster, he kept heaping the blame for the failure of his government on his coalition partners, while at the same time enumerating endless successes of that government.[66] Apart from the oddity of such claims and their inherent contradiction, al Mahdi did not realize that success ends when failure starts. Success is not a function of assertions subjectively made. It is invariably pegged to identifiable performance goals. Gauged by this measuring rod, al Mahdi has provenly the best claim for being Sudan's worst prime minister. His most awesome failure was delivering Sudan on a silver platter to the NIF. He could not see in his mind's eye the gathering storm, even when 21 deputies of his own party took issue with the inclusion of the NIF in government. Their protest was expressed in opposing Sadiq's nomination of one of the NIF's cadres for the speakership of Parliament. That was done at the cost of removing the former speaker, Mohamed Ibrahim Khalil, one of Sudan's best lawyers and highly respected politicians. He is also known for his staunch opposition to the NIF and their misguided Islamist policies. Thus Sadiq was ready to reward the NIF, even if that meant losing better brains within his own party. That Umma rebellion against Sadiq was also led by farsighted party stalwarts including the majority leader in Parliament, Salah A.Taha, and one of the most tenacious party workers, Abdulahi Abdel Rahman Nugd Alla. All the same, the Prime Minister refused to see the writing on the wall. Instead he sleepwalked over the cliff.

ENDNOTES

1. One Sudanese Scholar made the pertinent remark that 'Swar al Dhahab and his colleagues in the TMC were in fact Nimeiri's generals ... [and] as long as they did not abrogate the so-called September laws, i.e. the Islamic *shari'a* laws, then it was doubtful whether what has taken place was a revolution which changed a regime or a Palace *coup*', Harir, Sharif, *Short-cut to Decay*, p. 13.

2. For example, General Swar al Dhahab was appointed Chairman of the Islamic *D'awa* (call) organization which provides a humanitarian cover for the NIF's dabblings in a number of African countries. Those dabblings include the use of relief work in Sudan as a tool for religious conversion. His deputy, General Taj el Din Abdalla, was awarded with the chairmanship of a shady NIF paramilitary organization called *shabab al wattan* (Youth of the Homeland).

3. In his message Siwar al Dahab pledged 'the Armed Forces total support and firm stand [behind the September laws] which emanates from their faith in the establishment of an Islamic Society.' *Al Sahafa*, Khartoum, 13 September 1983.

4. *Al Sahafa*, 3 October 1983.

5. It was an open secret in Khartoum that all Sudanese doctors, on whose behalf Dafa'a Allah praised, and pledged support to, the Islamic penal laws, distanced themselves from the implementation of those punishments, given their 'cruel and inhumane nature within the bounds of the Universal Declaration on Human Rights'.

6. A British journalist, Andrew Lycette, wrote at the time that 'talking to the SPLM is fast developing into a symobl of political virility'. The Middle East, December, 1988.

7. Yousif was the only officer in the NDC to advise against the use of force against dissident battalions in the South in 1983, and around some of which the SPLA eventually nucleated. Siwar al Dahab, we recall, was one of the most bellicose in the NDC when the issue was debated.

8. In a Speech broadcast on 26--7 May 1985, Garang said: 'We did not organize the SPLM to fight for the restoration of the Addis Ababa Agreement or the unification of Southern Sudan, or for better concessions for Southerners. No, we organized the SPLM for much higher national objectives.' Garang, John, *The Call for Democracy*, pp. 48–76.

9. Ibid.

10. Ibid.

11. Ibid.

12. The Prime minister wrote to Garang: 'I know that the whole Sudan is your concern but there is a chronic bleeding sore in the South since 1955.' Garang, John, *Garang Speaks*, p. 87. Describing a war that had been raging for three decades and claimed the lives of nearly one

million persons as a 'bleeding sore' reflected a gross underestimation of the conflict.

13. Ibid.
14. Letter from Garang to Dafa'a Allah dated 1 September 1985. Garang, *The Call for Democracy*, p. 87.
15. Ibid.
16. Two of the MiGs crashed, one near Juba resulting in the death of its pilot; the other fell in SPLA hands together with its pilot. The pilot was later handed over to Libya through the intermediation of the Libyan ambassador in Addis Ababa.
17. Letter from Prime Minister Dafa'a Allah to Garang, *Call for Democracy*, 12 supra.
18. Literally, *Khazoug* is a piercing stake used to rip things apart; but generally the term signifies a dirty trick. It also implies a very difficult situation which, whatever way it is handled, shall result in some undesirable consequence. Nimeiri's statement revealed both his excessive cynicism and his contempt for the parties who succeeded him. To him, they have neither the temerity to impose this *khazoug* on the Sudan nor the daring to remove it after it has been imposed by him. Nimeiri must have had in mind those who vaunted that they would dispatch those laws to the 'dust bin of history'.
19. The three were all Muslim Southerners: Ali Tamim Fartak (Bahr el Ghazal), Ahmed Al Radhi Jabir (Upper Nile) and Amin Ismail Jula (Equatoria). That was the first time for the Islamists to capture parliamentary constituencies in the South.
20. *Al Musawar,* 20 February 1987.
21. Rycx, Jean Francois, The Islamization of Laws as a Political Stake in Sudan, in, *Sudan After Nimeiri,* (Woodward, Peter, ed.) p. 141.
22. General HQs SPLM/SPLA (20/8/1986): Minutes of the Meeting between the SPLM/SPLA Umma Party on, 31 July 1986.
23. When critizing Mahjoub for his excesses, al Mahdi did not spare a thought for the incidents of Bor during his premiership in which 24 chiefs were massacred while in custody of the army. The chiefs were rounded up from their homes shortly after a visit to the area by Prime Minister al Mahdi. Abel Alier appropriately described the revengeful nature of the vicious Bor killings as follows: 'as if the killings by mutineers in the 1950s were avenged by the army in the 1960s'. Alier, p. 9. To some observers, the Bor incident had been indirectly triggered by the Prime Minister's demeanour when he exhibited considerable emotion over the tomb of Lieutenant Zuhair Bayoumi killed by the *Anya Nya* in 1965. See, Malwal, Bona, *People and Power*, p. 42, and Khalid, M., *The Government They Deserve*, p. 231. Also, in fairness to Mahjoub's government, two members of his government (Sharif Hussein al Hindi and Abdulahi Nugd Alla) visited Juba and rebuked the army for the wanton killing of Southerners. They also scolded Northern merchants for their glee over the incidents.
24. Anderson, Norman, *Sudan in Crisis,* p. 107.

25. Ibid.
26. The Message was delivered by a low-ranking OAU officer, 24 supra, p. 100.
27. Lecture given at al Minhal Hotel, Riyadh, Saudi Arabia (October 1985). Al Mahdi also told an Egyptian weekly that Garang's call for the repeal of the September laws had nothing to do with religion, but was based on his Marxist ideology. *Al Mussawar*, 1 July 1987.
28. 24 supra, p. 83.
29. Ibid.
30. Lesch, p. 74, op. cit.
31. *Suna* 7 May 1986.
32. Following Nimeiri's demise, 48 parties emerged in the North. This was no a sign of political assertiveness, as some may wish to think, but a reflection of anarchy and cynicism. In both the North and South the majority of those parties withered away after the elections.
33. The registered Southern parties at the time were; Sudan African Peoples Congress (SAPCO), Sudan Peoples Federal Party (SPFP), Sudan African Congress (SAC), South Sudan Political Association (SSPA) and the Equatorian-based People's Progressive Party (PPP).
34. 24 supra, p. 125.
35. *Al Siyassa*, 15 May 1987.
36. *Al Dimograttia 'Aida wa Rajiha* (Democracy shall Triumphantly Return). Publication by the Umma Party Research Centre,
37. 24 supra, p. 205.
38. *Al Ahali*, 16 April 1986.
39. 24 supra, p. 103.
40. The Prime Minister received propositions from the Bar Association, the Judiciary, Attorney Ali Mahmoud Hassanein and the NIF.
41. *Suna* 28 September 1988.
42. *Sudan Times*, 12 May 1988.
43. Statement by Sid Ahmed al Hussein Deputy Secretary General, DUP, *Suna*, 31 April 1988.
44. Sadiq's government, in addition to Turabi, included ministers Abdel Majid Khalil, Ahmed Abdel Rahman, Ali al Haj, Mathew Abur, Aldo Ajo, Abdel Malik al Jaali, Mahmoud Bashir Jama'a, Bakri Adeel, Mirghani Abdel Rahman Suleiman, all of whom had served as ministers in Nimeiri's central or regional governments. Nevertheless, Sadiq al Mahdi opposed the nomination by his coalition partner (DUP) of Ahmed el Sayed Hamad for the membership of the Council of State, in view of his participation in Nimeiri's government.
45. Khalil and the twenty-two officers faced Nimeiri in the early 1980s with a litany of charges ranging from corruption to poor management of state affairs. They virtually asked the President to shape up or ship out. Garang, in a public statement, compared the position taken by Khalil to that of Swar al Dhahab, when the army challenged Nimeiri on the way he was running the country. Khalil and a group of 22 officers, said Garang, 'dared to give the dictator correct advice in the

national interest [while] Swar al Dhahab managed to stay in the army and buried his head in the sand'. Garang, John, *The Call for Democracy*, p. 170.

46. Ibid.
47. Khalil was replaced by General Mubarak Osman Rahama, a close friend of Nimeiri and a former Minister of Internal Trade in one of his governments.
48. 24 supra, p. 117.
49. Francis Deng told of the far-reaching impact of interventions by tribal elders to resolve conflicts on resources, not only on achieving an equitable apportionment of those resources, but also on the whole gamut of relationships between the Dinka and Misseriyya Arabs. Deng, Francis M., *Recollections of Babu Nimr, Khartoum*, 1995.
50. *Africa Watch*, November 1994.
51. Salih, M.A.M., *Tribal Militias, SPLM/SPLA and the Sudanese State.*
52. Ibid.
53. Letter addressed to Francis Deng by M.A. Mohammed Salih, Senior Lecturer in Politics of Alternative Development at the Hague Institute for International Studies. The letter was kindly made available to the author by the recipient.
54. Wingate, F.R., *Mahdism and the Egyptian Sudan*, p. 11.
55. Ushari, Mahmud and Baldo, Suleiman, *Dhaein Massacre.*
56. Negotiations between the DUP and SPLM commenced as early as 1987 in Addis Ababa; the main players on the side of the DUP were ministers Mohamed Tewfik (Foreign Affairs) and Sid Ahmed al Hussein (Interior). Both belonged to the secular fringe of the DUP.
57. *Al Watan al Arabi*, 26 April 1985.
58. 24 supra, p. 153.
59. Ibid.
60. Ibid., p. 155.
61. On casual reading, the Army's memorandum betrayed a sense that the army was only concerned with its own plight: equipping it better to win the war. However, by delving into non-military issues and being scathing in its criticism of the government's failure to stop economic decline, rampant corruption, collapse of security in Dar Fur and the blunders of the militias, the Army was, in effect, expressing its discontent with the way the country was run.
62. 24 supra, p. 97.
63. Ibid., p. 83.
64. The DUP left the government on 12 December 1988 and rejoined it on 25 March 1989. Two weeks after the formation of the new government, Turabi's draft law was withdrawn.
65. 24 supra, p.4
66. 36 supra.

CHAPTER SEVEN

The NIF: Ten Years out of the Twentieth Century 1989–1999

Earth groans beneath religions non age.
And priests dare babble of a God of peace
Even whilst their hands are red with
guiltless blood.
> **Percy Bysshe Shelley**
> **(Queen Mab)**

Introduction

On 30 June 1989, amidst a lot of fidgeting, political confusion and intrigue – these being the customary ingredients of traditional party politics in Sudan – Brigadier Omar Hassan Ahmad al Bashir put an end to Sadiq al Mahdi's government. Through his procrastination on the implementation of the peace agenda, and internal wranglings within his government, al Mahdi virtually handed the government over to the NIF. According to diplomatic observers who previously pinned their hopes on al Mahdi's government, 'popular disillusionment have reached the point where the average citizen was ready to welcome any rule replacing the ill-fated democracy'.[1] The regime was so ineffective and bereft of defenders that even the Prime Minister and the minister in charge of the regime's security ran for cover.[2]

Not only did Bashir turn the wavering of al Mahdi's government to good account; he also took advantage of that government's troubles. For instance, the first batch of *coup* plotters could not have been able to penetrate the army headquarters without duping the sentries that they were taking over the government on the instructions of the Army High Command, an eventuality that nobody, within or outside the army, discounted at the time. The plotters also penetrated al Mahdi's security apparatus to the point of recruiting its second most senior officer.[3] That was probably why the *coup* plotters did not pay much heed to the self-glorifying slogans of some Umma leaders to the effect that they were there to stay, come rain or sunshine.[4]

Bashir followed the customary process of military *coups*: he declared a bombastic sound bite as the name of the new *coup* – National Salvation Revolution. He also announced the creation of a National Salvation Revolutionary Command Council (NSRCC) including three Southerners, one Nuba and two from Dar Fur, with himself as Chairman. Some of those emerged to be a bunch of ill-educated despots. In addition,

Bashir suspended the constitution and banned political parties; though he avoided for a few days any utterance that could have revealed the true identity of the regime. Evidently, Bashir was still afraid of a rebound by the country's *'assiyad'*. The rest of the nation held its breath.

As is the case elsewhere, there are two kinds of *coups*: the type that is aimed basically at deposing an inept regime, house cleaning and paving the way for democracy; and the kind that aims at deposing an inept regime to replace it with a more inept and inauspicious one. Al Bashir's *coup* falls in the latter category. Once it had the rein of power firmly in hand, the regime pressed ahead to give itself a cloak of legitimacy: it hand-picked a transitional parliament in 1992 that was to hold fort until elections took place. That was mere garniture, the real power being wielded by an inner cabal of the NIF, known as the Council of Forty. Sham 'elections' were held in 1996 in which Bashir was returned as President and a parliament dominated by the NIF (the only political party to participate), was 'elected'. NIF leader Hassan al Turabi became Speaker of the new parliament. Following this counterfeit elections, the (NSRCC) 'dissolved itself' and transferred all powers to the by then self-promoted General al Bashir. This only happened after leading Southern members of the NSRCC, government or parliament as well as Northern members disheartened by the progression of events began deserting the NIF institutions. Some were discarded after being used and abused.[5] A new system of government, based on popular (Libyan style) congresses, was adopted as the system 'best suited' for Sudan as was a form of federalism according to which the Sudan was divided into 26 states. A National Congress (NC) was finally arrived at in 1996 as the only recognized party in Sudan.

In the meantime the government took over all the centres of power and wealth in the country and moved to fleece the economy and reshape the country to its Islamist image. It also monopolized all means of public outreach while continuing with tenacity to deny links with the NIF. In effect, six years after the *coup,* Turabi persisted in disavowing any relationship between the NIF and the *coup* plotters. In a statement to a press conference, galling in its cynicism, he disclaimed such a relationship and added 'I am an honest man, … all of you know me as a man who does not lie'.[6]

In their first five years in office, The NIF kept busy entrenching themselves in power, taking over the army, police, security agencies, banks, media, education, mosques, trade unions and anything that was left of the civil society. Having populated the judiciary, armed forces and the civil service with their supporters, the NIF proceeded to expunge from the services all those who posed a real or potential threat to the regime.[7] Some were arrested and detained. This preoccupation with security left little time to the government to attend to the 'secondary' role of governance (good or bad). In return, the NIF offered to the people of Sudan a so-called system of governance based on *Shar'a Allah* (Laws of God), conceived by their chief ideologist, Dr Hassan Turabi. Having founded his 'city on the hill', Sudan's Winthrop expected Sudanese Muslims to abandon their scruples and follow blindly the *soi-disant* Allah's laws even when they were inconsequential to the country's real problems. At the height of the collapse of totalitarianisms all over the world, the NIF unabashedly decided to establish its own totalitarianism vide a so-called *tamkin* (consolidation or capacitating) strategy. To that end, that domination tendency was crystallized in the creation of a ministry for social development as the regime's principal means of social control and, about a decade after Orwell's *1984*, the regime established its own version of the Ministry of Truth which monopolized the totality of the communication media (print, audio and visual). Characteristically, the full occupation of that intricate apparatus was disinformation, and behind the smoke screen of disinformation, truth dissipated. Besides, the regime used all public assets to ensconce itself in power and as the years passed it hardened to injustice and cynicism.

Nonetheless, despite all this cheerless history, one cannot ascribe to the NIF every Sudanese misfortune. There is abundant evidence in the previous chapters to show that this is not the case. The celebrated Sudanese novelist, Tayeb Salih, once wrote exclaiming about the NIF phenomenon. 'From where did those creatures emerge?' he asked. Salih may have found in some of the NIF practices the stuff of nightmare, but truthfully, the NIF has emerged from nowhere other than the polluted womb of Sudanese politics that had befouled politics for nearly half a century.

However, the NIF's main sin may be that it has made Sudan's polarization complete. That was especially true in its approach to the South question where the war continued unabated after unsuccessful attempts to incorporate the SPLM in the regime. Having failed in that endeavour, the NIF converted Sudan's uncivil civil war into an unholy holy war. Efforts to make peace with the SPLM nonetheless continued, but they were destined to fail because the NIF's bottom line was to achieve through negotiation's what it could not wrest in the battle field.

Bashir's government has been a personal triumph for Turabi and for the forces of Islamic fundamentalism in general. His 'revolution' was in fact an NIF *coup* all along, protestations to the contrary notwithstanding. In a sense, Turabi to Bashir was like Rasputin to the Tsar. For sure, Turabi is not a mad monk and unlike the Russian ignoramus, he is an urbane scholar. But his magnetism over Bashir – indeed over all the leadership of the NIF – was no less sweeping than that of the Russian magus over the Tsar. However, when Turabi and Bashir parted ways ten years later (December 1999), they made astounding revelations; both confessed that the *coup* was completely an NIF project. Turabi was more garrulous this time about his role in engineering the *coup* and blessing Bashir's leadership. He divulged that he had submitted himself voluntarily to confinement in prison with the opposition leaders in order to camouflage the identity of the *coup*.[8] That unwonted statement, coming from the 'honest man who does not lie', was mind-blowing.

Mythomaniacs invariably lose at the end, but in this case Turabi's and Bashir's greatest loss is that of future credibility and ability for moral persuasion. But then, in the world of equivocators, there is hardly a moral frame of reference. Eventually the schism between the two became irreparable and of the two, Turabi – the more ideological – started to edge towards a simple truth: the survival of political Islam in a country with multiple diversities like Sudan was only possible within the context of civil pluralism. As for Bashir, the supposedly less ideological, he nailed his colours to the Islamist mast and became more abrasive in his statements and actions. Probably he became hostage to the sheikh's leftovers who comprised some of the most intolerable elements within the regime. By so doing, Bashir could no longer claim that Turabi was the whole locus of evil.

Genesis and Political Evolution

To be properly understood, Islamic radicalism has to be placed within the right perspective. Sudan's NIF is a reincarnation of the *Ikhwan al Muslimeen* (Muslim Brothers), and as a political force, they are of recent provenance in historical terms.[9] And though they were organizationally linked to the *Ikhwan* of Egypt in earlier days, the Sudanese Brothers eventually matured into an independent entity. After a series of internal struggles for power, Hassan al Turabi established his ascendancy within the movement. As an accomplished lawyer[10] and a man who was not involved in the Brothers family feuds, he earned the support of younger elements within the movement. He was also highly respected within the international Islamist movement, though he remained an enigma to some of its leaders.[11]

Within Sudan, Turabi was not thoughtless in the beginning, of the country's complex multicultural realities. That was why he first settled for playing the game according to the rules. His assumed resignation to Nimeiri's wiles was part of that apprehension. During the regime of the parties in the 1950s and 1960s, Turabi paid court to the two Sayyids,[12] and endeared himself to sufi orders. Coming from a man whose pride passed belief, that was unusual. But Turabi's feigned humility was part of a calculated strategy, not out of obsequiousness. Furthermore, despite his visceral antipathy to the communists, Turabi was the first leader of the Brothers to replicate their tactics in organizing his followers within student groups and professional trades unions, particularly in the underground.[13] The two elitist-led movements were contending for support from the same social base, and conflict between them was contained within the bounds of schools, universities and trades unions. By the 1960s, sure of themselves, and emboldened by support that they were able to muster from the traditional parties, the Brothers came out in the open against the 'heretic' SCP and stoked a war fever against it.

The NIF, though, is not only a Sudanese political movement; it is also a cog in an intricate international network of political movements that claim to be 'Islamist'. The term refers to 'movements and ideologies that claim Islam, as they interpret it, as the basis for restructuring contemporary states and societies according to an idealized image of Islam's founding period 1,400 years ago'.[14] Those movements found a fertile soil in the Middle East in the wake of the humiliating Arab defeat of 1967 and the collapse of pan-Arab movements. Both events led to general disenchantment of the public with socialist and pseudo-socialist regimes in the Middle East and North Africa. The failure of pan-Arab and secular leftist movements in the region inexorably led to the erosion of their legitimacy. It also unveiled the inanity of the slogans they had raised for quarter of a century. That situation has left the ground wide open for all sorts of simplistic solutions and tractable slogans, especially the ones clad in the garb of *asala* (originality), revivalism, cultural regeneration etc. Religion throughout history has readily lent itself to oversimplification by zealots and undoubting salvationists. Patently, at a higher plane of thought, religion is to simplify life, render it intelligible and ascribe meaning to it. After H.G. Wells, religion saves us 'from the black misery of wounded and exploded pride, of thwarted desire, of futile conclusions'. 'It seems to me,' Wells said, 'that this desire to get the complex of life simplified is essentially what has been called the religious motive.'[15] But for zealots, religion is narrowed down to external forms, e.g. the way people are attired, what they eat and drink and how they conduct ritual practices. In setting great store by this formalistic approach to religion, Islamist zealots had effectively undermined the inner meaning of religion and the transcendental reality of faith. There is positively more to religion than those outward forms.

All the same, Islam became the most credible alternative to worldly ideologies in the Middle East, since submission to the divine messages had always been a powerful force among Muslims in general, and Middle Eastern Muslims in particular. Equally credible was the use of Islam as a weapon for undoing what Western colonial penetration has done to deform the Islamic identity and restoring to that identity its lost authenticity. To the majority of Muslims, Islam remains to be an unassailable bastion of cultural identity. A new set of religion-based slogans, therefore, began to occupy centre stage in the political discourse within the 'humiliated' Arab Middle East. Given the Islamists' hostility to secular nationalism and Western materialism, their slogans were apt to be potentially rejectionist of all things Western.

Conveniently, the neo-Islamists espoused the ideas of the most radical fringe of the Egyptian Muslim Brothers led by Sayyid Qotb. Qotb has denounced the whole modern society as 'infidel' and oppressive, and called for the destruction of its social and political structures through *jihad*.[16] To him, the modern society included capitalist, communist and Western liberal democracy. He also offered Islam as the only viable alternative to all those isms. With this imperial disposition and totalitarian vision, Qotb was set to conquer the world. He based that political construct on his own hermeneutics of the Qur'an. Romanticism might have had something to do with Qotb's quixotry, for it would be unfair to stigmatize such a learned person as being driven to that path by implacability. Before he became a 'second born' Muslim, Qotb was a celebrated literary critic and a disciple of the liberal thinker Abbas al Aqqad. He shared with his mentor a large part of his moral sensibility and some of his poetic frenzy. In reality, his first serious intellectual *rendez vous* with the Qur'an was at the literary level. His book, *Al Taswir al Fani fil Qur'an* (Artistic Figuration in the Qur'an), remains to be one of the most illuminating literary interpretations of the holy book. Imbued with Western culture (which included a period of training in the US), Qotb came out with another important work, *Al 'Adala al Ijtima ia fil Islam* (Social Justice in Islam). That work represents one of the few efforts by Islamist scholars to articulate a socio-economic Islamic philosophy. Qotb also dabbled with Nasserism in the early years of Nasser's rule, but that did not last long. He soon fell out with Nasser and was sent to prison. In the solitude of his prison, Qotb was introduced to the writings of Abu al A'la Maududi, an Indian Muslim scholar from Andrah Bradesh. Maududi appealed for the creation of a religion-based state for Indian Muslims and to that end sounded the trumpets of *jihad*.[17] Maududi justified *jihad* 'in the name of Allah against those who perpetrate oppression on all Muslims'. This line of thinking was not novel; it was shared by earlier Islamic scholars.[18] Surprisingly, the mainstream Moslem Brothers did not share Qotb's manifesto and, in rebuttal, produced their own, entitled *du'aat la qudat* (Preachers and not Judges). That document, which effectively shunned violence, was clandestinely circulated and only published in 1977 after Nasser's death.

Qotb, however, gave a universalistic twist to Maududi's India-based ideas. He concluded that all Muslim governments were heretical and should be forcibly removed. Likewise, he ruled that the whole world lived in the darkness of *Jahiliyya* (pre-Islamic non-enlightenment) and could only be saved through Islam via *jihad*. The choice before Muslims, Qotb claimed, was between Islam and *Jahiliyya*. Qotb's rejection of the Western isms, after forty years of Western scholarship, was total. His views on this were revelatory. ' I do not regret spending those forty years because they enabled me to see the true nature of the *jahiliyya* with all its disorientation and arrogance. I also learned that a Muslim cannot espouse the two cultures at the same time,'[19] he said. Positively, there was no middle way to Qotb. Radicals of this nature scarcely have any patience with those who do not share their vision even among fellow Muslims. Inherent in Qotb's message, however, were two things: first, the denunciation of attempts by staid Muslim scholars at the time – and indeed since Imam Mohamed Àbdu, the Grand Mufti of Egypt (died 1905) – to reconcile Islam with modernity; and second, was his uncritical belief in violence. Violence was predictably central to Qotb's message and was expounded in no uncertain terms in his 'Islamist Manifesto'.[20]

However, Qotb's message first served to organize the anger of the marginalized young in Cairo, of whom a large number came from rural Egypt. Apart from their grievances against an inhospitable urban society that won them to Qotb's damnation of that society, the fact they emanated from rural areas where superstition prevailed made them more susceptible to the uncritical acceptance of Qotb's dogmatics. It is interesting to note, however, that though Maududi's approach to Islam and society found a fertile soil in Egypt – via Qotb – it hardly found root within Pakistan, a state carved out of the Indian subcontinent on the basis of religion. This confirms the thesis that contemporary Islamic *suni* radicalism is largely an Arab Middle Eastern phenomenon that was eventually exported to other Muslim regions.

The neo-Islamists' rejection of the industrialized countries of the North, should not be confused with the smouldering resentment that the countries of the Third World (including Muslim countries) feel towards the North (US and Europe). That resentment is justified by the real or perceived economic marginalization of those countries by the North. For despite their abundant wealth in natural resources, the GDP of the totality of Muslim countries does not exceed 1,000 billion US dollars, while that of France, Germany and Japan alone stand respectively at 1,500, 2,500 and 5,500 thousands. As one scholar fittingly remarked: 'Muslims may protest with violence but they protest as aggrieved parties on the margins of a world system that they did not create and cannot control, but in which they participate and refuse not to be counted.'[21] In reality, neither have Muslim countries who are in the forefront of the struggle against the inordinate economic dominance of the North any false pretences as to their role in the world, nor does any of them assume a God-ordained role to change that world.[22] Over and above, neo-Islamism should not be lumped together with the liberation theology of South and Central America (for example Oscar Romero in Salvador and Cardinal Erenze in Brazil); theirs was a political revolt against authoritarianism in their countries as well as against the traditional church which supported authoritarian regimes. To the liberation theologists of the Americas, the established churches sinned by familiarizing theselves with, and condoning, despotic regimes. The South American liberation theologists never claimed for themselves a mission that transcended their countries of origin. Par contra, radical Islamists' did not resort to violence only to put right what was assumed to be wrong within the bounds of their countries of origin. They also aspired to impose a divinely ordained political dispensation on Muslims and non-Muslims beyond national borders. For achieving that end, any measure of violence was justified, especially against what Khomeini called *dwal al istikbar* (arrogant states). By that he means the West. Khomeini's first challenge of *dwal al istikbar* was reflected in the symbolic occupation of the American Embassy in Teheran. Besides, within the Islamic world, the radical Islamists believed that Muslims represented an *Umma* (Commonwealth) which knew no national boundaries. Based on that assumption, they arrogated to themselves the right to propagate and enforce in all Muslim countries their ideological end of the rainbow. With this level of intellectual narcissism, the Islamists' drive became a contraption of religious dogmatism, lust for power, violence and totalitarianism.

Another factor that helped the neo-Islamists' progression to prominence was the superpower rivalry, particularly during the Afghan war. Present-day Arab and Middle Eastern radical Islamic groups (including Sudanese) were nurtured by rich Arab countries and the United States as neutralizers to Nasserism and Communism throughout the decade of 1960S and early 1970. After Nasser's onslaught on the Brothers, anti-communism, and by extension anti-Nasserism, became the *raison d'être* of the Islamists' struggle in the region. The US provided Middle Eastern political Islam, *ab initio,* with the economic underpinnings that enabled it to expand beyond Arab lands. So too, was the military training and wherewithal it was endowed with, to a large extent, an outgrowth of their engagement in the Afghan war against the 'evil empire'. Incongruously, the erstwhile benefactor of radical Islamists became their all-purpose villain.

The controversy about political Islam should also be placed within its proper concomitant, it is neither about Islam as a system of belief, nor as a cultural force; it simply relates to the ravings of some elitist ideologues to develop and impose by force norms of governance and organization of society assumed to be derived from Islam. However, if the Islamists were to preach what they believed peacefully, that would have been tolerated, but their claims became preposterous when they made a bid to impose them violently. After all, Muslims, wherever they are (as much as Christians and Jews for that matter), had never abandoned their ascriptive Islamic roots, or failed to embody their religious values in daily life practices. Under the eye of heaven, they blend religious values and practices in their everyday life in both perceptible and subtle ways. Much too often religiosity is not expressed in rituals which are external forms of communion with God, but in the inner heart and the depth of conscience. That is what holds human beings together. Consequently, what ordinary Muslims reject in the pretensions of political Islam is, first, its claim to reconstruct Islam to its own image allegedly to revalidate its mission. Second, they take a dim view of its pretension that it is capable of providing a definitive solution to the problems of mankind. The shallowness of this pretension is demonstrated in the neo-Islamist's rigid and formalistic approach to *shari'a.* In practice, they produced less than sterling results to justify their contention. Their failure has been both political and intellectual. Over and above rancid corruption, sharp practices, under-the-counter dealings and deceit, added a moral dimension to the insufficiency of contemporary political Islam. For all the above, political Islam began to run out of steam and began a relentless spiral of recession. In Sudan it has commenced retrieving its steps from what was presumed to be God-given truths.

This insufficiency belies claims by some Western scholars and politicians who believed that the radical Islamic phenomenon is a new wave of cultural revival with which the world should learn to live. Based on empirical evidence, the so-called tidal religio-cultural wave of Islamic fundamentalism is neither a wave nor is it about religion and culture. To all intents and purposes, it is a pattern of religious neo-fascism that, in practice, owes more to Mussolini than to Mohammed. The hypothesis that this phenomenon represents the future is punctured by its failure in its own backyard to do better than any of the regimes it had wrested power from. Today, political Islam is in an unenviable position, because all that it has been able to offer as an 'Islamist' alternative model of governance, As Bashir's Sudan, Taliban's Afghanistan or the Iran of the *Ayatollahs* who are unable even to live with Khatemi's thoughtful, but mild reforms. Surprisingly, the inadequacy of the Iranian experience was not only in providing a better model of governance, but also in upholding moral values and codes of behaviour. Conformity to good morals, probity and virtuous conduct is the essence of all religions. For example, in Iran alone, the backlash against the dogmatism of the *Ayatollahs,* particularly among the young, was amazing. In a statement to an Arabic London weekly, Mohammed Ali Zam, Director for Cultural Affairs in Teheran Municipality, revealed that 80 per cent of the young do not follow their daily prayers, 60 per cent are given to pre-marital and extra-marital sex and 20 per cent are drug addicts.[23] Also, according to an Arabic London daily, Tehran alone, under its present Islamic rule, consumes fifty tons of opium daily. [24]Those are alarming figures in a country which many Islamists put on a pedestal as the model for an Islamic state.

In Sudan, the NIF did not fare better; Bashir, eleven years after usurping power with the professed purpose of delivering the nation from evil, made a startling confession when he said: 'we have failed to implant our values and ideals in the heart of society and essentially depended on the state organs and laws to impose those values and ideals'.[25] Regardless, the failure of the NIF project in Sudan was incontestably demonstrated in their moves (after the breakup between Bashir and Turabi) to revert to broadly based alliances with forces they had dismissed as heretic, infidel or apostate. In effect, after ten years during which they laboured hard to roll back the wheels of history, the NIF's *volte face* pointed out one thing, the high tide of the Islamists has come and receded. As one commentator reported, the 'fundamentalist life cycle as a revolutionary tool in the region is beginning to hamper, instead of benefit, the governments that used it to achieve power'.[26] In actuality, the only *Suni* radical Islamist movement that is still fervid and flaming is what came to be known as the republic of Londonstan, i.e. Islamists groups who took refuge in *dwal al istikbar* and are exhausting all the possibilities offered to them by that 'infidel' community.

The empathy of Western scholars and diplomats towards Turabi, in particular, has another side to it: self-paid homage. Despite all his sabre rattling against the West, those scholars and diplomats still see in Turabi's scholarliness and mastery of European languages an achievement of their own educational system. An American journalist who visited Turabi in Khartoum reported that Western diplomats he met in that city invariably described the Sheikh as 'urbane, erudite and beguiling'. On their part, the Sudanese whom the journalist met agreed with that praise but added other characterizations: 'evil, liar and dangerous'. To underscore their point, they told the visiting journalist: 'Turabi'll meet you as an American and convince you that he is not different than George Bush'.[27] The conclusions reached by those Western diplomats in Khartoum on Turabi, weighs heavily against their judgement. Seemingly, none of them saw or cared to see the hatred engendered among the Sudanese by Turabi's policies. Huffing and ruffling the dignity of the Sheikh, to the American journalist, was simply an expression of that hate.

Notwithstanding his avowed hatred of the West, Turabi has an ambivalent attitude towards it. With almost the pathological duality of Jeckyl and Hyde, Turabi, on the one hand decries everything Western in statements he makes inside Sudan and to the Arab media, while on the other, he appears almost apologetic for the excesses of the Islamists in enunciations he makes in Western fora. To those we shall refer in this chapter. Effectively, by absolving himself of those excesses in order to give satisfaction to his Western interlocutors, Turabi is unwittingly condemning his own civilizational project. For example, in an interview with a London Arabic magazine, *al Majala*, he had this to say: 'The West lives in a moral vacuum and it is our destiny to fill that vacuum. This is a trust that we have to fulfill.'[28] Nonetheless, following his decision to Arabicize education in Sudanese universities, Turabi ordered the recall of all students studying in the West on government grants in order to save them from 'Western cultural pollution', he still found no better place to send his youngest son for education than the University of Wales. One would think that his choice would have been Qom or Mashhad.[29] This ruckus of incongruity is nothing but a symptom of a torn soul; Turabi is desperately fighting a world that had produced him and wishes everybody to join him in that fight, excepting those close to him. In this Turabi is not alone. A dozen of NIF 'anti-Western' leaders are still unrestrainedly delighted with holding US, Canadian or British citizenship and have no qualms in allowing their families to enjoy the benefits accruing from that citizenship while their foreign passports remain freeze-dried for future use, just in case.

The greatest moment of the Brothers came during Nimeiri's regime, both as foes and supporters. In the first instance, the Brothers capitalized on Nimeiri's leftist radicalism of the early 1970s and fully exploited its potential threat to traditional Arab governments in the region offering their services to those governments so as to ward off the 'red' menace across the Red Sea. Later, they made themselves available to the 'secularist' opposition leader Sharif al Hindi and to a predisposed Sadiq al Mahdi when he finally settled in the opposition National Front. Apart from the fortune they were able to amass for their role in parrying the 'red' menace, they were also able militarily to train many of their cadres in the Libyan Desert under the aegis of the Front.[30] In the second instance, following their rapprochement with Nimeiri, the Brothers dexterously used their newly acquired position to organize their ranks, infest government departments with their supporters and consolidate their grassroots organizations. Funds availed to them from Islamic banks, particularly the Faisal Islamic Bank, immensely helped their mobilization drive among students and artisans for whom special windows of lending were established by that Bank and with which Turabi had very close relations.[31] In a statement to an Arabic London daily, Turabi confessed that the Brothers' cooperation with the Nimeiri regime was part of a stratagem to penetrate Sudanese rural society in general, and the South in particular, 'in view of the expansion of Nimeiri's regime into those societies'.[32]

By the mid-1980s the NIF had grown to become the richest politico-religious organization in Africa with investments under different guises in the Bahamas, Malaysia and Switzerland and a bevy of secret accounts in those and other countries. Unaffected by the political jostling, the Brothers extended their tentacles further in the country and entrenched themselves in the economy. In addition, through contacts with rich benevolent Arab individuals and voluntary organizations in the Gulf, the Brothers assumed the role of overseeing Islamic charity and humanitarian operations in Africa, by virtue of being Muslims and Africans. In their new incarnation as NIF, the Brothers were thus poised to play an important role in Sudanese and African politics. That was why, when the coalition government was reconstructed in May 1988, they managed to penetrate the cabinet with the appointment of their Secretary General, Hassan al Turabi, as Attorney-General despite his stunning defeat in parliamentary elections.

Another great opportunity for the NIF came (or was made to)[33] when Omar Hassan Ahmed al Bashir usurped power in 1989. That was indeed the greatest success for political Islam after Iran. But, as was to emerge later, the military regime was only a puppet, Bashir to Turabi, was a Tsar held hostage by a Sudanese Rasputin. From the outset, both Turabi and Bashir denied any connection between the *coup* and the NIF. Ten years later when he fell foul of Turabi, Bashir did not only confess the NIF's role in the *coup*, he also disclosed that he was a dyed-in-the-wool Muslim Brother since his secondary school days. Shockingly, it never dawned on the 'moralistic' crusader that presidents who lie to the public in the 'infidel' world the NIF was set to reform were impeached, chased out of office and disgraced. But in the NIF's world, assumedly ordained by Allah and answerable to Him, a barefaced lie is neither a sin nor an offence. Manifestly, there is structure to hypocrisy and deceit to the NIF's 'godly' commission.

NIF's Warped Vision of Sudan and Islam

Before assuming power, the NIF explained its 'vision' of Sudan in a party document entitled 'Sudan Charter: National Unity and Diversity' issued in January 1987. In that document, it justified the domination of the society by Muslims and Islam. Muslims, the Charter said, 'have a legitimate right, by virtue of their religious choice, demographic weight and as a matter of natural justice, to practice the values and rules of their faith to their full range in personal, familial, social and political affairs.' Accordingly, it saw the imposition of an Islamic way of government and life as its primary duty. Since Sudan is Islamic in terms of the statistical majority of its population, the charter affirmed that it was within the bounds of democracy that Islamic norms be the guiding principles of life in Sudan. For non-Muslims, the charter maintained that they had the right to practise their religions to the full, so long as they did so in their 'private, family or social set-ups'. The term 'social set-up' is misleading, for it neither includes political and economic institutions, nor laws governing relations among citizens which are obviously to be predicated on Islamic *shari'a*. Turabi's legal and constitutional template inevitably created two classes of citizens in the multireligious Sudan.

Turabi had no compunctions in describing this discriminatory system of governance as an 'original' model of democracy to be offered to the world.[34] As one Islamic scholar justifiably remarked, such a majoritarian model was indeed antithetical to democracy, because it condemned so-called minorities to a state of perpetual subservience to the 'majority'[35] It is doubtful, however, that Turabi, the Western-trained lawyer, really believed that a model of governance which condemned any group in society to second-class citizenship was anything close to democracy as the world knew it, or indeed to the democracy the Sudanese have practiced in the past and continued clamouring for. And because Turabi's model was entirely divorced from the Sudanese realities on the ground, the NIF ideologues came back full circle ten years later to admit the major flaw in their political thought. Speaking to a Cairo daily, a leading NIF ideologue, to his credit, said: 'We are in the stage of nation building and reconciliation. The solution for problems in a multi-ethnic and multicultural country is in recognizing the other and coexisting with him. John Garang, the Christian, is more important to us than any Islamic movement'[36]

In another document circulated in Khartoum in 1985 and entitled: 'The Southern Sudan Question: Review, Analysis and Proposals', the NIF computed South Sudan's population at a little over five million of whom '65 per cent are without religion'.[37] This statement patently reflects the NIF's benightedness on the issue of religion; African belief systems to which the 65 per cent adhere, are reduced by the NIF to non-religions. Religion, as commonly known, is the medium for man's communion with the sacred, spiritual or divine. Its most enduring contribution to civilization and mankind is reflected in commandments, injunctions and supreme precepts that edify justice, consecrate man's dignity, and exalt brotherly love and human charity. African belief systems are not shorn of those attributes. But, according to the NIF's relativist cultural scale, African cultures are synonymous with the *Jahiliyya*.[38] Evidently, people are prone to turn their backs on what does not fit in with their cultures without making the least effort to get the hang of what they reject. This warpped vision is not a monopoly of the Islamists, according to Evans-Pritchard: 'It is a remarkable fact that none of the anthropologists whose theories about primitive religions have been most influential, had ever been near primitive people … and relied on the stories of explorers, missionaries, administrators and traders.'[39] Fortunately, this condescending view of African belief systems in Sudan is not shared by all Sudanese Muslim scholars.[40]

Turabi, whether he believed it or not, initially considered his Islamist model as a working project. In an interview with an Iranian paper, he said: 'Sudan is an Islamic republic, for all effective purposes, regarding the implementation of injunctions in political, economic, social and cultural fields. At present Islam is ruling and Islamic values prevail in society'.[41] Equally, Turabi believed that his model of governance was ineradicable since it was 'more natural, authentic and deeply rooted than the process that produced Khomeini'.[42] To consider 'natural' a system of governance installed by force and sustained through violence is a tough logic to comprehend. Turabi, therefore, saw an international role for that rickety project, this time to 'fill up the vacuum created by the collapse of socialism and the bankruptcy of Western liberalism'. This vacuum, Turabi claimed, could only be filled by Islamic revivalism.[43] In another statement to an American journalist, he bumptiously took it upon himself to spearhead that revival: 'There is a vacuum now, that vacuum is being filled by an Islamist spirit. I just happened naturally to have been at the track where history is moving,' he said.[44] Whose and what history, one may ask? Turabi surely saw himself as a man of destiny entrusted with reviving Islam, but the Islam he sought to revive had nothing to do with the Islam the Sudan (his powerbase) knew. To the contrary, the Islam he yearned to reinvent, taken at face value, was an idealized and pristine Islam. The condolent would consequently say that Turabi was entrapped in his own ideological ravings; ideologues scarsely lived in the real world. As Havel avers, ideologies are 'a special way of relating to the world, they offer human beings the illusion of an identity, of dignity and of morality while making it easier for them to part with it'.[45]

It is perhaps because of this manner of defining ideology that Turabi always found it easy to talk in two tongues; one to Muslims in his own home ground, the other when he addressed a Western audience. To the latter, Turabi portrayed his brand of Islam in endearing philosophical terms, though every so often the truth came out chasing the lie. For example, he frequently described his model of democracy as unparalleled, but when asked once about multipartism he became bellicose and incoherent. Democracy, he said, 'does not require multiple parties, the right of any individual to stand for office or spend money campaigning for it, or the right to advocate a view that contradicts Qur'an'.[46] The reality is that Qur'an never defined a systems of governance, but only spelt out general guiding principles from which those who adhere to it drew inspiration.

The whole Islamic constitutional jurisprudence that had developed after the death of the Prophet (AD 632) was, in reality, the work of scholars who – with few exceptions – made concessions to political expediency. As An-N'aim avers, the contribution to constitutional law by those scholars is not divine law but a human understanding of divine law.[47] Undoubtedly, all standard treatises of *fiqh* dealt with 'governance as a divine instrument' and devoted space to its functions, how it was acquired and should be exercised and, in general, to the relationship between the ruler and the ruled.[48] However, those studies were every so often politically inspired and aimed at maintaining the cohesion of the Islamic state rather than delineating constitutional rights and duties or defining modalities for redress, checks and balances and sanctions against erring government agencies. Infrequently, the *fuqaha* deviated into theorizing on an Islamic model state and 'by theorizing exclusively on what *ought* to be the case, this group of *ule'ma* simply avoided the whole question of what happens when rulers fail to implement the ideal model'.[49] In fact, some of the most important treatises on constitutional law were mere apologia for authoritarianism.[50] In addition, despite its rich heritage in philosophy, *ilm al kalam* (scholastic theology), natural and abstract sciences and medicine, Islamic civilization was completely inattentive to political thought and science. Probably – with the exception of Farabi's work al *Madina al Fadhila* (Utopia)[51] – all major treatises on political philosophy were commentaries on Greek works.[52] Surely, if Turabi's archetype of Islamic governance was based on his restrictive interpretation of Islam's fundamental sources of legislation,[53] or on sources of dubious validity, then neither would Islam have a universal appeal, nor would many Muslims be comfortable with associating with it. As an accomplished lawyer and an unwavering believer in the excellence of his model for good governance as an alternative to contemporary models, Turabi obviously failed. A model that rolls back the margins of democracy as it is universally defined and as it has been practised in Sudan since independence would appeal to no one.

Turabi has often stated that he wanted to recreate in Sudan the Madina (city) of Prophet Mohammed.[54] His claims in this respect were sometimes hilarious. For instance, he told a Khartoum daily that 'we entered Khartoum the way prophet Mohamed entered Madina'.[55] The statement was as specious as it was disrespectful, for neither did Prophet Mohamed usurp power in the dusk (the way the NIF did on 30 June 1989), nor did he conquer his enemies through false pretences. Be that as it may, Turabi's model was premised on leaky assumptions; the Madina of the Prophet, in both spatial and annalistic terms, is an inappropriate model. First, the polity over which the prophet ruled was an extremely limited territory, and second, the span of time during which he 'reigned'[56] was also very limited (AD 622 to 661). The authority endowed upon him by divine will was unchallenged which by necessity made that model unique and inimitable. In this day and age the society of Madina (as it existed during the time of the Prophet) can neither be reinvented nor replicated in the Madina itself, let alone in a country besieged by a tumult of multiplicity: religious, cultural, ethnic, and political. Nor would that model fit in a world structured around national boundaries, governed by universal human rights covenants and, above all – as far as *realpolitik* is concerned – stablized (or destabilized) by balances of political, economic and military power. Besides, by reaching back to the society of Madina, Turabi was implicitly saying that political Islam since the days of the prophet was deteriorating and had nothing to offer.

The society of Madina undoubtedly exemplified tolerance within its historical context,[57] but it cannot be recreated to respond to man's political needs in today's world. Viewed through contemporary lenses, Madina was a male-dominated society which accommodated non-Muslims from *ahl al kitab* (people of the book, i.e. monotheist Christians and Jews who believed in Holy Scriptures) with limited social rights and no political rights whatsoever. Even those limited rights were only granted within the terms of an arrangement of *aman* (temporary sanctuary) in *Dar al Aman* (zone of peace) as opposed to *Dar al Harb* (zone of war). Obviously at the time, discrimination on the grounds of sex, race and religion was the general norm in all cultures and religions. Islam in this respect 'compared favourably' with those cultures and religions in its approach to those categories.[58] However, since the nineteenth century, Western concepts of civil and people's rights developed by leaps and bounds, while Islamic constitutional law in this field lagged behind 'the human and enlightened ideal its founders has envisaged'.[59] Without a thorough reformation of that law, on the basis of guiding principles of the Qur'an, Islam would not only lose its contemporaneousness, but also its relevance. For example, as An-N'aim opined, the formalistic application of the rules of the Madina to today's Sudan would presumably reduce Sudanese, whose traditional African beliefs would not qualify them as people of the Book by *shari'a* criteria, to the same status as those subjected to the charter of *dhimma* (mutual obligation). That charter affords protection to its subjects but denies them political rights.[60] Indeed, in launching *jihad* against the South, the name reserved by Turabi and the NIF for their 'enemies' (who were indigenous Sudanese citizens) was *al mushrikeen* (polytheists or idolaters). Within Turabi's own definition of war, this classification denied those citizens any political or civil rights, even as limited as those enjoyed by *ahl al kitab* under the terms of sanctuary.

To achieve his aim, however, Turabi embarked on a self-styled civilizational project. His objective was to remake Sudanese society and eventually take on the world. The building blocks for that edifice were reportedly drawn from *shari'a* (Islamic jurisprudence as it has been historically handed down by Islamic jurists). Turabi's dilemma, as well as that of other Islamic revivalists, was that they gave to *shari'a*, thus defined, a degree sanctity commensurate with that given to the main sources from which it was derived: the *Qur'an* and the *Suna*.[61] *Shari'a*, as religious edicts, applied to practical problems in day-to-day life, could not but be historically contextual and, in a sense, secular.[62] In his ecliptic way, Turabi surprisingly shared this view about the secularity of *shari'a*,[63] even though he maintained in 1968 during the deliberations on the Islamic Constitution in Parliament that secularism and *laicte* were alien to Islam.

The *shari'a* Turabi and other contemporary Islamists endeavour to apply to public policy is, to a large degree, derived from views inducted by the old *fuqaha* from the two original main sources of Islam: Qur'an and *Suna*, to respond to their contemporary realities. Without this process of inductive reasoning, Islamic normative rules would have been frozen in time. As time changed, new *fuqaha* like Turabi were expected to adumbrate new rules of general application based on the same main sources to meet evolving needs. By definition, the body of *shari'a* expounded, or inferred through *ijtihad,* by the old *fuqaha* to respond to problems in their time is today discrepant.

Nowhere is the discrepancy as glaring as it is in the area of universally upheld human rights. *Shari'a,* as applied and transmitted by the *fuqaha,* may have been adequate and progressive for their time, but not for addressing issues that emerged later: rules that impinge on universally upheld human rights such as women's and minorities rights or rights of association and conscience. This seeming riddle was brilliantly resolved by the Sudanese Muslim Scholar Mahmoud Mohammed Taha when he distinguished between the *Meccan Qur'an* (chapters and verses revealed in Mecca) which contained high moral precepts of equality, justice and dignity of man, and the *Madinan Qur'an* which dealt with practical situations within a specific historical conjuncture.[64] The elderly scholar was executed by Nimeiri at the behest, and to the utmost satisfaction, of the 'revivalist' Brothers.[65] Taha, nonetheless, was crucified alive and idealized dead.

Historical *shari'a* up till today maintains laws which, if applied formalistically, shall decidedly be repugnant to universally upheld human rights, e.g. amputations for theft in penal laws, restrictions on the rights of women in areas such as inheritance and the law of evidence, sanction of *jihad,* the toleration and regulation of slavery and denying non-Muslims the right to assume high officers in an Islamic state.[66] Turabi occasionally came out with very progressive views on various aspects of Islamic law, but also he often appeared to uphold some of the anachronisms inherent in *shari'a*.[67] Some of those anachronistic laws are positively enshrined in the Qur'an, but equally enshrined in the Qur'an are guiding principles that make it possible for Islam to be correspondent to ensuing human conditions. Agreeably, *shari'a's* historical formulations 'could not have provide ... institutional arrangements for the full range of civil rights in the modern sense of the world.'[68] Nevertheless, conformist adherence to those historical formulations would ineluctably abnegate the sempiternity of Islam. It is thus the height of fraudulence for Islamists to claim that original and historical *shari'a* had produced concepts on human rights akin to those articulated by western secular constitutions. Such contention reflects either 'distortion of facts relating to Islamic constitutional history or to that of Western constitutional thought'.[69]

Truly, were Sudan's Islamic 'revivalists' to say, like orthodox Islamists, that *shari'a* as they understood it, was Allah's immutable word and, therefore, had to be literally applied, things would have been much easier. Enlightened Islamists who also believe in the inherent dynamism of Islam and its capacity to chime in with man's evolving needs may have dismissed that rigidity as a reflection of intellectual inadequacy. However, Sudan's professed 'revivalists' were not only impervious to their intellectual insufficiency, they also remained unswerving in their belief that historical *shari'a* was a co-equal to universally acknowledged norms for good governance as well as to contemporary covenants on the rights of man. Good governance today is firmly predicated on recognition of popular will, rule of law, independence of the judiciary, peaceful transfer of power, accountability of the ruler to the ruled and respect for human rights as they are universally defined. There is nothing of the sort in historical Islamic constitutional thought or practice. The *shura* (consultation), which modern Islamists take for granted as synchronous with democracy, was limited to male Muslim elites. Women were never consulted (and less so non-Muslims) on who should rule them. Human rights were not universal. And there was no system for peaceful transfer of power. That was probably why, of the four caliphs who succeeded the Prophet, three were assassinated for political reasons. Indeed, the third Caliph, Uthman Ibn Àfan, told his challengers among the *Sahaba* (companions of the Prophet): 'How can I divest myself of a garb bestowed on me by Allah?' Uthman was referring to his right to continue ruling till he died. Effectively, after the battle of Safin between 'Ali and Muawiya in which, according to the historian Ibn Kathir, seventy thousand died, the Islamic caliphate was turned by the latter into a Byzantian state which was only Islamic in name. A cursory look at the 1998 constitution promulgated by the NIF regime and deemed to be accordant with *shari'a* reveals a similar perfidy. That constitution includes provisions relating to immunity of legislators, the right of citizens to content the president before constitutional courts, independence of judges, secular qualification of voters, etc. Nothing of the sort existed in *shari'a*, nor in the historical practices of governance in Islam.

As for human rights principles as they are now universally recognized, those too had no place in traditional *shari'a*. Today, there is no Muslim country, including Sudan,[70] that does not acknowledge those principles or generally accredit them as legally binding norms.[71] The universality of those principles and norms is implicit in the adhesion by those Muslim countries to the conventions in which they are enshrined. An-N'aim aptly traced the recognition by all nations of the world of those rights to the universal principle of reciprocity, also known as the Golden Rule. This rule, according to the scholar, indicates that since every person should treat others as s/he would like to be treated by them, s/he should concede to them the same civil rights s/he claims for herself or himself'.[72] In effect, the universality of those rights is such, that they can neither be territorialized, nor anchored on any specific religion, as some western Christians scholars may wish to think.[73] Western scholars, and not without reason, invariably trace back the origin of contemporary human rights laws – at the conceptual level – to the intellectual revolution in Europe from Locke to Rousseau, who postulated that those rights were basic and belonged to the *individual.* They are neither bestowed upon, nor conceded to, him.[74] Nevertheless, claims that the human rights principles solely had their origin in European philosophy are untenable. First, such claims are substantially inattentive to major trends in European thought that had never conceded the universalistic nature of those rights. For example, the treatment of non-Europeans by some European thinkers of the post-enligntment era as barbarians who were disentitled from enjoying such rights absolutely contradict those claims. That view was shared by European thinkers across the ideological spectrum, from John Stewart Mill to Friedrich Engels.[75] Second, Eurocentric scholars who sought to trace the intellectual origins of human rights entirely to the European elightment were, to say the least, completely oblivious to the contribution to the concept of the rights of man by other civilizations and religions including Judaism, Christianity and Islam. Neither Jesus of Nazareth nor Moses was a European, and both preached principles and ordained commandments that aimed at edifying the dignity of man. In Islam, however, nowhere is the sanctification of the right of man more encapsulated than in the Qur'anic verse: ' He who slays a soul not to retaliate for a soul slain, nor for corruption done in the land, shall be as if he had slain mankind altogether' (5:32).

Nevertheless, so long as Islamists equate it with *shari'a*, Islam shall be wanting in responding to the yearnings of modern man to liberty and human dignity. To be aligned with modern human rights concepts, Islam needs an inner renewal so as to 'harmonize, on a new basis, modern knowledge and experience with the principles of the faith'.[76] Contemporary human rights principles do not in any way contradict the normative values of Islam or, for that matter, of any other religion that bolsters the dignity of man. Jews and Christians were, to a great extent, inspired in their approach to human rights by the high moral values of Judeo-Christianism, though they never steeped themselves in interpretations of the holy books by the old fathers of the church. Islam, as a Sudanese Muslim scholar maintained, shall only be a liberating force and moderating influence it ceased to be interpreted 'in the light of static and deterministic views'.[77] This liberal and non-revisionist interpretation would lead to an 'overlapping consensus' between contemporary legally binding norms and related religious canons'.[78]

Turabi, at the intellectual level, came out with some progressive Islamic-based writings on issues relating to the renovation of faith, religion and arts and generally on Islamic revival. But as a practitioner he kept meandering between rigid and static views (whenever it suited him) and very liberal views when he thought that would please his audience. Some of Turabi's views on women, expressed in Western fora, were denounced by orthodox Muslims as heretical.[79] But sometimes he came out with very regressive views on women based on a literal interpretation of the holy book.[80] Clearly, there is no irreducible core to Turabi's Islamist thinking. The rigid approach gained full play during his term in office as exhibited in his views on war and peace, civil rights of non-Muslims, democracy and universally upheld human rights principles. On all those issues one discerns an element of expediency in Turabi's contradictory stances. Not infrequently, the NIF perversely exploited the 'harshness' of Islamic punishments, e.g. flogging and amputations, not so much in compliance with Allah's laws, but above all to overawe or humiliate opponents.[81] This was done irrespective of the psychic disorders those punishments inflicted on their subjects.[82] They are also applied at the cost of undermining the humane image of Islam which the Islamists often portray in their enunciations, especially in external fora. Such cynicism not only betrays disrespect for people's minds, but it also corrodes the humanistic nature of Islam.

In general, the NIF government brooked no criticism of the so-called 'God's Laws' *(Shar'a Allah)*, and when criticised, they invoked threats of blasphemy and warned that attempts to fight 'God's Laws' were reason enough for declaring *jihad* against the abjurers. Not even a national consensus, Turabi argued, could remove the laws of 'God'. Turabi was no longer resorting to his calculated wordplay of the 1960s, his rhetoric becoming incendiary and uncompromising. His words were more and more equated with the covenants of Islam. That left little margin for debate. Even democracy, under whose protection the Muslim Brothers thrived and expanded in the past, had to be reconstructed according to 'God's Laws' as interpreted by Turabi. So, by making himself the prime expositor of the words of God, Turabi introduced into *Suni* Islam, a concept alien to it, that of *Marja'a taqlid* (source of emulation) among the *Shi'a*. Quixotic aspirations apart, by contriving a conflict between Islam on the one side and democracy and universal human rights on the other, Turabi had virtually ruled that Muslims have an absolute imperative to live outside universally recognized norms of good governance.

Despite this flagrant intellectual inadequacy in relating Islam to the needs of contemporary society, Turabi continued to fantasize about his civilizational project both as an instrument for national regeneration and as a model to be emulated by the world. In an interview with an Arab London weekly, he stated that Europe and America were morally sick and spiritually penurious; their salvation lay only in Islam[83] (obviously, his own version). That was indeed Turabi's end of history; he wanted to be a *non pareil* innovator in this field. Excluding this effrontery, and Turabi's civilizational project was incoherent, jumbled and irrelevant, its ideological prototype utterly inconsequential to the ground needs of Sudanese society. What Sudan needed was peace, national unity, uplifting the economy, ensuring good neighbourly relations and enabling the country and its people occupy the place they deserve in the civilized community of nations. On all those issues, there was no original body of Islamic-inspired *ijtihad* by Turabi. Accordingly, the NIF faltered in every step on their way to the 'Madina'. The civilizational project boiled down to a self-serving concoction of moral exhortations and wishful thinking. This insufficiency in addressing real problems in the real world curtailed the NIF's ability to capture the imagination of Sudan's Muslims, and alienated further non-Muslims.

By the end of ten years in power, instead of remaking the Sudan in its own image, the NIF only recycled nostalgia in an attempt to retrieve a chimerical past. All the same, it persisted in considering its ideological mumbo-jumbo basic to the identity of the Sudanese nation. In their lingo, the Islamists called their ideological catchphrases *al thwabit*, i.e. fundamental principles to which every other thing was secondary. But the 'every other thing' was the stuff the nation was made of. The NIF utterly failed to comprehend a basic truth, that in a multicultural society, whatever your ascribed cultural heritage was, it would have to be indigenized if it was to be embraced by other citizens who do not share that culture. Inevitably, the endgame of the NIF politics of nostalgia was to turn Sudan into a cultural Jurassic Park.

Theocracy and the Mafia Syndicate

Although the NIF leaders persisted in claiming the pursuit of a lenient Islamic law that embraced principles of respect of human rights and religious tolerance, the reality of the regime proved to be very different. Their constitutional template neither allowed for the accommodation of 'non-believers' as defined by the NIF, nor for that matter, for any civil pluralism. Party activities, Turabi told an American interviewer, were 'divisive, sectarian and tribal',[84] a conclusion with which few would disagree. However, he continued to say that elections in Europe distorted the will of the people because they were completely influenced by financial powers. Turabi's view was not different from that purveyed by communists in the past against 'bourgeois' democarcy in order to justify their totalitarian model of governance. In the same interview, Turabi added that he would like 'to teach Europe a lesson on democracy,' and to that end 'he wouldn't care for the world'. 'For me this is an act of religion,' he said.[85] In place of what he considered to be a 'frayed' Western model of democracy, Turabi advocated an exclusionary system: 'I am a unitarian calling for unity of the Sudanese people ... our faith tells us that God is one, our party is one and our path to God is one.' Two absurdities are notable in this proposition: first, it is beyond comprehension that the standard-bearear of Islamic rejuvenation elects to advocate as a model for governance a monolithic system at a time when all totalitarianisms are collapsing, and second, it is also beyond belief that a man who has benefited from tolerance in the multi-party era, appears now be incapable of tolerating tolerance. Turabi's argument in favour of his monocratic system confused the sacred with the temporal, the religious with the political, and in one sweep divided the nation between *Hizbo-allah* (the party of God) and *Hizbo-al Shaytan* (the party of Satan).

In line with that thinking, those who challenged the NIF regime were summarily executed, ending six feet under the ground so that they were not heard of anymore. For example, in one of his revengeful spirals of violence, 28 army officers were executed by Bashir in April 1990 after a failed *counter-coup*. Their trial took less than two hours, two minutes were allowed for each accused. If that was Islamic justice, then the NIF had little to exult in. Others were tortured or held incommunicado in 'ghost houses'.[86] Those houses were normally guarded by hooded retainers so as to conceal their identity. This manner of bruising thuggery is unknown to law-abiding 'heathen' countries; the role of prison guards in those countries which Turabi wants to save from moral penury, is to detain, not to intimidate, to keep an eye an, not to torture. By no means does this dastardly *modus operendi* and perverse fascination with torture befit any self-respecting government, let alone one that is marketed by its proponents as Allah's heaven on Earth. Consequently, the regime's human rights abuses were criticized and amply catalogued by the international community over the years. Many Sudanese Muslims were increasingly critical of those practices which, in their view, did little honour to Islam. The regime was also consistently condemned by the United Nations Commission on Human Rights for gross abuses of human rights, including ethnic cleansing verging on genocide,[87] especially among the people of the Nuba Mountains.

Concerned with the Sudan government's shocking violations of human rights, the UN Commission appointed Gaspar Biro on 30 March 1993 as a Special Rapporteur to monitor the human rights situation in the country.[88] The rapporteur was also to investigate human rights abuses by other parties to Sudan conflict. In his 1997 report, Biro gave a grim picture of the human rights situation in the country.[89] His investigations grasped the essence of the regime's brutality and narrated cases of extrajudicial killings, summary executions, involuntary disappearances, torture and other cruel, inhuman, or degrading treatment, arbitrary arrests and reprisals. Among the reprisals, Biro reported the harsh treatment inflicted by the government security forces on Eliaba James Surur, a respected elderly Southern politician and leader of the Southern umbrella party organization, Union of Sudanese African Parties (USAP). Surur's crime was his refusal to be co-opted by the government.[90] In another incident, respectable Sudanese ladies were arrested in front of the UN offices and flogged, their offence being petitioning the UN on crimes committed by the government against women. Women may not have been treated as equals in the past and were certainly victims of inbred discrimination by former regimes in the social, political and economic spheres, but at no point of time were they publicly humiliated. Under the NIF, women were arrested, incarcerated and publicly lashed for conduct 'contrary to public morals'. Section 152 of the Sudan Penal Code (1991) prohibited wearing 'improper' clothes (which included jeans), or leaving the hair uncovered. Women were also forbidden to travel alone irrespective of their age, marital status or profession; they had always to be accompanied by a '*Muhrim*' (chaperon). Asked about those regressive laws, Turabi denied their existence. 'Dress,' he said, 'is a private matter.'[91] His questioner disagreeably reported that he talked to a Sudanese medical doctor who was treating three girls traumatized by being lashed publicly, forty lashes each. Their crime was being seen in public with their heads uncovered.[92] Despite Turabi's denials, the Governor of Khartoum prohibited, in January 1999, women from working in businesses that serve the public, e.g. coffee shops, petrol stations etc. Howbeit, some of those measures were not even applied by official security agents, but by NIF young molesters detailed to insure *al amr bil m'arouf wa al nahi 'an al munkar* (enjoining goodness or equity and inhibiting evil).[93] Those *enfants terribles* became a law unto themselves and the terror of neighbourhoods: eavesdropping on the localities, molesting young women, harassing men and disturbing the peace of couples in public as well as private places. Turabi justified the latter action by claiming that Islam prohibited contiguity between a man and a woman other than his wife, away from the public eyes.[94] In keeping with his regressive approach to women, it came as a surprise to nobody when Bashir refused to ratify the UN Convention on the Eradication of all Forms of Discrimination against women (CEDAW), despite UN urgings.[95]

From the start, Biro was subjected to a severe campaign of denigration, Sudan's Attorney General wrote to the Commission in February 1994 taking exception to the critique of the Special Rapporteur against Sudan's penal laws.[96] The rapporteur singled out sections of the penal law that were opposed to Human Rights Covenenats, particularly those relating to amputations, cross-amputations and *qasas* (retribution). The Attorney General, in a statement to press,[97] described this critique as a 'flagrant blasphemy and deliberate insult to Islam equal to Salman Rushdi's *Satanic Verses*'. By evoking Rushdi's name, the custodian of law in Sudan evidently wanted to whip Islamic sentiments against the UN official. Explaining his position on this issue to the *Washington Post*, Biro said that since Sudan had ratified the International Covenant on Civil and Political Rights, the Universal Declaration on Human Rights and the Convention on the Rights of Children, the 'cultural argument' that these laws (*shari'a*) were deeply rooted in the traditions of the country was irrelevant. Biro, who lived under a totalitarian communist regime in his country, added: 'I know how totalitarian governments operate.'[98] Earlier, Dr Ahmed al Mufti of Sudan's Ministry of Justice wrote to the UN categorically rejecting Biro's suggestion to the UN to complement his work with the presence of Human Rights observers inside Sudan. Such action, Mufti maintained, 'would constitute an unjustified escalation in total disregard of Sudan's cooperation with the special rapporteur'.[99] Khartoum, ostensibly, could live with the intermittent visits of the rapporteur, but not with the permanent presence of observers inside Sudan who might end up exposing skeletons in the government's cupboards.

The regime had every reason to be nervous about the presence of observers, as the pattern of the torture it had been practising was racking. Human Rights Watch (Africa) recounted in its 1994 report practices such as immersion of the head in cold water, hanging from the hands on cell bars, burning with cigarette ends, electric shocks, mock executions, rape and the pulling off of finger nails. Examples of cruel or degrading treatment comprised insults, beatings or requiring a person to imitate animal sounds. The regime also confiscated the property of opposition leaders, arrested leaders of labour unions and made pawns of the professional societies, including the Sudan Human Rights Organisation. Besides, it put down protests at Khartoum University with armed riot police who shot and killed students, and fired dozens of professors and instituted periodic police sweeps to arrest campus 'troublemakers'. The students were clearly turning against the regime because of its harsh policies and despite the indefatigable efforts of the NIF, during the Nimeiri regime and that of the parties, to woo them to its side. University students in Sudan are a barometer of Sudanese politics.[100]

Markedly, the aim of the regime's repressive policy was not revenge; it was above all, to destroy the citizens' self-respect through demoralization, intimidation and dehumanization. As if drawing a leaf from Machiavelli's *The Prince*,[101] the regime did not seek from people loyalty but obedience; not allegiance but subservience. With the technical help of Iran, the regime perfected suppression to an art form. In mid-December 1991 the *New York Times* reported that Iran had sent 2,000 revolutionary guards. Two weeks later the *Washington Post* reported that Sudan, with the help of Iranian money and expertise, had emerged as a new base of terrorism.[102] It was common knowledge in Khartoum that the NIF chief of security, Nafie Ali Nafie (previously a lecturer in the Khartoum University Faculty of Agriculture), received an intensive training in Teheran on the crafts of intelligence a *l'iranienne*; his butchery mission was undertaken before the NIF's assumption of power under the benign remissness of the government of the day and of the University administration.[103]

Nevertheless, in an intellectual debate at the University of Florida (1993), Turabi declared that 'Iran has nothing to teach the Sudan, since the Sudanese Islamic movement is older than that of Khomeini.'[104] That was an economy of truth, as Iran obviously had something to teach the NIF. Asked at the same debate about the relationship between the NIF and Iran, Turabi tried to give an ideological veneer to that relationship. His mission, he said, was to end the senseless 14 centuries cleavage between the *Suna* and the *Shi'a*. Till today, in neither his extensive writings nor dialogues, did Turabi venture to reconcile the differences that had torn the two schools apart. Not even the efforts of President Khatemi to give a human face to Islam were matters of political or intellectual concern to him. The NIF's real concern was seemingly elsewhere, using the prowess of the Pasadran in suppressing his opponents. To its credit, Iran has produced, from the bosom of its Islamic movement, leaders and scholars who denounced the excesses of the regime, such as Ayatollah Muntaziri and professor Hashim Aghagiri who declared that a government that suppressed people in the name of religion had nothing to do with religion.[105]

In light of all those heinous practices, the description of the regime by an American journalist who visited Khartoum and met with Turabi, was both opportune and well directed; the NIF regime, he said, 'is an ingenuous hybrid between a theocracy and a Mafia Syndicate'.[106] No question, the term theocracy may not be a fitting description for the NIF elite who were trained in the West, walk and talk like westerners and immensely enjoy (together with their families) Western goodies. The term mafia may also not be the most suited appellation to Sudan's tyrannicides with a cause, '*Cosa nostra*' (our thing or cause) would be more germane. However, the 'mafiosi' inclination, more than anything else, explains the NIF's deviation from the historical Islam to which they are allegedly committed. For nowhere in *shari'a* – despite all its deficiencies – do we find a justification for the bloodlust and acts of inhumanity in which the NIF hatchet men have become engrossed with arrogant impunity. In historical Islam, the presumption of innocence is the golden thread that runs through the whole criminal justice system. But for all to see, the *mafiosi* part got the better of the religious and reduced the regime into an abstraction of evil. The NIF may have thought that it had created virtuous *Leviathan*, but seemingly the building blocks for that edifice were borrowed from Thomas Hobbs, not Islam. Only Hobbs posited that force and fraud are the only two cardinal virtues.

Not only were the NIF practices in governance repugnant to the teachings of Islam, but also their puritanical approach to so-called social ills like drinking, promiscuity, women's 'immodest' dress, were both hypocritical and on the wrong side of the realities of Sudanese Muslims society. For one, in a regime that crawled with liars, exterminators and purloiners of public funds, the NIF's pietism was stupyfingly grotesque. On the other hand, Sudanese Muslims for decades had taken for granted many practices that would appall orthodox Muslims, e.g. drinking of alcoholic beverages in nearly all parts of Northern Sudan is as pervasive in normal daily living as during social events.[107] Northern Muslims who savour those drinks (prohibited by Islam) hardly consider their indulgence incompatibe with their religious belief. More interesting is the condonation of promiscuity by some Muslim tribes in Western Sudan, reflected in the institution of *hiddana* (amatorial embrace).[108] To orthodox Islam this practice is tantamount to sexual delinquency, but to the tribe that engages in it, it is more or less a prelude to tying the knot. This social relaxation of religions strictures was not unknown to a string of *fuqaha* and religious leaders to whom those tribes owed absolute obedience; but in their ripe wisdom, the religious leaders knew that social habits could never be changed by fiat; Jesus, after all, did not regenerate Mary Magdalene by sending her away with a flea in the ear. So, irrespective of their feigned desire to cleanse society from vices, their claim that their legitimacy is derived from their representativity of the conscience of Sudanese Muslims is less than honest. The Islam they claim to represent is not the Islam Sudanese know and practise, but a fraudulently varnished version of it. That is why Sudanese Muslims do not see in the NIF's project anything less than an attempt to reislamicize Islam.

As a result of the pervading culture of violence initiated by the NIF, phenomena unknown to Sudan's popular Islam broke out. For example, in December 2000 a gruesome attack was launched by an Islamist lunatic on a peacefully praying crowd of *Ansar al Suna al Muhammadiya* (adherents of Mohamed's path) at the Garaffa mosque outside Khartoum. Twenty-three persons were killed and a number seriously injured. The killer belonged to a fringe extremist group calling itself *al takfir wal hijra* (denouncing infidelity and retreating from society). That group is guided by an antisocial philosophy which calls for punishing those who deviate from the path of Islam and preaches retreat from the 'infidel' community. The incident of December was not the first; *Ansar al Suna* were subjected to the same treatment in 1994 when the leader of that group, Mohamed al Halifi who held dual Libyan-Tunisian nationality, attacked a mosque in Omdurman and killed 20 worshipers. Surprisingly, the killer of Garaffa, Abbas al Baqir, was among the accused in the first murderous ouslaught; he was arrested and then released. More important was the fact that he got his slaughterous training within the ranks of the NIF militias, including a tour of duty in the South. In place of addressing the underlying causes of this pervasive culture of violence unknown to Muslims in Sudan, the government chose to tinker with the security aspect of the problem; it amended the National Security Act (Section 21) to empower Security Agencies (the very agencies that instituted that culture in the first place) to deal with *al Zwahir al Shaza* (anomalous phenomena). To that end, the agencies were empowered to hold in custody for six months without trial, any person accused of those 'anomalies', whatever the term meant. The NIF regime failed to realize that the real anomaly was the policies it had instituted. Effectively, the line between *jihad* and ritual killing became very thin when the NIF opened the country's gates to scatterbrained anarchists from all over the world, called for *jihad* against every opponent they assumed to be an infidel and invited all and sundry to engage into it.

Bestiality, however, has its own dynamics; it invariably consumes its perpetrators. This reality dawned at long last on Turabi when the illusion of his regime's invincibility was punctured by the chain of defeats it had suffered at the battlefront, as well as in the face of sustained internal uprisings. When his wings were further clipped by Bashir, Turabi reinvented himself as the doughtiest champion of democracy and principal opponent to abuses against democracy and human rights by the very regime he had built. But before snapping up the mantle of democracy to himself after his break-up with Bashir, Turabi began a calculated retreat from his absolutist position. In a specious cosmetic operation, he drafted a new constitution in 1998 to cater for Sudan's multiple pluralisms. The draft omitted any reference to a state religion, a matter for which Turabi had fought tooth and nail during the debate for the adoption of the 1968 constitution. Those who opposed the proposition then were condemned as 'secularists' and atheists. It also posited rights of citizens on *muwatana* (citizenship), the presumption being that religion was no longer the determining factor of constitutional rights and duties. Coming from the same *faqih* who told Ghabboush in 1968 that non-Muslims could never aspire to be head of state in Sudan's Islamic Republic, that was indeed an impressive retreat.

The constitution promulgated by Turabi, however, came after his rejection of another draft constitution that addressed the main issues more forthrightly. That draft was drawn by a constitutional committee that brought together a number of independent lawyers and professionals. The chairman of that committee, former Chief Justice, Khalaf Allah al Rasheed, told a Cairo daily that he was surprised to observe that out of the 206 articles proposed in his committee's draft, only 144 were adopted. The changes, he said, related to parts of the constitution that upheld the rule of law and civil rights.[109] Turabi, who was apparently aggravated by the high-handedness of his colleagues in government, was addressing two constituencies: the opposition and the NIF rank and file. His double-tongued document was, therefore, meant to water down the committee's draft while giving it an Islamic veneer. For instance, Turabi's constitution stipulated in Article 4 that *hakimiyya* (supremacy) in the state was for God, the creator of man, and that sovereignty shall be bestowed on his vice-regents, the people of Sudan who 'practise it as worship of God, bearing the trust, building up the country and spreading justice, freedom and public consultation'. This was meant to convey, in a convoluted way, the concept of people's supremacy. In the meantime, Article 65 ruled that *shari'a* and *ijma'a al umma* (consensus of the nation) were the sources of legislation. Regardless, the term *ijma'a* is meaningless since the word of God cannot be contradicted by the will of man even when the whole Nation of Islam was at one on an issue that was unconformable to Allah's word. This, we recall, was Turabi's argument against the deprecators of his so-called Islamic project. Albeit in both cases, *shari'a* and God's words were to be explicated by men: the *fuqaha*; with Turabi as the chief of the pack. Furthermore, the concept of 'consensus' has no place in multi-party democracy; multipartism is posited on the respect of the will of the majority, which normally prevails within a constitutionally defined time frame.

Turabi removed from the draft prepared by the committee all stipulations that enshrined precepts of democracy as they were universally acknowledged and commonly applied in Sudan. For example, Article 41 of the committee's draft relating to freedom of association was replaced by Article 26 in his document on the so-called al *tawali* (solidarity); the term has no meaning in constitutional literature or Islamic jurisprudence.[110] The most shocking malapropism in that article was its stipulation that political organization under *tawali* would only be authorized subject to commitment to peaceful advocacy and the shunning of physical force. Coming from the political party that had made physical violence an instrument of policy, the stipulation was indeed nettling. Further, Article 25 of the committee's draft, which prohibited the deprivation of citizens of constitutional rights save through due process of the law, was replaced by another stipulation (Article 23) that curtailed legal protection for those subjected to extra-legal detention, thus denying this group constitutionally guaranteed protection.

On the other hand, Turabi was reported to have been unhappy with the predominance of the military wing within the NIF. That was why he urged the NSRCC to dissolve itself and called for the replacement of the NIF by a broadly based National Congress (NC). The prefix 'Islamic' disappeared from the name of the new party, but not the Islamist slogans and battlecries. The NC, in effect, is no more than a façade for the monopolization of power by a hegemonistic minority party. Thus, the NIF slogans remained very much alive in the NC's meetings, even though the NC comprised within its top hierarchy non-Muslims. Turabi's future moves towards Bashir were all motivated by political expediency, particularly when the General grew too big for his shoes. Thus, by removing any reference to a state religion and the predication of constitutional rights on 'citizenship', Turabi addressed, and sought to appease, non-Muslims as well as to hoodwink the Western world. While the term *tawali* was disingenuously cooked up to persuade NIF followers that he was not abandoning his civilizational project, but only authenticating the Western concept of democracy and implanting it in the soil of Islam. In reality, that sham multipartism was, by its nature, the antithesis of multi-party democracy which guaranteed an all-inclusive and open-ended right for political organization, save for regulatory limitations on which all parties agreed. *Al tawali,* by the remotest definition of pluralistic democracy, did not qualify as a viable alternative to multipartism.

Turabi's constitution was also bespangled with references to *shari'a* and *usul al ahkam* (fundamental principles of Islamic jurisprudence) as the definitive source of legislation. That made a mockery of the idea of the nation's sovereignty as understood in contemporary constitutional law. Sovereignty, according to Turabi's schema, was subject to God's dominion, obviously as interpreted by his vicars on earth. Consequently, Turabi's *tawali* did not delude more than a few artificial parties created by the regime and a ragtag assortment of traditional party dissidents, whose combined force did not add up to more than the square root of zero. The NDA, including Sudan's major political parties and Southern political organizations rejected that counterfeit 'democratic' constitution. The NIF's political test tube parties were no different than the five political parties created by Sani Abacha in his later years which invited Bola Ige's (presently Nigeria's Attorney General) sardonic description: 'the five fingers of a leprous hand'.

External Exploits of Khartoum's Al Capone

The NIF's mafiocracy did not stop at Sudan; outside Sudan, the NIF's central policy was destabilization. The NIF was clearly in no doubt that once it had established its doctrinal precedence, uprooted traditional Islam in Sudan and reshaped the devotional culture of Sudanese Muslims, it could comfortably take on the world. Having seduced the whole country, excepting a few unbelieving recusants (or so it thought), the regime proceeded to challenge the world. As we have seen earlier, Turabi neither had any doubt about his messianic world role, nor did he have any compunctions about declaring his intent to transform the world to his image. In the summer of 1991 he initiated the Popular Arab Islamic Congress (PAIC)[111] with himself as Secretary General. The Congress brought together a consortium of extremists, each with his own revolutionist agenda. According to a Congressional report the exact character of, and mandate for, the PAIC were decided in a meeting at Turabi's house in *al Manshiyya*, a suburb of Khartoum.[112] Out of that meeting a decision emerged to make available 12 million US dollars to the Islamic Salvation Front (FIS) in Algeria. The funds were channelled through the Faisal Islamic Bank in Khartoum. The report also enumerated a number of camps for terrorist training in Sudan based at Kadaro, Jabal Awliya and Kamleen as well as the formation of a task force as a nucleus for 'Islamic' political action in Europe.[113] Sudan was thus turned by the NIF into a hotbed for international terrorism, a centre for terrorist training and a conduit for smuggling arms and channelling funds through its banking system to sympathetic political groups across the world.

Egypt and Libya were among the first Arab countries to be targeted by the regime. Surprisingly, both countries were supportive of the regime at its inception; Libya gave the NIF regime material support including badly needed fuel supplies, and Egypt virtually marketed Bashir to the Arab world and Europe as a well-meaning nationalist reformer. Turabi, nonetheless, believed that Libya was the weakest link in the chain and that conquering it via Libyan Islamists would avail to him the resources he needed to control North Africa and make inroads towards Europe. Turabi's quixotic aspirations must have by now reached a megalomaniac dimension. According to the Congressional report, Turabi met with Libyan dissidents to plan the takeover of the *Jamahiriyya*.[114] He was apparently convinced that the march to Tripoli would be easy; in an interview with an American journalist he said, 'Qaddafi has of late pointedly and publicly lectured the Sudanese government of the inadvisability of mixing politics with religion ... Qaddafi is so worried. The Islamic phenomenon is all around him.'[115] However, what Turabi thought to be light work became an arduous job. His adventure was short-lived, as Ghaddafi rounded up all Muslim Brothers in Libya and had them executed after the failure of their bid to overthrow his regime. He also stopped providing the NIF regime with oil supplies. To the far west, the NIF extended its tentacles to peaceful Mauritania. On 3 October 1994, *Mauritanie Nouvelle* reported the arrest of five persons belonging to Islamic Jihad while organizing a campaign of terror in the country with a view to destabilizing the regime. The group, according to the report, was traced to Sudan.

The NIF gravest external adventure, though, was their support to the Iraqi invasion of Kuwait despite Turabi's professed disdain for Saddam. In the University of Florida seminar, Turabi described Saddam as the enemy of the Islamists who would never be hoodwinked by his calls for *jihad'*.[116] In effect, while Turabi was denouncing Saddam at Tampa, Florida, his government back home was using Sudan as an 'offshore piece of real estate' to keep Iraq's weapons of mass destruction away from the onslaught of the Allied Forces on Iraq.[117] In his wishful way of thinking, Turabi may have thought that Saddam would march up to Saudi Arabia. The shouts on the streets of Khartoum orchestrated by the NIF at that time supported this conclusion.[118] Turabi's contemptuous remarks about Saddam in that seminar were only paired off with the disparaging remarks about Saudi Arabia and its ruling family, which he intimated to an American pen-woman. Turabi told Judith Miller that 'the Saudi rulers are neither Muslim fundamentalists, nor Muslims... their monarchy and secular laws and elites have propagated a very conservative Islam through the Middle East for years'.[119] In effect, without backward glance, Turabi told the Tampa audience that he was in contact with young elements in Saudi Arabia who wanted to see the Saudi monarchy removed.[120] Turabi may have conjured up the vision that Saddam and his secular *Baath* party would under no circumstances be able to hold on to the land of the holy shrines, and that the Saudi fundamentalists would be the potential heirs and, he (Turabi), their ideological guide and philosopher. This was the same reasoning that led him to support the atrocious Algerian Islamic groups of whose final victory he was sure. Convinced of his ability to realize those giant aspirations, Turabi believed that sticking out for Ethiopia and Eritrea would only be an outdoor meal. The regime learned otherwise after badly bloodying its nose. Regardless, it was mind-boggling to see such an uncivilized behavior that went in every way against the principles of comity of nations emanating from a man steeped in the law of nations.

The attempted assassination of President Mubarak was an action of which future evidence may absolve Bashir and Turabi, but accusatory fingers were pointed at elements that were then closer to Turabi's inner circles and now equally close to Bashir himself after he parted ways with

Turabi. The evidence accumulated by Ethiopian investigators proved beyond reasonable doubt the involvement of the NIF regime in the attempt on Mubarak's life, particularly through the facilities it had provided for the Egyptian assassins. The subsequent harbouring in Sudan of the accused persons after their failed attempt, and the help that was given to them by the extensive network of NIF-sponsored Islamic charity organizations in Ethiopia, was further proof of the regime's complicity. Thirteen of those organizations were closed down by the Ethiopian authorities. On the strength of that evidence, the UN Security Council adopted Resolution 1054 (1996) in which the Sudan government was condemned and ordered to take immediate measures to extradite to Ethiopia three suspects who took refuge in Sudan. The Council also imposed sanctions on Sudan under Chapter VII of the UN Charter. Sudan thus stood condemned by the UN, not only for its human rights violations, also for disturbing international peace.

Though Turabi had no hand in the attempt on Mubarak's life, he was nonetheless overjoyed by the attempt. To the US ambassador in Khartoum he had this to say: 'When Mubarak dared to go to Addis Ababa to attend the OAU Summit, the sons of prophet Moses, the Muslims, rose up against him, confounded his plans and sent him back to his country'.[121] Evidently, the name of Moses evokes that of Pharaoh. Berating Mubarak in a manner vexing in its impertinence and presumptuousness, Turabi added: 'I found the man to be very far below my level of thinking and views and too stupid to understand my pronouncement.'[122] Turabi, following his conflict with Bashir, completely disowned responsibility for the heinous crime against Mubarak. Responding to a question by a Cairo weekly on his role in the attempted assassination, he said; 'This question should be addressed to the government, I am only a thinker and preacher.'[123] Turabi had reason not to take the flack for that crime, but his enunciations after the fact made of him a willing accomplice. One reason for hailing a heinous act he did not commit might have been his ill feeling towards Egypt which hid neither its detestation of Mubarak nor its desire to see Bashir getting rid of him.

The attempt on the life of Mubarak crowned numerous distabilizing acts by the NIF against Egypt, including smuggling of arms to Islamist groups, giving succour to fugitives from justice, providing them with travel documents etc. Yet the assassination attempt brought the whole house of cards crumbling; Ethiopia, injured by the incident, would not relent. Egypt, on its part, went along with pressures to take up the matter to the Security Council, a matter that put the regime in a total fix. If there was one moment at all in the history of the NIF regime that made it rethink its adventurous policy, that was the one. Bashir undertook a limited clean-up exercise in the security apparatus, but his actions were inadequate and the clean-up was not sufficiently sweeping. Turabi, on his part, continued to hail the attempt and vowed to continue with similar actions 'till Egypt is cleansed from impurities'.[124] He also threatened to stop the flow of the Nile's water into Egypt.[125] Turabi, clearly wanted to be the thug of the region, without realizing that there were mightier powers out there.

Sudan's neighbours to the east, we noted, were not shielded from the NIF's adventures. Even before the failed Addis Ababa attempt on the life of Mubarak, both Ethiopia and Eritrea were sufficiently aggravated by Khartoum's adventures to the point of warning Bashir. In July 1994, Presidents Afwerki of Eritrea and Zenawi of Ethiopia met with Bashir in the Ethiopian capital; their joint message to him took the form of an ultimatum: 'stop meddling with our Muslims and keep your brand of Islam within the borders of Sudan'. Bashir denied any wrongdoing. As likely as not, the President of Sudan was not aware of Turabi's designs for the Horn of Africa. Turabi, two years before Bashir's meeting with his peers in Addis Ababa, told a visiting journalist that much of the Horn – Sudan, Somalia, Ethiopia and Eritrea – would be, like the European Community, one Islamic Community and borders would disappear.[126] Those who do not profess Islam in those countries must have had a chill down their spines. The journalist incorrectly observed that there was nothing inherently alarming about Turabi's vision; 'what is troubling ... is how he is going about making it a reality'.[127] We know how, and the region surely gained an inkling of Turabi's *modus operandi* to concretize his Islamic community when the Eritrean security forces intercepted and killed 20 infiltrators from the Eritrean Islamic *Jihad.* The group included Moroccan, Eritrean, Tunisian, Afghani and Pakistani elements, and certainly was not driven by a desire to create an East African Community. On the 1 January 1995 Eritrea severed diplomatic relations with Sudan.

Turabi's analogy between the Horn and the European Community (EC) was ill-advised, for the EC is a voluntary union based on respect for diversity, commitment to common ideals and endorsement by popular will.[128] That community was also founded on liberal democratic ethics, and accordingly countries that were not respectful of those ethics were barred from it. They were only admitted to the family when they came to adopt liberal democratic ideals, e.g. Greece of the Colonels (1976), Franco's Spain (1975) and the Portugal of Salazar (1974). Equally, though driven initially by the engine of two states, (France and Germany),[129] those two states were wise enough not to throw their weight around. Verily, Turabi did no justice to European union by citing it as an example for his desired Islamic community of the Horn; his approach to that unity was no different than that of wrongheaded Arab nationalists who strove to impose Arab unity from the top with disastrous consequences.

Uganda, though not part of Turabi's proposed Islamic Commonwealth, was also a target of Sudan's destabilization efforts, allegedly because of its purported support to the SPLM/A. Curiously, President Museveni was one of the first regional leaders to use his good offices to bring Sudan's warring parties together. All the same, the NIF's methods of intervention in Uganda were bizarre. On the one hand they exploited Islamic charity organizations to incite Muslim groups against their non-Muslim co-citizens in a manner that threatened the social fabric of

Uganda.[130] On the other, the NIF regime embraced the Lord's Resistance Army (LRA), a primitive Christian fundamentalist group known for profane practices such as the slaughter of children as an offering to their deities, while calling, at the same time, for strict adherence to the Ten Commandments.[131] Clearly, the NIF had not aligned itself with this barbaric Christian fundamentalist group for the sake of Islam. This was yet another example where the NIF had sacrificed its presumed golden rules at the altar of political expediency. Several attempts were made to mend fences between Uganda and Sudan, including one by former US President, Jimmy Carter, but they were not met with success.[132] Uganda's irritation with Bashir's double-talk reached a high-point, leading President Museveni to say: 'I have negotiated with Bashir; we want him to stop Kony … if he didn't we will stop him ourselves. Bashir has no right to kill our children.'[133] Museveni's suspicions on Sudan were confirmed by the European Union (EU). An EU delegation that visited Northern Uganda (Gulu and Kitgum) in March 2001 stated that the Sudan 'has not cooperated [and therefore] remedial action should be taken now to ensure that peace prevails'.[134]

Moreover, in contempt of its professed commitment to African liberation and unity, the NIF regime sought to build bridges with the apartheid regime in South Africa before its demise. In the early 1990s, before the installation of the Transitional Executive Council (TEC) in South Africa, the NIF established contacts with Armscor, the South African corporation in charge of arm sales, with a view to securing arm supplies. As a result, a virtual air bridge was established between Khartoum and Johannesburg to ferry arms to Khartoum; the flights were run by a Sudanese carrier and South Africa's Atlas Aviation. South African officers were also dispatched to Sudan to help in maintaining old helicopters and train the Sudanese military on the use of new arms. The issue came into the open when Pax Christi, Holland, and the Oslo-based World Campaign against Military and Nuclear Collaboration with South Africa, sounded the alarm bells. The campaign was soon taken over by the South African Bishops' Conference (SABC), leading to a public outcry.[135] The matter became an embarrassment to TEC (the incoming national reconciliation government) and led to a decision by South Africa's new Minister of Defence, Joe Modise, to stop all sale of arms to Sudan. He also formed a commission headed by Justice Edwin Cameron to investigate shady deals by Armscor. Having gone to that level of duplicity and treachery, it surprised nobody that the regime received in Khartoum, on 22 May 1994, Mobuto's minister of defence to coordinate with his regime's plans on intelligence gathering, including information on the whereabouts of Garang with a view to kidnapping him.

In view of those wanton adventures, it was not long before Sudan was included by the US government in the infamous league of terrorist states. The decision was certainly hastened by the indirect association of the NIF with the bombing of the World Trade Center in New York,[136] and its direct role in the harbouring of, and giving sustenance to, infamous terrorists from Egypt and Saudi Arabia, including Osama bin Laden who established a vast network of economic enterprises in the Sudan as front organizations for his political activities.[137] Later revelations during the trial in Manhattan of the alleged perpetrators of the bombing of the US embassies in Nairobi and Dar-es-Salaam threw the NIF's support to bin Laden's activities into greater relief.[138] The regime's reaction to the revelations was stunning. In a statement to the press, Foreign Minister Mustafa Osman Ismail said, 'Those reports refer to a previous period in history … many changes have taken place in Sudan. Bin Laden is not in Sudan and anything connected with him is history.'[139] The Minister may be right in saying that many changes had taken place in Sudan, but what faded from his mind was the regime's consistent denials in the past of any connection with bin Laden; invariably the NIF maintained that accusations relating to bin Laden's connection with the regime were framed by foreign governments who resented the success of its civilizational project.In no circumstance did the regime respond to the specific accusations levelled against it by Egypt and the US on the activities of bin Laden and his nightmares.

The regime's allegation that the West was only exasperated by its Islamic orientation was made notwithstanding assertions to the contrary in a US memorandum, signed by Warren Christopher in August 1993, which designated Sudan as a state sponsoring terrorism.[140] That memorandum came after several notices served on Khartoum by the US administration expressing utmost concern at Khartoum's behaviour.[141] Khartoum rulers were so self-satisfied that they concluded that the US and the world would eventually accept them for what they were.[142] That was indeed obtuseness pleased with itself. The NIF often vaunted that it had put Sudan on the world map; to be sure it had, but only in the way Al Capone did for Chicago. In no circumstance did the regime respond to the specific accusations levelled against it by Egypt and the US on the activities of those nightmares.

The NIF finally realized that lawlessness was costly, and commenced a campaign of allurement in the very West it claimed that it was out to destroy, and that campaign intensified after the break between Turabi and Bashir. Bashir, on his part, moved fast to mend fences with neighbours, and to allay the fears of the US. To achieve the latter, he welcomed a US intelligence mission to investigate claims about the regime's terrorist activities. Believing their own lies, the regime thought that by smoothness and sweet talk it would take the world for a ride. However, the artlessness of the Khartoum rulers was such that they doubled their bid by presenting Sudan for an African seat in the UN Security Council, Surely it was encouraged by what it assumed to be the success of its siren songs in Africa and the Arab countries. That audacity raised the temperature of the regime's opposition and provoked the US and human rights organizations all over the world; how, many asked, could a regime that has abused all internationally recognized norms of decency be rewarded with a seat in the Security Council? The views of those dissenters were succinctly summed up in the title of an article by Eric Reeves: 'A UN seat for Genocide'. Reeves, a scholar dedicated to the causes of democracy and human rights in Sudan, wrote: 'it is beyond disgrace and moral conception that [the government of Sudan] will smugly take [its] place at the table of the world's governing body'.[143] The US, on the other hand, raised three reasons for debarring the government of Sudan from membership in the Security Council: that the government was still under UN sanctions; that it had deliberately attacked a UN relief plane in South Sudan and that it was incessantly engaged in aerial bombardment of civilian targets in South and East Sudan. In view of all those pressures Sudan was denied membership of the Security Council by two-thirds of the membership of the UN General Assembly.

The NIF and War

The civil war in the South and the Nuba Mountains, we now know, was transformed into a religious war in which *jihad*, which essentially means sacrificing one's soul to achieve a divine will, became the main ideological vector. But when asked about the meaning of *jihad* at the Florida symposium,[144] without misdoubt, Turabi opined that *jihad* was a defensive, rather than an offensive concept in Islam. Islam, he said, eschewed *baghi* (injustice) and *Ùdwan* (infringement or aggression) and, to that end, enunciated laws that govern the conduct of war, very much like the ones upheld by contemporary international law.[145] But neither in his extensive writings and utterances, nor in practice, did Turabi give credence to this thesis. On the contrary, his *fatwas* (authoritative legal opinion) on *jihad* were so inflammatory and demagogic that some thought Turabi was desecrating Islam.

Jihad was reputably used by Muslim zealots to wage wars against so-called unbelievers, using and misusing Qur'anic sanctions. The Qur'an, like other holy books, has invariably been subject to exegesis by men whose intentions were not infrequently to transfigure the words of the Lord to suite mortal ends. However, the Qur'an, like the Holy Scriptures, is a spiritual book that reflects the human condition with all its contradictions. Accordingly, it is apt to be contradictory while seeking to rationalize the contradictions of this world by promising a consistent and virtuous life in the world hereafter. In the two books, one may come across bafflingly irreconcilable enjoinments. For example, in one *sūra* (chapter) of the Qur'an Allah's revealed word enjoins Muslims as follows: 'when you people encounter those who denied God in combat, strike upon their necks and when you have brought death upon most of them, keep them in confinement': (Muhammad 47/7). In another chapter the revealed words read: 'Compulsion is incompatible with religion. Now has the path of rectitude been distinct from the path of error. Therefore, he who rejects false beliefs and turns to God will have grasped the most secure hand-hold which shall never break': (*Al Baqara*) (The Cow 2/256). The combative and non-reconciliatory language of the first verse is flagrantly at odds with the placatory indulgence of the second. Also, in the Meccan Qur'an, *jihad* was described as intellectual rather than violent warfare. For instance, in one *sura* Allah instructed the Prophet as follows: 'Do not yield (O'Muhammad) to the infidels and wage against them a spiritual warfare by divine means' (the Qur'an): *Al Furqān* (The Criterion, 25/52). Similar irreconcilable versicles are to be found in the Bible; for example in Matthew Jesus says: 'Do not think that I have come to bring peace to the world. No, I did not come to bring peace, but a sword' (Matthew 10:34 in the Good News Bible for Catholics). While in Luke he says: 'The son of Man is not to destroy men's lives but to save them' (New American Standard Bible, Luke 9:56). A British commentator correctly pointed out that some verses of the Book, read through today's prism, would amount to nothing short of a call for genocide.[146] The holy scriptures, therefore, give rise to a wide margin for interpretation as well as misconstruction. People read in them what they want to read. So, drawing conclusions from this or that verse of the Qur'an or the Bible – read out of their historical context and in complete disregard of the humanistic imperatives of religion – does no justice to religion. Religion, when all is said and done, is essentially an ethical investment, so any religion that is taken to encourage violence should be presumed to have no sensitivity to evil.

The Qur'an particularly in its Medinan-revealed verses, is sated with injunctions against befriending or favouring the tutelage of Jews and Christians. Muslims who favour that tutelage 'shall be counted as part of them' (Jews and Christians).[147] This seeming propensity to animosity against people of other faiths was justified by a Muslim scholar as a means of providing to the early Muslim community 'the necessary psychological support for the cohesion of that vulnerable community who was trying to survive in a hostile and violent social and natural environment'.[148] But irrespective of the verisimilitude of this explanation it would be beyond reason to apply literally Allah's word as it was revealed in the seventh century on today's communities within or outside Sudan. To do so would be tantamount to a campaign of hate that might demolish the meaning of other Qur'anic calls for peoples of all races to know and coexist with each other. And here lies the rub: how to reconcile universal values enshrined in the Qur'an with the evolving demands and ethos of modern society. Being stuck fast to the words of the scriptures shall not facilitate this process. That was where the NIF failed and where its dilemma lay. Though passing itself off as a modernizing Islamist movement, the NIF continued to be literally wedded to a bygone world. In addition to their retrograde and contradictory positions on women rights, nowhere was their regressiveness more glaring than in their hilarious approach to *jihad*. In effect, one year and a half after Turabi's departure, and in the middle of the Islamists' so-called drive towards a just peace, the Islamic Fiqh Complex in Khartoum, on the promptings of the regime, declared that *jihad* was a fardh *àin* (absolute compulsory obligan) on all Muslims.[149]

In the NIF's version of *jihad,* however, NIF warriors are elevated to *Shuhada* (martyrs), while those on the SPLA side are discounted as a'*ada allah* (enemies of God). Thus, while Muslims who did not subscribe to the NIF vision of Islam became second class citizens in their own country, non-Muslim Southern Sudanese were to be reduced to an endangered subspecies. With this diabolical approach to war, the NIF accentuated the Southern problem and escalated war to unprecedented levels, thereby adding a new dimension to the conflict. It also dealt a mortal blow to the country's unity. The idea behind *jihad,*of course, is to dehumanize if not demonize the 'enemy' so as to justify his eradication. Indeed, gross violations of human rights, according to Mazrui, are invariably preceded by a process of psychic subhumanization: 'the violator subhumanizes his victim in his own imagination,'[150] but not completely. Mazrui aptly observes that grave abuses of human rights also encompass an element of hate of the victim. Accordingly, few human attributes should be left for the victim for him to be hated. One cannot, for example, hate a rock or a tree.

Four serious developments, however, ensued from the sanctification of war: the farcical manner in which the 'erudite' Turabi went in his *ijtihad* to justify the mobilization of Muslims for *jihad*; the escalation of violence to levels impermissible under the law of nations and even *shari'a* itself; the degeneration of tribal militia wars into tribal pogroms and slavery and the ruinous economic cost of war to the point that the whole country was brought to its knees. *Jihad* was elevated by the NIF to a *fardh* (religious obligation) to which every Muslim was subjected.[151] Accordingly, all government civil servants (including senior officials of whom some were in their fifties and sixties) were compulsorily subjected to military training. Those who refused were retired from service. Even non-Muslim civil servants were not exempted from that 'Islamic' edict. Young school boys were also not absolved from the ordeal, laws being passed obliging all young men from age 18 to undertake military training and have a tour of 'Islamic' duty in the war zone. Those among them who were enrolled in schools were denied admission to university or receipt of their highschool leaving certificates, unless they completed that tour of duty. As a result, families withdrew their children from schools to the safety of their homes at the cost of depriving them from the opportunity to complete their education. Those who had the means sneaked their children out of the country. Nevertheless, the NIF continued raiding homes in search of children e taking shelter in their own abodes. The practice was so notorious that both UNICEF and the UN Special Human Rights Rapporteur asked the government to desist from it.[152]

To beguile children and their parents, NIF preachers and schoolteachers bombarded the public with sermons on the virtues of *jihad,* and about holy spirits who fought alongside the *mujahideen*. More absurd were claims that those who died in the course of *jihad* would be rewarded instantaneously in heaven with uncontaminated virgins, seventy of them. Sudan TV, in a programme called *Sahat al fida'a* (fields of sacrifice) showed nightly, with doctored footages from battles in the South, fresh martyrs. Garang and other opposition leaders were constantly drubbed in those shows and equated with vampires. Turabi habitually officiated the betrothal of the martyrs to their intangible virgin wives. Theatrics apart, scenes like that had more to do with voodooism and magic lore, than with Islam and the Sorbonne. One parent, according to a British journalist who met him, had the courage to stand up to this sorcery and called its perpetrators by their name: 'crazy'. Professor Omar al Agr'a, a man 'of shining yet unassuming integrity', as the journalist described him, resigned from the University of Khartoum on principle when it was taken over by the NIF. His young son, Hassan, was an Islamist who purportedly joined a relief convoy to the South as an officer in charge of that convoy. 'This is what they told him, I don't think he really wanted to fight, but in the end he died for those crazy people,' said the father. In place of leaving the bereaved father to nurse his sorrows in quiet, NIF gangs descended on him to 'congratulate' him for the loss of his son who had joined seventy virgins in heaven. The father, even in that hour of grief, did not lose his sense of humour; he deplored the exploitation of his son's death for political ends and derisively told 'the crazy people', 'Then as a married man with a little daughter he must have committed adultery.'[153]

The NIF's *jihad* against the 'infidels' was most unholy in its conduct. Even within its historical Islamic context, *jihad* was circumscribed by interdicts that demanded forbearance in favour of the vulnerable and leniency towards prisoners of war. Those principles today are enshrined in the international law of war by which Sudan is obligated.[154] Among those laws is the Geneva Convention Relative to the Protection of Civilian Persons in Time of War which binds governments to search for, and prosecute, offenders who commit gross violations against civilians in the time of war. The Third and Fourth Convention cover treatment of war prisoners (POWs) as well as civilians. The Sudan governments, in the past, had not been consistently observant of those rules as we have seen from the flagrant excesses by the army in the conduct of war, particularly in the period that followed the October uprising. Nonetheless, when those excesses were discovered, they were publicly exposed by the independent media and castigated by civil society organizations. Under the NIF, things had foreseeably changed. For instance, it is out of the ordinary that throughout its 18 years of war with the SPLA, the Sudanese army had failed to capture a single prisoner of war from the SPLA. The Sudanese army could not be that inefficient in war. The reality is that to the government, the only good SPLA warrior is a dead one. This is what the politics of hate leads to. Surprisingly, the SPLA – since the early 1990s and up to 1999 – had in its custody over 3,000 POWs from the Sudanese army. Of those, nearly two-thirds were released on the mediation of the National Professional Alliance in 1986, the NDA in 1999 and voluntarily in numerous national occasions. All those POWs were also given access to their families through the ICRC. But if the NIF regime had broken every rule in the book in the way it treated Muslims in *Dar al Islam*, why should they be expected to mete out better treatment to 'non-believers' in *Dar al Harb*?

As a result of all those practices, it was not only the NIF victims who suffered, but also its civilizational project which was presented as an idealized model of justice, rectitude and sinlessness. Even by the standards of historical Islamic laws to which it claims to be attached, and which it feigns emulating, the NIF regime erred by a wide margin. The NIF regime had reincarnated the Prophet's theatre of war, only by assigning to their military offensives names of historic Islamic battles or military leaders. Apart from this symbolism, the NIF's conduct of war had nothing Islamic about it. It was no less brutal than any war waged by fascist or racist regimes. Their offensives often included scorch-earth tactics, bombardment of civilian targets, destruction of religious institutions and forcing young men against their will into *jihad*. Evidently, the Islamist warriors who reduced the 'Islamization' of war to puerile symbolism never came across the tolerant, humanistic and environmentally conscious injunctions of Caliph Abu Bakr (the first Caliph after Muhammad) to the *mujahideen*. Said Abu Bakr, 'Oh people, I charge you with ten rules; learn them well. Do not betray, or misappropriate any part of the booty. Do not practice treachery or mutilation. Do not kill a young child, an old man or a woman. Do not uproot a palm tree or cut fruitful trees. Do not slaughter a sheep, a cow or a camel except for food. You will meet people who have set themselves apart in hermitage, leave them to accomplish the purpose for which they have done this. You will come upon people who will bring you various kinds of food. If you partake of them, pronounce God's name over what you eat. You will meet people who have shaved the crown of their heads, leaving a band of hair around it. Strike them with the Sword.'[155] Ironically, in no time in the history of Sudan's civil war before the NIF's era, were civilians made a regular target of attack as a matter of policy. Whole populations were subjected to slow but sure ethnic cleansing. Without wasting words, an acute Sudan observer described the NIF's method of genocide as lacking 'the blood lust of Rwanda or the frightening enforced *eugenics* of the Nazi holocaust', but 'it is every bit as brutal'.[156] Furthermore, government instigated tribal wars degenerated into slave hunting, and food aid was turned into a weapon for forcible conversion to Islam. Non-Muslims who refused to be dragged into the NIF's dubious *jihad* were subjected to no less brutal treatment.[157]

The Nuba were perhaps the group who suffered most from the NIF's policies of ethinic cleansing, probably because they represented the largest cohesive non-Muslim ethnic group within the geographic North. The aim of the NIF's policy was to expunge the way of life of non-Muslim Nubas, even if it took physical liquidation.[158] And though a large number of the Nuba had for generations adhered to Islam, the familial and tribal bonds remained stronger than the religious ones. According to a

Sudanese scholar of Nuba origin,[159] allegiance within the Nuba community is principally to family and tribe across religious divides and not to religion; that is why the Nuba never knew religious wars. Unlike Islam and Christianity, the scholar maintains, the Nuba traditional practices are informed by tribal norms that are characterized by 'immediacy'; there is no expectation of reward in the life hereafter but immediate community sanctions for the transgression of the tribal code. Evidently, the aim of the NIF's policy towards the Nuba was to annihilate the remaining vestiges of tribal society and destroy the unity of the tribe by inciting Muslim zealots against the *'Kufar'*, i.e. non-Muslims among the Nuba, even when both belonged to the same family. Muslims who did not heed the NIF's call were, therefore, condemned as *murtadeen* (apostates).[160] The Islamists were not guarded even against burning mosques in Nubaland, as long as those were used by Nuba Muslims supporting the SPLA. One Nuba Muslim officer related to a visiting catholic priest (Fr Kizito) how the government troops raided and erased a mosque in Kauda village for no other reason than that the inhabitants of the village were SPLA supporters.[161] Kauda, as we shall see in numerous instances, became a permanent target of the NIF's aerial bombardment.

The manner of torture to which the Nuba were subjected was sufficiently recorded by human rights organizations and monitors. A special United Nations mission that visited Sudan in October 1994 reported, on the basis testimonies collected from those who escaped torture, harrowing stories of extrajudicial killings and summary executions of Nuba elite. According to the report, 'Between 40 and 50 prisoners (primarily educated professionals), were held in a secret detention centre in Kadugli between June and August 1992. Small groups of four or five were taken each day in the afternoon or at midnight to a place called *El-Saraf Al Ahmar*, approximately three kilometres South of Kadugli, where they were executed. Usually, at least one man was allowed to return to the detention camp to tell the others the story.'[162] Those executed were accused of cooperating with the SPLA. To conceal those atrocities, the Nuba region was completely sealed off from international observers and relief agencies. As a discerning observer wrote, the NIF imposed on the Nuba people a virtual *cordon sanitaire* and excluded them from all relief operations.[163]

This brutality against the Nuba was more than matched by policies of cultural uprooting applied by the regime to young displaced boys and girls from the South. The children were removed from their families in the ghettos around Khartoum and taken to Quranic schools where they were given Muslim names to obscure their ethnic patronyms.[164] That gross infringement on human rights impelled investigations by a fact-finding mission led by Dr Kevin Vigilante, Assistant Professor of Medicine at Brown University, accompanied by a Dutch member of parliament. Vigilante presented a report to the UN Commission on Human Rights in which he listed camps to which the abducted children were relocated. On his part, Gaspar Biro undertook a thorough investigation on displaced children and reported five camps in different locations of Sudan where children were forcibly converted to Islam and made to undertake military drill.[165] One of the tools brazenly used by the NIF forcibly to convert children to Islam was food; relief supplies, including those provided by the UN and Western European NGOs were only made available to displaced persons who were willing to become Muslims. The practice became so discomforting that the SPLM had to bring it up as an issue of major concern in meetings with the government that were meant to discuss the facilitation of timely distribution of humanitarian relief assistance.[166]

Equally alarming was the NIF government's increasing resort to aerial bombardments, which were not as common in the past. At first, bombardment by high-attitude flying objects was probably meant to provide cover for ground forces, but afterwards they became a tool of destabilization. By engaging in those abominable assaults against civilians, the meritless regime had crossed all the bounds of the rules of engagment. The US Committee for Refugees compiled a detailed and adequately substantiated register of those bombardments for a period of 15 years, long before the NIF took over power.[167] According to the report, sorties during this period numbered in the thousands and the persons attacked in hundreds of thousands, generating in their wake wide displacements. The author of the report concluded that the 'widespread use of aircraft to attack civilian targets indicated that Khartoum had declared war, not just on John Garang and his SPLA, but on its own people … the NSRCC was ready to commit any war crime in order to end the rebellion.'[168]

This policy of annihilation was deliberate from the start. In November 1989 – a few months after the NSRCC assumed power – 55 bombs were dropped at Yirol town. The attack was denounced by the International Committee of the Red Cross (ICRC). For daring to denounce the government, the ICRC was threatened with expulsion. Obviously, the government, would have preferred witnesses who saw nothing, heared nothing and said nothing. In the light of those attacks on civilians, UN Secretary General Javier Perez de Cuellar demanded an explanation from the government as to why civilian targets were bombed. His protestation was brushed off by the Khartoum regime. As if that was not searing enough, the NIF engaged in the late 1990s in regular attacks on civilian installations like hospitals and schools in South Sudan. Ostensibly, the government's aim was not to destroy the enemy, but to disturb communal peace and destabilize settled communities within the liberated areas. Those recent attacks were widely reported by the media, especially when they became a weekly occurrence in 1999,[169] despite President Clinton's warning on 15 February 2000. In that warning President Clinton stated that: 'It is an outrage that such egregious abuses against innocent Sudanese citizens have become commonplace in the ongoing civil war in Sudan.' He called on the government of Sudan to cease all aerial bombardment and to refrain from any attacks on civilian targets.[170] That warning came after the dastardly attack on a catholic primary school in the Nuba region. The attack prompted Bishop Makram Max Gassis, responsible for the Nuba diocese, to take up the matter to the US Commission on Religious Freedoms established by Congress.[171] Typically, the regime, despite all evidence to the contrary, persisted in describing the school as a military target. The government's calousness was exemplary. A Sudanese diplomat in Nairobi, obeying the reign, told a newspaperman who visited the site of the attack that the government was sure of hitting a military target. The journalist, with evidence in hand challenged the diplomat and presented him a seven minutes of video clips showing a civilian area, no soldiers or arms but scattered books, terrified children fleeing, a blackboard with an ongoing lesson, benches and corpses.[172] As if it cared less, the same village was targeted, not once or twice, but regularly by Sudan airforce. The area has no strategic advantage though it is a centre for religious preaching and teaching. Clearly, the NIF leaders who claimed in the early 1990s to be the apostles of universal Islamism had degenerated by the end of the decade to religious bigots and ethnic nationalists.

Observers began to see clearly the government's strategem behind aerial bombardments. They were not just acts of war, but reflection of a more sinister policy to terrorize and destroy people. One observer asked, 'Why these soft targets? Is it because the defenceless civilians are not likely to put up a resistance or is it just part of Khartoum's strategy to terrify the civilians and ensure that their lives remain a long stretch of misery. Could the government be having an agenda to annihilate the population in the rebel territory?'[173] However, two aerial attacks caused tremors. The first was the attack on Lui hospital (6 March 2000). The hospital is run by the American NGO, Samaritan Purse. To make things worse it took place when President Clinton's Special Envoy to Sudan (Harry Johnston) was visiting Khartoum for the first time since his appointment. The other attack targeted relief agencies and thus denied access to vulnerable groups.[174] The attacks were denounced by the World Food Programme (WFP) Executive Director, Catherine Bertini. In her words, 'these violent attacks are totally unacceptable and we strongly condemn them. They show that there is no respect for aid workers trying to help innocent Sudanese.'[175] Despite the uproar, the attacks continued unabated.[176] That was probably what impelled Thiery Durand, Director of operations of MSF, to come out with a damning report against the government's targeting of schools and hospitals, including clinics that were under its own supervision. Durand added another dimension to the attacks; he stated that 'evidence has been found and serious allegations have been made that weapons of internationally prohibited nature are regularly employed against civilians.'[177]

This allegation was corroborated by evidence given by an Iraqi Kurdish doctor, Hassan Abdul Salam, who took refuge in Denmark. Abdul Salam was debriefed by Interpol and the Danish Intelligence Services. To his investigators, he reported about joint Iraqi-Sudanese efforts to manfacture weapons of mass destruction, adding that: 'Those poor people of South Sudan are worse off than the Kurds.'[178] It was also reported in April 2001, following the crash in Southern Sudan of an Antonov aircraft carrying Sudan's State Minister of Defence and a contingent of senior army officers, that both the pilot and co-pilot of the aircraft were Iraqis. Thirteen officers, including the Minister perished in the crash, while the pilot, co-pilot and over twenty other passengers survived. Contrary to established customs in such accidents, neither the pilot nor co-pilot was allowed to make public statements on what had happened. The government surely sought to hide their identity.

The reckless onslaught on civilians invited a broad-based campaign in the US, demanding the administration to intervene and impose a no-fly zone in South Sudan. Also, towards the end of the year 2000, the New Sudan Council of Churches (NSCC) called on the international community to take action against the government in view of its targeting of civilians in air offensives and called on the UN Security Council to impose a no-fly zone over South Sudan, Nuba Mountains and Southern Blue Nile. Paradoxically, those offensives intensified at the very time when the regime escalated its charm offensive, particularly in Europe. This was neither the way to pursue an endearment campaign nor to demonstrate a will to achieve peace. Astonishingly, countries of the European Union (EU) were reluctant to denounce expressly the aerial bombardment of civilian targets including hospitals, schools, women and children.[179] As a result of this willful oversight, the EU countries created the perception that aerial bombardments could be tolerated. People surmised that this remission was only attributable to the fact that aerial bombardments were carried out in order to clear areas where petroleum was produced by European oil companies. That conjecture was made probable by reports of independent journalists and NGOs. So, if the European 'peacemakers' did not know why the government was targeting civilians in certain areas in the South, the rest of the world, including European NGOs, knew. And so did people who were incessantly subjected to those aerial bombardments. In response to a question by Andrew Harding of the BBC about why they were targeted by the regime, John Wijial, a senior citizen in the regions, answered: 'The government found oil beneath our village. They want the oil, but they don't want us.'[180]

The government's most odious war crime was the tribalization of the armed conflict. Admittedly, tribal militias were used since 1985 to create a buffer zone between combatants, but in the late years of al Mahdi's government and all through the NIF era, they became more vicious, as tribes were armed to the teeth and set loose on the 'enemy'. The militias were also given a free rein to freelance in looting and abduction. In an interview with the *Baltimore Sun*, a militia commander told a newsman: 'We are people of a great noble family; whatever one of us says is going to be accepted by everybody. That is what got me the commander's job.'[181] The 'commander' said that he was recruited by Colonel Babiker el Sid to fight 'infidel' SPLA rebels. In return, he said, the militias were given freedom to loot property and enslave children because 'we are not given any salary; our incentive is looting'.[182] The *Sun* had dispatched two newsmen to investigate cases of alleged slavery who went deep into the border zone and came back with chilling stories of tribal raids by the Rizeigat against the Dinka. The stories were based on interviews they have had with both victims and abductors. The journalists named places and middlemen and reported how the raiders were rapturously received with chants and dances by their kinsmen who celebrated the success of the raids. In addition to abductions, the militias were not constrained by their minders from attacking relief centres. One such case was when hundreds of horseback militias raided and looted the Red Cross clinic in the village of Chelkon; tents were destroyed, vehicles burned and other moveables looted.[183] As it turned out, neither were the brutish tribal 'commanders' concerned with the bad name they were giving to their tribe, nor was the government troubled with the pain caused to innocent civilians.

The NIF and Slavery

So slavery was back again, almost a century after the freeing of slaves by the British. The government and its apologists bent over backwards to explain this odium, first by distancing themselves from the actions of the tribal militias. Sudan's ambassador to Washington trivialized the issue, claiming that slavery was an anathema in Sudan and contrary to traditions of Islam. The two journalists described his response to the accusation as 'unctuous and disingenuous', he acted as though the two newsmen 'knew none of the history of slavery in Africa and in Sudan' or he was talking to 'Beavis and Butthead'.[184] Apparently, NIF diplomats, like their leaders, have scant respect for other people's intelligence. The ambassador was not alone in skulking such an important issue; his mentor, Turabi, was even harder to catch. Asked by a group of scholars at the Florida seminar about slavery in Sudan, Turabi said that it 'was not known to the country till the coming of Mohamed Ali and his European friends'.[185] In the company of scholars whom he should have presumed to know better, Turabi was not only evasive about contemporary events, but was also misleading on presenting historical events. For example, he could not have been unaware of the fact that slavery was a recognized institution in old Sudanese society, as indeed it was in other old societies. More importantly he could not have been unacquainted with the fact that the first external enslaver of Sudanese was not 'Mohamed Ali and his European friends', but Àbdullahi ibn abi al Sarh who conquered Nubia in the name of Caliph Amr ibn il As. Nor could the knowledgable jurist have been ignorant of *al baqt* agreement which is regarded as a *locus classicus* by all jurists.[186] But, to cheer up his audience and exonerate historical Islam, Turabi had no problem to make reverses of the truth. Turabi, however, passed from the sublime to the ridiculous when he told Chevalérias that Islam permitted concubage as long as the woman slave fell into the hands of a Muslim warrior in the course of *jihad* or was entrusted to his care during battle.[187] With an edict like this, the fate of women captured in the course of Turabi's *jihad* in the South was sealed. Sexual enslavement, according to this interpretation of Qur'anic edicts, is thus justified in this day and age.

Secondly, in their guileful attempt to draw a distinction between slavery and forcible abduction of 'captives for ransom', the NIF apologists were not aware that they have been overtaken by events. Truly, in the present war induced enslavement is not comparable in any manner or form to the nineteenth-century structured institution of slave trade, but the issue here is not one of legal niceties, whatever way you look at it. It relates to kidnapping persons and engaging them in work against their will, using women as concubines or exchanging human beings for pecuniary reward. All those are ingredients of a slavery of sorts that the government is legally bound to discourage and stop. As one observer wrote: 'It is true that the government cannot be described as having directly participated in slavery, [but] they have engineered and profited from the social chaos out of which slavery has reappeared.'[188] The government knew very well that children and women were legitimate war booty for the militias it had unleashed to destabilize areas whose population was thought to be sympathetic to the SPLM. However, on the strength of the international law of war alone, the government cannot escape reprobation; the Hague Conventions (1899 and 1907) stipulate that laws and customs of war protect civilians from enslavement or forced labour. Also, the statutes of the International Court of Justice (ICJ) rule that slavery and slave-related practices and forced labour constitute a war crime if committed by a belligerent, and a crime against humanity if committed by public officials against any person irrespective of the circumstances.[189] Over and above, the Geneva Convention Relative to the Protection of Civilian Persons in Time of War obligates states to seek offenders in slavery-related crimes and prosecute them (Article 147). As well, the ILO Convention 182, which went into effect in November 2000, deals mainly with the worst forms of child labour, and the government could not be unaware of the obligations imposed by that convention on governments.

But war or no war, the law of nations has evolved to the point that slavery now comprises a multitude of malpractices: debt bondage, forced labour, sexual and physical abuse of immigrant domestic workers, trafficking in people for purposes of prostitution etc.[190] Not only are states required to respect those rules, they are also duty-bound to provide the abused victims with effective judicial recourse against the outlawed practices. In addition, the Sudan was signatory to the 1981 Africa Charter on Human and Peoples Rights of which Article 5 prohibits all forms of exploitation and degradation of man, particularly slavery and slave trade. Effectively, even the laws of Sudan (Sudan Penal Code) amply cater for such offences, e.g. Sections 161 on abduction, 162 on kidnapping, 163 on forced labour and 164 on unlawful confinement. The government of Sudan has, therefore, no place to run for cover. Defensive self-advertising by brandishing the prohibition of slavery by Islam is not a good enough alibi. Whether Islam prohibits slavery or condones it is not the issue; the issue is what the government has done, and is doing, to enforce its own laws as well as the laws of nations to which Sudan has subscribed. Besides, evasiveness and weasel words would do good neither to Islam nor to the government. The government, if it only cared, should have investigated the reported incidents and prosecuted the offenders. Unfortunately for the NIF, the accusations did not only come from two hapless university professors, but from high-powered congressmen, investigative journalists[191] and human rights groups including the Sudan Human Rights Organization (SHRO) in Cairo. SHRO carried out its own independent investigation and produced inconvertible evidence of cases of abduction and trade in humans leading to the conclusion that 'acts of slavery are widely practised with direct support from the authorities.'[192] Indeed, an authoritative UN agency estimated that between 12,000 to 15,000 people were held in bondage in Sudan.[193] In the face of those government tolerated or sponsored acts and the embarrassing international campaign they engendered, Sudanese of all colour or race cannot afford to watch the abhorrent practice of slavery – under whatever guise it is committed – and remain silent. They should follow the footsteps of SHRO and speak out. Those who do not are as much culpable of the offence as are those who commit it.

Furthermore, the slavery issue, to the dismay of self-respecting Sudanese, became a *cause celebre* among Afro-Americans in the US. In May 2000, the Salvation Army, Family Research Council and chapters of the Urban League as well as Coretta Scott, the widow of the late Martin Luther King, launched a campaign to end slavery in the Sudan.[194] Reverend Walter Fauntroy of the National Black Leadership (a Washington-based group which includes heads of 200 national black organizations), described the initiative as a 'catalyst to bring together spirited descendants of Harriet Tubman, Lloyd Garrison and John Brown in the twenty-first-century abolition movement'.[195] An Afro-American Washington talk-radio host who visited Sudan gave a stark picture of what he had seen: 'I am an Afro-American, the descendant of slaves. It was like I was in a time machine, watching my own ancestors in slavery. Only this is real and it's happening.'[196] Madison, the talk-show host, went on to say, 'For black Americans in particular, slavery is a huge emotional issue. We very readily find it easier to accept the slaughter of the Dinka man of South Sudan, than the enslavement of Dinka women and children.'[197] After a visit to South Sudan, Fauntroy and Madison threatened to resort to tactics similar to those led by Afro-Americans in the 1980s against aprtheid.[198] Madison's campaign registered astounding successes.[199]

The cynicism of the NIF regime reached its utmost high when Foreign Minister Mustafa Osman Ismail told the 55th session of the UN General Assembly (19 September) that Sudan looked forward to participating 'effectively' in the UN International Conference on Racism due to be held in South Africa in the year 2001. Instead of Sudan's 'effective' participation in the UN Conference on Racism, the whole world was looking forward to its response to the ear-splitting shrieks of Majak Bok Majak. Mijak, a Dinka woman carrying a 14-month-old boy, was camping together with a crowd of supporters outside the UN building in New York, in protest against Bashir's visit to the city to address the Millennium Summit. According to her story, the young lady was captured in 1987 by tribal horsemen and remained in captivity till she escaped in 1997. She told a newsman: 'I demand the arrest of Bashir who is now walking freely in the streets of New York because he directed the forces that created slaves.'[200]

Sudan's position on the issue of slavery was not made easier by the reports of the UN human rights monitors in one of his recent reports to the effect that cases of involuntary servitude existed on a large scale in Sudan.[201] In addition, he reported that he 'cannot but conclude the existence of abduction of persons, mainly women and children, belonging to racial, ethnic or religious minorities from South Sudan, the Nuba Mountains and the Ingassana Hills'.[202] In an earlier document (1995), Biro reported the abduction of 217 Dinka youth from villages along the railroad between Babanusa and Wau; the government in that instance, he said, did not deny the abduction but described the accusation of slavery as baseless. Nonetheless, Biro deemed those actions as a transgression of international conventions to which Sudan had adhered.[203] In his last report before relinquishing his job, Leonardo Franko reported with dismay that 'no serious investigation had taken place of the root causes of the practice, possibly because of the lack of engagement of the top political leadership in the process or reluctance to cooperate'.[204]

Equally, as a result of the war-induced exodus of displaced persons from the South into Northern towns, ethnic-based fears reaching the level of phobia reared their ugly head again. Those unmistakably racist fears took one back to the 1920s, to the cantonments around the capital where displaced persons from the South and Nuba Mountains lived. The present day cantonments are hushedly referred to by unrepentant racists as al *hizam al aswad* (the black belt). The South African white supremacists had at least the courage of their decaying conviction when they openly talked of the *swart gevaar* (black peril). Seemingly, it did not matter the least to the detractors of those *aswads* (blacks), that within the Arabicised *macchiatos* of the North there were many groups who were no less 'disgraced' by the dark tincture and physical features they abhored most in their Southern co-citizens. Presented in this tawdry manner, the issue ceases to be one of *racial* differentiation. It is *racist* in every sense of the word. Racism is reflective of a mindset that is generally not blessed with any aptitude for judicious discernment. For how many white Americans call some of their co-citizens 'black', based on a binary classification of people into black and white, when almost nine-tenths of the blood of those is 'white' (if such a thing exists). In a closed system of prejudice, people never realize how racist they are,[205] nor do they readily admit it. To those, we have nothing but wishes for a quick recovery.

Sudan's 'invisible' racists, nevertheless, become more grotesque when they conjured up dangers inherent in the swelling masses of 'black' citizens in Khartoum, supposedly the capital city of the country to which those wretched of the earth belong. Sometimes the grotesqueness verges on hallucination. One such example is the not so infrequent reference by some Khartoumese of Arab extraction to the incidents of Zanzibar (1964), and to which the author was privy. Those incidents set Zanzibari 'blacks' against 'Arabs'.[206] Perplexingly, those who nurse such absurd views include elements who frequently vaunt libertarian democratic tendencies. Regrettably, one of those is Sadiq al Mahdi. During a Ramadhan *Iftar* (breaking the fast) in December 2000, he told Arab diplomats in Khartoum that Sudan was threatened by a Zanzibar-like revolt.[207] By recalling the Zanzibar episode out of its historical context, the 'libertarians' not only revealed a lack of contextual understanding of the history they related, but also exhibited a tendentious racist disposition.[208] Summoning up the Zanzibar events with attendant insinuations about the gang bangs that were reportedly associated with those events, was evidently meant to trump up fears and undermost sentiments within the North. Those broad hints and half-spoken remarks about the dangers posed by the 'black' displaced in *al hizam al aswad* on the fair sex in the North cast one's mind back to Martin Luther King's stroke of wit addressed to white supremacists in the US: 'I want to be the white man's brother, not his brother-in-law,'[209] said the apostle of racial equality.

Attitudes like this are, without doubt, meant to generate heterophobia against Southerners living in the North. As Cohen stated, fear of the unknown and heterophobia (fear of difference) are both marked by a psychological state of unease, extreme anxiety, discomfort and a sense of loss of control'.[210] However, that attitude also disbosoms the length of puffery to which some people would go to foment hate and provoke a psychosis of fear in a society where the average Northerner and Southerner live peacefully together. Sudan is no Rwanda, nor has it been afflicted by the type of racial hatred that, for example, pitted Hausas against Yourabas in Nigeria. But even in those countries, the horrifying massacres that tormented both countries would not have taken place without instigations by perverse gang leaders. Wayward politicians and self-serving pseudo-intellectuals have always been the initiators of the pedagogics of hatred. Regardless, the majority of those 'threatening' displaced persons in the North would rather go back to their hamlets in the South and the Nuba Mountains, than live in a 'united Sudan' in which they were perpetually seen as an imminent danger. This foul hitting and paltering with truth confutes claims by underhand political players that Sudan belonged to all its *muatineen* (citizens). The struggle of the marginalized, need we recall, is about equality and not ravishment, about fairness and not enrapturement. Facing those issues frontally is an eventuality that some are not yet ready to envisage. As it were, they would rather go along with the adage: 'Give the dog a bad name and hang it.'

The Tsar Revolts against his Rasputin

In the mid-1990s a member of the country's rubber-stamp transitional National Assembly said: 'Under the Islamic umbrella, some have too free a hand to creep all over the place. They think that they can do anything because they have beards. But being a devout Muslim doesn't depend on pieces of hair hanging from your face. They are doing Islam and Sudan a great disservice – and putting people who believe that Islam is humane in a very difficult situation.'[211] Those excessive reactions, even by one of the NIF assumed supporters, were a direct result of the regime's excesses, insubstantiality and assumed presumption of infallibility.

The gap between fancy and reality dismayed even some of the otherwise pertinacious Islamists who spoke openly and mainly against the NIF's way of doing things. Among those critics were militants groomed by Turabi, such as Abdel Wahab el Affendi and independent-minded Islamist scholars such as Hassan Mekki and Tayeb Zein al Abdin. The latter two clearly saw the dead end to which the NIF has led Sudan. El Affendi, on the other side, wrote a scathing article in which he advised Turabi to retire from political life, if he was to have any chance in playing an indirect role in the future.[212] However, some of his earlier writings revealed a hard to understand daydreaming about maintaining Turabism without Turabi. Evidently, the belief of Turabi's critics in the religious verities of political Islam did not wane, but some had the wisdom to realize that the time for the NIF regime was up, while others believed that they could still have it both ways. For example, in a work purported to be an objective critique of the NIF's misgovernance, el Affendi maintained that if there were to be any political liberalization or constitutional restructuring in Sudan, it 'must begin with gradual permission of political pluralism and only after the consolidation of the new Islamist movement and the promulgation of a constitution that governs political action and curtails sectarian, tribal and regional polarizations'.[213] Put another way, el Affendi wanted Sudan to be kept hostage to the Islamists' ravings, trials and errors. Happily, a few years later, el Affendi surprised friends and foe by acknowledging the failure of the NIF model to measure up to either the Islamic pristine model or contemporary democracies.[214] He considered the regime's oppression and coercion as tantamount to fascism. The Islamic state, at the end of the day, cannot be anything but democratic, he said.[215] This is not just a volte face but a well reasoned and courageous self-criticism by an Islamist intellectual who was born and bred within the Sudanese Islamist movement. Affendi patently sobered up to the fact that no noble mission could be achieved through unnoble means. But within the rank and file of the NIF there are still brainwashed footsoldiers who believe in the NIF's infallibility and are ready to die for it. In defiance of the total ruin brought on Sudan by the NIF's grand design (except perhaps for the NIF and its adherents), they comfort themselves with the fiction that if the exigencies of the real world do not respond to the coinages of the Sheikh's brain, then something must be wrong with the real world. However, after the split between Turabi and Bashir, even among those foot soldiers, support for the NIF cadres began to waver.

Ten years after Turabi had launched his ideological *Leviathan,* some of his erstwhile sycophants decided to change horses in the middle of the race. With Turabi's clone and second-in-command, Ali Osman Mohamed Taha, at their head, ten NIF apparatchiks joined hands with Bashir against the Sheikh. Their aim was to curtail his authority within the NC. Taha orchestrated the group from behind the scenes. Some of the plotters had obviously had enough of their mentor, others were only disgruntled with him for cold shouldering them in the NIF's power struggle. Turabi was unsparing in his contempt for his long-serving dupes. In an interview with the *Economist* he described them as clerks, time servers and double dealers.[216] The Sudan's messiah was clearly traumatized by the treachery of his disciples, particular that there were ten and not only one Judas among them. But despite the denunciation of their mentor, none of them saw the *huis clos* to which the NIF's politics had led the country. Nor could they recognize, like some of their colleagues, the depth of ignominy to which the regime has sunk.

The rebel gang included some of the most culpable elements of the regime and the most publicly hated, either for atrocities they committed within the security agencies or for their strident style in public discourse. In sober recognition of the serious abuses against human rights which were amply explained, some of them were, at bottom, just criminals. Albeit, the gang of ten stopped short of removing Turabi from his only official position, the speakership of Parliament, though the measure had been debated. That proved to be a fatal mistake. Turabi accepted his fate with assumed open-handedness, but went on surreptitiously to plan his next move on three fronts: the party, Parliament and, surprisingly, peacemaking. For a number of months, Turabi gallivanted around the country to garner support for himself within the grassroots in preparation for a showdown with Bashir at the convention of the NC. The meeting took place in mid-1999 and, after a heated debate, Turabi's powers were reinforced and the ten rebels voted out of office within the NC.

His second move was more subterfuge. Without the knowledge of Bashir, he organized in the beginning of May, 1999 a meeting with Sadiq al Mahdi in Geneva to discuss rapprochement and reconciliation. That meeting took place at the World Intellectual Property Organization (WIPO) and was facilitated by its Sudanese Director-General, Dr Kamil el Tayeb. In this instance, the SPLM bailed out al Mahdi in the face of criticism from NDA elements. His, the SPLM declared, was an exploratory initiative which Sadiq and his party were entitled to undertake just as the SPLM was engaged in negotiations with the regime.

In political terms, the similarities between Sadiq and Turabi outweigh the differences. Foremost, is that both are spurred by an almost Macbethan ambition, a 'vaulting ambition which o'er leaps itself and falls on the other'. Also, the two are committed to the religionization of politics. Nevertheless, to give leeway to Sadiq, both the DUP and SPLM, who described the meeting as exploratory, looked forward for a brief from the Umma leader about the results of the Geneva meeting. But Sadiq al Mahdi was cagey in reporting to his NDA colleagues the results of the meeting with his brother-in-law. This gave ground to the not so unreasonable conjecture that Turabi wanted to recreate the old alliance between himself and al Mahdi. There was a confluence of minds between the two leaders to justify that conjecture. Turabi wanted to sidestep Bashir and save the Islamist movement that he had been building for forty years and which, to all appearances, came to grief. On his side, al Mahdi, the 'legitimate prime minister' wanted to recover his lost position following a route of least resistance. The success of Turabi's stratagem hinged on another thing: using al Mahdi to persuade al Mirghani and Garang to go along with it. His intention, it would appear, was to dispossess the NDA of the two major Northern parties (Umma and DUP) as well as its major fighting force: the SPLA. This way the NDA would have been destroyed as a unified opposition force. Failing to do that, the second option would be to bring al Mirghani into the fold so as to create a Muslim Northern bloc against a Southern non-Muslim one. This was in line with al Mahdi's own strategy to unify *ahl al qiblatain* (people of the two *qiblas*, i.e. followers of the two heavenly religions).[217] Unfortunately for the Geneva duo, neither al Mirghani nor Garang would have anything to do with that ruse. Together with other members of the NDA, they criticized the Geneva secret agreement and affirmed the NDA's position of no peace talks with the regime till it came out clearly on fundamental issues of war and peace: pluralistic democracy, interim arrangements, religion and the state and respect for universal human rights.

Future revelations proved the worst fears of the NDA. According to those very close to Turabi, the Geneva meeting was crowned with an agreement by the two leaders which was reduced to writing in two copies, one copy kept by Turabi, the other by Sadiq. Sadiq al Mahdi denied the existence of any agreement between himself and Turabi. The upshot of the agreement was that both parties would join forces to dismantle Bashir's regime through mass action. In consequence, the two parties would inherit the earth and impose their terms on others, including the NDA. That was why Turabi engaged upon his return from Geneva in his last and fatal move: using Parliament to clip Bashir's wings and prepare the ground for the implementation of the Geneva agenda.

As the Speaker of Parliament, Turabi engineered, in November 1999, a motion to amend the constitution in order to create the position of prime minister responsible only to parliament. Bashir would thereby be reduced to a ceremonial president at the initial stage before he was shipped into oblivion. But in fairness to Turabi, his strategy also aimed at ending the hegemony by the military and its civilian helpmates and creating a pluralist system tailored by him. Turabi's proposal to make the head of government accountable to parliament and to have governors of federal states elected was part of that grand design. Clearly, he knew that in any fair and free elections neither Bashir nor his helpmates stood a chance.

As for the duo (Turabi and Sadiq), the Arab press close to the NIF reported that Turabi had in mind his own plan for the presidency and the prime minister's post. Its aim was to woo Sadiq who often declared his preference for a system of governance similar to that of France where executive power was apportioned between the president and the prime minister.[218] Turabi was ready to accede to Sadiq's demand. In that scheme of things, Turabi would allocate the prime minister's post for al Mahdi, while he assumed the presidency *'a la francais'*. Like al Mahdi, Turabi favoured that system of government despite its shortcomings and inadaptability to the Sudanese situation.[219] Given Sudan's political diversity and deeply entrenched interests, the Sudanese political class had opted since independence for a system of rule wherein the executive and legislature were constructed as counterweights. Turabi, the French-educated lawyer, knew very well what the French system held in store for him. Talking to President Nixon, Francois Mitterand described that system initiated by De Gaulle as a 'constant *coup d'état'*. But, he added: 'we did not like it when he was in, but now that we are in we like it very much'.[220] Bashir, on his side, was totally opposed to the idea of creating a prime minister's post independent of the presidency, so he appealed to parliament to postpone debating the motion. To that appeal, Turabi haughtily replied, 'We do not expect the President to comment on a parliamentary motion, he can only make his comments if he wishes.'[221]

The schism between the two became beyond repair. On 12 December, Bashir, clad in full military uniform, faced the nation to announce the dissolution of parliament and the imposition of a state of emergency for three months. He also engaged in an impetuous castigation of the NC, his own party. Thereafter, Bashir met with senior officers of the armed forces and police (not the NIF's grassroots committees). The irony of this episode was that, after a decade of usurping power in the name of the armed forces (not the NIF), Bashir came back full circle, first and foremost, to seek support from the very army which he had fraudulently cajoled and led into a *coup* that it did not foreplan or contemplate. The forces, however, were reported to have told Bashir that the move against Turabi was long overdue; the army (or whatever was left of Sudan's professional army) was evidently fed up with the way the NIF was doing things, including the meddling by the militias in military affairs. The imposition of the state of emergency, rather than widening the margin of liberties, entailed more ultrajudicial powers to the security agencies.

Bashir's statement was objectionable both in tone and substance. He unrepentantly reiterated all the tired slogans of the NIF: civilizational project, adherence to *shari'a* and commitment to the guiding principles of the *ingaz* (salvation), the name by which the regime came to be known. Turabi's *thawabit* loomed large through Bashir's address. He also went into a vigorous exhortation of the Sudanese people to unite in the face of 'external threats'. America, he said, has declared war on Sudan and 'Madeleine Albright would not sleep until the Khartoum government is overthrown'.[222] Probably, the reaction of those who were listening to him inside Sudan, was: 'we wish she did'. However, Bashir's hollow jingoism and strained beseeching was only meant to comfort whoever was left of the faithful. Manifestly, out of the ideological wreckage of Turabi's civilizational project, the only spar left for Bashir to hang on was sloganism.

Bashir's words on the party and government were astonishing: 'we are one system, one party in government (NC) and in the Assembly (Parliament)'. This was the same man who was boasting after a sham election a few years before, of wide-based popular support to his government that went beyond the NIF. Bashir related a catalogue of accusations against both the NC and the Assembly: 'when the President of the Republic decides to hold a meeting with the Assembly members, his request is refused; and when he wants to deliver a message to the chair of that body, his request is refused and the chair declares in a press conference that he is not obliged to coordinate anything with the executive'. On the NC, Bashir lamented what he called 'broad practices that resulted in shaking the authority and standing of government'. Consequently, he said, 'Rival power shall not be tolerated anymore.'[223] Behind Bashir's simulated perseverance in his crusading cause, four messages clearly emerged: repelling a fictitious external threat, stopping the war, ending dualism within the NIF power structures and continuing with reconciliation. Bashir could have been better served if he came out for ending the war and reconciliation as his main commission. By focusing on the power struggle within the NIF and impressing on the whole world that he was better equipped than Turabi to carry on with the Islamists agenda, he made himself needless for the process of attaining a just peace and genuine reconciliation.

Predictably, the NDA reacted negatively to Bashir's calls. The Alliance wanted palpable change of policy, not simply a change of guard. The SPLM's reaction was also forthright. In a statement on 17 December, Garang said: 'Bashir's coup of 12 December 1999 is an internal crisis within the NIF and represents no change in the regime.' Indeed, the Ali Osman Bashir [224] faction of the NIF is even more hardline. Nonetheless, the SPLM welcomed the events of 12 December 'as they put the struggle of the Sudanese people on a new higher and positive threshold'. That may have been true to a point, but the schism was real, though it was more personal than ideological. Bashir, wishing to outdo his rival, persevered in hurling Islamic rhetoric against Turabi. The SPLM also appealed to the Sudanese people to 'remain vigilant and use the crisis within the NIF to bring about full and real change in the country'. It also appealed to the army to move against the regime: 'They know that what might not have been possible before 12 December is now possible.' Garang, in addition, declared that the SPLM and the Unified Military Command of the NDA (which he heads) shall establish appropriate contacts and closely monitor the situation. Albeit, the schism was the end of the road for the NIF; any crack within a cultist group inevitably leads to complete rupture and explosion or implosion. The NIF, which had survived on creating cleavages among other parties, were now having a taste of their own cleavages.

Having lost the battle within the NC, Turabi soon moved to establish his own party, the Popular National Congress (PNC). Despite all the 'Islamist' slogans and rhetoric, the word Islam did not figure in the name of that party, as indeed it did not fiqure in the name of Bashir's, the NC. This equivocation was not new,[225] but this time Turabi over-excelled himself. Farcicality was at its highest, though, when he explained the reasons for forming his own party. The party's mission, he said, was to fight military dictatorship, restore power to the people and stop the deviation towards secularism.[226] Turabi's assault on Bashir became a little *de trop*, when he and his disciples engaged in washing the NIF's dirty linen in public. Blowing his own trumpet, Turabi revealed his role in securing financial support to the regime from the international Islamic movement and Iraq as well as from Anwar Ibrahim, the former Malaysian Deputy Prime Minister. Those funds, he claimed, went into the enhancement of petroleum production and arms industries.[227] His deputy, Ali al Haj, repeated the same statement, adding another accusation to his former colleagues in Bashir's camp of misusing the returns from petroleum sales.[228] He also dared them to tell the Sudanese people where the funds had gone.[229]

In lieu of accepting that their time was up, both parties in the NIF conflict went into a not-so-clever enterprise of trying to woo the opposition back to the fold, while saving as much as they could of their agenda. The Islamists reached the end of the road, but that they didn't know it or pretended not to. That reality, however, has dawned on Islamic movements elsewhere; a Cairo weekly revealed an internal evaluation document emanating from the Jordanian Muslim Brothers in which they attributed the failure of the Sudanese experiment to addiction to power and lack of a mechanism for its peaceful transfer. The Jordanians, according to the Cairo paper, maintained that schisms within the NIF would have an impact on the Islamic Movement as a whole.[230] Bashir's faction, nonetheless, came up with an unsophisticated trick to dower himself with popular legitimacy against Turabi and probably the opposition. He declared an early presidential election and dared all parties (including Turabi's) to run against him. All parties boycotted the sham election. Unsurprisingly, Bashir was re-elected but his ingenuity in rigging the elections was such that he was returned with the support of 7,750,743 voters. We recall that the totality of voters in the 1986 election (including those who voted for a unified NIF) did not exceed 5,413,642 voters. Also, in the 1986 elections the totality of those who voted for the NIF in a free and fair election was about 700,000 voters. Evidently, as in the Southern war, Bashir must have been able to increase the NIF's support 10-folds, with the help of a few million holy ghosts in Sudan's fairyland.

Bashir scored some points against Turabi in the external front; Egypt [231] and other Arab countries welcomed the move against Turabi and encouraged Bashir to do more. Turabi, on the other hand, went haywire, and accused Bashir of dictatorship (as if what Bashir had been overseeing for over ten years in cooperation with Turabi had been blissful liberalism). He also became a self-appointed advisor to the opposition. Turabi warned the opposition against Bashir by saying 'How would a man who betrayed those who brought him to power treat you?'[232] The opposition took Turabi's advice on face value, but also added: 'we don't trust you either'.

Turabi's most puzzling contributions were on the intellectual front; anchoring his neo-liberal views on Islam once again, he called for unbridled democracy since 'Allah has decreed liberty for man to enjoy it to the point of *Kufr* (unbelieving) in God or in *gha'ib* (the transcendental).'[233] Could this be the same man who engineered in 1988 and maintained afterwards in Sudan's penal laws, Section 126 which reads: 'Any Muslim who abandons the faith of Islam or declares by a categorical act that he abandons the faith of Islam is punishable with death.' But that was not the first time Turabi came up with contradictory statements on this issue; in 1995 he told Milton Viorst that conversion by a Muslim to another religion is not apostasy.[234] Evidently, the multi-shaded verses of the Quran offers Turabi, when he wishes, easy escape routes. For though the revealed words sanction *jihad* against infidels in some of its verses, as we have seen, it also enjoins Prophet Mohamed in others to give scope to non-believers. For example one verse reads: 'And say to them (O Mohammed) Gods truth has come to guide us into all truth and he who wishes to acknowledge it is free to do so and he who wishes to reject it is free to do so' (*Al Kahf* The Cave 18/29). That is why non-NIF Sudanese Muslims were not amused by Turabi's complex circularity in all matters religious. Some described his *fatwas* as *fiqh al dharura* (jurisprudence of necessity or convenience). One such case is Turabi's condemnation of *jihad* and the forcible conscription of young boys in war: 'Where is your army?' he asked Bashir.[235] And what about your old *fatwas* on *jihad*, might have been the answer of Bashir and his footmen.

Turabi's playing with the word of God reached the limit when he advised NIF militia's that the war they were fighting was not *jihad* but an unjust war in support of tyranny. Who could ever have guessed that the Pope would turn into a Luther? Indeed, in a press conference on 28 October, the unfathomable Turabi crossed the rubicon when he claimed that negotiations were afoot between him and the SPLM, because Garang was a 'unionist and the war he was fighting was a just war'. That was the same war which Turabi, since 1988, bent over backward to see consummated to the bitter end. Rather than being mute about this statement that came like a bolt from the blue, the SPLM responded in a seven-point press statement.

i. The SPLM has been negotiating with all governments of the day in Khartoum, from Turabi to Bashir. Two landmarks in those negotiations were the KDD and the Mirghani–Garang agreement,which were eventually crowned with the creation of the NDA. The NDA was Sudan's only hope for consecrating national unity.

ii. The SPLM negotiated with the leadership of the NIF, of which Turabi's group was part and parcel.

iii. After the cleavage within the NIF, the SPLM continued to negotiate with Bashir's faction and there was, therefore, nothing that hindered negotiation with Turabi's party so long as those negotiations were geared towards a comprehensive political settlement for Sudan's crisis.

iv. Turabi's new declarations condemning *jihad* and his appreciation of the SPLM's unionist vocation evinced a positive stance that could be further developed.

v. The SPLM believed that the present totalitarian system should be dismantled and replaced by a system that respected Sudan's ethnic, religious and cultural diversity. Equally the SPLM recognized political Islam as a legitimate trend with which it was ready to engage in a debate so as to achieve a national consensus.

vi. The SPLM pledged itself to achieving unity on a new basis and to holding any group accountable for their misdeeds since 1956, particularly crimes against humanity committed during the NIF era. In this, the SPLM would be guided by the NDA resolutions on this matter.

vii. The NIF's so-called civilizational project should be abandoned, since it had threatened Sudan's unity and destabilized the region and the world.[236]

Conclusion

The NIF usurped power in 1989 allegedly to save the nation from the bedlam caused by the parties. Ten years later, the NIF's salvation turned out to be Sudan's damnation. Unlike Nimeiri's imamate, the ten years of the NIF were not an episode in Sudan's transmutable history, but a failed plan to undo the country. In the process of implementing that plan, the NIF made Sudan walk ten years out of the twentieth century. The NIF's civilizational project turned out to be an adventure to civilizationize the Sudan we knew out of existence. In the whole decade of the 1990s the NIF applied all its energy to destroy institutions and extirpate from people's minds the received wisdom of the past. Their project, in essence, was not a cultural revolution, but a counter-revolution. Hence, whatever the NIF claimed to be doing in Allah's name, Muslim Sudanese thought not.

The NIF's preoccupation with *jihad* in the South and with security all over the country had devastating effects on the Sudanese economy. The main economic project for the NIF was not the civilizational project – as one would have expected – but funding war. Inflation in Sudan was in the 70 per cent range and the public debt stood at US$ 20 billion in 1999. That was more than twice the country's GNP. This economic disaster had been particularly grave for the South. 'Undesirable' Southerners were driven out of jobs and loyalty to the ruling party replaced any test of competence. On the other hand, the NIF proceeded to plunder the nation with abandon. Government contracts were no longer open to tender they only went to businessmen approved of by the party. Even established Northern businessmen were chased out of the market to the point that the rich became poor and the poor starved. The NIF established its own business network and granted it all manner of tax exemptions including exemption from customs duties. Graft thus became a structured government policy and money and religion ranked *pari passu* in the NIF's 'Islamic' Republic. Still, despite all those ungodly practices by its cadres, the NIF continued to dissemble puritanism. In such an environment *bona fide* businessmen had to pack up and leave, after having exhausted all their assets. The NIF, undeterred by this dismal picture, continued to apotheosize Sudan as Allah's heaven on earth even when feeding the citizens of Allah's commonwealth was left for Caritas, Oxfam, Norwegian Christian Aid and a host of other 'ungodly' NGOs. Famines, rather than being addressed as natural or often man-made disasters, were generally described as a wrath visited by Allah on the unbelieving. The Mahdi used the same argument in the nineteenth century, as did Nimeiri in his autumn years. One would have expected the NIF's highly educated cadres, who took it upon themselves to change the world to the better, to be more at home with the socio-economic factors that produced certain physical phenomena. There was nothing metaphysical about Sudan's economic collapse. And as if he didn't have a care in the world, their leader, Turabi, devised an improbable economic theory. In an interview with Al Jazira TV, he said that economic well-being was a psychological condition. Such were the unreal realities of the NIF's Sudan.

Turabi himself, despite all his 'Islamic' mumbo-jumbo, was clearly not an ardent believer in many of the things he was saying. His pragmatism is undisputably monumental. In his meetings in Western academic circles, he claimed that there were no abuses of human rights; that *jihad* was not what it was presented to be; that women were not segregated from men; that Islam was very tolerant to other religions and that the South could go its own way if it so wished. As for the accusation of harbouring terrorists, Sudan, he said, was only giving refuge to law-abiding Muslims. Apart from the absurdity of saying this to people who had the capacity to see through walls, repetition of those inveracities undermined Turabi's own scheme. Indeed, by telling the Western world that he was respecting all of its benchmarks – even when those benchmarks were contrary to the normative values he pleaded and the policies his regime was following – Turabi sabotaged his own civilizational project.

In the exercise of power, Turabi, like all ideologues, was disappointing, particularly to those who held him in high regard. Notwithstanding his many academic achievements and excellent training, he failed to wield power wisely. For example, wanton foreign adventures, (whether he initiated or condoned them) debilitated the regime and eventually brought Sudan to its knees. They also made the country an international pariah state. Turabi and other NIF leaders, despite advice to the contrary from many foreign quarters and friends, might have believed that they could be the playground bullies. They did not realize, or cared to realize, that high-risk lawlessness had a price that the Sudan was neither capable nor willing to pay. One reason for Turabi's excesses may have been his lack of humility. And where absolute earthly power is conjoined with transcendental claims, the line between arrogance and megalomania becomes transparently thin. Because of this, Turabi's recent conversion to democracy was not readily accepted by many Sudanese who continued to believe that the intensity with which he pleaded for democracy today, was inversely proportional to his belief in it. This may be an unfair judgement on the very versatile and pragmatic Turabi. He surely is not peerless in this type of somersault. For who would have expected that the collapse of the Leninist system would come at the hands, of all people, of the Secretary General of the Communist Pary of the USSR?

Bashir, who is no ideologue and hardly vain, is no less duplicitous. That is not an unkind remark on the man. After all, for the whole decade of the 1990s (up to December 1999), he took the country and the world for a ride by abnegating any link between his *ingaz* (salvation) and the NIF. No more evidence is thus needed to prove the man's capacity for deceit and disrespect for the Sudanese people. The test of his credibility, therefore, lies in his ability to admit that Sudan cannot suffer another decade of ignominy under the NIF. Furthermore, when the two parted ways, Bashir virtually attributed all the regime's crimes and misadventures to Turabi. But more than a year after Turabi's removal from the NIF power structures, the regime continued to sink in iniquity. Even human rights activists were not saved from the regime's brutality.[237] The UN Human Rights Rapporteur was among the first to acknowledge this.[238] Bashir, therefore, should not count on the opposition to take him at his word, nor should he hope for any reconciliation by it with the NIF while business went as usual in the Sudan, e.g. mobilizing more children for *jihad,* pretending that the problem of the South is a figment of Garang's imagination, bombarding civilian targets, arresting and intimidating dissidents including the NDA leadership in Khartoum, closing down newspapers that do not share the regime's vision and imposing censorship on others, harassing Christian priests and playing one peace initiative against the other. His situation is made more complicated by the apparent fragility of his regime in the face of Turabi's defiance. The battle with Turabi has all the makings of a long-drawn one.

It took the Russian Tsar shooting, poisoning by cyanide and dumping in the Malaya Nevka to get rid of his Rasputin. How long will it take Khartoum's tsar to get rid of his, if at all?

Bashir's salvation only lies in edging away from the unworkable muddle he has started. He should not believe that having succeeded in presiding over decline, he would be allowed to position himself to preside over collapse. Also, with the sorcerer gone from the NIF power structures, Bashir may still have to tame the sorcerer's apprentices around him. He would commit a grave mistake if he thought that all what he needed was time to calm the nerves and hoodwink the world. He would also stray from the straight and narrow if he deluded himself that he could survive with the help of Allah and, to boot, returns from oil resources. For even if he is given all the time in the world he wants on the drivers seat, there is very little that he and his NC alone can do with the skeletal remains of the country they are now governing and, appallingly, continue to pulverize. The way out for Bashir, indeed for the Sudan, is to trace his steps back to where he had taken the country from. That is the point where all Sudanese, save for the NIF, had agreed on a *modus vivendi* on 16 November 1988.

ENDNOTES

1. Anderson, Norman, *Sudan in Crisis*, p. 6.
2. Al Mahdi was in hiding in Omdurman west when the other political leaders were taken for custody from their habitual residences. So when the Minister of the Interior (Mubarak al Mahdi) took refuge in a suburb of Kharoum Mubarak was reputed to be al Mahdi's strongman. A few days later, al Mahdi sent a message to al Bashir , incredibly transmitted by his (al Mahdi's) chief of security, Abdel Rahman Farah. In that message the former Prime Minister offered to surrender to the authorities on condition that he be treated the way other political detainees were. Unmistakably, he was apprehensive that he may have been ill treated by the regime. In that message he made a puzzlingly bizarre statement. He told the new ruler that he was waiting to see whether the *coup* was nationally inspired or foreign-led (as if that made a difference in the removal of a freely elected government by a military junta). He also called for a debate between those who had popular legitimacy (himself) and those whose legitimacy rested on might. Even in the throes of adversity, al Mahdi still wanted to debate and philosophize. However, by sending that letter, the deposed ruler offered a shield of legitimacy to those who wrenched power from him.
3. Ibrahim Nayel Idam, an officer from the Nuba Mountains region, was deputy to the chief of security in al Mahdi's government. Under Bashir, he became a member of the ruling military junta and was later rewarded with a ministerial portfolio.
4. The battle cry of the Umma Party was, as now is, the ill-advised slogan *al balad baladna wa nihna assiyadha* (The country is ours and we are its masters). This is hardly the slogan of a democratic party. No democratic party committed to people's supremacy would claim dominion over the whole nation and treat its people as supplicants.
5. A member of the NSRCC, Martin Malwal was removed after he expressed disillusionment with the regime (March 1992). The regime alleged that he was sacked because of corrupt practices. However, eight years later he rejoined the government, but nothing was heard of the alleged crime of corruption. Also, the former Catholic priest George Kinga left his position as Minister of Labour while on mission to the ILO, Geneva (July 1992), and so did Aldo Ajo, the Deputy Speaker of Parliament, who defected in 1994 after having represented the regime in one of the sessions of the UN Human Rights Commission. The leading NIF Northerner to leave the NSRCC was Osman Hassan Ahmed who was reported to have been Bashir's rival for the chairmanship of the junta council. Ahmed reportedly left the council in view of the inordinate role of the NIF in government.
6. *Sudan Monitor*, vol. 14, February 1994.
7. According to a reliable Sudanese investigative journalist, 73,640 civil servants were dismissed by the NIF in the period June 1989 to

September 1993, while the total number of civil servants pensioned off from the colonial days (1904) to 1989 when the NIF assumed power did not exceed 32,419. Ahmed, Sir Sid, *Al Shark Al Awsat*, 19 May 2001. On the other hand, based on statistics compiled by the Arab Lawyers Association and American Lawyers Committee on Human Rights, eighty per cent of the judges in office at the time of the NIF *coup* were purged within two years. An-N'aim: *Reforming Islam*, p. 64.

8. *Al Shark al Awsat*, 14 December 1999. Also following his dismissal as Secretary General of the National Congress (26 June 2000), Turabi told the Arabic service of the BBC (29 June 2000) that he had engineered the NIF *coup*, recruited Bashir and camouflaged his action in order to 'hoodwink the Americans and the communists'. In a pointed threat to Bashir, he told the BBC that he was capable of doing the same thing again.

9. The first cells of Muslim Brothers were formed by Sudanese graduates of Egyptian universities who joined the Brothers in Cairo, particularly in the mid-1950s. For details on the evolution of the *iakhwan* see el Affendi, *Turabi's Revolution*, pp. 48–68.

10. Turabi studied law at the University of Khartoum and completed his graduate studies in the Universities of London and Paris. Thereafter he joined the teaching staff of the Faculty of Law in Khartoum University. Both as a student and teacher he had an unblemished academic career.

11. Mohamed Mahdi 'Akif, represntative of the Intenational Islamist Movement in Europe, told an Arabic weekly that the movement disapproved Turabi's *modus operandi* and did not share many of his views. *Al Wattan al Arabi*, 2 April 2001.

12. In the course of those blandishments, Turabi married the daughter of the Imam of the *Ansar,* sister of Sadiq al Mahdi. In addition to ideological affinity that brought the two closer together, Sadiq might have thought to exploit Islmists activists for his own ends. However, the astute Turabi had other plans. He was reported to have told one of his confidants that the 'fool' (meaning Sadiq) thought that may only purpose in marrying his sister was to become a minister in his government.

13. Turabi, H., *Al Haraka al islamiyya, fil Sudan*, pp 144–8.

14. Karawan, Ibrahim, *The Islamic Impasse*, p. 7.

15. Idowa, Bolajc, *African Traditional Religions*, p. 2, op. cit.

16. Qotb, Sayyid, *Ma'alim fil Tarig* (Sign posts on the Pathway). Qotb, alongside two of his colleagues (Abdel Fatah Ismail and Mohammed Yousif Hawash) was executed by Nasser for 'seditious' activities. Amazingly, Qotb cooperated with Nasser in the early years of his rule as an education adviser to the Revolutionary Council.

17. Maududi, A.A., *Towards Understanding Islam*, p. 107.

18. Exegetes and expounders of the Qur'an like al _abari and al *Shafi'e* interpreted some verses of the Qur'an as a licence to Muslims to spread enlightenment on the whole world. One such example were

Suras 31 and 32 in *Al Tawba* (Repentance): 'They wish to quench the light of God by word of mouth but God shall continue sending his illumination until enlightenment has prevailed, albeit this be hateful to non-believers. It is he who has sent his apostle with the spirit of guidance and true faith that shall succeed all other faiths, albeit this is hateful to polytheists'. That view was shared by Ibn Taimiyya who justified *jihad* even against hypocrites (non-believers who feign Islam). *Al Siyyasa al Shariyya.*

19. *Ma'alim* , 16 supra, p. 144. Qotb effectively called for the rejection of all Western tools of analysis because they would blur one's vision to understand Islam properly.
20. *Ma'alim* virtually became the political manifesto of the Islamists in the Middle East and, together with Maududi's printed words, their main works of reference.
21. Lawrence, Bruce, *Chattering the Myth*, p. 153.
22. Since the mid-1970s Muslim countries such as Algeria, Egypt, Malaysia and Indonesia coalesced with non-Muslem countries in Asia, Africa and Latin America to challenge the inequities of the prevailing international economic order in fora like the Group of 77 at the UN, UNCTAD and the Non-Aligned Movement.
23. *Al Wasat*, 24 July 2000.
24. *Al Hayat*, 4 October 2000.
25. *Al Hayat*, 7 February 2001.
26. Eltheridge, Jaimie, *Fundamentalism on the Wane*, Special Report to ABC News com. 17 November 2000.
27. Bonner, Raymond, The *New Yorker*, 13 July 1992.
28. *Al Majala*, 23 March 1997.
29. Turabi told an Arab journalist that his son was studying in Sudan but a member of the family took him to study in Britian. Interview by Ghassan Shirbil, *al Shark Awsat*, 5 March 199. That response did not address the issue the journalist wanted him to explain: Turabi's decision to bar other Sudanese students from studying in the West in order to save them from western cultural pollution. Surely, he did not send his own son to Western universities to be culturally 'polluted'.
30. A number of the present NIF leaders were trained as part of the National Front forces in *Kufra*, Libya (Ghazi Salah el Din, Ibrahim el Sanousi. Mahdi Ibrahim). The National Front was originally established by Sharif al Hindi (DUP) and the remnants of the supporters of the late Imam of the *Ansar*, as a political opposition force against Nimeiri with no defined ideological tag.
31. Turabi is one of the founders and key advisors of *Dar al Mal al Islami* based in Geneva. *Dar al Mal* is the external holding company of Faisal Islamic Banks.
32. *Al Shark al Awsat*, 3 July 1988.
33. The NIF started planning the *coup a* few years before it took place. Hassan Mekki, a leading member of the NIF *Shura* Council (the highest NIF consultative body) affirmed that the idea of a military

takeover had been mooted since 1969. *Al Khartoum,* 19 February 2000.

34. In an interview by *Newsweek,* 3 June 1996, Turabi said that his role was to mobilize religious energy for economic and political development, social unity, democracy and justice. He added that he wanted to play a role in the world: 'You've to contribute something original otherwise you'll become nobody, only following some other model.'

35. 'The moral justification of adherence to the principle that the majority view should prevail in public affairs, is that the minority must have the legal and practical opportunity to become the majority so that its view may one day prevail. For this to be possible, the majority and minority should not be constituted in terms of permanent incidental factors, such as race or gender, which an individual person is unable to change.' An-N'aim, Abdullahi A., *Constitutional Discourse,* p. 99.

36. Interview by *Al Khartoum* with Hassan Mekki, 19 February 2000. Mekki represents, within the Brothers, a group of flexible Islamists who advocate a more accommodative political Islam. However, in the euphoria evoked by their success in June 1989, even this group acquiesced to some of the most heinous and un-Islamic excesses perpetrated by their 'Islamic' regime.

37. Warburg, G., *Discord,* op. cit., p. 143.

38. Within a cultural historical context, even the so-called pre-Islamic *Jahiliyya* was not as dusky and recondite as it is portrayed in the Islamist literature. Heathen as it may have been in their estimation, the *jahiliyya* also produced for Arabic culture some of its finest poets and dissertators.

39. Evans-Pritchard, E.E., *Theories of Primitive Religion,* p. 6.

40. In a preface to one of Francis Deng's novels (*Cry of the Owl*), `Abdullahi An-N'aim, a respected Muslim scholar (presently Professor of Law at Amory University), wrote: 'beside confronting me with my own ignorance of this profound tradition so close to home ... I came to a greater appreciation of what you mean when you say that the so-called animists of the Sudan are as religious, if not more so, than the adherents of Islam and Christianity'. Warburg, *Discord,* op. cit., p. 172.

41. *Keyhan,* Tehran, 24 April 1992.

42. Hurst, David, *Dark Times Loom for Visionary Sudan,* The *Guardian,* London, 26 May 1997.

43. Bonner, Raymond, *Letter from Sudan, The New Yorker,* 13 July 1992.

44. Interview by Bill Berkley, *New York Times Magazine,* 3 March 1996.

45. Havel, Vaclav, *Living in Truth.*

46. Miller, Judith, *Faces of Fundamentalism, Foreign Affairs,* November/December 1994, p. 137.

47. An-N'aim: *Reforming Islam,* p. 25.

48. Lewis, Bernard, *The Political Language of Islam,* pp. 25–6.

49. An-N'aim, *Civil Rights in the Islamic Constitutional Tradition,* pp. 282–3.

50. Islamists frequently seek inspiration from particular classical works

on al *Siyassa al Shar'iya* (religion-based politics) to vindicate their contemporary political constructs. All those works, to a large degree, were written to legitimize authoritarianism or to validate competing claims over power. For example works by al Mawardi (*Al Ahkam al _ultaniya*) and Al Ghazali *(Na_ihat al Mul_k)*.

51. Abu Nasr Al Farabi, *Ar_a ahl al Mad_na al Fadhila.* Farabi's contribution to political philosophy and his pre-eminence in the field compared to so-called Muslim political scholars, was ably analysed by President Khatemi in a series of lectures recently published under the title *Al D_n wa al Fikr fi Fakh al Istibdad* (Religion and Thought in the Trap of Authoritarianism). Khatemi averred that with the death of Farabi the age of reason in the field of political philosophy came to a close.

52. Works by Avecina and particularly Averoce's *Jawami'a Siyyast Aflatoun* (Summa of Plato's *Politics*).

53. The fundamental sources of legislation in Islam are the *Quran*, the *Hadith* (sayings verifiably attributed to the prophet), *ijtihad* (literally the term connotes endeavour, but here it refers to endeavours by learned men to identify Islamic solutions to emerging problems on the basis of the first two sources). *Ijtihad* is central to the *Suni* creed.

54. Miller, Judith, 46 supra.

55. *Al Anba'a,* 11 July 1999, Khartoum.

56. 'In modern constitutional terms the Prophet was the original sovereign and sole human source of law and political authority.' An-N'aim, *The Contingent Universality of Human Rights,* p. 279.

57. Within its historical frame, of reference, the society of Madina had shown tolerance to Christians and greater tolerance to Jews, much more than old Christian societies have had done.

58. An-N'aim, *Reforming Islam,* p. 25.

59. Ibid.

60. Abdullahi An-N'aim opines that this sanctuary or safe-conduct defines the status of the beneficiaries in terms of the reason of their temporary stay in the territory of the Islamic state'. It did not bestow on these non-Muslims political rights similar to those enjoyed by Muslims, let alone contemporary rights in the light of the Universal Declaration. *Constitutional Discourse,* p. 105.

61. '*Shari'a* is not the totality of Islam ... [it] is simply the version of Islamic law developed by early Muslim jurists who interpreted the sources of Islam for their own time and place, as distinguished from the sources themselves.' An-N'aim, Ibid.

62. In effect 'while *shari'a* is essentially religious, it is also profoundly secular in that it deals with the orderly and proper conduct of Islamic society and from its very beginning it has dealt with practical problems.' Lobban, Carolyn Fluehr, *Islamic Law and Society in Sudan,* p. 2.

63. Asked by Alain Chevalérias about laicté, Turabi said that he did not oppose it because in Islam there was neither a church nor a religious

hierarchy that challenged the state. As such, Turabi said, the Islamic state is laic. When asked by Chevalérias about Iran where a religions hierarchy assumed political and constitutional powers above those enjoyed by the head of state, he evaded the issue by saying that Sudan was not a *Shiite* country. As for his own role in Sudan, Turabi said that he was not a Pope, but only a thinker who endeavoured to show the way of God. Islam, *Avenir de Monde*. pp. 87–9.

64. See Taha, M.M., *The Second Message of Islam*. The book was translated into English by A. An-N'aim. See also Afif, Bagir al, *Toward an Islamic Reformation*, in *Ruwaq Arabi and* Lobban, Fluehr, 62 supra, p. 247.

65. Turabi continued to gloat over Taha's execution, even after Sudan's Supreme Court had posthumously quashed the sentence against him on 11 November 1986. In a statement to a Khartoum paper Turabi said: 'I have totally no regrets that Taha was executed.' This is hardly the language of compassion and forebearance that epitomizes Islam. *Al Watan*, Khartoum, 30 April 1988.

66. For example, in the field of penal law the Quran ordained a retributive system of justice *(lex talionis)*, while in other fields it included injunctions that would be disadvantageous to women and non-Muslims in the laws of inheritance, evidence and constitutional rights. On the latter, a restrictive reading of those edicts would preclude non-Muslims and women in general, from *Al wilaya al kubra* (high public offices) including the presidency of the state.

67. See Chapter Four (debate on the Islamic Constitution in 1968). Turabi's views on the disqualification of non-Muslims from the assumption of the presidency of the republic was based on a restrictive interpretation of *shari'a* which reserved that right to adult male Muslims.

68. An-N'aim, *The Contingent Universality*, p. 270.

69. Ibid.

70. The Preamble to the Universal Declaration of Human Rights. General Assemly Resolution 217 A, III. Adherence to the Declaration is a condition precedent to admission of any government to the UN.

71. Bielefeldt, Heiner, *Muslim Voices*, p. 591.

72. An-N'aim, *The Contingent Universality*, p. 272.

73. Ibid., p. 591. The writer correctly maintains that revolving human rights on Christian tradition, as some Christian writers presume is problematic since the universality of those rights 'becomes tantamount to the universal religious mission of Christianity'.

74. Ricoeur, Paul, (ed.) *The Philosophical Foundations of Human Rights*, Introduction.

75. Mill maintained that barbarians had no right as nations except the right to be converted to civilization, *A few words on Non-intervention*, op. cit., Mazrui in *The Philosophical Foundation of Human Rights*. As for Engels, he blatantly welcomed the French occupation of Algeria because, in his view, it would allow Algeria, Tunisia and Moroco 'to enter upon the path of civilization'. He further said that, although

those countries are 'nations of barbarians who look very proud, noble, glorious at a distance' they are still 'ruled with the lust of Cain'. Article for the *Northern Star* (English Chartists publication), Vol. XI, 22 January 1848.
76. 74 supra, Mohamed Àllal Sinaceur.
77. An-N'aim, commentary on New Islamic Politics, Faith and Human Rights in the Middle East, *Foreign Affairs,* May–June, 1996.
78. Ibid.
79. In a seminar in Washington (1993) Turabi, contrary to the letter of the Qur'an and traditional *shari'a,* declared that a Muslim woman had the right to marry a non-Muslim. That statement caused a furor in Sudan and Saudi Arabia. Nonetheless, in his *Risala fil Mara'a* (Message on Woman), a small booklet published in Sudan in 1973, Turabi evaded this issue as well as other issues relating to women's rights in inheritance, law of evidence and political participation.
80. The Islamic law of evidence glaringly abridges the rights of women. For example, women are denied testimonial competence in criminal law, while in civil actions evidence by a male witness can only be rebutted by that of two women. Turabi gave the most absurd explanation to that abridgment when he told an interviewer that the stipulation was justified by women's physical limitations, e.g. pregnancy or menstrual cycles. Those conditions, he said, might hinder their appearance before justice when they were called upon to make a diposition. Chevalérias, p. 38.
81. In the mid-1990s a former *shari'a* judge (Sheikh Majdoub Kamal el Din), a respected ophthalmologist (Abdel Gadir Hassan Ishag) and the son of former prime minister Mohamed Ahmed Mahjoub, were publicly flogged on a framed charge of drinking. The three were known for their opposition to the regime. Paradoxically, the Attorney General, who prosecuted the three and was a close friend of Turabi, was known to be a notorious boozer.
82. Magdi Ishag Ahmed, a Sudanese mental health doctor, retold his personal experience when he served at Kober Prison. In a letter circulated through electronic mail (Sudan@listserv.cc.Emory.edu), stated that all those who were subjected to amputations ended with some form of psychiatric disorder: depressive disorders or antisocial personality disorder. The doctor wondered and asked a very pertinent question: 'Why anytime they [the Islamists] talk about the implementation of Islamic rules, the first thing their attention goes to is flogging and imputations.' Ironically, Omar ibn al Khatab, the second caliph after the Prophet, froze the punishment of amputation which was explicitly provided for in the Qur'an when famine stalked the land. He argued that in a period of penury and destitution, theft might be tolerated.
83. *Al Majala,* 23 March 1997.
84. Interview by James McKinley Jr, *New York Times,* 10 March 1996
85. Ibid.

86. 'Ghost houses' is the popular name given to secluded security houses that were used by the NIF security agencies for detention or torture of political detainees. One of the visitors to those houses, a professor of Botany in the University of Khartoum, wrote to Bashir describing the ordeal he had gone through during his two weeks of incarceration. Professor Faroug Mohamed Ibrahim took Bashir's recent liberalization measures on face value and thus appealed to him to investigate the harrowing experiences he had gone through, naming his persecutors, of whom some occupied ministerial positions in Bashir's government. *Al Khartoum*, 19 November 2000.

87. Though the international media and many human rights workers equated that practice with genocide, there were still doubts in the minds of others whether the NIF's ethnic cleansing constituted genocide within the meaning of the 1948 Convention on the Prevention and Punishment of the crime of Genocide or its Implementation Act which requires 'the specific intent to destroy, in whole or in substantial part, a national, ethnic, racial or religious group as such'. Report by the US Commission on International Religions : Religious Freedom in Sudan, China and Russia, May 2001, p. 7.

88. Dr Gaspar Biro, a Hungarian jurist, was appointed on 30 March 1993 as a UN Human Rights Special Rapporteur in Sudan. On completion of his mission, Leonardo Franco (Argentina) replaced him to follow up his work. Franco, in turn, was replaced by Gerhart Baum (Germany).

89. In that report, Biro concluded that 'all Sudanese citizens living in the areas controlled by the government of Sudan are potential victims of human rights violations and abuses'. The report called on the government 'to bring an end to the violations and to hold the perpetrators responsible'. Those admonitions were consistently ignored by the government according to Biro. P. 64.

90. Surur was evidently under imminent threat in view of his non-cooperation with the regime. Before his detention (12 September 1993) Surur met Biro who cautioned him to keep out of harms way by being careful about who he met and what he said. Biro, 1993 Report, p. 15.

91. Bonner, Raymomd, *Letter from Sudan*, 27 supra. Turabi repeated the same view in a seminar at an American University (104 infra). When asked about imposing an 'Islamic' dress on women, he responded that Islam did not enjoin women to wear a specific dress, but that dress was only *mustahab* (commendable).

92. Ibid.

93. The divine call for *al amr bil m'arouf wa al nahi 'an al munkar* was addressed to the Prophet: 'Those who acknowledge the mission of the unlettered Apostle and which they [people of the Book] find inscribed in the Torah and the Gospel. He shall enjoin them equity and forbid evil…' (*Al A'raf*, 7/157). However, this command was repeated in other verses of the Qur'an (*Al 'Imran*, 3/104, and 110 and *al Tawba* 71.

The Prophet was also reported a *hadith* to have commanded Muslims who come across a *munkar* (objectionable or forbidden act) to rectify it. It is on the basis of those cautionary words and Qur'anic signals that groups claiming to be engaged in *al amr bil M'arouf* had mushroomed in Saudi Arabia under the Wahabites. In Sudan, though, the censurable Munkar addressed by those groups was strictly limited to drinking, alleged unchastity and acts of assumed debauchery. Pervasive poverty alongside the existence of islets of superfluity, corruption of rulers and excessive repression of citizens in a so-called Islamic state, were matters of no concern to the Islamists 'do-gooders'. This gainsays the trustworthiness of those groups. In reality they are nothing but tools of intimidation against 'undesirable' opponents. Their function is neither to uphold Islamic values, or cleanse the society from vice, but only to protect state interest or overawe and humiliate opponents through framed up charges.

94. Chevalérias, Alain, p. 43.
95. *SUNA*, Khartoum, 14 January 2001. Bashir, despite urgings by Karin Shan Poo, Deputy Director of UNICEF to ratify the agreement, refused to budge, claiming that the convention contradicts 'national traditions'.
96. Sections 59, 60 and 133 of Biro's report, E, CN4, 1994.
97. *Al Khartoum*, 2 February 1994, the *Washington Post*, 26 March 1994.
98. The *Washington Post*, 26 March 1994.
99. DNA/QA/Rapporteur/64, Khartoum , Ministry of Justice, 29 December 1993.
100. Professor Adlan Hardalo, Interview by Julie Flint, Africa Report, May 1995 Vol. 40, Issue 3, p. 34. Similar incidents were reported in Ahliyya University, Omdurman; Gezira University Wad Medani etc.
101. In one of Machiavelli's advices to the Prince: 'Men ought to be treated well or crushed, because they can avenge themselves of lighter injuries of the more serious ones they cannot'.
102. 91 supra.
103. Sudan's would-be Beria was presumed to be on a sabbatical leave to pursue studies in agriculture. It never dawned on anyone in either the government or the university, that Teheran was not the most obvious place for the pursuit of studies in agronomy. That was the degree of laxity and ineptness in government that made the NIF triumph without really trying.
104. Lecture on Islam, Democracy, the State and the West, World and Islam Studies Enterprise, University of Florida, Tampa, 1993.
105. *IHT*, 5 August 2000.
106. Berkely, Bill, 44 supra.
107. Drinking *araki* (an alcohol made from dates in Northern Sudan, and sorghum in other parts of Sudan) is extensive in the Muslim North, probably excepting the *Beja* region. More extensive is the drinking of *marissa* (an intoxicating brew based on sorghum) all over the riverain North and the West. The Dar Furians call it *Kira* of which a milder

brew known as *rututu* is drunk by the *fuqaha*. Surprisingly, alcoholic drinks are not traditionally known among the Nilotes of the South.

108. Boys and girls in those tribes, who are destined to marry each other, are allowed to sleep together once they have reached the age of puberty, the only caveat is that the girl should not be impregnated by her suitor.

109. *Al Khartoum,* 18 November 2000.

110. The term was artfully concocted by Turabi, claiming its derivation from Quran so as to give an Islamic veneer to his so-called multipartism. Turabi posited this concoction on a Quranic edict reflected in a number of *suras,* e.g. 'Those who conformed to Islam and emigrated to where they would best serve God with their wealth and their souls are *awliyyau baad ihim'*, i.e. joined one to another in mutual intimacy. *Al Anfal,* (The Spoils of War) 8/72. But wherever the term *awliyyau* (people joined together), was cited by Quran in a commendable sense, reference was made to the believers. In effect the Qur'an textually proscribed any *tawali* between Muslims and non-Muslims (*Al Maida,* (The Festive Table) 5/51 and 57.

111. The Congress was initially called the Popular Islamic Congress but subsequently changed to Popular Arab Islamic Congress after the incorporation, within in its members, of two die-hard Palestinian radical politicians (George Habbash and Nayef Hwatmeh), both Christians. Their inclusion pointed out clearly that the main objective of the Congress was not Islamic revival, but the destabilization of the region through a medley of angry men.

112. The inaugural meeting of the Congress was attended, along with Turabi, by General Bashir; Abbasi Medani (Algeria); Rachid al Ghanoushi (Tunisia) and Mahdi Ibrahim (NIF). Report by the Task Force on Terrorism and Undercover Warfare, House Republican Research Committee, US House of Representatives, 3 February 1992.

113. The nucleus comprised twenty-five Algerians and ten Tunisians detailed for political action in France; twelve Algerians and eight Tunisians for Belgium; five Algerians and two Tunisians for Holland, in addition to thirteen Egyptians dispatched to work among different radical Islamist groups in Europe. Ibid.

114. Libyan Muslim Brothers Fayez Mohamed, Juma'a Ali Ramadan, Abu Zuluk and Kamal Shami met with Turabi to discuss strategies for the military takeover. The meeting was attended by two NIF cadres, Mahdi Ibrahim and Taj al Sir Mustafa. Report of the Task Force, p.11.

115. Bonner, Raymond, 27 supra. Amazingly, Turabi confided to Bonner that he was once part of a CIA covert operation against Qaddafi during the Nimeri era. No denial of that report was ever made by Turabi.

116. 104 supra.

117. Stone, Barbara, *ABC News,* Washington, 10 August 2000.

118. During the Iraqi invasion of Kuwait, the NIF organized rowdy demonstrations in Khartoum in support of the invasion and against the US and her 'treacherous' Arab allies. The slogan incessantaly

shouted at that demonstrations was *ila al amam ya Saddam, min al kwait ila al Damam*; ('forward, forward Saddam, from Kuwait to Dammam'.)

119. Miller, Judith, 46 supra , p. 219.
120. 91 supra. That was the time when the NIF welcomed the Saudi dissident Usama bin Laden. Conjointly, the regime's disdain for the monarchy was publicly expressed in the NIF-sponsored demonstrations during the Gulf War; the street shouts by NIF activists were both racist and abusive: *Yahood, Yahoold Al Saud* (Jews, Jews, Saudi family).
121. Peterson, Donald, *Inside Sudan*, p. 179.
122. Ibid.
123. Interview by Hamdi Rizq, *Al Musawar*, Donald, November 24 1999.
124. Turabi told a London Arabic daily that 'Egypt is today experiencing drought in faith and religion … [but] Allah wants Islam to be revived from Sudan and flow along with the waters of the Nile to purge Egypt from obscenity', Al *Shark al Awsat*, 6 July 1995.
125. *Reuters,* 9 July 1995. Turabi's threats impelled Egypt's Minister of Works and Water Resources to describe him as irresponsible. *Akhir Sa'a*, 13 July 1995.
126. Bonner, Raymond, 43 supra.
127. Ibid.
128. The Mastricht treaty made popular sanction through a referendum mandatory for adhesion by any country to the community.
129. General de Gaulle was reported to have said that Europe is France and Germany, *'la reste c'est la garniture'* (the rest is simply a decoration). Nonetheless none of the two countries assumed to be the driving engines of European unity applied its comparative advantage to impose unity on its terms.
130. The NIF was accused by Uganda of supporting a shady Muslim group *Tabligh* (conveyance of divine message). After several notices served on Khartoum, Uganda severed diplomatic relations with Sudan and curtailed the activities of Islamic relief organizations. The NIF's complots in Uganda made Kenya wary. It imposed strict controls on all Sudanese visiting the country and eventually moved against Islamic charity organizations after the bombing of the US embassy in Nairobi allegedly by a bin Laden group. The Kenyan action, however, was not unjustified. As it transpired later, the representative of those charity organizations in Kenya, Dr Mutrif Siddiqs, emerged as a senior officer in the NIF's intelligence community. In addition, in late January 2001, Kenya deported six Sudanese citizens claiming to be businessmen, on the strength of evidences that proved their association with bin Laden. According to Prosecutor Horace Okume they were 'dangerous people linked to international terrorist'. *AP*, 26 January 2001.
131. The LRA struggles to take over government and establish in Uganda a system of rule based on the Ten Commandments. For details see Ofcansky, O., Warfare and Instability along the Sudan–Uganda Borders, in *Black Blood*, pp. 195–208.

132. President Museveni told the *East African*, (13 March 2000.) why mediation efforts had failed. 'Southern Sudanese are being oppressed and made second class citizens ... and when black people run away, we cannot throw them out ... there are 300,000 of them in Uganda. When they are fighting inside their country for their freedom, Northerners want us to blockade them. If they want to blockade them they should blockade them from the North', said Museveni.

133. *Reuters*, 26 January 2001.

134. *Xinhua*, 23 March 2001. The EU mission comprised Ambassadors Luigi Napolitano (Italy) and Hans Anderson (Sweden). However, as a concession to President Qaddafi, the Ugandan President agreed in May of the same year to resume diplomatic relations with Sudan at the level of chargé d'affaires.

135. The *Johannesburg Citizen* reported the matter on 25 January 1995 under the headline 'South Africa's role in Sudan civil war'. Nearly a year before, the South African press published a statement by the spokesman of Armscor in which he confessed to the collaboration between Sudan and Armscor with the knowledge of South Africa's Ministry of Defence. *Business Day*, Johannesburg, 30 March 1994.

136. The name of a certain Mr Siraj, a second secretary in Sudan's Mission to the UN, was mentioned as a collaborator in the plot to bomb the UN headquarters building in New York. No sooner had his name appeared in the media, than he was spirited from New York under the cover of his diplomatic immunity. Siraj was rewarded by the NIF with an appointment as the chairman of the Human Rights Committee in the NIF parliament. The NIF's cynicism knew no bounds.

137. Bin Laden established a number of commercial outfits in Sudan that were involved in multifarious activities: a financial organization known as *Wadi al Aqiq*, an agricultural company called al *thimar al Mubaraka* (blessed fruits), a corporation involved in the tanning industry and another engaged in road construction. All the so-called economic corporations collapsed financially, or indeed withered away after having served their purpose as a conduit for funds to finance terrorist activities. In a recent report by a leading London Arab daily, the financial manager of bin Laden's establishments in Sudan (Abu Hajir al Iraqi), was arrested in Munich and handed over to the US authorities in view of his alleged participation in the bombing of the US Embassies in Nairobi and Dar-es-Salaam. According to the report, Abu Hajir was an alias, his real name being Mamdouh Mahmoud Salim, and he used to travel on a Sudanese passport. *Al Shark al Awsat*, 19 November 2000.

138. Defendant Jamal Ahmed al Fadl (who turned into a star witness) gave a detailed discription of bin Laden's activities in Sudan including the importation into Sudan of rockets from Afghanistan, smuggling of weapons through Port Sudan to Aden to fight South Yemen's 'communists regime', financial support to the Eritrean Islamic Jihad, training of military cadres in Damazin on the Blue Nile etc. However, one of his most startling confessions were about bin Laden's attempts to

acquire uranium smuggled into Sudan and a joint programme with the NIF to produce chemical weapons. The defendants named Colonel Abdel Basit Hamza of the Sudanese army as the NIF's counterpart in that operation. Besides, he revealed to the court the existence of written instructions from Bashir ordering customs authorities to allow unimpeded passage for all imports in the name of bin Laden's companies.

139. *Al Shark al Awsat*, 16 February 2001.

140. Christopher's memorandum stated that the decision 'reflects an assessment of facts, not a bias against Sudan because of the ideological or religious orientation of its government'.

141. In addition to several cautionary notes by US diplomats in Khartoum, notices were also served on Sudan by Ambassdor Robert Houdek, Deputy Assistant Secretary for Africa and US Ambassador to the UN, Madleine Albright, when she visited Sudan on 31 March 1994.

142. US Ambassador Donald Peterson wrote that, 'Turabi believed that the world shall accept the inevitable … Our discussion didn't indicate that the Sudanese really understood the depth of our difference'. Peterson, Donald, *Inside Sudan*, p. 15.

143. Reeves enumerated the regime's crimes against humanity, especially ethnic cleansing, targeting civilians in war and deliberately destroying schools, hospitals, relief feeding centres etc. the *Washington Post*, 15 August 2000.

144. 104 supra.

145. Ibid.

146. Samuel Brittan, in a lecture to the Jewish Society at Oxford, challenged the myth that Christianity was much gentler than Islamic fundamentalism. He drew attention to the mild treatment by Islamic kingdoms in medieval Islam to Jews in Spain, while Christians who conquered that country put to the sword all those who did not accept their religion. In that connection, Brittan quoted Elijah's order against the priests of Baal: 'now go and smite the Amalikites and utterly destroy all they have and spare them not: both man and woman; infant and suckling, ox and sheep, camel and ass'. *The Spectator*, 25 March 2000.

147. *Al Maida* 5/51. Similar verse are to be found in *Al 'Umran* 28, *Al Tawba* 23, *Al Nisa* 144, *Al _nfal* 73.

148. An-N'aim, *Islamic Ambivalence to Political Violence*, p. 325.

149. *Rai al Àm*, 10 June 2001. That declaration came at the height of the war fever in Khartoum, triggered by its military defeat in Western Bahr el Ghazal.

150. 74 supra, p. 243.

151. In its first years in office, the NIF organized a major conference to map out its strategy for remaking the Sudan. One of the conclusions of the conference was that *jihad* against internal and external threats is a religious obligation in a system based on subservience to Allah', Minutes of the National Founding Conference for the Political System

(April–May 1991), Khartoum.

152. Biro, 1997 report, p. 13.

153. Hurst, David, the *Guardian*, London, 26 May 1997.

154. Since 23 September 1957, Sudan became party to the four Geneva Conventions of 1949 encompassing humanitarian rules on armed conflict.

155. *Tarikh al Tabari*, translated by Bernard Lewis, *The Multiple Identity*, p. 76. Lewis noted that while Abu Bakr was tolerant to monks, he was decidedly against tonsures.

156. Middleton, Mel, *The Report on Line Story*, 31 January 2000.

157. Biro reported the dolorous story of Camilio Odongi Loyun, an elderly former army officer from the South,who was persuaded by the NIF to join in the *jihad* against his kith and kin. When he refused to do so he was 'tied to the bars of a window with his arms and legs apart. A rope with a noose was then tightened around his testicles and was beaten to death'. Biro, 1993 report, p. 13.

158. Africa Rights compiled an extensive report on this subject after a field mission to the area. According to the authors of the report 'the government's intentions are clear, it is involved in a war to culturally cleanse the Nuba and do so by physical liquidation if necessary' Facing Genocide, the Nuba of Sudan. Report by R. Omaar and Alex de Waal, 1995, p. 193.

159. Hunud Abia Kadouf, Nafir, *Newsletter of the Nuba Mountains*, January 2000.

160. On 27 April 1993, a *fatwa* (religious edict) was issued by imams in El Obeid mosque in a meeting held at the Popular Committee Hall (seat of the NIF-based local government). The *fatwa* ruled that the lives of 'infidels' in Kordofan who opposed *jihad* should not be spared and their children, property and wives were free for all Muslims. Also, Muslims who sided with those infidels were deemed apostates who should receive the same fate. *Sudan Update*, 4:21, 8 October 1993.

161. *The Sunday Nation*, Nairobi, 7 January 2001.

162. In the Name of God, Human Rights Watch, Africa. vol. 6 no. 9, November 1994.

163. Winter, Roger, The Nuba People, in *Black Blood*, pp. 183–194.

164. Sudan Invisible Citizens; the Politics of Abuse against Displaced Persons in the North, Africa Rights, 1995.

165. Biro reported the existence of five camps in different locations in Sudan, i.e. Abu Radom, Faroug and Jaz near the Rahad scheme, Durdeib in Eastern Sudan and Hantoub across the Blue Nile from Wad Medani.

166. The issue was raised at the UNESCO Seminar on the Culture of Peace, The Hague, Holland, 20 May 1996.

167. Quantifying Genocide in Southern Sudan and the Nuba Mountains (1983–98) complied by Millard Burr, US Committee for Refuges, Washington DC.

168. Ibid., p. 12.

169. Sudan Catholic Information Office (SCIO) reported the dropping of 12 bombs on Nimule school killing, one and injuring 12, which was witnessed by a German church delegation. The attack hit the Episcopal church and reduced it to rubble. Aerial attacks on civilians were also reported in Yirol, Kotobi and Kaya on the Sudan–Ugandan Border. *East African Standard*, 4 April 2000.

170. White House Press Office, Washington DC, 15 February 2000.

171. Dancy, Shelvia, C2000, Religion News Service, 21 February 2000. Bishop Makram called on his colleagues and the media not to hide their heads in the sand and describe what was happening in Sudan as merely a political issue. The situation in Sudan, he said, was no less disastrous than that in Kosovo.

172. Amin, Stephen, *African News*, Issue 47, February 2000.

173. Charles Omondi (SCIO), Ibid.

174. In July 2000, 14 bombs were dropped on an airstrip used by the ICRC. Shrapnel penetrated the tail of a plane belonging to that organization. Horn of Africa, IRIN Update, 18 July 2000. Shockingly, the government accused UN planes of ferrying arms to the 'rebels'. The accusation invited protest by all NGOs operating under OLS. The NGO issued a statement condemning the bombings and adding that 'the specific targeting of NGO compounds and both OLS and ICRC planes, which have legally negotiated access to South Sudan, has had a significant impact on the level and quality of aid being distributed and is in direct violation of international agreements'. The 'NGO members of the OLS consortium have a strong philosophy that includes neutrality, impartiality and transparency', said the statement.

175. *The East African Standard*, Nairobi, 9 August 2000.

176. The US Committee for Refugees reported on 30 March 2000 that aerial bombardments of civilian targets, hit nine targets within a couple of months Those were Comboni Primary School in Kauda (Nuba Mountains) on 7 February; The Samaritan Purse Hospital at Lui (South Sudan) 7 March; Concern World-Wide Relief Centre at Yirol (South Sudan), 6 March; Samaritan Purse Hospital again, 7 March; Voice of Martyr's Hospital, 14 March; The Diocese of Torit Hospital at Nimule, 14 March; Displaced Persons Camp at Kotbi (South Sudan), 25 March and the Samaritan Purse Hospital for the third time on 23 March. US Newswire, www.refugees. org, March 2000.

177. A report by a US NGO drew attention to the astounding coincidence that the MSF's clinic in Kaju Keji was targeted ten times by the NIF regime in 1999, the same year MSF was awarded the Nobel Prize for Peace. *Temoinage* (witnessing) is part of the mission of MSF and accordingly they regularly report human rights violations, displacements and genocide crimes. Religious Freedom in Sudan, China and Russia, Report by US Commission on International Religious Freedom, 1 May 2000.

178. Baido, Anthony Lo, *World Net Daily. Com*

179. Though the EU countries made an issue of the alleged use of children in SPLA camps in the course of the meetings of the UN Commission on Human Rights in Geneva (April 2001), they were wary of denouncing aerial bombardment of civilian targets in the South. Astonishingly, a programme to deal with the issue of children was already under way under the aegis of UNICEF. The SPLA has admitted that hundreds of children were to be found within its camps, not as combatants but as aids carrying out non-military duties. It also told concerned NGOs that the children were either orphans or separated from their families because of war and had no place to find solace other then military camps. Accordingly, the SPLM called upon NGO' to facilitate the children's integration with their families (if those could be identified) or take charge of them with a view to providing them with better living conditions. UNICEF undertook that responsibility. No similar action was taken by the government regarding aerial bombardment of civilians up to that date, with or without NGO intervention.

180. Harding , Andrew, *BBC News,* 21 April 2001.

181. The *Balitmore Sun*, Gilbert A Lewthwaite and Gregory Kane, 14 June 1996. Interview with Faraj allah wad Mattar, a Rizeigat tribesman.

182. Ibid.

183. *Reuters,* 19 January 2001.

184. Tales of Slavery Contradicted by Sudan Diplomat, the *Baltimore Sun,* 16 June 1996.

185. 104 supra.

186. Àbdullahi conquered Nubia and concluded with its Christian King the *Baqt* agreement (probably from the Latin word *Pact*) to regulate relations between the Islamic Caliph in Cairo and the Christian Nubian kingdom. According to that agreement, the Nubians were to remain in their religion but, in return, they were to provide the Caliph with 336 slaves annually by way of tribute, one for each day of the year. The *Baqt* stipulated that the slaves should comprise women, obviously for purposes of concubage. Since slavery was unknown to the Nubians, they often failed to abide by the terms of the agreement, which led to their subjection to several punitive raids from the North.

187. Chevalérias, p. 31.

188. Verney, Peter, *Slavery in Sudan,*

189. Bassiouni, Cherif, Enslavement as an International Crime, *New York University Journal of International Law and Politics*, vol. 23, Winter 1991, pp. 445–517.

190. Rassan, Yasmine, Contemporary Forms of Slavery and the Evolution of the Prohibition of Slavery and Slave Trade under Customary International Law, *Virginia Journal of International Law*, vol. 39, Winter 1999, pp. 305–6.

191. The *Baltimore Sun, Washinton Post, Corierra dela Sera, Guardian* etc.

192. *Sudan Human Rights Quarterly* No. 9, February 2000.

193. Gedda, George, *AP*, Washington, 3 May 2001.

194. Chaddock, Gail Russel, The *Christian Science Monitor*, 5 October 2000.
195. Ibid.
196. Ibid.
197. Raspberry, William, The *Boston Globe*, 4 October 2000.
198. Revd Walter Fauntroy, former Congressional delegate, talk-show host Madison and Hudson Institute fellow, Michael Horowitz, chained themselves to the entrance of the Sudan Embassy on Good Friday, 13 April 2001. Madison refused to post bail and remained in jail for the weekend. They appealed to others to engage in similar action 'for however long it takes' till the Bush administration do something to change Sudan government's policies. Mufson, Steven, The *Washington Post*, 14 April 2001.
199. In a statement to the Washington Post he said: 'We've got left and right, black and white. We've got white evangelists and civic rights activists. We've got white evangelists and civic rights activist. We've got people like Sam Brownback and Dick Armey and Charlie Rangel. At a news conference Rangel came on and said that in his thirty years in Congress this was the first time he had been on the same platform with Armey on anything. Raspbery, William, The *Washington Post*, 7 May 2001.
200. *AFP*, September 2000.
201. Human Rights Monitor Leonardo Franco recommended that Sudan government should be prevailed upon to cease support to militias, prohibit raids against civilians, punish perpetrators of abduction of persons and establish a joint Sudan–international mechanism for the purpose of tracing abducted persons and allow investigation into all cases of slavery. Report to the 53rd session of the Commission.
202. Biro Report 1997, p. 18.
203. The report recalled Article 1 of the 1926 Slavery Convention and Article 1 of the 1956 Supplementary Convention on the Abolition of Slavery, Slave Trade and Institutions and Practices Similar to Slavery, e.g. serfdom, delivery of children to others for the purposes of exploitation etc ECOSOC /E/CN/4/1995. Sudan is signatory to those conventions and was, therefore, bound by their stipulations.
204. UN, A/55/374, 11 September 2000.
205. For example, in a recent poll in Brazil conducted by the Center of United Marginalized People, 87 per cent of the Brazilian whites polled denied that they were racists. At the same time, the majority of this group admitted in the same poll that race was a societal problem. Commenting on the results of the poll, the Executive Secretary of the Centre, made a piercing remark: 'Apparently we are fighting an invisible enemy' International Herald Tribune, 13 June 2000.
206. In 1964, Abeid Karume and Abdel Rahman Babu led a rebolt by the descendants of African slaves against the ruling Afro-Arab masters, the Busaidis. The uprising was marked by wanton killings and alleged gang rapes of 'Arab' women.
207. *Al Shark al Awsat*, 12 December 2000. Sadiq al Mahdi also accused the

US of being the prime mover of that policy.

208. The revolt in Zanzibar was one of serfs against their feudal overloads; race was not the issue. When President Nasser was asked by some Gulf Arabs to intervene in favour of the deposed Sultan, Nasser replied: 'You do not expect a man leading the struggle for African liberation to support feudal lords against their thralls'.

209. *New York Journal American,* 1962.

210. Cohen, Robin, *The Making of Ethnicity,* p. 9.

211. Flint, Julie, *Africa Report,* May 1995, vol. 40, p. 34.

212. *Al Qods al Arabi,* 4 August 2000.

213. El Affendi, *Al Thawara wa al Islah al Siyyasi,* p. 234.

214. El Affendi: *Al Islam wa al Dawla al Haditha* (Islam and the Modern State), p. 38.

215. Ibid., pp. 174–5

216. The *Economist,* 19 August 2000. Talking about one of Bashir's ministers whose name was not divulged by the magazine, Turabi said that the man was 'a time-server, pathetic figure, a mere clerk, ambitious, weak', then intriguingly added: 'Al, he is still close to us.'

217. *Qibla* is the direction towards which Muslims turn during prayers. Before Muslims were commanded to turn to the direction of Mecca for prayers, their *qibla* was Jerusalem. Indeed Islam recognized both historical Judaism and Christianity as well as the holy books of the two religions: the *Tawrat* (Pentateuch) brought by Moses, the *Zabour* (Psalms) brought by David and the *Injil* (Gospels) brought by Jesus. Muhammad also stated that he was not establishing a new religion, but his mission was a confirmation of the old religions (all attributed to Abraham) and a closure of all divine missions. Al Mahdi, in his cryptic way, was thus calling for unity between Muslims and Christians. This scheme, evidently, does not include Sudanese who do not belong to either faith.

218. The London *Al Qods Al Arabi* reported at the time that the new post was to be offered to al Mahdi while Turabi would assume the presidency, in the French style. If that happened, the paper continued, 'Umma and NIF shall rule Sudan forever'. Al Mahdi, however, had often urged his colleagues in the NDA to adopt the French system in the post-Bashir Sudan, but his urgings were rejected.

219. The system initiated by General De Gaulle worked well when both the legislature and executive were controlled by the same party. Cracks in the system always appeared when the opposition controlled the legislature, as was the case under President Mitterand (conflict with Prime Minister, Balldur) and later during the Chirac presidency (conflicts with Prime Minister Jospin). Mitterand coined the term *cohabitation* to describe the uneasy relationship between the two branches of the state. As a result of this awkward system, France became the only country within the European Union where the head of state and head of the executive combine in one person. Evidently, France was able to weather political conflicts at the top because of its

strong and able civil service; there is nothing of the sort in Sudan.

220. Nixon, Richard, *In the Arena*, p.

221. *Suna,* 11 December 1999.

222. *Suna,* 12 December 1999.

223. Ibid.

224. Turabi, in fact, accused Ali Osman M. Taha, the First Vice-President and his deputy in the NC, of masterminding the coup. The NIF's media support of the Turabi faction portrayed Taha as Turabi's Judas Iscariot.

225. Turabi paid a visit to Uganda in his capacity of Deputy Prime Minsiter (during Sadiq's rule) to represent the government on the occasion of the anniversary of Museveni's ascension to power. The Ugandan President sarcastically presented Turabi as the head of a party of which he was not qualified to be a member because of his religion. To that statement, Turabi retorted that his party, the National Islamic Front, had advisedly given precedence to its national over religious character.

226. *Al Bayan*, Dubai, 28 June 2000.

227. *Al Shark al Awsat*, 20 July 2000.

228. *Al Khartoum*, Cairo, 18 July 2000

229. *Al Khartoum*, Cairo, 16 July 2000.

230. *Al Qahira*, 11 July 2000.

231. Foreign Minister Amr Musa told a Saudi paper: 'we are accused of supporting the recent move by Bashir.. we actually do, but we do not interfere in Sudan's domestic affairs' *Okaz*, 18 December 1999.

232. *Al Shark al Awsat*, 13 June 2000.

233. *Al Shark al Awsat*, 22 December 1999.

234. Viorst, Milton, Fundamentalism, in Power: Sudan's Islamic Experiment, *Foreign Affairs*, 74 No 3, May/June 1995. In that statement Turabi told his interviewer that: 'If a Muslim wakes up in the morning and says he doesn't believe any more why that is his business.'

235. *Al Shark al Awsat*, July 2000.

236. Statement by SPLM spokesman, Yassir Arman, 30 October 2000.

237. In January 2001, lawyer Ghazi Suliman was arrested and kept *in communicado* for nearly two months. During his incarceration he was beaten on the head by the NIF thugs guarding him leading to a concussion from which he only partly recovered after 12 days. By treating in this way Suliman, the foremost human rights worker inside Sudan, the regime was saying loud and clear that none was immune from its wrath.

238. Gerhart Baum, the new UN Human Rights Rapporteur stated that there was a wide gap between the written laws and declared policies and the reality in Sudan. *Al Hayat*, 13 March 2001, and AFP, 12 March. Baum was also denied permission to meet with Turabi in prison.

PART FOUR

Toward a National Identity

CHAPTER EIGHT

The Conundrum of Sudanese National Identity

> *The Sudan holds Africa's destiny in her hands. If she can succeed in reconciling the two elements in her own population, she will have done a piece of constructive pioneer work for the continent as a whole. If the conflict in the Sudan becomes acute and chronic, this will heighten the tension between the two Africa's everywhere and, sooner or later, the South Sudan will become a focus for Negro Africa's latent resentment against North Africa.*
>
> *Arnold Toynbee* [1]

Introduction

Geophysically, modern Sudan is an immense plain through which the Nile snakes from south to north. The Nile, in more than a metaphysical sense, is an umbilical cord that joins the heartland of Africa to the north of the continent and the Mediterranean. To the north, Sudan roughly lies between the capital city, Khartoum, and the Egyptian border, a sparsely inhabited harsh land of desert and semi-desert. To the middle is situated the area which is drained by the two Niles, the Blue and White, and is of a somewhat milder climate. In a general sense, this is the homeland of the Arabicized Northern Sudanese, although the area is also home to other non-Arabicized Muslims: Beja in the East, Fur, Zaghawa, Masalit etc. in the West and Funj tribes in the Southeast. To the South is to be found a wetter, less accessible and swampier region inhabited by the Nilo-Hamitic Sudanese, the majority of whom adhere to African belief systems. In addition, it has to be borne in mind that Sudan is a vast country, the largest in Africa[2] and probably the African country with the most extensive racial, religious, cultural and social intermixtures. Sudan, therefore, cannot be deemed to be a product of one culture. Those prolific intermixtures, together with its abounding natural endowments, should have made of Sudan a model country in Africa, if they were harnessed for the good of its people and other peoples in the continent. Woefully, the Sudanese remain a divided people with enduring ethnic, linguistic and cultural dichotomies. For that division, the Sudanese have no body to blame but themselves.

As regards racial composition, both the Arabicized Hamitic Northerners and the Negroid or Nilo-Hamitic Southerners would each present itself as a thoroughbred race with a high level of homogeneity. This is a fallacy. Northerners and Southerners, to one extent or the other, are hybridized. The issue has been abundantly debated by scholars from both the North and South,[3] but while a lot of the arguments adduced, and the images evoked are potent, they often elude the main issue. Sudan's conflict since its inception had more to do with political and economic hegemony than with ethnicity, whether that was biologically determined or fictitiously contrived. From its inception, the Southern struggle has been one for political and economic empowerment. Nevertheless, the issue of ethnic identification became a factor in North/South relations, the moment belonging to a particular ethnic origin evolved into a tool of legitimizing historical hegemony by one group (the riverain Northerners) over the others (people of the peripheries), the majority of whom happened to be non-Arab. This was not the case with the universalistic Islamists in the North who should be credited with transcending ethnic barriers in the allocation of roles in public life. This was as true of the first Mahdism (the second Mahdism developed into a self-perpetuating dynastic plenipotency), as to some degree with the NIF. Ethnic origin, for instance, was never a barrier to political promotion during the *Mahdiyya*.[4] If any thing, Mahdism was denounced by its riverain Northern leaders for its alleged favouritism towards the hitherto marginalized people of the West.[5] In the case of today's Islamists, ethnic origin, by and large, has not been a determinant factor in elevation of party workers to the higher power structures of the NIF, notwithstanding complaints by the Dar Furians about subtle favoritism towards riverain Northerners in the apportionment of high offices. This was revealed in a document circulated by that group and entitled *al Kitab al Aswad* (The Black Book).[6] Scandalously, one of the recurrent recriminations against Turabi by his detractors – even those within his own party who hail from the riverain North – was his alleged *itijahat unsuriya* (racist tendencies). That is an euphemism for Turabi's embracing and promotion of the *gharaba* (Westerners) within the NIF power structures.[7] If that was the case, then Turabi, with all his assumed political misdeeds, was being flailed for one of his few saving graces.

However, the problem with both the *Mahdiyya* and the neo-Islamists lay in their use of religion as a tool of both identification and apportionment of rights and duties. This has led to another kind of marginalization based on religious affiliation. The NIF's tolerance towards Muslims, irrespective of their ethnic origin, did not extend to non-Muslims. Consequently, Southern non-Muslims suffered under both Islamist and quasi-secularist regimes. For if they were derided by some Northerners in the past as inadequate for certain jobs because of the 'backwardness' from which they needed to be uplifted, they were also reviled by Islamists as 'pagan' and ungodly. Their conversion to Islam, therefore, became an act of redemption. Paradoxically, it was precisely this patronizing messianism that frightened away Southern non-Muslims from Islam, especially during the *Mahdiyya* and the NIF era.

The case was different when submission to the faith was voluntary and uncoerced.

Reputably, ethnic groups, whether in the North or South, stake claims to their identities based on subjective notions of inborn excellence and superiority. Nonetheless, myths of racial superiority in the North might not have been as threatening had it not been for their deleterious consequences. Foremost among those consequences was the assignment of roles in society on the basis of a predetermined ethno-cultural stratification that through time perpetuated inequalities. Those inequalities were buttressed and justified by an elaborate cultural infrastructure saddled with its own myths about the self and the other. Ergo, a whole subculture and value system developed around this insidious stratification. That subculture developed its own aphorisms intended to give credence to the claim that certain people were only made for certain jobs. Imagine! *Sajam al hilla al dalila abid* (woe on a village whose steersman is a slave); or *al a'bid kūlū ma zad 'umru qalat qīmtu* (the older the slave gets, the less prized he becomes). Those aphorisms may have been put up with during the slavery era as appurtenances of that disreputable institution. Not so when they are wantonly purveyed in relation to those who are set down as descendants of slaves long after the slavery era. The myths of superiority, however, were hardened by policies that were in no way devised to unravel the myths, but on the contrary to sustain them.

Sudan: A State or a Nation?

But before delving into defining the ingredients of the Sudanese *national* identity, it will be appropriate to explore whether there is at all a Sudanese nation. In common parlance, the term nation is frequently taken to be synonymous with a state. This confusion goes beyond plebeian talk; even major international political institutions come in for a share in it. As Connor[8] observed, even the principal world organization which is essentially a confederation of states was baptized the United *Nations*. Remarkably, the UN Charter itself was conceived as a peoples' charter, not a charter of nations or states. Its preamble commences with: 'We the People of the United Nations'. However, in furtherance to our earlier reference to the issue of nationhood (Chapter Two), there is need to elaborate on the question of nationalism as a defining mark of identity. Political science dictionaries make a clear distinction between nations and states.[9] On the one hand, a state is defined as a 'legal concept describing a social group that occupies a defined territory and is organized under common political institutions and an effective government'. On the other, a nation is defined as a 'social group which shares a common ideology, common institutions and customs and a sense of homogeneity'. Based on this definition, it would appear that nationalism, as an ideology or a group behaviour, is basically a subjective notion, i.e. a notion based on individual choice propped up by a fervid imagination. But inherent in nationalism, there are also objective attributes. The state, on the other hand, is both a legal concept and a political institution that is defined solely by objective politico-legal criteria. Anthony Smith[10] describes a nation as 'a named human population sharing an historic territory, common myths and memories, a mass public culture, a single economy and common rights and duties for all members'. On the other hand, he defines a state as a 'public institution of coercion and extraction within a recognized territory'. How do all those considerations apply to Sudan.

As we have shown in Chapter One of this book, a state that brought the totality of the country within the purview of its control had existed since the time of Mohamed Ali. But as we have also endeavoured to explain in previous chapters, peoples within that state were never allowed to mutate naturally into a nation. Sudan's disparate peoples remained separated by deliberate policies of division, hegemony, sustained attempts of domination by one group over the others and in earlier days the syndrome of master/slave relationship. This process continued even in the post-independence era, despite the tiresome drumming up of *al mwatana* (citizenship) as a unifying force. Clearly, for *al muatana* to have any meaning, diversity in all its forms must be recognized and not only tolerated. It should also be given expression in policies, laws and practices. David Miller[11] succinctly defines three conditions for this to happen:

i. The political sphere must be purged of procedures, symbols and norms which embody the values of the group that have hitherto dominated it.
ii. Groups should participate in the political realm on an equal basis and should be encouraged to affirm their distinct identity and perspectives.
iii. The policies that emerge from the decisionmaking forums should be sensitive to group differences.

A citizenship that is not inclusive and does not come with tangible benefits is meaningless, Miller affirmed.[12]

Like all dominant groups who marginalize other groups, the Northern political class and elite every so often justified their assumed right to dominate others in the name of majoritarian politics. However, the term 'majority' is a statistical term that carries no meaning without being pegged to a specific frame of reference, e.g. racial origin, religion, economic status etc. And where there are competing claims regarding identity, this frame of reference cannot be subjectively determined. As An-N'aim rightly observed: 'Nations usually subsume many nations, some of whom dominate and oppress others and the ideal of integration and unity often imply the assimilation of minority peoples (who may be, in aggregate, the numerical majority of the population of the state as a whole) into the dominant culture.'[13] Besides, in majoritarian politics (whatever definition one gave to that majority), countries that were plagued with diversities such as Canada (linguistic diversity), India (religious and cultural diversity), Nigeria (ethnic, cultural and religious diversity) and Lebanon (religious and sectarian diversity) would never have been able to remain united. In Sudan, majoritarianism has always been raised as a justification for the dominance of Arabo-Islamic culture over the rest of the country. But even if one conceded that imposed assimilation was accepted in the past as a tool for achieving unity, things had drastically changed in the contemporary world. Sudan is now obligated by both international and regional covenants to which it had adhered, to respect certain principles concerning the rights of 'minorities'. For example, Article 27 of the International Covenant on Civil and Political Rights states that 'in those states in which ethnic, religious or linguistic minorities exist, persons belonging to such minorities shall not be denied the right, in community with the other members of their group, to enjoy their culture, to profess and practise their own religion or to use their own language'. Also Article 22.1 of the African Charter on Human and Peoples Rights affirms that 'all peoples shall have the right to their economic, social and cultural development with due regard to their freedom and identity and in equal enjoyment of the common heritage of mankind.' The Northern Sudanese political class and elite can no longer behave as if they are not part of the world, or that they can trample with impunity on international conventions.

Roots of Ethno-politics in Sudan

Admittedly, as Francis Deng suggests, if the concept of identity in Sudan entailed a simple tag, an objective label by which people were known, the road towards creating a stable and united nation would have been considerably shorter. But after Deng; 'Identity is not always a descriptive portrayal of neutral facts, but often a judgemental designation with consequences on one's place in society. It is a starting point to understanding who gets what, occupies what position or plays what role in the political, economic, social and cultural life.'[14] This situation, *de rigeur,* gave rise to the emergence of 'complex ethno-politics, ... in which political leaders seek to control the actions of members of their ethnic group and to affect the relative power and position of their group *via-à-vis* others.'[15] In turn, the 'others' did not only challenge the existing political superstructures, they also looked askance at the infrastructure that sustained them. Moreover, they played on the basest instincts of their own ethnic constituency, summoning up the worst memories of the past: the slavery era. Looked at objectively within its historical framework, slavery was an expression of imbalances in power. But such cool analysis and understanding is not possible in the presence of residual manifestations of the slave culture reflected in the supercilious attitudes that are subtly demonstrated (and sometimes without pretence at subtlety), by one section of the society against another. Rarely if at all, do Northerners muse upon the relevance of such attitudes to Sudan's political crisis, or contemplate the contribution that forswearing those odious attitudes shall make to the creation of an enabling environment for the two parts of the country to live together in peace. The issue of ethnicity, therefore, became germane to Sudan's political conflict and started to occupy an important place in contemporary debate.

What matters for the purposes of our thesis is, first, the scars that slavery has left glaringly etched in the collective memory of Southerners. And second, the insensitivity of Northerners to the pain that those scars had left in the psyche of Southerners. Those memories would not have survived for so long were it not for the aforementioned attitudes passed down to modern-day Northern Sudanese, and reflected in overt and covert actions and utterances. One such example is racial slurs. Racial slurs are, of course, as pervasive in Northern Sudanese parlance as they are in the South. In the North, however, they are ascribed to others according to the colour of their skin, regional provenance or ethnic origin. For example, Sudanese with a very light skin (probably having their roots in Egypt or Turkey) are often referred to as *'hallabi'*, i.e. gypsy. Northern nomad pastoralists are surprisingly depicted by townees as 'Arabs' (meaning by that Bedouins), while those who hail from western Sudan are dismissed disdainfully by riverain Northerners as *'gharaba'* (Westerners). As for those who belong to the South or Nuba Mountains, they are habitually disgraced with the term *'abid'*, i.e. slaves.

Abominable as they are, racial slurs are not uncommon to all cultures and are inadvertently exchanged behind the back of their objects even among persons who should normally be immune from racism. Segal describes the pervasiveness of this cowardly behaviour as the institutionalization of hypocrisy.[16] Things become different, however, when the slurs and innuendoes categorically exhibit remnants of slave culture. As such, they recall in the minds of their objects a history they wish to forget, history of ancestors who were bought as chattel in chains and equated to animals.[17] Today, it is those slurs and the vision that informs them – more than direct affront – which makes the 'slaveable' frazzled and vulnerable. Consciously or subconsciously, Northerners never think of their degraded brethren as Sudanese citizens with equal political, cultural and social rights like themselves. Their culture is dismissed as unworthy, their legitimate political aspirations are considered overblown and their desire to have a say in the affairs of the nation is mocked at as pretentious. In effect, the Arabicized Northerners are scarcely mindful – as Muslims – of Prophet Muhammad's admonition to the *umma* in his farewell sermon: 'No Arab has any priority over a non-Arab, and no white over a black except in righteousness.' Also, once in a month of Sundays do they remember the Qur'an counsel on coexistence among peoples: 'Oh mankind, we have created you male and female, and appointed you races and tribes, that you may know one another. Surely, the noblest among you in the sight of God is the most God fearing of you' (*Al Hujurat* 49/13). Whatever way you look at it, therefore, the attitude of Arabicized Sudanese Muslims towards indigenous black non-Muslims (and sometimes Muslims) is not only racist, it is also basically anti-Islam.

Not even the tortured expression, *al mwuatana*,[18] we reaffirm, could cover up this racist state of mind. Northern politicians and researchers who have down-played the issue of slavery and its remnants in contemporary society may have found an easy alibi for this amnesia in the mischief caused by missionaries through their hypocritical sponsorship of the issue of slavery. The question was thus uncritically dismissed as a contrivance by missionaries, if not a shadow without substance. The question was never asked, why did that issue abide and why the effects of slavery endured for so long in the collective memory of large groups in the South. In other parts of Africa, the memories of this ugly page of history had almost faded away and became mainly a matter of interest to historians. One reason is certainly false pride to own up to past misdeeds of our forefathers. But one shall not be off target to say that the most important reason for the inveteracy of the phenomenon is the perpetuation of myths about superior master races and inferior enslaveable ones to justify a syndrome of subjugation.

Frequently, the author was asked by supposedly right-thinking Northern friends: 'Do you really expect Garang to be President of Sudan?' Apart from the fact that the author is not in the business of deciding for the people of Sudan who shall rule them, the question is rich in overtones, particularly when it comes from people who had suffered gladly all manner of fools at the helm of government, both under Northern civilian and military leaders. Clearly, the question uppermost in the questioners' minds was neither good governance nor personal qualities and attributes of leaders. It was about the 'inferior stock' of the presumed aspirant. In the particular case of Garang, in all likelihood, the questioner's foreboding may have also had another reason for it beside the man's origin and faith:[19] the iconoclastic nature of his vision. Garang, surely, cut through the mumbo-jumbo of *muuattana* and *wahdat al watan* (unity of the homeland) to reach out to the real meaning of the term and its implications on political, social, economic and cultural policies.

The slavery phase of North/South relations could have been complaisantly overlooked by Northerners in general as a passing phase in the country's history and treated by Northern historians as a footnote in that history, as some have done,[20] if post-independence governments had succeeded in erasing historical and contemporary injustices. Having failed to do that, there was no way for that shaming page of Sudan's history to be extirpated from today's political debate, especially when its barefaced vestiges accosted their victims every day. It is, therefore, in the interest of both peace and unity that the Sudanese face the issue head on. This, perhaps, is what prompted Francis M. Deng's felicitous expression: 'It is not what is said but what is unsaid that divides.'[21] This indifference to the sordid antecedents of the North/South relations endured, despite the cautionary remarks made since the Juba conference by political pace-setters. Those pace-setters, whose role has not been sufficiently highlighted by political historians, were obviously racked by self-doubt. Because of their moral integrity, they were able to come out clear on the issue of historic slavery and the fears it continued to engender among present day Southerners. They were few and far between, but their contribution should be underlined, not least to point out that it was not for lack of alternative options that the ruling class of yesteryears took the perilous route it had taken.

Who are the Sudanese Then?

As demonstrated earlier, the ruling establishment in the North and a large section of the Northern elite were inimical to Sudanese cultures other than the Arabo-Islamic to which those cultures were deemed inferior. To make things worse Arabism, in the minds of its political protagonists, was often defined (or seemed to be defined) as a racial lineament, not a cultural procurement. In a multi-ethnic and multicultural country, such parochialism is both stultifying and misplaced. Also, relativism in matters cultural is, generally speaking, ill judged. All people take pride in their culture, no matter what the others think of it. Like Europeans in general, Arabs have historically sneered at African cultures and caricatured them as crude and unrefined. To the European eyes and ears, African art is naive, its music cacophonous and its dance lascivious.[22] Culture, obviously, has more to it than highbrow *belles letters*. It is a complex whole that encompasses a man's whole universe of knowledge and wisdom including belief systems, customs, normative values, social structures, religion, visual arts, music and dance, fables, oral traditions and indigenous sciences.

The older Sudanese elite, by and large, visualized African cultures in the same light as Europeans and classical Arab writers perceived *al Sudan* (blacks). To all appearances, they may have sought to create a Sudanese trans-ethnic identity based on the 'superior' Arabo-Islamic culture and reinforced by processes of education, public information and Islamic proselytization. However, the excessive zeal with which that policy was prosecuted, not only worked against its implementation, but also proved the worst fears of the South. Fancy this! 'Sudan is an Arab country and whoever does not feel Arab should quit.'[23] This injudicious enunciation was made by a Sudanese minister in the first parliament in response to a request by a Southern member in the same parliament for the adoption of English as the official language of the South. The minister's statement was not only flauntingly offensive, but also unwarranted.[24] It is to statements like this that Southern commentators often hark back. More direful was the emanation of such a statement from the minister of education. Two years after that ominous statement by Sudan's minister of education, African ministers of education, at the behest of UNESCO, adopted at Addis Ababa the Convention against Discrimination in Education (1960). That Convention guaranteed minorities the right to establish their own educational systems and teach in their languages, 'without preventing them from understanding the language of the community as a whole'. The Convention, therefore, not only protected the different groups cultural attributes and peculiarities within a community, but also upheld the community's right to consolidate its unity through a common language. Those nuances have no doubt eluded cultural hegemonists within Sudan's elite and ruling class. In reality, by recognizing people for what they are and respecting their cultural attributes, as Francis Deng maintained after the Addis Ababa agreement, people 'are more willing to adopt the cultural pattern of the people with whom they interact than they would otherwise'.[25]

Contradistinct from all other Arab countries, Sudan is the only country in the Arab region where 130 indigenous languages are spoken.[26] Those languages survived even among people who were among the first to be Islamicized in Sudan, e.g. Nubians and Beja. In all other Arab countries, excepting those in North Africa where pockets of Berber language and culture still exist and Iraq where Kurds maintain their culture and language as a distinctive badge of identification, indigenous languages were for all practical purposes obliterated. Even in Egypt, a country known before Islam as the country of the Copts, the Coptic language had ceased to have a role in everyday life. That country was extensively Arabicized after the Islamic conquest and more so after the fall of the Abbasid dynasty in the hands of the Tartars when thousands of Arab families were reported to have migrated to Egypt. The process continued under the Fatimids and the Ayyubids. By that time, not only Copts but also the Berbers, Kurds and Circassians living in Egypt were totally Arabicized. No such process took place in Sudan, despite the conversion of the totality of Northern Sudanese to Islam.

However, Sudan is not the only multilingual nation in the world. The approach of other multilingual nations to linguistic pluralism may, therefore, be instructive. For example, neither the US constitution nor that of the old Soviet Union contained a clause on a national language. Nor did the Italian constitution up to 26 July 2000.[27] On the other hand, a number of multilingual countries, irrespective of the numerical weight of linguistic groups, have adopted more than one official language: English and French in Canada, French, German, Italian and Romansch in Switzerland and 17 languages alongside English and Hindu in India. But for whatever reason, both rulers and elite in Northern Sudan behaved as if Sudan was unique. They seemingly assumed that it had nothing to learn from the rest of the world. And while one may find an excuse for the older intelligentsia who only saw non-Arabs with a gaze of cultural superiority, no excuse is readily available for today's ruling and intellectual elites. Indeed, the modern elite has no reason to be oblivious to the resolution of the OAU Summit in June 1985 (to which Sudan was a party) relating to the development of African languages and building a feeling of worth to them. Nor should they be insensitive to UNESCO's decision in 1995 (dubbed the year of illiteracy) on the encouragement of indigenous languages as a medium for combating illiteracy. Effectively, the UNESCO African Regional Bureau in Dakar cited more than one hundred African languages (including Arabic) that may readily be used as media for education. Also in January 2000, top African writers, led by the OAU, met in Asmara, Eritrea, to deliberate on African languages and culture in the twenty-first century. Out of that meeting emerged the Asmara Declaration on African Languages and Literature which reaffirmed the 'legitimacy of languages and their entitlement to acceptance as critical components of the African character'. Their preservation, according to the Declaration, 'is a prerequisite for African unity and socio-cultural evolution'.

Africa has in reality known indigenous cultures that had evolved into recognizable civilizations, e.g. Nubia, Kanem, Mali, Songhay, Ghana, Benin etc. Those cultures were endowed with the four basic elements that constituted a civilization: a system of social organization, art, religion and laws. European scholarship was not only unmindful of those cultures, but it also treated Africans themselves as the retarded children of the world. This racist perception was principally held so as to justify domination. It was not a mistake, misunderstanding accident of human error or deviation from proper norms of behaviour, as Davidson maintained.[28] Davidson attributes the European perception of Black Africa as a moral justification for dominance by Whites over Blacks. It is in this light that we also see the outrageous condemnations of Blacks by Arab historians like Ibn Khaldoun, otherwise the eminent Muslim historian would not have held such a view that went completely against the teachings of Islam. Given all those racist and domineering impulses that helped form the European and early Arab perception about Black Africa, it is astounding to see Northern Sudanese partaking of the same perception. Nonetheless, it is to the contribution of those undervalued cultures to human civilization that Africans look back in glory. Amilcar Cabral equated cultural rejuvenation with national liberation struggle. Addressing a UNESCO meeting in 1972 he had this to say: 'African culture has taken refuge in its villages, in the forests and in the souls of the victims of oppression. It has survived all trials and, thanks to the struggle for liberation, it has regained the capacity for new life. The struggle for liberation is not simply a consequence of culture, it also determines culture.'[29] To one's disbelieving surprise, African sociocultural evolution remains to theme to which the Sudanese Northern elite often pledge adherence. But like in the case of the *muwatana*, it is only a lip-service adherence. Perplexingly, the attitude of this elite to the cultural claims of the 'Africa' in their midst (South Sudan) reveals that their recognition of Africa's cultures as much as that of cultural diversity within Sudan is a sham. Over and above, the disparagement of any culture tells more about the disparager than about the disparaged culture.

But not all Northern Sudanese politicians of the post-independence era were contaminated with this misguided self-satisfaction. For example, the Secretary General of the SCP, Abdel Khaliq Mahjoub, in a discourse on the question of nationalities, called for the development of indigenous languages and their adoption as a medium for education.[30] A scholar who shared Mahjoub's vision credibly maintained that the pre-eminence of the Arabic language should be determined by its cardinal role in real life as a medium of trade, communication and social interaction amongst Sudan's disparate peoples, and not by constitutional stipulations that may be marred by chauvinistic supremacist undertones.[31] People rationally and voluntarily choose the most appropriate medium for intercommunication among themselves. For example, Nigeria with its 400 languages and dialects settled, of its own volition, for English as its *lingua franca*, in view of its pervasive use by Nigerians. Also, *Swahili*, a language that was greatly influenced by Arabic, was chosen by East Africans (particularly in Kenya and Tanzania) as their *lingua franca*. However, attempts by any group to impose its language on another group would ineluctably backfire. At times it drives people to absurd extremes in their reaction. For example, as an expression of their revulsion of russification, the Azerbaijan, Turkmenistan and Uzbekistan nationalities turned to Latin characters instead of Cyrillic, while the Tajikistan chose to replace Cyrillic by Arabic characters. Even in the United States, which is one of the most culturally homogeneous societies, new waves of immigrants who voluntarily adopted American culture as their own are now claiming a place for their ancestral cultures within that country's cultural matrix. An education expert directing ethnic-cultures' schools attributed the move as a reaction to America's very vocal English only movement.[32]

In Sudan, Arabic had historically dominated the Sudanese economic, social and cultural landscape. No natural or man-made barrier was powerful enough to stop processes of natural osmosis. That was, first, because of the advantage bestowed by that language on people in their day-to-day life. Second, the mind of man is a thoroughfare through which bodies of opinion, formulated beliefs and thought processes flow unhindered. Talking about Sudan, Douglas H. Johnson pertinently said, 'the formidable geographic barriers which hinder movements of armies, flotillas and caravans were no hindrance to the movement of people and even less to the flow of languages, cultures and ideas'.[33] The hopeless attempts by missionaries and colonialists to curtail Arabic in the South should have been proof enough to the protagonists of forced acculturation of the futility of their efforts. In effect, the process of cultural diffusion and permeation was often times achieved through subtle non-politicized processes, e.g. music and songs. How right was John Voll when he said: 'In the long run ... the future of Sudan rests on the ability of the Sudanese to transform unstable balances into a more national synthesis. The poets and musicians lead the way. It remains to be seen whether the political leadership, both in the government and opposition can follow the lead of artists.'[34] Arabic culture would be in a good stead if they did.

Be that as it may, attempts to obliterate Sudanese cultures – other than Arabic – proved to be counter-productive. In a multicultural country that wished to be united, policies adopted by one group deliberately to obliterate the cultures of another group invariably lead to a cultural *pro partia* and insularity by the other. As history has it, cultural nationalism wherever it has originated always 'assumed manic dimensions.'[35] Given the economic and political injustices they suffered, Southerners, we repeat, no longer viewed the use of Arabic in the South for what it had always been at the level of the common man: a medium of communication with other Sudanese in daily life and a rich African language in its own right. To their mind, it has become the language of a domineering North which was using it as another tool of hegemony. The vulnerability of Southerners to all things 'Arab' was, therefore, enhanced by imprudent cultural policies. Though we firmly believe that the Arabic language can and should play a cardinal role in the country's cultural homogenization as it has done through the ages, we also postulate that cultural unity cannot be achieved through forcing uniformity; only by allowing diversity to flourish and cross fertilize would cultural homogenization be achieved. Homogenization is not hegemonization. In reality, it was the intellectual mutation of cultural differences that gave the culture of the North itself a special Sudanese character.

Identity in Sudan, however, has generally been shrouded in genealogical myths: myths of pedigree, parentage and bloodlines. Those myths played an important role in defining ethnic identity in both North and South Sudan. Within the two regions there were visible forms of identification such as dress, skin colour and names, that distinguished one group from the other. In general the 'creation of boundaries between the self and the other was an important aspect of building and reinforcing an ethnic identity'.[36] Even so, genealogies in Sudan, according to Cunnison, were not static; alterations in them were characterized by 'elision of generations, the merging together of collateral branches, the incorporation of total strangers, the exclusion of groups who, having moved away, are no longer relevant'.[37] In spite of those dynamic changes among groups, the myths of genealogical purity persisted. Among the Arabicized Sudanese, some groups often traced their origins 'back in time beyond the name of the tribal ancestor to reach to names associated with an ancient cradle land, in this case Arabia'.[38] This mythologization of pedigree (claiming patrilineal descent from distinguished Arab ancestors) is not peculiar to the Arabicized Northerners. In fact, Cunnison aligns the process functionally with the type of genealogy records from African people in which the ancestor of the group is connected with God or with some miraculous event at the beginning of the world or society'.[39] In the Arabicized North, however, the religious impulse (claiming derivation from the Prophet's family and not just any Arab ancestor) was certainly the driving force for the contrivance of mythical genealogies by many Sudanese holy and not so holy families.[40] Could it be that this addiction of the Arabicized Sudanese to tracing their roots back in time is a result of a curse on all the sons of Abraham. Jorges Luis Borges, in his well-turned language, wrote a feuilleton entitled: 'I, a Jew'. He said 'Never Phoenicians, Garamantes, Scythians, Babylonians, Persians, Egyptians, Huns, Vandals, Ostrogoths, Ethiopians, Berbers, Britorns ... the nights of Alexandria, of Babylon, of Carthage, of Memphis, never succeeded in engendering a single grandfather. It was only to the tribes of the bituminous Dead Sea that this gift was granted.'[41] To the tribes of the 'bituminous' Dead Sea, one may also add those of Arabia Deserta and their 'lost tribes'.

Beyond religious and ethnic impulses, the perpetuation of genealogical fiction had more to do with earthly designs such as eternalizing an advantageous position (political or economic) or maintaining vested interests. Thus, by subjectively distinguishing themselves as a superior race, the supremacists built around this fiction self-perceptions and legends that justify subjugating the other. That was probably why calls for an all-encompassing Sudanese identity were innately rejected by groups who only saw in them attempts to undermine the way they had always perceived themselves as superior. In the face of competing claims by indigenous Sudanese, this perverse way of self-preservation would undoubtedly subvert assertions by Arabicized Northerners of their right as the principal owners of the land. In the words of a weather-wise Northern scholar, 'the use of history to prove or disprove to whom ... the whole Sudan belongs (or belonged) is self-defeating, particularly for these who claim to have originated in Arabia'.[42] To make things worse, assumed ethnic superiority in the North turned out to be contagious. Within the North itself, some decidedly non-Arab groups fabricated an 'Arabo-Islamic' origin only to validate their ascendancy relative to 'lowly' divisions within their group.[43] By the same token, many descendants of ex-slaves residing in the North were driven to abnegate their ethnocultural origin and assume Arabo-Islamic marks of identification. That would have been understandable as a means of facilitating their integration into Northern society, but not when it conveyed a desire to distinguish themselves from their 'inferior' precursors. In the complex Sudan, it would appear that for every underdog there is not only an overdog but also another underdog.

From our narration of Sudan's post-independence history, it is evident that Arabo-Islamism had decreed itself not only as a superior identity but also as the only identity of Sudan. This may have theoretically worked out were it not for the obtaining economic and social cleavages that virtually made of Sudan two countries. Though initially fomented by colonial policies, those cleavages were maintained and intensified after independence by successive governments in Khartoum. Those policies ordained that the bulk of the national 'goodies' go to the riverain 'Arabo-Islamic' North to the detriment of the marginalized regions who continued to eke out a life of wretchedness. Since the majority among those groups happened to be non-Arabicized, a perception that the North has claimed the nation as its own was created.

Among Southerners, as we maintained earlier, there are groups who overstress the issue of domination to the point of indicting the whole North for the mistakes of its ruling and intellectual elites. Within those groups, some went to all lengths to deny Northern 'Arabism'. Northerners, they claim, have no right to call themselves Arabs. Decidedly, this view fell short in perceiving the impact of three centuries of Islamization and Arabicization by the Funj kingdom on the totality of northern and central Sudan. Apart from genealogical myths, Arabo-Islamism became a self-evident feature of the northern cultural identity. In this regard Sudanese were no different from other Arabicized people in Northern Africa, e.g. the people of the Maghreb. Though, largely Berbers, genetically speaking, the Maghrebans had culturally evolved into an Arabo-Islamic group because their whole intellectual universe was shaped by Arabic culture and Islamic civilization. Neither the Phoenicians, nor the Romans nor Vandals were able to have such a lasting impact on the Berbers. In effect the name *amazigh*, which the so-called Berbers gave to themselves, means free people, i.e. people who refused to be incorporated into the Phoenician, Vandal and Roman communities. What else could one describe people whose mother tongue and all their mental processes and stream of consciousness had been defined for centuries by Arabic culture? Actually, the total of the Arab military forces that had invaded *afriqia* (the name given by Arab geographers to Cyrenaica and the Maghreb) did not exceed tens of thousands. As in the case of Sudan, hordes of migrants, preachers, traders and soldiers of fortune moved into the Maghreb, settled there and intermarried with the indigenous population, particularly within the *baranis* (sedentary coastal Berbers). Those were fairly developed in view of their contact with the Carthaginians. The process of Islamization among the Berbers, similar to what happened in Sudan, was marked with a high degree of tolerance and respect of local customs. That was especially the case during the Ummayyad reign of Omar ibn Abdel Aziz who was known for his conciliatory approach to people of other faiths. Indeed, from the midst of those Arabicized Berbers emerged some of the most celebrated Islamic *fuqaha* like Assad ibn al Furat, Habib Ibn S'aid and Sahnoun. Nonetheless, in this era of cultural renaissance among all indigenous groups, the *Amazigh* began to assert their own identity. One reason for that may be the polarization created by Algerian radical Islamists as a result of which the 'Berbers' suffered immensely.

On the other hand, Northern Sudanese could not be approximated to African people, e.g. people of the eastern coast of Africa or the Sahel who adopted Islam as a faith, but maintained their indigenous cultural characteristics.[44] Despite their conversion to Islam, none of those African peoples had ever adopted Arabic as a language or were totally influenced by Arabic culture as Northern Sudan and the Maghreb had been. In addition, Sudan's contiguity to the Arab world – especially Egypt – had a considerable impact on the process of Arabicization in Sudan and in the intensification of the feeling of Arab belonging among Northern Sudanese, no matter what the antecedents of their Arabism were, and however nebulous the myth built around it was. Arabo-Islamism, accordingly, assumed a life of its own in Sudan. In general, being connected to a community by indissoluble and impalpable ties of common language, historical memory, habit, tradition and feeling is what makes an identity, according to Isaiah Berlin. Such fellowship, Berlin avers, 'is a basic human need, no less natural than that of food or drink or security or procreation'.[45]

Southern intellectuals who deny Northern Sudan's Arabo-Islamic belonging have thus missed the reality by a wide mark. Manifestly, there is an element of self-contradiction in the postulations of extremist groups in both North and South. Those who plead for an exclusive Sudanese Africanity in which there was no place for groups who identify with, or take pride in, Arabo-Islamic culture, are basically anti-African. Africa is a crucible in which varied ethnic groups and cultures interact. That is, of course, if Africanity is not equated with *negritude*. On the other hand, Northern Sudanese who virtually reject the African cultural component of their 'national' identity are indeed denying a significant ingredient in their own physical and cultural constitution.

Howbeit, the way the older of Northern intelligentsia conceived cultural identity spoke volumes of their cultural insularity. Mohamed Ahmed Mahjoub, one of the main components of Sudan's cultural revival in the 1940s (later foreign minister and prime minister) was the knight in shining armour of that generation. This is why writers often exhume his writings to reach to the depth of that generation's thinking. Mahjoub proffered that a *distinct* Sudanese culture should be 'based on Arabo-Islamic heritage enriched by European thought and aimed at developing a *truly national* literature which derived its character and inspiration from the character and traditions of the people of this country, its deserts and jungles'.[46] Those views were encapsulated in an oft-cited lecture which he delivered in 1940 entitled, 'The Sudanese Intellectual Movement, whither?'[47] The purpose of Mahjoub's lecture was to indicate which way the Sudanese intellectual movement should take. So what were Mahjoub's signposts on that way? The lecture came under three subheadings: Sudan's distant and not so distant past, the influences of Islam and Arabic culture and the ecological impact on culture. On the first issue, the Northern luminary abridged Sudan's glorious Nubian history to an era influenced by Pharaonic civilization, paganism and 'other heavenly religions'.[48] The other 'heavenly religion' he left unnamed was Christianity which had held sway over North (not South) Sudan for seven centuries. And probably neither the Arabo-Islamist of Mahjoub's generation nor today's traditional as well as neo-Islamists are aware that the first gentile ever to be baptized was a Sudanese.[49] Besides, his relegation of the first indigenous Sudanese, indeed African civilization, to a footnote in history, showed how warped was the historical memory of pre-independence intellectuals. The Nubian civilization which flourished as an African civilization from 350 BC to AD 350, alongside the Roman and Hellenistic Egyptian civilizations, should have been an object of glorification by all Sudanese. However, with such indifference to Sudan's glorious ancient civilizations (Kush and Meroë), heaping scorn on contemporary and not-so-glorious African cultures was a foregone conclusion. This attitude betrayed an amazing lapse of sense of history. Sudan is not more wedded to Islam than the countries of the Maghreb. If anything, it was through the Maghreb that the most popular *Sufi* orders found their way to Sudan, e.g. *Qadiriyya* and *Tijananiyya*. Nonetheless, Algeria, which is an exclusively Muslim country that is still traumatized by an ugly spell of Islamist radicalism, astounded the world by reclaiming St Augustine the African as her own. Opening a seminar on St Augustine organized by the *Haut Conseil Islamique* of Algeria and the Universite' de Friburg, President Bouteflika said: 'That Augustine lived and developed his thinking before the revelation of the Qur'an does not disqualify his works as a *point d'appui* to the divine revelations from Abraham to Moses to Jesus.' By celebrating Augustine, the President said, 'Algeria is retrieving an important part of its history.'[50] Sudan is also not more Arab than Syria and Iraq. But neither did Syria fail to ascribe importance to its Roman heritage exhibited in Palmyra in the eras of Odaenathus of Palmyra and his wife Zenobia, nor did Iraq abandon its Assyrian and Babylonian history. Indeed Syria of late did its heart good by honouring its Christian history,[51] and Iraq never ceased in writing its Babylonian history in letters of gold. But in Sudan, the glorious Nubian civilization was disowned by its heirs not so much because it was distant and remote (which was not good enough reason), as in view of its so-called paganism. It is the more surprising that the Northern riverain intelligentsia, who always looked to Egypt for intellectual inspiration, were never illuminated by the outlook of many of their Egyptian role models towards Egypt's Pharaonic heritage.[52] The intemperance of that generation in asserting Arabo-Islamic cultural identity at the expense of all other cultural strands in the Sudanese cultural fabric was completely inadvertent to historical and contemporary realities. One is thus persuaded to hypothesize that the older generation of Northern elite, and to one's utter despair some of today's elite, are not comfortable with being at the peripheries of Islam and Arabism in both geographic and chronological terms. Following upon that, they raised their eyes to, if not flattered themselves with, being more Arab and Muslim than those who were at the centre of attraction of Arabo-Islamism.

Mahjoub furthermore asserted that Sudan was an attracting pole to waves of migrants from Yemen, Hidjaz and Abyssinia who settled in the land, intermarried with its indigenous women and eventually chased away the *indigene* further south where they continued to preserve their native cultures. That of course was how human settlements of the post-Nubian civilization came to be created. But Mahjoub's fleeting remark on centuries of communion among peoples and cultural convergences in the country, notably glossed over centuries of hybridization of ethnic groups, cross fertilization of cultures and interweaving of lifestyles and mores. Nowhere were those historical processes that shaped Sudanese identity to be found in Mahjoub's cultural map, except probably in one thing: ecology. In reality, Mahjoub reduced the non-Arab African component in the Sudanese identity to an ecological phenomenon symbolized by the jungle. But countries are not pieces of real estate, they are real estate furnished with people who have their own attributes and different ways of expressing human values. Apparently, some Northern intellectuals would prefer that piece of real estate unfurnished.

The wilful lack of interest in Sudanese 'African' cultures is compounded with another dubiety. Since Sudan's independence, all constitutions and policy documents were adorned with clauses on respect for the country's cultural pluralism. But the history we have just narrated proved that this too was an open question. Nowhere in Sudan's school curricula, mass media programmes, archaeological excavations or the performing arts was there a place for those diverse cultures. If at all, the only place reserved for them, as one acute observer maintained, was in a decrepit ethnographic museum in Khartoum.[53] Inconsistencies of this nature not only convey intellectual fickleness, but also evince a high level of moral deficit. For how can one ever laud cultural pluralism while, at the same time, deliberately seeks to annihilate all cultures other than the dominant one in order to impose uniformity. Constitutional edicts on the recognition of cultural diversity are meaningless, so long as premeditated policies and practices countermine them.

Another Northern intellectual who contributed immensely to the literature averred that Arabism and Africanism were completely fused in Northern Sudan to the extent that North, more than South, Sudan was more representative of Africa.[54] This is a view with which one would only concur if its proponent recognized any worth in Sudan's African cultures. Not when he maintained that contemporary African cultures, traditional beliefs and even historical 'pagan' civilizations like the Pharaonic and Nubian were 'not objects of glorification'.[55] To that Northern Sudanese intelligentsia, it seemed African cultures were patently primitive because they did not conform to their cultural pattern or to accepted Western cultural patterns. But as Evans-Pritchard opined the term primitive has both logical and chronological senses. The 'two senses have sometimes not been kept distinct even in the minds of good scholars.'[56] That intelligentsia, though decidedly African, took for granted the way Western Europeans and classical Arab historians viewed Africa. Ever and anon, did those 'Africans' ponder the contradiction inherent in that postulation was it to be applied to them. Sudan's intelligentsia in effect reconciled themselves with a charade. Sudan's history, they assumed, only began with the coming of Arabs to Sudan. They thus left the commemoration of their country's glorious past to bards from distant lands who were more conscious of its contribution to African heritage and to human civilization.[57] With this level of cultural insularity and misguided *amour propre*, the Northern intelligentsia burned both ends of the candle. They never grieved from an identity crisis, let alone a crisis of conscience.

Sudan's Arabo-Islamic-Africanists were lately joined by Turabi. In a statement to an American reporter, he said that Sudan is a microcosm of Africa. 'Eastern Sudan is part of the Horn of Africa, Western Sudan is part of West Africa and Northern Sudan is part of North Africa. So Sudan is well situated to relate to all Africa,' said he.[58] This, undeniably, is true as far as geography goes, but where was Africa's place in Turabi's cultural map? In another press interview, Turabi told the interviewer that Sudan's Islam was threatened both by America 'which understands nothing of the world' and Africans whose views only 'reflect their primitive nature'.[59] Turabi, and for that matter any Sudanese of his mindset, should not go into ecstasies for being a microcosm of primitiveness. What is more shocking is the belief of Sudanese leaders who speak with two voices that they can get away with their synthetic yarn. Hardly, if ever, do they ponder the impact of their apish approach to non-Arab African cultures on the unity of Africa of which Sudan is purportedly a microcosm. How on earth shall a country that determines its own unity on restricted and exclusivist cultural parameters claim to be part of a continent whose unity can only be predicated on recognition of multiple pluralities? Another white sepulchre is reflected in the 1998 NIF constitution drafted by Turabi. Article 27 of that constitution, entitled Sanctity of Cultural Communities reads: 'There shall be guaranteed for every community or group of citizens the right to preserve their particular culture, language or religion … freely within the framework of their particularity, and the same shall not by coercion be effaced.' Very nice words indeed, but the reality is different. Need we recall, in the face of this constitutional edict, that young Southerners living in the North were forcibly converted to Islam, that food aid was used as a tool of conversion, that war was launched not under the pretext of preserving the territorial integrity of the country but as an onslaught ordained by Allah, against heathens, that whole Muslim communities who refused to conform to the NIF line (Nuba) were virtually decimated and that all state-controlled audio-visual media became a one-issue medium: spreading the faith of Islam. Obviously, Muslims have every right to propagate their faith, but not a state that claims to belong to Muslim and non-Muslim alike. And certainly not when that state brandishes its commitment to the respect of the cultures and religions of all its citizens. One very revealing incident took place in 2000 and revealed the hypocrisy of the NIF regime, indeed its utter insensitivity to other faiths. On 1 October of that year, Pope John Paul II canonized Josephina Bakhita, a native of South Sudan. Bakhita, who suffered immensely under servitude and was later sold to the Italian Consul, ended by joining the Canossian sisters in Italy. Most of her life was spent with the Conossians in Venice and reportedly residents of Schio often invoked her protection from bombings during the Second World War. Before her canonization, Bakhita was beatified in 1992 for her humanitarian services. The canonization of a daughter of the land is not an event that should go unnoticed by a country that treasures its own. Deplorably, neither was the event reported in the government media, nor was it a subject of interest to Khartoum's investigative journalism. Manifestly, to both, the stunning journey made by that unique Sudanese lady from slavery to sainthood, was nothing to write home about. Bakhita ostensibly belonged to the wrong country and the wrong faith.

In the early post-independence years, British historian Arnold Toynbee visited five African countries: Nigeria, Sudan, Ethiopia, Egypt and Libya. The declared purpose of his visit was to study rival claims of Arabism and *negritude* in the continent. To the advocates of the latter (who were equally insularist), the real Africa was Negro Africa. Black Africa's cultures, in their estimation, are its own independent creation with no influences whatsoever radiating from the North. Toynbee challenged this thesis by asking: 'Has not Egypt played a leading part in history since the dawn of civilization? Isn't Egypt part of Africa as a matter of course?'[60] In the meantime, Toynbee cautioned against attempts by North Sudan to assimilate forcibly the South to the Northern way of life. 'That ought not to be,' he said. The eminent historian added that 'the South cannot be held with the North except by [its] free consent and on a footing of equality'. The problem of Africa, Toynbee asseverated, was the problem of two Sudans. He clearly saw Sudan's rich contribution to African cultures (Kush and Meroë), as well as its *pot pourri* of African cultures, as an epitome of the continent. Both Sudan's dogmatic 'Arabists' of the North, and 'Africanists' of the South are neither conscious of the nuances in this correlation nor heedful of the richness inherent in their country's multi-hued diversity.

So who are the Sudanese? Are they Arabs whose authenticity and cultural originality is best expressed through Arabism, as a large section of the Northern elite think? Or are they Africans whose destiny is closely interlinked with that of the rest of Africa south of the Sahara, as some Southern elites think the case to be? Even with such an ambiguity, conflict on identity would not have necessarily led to a hardening of positions to the extent of war, were it not for the impingement of identification on the public domain: who is to get or be what, according to his religion or pedigree. The politico-economic underpinnings of the identity crisis, therefore, explain the obduracy, more than any other factor.

Religion and Cultural Identity

It is obvious from the above that not only Arabism, but also Islamic faith, is assumed to be a defining variable of Northern Sudanese identity. This is the type of judgment that the Islamists would want stamped on the budding nation: a mark by which Sudanese are universally identified. But, as alluded to earlier, the hypothesis that the whole Muslim North shared such vision is both conceptually and empirically untrue. And though one agrees at the conceptual level that Islam is both a religion and a culture, it does not necessarily follow that Muslims who are beholden to the faith of Islam believe that its edicts and injunctions, as they had been applied in Sudan since the nineteenth century and more so under the NIF, should apply to the public domain. On the practical side, Sudan's experiences in the nineteenth century were surfeit with stories of Sufi sheikhs who spurned the *Mahdiyya,* precisely because of its religious excesses and monopolization of truth. As a result of its inordinately demanding religious radicalism, Mahdism became, as noted earlier, a source of social convulsion and dislocation. This was surely less than an unbeatable achievement for radical Islam in that era. As for contemporary experiences, Muslim Sudanese ridiculed Nimeiri's imamate and condemned Bashir's 'mafiocracy' for their incontinent approach to religion. Neither of the two twentieth-century 'Islamist' leaders could claim that their policies had engendered a groundswell of popular support among Muslims. It was only through brute force that they were able to impose a so-called Islamic system of governance on a people known for their undogmatic religiosity. This belies claims to the contrary by Sudanese political commentators as well as Western scholars who fell prey to the NIF's flummery. The Islamization drive, according to those commentators, was a response to the yearnings by Sudanese Muslims for the resurrection of *shari'a*. Obviously, you don't resort to brute force to impose on people a project to which they so dearly 'yearn'. The argument is as flimsy as it is deceptive. Those commentators blatantly passed over relevant experiences of contemporary Sudan, e.g. the resurrection of the quasi-secular 1956 constitution in October 1964 as the only document on which a measure of consensus was possible, the adoption by Nimeiri of an equally quasi-secular constitution in 1973 that remained valid for ten years and without which peace could not have lasted for as long as it had, the abrogation of Nimeiri's so-called Islamic laws by religious-based Northern political parties and, eventually, the new dispensation on religion and politics adopted at Asmara in 1995. We should also add the deceptive clauses in the NIF constitution (1998) which are contrary to all the benchmarks established by Turabi in 1968 as condition's precedent for the conclusion of a permanent constitution for Sudan.

The emergence of the NIF, nevertheless, was a blessing in disguise since their pattern of extremism forced the issue of identity wide open in Sudan. Polarity became complete and contrapositions became more pronounced. In addition to the country's manifold horizontal cleavages, the NIF imposed a vertical divide. In effect, a Sudanese scholar believes that by rejecting secularism, the NIF has in reality rejected democracy to which Sudanese are innately prone. Democracy, the scholar contended, is based on 'human reason and experience [where] social problems are solved by trial and error and not by an elite claiming possession of the absolute truth. There is no place in a modern democracy for such dogma or absolute truth.'[61] It would appear therefore, that for peace and stability to prevail in Sudan, Sudanese must evolve an all-inclusive national identity in place of the obtaining restrictive parameters for national identification. In other words, parameters of national identity must be refashioned to be more accommodative of other competing identities. That is, if the Sudanese want to see their country united in peace. Nowhere is this more urgent than in the area of religion, as the experiences of the last two centuries have shown. That would only be achieved through a form of constitutional separation between religion (*shari'a*) and the state and the creation of a pluralistic substratum that would provide space for all religions and political philosophies to coexist and compete in peace. The religion-based state, as it has been historically constructed, and more so as it has contemporarily developed from Iran to Sudan, is a monolithic and totalitarian system that leaves no political space for non-Muslims or non-religious Muslim. It is indeed the height of insincerity and fraud that Islamists living in Western countries (e.g. Londonstan) fight tooth and nail to enjoy civic rights guaranteed to them by the constitutions of those 'infidel' countries, while they deny the same rights to citizens of their own countries.

The dichotomy, however, between Sudanese 'secularists' (like the aforementioned scholar) and Islamists is artificial. It is deliberately accentuated by one elitists group (the neo-Islamists) against another elitist group comprising liberal democrats and 'leftist' with the SCP as their arch-chief in the North. The essence of the conflict is political and not religious. Since 1968, the Muslim Brothers had woven a plot whereby secularism was equated with atheism. The fallout of that artificial cleavage poisoned the political environment and led to hardened political positions. Substantially, no party in either the North or South has ever advocated the abnegation of religion in society, as the Islamists seem to suggest. What the secularists rejected was the centrality to governance and politics of one religion in a multireligious society. This is a conclusion to which the NIF itself has virtually come despite the clamour that 'their' Islamic principles were fundamental rules that cannot be abandoned. In less than a decade in government, the central myth of the NIF became so strained that they apparently became much wiser. Despite all fire and fury, it realized that in a multireligious society public policy could not be constructed on the basis of one religion. Whether the NIF genuinely believed in this and was ready to face the odds, or was just exhibiting borrowed plumes, the removal from their anodyne constitution drafted by Turabi himself of any reference to a state religion or to the religion of the head of state, proved that their *thawabit* (fundamentals) were far from being fundamental. Regardless, it would still be possible to make the argument that the retention of *shari'a* as a source of legislation is tantamount to a carte blanche for full fledged Islaization of state and politics. Such cavil proved one thing: the NIF's so-called religious verities were not about the 'immutable' words of God, but about politics pure and simple.

Political Islam, in the course of three decades (from the 1960s up to the 1990s) has threatened the corporate existence of a very soft country. Now that the country has reached the end of its tether, it should have become clear to everybody that the counter-thesis for forced acculturation is the dismemberment of Sudan. Fortunately, with the right alignment of forces, people change and what was deemed to be an absolute truth yesterday becomes relative today. So far, all Sudanese Muslims and non-Muslims – excepting Bashir's faction of the NIF – aspire for nothing less than the complete eradication of the NIF's politico-religious agenda, as they have lived through it in the last decade. Sudan has lived, and still lives, with political parties that derive inspiration from their ascribed religious beliefs, but it can hardly live with an elitist group that claims the monopoly of truth and pretends that it is endowed with a God-given mission to control man's body and soul.

But despite all the ruin it has wrought on Sudan, and the total collapse of its ideological *thawabit*, the NIF, remains intricately self-absorbed in its delusions in a way that makes it succumb easily to a mirage of infallibility. Even the looking all ways among the NIF advocates had readily come to the conclusion that their regime was there to stay and should continue calling the tune. With cockeyed self-indulgence, those advocates assumed that every Sudanese had no choice but to fall into line. One of those advocates made a not so clever comparison when he likened Sudan's North/South cleavage with the situation of Afro-Americans in the US. The writer drew a staggering parallel between, on the one hand, General Colin Powell whom he claimed, was recognized by 'white' Americans as their equal to the extent of considering him suitable for the presidency; and on the other, Louis Farrakhan who shunned 'white' America's institutions and ethos and was, according to the writer, 'ostracized'. 'All that Farrakhan could hope for his independence,' the writer said, 'was to live with those who support him in a small corner of America or go into exile with them.'[62] The moral of the story, of course, is that the choice for Sudan's Farrakhan (Garang) and his Southern supporters is between accepting to live in their 'small corner' within Sudan in the manner defined by the NIF, or 'exile' themselves to the South. Surely, such 'exile' has always been on the cards and could have been determined by Southerners themselves if they so wanted. They don't need to beg leave from the NIF or anybody else for that matter. But neither did the majority of them apparently wanted it, nor were those who wanted it, allowed to do so by Big Brother in the North who moved heaven and earth to keep the country united.

Notwithstanding, the correlation, on the one side, of two individuals living peaceably within the framework of a liberal society that, despite all its inadequacies, guaranteed them all natural and civic civil rights and, on the other, of more than one-third of the population of a country who were struggling for, and denied, those rights for almost half a century, was beyond the comprehension of mortals. Farrakhan, for example, was able to mobilize one million demonstrators in his nation's capital under the eyes, and with the protection of, the law. How many Southerners could dare organize a demonstration in Khartoum, their nation's capital, without being called *'mudabiri mua'mra unsurya'* (fomentors of a racial complot).[63] The thesis propounded by the Islamic writer is deformed on two counts. The first was the presumption that the identity of over one-third of the nation could be reshaped at will. Amazingly, the author himself was aware of the inherent difficulties in seeing through such an enterprise.[64] Second, the presumption that unless citizens belonging to one group abandoned their connate cultural traits and adopted the dominant culture, they would have no place in their own country was maladroit to the extreme. Presumptions like this could have been tolerated if they came from missionaries, not from political thinkers, much less from adherents to 'a national salvation' movement who should be aware of the fluidity of the composition of the so-called nation as well as of the processes of nation formation.

Truly, the approach of the Islamists to the South was no different than that of the Christian missionaries they deride. Given their pietistic Victorian values and their misguided confusion of Western illumination with Christianity, European missionaries of the nineteenth century fantacized that their main role in Africa was to save its people from the 'uncivilized aspects of native culture'.[65] Sudan's 'missionary' politicians were no less unbending and self-righteous. Even in their new 'liberal' guise, and after the virtual abandonment of all their rallying cries, the Islamists believed, without rhyme or reason, that they still held the keys to the gates of heaven and were divinely ordained to shepherd into it Sudanese Muslims and Christians alike. If this is the way the 'enlightened' and self-critical Islamists view political liberalization, then faith in the not so enlightened would be a hopeless hope.

This haughty patronization and perverse inclination by the Islamists to recondition and socially engineer the Sudanese, including those who do not share their faith, makes all non-Muslims in Africa – not only its direct objects in Sudan – heave in disbelief. A South African correspondent told the story about his visit to Chatham House in London to listen to Sadiq al Mahdi who was 'touted as an Oxford-educated political mastermind who will succeed where the soldiers had failed'.[66] Al Mahdi gave the correspondent the shock of his life because his views on reconditioning Sudanese non-Muslims were no less strident than those of the regime the correspondent dreaded most: apartheid South Africa. Al Mahdi, the South African correspondent said, 'sent a cold shudder down my spine when he postulated as his solution to the Southern problem: social engineering'. Africa has known all brands of civilizational missionaries descending on it from different colonial metropolises; but not a home-grown *'mission civilizatrice'*, except probably in the correspondent's country.

Palpably, the Islamists are ignorant of the nature of African belief systems including those practised in their own Sudan. Terms like *shirk* (idolatry) and *wathaniyya* (paganism) abound in their discourses on those belief systems. Carried to its logical conclusion, that postulation ordains that African systems should be forcibly eradicated. Instead of analyzing religious beliefs in Sudan as they have historically developed, and as they are now practised, the Islamists approached them in a condescending and messianic way. In effect, religion is a generic phenomenon that has been ubiquitous in all cultures through out history. To a great measure, religion provides man with an ability (however illusionary) to make a sense of life and bring order to its discordance. Without the numinous experiences of faith, men probably could not have been able to make sense of life. The return with venom by former communist countries to religion after over half a century of agnosticism proves beyond doubt man's desire to subject himself to ethical imperatives determined by a transcendental order. African belief systems are no exception to this general rule. But in no instance did the Islamists and religio-social engineers apply themselves to reach to the real meaning of those belief systems within Sudan so as to discover their innate spirituality and the high moral standards they set for their adherents. This understanding is necessary since to many Northerners (lettered and uninitiated alike) African belief systems are 'animistic' beliefs associated with sorcery, black magic and voodoism, and nothing else. In reality, the term 'animism' itself, coined by E.B. Tylor in his renowned work *Primitive Culture* (1871), was predicated on the belief that there are different levels of spirituality shared by all religions. To Tylor, the rudimentary 'animist' religion or spiritualism treats objects and non-human beings as having power and feeling like men. But like all religions, 'animistic' beliefs, in addition to moral values, are also endowed with the same characteristic feelings of reverence, awe and wonderment that are exhibited in other religions. The moral values, as is the case with other religions, are not only presented in terms of right and wrong, but also as godly and ungodly.

African belief systems in Sudan, especially among the Nilotes, uphold high moral and aesthetic values. By way of example, the concept of *cuong* among the Nuer prescribes an extramundane human act when it calls on every man to be in the right with his fellow men, in order for him to be right with God. All Nilotes also believe in, and communicate with, an omnipotent supreme God, a transcendental father that fashioned man.[67] Further, African belief systems are perhaps more nature-friendly than many established religions, since they are based on the unity of the cosmos and the continuum of life. For instance, among all the Nilotes the community does not include only the living, but also the ancestors and those yet to be born. Hence, the African adage to which many environmentalists refer when they discuss sustained development: 'It is not from our ancestors that we have inherited the land, but to the benefit of those who are yet to be born that we are conserving it.'

'Animism' is also derided for its totemism that makes certain objects a focal symbol of life and calls for the veneration to, and adulation of, animate and inanimate objects. But one knows of no established religion that does not include processes of sacralization of objects, days and events, or of veneration of things, images and symbols. In reality, there is absolutely no rational explanation to the symbolic meaning of liturgical vestments in Christianity, the veneration of the lamb's horn by Jews, the esteem Muslims give to *al Hajar al aswad* (black stone),[68] the association by Jews, Christians and Muslims, of blackness with evil. In this regard one can easily equate the rite of body painting in some African belief systems with the eucharistic vestments among Christians. Surely no rational or philosophical explanation can be given to those unintelligible symbols, since their unintelligibility lies in their mysteriousness. Authoritative religious edicts and symbols can never be analysed philosophically, because in philosophy arguments from authority are worthless and there is no finality in philosophical thought.

Be that as it may, the NIF despite its condescending attitude towards African cultures has of late assumed an African mantle so as to wriggle out of its isolation. The regime declared, within the community of the countries of the Sahara and Sahel of which it became member, its desire to play a leading role. A summit for that group was organized in Khartoum in February 2001. Reporting to the press on the *injazat* (achievements) of the meeting, Sudan's Foreign Minister, Mustafa Osman Ismail, reported among those *injazat* the adoption of projects 'to consolidate African cultures with full participation of educational institutions and the media.'[69] Coming from one of the leaders of a regime that made a religious mission of the annihilation of African cultures within their own country, that was the height of chicanery. Africans would rightly ask, how much of the consolidation of African cultures is reflected in the NIF's school curricula or media programmes? They would also ask how many 'African' non-Muslims Sudanese can see themselves in those programmes? Besides, it is most improbable that the regime that excelled in portraying the civil war pitting one Sudanese against another as an Arabo-African cultural war, would have any time for African cultures, let alone working to conserve them.[70]

No less shocking is the assumption inherent in the NIF's core message that if the South does not change to its liking, then the South has to go or accept the 'corner' to which it shall be assigned in the Sudan. It is of course one thing if both North and South decided mutually and voluntarily to separate because they have failed to cohabit. It is quite another when a minority elitist group claiming to be the guardian of the 'nation's conscience' decides, through the argument of force and not the force of argument, either to impose a subjectively defined identity on all Sudanese or to dismember the country. That is the more worrisome, when it is realized that all the other Sudanese political players are inclined to disavow exclusionary visions of identity and ready to espouse a mutually accommodative political framework based on civil pluralism.

The Arabist Dilemma

In reality, the concept of nationhood, in the sense of man's owing supreme secular loyalty and political allegiance to a defined territory, is a relatively new concept in historical terms. Before the rise of nation states, 'citizens' in Europe, where the concept evolved, owed their allegiance to a parochial community or a religious commonwealth, e.g. the Christian Roman Empire. Rousseau, inspired by the Greek city states, envisaged the nation state as a focal point for human activities but stressed the contribution of all citizens to the general will as well as the need to make political constitutions that reflected the peculiarities of each community from which they were drawn up.'[71] For the two centuries that succeeded the French Revolution, nation states with defined geographic borders became the centre of attraction to diverse indigenous peoples and a foundry for moulding multiform languages and cultures. They also became nerve centres for 'national' activities. The invention of the printing press played an important rule in enhancing cultural affinities of people sharing the same culture and language and thereby strengthened solidarity of people within nation states. And though the increasing feeling of interdependence among Europeans attenuated nationalist passions in the post-Second World War era, especially after the end of the Cold War and the lifting of the Stalinist lid, those feelings re-emerged. For all to see, they intensified in nearly all European countries where ethnic or religious cleavages persisted, e.g. the Balkans and the Russian Commonwealth. The idea of the nation state, however, caught on beyond Europe, particularly in the decolonization era. In Africa, the process was marred from the start by troubles and tribulations. African emerging nation states did not mutate naturally through a historical process to nationhood, but were set up by the colonialists with fictitiously drawn borders based on tribal or ethnic conglomerations. In their wisdom, African leaders decided in the Second OAU Summit (Cairo, 1964) to maintain national borders as they had been handed over by the departing colonialists. This was a source of recurring inter-state conflicts among a number of African nation states where the fictitious boundaries did not accord with political realities on the ground.

Sudan, nonetheless, was fortunate in that its present-day borders had been delineated since the nineteenth century by the Turks, so its problem lay elsewhere. Unlike other African countries, Sudan's evolution into a nation was frustrated by two impediments; one political, the other religious. Within the political sphere, Sudanese Arabists – up to the late 1980s – and Arabs in general, had no patience with legitimate Southern claims for autonomy, even though those claims were dictated by obvious sociocultural considerations. The South's legitimate claims were assumed by Arabists to be no more than colonially inspired obstructive devices to wheel-clamp the march towards consolidating a putative 'Arab nationalism'. Arabists, since the demise of the Ottoman caliphate, riveted their attention on the 'restoration' of the grandeur of that putative nation. This nation, though, was at the time limited to the Near East and Arabia, while in Egypt the issue was highly debatable.[72] During the Ottoman era, however, the concept of a pan-Arab nation never existed; Arabs and non-Arabs within the bounds of that Empire identified with, and pledged allegiance to, the Islamic caliphate. And so was the case with earlier caliphates from the time of Omar Ibn al Khatab (the second Caliph after Prophet Mohammed). That was the time when Islamic universalism held sway and deflated nationalist sentiments. But as the Arab resistance against the decaying and increasingly despotic Ottoman regime accelerated after the First World War, Arab nationalist feelings in the Near East were inflamed. The slogan of Arab nationalism was indisputably a handy tool of struggle against the Turks as well as a means for legitimizing the budding nationalist movement. That anti-Ottoman feeling was not necessarily shared by all Arabs. For instance, the Arabs of the Maghreb to whom Islam was the only badge of identification from the French, were more wedded to the Muslim caliphate for that reason.[73] Still and all, the idea of restoring a hitherto non-existent Arab nation gained momentum in the Near East and was soon to be ideologized if not mythologized by a number of Arab writers from that region,[74] positing that 'nationalism' on common language and shared historical experiences, probably drawing their inspiration from Bismarck's Germany.

Two developments intervened in the second half of the twentieth century with a great impact on the evolution of the idea of pan-Arabism. The first was the emergence of the state of Israel in 1948 and the ensuing Arab–Israeli wars. That not only heighten awareness of Arab identity, but also made of it a rallying point to galvanize Arab people to pool their resources against this new enemy. Accordingly, calls for Arab unity became a medium for stirring nationalistic fervour and was soon to be transformed into a potent political ideology that transcended the Near East. It also radicalized politics and assumed an anti-Western stance in view of the unconditional western support to Israel. Arab nationalism thus evolved into an ideology for both 'national' regeneration and anti-colonial struggle, while the idea of Arab solidarity became a corollary of Arab unity. With the accession of Nasser to power in the 1950s, pan-Arab 'ideology' engulfed the whole Arab world 'from the Gulf to the Ocean'. The only Arab leader who took issue with the Nasserian construct on Arab nationalism was Habib Bourgiba of Tunisia.

It did not take long though, before the 'ideology' of Arabism became a tool of domestic legitimization of radical Arab regimes that had invariably come to power through subverting democracy. Military coups became a legitimate vehicle of change at a great cost to the people of the region. For example, issues of major concern to Arab communities, e.g. development, democracy and the social well-being of nation states, were retrenched. Those who pleaded for democracy and human rights were denounced as 'enemies of the people.' Notwithstanding, the Arab defeat in 1967 became a turning point for the fortunes of Arab nationalists. That was not only because of the humiliation ensuing from that defeat, but also as a result of the cascade of schisms within Arabist ideological groups. Those schisms led to mutual excommunications based on the way each of those groups analysed the causes of defeat. The defeat, which was understated as the *naksa* (relapse), made one of the staunchest advocates of pan-Arabism, Kostantin Zureiq, much wiser.[75] It also inspired him to make an interesting confession in a later work.[76] In that work Zureiq confessed that he was persuaded to avoid using the term 'Arab Unity', which was the mainstay of his earlier works, because the idea did not tally with realities on the ground. Instead, he said, the term Arab societies was a more apt description of the reality, given the complex peculiarities of those societies. Eventually, the last nail in the coffin of ideologically conceived Arab nationalism was driven by the Iraqi invasion of Kuwait in 1990.

On the other hand, many Arab-related countries (ethnically or culturally) emerged in the wake of decolonization as independent countries, each with its own local proclivities. At the political level those countries voluntarily joined the League of Arab States which was created in 1945. Sudan joined that body in the morrow of its independence in 1956. As a matter of course, if the Arab countries pursued the steps of the fathers of the Arab League to consecrate unity on the basis of enlightened self-interest, the outcome might have been different. But Arabist ideologues persevered in their chimerical search of a one Arab nation, transcending all national proclivities and enforced through a top-down approach. Apart from the fact that the idea of an archetypal or foundational Arab nation was simply fictitious (if anything from the Ummiyyads to the Fatemides to the Ottomans), inadvertence to contemporary realities in the different component parts of the 'Arab Nation' worked against the legitimate cause of Arab interdependence. Moreover, obliviousness to those realities by Arab ideologues was incredible. From the early 1960s there was a virtual Arab cold war between so-called progressive and reactionary states, right and left, and Arab nationalists and assumedly insular 'anti-Arabsists' like Bourgiba. In addition, since the 1930s there had been at least five inter-Arab wars or conflicts over borders or shared resources among countries where no ethnic or cultural cleavages existed: Saudi Arabia and Yemen (1934), Algeria and Morocco (1963), Kuwait and Iraq (1990) Sudan and Egypt over Halaib (1957 and 1995), Qatar and Bahrain (1999), alongside similar disputes between Abu Dhabi and Oman, Oman and Yemen and Abu Dhabi and Saudi Arabia over oil resources. Paradoxically, none of those conflicts was resolved through intermediation by pan-Arab institutions, only through external mediation and adjudication or bilateral reconciliation. For instance, the 1963 conflict between Algeria and Morocco was resolved by the OAU, Iraq and Kuwait by the UN Security Council and Qatar and Bahrain by the International Court of Justice.

For sure, were the Arab states to follow the path of European countries who sought to minimize frictions in their midst through the articulation of progressive union based on sociocultural commonalities and shared future expectations, they would have made long strides towards unity. In the light of this assumption, Sudanese pan-Arabists would have been on target if they pleaded for Arab unity based on the commonality of language and culture, geographic continuity and economic interests. That would have been a plausible proposition. After all, commonality of language and culture had brought together disparate countries that had nothing else in common, e.g. the British Commonwealth and the Organization International de la Fracophonie (OIF). Moreover, geographic continuity, common economic interests and a shared political culture also drew together the countries of Europe, despite protracted wars amongst them up to the last century. This approach is a far cry from claims staked by pan-Arab ideologues all through the decades of the 1960s up to the late 1980s[77] that all countries within the League of Arab States (including Sudan) are unadulteratedly Arab, notwithstanding their cultural peculiarities. In this regard, African cultures were simply scoffed at and classical non-Arab cultures (Cushite and Nubian Christian) were only considered of museum value.

Arabs in general, and Sudanese Arabists in particular, have, therefore, failed since the 1960s to take the country for what it was. That had dire results to Sudan's own unity. They also failed to appreciate that a voluntarily united Sudan could have been a strong retaining wall to the virtual and non-concretized 'Arab Nation'. Moreover, the claim that existing nation states within the Arab world are fictitious creations – though factual – can be rebutted by the fact that nearly all states, in one way or another, are fictitiously created. But one fiction cannot be supplanted with another: an ideologically contrived fantasy of an all-embracing and undifferentiated 'Arab Nation'. On the positive side, however, Sudanese Baathists had engaged of late in a healthy debate on what they had taken to be an article of faith since the 1960s: the figmental distinction between *qaumiya* and *wataniya*,[78] and the belief that democracy within nation states can be put on a back burner pending the creation of the all-embracing Arab Nation.

A New Beginning: NIF Dividend

The breakdown of the process of transmutation into one nation has been further exacerbated in Sudan by the emergence of the NIF as a political player. New perspectives of the Sudanese problem began to unfold. As others would possibly view it, the NIF has created a new challenge that has shaken the rest of the country into re-evaluating its views on the Sudanese problem. The NIF, as indeed all political Islamists, claim to be against nation states. We referred earlier to the NIF's assumed aversion to political stratifications based on ethnic, cultural or geographic particularisms. The only fellowship they recognize is the community of Muslims. All Muslims, whatever their racial origin, language, culture and birthplace were assumed to be part of one nation: the Nation of Islam. The Islamists thus reject in theory, the idea of a nation state or citizenship and supplant it with the community of believers (*mu'mineen*, sing. *mu'min*). The state encompassing those believers derives its legitimacy from submission to Allah. It was for this reason that the NIF in 1992 changed the Sudanese Nationality Law, making that nationality a right for any Muslim. No Islamic state in modern history had done that. So, the concept of citizenship as an organic relation between an authentic native and the state in which he was domiciled and which imbued him with constitutionally guaranteed rights and imposed on him or her identifiable obligation, became meaningless in the NIF's Sudan. Paradoxically, Turabi himself defined citizenship in one of his works as attachement to the fatherland and loyalty to ancestors.[79] Nevertheless, Bashir told those who criticized the granting of Sudanese nationality to non-Sudanese that the only qualification for Sudanese nationality was the *shihada* (attestation that God is one and Mohammed is his Prophet). By enacting that miscalculated legislation to satisfy its swollen-headedness, the NIF regime had gone against all norms that govern citizenship in all states of the world including contemporary Muslim states. How much then could such

305

know-alls be entrusted with nation building. But the NIF lawyers were not naive, for under that dispensation which granted Sudanese nationality to every mother's son, the floodgates were opened to non-Sudanese Islamists of every description. Those 'citizens' were not just Muslims; they were above all radical Islamists of whom many were *persona non grata* in their countries of origin. Subsequently, that unfitting stipulation in the laws of Sudan was removed, *al Shihada* notwithstanding. That came after the adherence of Sudan to the African Convention on Combating Terrorism in Algiers in 1999 which Sudan and its Arab counterrparts signed in Cairo in 1998. During the negotiations on both conventions, the NIF was faced with a list of 'wanted' terrorists who either resided in Sudan, or were travelling on Sudanese documents. As a result, the NIF not only went back in 1997 to the idea of citizenship as it had been traditionally enunciated in the laws of Sudan, but it also made that citizenship the sole defining factor of constitutional rights and duties to Muslims and non-Muslims in Sudan. That was yet another instance where the NIF defrauded religion and transformed the country and its laws into a laboratory for testing its ideologically based compounds.

The NIF, we maintain, had done some good to Sudan. It brought to an end the blurring of the battle lines. First, in the North, the NIF was isolated. And whereas it persisted in its agenda of cultural, political and religious domination, the Northern political class (including traditional parties) began to see the future of Sudan as one in which equality, participation and justice held a greater promise of survival. Second, as a result of the above, there was a substantial retreat of the reactive secessionist mould of the South and movement towards a vision of unity, democracy and reform for the whole of Sudan as exemplified by the SPLM/A's call for a New Sudan and the Asmara resolutions. This disposition may not be shared by some Southern political old-timers who had weaned themselves off the concept of Sudan's unity. However, it is more observable among younger elements who liberated themselves from the underdog syndrome and moved forward to claim that Sudan belonged to them too. Inferiority, like superiority complex is a mental state. This regeneration is best expressed by the confluence of the SPLM/A and all other political and social forces under the umbrella of the NDA.

View from the North: Assimilation and Discrimination

Since the government of Ismail el Azhari, all through to that of Nimeiri up to 1983, Northern Sudanese as a whole could not really claim to have suffered under the hands of governments in Khartoum. On a religious basis, the governments were generally Muslim in composition, and tolerance of views within the religion was wide. Economically, development was concentrated in the riverain North and all Northerners were basically, to one extent or other, beneficiaries of this inclination. Even though government shifted between the traditional parties, on the one hand, and between the parties and the military on the other, Northerners could be said to have enjoyed a minimum amount of benefit from the fact that a Northern government was in power.

With the NIF this was no longer so. Though basically a Northern and purely Islamic government, the NIF has worked against both North and South alike. The only beneficiaries of the regime were its adherents. Even in war, the agony that was in the past mainly felt by Southerners was now shared by the North. In the past, the majority of Northern Sudanese perceived war as a distant fire in the backwoods. The NIF regime not only religionized war, but forcibly drafted young Northern Sudanese into it. Besides, the NIF's was the first Sudanese government since independence to transform the whole national economy into a war economy and bring war nearer home by pushing the Northern opposition to carry arms. Furthermore, the pervasiveness of the NIF's control of all walks of life made Northern non-supporters of the regime strangers in their own country. A Congressional Research Service Report published in 1995 stated:[80] 'NIF's cohesiveness, organizational discipline, and control over government machinery is another contributing factor to the Front's strength. NIF members occupy key positions in Omar el Bashir's government, especially in foreign affairs and the financial sector.' Though legally banned along with other parties since 1989, the NIF according to the report had infiltrated civil institutions by purging 'disloyal' civil servants and teachers and 5,000 military officers. As we have seen in Chapter Seven, the number has since increased. Most importantly, the report went on to say, 'the NIF has established parallel institutions to insure its stay in power, such as the NIF-controlled militia, known as the Popular Defense Force (PDF) which is almost equal in number to that of the regular military'. In addition, the 'NIF has its own security apparatus, and senior members of the current government occupy key positions in the security hierarchy'.[81] To strengthen its control of people's life, the regime eavesdroped on private conversations through the central telephone system, and went on to monopolize all commercial telephone exchange centres in the Sudan. All those centres are owned and run by security agencies. Evidently, the NIF was not mindful even of the commands of its own constitution. Article 29 of that constitution (1998) ensures the inviolability and privacy of communications.

This picture was also backed by the report of the Human Rights Watch/Africa, in its publication entitled 'Behind the Red Line'.[82] Interestingly, that title was drawn from a brazen speech by Bashir in January 1996 in which he said: 'When we talk of handing power to the people, we mean the people will be within certain limits but no one will cross the red lines which are aimed at the interest of the nation.'[83] Bashir's powers obviously admit no limitation. However, in analysing the political situation in Sudan, Human Rights Watch (Africa) said, that 'being a Muslim does not guarantee freedom of religion in Sudan's Islamic State since the two largest Muslim sects (*Ansar* and the *Khattmiyya*) from which in the past the two largest political parties drew their members were subjected to government attempts at control and confiscation of their mosques. Other Muslim groups who were critical of the NIF were deemed 'insufficiently religious' and consequently subjected to harassment. Imams (prayer leaders) who were considered too critical or ideologically out of line with the NIF's policies (even if the criticism did not impinge on doctrinal issues)[84] were also clamped down upon. The religious responsibility of those Imams oblige them to advise their flock and ethicize on worldly as well as on spiritual matters, but Sudan's 'Islamic' government viewed criticism as a challenge to its legitimacy. The government's response to the Imams' sermons, according to the report, had often been repressive and inordinate. Eventually, the government resolved to bring all prayer leaders under one broad umbrella, an association of Imams, controlled by the NIF. Those were Bashir's red lines that were meant to delineate the boundaries of national interest.

After facing the reality of this type of oppression by the NIF, many Northern Sudanese have begun to appreciate the predicament of exclusion to which Southerners were subjected. While previously it was the South that was denied the freedom of religion, today this freedom is denied even to fellow Muslims who did not adhere to the NIF dogma. Previously it was the South that was denied freedom of association. Today Northerners have been denied that too. Even the right of equal opportunity in economic activity was denied to Northerners who were not allied to the NIF in the same way it has always been denied to Southerners.

The current dilemma of a large segment of the Northern elite, therefore, is whether it is justified to fight for freedoms from the NIF government and yet maintain that the same freedoms continue to be denied to others. Obviously, by insisting that they have a right to freedom of religion, Northerners have no way but to support similar demands that have always been made by Southerners. By insisting on equal opportunity in economic activity, the Northerners have given credence to the same demand for equal development of all regions that has always been made by the economically marginalized.

View from the South: From Separatism to Unity

Faced with the assimilative excesses of the ruling classes in the North, the South has experimented with the entire spectrum of resistance, from a political crusade to be recognized as having their own authenticity and rights as citizens of the Sudan, to carrying arms. Armed rebellion in the South started in 1955, four months before independence in January,1956. That no lasting solution has been found decades down the line is perhaps an indication not only of the short-sightedness of the ruling establishment, but also of the complexity of the emotions that were involved. What needs to be re-emphasized, though, is that Southern feelings are now maturing and the South, through participation in the NDA and insistence on a voluntarily united democratic Sudan, can be said to be taking the lead in the efforts to create a more just and prosperous environment for future generations.

The SPLM/A was born at a time when the political environment in Sudan was particularly disheartening. Nimeiri's imamate and unilateral abrogation of the Addis Ababa Accord not only betrayed the South, but also embittered with disappointment the whole of Sudan. By cutting the feet from beneath peace, Nimeiri led the whole country into inevitable conflict and bloodshed. This is not to suggest in any way that the reinstatement of the Addis Ababa Accord would *per se* bring the ongoing conflict to an end. On the formation of the SPLM, its leader made an appeal to all Sudanese people in which he expressed a radical view of the country's crisis. Radical because it was a departure from the hackneyed clichés of the past that only saw the surface differences, not the underlying confluence. It was also radical in that it transcended the inferiority complex of many Southern leaders who were either content with the position of second class citizenry within a united Sudan writ small, or completely lost hope in achieving unity and, therefore, lowered their horizons to solving 'the problem of the South'. Garang recognized that it was the central authority (whether colonial, parliamentary, military or religious fundamentalist) that had put the knife to the bonds that held the Sudanese together, so that the nation stood divided into 'Northerners and Southerners, Westerners and Easterners, Halfawieen and the so-called *Awlad al Balad*' while to the South fragmentation according to tribe, has been prosecuted most strenuously; no doubt to the satisfaction of the coercionists and to the detriment of the abused.[85]

It is out of this deliberate segmentation of the country that the drive for secession arose. But whereas the South had hitherto been limited to seeing the cause of all their troubles as the impositions, the betrayals and the hegemony by Northern governments, Garang cut through the prejudices, the years of villainy and calumny and saw the problem for what it actually was. After years of perverted rule in Khartoum, the very ethos of state policies, the economy, religion and culture had in turn been perverted and thwarted. And though the depravity of the rulers in Khartoum affected everybody, its visitations on the South were more ruthless and telling because the South was different culturally and religiously and, thus, the forces of racial and religious bigotry found a readier home there.

Building Bridges between North and South

The collective realization of the need to create a new Sudan, other than for the NIF with its present agenda, is now almost universal. Garang, when addressing the first SPLM/A National Convention in March/April 1994, enunciated the vision of the movement for a united Sudan in the following words: 'The political discourse of the SPLM/A was directed at all the oppressed and exploited Sudanese people regardless of region, tribe, religion or cultural background. That was a call for a struggle to address and solve the fundamental problems of the country; its overriding aim was to bring about fundamental change.'

Having established his leadership in the South, Garang moved at the national level on three fronts: continuation of the political and armed struggle against the NIF, consolidation of the NDA as a viable alternative to the Khartoum regime and winning the battle of minds for the New Sudan concept. To provide a forum for the promotion of that concept, Garang floated in the early 1990s the idea of the New Sudan Brigade (NSB) as an engine for political and social change and a forum for intellectual debate on the import of, and modalities to bring about, the New Sudan. The NSB was meant to draw together all partisan and non-partisan individuals who were opposed to hegemonistic tendencies (now epitomized by the NIF regime), and shared the vision of creating a New Sudan. One other undeclared reason for the creation of the NSB was to provide a Northern-based fighting force closer to the centre of power in order to expedite Sudan's 'salvation' from the NIF'S 'Salvationist' regime. Two factors were at play when the idea was launched. The first was to neutralize rumblings among some elements within the SPLA who were wondering why it was they alone who continued to shed blood in order to bring about this New Sudan. The second was the realization by the SPLM that, unlike Abboud's military junta or the armed forces under Nimeiri, the NIF regime was utterly insensitive to the ruination they have wrought on the whole Sudan. And so long as they managed to control the citadel of power in Khartoum and its environs, they would never give in or give up. Their inspiration must have come from the pre-Taliban Mullahs of Afghanistan who pretended that whoever of them controlled Kabul controlled the whole country. Unsurprisingly the idea of the NSB caught on with younger Northern elements. A fighting force was formed on the eastern front bringing together a rainbow of adherents from different regions of Sudan. Today that force represents the largest fighting unit within the NDA forces on that front.

In a memorandum entitled 'The New Sudan Brigade, the Working Programme' Garang wrote, 'the concept of the New Sudan and New Sudanism must be operationalized and nurtured to become a living ideological weapon of struggle for nation formation, national renaissance and unity of the Sudanese people'. Garang advised that the concept of a new Sudanese nation, proud of its rich multicoloured past and aware of its historical mission and destiny, 'must be taught in all our schools and reflected in our outlook'. In defining Sudan's 'historical past' he did not reach out to the kingdoms of Ghana and Benin, but to Sudan's authentic African contribution to human civilization and its implications on the creation of contemporary Sudan. That history, Garang proffered, extended to Biblical times,[86] Nubia and Islamic kingdoms Sudan's current diversity. Those were the chapters of Sudan history of which the pre-independence intelligentsia was willing to forget. As for the Islamists (from Sadiq al Mahdi to the Bashir/Turabi regime), they were ready and willing to do away with that history and dismantle its remnants. In fact, it was during Sadiq al Mahdi's government that the minister of culture ordered Nubian and Coptic monuments removed from Sudan's national museum. Excepting for the furor caused among curators, the minister was never reprimanded for that grotesque act. Those monuments, the minister was reported to have said, did not reflect Sudan's true history. Obviously, history to that raw recruit began with the entry of the Arabs in Sudan. Little did that minister of 'culture' know, but Nubian treasures were celebrated all over the world. Indeed, few years after the minister's unpardonable error, an exhibition of Nubian monuments became a moving feast from Germany to France. Moreover, Nubians, of all people of Sudan, are reported on authority to be the most lifelike of modern Northern Sudanese both in features and skin colour.[87] How incredible for any man to erase with a stroke of the pen, for dubious ideological considerations, the history of the original owners of the land.

Garang was, therefore, on track when he lambasted the bigotry of the old Sudan. In the old Sudan, he said, 'national identity, nation building and national unity were only slogans camouflaging policies of political oppression and religious bigotry'. He said further the Sudanese nation, 'has not developed through a trajectory determined by its past and present realities, rather through an unrealistic trajectory imposed by speculators and vested interest groups with visions limited by these narrow, parochial interests'. Indeed, by reckoning back to mediaeval Nubia, while recognizing early Islamic kingdoms, Garang, as likely as not, did not seek to create for Sudan a mythical proto-nationalism, inasmuch as he was pleading to the Sudanese not to dispossess themselves of the variegated cultural strands of their rich history. Besides, by recalling the impact of Nubian culture on the rest of Africa he surely wanted to extinguish the false dichotomization prevalent in the minds of the proponents of *negritude* within Sudan. Nubians, for all ends and purposes, were Africans.[88]

Things in Sudan, however, are not as easy as one would like them to be. The failure of the NSB to create the groundswell support from Northern elements, particularly those who should have been naturally drawn to it, was stunning. This, to a large degree, applied to the educated elite who were neither satisfied with old party politics, nor with the political culture that sustained it. One understandable reason for the failure was the reluctance of Northerners to identify with the NSB in view of the military connotations inherent in the word brigade. To others, joining an organization that was sworn to overthrow the government by force was an act of sedition they were not as yet sure to undertake. Furthermore, Northerners laboured under the psychological blackmail of the NIF, so joining the NSB would have been portrayed as joining 'Christian' forces bent on conquering the Islamic faith in Sudan.[89] This type of blackmail was not just an NIF shenanigan. During the regime of the parties, intellectuals who chose to identify with the SPLM/A were regularly depicted by al Mahdi's government (1986–89) as fifth columnists.

There was also another factor that should not be minimized: the self-perceived pre-eminence by a not so insignificant slice of the 'new forces'. The fact that the vision of a New Sudan was articulated by a political leader from the South seemingly intimidated those groups. Like Southern separatists who were more comfortable with the old schisms (Arab versus non-Arab and Muslim versus Christian), the 'modernists', too, would have been much more at ease with an SPLM that lowered its horizons to the resolution of the Southern problem, while throwing its full weight behind them at the national level. Thus, while a sector of the 'modern forces' kept its distance from the SPLM because it was impolitic to 'follow' a Southern non-Muslim leader, many of those who got on the right side of the movement remained reluctant to recognize its leading role in the struggle for a New

Sudan.[90] Surely, neither the SPLM, nor the NSB wanted to take precedence over, or queue jump, other leaders at the national level. If anything, they only sought cooperation among like-minded political groups both within and outside the NDA, the SPLM had willingly cooperated with Northern-based political organizations as an equal partner.

On the other hand, any assumption that the SPLM, only by the dint of its Southern origin, should vacate its national leadership role for Northern 'prefects' would not be but presumptuous. Groups who entertained such notions had completely misread the political road map, for what made the SPLM different than any Southern-originated political movement were, first, the vision it has formulated, second, the targets it has set to achieve, third, the struggle it has launched, fourth, the wherewithal it has mobilized for consumating that struggle and achieving those targets, and fifth, the successes it has scored on the ground politically, militarily and intellectually. If all that the SPLM had come up with was its manifesto, very few people would have remembered it or cared for it; in politics Good Samaritanism is not the name of the game. Even so, no one would have remembered the Good Samaritan, according to Margaret Thatcher, 'if he'd only had good intentions. He had money as well.'

In addition, if all the SPLM's might and main was directed towards resolving the Southern problem, the 'modern forces' would have not been as buoyed up with it. For that reason, the 'modern forces' who have pertinaciously struggled for political renewal in Sudan, but failed to create the appropriate alignment of the forces to generate that change, endorsed the SPLM's vision of the New Sudan as well as the modalities it proposed to enact it. Regrettably, some of those 'modernists' went on to do exactly what they deplored most in the traditional parties: assuming political leadership for themselves as if by right of birth. There was indeed a time when some of those 'born leaders' expected the SPLM to break ranks with the traditional parties and coalesce with the modern forces – amorphous and undefined as they were – against those parties. In other words, they wanted to come to power on the SPLM/A's coattails without recognizing its leadership role even as *primus inter pares*. Apart from the unwelcome thought of cheating a political movement out of history, this stance lacked both historical perspective and contextual understanding of the alignment of forces on the ground.

To the SPLM/A, building a new Sudan can never be predicated on exclusion, only through inclusion and making everybody (including the traditional forces) face the stark realities of the Sudanese situation. That is, if Sudan is to remain united. The success of KDD and the Sudanese Peace Initiative was based on this strategy. In consequence, those who called for ideologically centred alliances erred on three reckonings. First they failed to see the NSB for what it was: a sparkplug for triggering change and transformation. Such change could not have been possible without the persuasiveness of the SPLM and the disuasiveness of the SPLA. Second, if Sudan's unity is what the 'modern forces' aim at, then the last chance for achieving it shall only come through the political dispensation triggered off by the SPLM and accepted by the majority of political forces since Koka Dam. The actualization of that dispensation depends entirely on the SPLM/A's full and direct participation in it, and not by proxy. Third, the creation of the New Sudan is not an episode; it is a process. This process entails engaging all political players away from the overplayed jingles of right and left, new and traditional. After all, among those who are shedding their blood to build the New Sudan are warriors belonging to tribal or ethnic-based formations (Beja, Rashaida, Nuba, Funj). What brought this consortium together were not ideologically based affinities but the afflictions they had suffered in the old Sudan.

Jump-starting the Brigade, therefore, showed how slowly change was accepted, and how grudgingly people lay down prejudices and self-perceived virtues. Perceptions that are woven into a man's whole life are evidently hard to shift. So are prejudices as attitudes of mind; they cannot be changed overnight. Further, habits of mind cannot be legislated away, but only through a long process of education and enlightenment shall they dwindle to vanishing point. For someone not acquainted with the complexity of the Sudanese situation it would appear that there were still some Northern Sudanese who would prefer Northern-born repression to Southern-led freedom. Francis Deng, delving on this issue in an address to a Sudanese symposium held in Cairo asked: 'Are we Sudanese racists or cultural chauvinists? We are both,' he answered.[91] Disagreeably, this author tends partly to agree with that reprobative and unpalatable conclusion.

Conclusion

To keep their country intact, the people of Sudan have no way but to reconceptualize the 'Sudanese nation'. Forty-four years of trial and error at establishing a stable country have resulted in a total breakdown in relations between the communities living within the geographical frontiers that denote Sudan. The breakdown is so grave that possibly not one of these societies can claim to be in a better situation today than it was during the Condominium. The greatest failure, as we and other writers have argued, is that Sudanese have no concept of what 'Sudanism' encompasses. Instead the country continued to be besieged by two parallel visions of identity. Reconciliation of the two visions would not have been an issue were the South to go its way, but it is when both Northerners and Southerners claimed that they wanted to live as one nation. The onus on the North is greater, since it was the one who resorted to force in the first place to maintain that unity. Also, the ideas that have militated against the nucleation of Sudan as a nation had their origin in the North.

But alongside Sudan's unpropitious adversarial politics in the North, and internecine wars between the North and South, the country was made to suffer another crisis: that of cultural identity. This often translated into the reductive and simplistic stereotypes of Arab North and African South. Reductive and simplistic because Sudan is an integral part of Africa, not only in a geopolitical terms, but also in a cultural sense. The intercommunication between the people of Sudan through the years, and particularly since the fourteenth century, was not only dominated by geographical and environmental variables. Other cultural, social and human parameters were also at play. Not even the daunting geographic barriers stopped the flow of culture from Nubia to nearly all the East Sudanic belt, or the flow of Arabic language to the deep recesses of the South. This happened through a process of cultural transudation that was only hindered by messianic do-gooders, from the religious zealots of the nineteenth century to the Christian missionaries of the twentieth century up to the NIF fanatics of today. Nevertheless, this historical process of cultural cross-fertilization has produced an identifiable multifaceted and composite Sudanese culture. Professor Mazrui rightly observed that the Arab–African divide in Sudan is not dichotomous but has the complexity of a continuum.[92] Sudan, he maintained, has made a singular contribution to Africa by adding a Negro dimension to Arabism. As such, Sudan had emerged as a paradigm case for an Afro-Arab dual identity. Indeed, were the Sudanese to grow up as one united people, they need not re-imagine themselves, but see themselves for what they are. If united in a vision bigger than that of its disparate fragments, Sudan would evolve into an entity bigger than the sum total of its component parts. But then, as Mazrui contends, 'national integration implies transcending ethnic and cultural partial peculiarities and coalescing around a new trans-ethnic identity'.[93] Tellingly, neither blood and soil relationship nor religion were strong enough bonds to keep together nations characterized by other diffusive pluralities. There is no nation in Africa which is ethnically more homogeneous than Somalia. Yet the adversities through which that country had gone for nearly two decades should make many scholars rethink their conclusions as to what made a nation in Africa. Neither ethnicity nor common culture and religion kept Somalia together. On the other hand, the politically motivated secession of Bangladesh from the 'Islamic' Republic of Pakistan exposed the flimsiness of the idea of a Nation of Islam. It should have served notice on the political missionaries who advocated that idea in Sudan. Nations cannot live by religion alone. The disintegration of a republic which was confectioned from scratch on the basis of religion was, for all ends and purposes, propelled by political concerns: the perceived economic injustices suffered by the Bengalese at the hands of the Sindis.

In Sudan, distortions of the meaning and quintessence of identity deepened the country's crisis. Reasons for the distortion, as we have demonstrated, vary. On the one hand, there was the deliberate disfiguration of historical and contemporary realities either to bolster dominance, or to give credence to elitist quixotic yearnings. On the other, the syndrome of denial ensuing from this dominance triggered off exasperated reactions. In the face of denial of their worth by others, people generally become inward-looking. The American playwright, Arthur Miller, hit the nail on the head when he told the English weekly, *The Observer*: 'If there weren't any anti-semitism, I'd not think of myself as Jewish'.

At the end, in the face of all the above irrational claims, we are left no wiser about the essence of the multifaceted Sudanese identity. Nevertheless, the emergence of the NIF and its complete polarization of Sudan's identity crisis, and the emanation of the SPLM and its conceptualization of a New Sudan, forced the alternatives out in the open. The SPLM's new conceptualization of identity has evidently daunted many Northerners, if only because the so-called 'slave' half of the equation had now the temerity to take a position on what Sudanism is about. John Garang phrases it as follows: 'Our major problem is that Sudan has been looking and is still looking for its soul, for its true identity. Failing to find it, the Sudanese take refuge in Arabism. Failing this they find refuge in Islam as a uniting factor. Others get frustrated as they fail to see how they could become Arabs, when their creator thought otherwise, and they take refuge in separation. In all this, there is a lot of mystification and distortion to suit the various sectarian interests.'[94] This is as accurate a reading of the Sudanese identity dilemma as one is likely to encounter.

Cynics may say it is too late to consolidate a coherent nation within Sudan's geographic mass. To the incredulous, the country is beyond redemption. But those who are struggling for Sudan's unity on a new basis are moving mountains and they know it. Some may therefore ask: 'Is it a worthwhile endeavour, despite the cost involved?' Our answer is yes, because if you believe in the unity of Africa and the solidarity of the countries of the global South in a world which is increasingly segmented between have-lots and have-nots, then it would be ill-considered to encourage the dismemberment of existing units within that South.. To this vision, all political schools in Africa are professedly committed. However, the actualization of that vision does not only presuppose a sense of history on the part of those who subscribe to it, but it also requires stamina to continue the race. In the race for the creation of a New Sudan larger than the sum total of its parts, Garang proved to be a long-distance runner. Leaders of this mettle, without respite, refuse to be disappointed in the future.

In this marathon race, two things are to Garang's credit: first, he had liberated himself from the idea of an insular SPLM/A conceived by secessionists; second, he successfully challenged assumptions by Northern politicians that Southern politicians should remain fossilized as a regional subspecies. By so doing he turned the whole nation's politics on its head. It is perhaps this *boulversement* – more than any other factor – that annoyed his unyielding critics in the North. This need not be the case. Those critics would have done their country some good if they reconciled themselves with the contemporary realities that nationally, regionally and internationally besiege Sudan. Those who fail to liberate themselves from the fetters of the past shall have no future, their future shall always be their past thrown in front of them. In a Proustian sense, they shall always remain in search of things past.

In the end, Garang, to a fashion, may be the catalyst for, if not the midwife of, a New Sudan. Extraordinarily, his best Northern counterparts in seeking to remould Sudan are those who are viscerally anti-South, anti-

SPLM and anti-modernity (as the rest of mankind understands it): the NIF. The NIF, like the SPLM, is engaged in remoulding the Sudan in a new image. This perhaps explains why the NIF, while depicting Garang in their media as the devil incarnate, still pursues him in all peace negotiations as the most desired bedfellow.

However, there are two basic differences between the two visions that the NIF had failed to concede, or indeed conceive. The first is that the SPLM's paradigm is posited on popular acceptance of a new political dispensation for the whole Sudan through a national constitutional conference, and for the South, through the exercise of self-determination by its people. Hence the SPLM's scheme is not a prepackaged programme to be rammed down the throats of Sudanese, least through the barrel of the gun. The second is that religion, of whatever denomination, should never be transformed into an instrument of hate or allowed to degenerate into a persuasion to destruction. Truly, the exploitation of religion for political ends is not a brand name for Sudan's Islamists. The unscrupulous use of religion as an opportune tool to achieve earthly ends has been with us since time immemorial. In his *Decline and Fall of the Roman Empire*, Edward Gibbon put it succinctly; the different modes of worship within the Empire, he said, 'were all considered by the people as true, the philosopher as false, and the magistrate as useful.'[95] But the world has changed since the days of the Roman magistrates, and is increasingly changing. In Sudan, if the forty-four years of agony that elapsed since the declaration of the country's independence were not lesson enough to the Sudanese, the last ten years under the NIF should have opened the eyes of the Islamists and traditional neo-Islamists to a simple reality. Their own self-interest dictates that they adhere to the demands of civil pluralism. That is also the godly thing to do, for 'nothing is more acceptable to God than an enlightened view of our own self interest'.[96]

ENDNOTES

1. Toynbee, Arnold J., *Between the Niger and the Nile*, p. 6.
2. Sudan occupies a surface area of approximately 2.5 million square kilometres (about one million square miles), which is equivalent to that of Italy, Portugal, UK, France, Denmark, Norway and Sweden put together, or that of the territorial US, east of the Mississipi.
3. Abdel Rahim, M., *Imperialism and Nationalism*; and Deng, F.M., *War of Visions*.
4. By selecting his caliph from amongst supporters from the marginalized West and not his own kinship, al Mahdi transcended in one *coup* the biases of riverain Sudanese against those of the peripheries. This non-ethnic-based approach to policy decision was also evident in the Mahdi's appointment of his top generals such as Hamdan Abu Anja (Nuba).
5. As observed earlier, the contumely of the riverain notables against the Khalifa and his *gharaba* ruling clan, led to plots for his removal for which they paid dearly. The riverain notables assumed that ascendancy to the highest echelons of power should have been theirs by right of birth.
6. The book enumerated cases of political disempowerment suffered by Dar Furians, particularly in senior government posts. This type of complaint was in the past only limited to Southerners. Turabi welcomed the book and associated himself with the Dar Furian complaints. So did Ali al Haj, Turabi's deputy. *Al Khartoum*, 16 July 2000.
7. Skilfully exploiting his position as SSU political commissar of Dar Fur during the Nimeiri era, Turabi built in that province intricate nests of Muslim Brothers supporters, rather than consolidating the SSU grassroots. The Dar Furian Islamists remained loyal to Turabi, even after his schism with Bashir.
8. Connor, Walker, *Ethnonationlism*, p. 40.
9. Ibid., op. cit.
10. Smith, Anthony D., Professor of Politics at London School of Economics, in *People, Nation and State*, Edward Mortimer *et al.* eds, p. 39.
11. Miller, David, Fellow in Social and Political Theory, Nuffield College, Oxford, *Citizenship and National Identity*, pp. 63–4.
12. Ibid.
13. An-N'aim, *The National Question, Secession and Constitutionalism*, p. 105.
14. Deng and Gifford, *The Search for Peace*, p. 63.
15. Lesch, Ann Mosely, *Sudan, Contested National Identities*, p. 4.
16. Segal, *Islam and Black Slaves*, p. 8. Segal was referring to the prevalence in the US, up to the 1960s, of the adjective Negroes or nigger in

describing Afro-Americans, despite the country's political culture which asserts its particular contribution to civilized development, its devotion to the national, the democratic and the liberal.

17. In the *Mahdiyya* documents reviewed by M.I. Nugud, slaves captured in war were catalogued in lists of the treasury *(beit al mal)* alongside goats and sheep. J. Spaulding also uncovered private family papers of the Funj era in which properties owned by those families were enlisted, and in which slaves were neither described by their names nor tribes, but were derogatorily called *hayawan natig* (talking animal). Spaulding, *Slavery, Land Tenure and Social Class*, p. 12.

18. The term was coined by advocates of a new Sudanese identity based on the only attributes that unite Sudanese, not those that divide them like religion or ethnic origin. Manifestly, the NIF had adopted the term in order to attenuate fears expressed by non-Muslims against its religioun-based constitution. Priorly, the Islamists espoused a constitutional model that excluded those groups from high offices. The *muwattana* is thus meant to ensure that constitutional rights and duties shall only be determined on the basis of citizenship irrespective of religion, gender, or ethnic origin. However, a cursory look at the way in which offices at the higher echelons of government, judiciary, the army and parliament were allocated in the past and up to the present, reveals a different reality.

19. *Alwan*, an organ of the NIF, published on 7 April 2000 a virulent editorial on the author whom they apparently chose to box within the confines of ethnicity and faith. Pandering to the prejudices of Northern Muslims, the article accused its target of the 'sin' of seeking to impose on Sudan a Christian president. The NIF organ, nonetheless, never ceased to laud the openness of the NIF's brand of Islam and the broadmindedness of Turabi's 'Islamic' constitution which anchored constitutional rights and duties on *muaattana* and not religion.

20. M.O. Beshir, a Sudanese political historian who did more than any of his peers to educate the North on the problem of the South, had an interesting view on slavery. Slavery, he said, 'ceased in the Sudan long before the conquest. What remained were a few cases of forced capture of individuals when tribes fought against each other and the existence of "slaves" captured in the old days were employed in certain areas by a few individuals as in agriculture or as domestic servants'. *Background to Conflict*, p. 20.

21. Bergen workshop on the Management of Crisis in Sudan.

22. Shyllon, Folarin, *Cultural, Rights and Wrongs*, UNESCO, p.103.

23. Statement by Sudan's Minister of Education, Ali Abdel Rahman, Second Sitting, First Session, Sudan Parliament Records, 1958.

24. The minister did not have to go into a blood-and-thunder speech about the use of English as a working language for the South, because in the same parliament in which the statement was made, English was

recognized as a working language for the benefit of Southern members, like the questioner, who were not versed in Arabic.

25. Deng, F., *Dynamics of Identification*, p. ix.
26. *The Ethnologue,* 13th Edition, Barbara F. Grimes (ed.), 1996 summer Institute of Linguistics.
27. It took Italy a century and a half after its unification by Cavour, to declare Italian as the official language of the republic. Nevertheless, the draft law was vehemently opposed by the communists and all representatives of linguistic minorities, though invariably they use Italian as an official language.
28. Davidson, Basil, *African Civilization Revisited*, p. 3.
29. Op. cit., Davidson, Basil, *The Search for Africa*, p. 261.
30. Ibrahim, 'Abdullahi A., *Al Marxia wa masa'lat al Lugha*, p.7.
31. Ibid.
32. Kuchment, Anna, *Newsweek*, 2 April 2001.
33. Johnson, Douglas H., *The Future of Southern Sudan's Past*, p. 39.
34. Voll, John and Sarah, *The Sudan Unity in Diversity*, p. 159.
35. O'Brien, Conor Cruise, *Passion and Cunning, Essays on Nationalism*, p. 193.
36. Lesch, Ann Mosley, 15 supra, p. 5.
37. Cunnison, Ian, *Sudan in Africa*, p. 189.
38. Ibid.
39. Ibid.
40. The Funj kings, for instance, promulgated an *Ummayyad* pedigree despite their Hamitic (and some historians claim *Shilluk*) origin. See Holt, P.M., *The Sudan of the Three Niles, Funj Chronicles*.
41. Borges, J.L., *The Total Library*, p. 111.
42. Chapter Six supra, note 53.
43. The forefathers of the Berta of Southern Blue Nile, composed of Northern traders who moved to the region after the conquest of Beni Shengul by Mohammed Ali Pasha, intermarried with the indigenous Berta and were incorporated in their community. Still, five generations later, those among them who continued to describe themselves as *Ja'alis* or *Dungulawis* were subject to ridicule by the Berta to the point that they decided to hide themselves by day and only emerge at night. As a result they were derogatorily called *Watawit* (bats). James, Wendy R., *Sudan in Africa*, p. 207.
44. Deng, F.M., *War of Visions*.
45. Berlin, Isaiah, *The Counter Enlightment*.
46. Op. cit., Abdel Rahim, M., *Imperialism and Nationalism*, p. 113 and Deng F.M., *War of Visions*, p. 115.
47. Mahjoub, M.A., *Al Haraka al Fikriyya wa ila ayna yajib an-tatajih*.
48. Ibid.
49. The man was a 'eunuch of great authority under Candace the Queen of Ethiopians who had charge of all her treasury and had come to Jerusalem to worship'. Acts 8–26 / 34. Candace was the queen of

Nubia and oftentimes all the area south of the first cataract on the Nile was described in the Bible as Ethiopian.

50. *Nouvelle Economie,* Algiers, 11 March 2001.
51. Syria received the Holy Father in May 2001. One of the most important sites he visited, in the footsteps of St Paul, was the *Umawy* mosque where John the Baptist, revered by both Muslims and Christians, is buried.
52. Some of Ahmed Shawqi's finest poetry and Tawfiq al Hakim's and Naguib Mahfouz's most celebrated novels immortalized Egypt's Pharaonic history.
53. Jama'a, Fideili, *Race and Culture,* Centre for Sudanese Studies.
54. Rahim, Abdel, op. cit., Warburg, Gabriel. R., *Historical Discord,* p. 155.
55. Ibid.
56. Evans-Pritchard, *Theories of Primitive Religion,* p. 18.
57. Paul Breman, the west Indian poet wrote:
    I smelted iron in Nubia when your generations still ploughed with hard wood,
    I cast bronze in Benin when London was marshaland,
    I built Timbuktou and made it a refuge for learning,
    When in the choirs of Oxford unlettered monks shivered unwashed.
    Paul Breman (1973), *You Better Believe it: Black Verse in English*
58. Bonner, Raymond, *The New Yorker,* 13 July 1992.
59. *Daily Telegraph,* London, February 1999.
60. 1 supra.
61. Al Bashir, A.E. in Deng and Gifford, p.155.
62. El Affendi, Abdel Wahab, Commentary on Francis Deng's book *War of Visions. Al Qods al Arabi,* London. Those views, however, were written before el Affendi reached his bold and thoughtful conclusion on the non-feasibility of the NIF's Islamist model. See Chapter 7 notes 204 and 205.
63. The term is reserved in the North for any legitimate uprising against the central authority by Sudanese who belong to the geographic or ethnic margins. In essence, the term suggests that there is only one ethnic community in Sudan to which all others are subsidiary. The remark also evokes the concept of *Shu'ubi* and *shu'ubiyya* which the Arabs gave to individuals and groups who belonged to other cultures or ethnic origins and were loath to recognize the prominence of Arab people and culture over their own.
64. In another article, el Affendi maintained that 'there was a general feeling to make up for lost time by spreading the national culture (Arabo-Islamic) in the South as a basis for unity. This conception presupposed that the South would act as an inert mass, wanting to be reshaped anew'. El Affendi, *Discovering the South,* p. 372.
65. Mair, Lucy, *An African People,* p.3.
66. Dondon, John Cameroun, *The Mail and Guardian,* 21 January 2000.

67. *Nhialic* among the Dinka and Kwoth among the Nuers. See Lienhardt, Geodfrey, *Divinity and Experience*, Evans-Pritchard, *Nuer Religion* and Edward B. Tylor, *Primitive Cultures*.
68. As its name suggests, it is simply a black stone situated in the Ka'aba. Muslims who visit that shrine automatically kiss that stone. Interestingly, Omar Ibn al Khatab, the second Caliph, announced on kissing it: 'I know you are a stone that shall do no harm or good to me. Haven't I seen Prophet Mohammed kissing you, I would not have done so.'
69. *Al Sharq al Awsat*, 26 February 2001.
70. Addressing the Arab Parliaments' Union, Sudan's Deputy Speaker, Abdel Aziz Shiddo, told the Union's meeting in Cairo that Islamic system must be supported because it protects Islam and Arabism from an African Christian onslaught'. *Al Khartoum*, Sunday 18 May 1997.
71. *The Encyclopaedia Britannica*, vol 8. Micropaedea, p. 552.
72. A very influential Egyptian school of thought at the time advocated closer links between Egypt and countries of the Northern Mediterranean: Taha Hussein, *Mustaqbal al Thaqafa fi Misr* (Prospect for culture in Egypt), while another looked with pride to Egypt's past before the advent of the Arabs, e.g. Tewfiq al Hakim.
73. Islam, more than Arabism, continued to be the badge of identification by which the Muslim population distinguished themselves from the French. Interestingly, the French themselves often described the native population as Mohamedans (followers of Mohammed). In their turn, the Maghrebans called the French *Room* (Literally Romans or Europeans), or pejoratively described them by the Turkish adjective *Ghawri* (foreigner).
74. Sati'a al Hussary, Kostantin Zuraiq, Michel 'Aflag, Salah al Bitar etc.
75. Constantin Zureiq wrote his chef-d'oeuvre *Maa'na al Nakba* (The Essence of the Calamity) in 1948 following the first Arab–Israeli war. In that work he argued for the consolidation of Arab nationalism as the only viable strategy to face the 'enemy'. Two decades later (after the June 1967 Arab–Israeli war), Zureiq revisited the issue, addressing this time the enemy from within. In *Ma'ana al Nakba Mujadadan* (The Essence of Clamity Revisited), Zureiq, attributed the *naksa* to lack of democracy, abridgement of human rights and unbridled authoritarianism in the region.
76. Zureiq, Kostantin, *Ma al'aml* (What to Do).
77. The invasion of Kuwait, and the disintegration of the Arab community that ensued from it, became a defining moment for Sudanese Baathists. The fallout of the Iraqi adventure threw the mask off the contrived distinction between *qaumiyya* and *wattananiyya*.
78. Leading Sudanese Baathists challenged the idea of political change through military *coups* which was central to the Baath creed. In a courageous confession, Sudanese Baathists admitted their past

mistakes in this regard. Mohamed Ali Jaden, *Al Bayan*, Dubai, 22 November 2000.

79. Turabi, *Al Mustalahat al Siyyasia fil Islam*, p. 39.
80. CRS Report for congress by Theodoros Dagne, 14 November 1995.
81. Ibid.
82. Human Rights Watch/Africa, *Behind the Red Line: Political Repression in Sudan*.
83. Harker, John, *Report on Human Security in Sudan*, op. cit., p. 23.
84. Prayer leaders sometimes criticized in mosques government policies in so far as they relate to worldly affairs, such as the high cost of living and deterioration of public services.
85. Garang, John, The Call For Democracy, p.127.
86. Garang quoted 2 Chronicles, Ch. 14, Verses 8–12 (story of Zerah the Ethiopian king and king Asa's invocation of God on him and his army). The term Ethiopia also referred to Cush. According to the Good News Bible, Cush was the term by which the Old Testament designated the area from the first cataract of the Nile at Aswan. That area was also known in Graeco-Roman times as Ethiopia and later as Nubia. Garang also recalled in 2 Kings, 19:9 where reference is made to Tirhaka the Nubian Cushite. Tirhaka was described in the new King's James version as an Abyssinian. Other citations on Nubian Sudan are also to be found in the Book of Numbers, 12:1 where reference was made to Moses's marriage to Zefra, the Cushite. Moses was criticized by Miriam and Aaron for marrying that *lowly* women but they were reprimanded by God, Number 12:8. Zefra's father, Jethro (though described as a Midian in Exodus 18:1) was Mose's instructor on law and public administration, Exodus 18: 13–27.
87. Adams, William Y., *Nubia, Corridor to Africa*, Princeton University Press, 1977 and Shinie, P., *Meroe, A Civilization of Sudan*, London, 1967.
88. Shinie, P.L, a leading authority on the history of Nubian civilization, took issue with the title given to the paper he was commissioned to write at a University of Khartoum seminar on Sudan in Africa. The title was 'The Culture of Mediaeval Nubia and its Impact on Sudan'. Shinie thought the question was misleading 'since it implies that Nubia stands outside Africa, whereas the opposite is the case. Its geographic location sufficiently makes the point. Its population by definition is African and the language of Nubia is part of the large East Sudanic group.' *Sudan in Africa*, pp. 42–50.
89. Despite all protestations to the contrary in Western capitals, the NIF never relented in its popular mobilization campaigns to depict the war with the SPLA as a religious war against infidels. As recent as the last week of March, 2000, and at the height of its sales promotion in the West, the NIF sought to make mileage from the capture by NDA forces of Hamashkoreib, a small town in Eastern Sudan. The town is reputed as centre of Qur'anic teaching in Beja land and the attack on it was conducted by an NDA detachment including a large number of Beja fighters. Rather than treating their defeat as a normal military

reversal, the NIF used to advantage the fact that Garang, the Christian, was the over-all commander of those forces. Inciting the lowest common denominator in Muslim impulses, the NIF government took to the streets to galvanize Muslims against an alleged onslaught by 'infidels' on Islamic shrines.

90. Since the NIF's assumption of power, at least ten political groups belonging to the 'modern forces' approached, some time or the other, the SPLM seeking 'cooperation' with it. In one of those cases, the totality of the membership of the group did not exceed the delegation that met with the SPLM. Those groups generally lacked identifiable popular bases within Sudan. At best, they represented a constellation of like-minded intellectuals. Sometimes they were made of intellectuals who found themselves by accident in a near or distant world capital. Surprisingly, not one of those minuscule groups proposed to join the SPLM. They always indicated a desire to keep their own identity, and still benefit from the SPLM political presence and military might. That, of course, is understandable in the case of political organizaitons with an identifiable core of popular support and a historical presence within Sudan's political landscape, but not in the case of weightless political groups.

91. Deng, Francis, *Race and Culture*, Cairo, August, 1999.
92. Mazrui, A., *Sudan in Africa*, p. 242.
93. Ibid.
94. Garang, John, *The Call for Democracy*, p. 127.
95. Gibbon, Edward, *Decline and Fall of the Roman Empire*, p.
96. Butler, Samuel, *The Way of All Flesh*, p.

CHAPTER NINE

Peace, Mediation and Conflict Resolution

I have many times asked myself whether there can be more potent advocates of peace upon earth through the years to come than this massed multitude of silent witnesses to the desolation of war.
George V at the Cemetery in Flanders, 1922

Introduction

One amazing feature of the Sudanese conflict is its tenacity. Despite the annihilation of two million Southern Sudanese either in the battlefield or through war-related hazards, and the dislocation of twice that number, there is still no end in sight for the infernal war. The statistics of death alone were a sufficient indicator of the desolation of war. But Sudan's war continued to defy the battlefield and elude, for decades, mediation efforts for peaceful resolution. Like the mythical phoenix, whenever the flames of war die down, it surprises friend and foe by emerging from the ashes; reinvigorated, more vicious and ready to inflict greater casualties and economic damage on a nation that by all accounts has had more than its fair share of suffering and division. Even during periods of relative calm, the prospects for renewed conflagration were always there, simmering below the surface like a hellish ghoul. Sadly, none of the root causes of the war was unknown to the belligerents, nor were the solutions obscure. The tardy recognition by Sudanese political leaders of the entrenched causes of the crisis, after almost half a century, speaks volumes of the quality of that leadership.

The cycle of conflict that started with the 1955 mutiny was followed by half-hearted efforts on peacemaking, alongside concerted destruction and bloodshed that climaxed with the Nimeiri *coup* in 1969. A peace of sorts was worked out in 1972, but shattered in 1983 into fragments of conflict that were more violent than at any other time in the history of the country. Sudan, by the end of the century, was almost back to where it was at its dawn. G.W. Steevens, a journalist accompanying Lord Kitchener then wrote: 'The Sudan is a desert, and a depopulated desert. Northward of Khartoum, it is wilderness; southward it is a devastation.'[1]

Today, the scale of war is unprecedented It does not merely pit the North against the South, but virtually the whole of Sudan against itself: South against South, North against South and North against North. And whereas the fundamental causes of the North–South conflict are sustained; within the South the SPLA has fought amongst itself, and the NDA forces are fighting a Northern 'Muslim' regime in the East. There is a certain self-sustaining rhythm to this conflict that suggests that perhaps now that the intensity of animosity is at a fever pitch, now that the war has built itself into a climax and assumed a self-sustaining momentum, then the moment is ripe for a negotiated and hopefully this time, permanent peace.

But before we can hope for such a miracle, we need to understand the dynamics of this monstrosity. Contrary to the simplification that is quite often pursued for ease of analysis, we repeat, the Sudanese conflict goes well beyond an NIF versus SPLM/A, Arabs against Africans, Christian killing Muslim, type of dichotomy. True enough, those are critical dimensions, but in reality the conflict is like an onion; it is multi-layered, and each layer has subtle subsets of causative variables, each working to fan the fires of conflagration. But one thing is sure and can be summed up in a few words: the old political Sudan is caducous with one foot on the grave, and the new is yet to emerge. This is clearly a definition of crisis.

The Conflict and its Many Faces

At one level, the war in Sudan is a straightforward rebellion by the South against the North, a defiance of the centre by the periphery. As we have established elsewhere, there is no denying that at the heart of the sources of war is the consistent effort over the years by successive governments in Khartoum to impose hegemony over the South. Another level involves the absurdly mundane but no less violent and destructive power struggle between the dominant political forces in the North. Here, the traditional political parties cobbled together power structures that tapped support from religious sympathies. Here, also, the Islamic fundamentalists of the NIF proposed and went ahead to carry out a violent and radical application of Islam that challenged the authority and power base of the established Islamic fraternities. Here too, are the 'modern forces': trades unions, intellectual groups etc. an amorphous, though potentially influential segment of society, without the organizational facility or the democratic space within which to evolve into a politically significant player. And like the others, the most vociferous among them ended being locked in an unscrupulous struggle for state power.

The other level is international, as inevitably when two people take on each other, there is always a third, either urging them for ulterior motives to go on fighting, or trying to draw them apart. Since the demise of Nimeiri, efforts for intermediation, exploration of prospects for peace, facilitation of dialogue and intellectual probing went unabated. To some of those we shall refer, but the point to underscore at this stage is that even peace- making in Sudan has eventually degenerated into an industry in which all and sundry are trying their hand. Regardless, the onset of the NIF rule has added other dimensions to the conflict that made external intervention inescapable.

To start with, the regime's messianic zeal in forcing its brand of Islam onto adherents to other faiths within Sudan created its own problems. Christians and adherents of African belief systems were regularly harassed and coerced ant at times coaxed into converting to Islam. On the other hand, the regime served notice on neighbouring countries that its religious mission extended beyond Sudan's borders, a matter that caused alarm among some neighbours. As the regime's interference in the internal affairs of neighbours increased, so did the worry and anger of those neighbours as well as that of the international community. Furthermore, the degeneration of both civil war and the internecine South–South conflict to unbearable limits caused an unprecedented humanitarian crisis. That crisis weighed heavily on the spirit of the international community and spurred it into collective action to alleviate suffering. All those factors combined, made external intervention a matter of course.

Other factors also turned the war into a self-perpetuating phenomenon. In addition to the old cultural, religious and political animus, new battlefield realities made the continuation of the conflict a matter of material benefit to some combatants. To those, war turned into an enduring state of 'normalcy'. For instance, areas in the Nuba Mountains, which were systematically ethnically cleansed of indigenous population, became a source of ready wealth for an unholy alliance of government soldiers and merchants. Also, cattle rustling, smuggling of ivory, gold and semi-precious stones, hoarding of goods, profiteering in garrison towns, trade in arms among tribal militias, as well as a host of other unscrupulous and nefarious moneymaking ventures, made war a very profitable business for soldiers of fortune. Given that the fighters of the SPLA also lived off the land, an environmental dimension was added to the conflict, and a dangerous one at that, since it portended a violent competition over limited natural resources. The fauna of the Savannah became a major source of military logistics. Those factors, put together, complicated the equation of war and threatened the natural resource base. There is yet another layer: prized resources. In any other country, the discovery of oil would have been an occasion for rejoicing and one that could hold nothing but the promise of prosperity. Not so in Sudan where oil has just become one more weapon of war, one more reason to fight. It is in this context that the burgeoning war became a hydra-headed conflict.

It is to the dynamics of those interrelated ramifications, political, economic and humanitarian (each with its own international dimension), that we shall now turn. That is the map of the conflict as it is today. A negotiated settlement must take into account every contour, and must arrive not merely at a cessation of hostilities (which is difficult enough), but at a sustainable peace. Such peace encompasses the removal of historic political and economic injustices, solutions to the war-generated humanitarian crisis as well as issues related to the exploitation of, and competition over, natural resources (oil, mining, water and pastures). The solution should also address the amplitude of the destruction caused by war on the natural resource base on which economic development depends, in addition to all manner of social ills spawned by the culture of war.

Religion as a Factor of War

At the outset, as the transformation of Sudan's civil war into a *jihad* made the Nile foam with blood, so did it make Christians, within and outside the country, froth with indignation. In the last three decades, particularly following the Addis Ababa agreement, world Christian institutions[2] were, for the most part, involved in helping Sudan cope with its humanitarian crisis. After the emergence of the NIF regime the situation changed; Christian institutions began sounding their horns not so much because they were affrighted by the regime's religious orientation – as the regime often claimed – but because of its dogmatism and intolerance towards other faiths. With every Christian denomination waiting for the axe to fall, Sudan's Muslim fundamentalists had no reason to be jolted by the Christian counter-rebuff generated by its policies. For example, in the course of the decade of the 1990s, Sudan received for the first time in its history two leading Christian pontiffs: Pope John Paul II (February 1993) and the Archbishop of Canterbury (January, 1995).[3] Both pontiffs came to Sudan to deliver a message of peace, but more importantly to counsel the regime that no religion should be a persuasion to evil. The Pope, for example, held an open-air mass in Khartoum in the course of which he appealed for religious tolerance. On the other hand, the Archbishop announced to a congregation at Juba on 28April: 'I do not believe there is any reason either here in Sudan or anywhere else in the world for Christians and Muslims to commit violence against one another.' The Archibishop's concerns were conveyed before his first visit to Sudan by Peter Vaughan, the Bishop of Ramsbury. Vaughn saw the NIF for what it was and, without mincing his words, castigated the regime for its excesses. 'Both Christians and Muslims in Sudan are crucified as a matter of course to instill fear in their hearts,' he told a London weekly.[4]

The regime belatedly engaged in intensive lobbying with the high and mighty in the Christian world, but lobbying outside Sudan had nothing to do with realities inside it. Contemptible to its own claims about tolerance of Islam to other faiths, the regime adopted a series of repressive measures against Christians and Christian institutions, leading the Sudanese Catholic Bishops Conference to write to the United Nations Secretary General, Boutros Boutros Ghali, in September 1992 complainig about the harassment they were increasingly subjected to. On 6 October 1992, the Sudanese Catholic bishops took advantage of their quinqennial visit to the Holy Father known as *Visita ad lumina* to raise the alarm bells. In a strongly worded appeal, the bishops told the Vatican: 'We are spiritual leaders and shepherds and in no way statesmen or politicians. Therefore, our defense of human rights must be seen as part and parcel of our vocation and mission.' The bishops message was 'an appeal for peace and respect for human rights'; but peace, they said, 'was unattainable without justice and respect for human rights'. Elaborating on the matter, the bishops added: 'Under the present regime basic freedoms, including the right to life, right to free speech, right to education and right to profess ones faith are totally and integrally denied.' The suppression of Christians took different forms, from demolition of places of worship to persecution of bishops. For instance in December 1996, the regime demolished the Catholic Multipurpose and Prayer Centres in Douroushab; in March 1997 a similar centre in Teria was razed; on 7 April of the same year another centre in Kalakla al Guba was also destroyed, as was the one in Jebel Aulia dismantled in July.[5] The government's flimsy argument that those centres were a source of public nuisance because they were estabilshed in residential areas was astounding, as if places of worship were deemed to be located in industrial areas. No such requirement was envisaged for the construction of mosques. On the other hand, the Anglican Bishop of Khartoum was sentenced to public flogging on a charge of adultery. Apart from the fact that non-Muslims were not subject to Islamic penal laws, the very stringent rules of Islamic evidence that required the presence of four witnesses, who should have simultaneously watched the guilty act committed, was not observed by the NIF judge. Obviously, the idea was not the application of God's laws in as much as it was to humiliate the bishop who refused to keep his mouth shut.

Hardly at all did the regime address the legitimate demands made by Christians inside and outside Sudan; on the contrary, it went on befooling the Christian world outside about its tolerance of other faiths, while the policy of persecuting and harassing non-Muslims inside Sudan went ahead. The regime nevertheless exerted itself to cover up for its religious excesses against Christians through fraudulent Muslim–Christian dialogues, the first of which was held in Khartoum in 1994. The purpose of that meeting was to create a broad Islamo-Christian front to work together, of all things, for restructuring the UN. Turabi, who led the debate, was indubitably on cloud nine, while those whom he was addressing were very much down to earth. One of those, John Isaiah, a teacher of Christian studies in Dongola (North Sudan), challenged Turabi, arguing that before restructuring the UN, 'we should think of restructuring our own house'. In that respect, Isaiah referred to the harassment to which he was subjected in his school. That statement invited a violent response from the Secretary General of the NIF, Ghazi Salah el Din. 'If there were pressures on Christians, people like you would not have been allowed to say what they said,' said Ghazi.[6] That statement alone summed up the NIF's perception of religious tolerance as well as the way its leaders understood the meaning of freedoms of conscience and thought. The two freedoms are intertwined and it was not without reason that the article on freedom of conscience in the Universal Declaration (Article 18) was immediately followed by that on freedom of thought and expression (Article 19). However, the regime's cynicism was such that at the height of its aerial bombardment of Christian places of worship in South Sudan (July 2000), Foreign Minister Ismail visited the Vatican to enlist its support for the ongoing peacemaking efforts. It was at that period, too, that the regime refused to budge from its position on religion and politics at the IGAD negotiations. Nonetheless, with a steady pulse, the Minister told Monseigneur Jean-Louis Tauran during that visit, that the Sudan government was committed to religious tolerance, peaceful coexistence among religions and respect for cultural pluralities.[7] Unmistakably, there is no limit to the NIF's disregard for human intelligence, or to their unbelievably false front. The policy of religious discrimination and persecution continued, therefore, in defiance of the government's own inducements to Christendom.

That eventually led Sudanese Catholic bishops, together with the US Catholic Conference, to issue an appeal in Washington on 14 November 2000, entitled 'Cry for Peace'. The appeal left nothing unsaid. 'A government that does not represent the people of Sudan,' said the document, 'has waged a systematic campaign of terror against Christians, practitioners of traditional African religions, and non-Arabs in the South and Eastern parts of the country, while in the North, Christian churches have been destroyed and voices of opposition have been brutally repressed' To underline their non-partisan approach to the intractability of conflict, the bishops added that it was clear to them that 'all sides are implicated in egregious human rights abuses, including the SPLM/A but the Sudan government 'bears the greatest responsibility for abuses against civilian population, slavery, tortures, executions, religions persecution, discriminatory laws, unconscionable restrictions to aid to populations threatened with famine, indiscriminate bombing of churches, hospitals and schools and the systematic destruction and expropriation of church property'. In an earlier hearing before the US Commission on International Religious Freedom Dan Eiffe made a damning statement on the regime. Said he: 'I was a priest in South Africa and detained under apartheid as a priest fighting for Black rights. South Africa's apartheid, at its worst, is nothing compared to Sudan. Sudan is the hell of the world; there is no question about that – it is the hell of the world, and this suffering should not be allowed to continue.'[8]

One would have thought that those denunciations would make the regime see the error of its ways. Not in the least. For example, during Easter celebrations (April 2001) security forces of the regime clashed with thousands of worshipers belonging to Sudan's Episcopal Church who gathered to listen to a German evangelist, Reinhard Bonnke. As a result of the clash some were reported dead or severely injured, others arrested including former Vice-President Abel Alier, BBC correspondent, Alfred Taaban and the Secretary General of the Church, Ezekiel Kondo. Amnesty

International called on the regime 'to conduct an impartial and independent investigation into the incident, and those responsible for unlawful shooting should be brought promptly to justice'.[9] Amazingly, this happened at the time when the UN Human Rights Commission was discussing in Geneva Sudan's human rights violations, including religious persecution. No more evidence is thus needed to prove the government's political stupor and moral insensitivity. Startlingly, the government gave an absurd excuse for the interdiction of that peaceful Easter gathering. It claimed that radical Islamists planned to attack the Christian congregation and thus advised that the congregation should take place in another venue, which was not prepared for the occasion anyway. No details were given on who those radicals were, nor were any arrests made of the shady group that was set to disturb peace and tranquility.

As if that was not enough, the government attacked during Easter celebrations Kauda village in the Nuba Mountains. That was the same village whose attack prompted President Clinton's denunciation of aerial bombardments a few years earlier. In that aerial attack, the government used its instrument of choice: Antonov bombers throwing old barrels containing ammunitions studded with nails. Not even Mussolini resorted to such hell-born measures against citizens of his own country. But as we have elaborately shown, to the NIF and people of its mindset, the Nuba and those of their ilk were not fit to hold a candle to. Some believe that the attack might have been targeting Fr Makram Max Gassis who was visititng the area to celebrate Holy Week with his flock. According to some news reports, the government would never forgive Gassis for his 'pioneering efforts to establish and maintain civic and religious institutions ... even in the midst of war'. Those efforts, the report said, are 'a major thorn in the side of a regime bent on depopulating resource-rich Nuba Mountains and weakening, if not destroying, the influence of non-Islamic institutions in Sudanese life'.[10] In light of all the above, the NIF had no reason to think that grievous abuses of this size would not provoke the anger of Christians inside Sudan who are tormented by them, or stir the emotions of groups outside Sudan who have zero tolerance for human rights violations of such magnitude.

Not content with its religious intolerance at home, the regime intensified its efforts to export its ideology to neighbouring countries, giving rise to anxieties at the regional level. The regime's intrepidity and derring-do made those misguided external intrusions more intimidating. For example, during one of the early sessions of the IGAD mediation in Nairobi, the NIF emissary shocked mediators when he said without qualms that the NIF's mission was not merely to implant Islam in the Sudan, but also to carry the torch of fundamentalist Islam to the rest of Africa.[11] A public declaration of that nature was likely to make Sudan's neighbours very nervous, and they may have felt that it was in their national interest to influence the course of events in the war.

Cleavages in the South: A Conflict within the Conflict

Another layer added to the conflict was ethnic antagonisms in both the North and South.[12] In the South, those predatory conflicts set Southerner against Southerner as well as Southerner against Northerner. The pangs of the latter conflicts were more felt in Bahr el Ghazal. The antagonisms took the form of raids, killings, plundering of assets and forcible abduction of young boys and girls that ignited racism at its most virulent. On the other side, the intra-South conflict, which was an excrescence of Khartoum's policy of divide and rule, was made easy by the unscrupulousness of some Southern politicians. Whereas it is easy, for the sake of analysis, to see the South as unified and one, there actually had always been differentiations among Southern elite and among the Southern people themselves, either of vision or of a more primordial nature such as tribe and kinship. Those differentiations rarely culminated in armed confrontation in the past. But come 1991, and the SPLM/A experienced an extreme internal fissure resulting in the breakup of the movement into, on the one hand, the mainstream SPLM/A led by John Garang, and on the other, a loose alliance under Riek Machar. There were serious personality and ethnic differences that have worked against the unity of the South.[13] On 28 August 1991, rivalry and blind ambition within the leadership of the SPLM/A culminated in an announcement at Nasir by Riek Machar that he had overthrown Garang as leader of the SPLM/A. Machar was supported by Commanders Lam Akol and Gordon Kong. In justification of his alleged *coup*, Machar cited the following grievances:

  i. That the movement was lacking in democracy.
  ii. The Movement, instead of fighting for the creation of a united, secular and democratic Sudan, should fight for self-determination, or what he termed a trial separation.
  iii. The Movement had violated human rights and lacked formal structures and institutions.

Some of Machar's grievances were not completely devoid of merit. In the brutality of war against a cruel, ruthless and sometimes stronger enemy, the Movement could not, at the best of times, pass itself off for the epitome of democracy and respect for individual liberties. But as often happens, adversity becomes a source of new strength and rejuvenation. So, as regards the third point in Machar's list of grievances, the attempted *coup* might have been a wake-up call. Riek for various reasons omitted any mention of his and his lieutenants being in any way associated with the alleged human rights violations and autocratic style of leadership.

The people of the South since that date suffered as much, if not more, from internecine fighting between the two factions as from the war with Khartoum. In October/November of that year, government-led Nuer tribesmen mobilized by Machar attacked Dinkas at Bor and Kongor, forcing 200,000 of them to flee with only 50,000 out of their 400,000 cattle.[14] Khartoum obviously relished the conflict, and with gusto fanned the flames into a blaze. What made the split in the SPLM/A even more unfortunate was its impact on the peace process; conducted along three lines, the process was bogged down and became intractable.

Following the Machar debacle, the SPLM/A embarked on the course of reforms which, in theory at least, transformed it to (a) an army of liberation that did not merely live off the people but was integrated in the community for which it fought through the evolution of an administration and other governance structures at the grassroots, (b) the Movement also incorporated within its structures a keener awareness of the rights and freedoms of the individual,[15] (c) the SPLM Convention held in Chukdum between 2–14 April 1994 and followed by the Conference on Civil Society and Organization of Civil Authority in April/May 1996, served to set off the beginning of a more democratic and participatory way of conducting governance in the liberated areas and (d) economic development of the liberated areas became part and parcel of the agenda of the SPLM.[16] Strictly speaking, all those meetings were triggered off by the Torit meeting held between 7–12 September 1991 and attended by ten SPLA commanders who confirmed Garang's leadership and adopted 18 resolutions covering a wide gamut of subjects: assessment of current peace initiatives, the role of the SPLM within the NDA, civil administration in the liberated areas, the economy, foreign policy of the SPLM, humanitarian relief, ideology, codes of conduct for combatants, human rights and civil liberties, gender issues and protection of wild-life and the environment.[17] Out of the Torit meeting also emerged the idea of the new administrative structures for the liberated areas known as the Civil Authority for the New Sudan (CANS), the term authority rather than government was deemed less vexatious to Northerners including some of the SPLM allies, who may have perceived such an appellation as a prelude to separation. The policy adjustments in Torit were both a reaction to the extremists policies of the regime as well as an attempt to fend off rebellion within the ranks. The Nasir incident came as no surprise to the leadership.

Verily, Machar's reasons for the *coup* were not sincere; they were only part of a strategy that masked a hunger for power cloaked in concern for human rights and democracy. By brandishing buzzwords like democracy and human rights, Machar was playing up to external lobbies, including some NGOs serving in the South. Those NGOs who looked askance at Garang for his assumed lack of malleability, and were ready to have their knife into him. Accordingly, they promised Machar support were he to succeed in removing Garang. Despite their non-political vocation, the NGOs in question had their own political agenda for the South. To them North was North and South was South and the two would never meet. Ostensibly, the 'non-pliant' Garang did not do the needful by refusing to run in a groove, as they wanted him to. That was enough reason for the meddling NGOs to seek the removal of a 'stumbling block' that kept frustrating their plans. In reality, some of those NGOs transformed Sudan's civil war into an industry. One such NGO degenerated into a one-issue advocate: removing Garang. Objectively that NGO became the NIF's best ally. Worse still, that NGO was so irked by Garang's assumed obduracy that it laboured hard to dismember the SPLM by concocting an alliance bringing together the late Yusif Kuwa of the Nuba Mountains, Malik Aqqar of Southern Blue Nile (both SPLA Commanders) and Lam Akol of Upper Nile. Akol at that point was already part of the regime. This peripheral NGO continued to make capital of the purported excesses of the SPLA, equating them with those of the regime. Certainly, violations of human rights by wayward commanders and combatants are undeniable and should be identified and condemned. Disinterested NGOs who had no axe to grind never shied away from drawing the SPLM's attention to such violations without making a moral comparison between such violations and those of the government. For example, the US Commission on International Religious Freedom reported that 'while the SPLA is responsible for committing atrocities, it would be incorrect to suggest that there is a moral equivalence between the magnitude of the human rights violations committed by the Government and those by the SPLA.' [18]

However, neither the relative standing of the three musketeers within the Movement, nor the unsubstantiality of the professed influence of the politicized NGOs, over the international community, made it possible for the *coup* to succeed. Hence the plotters were left with no choice but to resort to appeals to the primitive instincts of tribal consciousness to forge a credible bargaining chip. In effect, by 1994, there were no substantive ideological differences between the SPLM and the rebel factions. The SPLM, following the Torit meeting, had affirmed the idea of the New Sudan based on a new political dispensation, failing which all other options should be open to the South. The meeting equally endorsed the SPLM's adherence to the NDA, resharpened its position to favour self-determination and consolidated its ranks. And though the essence of New Sudanism was maintained, the SPLM also satisfied those within its ranks who might have been duped by the secessionists into thinking that the leadership had abandoned the genuine interests of the South. Machar and company were of the view that the Northern traditional parties with whom Garang was cooperating in the NDA were not different from the NIF. In response to that allegation the SPLM retorted that it was the government of the day, and not the former governing parties, which was circumventing the realization of the South's legitimate rights at the moment, and it was thus against that government that Southerners should focus the struggle.

One would have thought that after this clarification of positions, the gulf between the two factions would become bridgeable, but subsequent meetings between them further reinforced apprehensions that the source of the difference was purely on the leadership of the SPLM/A, with Machar presuming to be best suited to lead. To this belief he held so firmly that he intimated to mediators that the factions would only unite after the death of either himself or Garang. And although the desire for reunification was strong, there was considerable disquiet in the SPLM/A over a peaceful deal that would retain Garang as the leader, with Machar being offered the position of his deputy, the kind of settlement that Machar might not have been averse to. The argument against this proposition was that to buy unity by accepting Machar back as Garang's deputy would be to reward insubordination and rebellion, a course of action that would have impacted negatively on military discipline. On his part, Machar buttressed his hand with the curious logic that his Nuer tribe would rather accept an alliance with the NIF than be in a movement under a leadership other than his own.

For a number of reasons, the crisis portended danger for the cause of the South as well as for democracy in the Sudan as a whole. For one, the South became a house divided against itself. This not only played into the hands of the NIF whose dream was to divide the Southern forces and conquer them, but also decimated the diplomatic, political and military credibility of Southern fighters. On the other hand, Machar applied himself to fanning tribal animosity against the SPLM/A in an effort to strengthen his own position as the leader of the Nuer. In so doing, he let loose the tribal *genie*, the ever-present danger of Balkanizing the hitherto united resolve of the South, however tenuous that might have been. Furthermore, in jostling for military advantage in the field, factional fighting caused untold suffering to civilians. Fully 20,000 civilians were estimated to have died from internecine fighting. The factional fighting in turn cost the liberation struggle invaluable support from communities within which they lived and fought, as well as from the wider international community which viewed the struggle as lacking in seriousness and in will to unite for a worthy cause. The question that has been asked as a result was, if the SPLM/A could not unite to fight the enemy without, how could it seriously be reckoned with as a credible alternative government, one that would heal a seriously divided country? There was also the real danger that, inevitably, one of the factions would seek the help of the 'enemy' in Khartoum in order to defeat the other. Eventually, Machar, first on the sly, capitulated to the NIF and fully joined in the war against the SPLA. Nevertheless, Machar and the satellite factions that gravitated towards him maintained a patina of rebellion, and quite apart from the sham of diplomatic contacts and the so-called peace talks such as the Frankfurt process,[19] the war the group fought against the SPLA was a war by proxy, a war on behalf of the NIF, which began to provide Machar with war materiel, and sometimes, with officers and soldiers.

Soon thereafter, Machar and other factional leaders allied to him were confronted with a stark choice: to rejoin the SPLM, humbled and in disgrace, or pitch their tent with the NIF in the hope of trampling their perceived rivals in the mother movement. Machar, reportedly under considerable pressure from some of his commanders, chose the latter course. As a matter of fact, by 1994 Machar's army commanders were routinely requisitioning their arms from the Sudan army headquarters in Malakal. Open surrender to the NIF was, of course, a political suicide; consequently a framework that would be sufficiently negotiative was needed to allow Machar to save face, while at the same time ensure that the NIF's positions on religion and state as well as self-determination were in no way assailed. By this time the regime felt it had recruited influential Southern politicians in its programme; the federal structure that was marketed vigorously by the regime turned out to be an inferior product. It is through this prism that the NIF's 'peace from within' initiatives should be viewed. Incredibly, Machar's teaming up with the NIF came after two important milestones. First, his adherence on 22 October 1993 to a solemn declaration worked out by Congressman Harry Johnston, Chairman of the Africa Subcommittee in the US House of Representatives, which asserted three principles: right of self-determination for the South, Nuba Mountain and Southern Blue Nile, cessation of hostilities between the two factions and opposition to the policies of the NIF or any subsequent regime that denied the South the right of self-determination. The agreement was not signed by the parties. Garang refused the appelation by the authors of the draft of the party he led as SPLM/A (Mainstream), while Machar's group was called SPLM/A (United).[20] To Garang there was only one SPLM/A. The second milestone was the recreation of Machar's group into an undisguised separatist movement.

A *coup* devoid of principle or strategy was apt to disintegrate. Lam Akol soon fell out with Machar and the two parted ways with Machar, the stronger party, christening his movement South Sudan Independence Movement/Army (SSIM/A) and Akol maintaining both the name of SPLM/United and the rallying cry of that organization: separation of the South. Of the two, Machar was the one who had an identifiable grass-roots support and a semblance of military support. As for Akol who seceded from the secessionists, he eventually ended as a *shari'a* law-abiding minister in Bashir's government after another face-saving peace conference with the government held at Fashoda.[21] The Fashoda meeting came after a short stint in which Akol was a unionist on odd, and a separatist on even, days. In effect as late as March 1997, Akol told an African weekly that 'Garang wanted a united Sudan but SPLM/United called for self-determination so that the South should decide for itself whether it wanted unity or separation'.[22] Akol knew that the announcement of the Torit resolutions would pull the rug from under his feet. He, therefore, ran out with them to an anxious public. Paradoxically, two years earlier Akol sought to join the NDA and told its Chairman, al Mirghani in London, that he was whole-heartedly behind Sudan's unity.[23]

Terms of Surrender: The Political Charter, 1996

After years of collaboration, military cooperation, and diplomatic stunts that convinced no one, the NIF government and Riek Machar, Chairman and Commander (SSIM/A), and Lt Col Kerubino Kwanyin Bol, Commander of the Sudan People's Liberation Movement and Army (Bahr el Ghazal Group) (SPLM/A-BGG), affixed their signatures to what was termed the Political Charter.[24] On 21 April 1997, Lam was not a signatory; his turn came later. In that Charter the parties pledged themselves, *inter alia*, to:

   i. Affirm the territorial integrity of the Sudan 'within its known borders' and commit themselves to protect it against internal or external aggression within the established constitutional regime, i.e. that of the NIF.

   ii. Recognize and affirm the constitutional arrangement and the federal and political system devised by the (NIF) government.

   iii. Conduct a referendum in the South after full establishment of peace and stability and after a reasonable level of social development in the South is achieved.

   iv. Make *shari'a* and custom the sources of legislation.

   v. Acknowledge the cultural diversity of the Sudan and observe religious freedoms.

   vi. Establish a Coordinating Council to oversee the implementation of the Charter and subsequent agreements.

   vii. Acknowledge that citizenship shall be the basis of civil and political rights.

Inherent in the above and the rest of the 14-point charter were glaring inconsistencies upon which we base our conclusion that Khartoum's initiative was nothing more than a face-saving device to enable the rebel factions to join the NIF government; their contribution to the search for peace in Sudan was, therefore, dubious in the extreme. First, in his attempted *coup* against Garang, Machar said he disagreed with the Movement's determination to sustain the Sudan as a unitary state and presented himself as a champion of self-determination, leading to the secession of the South. In effect Machar and his aides told the US Ambassador, Donald Peterson, in a meeting in Ulang village that he and his faction would never budge from insisting on total separation of the South from the North.[25] But in the Charter, the Machar axis turned around and pledged themselves to the territorial integrity of Sudan as defined by the NIF government, clearly a position antithetical to the founding concept and even name of his movement. Also by singularly accepting unity, he usurped the sovereign right of the South whose onus it was to determine whether it wished to be part of the Sudan in an open and free referendum. Furthermore, one of Machar's objections to the SPLM leadership was its alleged undemocratic tendencies and 'collusion' with 'discredited traditional parties of the North. But, by his accommodation with the most odious and hegemonistic regime in Sudan's modern history, democrat Machar belied his professed grief for lack of democracy within the SPLM as well as his denunciation of former regimes. Indeed, by aligning himself with the NIF regime, while all its laws and institutions of terror remained, Machar exposed the untruthfulness of his commitment to upholding human rights. Those points, more than anything else, undermined Machar's credibility and claim that his open defiance of the authority and leadership of the Movement had a basis in principle. It, therefore, did not surprise anybody when Machar renamed his South Sudan Independence Movement, the United Democratic Salvation Front (UDSF), patently taking his inspiration from Bashir's National Salvation Movement.

Other parts of the charter gave the NIF government an inordinate amount of leeway to opt out of commitments. The implementation and enforcement of the charter was solely predicated on the goodwill of a government that lived by its wits. An example is the question of 'known boundaries'. Over the years, the boundaries of the South have been fluid and frequently gerrymandered to annex mineral rich regions to the North. For the Machar axis to be party to an agreement that gave away lands of the South, which he had sworn and actually fought to defend and liberate, went beyond benign irony. Those lands included Bentiu, from which Machar himself originally came. Another sticking point was that the charter committed the Machar axis to accept the constitutional order in the Sudan as it existed at the time of signing. As Abel Alier argued, the axis committed itself to live under, and defend, the legal pillars of a radical Islamic State. These, according to Alier,[26] had introduced an Islamic system of government, robbed the judiciary of its independence and made the Sudan army and other security organs and institutions for *jihad* and guardians of Islamic civilization.[27]

Why, the rational man wonders, did Machar and his comrades sign away the essence of what they have spent a considerable part of their adult lives fighting for? The point to be made is that the political charter, in the light of the reasons advanced for the breakup of the SPLM would not stand the test of scrutiny. It amounted to one of the most significant betrayals of the cause for peace and democracy in the country. Two more points can also be made about the charter:

i.   Whereas it proclaimed *hari'a* and custom to be the sources of legislation, the convoluted way in which the constitution was drafted not only gave pre-eminence to, but explicitly required the courts to be solely guided by *shari'a* as the main source of legislation. This concept was maintained in Turabi's constitution passed one year after Machar's incorporation into the NIF regime. For example, Article 65 on the sources of legislation in the 1998 Constitution was guilefully drafted with a view to obfuscate, not enlighten, the reader.[28]The double-talk in that article about the will of the nation, opinions of scholars etc. as sources of legislation, was a conjuration meant to make opaque the article's real meaning, since the will of man, according to Turabi, shall in no way or manner supersede or negate the word of God. This, necessarily, renders nugatory provisions of the charter relating to the exercise of popular will.

ii.   The charter also stated that a referendum shall be held in the South 'after full establishment of peace and stability and a reasonable level of social development in the South were achieved'. It is this kind of defectively open-ended provision that, economically speaking, would apply with equal facility and legitimacy to any of Rostow's levels of economic development, and socially, to any of Marx's stages of human civilization. It is, therefore, worthless for all practical purposes.

To the NIF regime, deception is evidently the name of the game. From the start the regime had no doubt as to the real significance of the agreement. It, therefore, came as a shock to no one when Sudan's First Vice-President, Ali Osman Mohamed Taha, told a London Arabic daily that 'there is no defined time for self-determination. The peace-from-within agreement only said that self-determination shall be undertaken after the realization of a certain degree of stability and development that shall enable Southerners exercise that right.'[29] In addition, exactly four years after the signining of the peace-from-within agreement, Sudan's minister in charge of peace, Mekki Ali Balayel, declared that the agreement was unimplementable because the SPLM remained outside it.[30] That statement drew Peter Abdel Rahman Sule, Chairman of the UDSF, to say that the government had lost all credibility.[31] It is thus inconceivable that the parties to the charter, being politicians and soldiers of experience, did not see that the vagueness of, and contradictions in, the agreement were deliberately intended to make it unenforceable. Without doubt, the Southern signatories did not append their signatures, believing that they were involved in a genuine process to bring lasting peace, or that working with the NIF in this way was no different from the SPLM/A working with the NDA. They did so out of desperation since they discovered that they had neither the military wherewithal nor the logistical infrastructure to exist as a distinct and credible force in South Sudan.

Hence it was by openly collaborating with Khartoum to destroy the SPLM/A and virtually undermine the genuine aspirations of the South that Machar and his inner curia of collaborators put greater store to their personal political interests and ambitions than to the ideals of liberation. And to lay to rest the tribal bogeyman that Machar had conjured up to justify his *coup*, many from his tribe openly championed the reunification of the Movement and the cutting of links with the NIF. As a result, on March 1995, Nuer members of the SSIM/A met in Nairobi and unanimously resolved that collaboration with the NIF was blatant treason and demanded that those guilty be kicked out of the SSIM/A. Machar ignored the pleas.

Unity of the South: Reunification and After

On 27 April 1995, the SPLM/A and the SSIM/A became conscious of the damage that their estrangement had caused not only to the Southern cause, but also to the cause of democracy in Sudan. Out of that consciousness came the Lafon Declaration in which the two pledged themselves to a cease fire, reconciliation of all the peoples of the South, reunification of the Movement, integration of the armies and restoration of peace in the South. On Labour Day 1995, an emergency session of the SPLM/A National Executive Council (NEC) met. Top on the agenda of the new leadership was unity of the Movement and a commitment to the course taken by the NDA. The meeting unanimously endorsed the Lafon Declaration, pledging itself to its letter and spirit. It also invited the still recalcitrant to join in the reconciliation. NEC also authorized the integration of hitherto rebels within the SPLM. A few months later,[32] while commanders of the SSIM/A mounted a *coup* of their own against Riek Machar, accusing him of a lack of vision and 'unpatriotic stand against the unity of the Movement and the people of South Sudan' and for 'instigating tribal and factional fighting for his selfish interests'. That accusation was confirmed by independent observers.[33]

A year after the Lafon Declaration, Cmdr Salva Kiir Mayardit, SPLA Chief of General Staff, and John Luk Jok, Commander-in-Chief of a breakaway SSIM/A (who by then was in control of Akobo), signed a treaty of unification in Nairobi, the highlights of which were:

   i.   The unified Movement would retain the name SPLM/A and John Garang would be its leader.
   ii. Affirmation of the principles of the SPLM/A, notably self-determination for the marginalized peoples of the Sudan, equality and justice as well as democracy and respect for human rights.
   iii. Integration of administrative and political structures of the two organizations and the merging of the armies.

The reunification was important for the cause of peace in many ways. First, the South could speak in one voice and negotiate as a block. Second, it restored the credibility of the SPLM/A both on the battlefield and in the eyes of the world.

But fratricidal conflicts in the South are just one of the many complications on the path of a negotiated peace. Sprouting from those conflicts at the top were also substrata affrays that were cause of concern to many, not least church and grassroots communities in the South. Hence, on the initiative of the New Sudan Council of Churches (NSCC) and through facilitation by the SPLM, two people-to-people meetings were held in the course of 1999 to end the Southern fratricidal conflict. In March, under the aegis of the NSCC, a meeting was held in Wunlit, Bahr el Ghazal, and attended by tribal chiefs, church and community leaders and administrators, as part of an effort by the Southerners themselves to engage in grassroots peacemaking. The successful conclusion of that meeting proved beneficial to the community as it ensured unhindered access to shared grazing areas, farmland and fishing sites. A council of elders was formed to mediate disputes over resources among the population. Wunlit was not only a major achievement in terms of peaceful and harmonious coexistence between the Nuer and Dinka ethnic groups, it also could not have come at a better time. Thanks to Wunlit, it was possible later for thousands of civilians who had been displaced from Western Upper Nile as a result of constant bombardment by government Antonovs and helicopter gunships to seek sanctuary among Dinka communities in Eastern Bahr el Ghazal.

Encouraged by its success in Wunlit, the NSCC in November of the same year engaged in another mediation exercise among the Lou Nuer of Upper Nile in the areas of Waat, Akobo, Yuat and Langkien. Conflict among the Nuer sections had raged since the assassination of William Nyuon Bany who was punished by Machar and the Khartoum government for rejoining the SPLM/A after the Lafon Declaration. The conflict was of such intensity that all humanitarian aid agencies withdrew from the area. The Nuer Peace and Governance meeting, like Wunlit before it, was a resounding success. On concluding the meeting, the parties to it solemnly declared: 'We will protect this peace against anyone from within our ranks or who would come against us from the outside attempting to destroy our unity and peace. For this peace we are willing to die so that our children may live in peace and enjoy the good land that God has given us'. By mid-1999, therefore, it was clear to all in the South that the war within was simply unsustainable and, with the exception of Machar, Kerubino and Lam and their inner circle, the dissidents had accepted that salvation only rested in reunification.

Within the NIF circles, Machar and company were increasingly discounted as of no consequence other than a nuisance value. Like the *uvula* drooping from a man's throat, they served no function other than making noise. This was a situation proud Machar could not accept for himself, but having refused to heed the advice of his friends,[34] he only had himself to blame. Evidently, Machar never came across the saying that: 'He who dances with the wolves must always count his toes.' Machar eventually deserted the sinking ship, bruised and abused. After a number of collisions and altercations with the regime, he opted out and resigned his post as Assistant to the President. In his letter of resignation he accused the government of violating the terms of the Khartoum peace agreement and failing to implement vital articles in it. He also deplored the dismissal and appointment of governors of Southern states at will and accused the regime of sponsoring anarchy and terrorism among Southerners and pursuing a policy of divide and rule in the South. The government's delinquency in abiding by its words should not have caught Machar unaware.

The greatest tragedy of the Lam–Rieck misadventure is that they rained on their own parade. Having identified the failures of the SPLM/SPLA and its leader John Garang, the reformers proceeded to duplicate Garang's assumed negatives and to ignore his positives. The Nasir trio duplicated the SPLM/SPLA formula with a contradictory surfix (united). Even after they split, Lam ran away with this meaningless name and Machar, incapable of conjuring anything new, gave his group another double name South Sudan Independence Movement/Army (SSIM/A). As if this was not enough, when time came for the registration of political parties under the *tawali* law is Khartoum, Riek Machar copied Omar Bashir's buzzword *ingaz* (salvation) and renamed his party accordingly.

In more substantive matters, Riek Machar duplicated the organizational model of the SPLM/SPLA where the political dimension became virtually a tool of the military. This is the most vulnerable aspect of the movement against which Riek and Lam Akol rebelled. They could have earned many political dividends in the South (their purported zone of concern) if they segregated the army from politicians, even if they did not go so far as to subject the army to civilitian control as is the convention in a democracy. Manifestly, within a liberation movement such distinction is not readily attainable since the combatants are, in reality, politicians in arms. Nevertheless, like the SPLM/SPLA they condemned, Riek Machar and Lam Akol constructed a model with a single engine in one wing. The other wing (civilian) was superficially affixed for cosmetic benefits. While John Garang has left himself open to criticism for adopting this framework, he nevertheless deserved credit for novelty, creativity and originality. That his sworn enemies could not think of an alternative structure completely exonerates him and annuls the rational of the rebellion against him, at least in so far as the segregation of civil administration from military control.

On the other hand, even John Garang's worst enemies cannot fault him on his stamina and skills in giving whoever assumed power in Khartoum a hard time. Whether you liked him or not, he had always been consistent. Some say he is dubious. A better description may be that he is a man who always keeps his cards up his sleeves, especially when he is dealing with politicians who never honour a word or with a regime whose leitmotif, from its inception, is lies, lies and more lies. To be consistent, however, one must have conviction and a fair perception of the endgame. If Riek Machar and Lam Akol had a genuine conviction that the North as a whole were enemies of the South and that they had a calling to struggle for the independence of the South, they would not have lacked a political platform and a physical space. If only they had, between August and December 1991, used their arsenal against government garrisons in Upper Nile, their faction could have won a lot of hearts in the South. The Frankfurt agreement of February 1992, and the mounting evidence on their military cooperation with the 'enemy', together with the massacres they committed in Jonglei province disqualified their credentials as liberators. For while SPLA (United) devastated Jonglei, the government army was granted the corridor they needed to dislodge the SPLA from Eastern Equatoria.

Equatorians had not always been overly enthusiastic supporters of the SPLM/A. They had their reasons, particularly as regards what they assumed to be a Dinka domination. That assumption, as we explained earlier, was not totally justified. However, things changed after 1992. Riek and Lam forced Garang's Equatorian critics to recognize him as firm protector of Southern interests in the Sudan. Many of those were professionals who hitherto either sat on the fence or vocally complained about a range of concerns including the objectives and conduct of war. Thanks to Riek Machar's betrayal, they rallied behind John Garang and joined him in the positive effort to revitalize and strengthen the SPLM/SPLA. To that conclusion also came Machar's commanders and men, with Taban deng Gai, Machar's second-in-command at their head. In late May 2001, Gai on behalf of SSIM/A signed with Dr Justin Yac Arop, on behalf of the SPLM/A, an agreement to reintegrate Machar's movement in the SPLM and merge the forces of the two armies.

Riek Machar also squandered the huge diplomatic capital he inherited in 1992. His late wife Emma McCune had mobilized the NGO community behind him for whatever reasons she had. He had also the US-based Presbyterian Church ready to fund and promote his agenda abroad. Together with the spokesmen of the SPLM in London (John Luk) and Washington (Paul Anadi) on his side they could have weakened, if not erased, all the supportive fences Garang had in the West. But, in a matter of months, Riek was in bed with Omer Bashir's regime and that was enough to make all his diplomatic gains evaporate into thin air.

It is very hard to comprehend why two well-educated, urbane, and modern Southern intellectuals behaved much worse than Southern opportunists who joined Bashir from the start. Perhaps education is not the source of wisdom and patriotism. But the minimum education should enhance common sense and good judgement. If it does not, then its value is questionable. But Lam Akol and Riek Machar have their counterparts in Turabi and Sadiq al Mahdi. These too are well known for their good Western education and poor judgement. They had the opportunity to build a strong state on the Nile basin; instead they destroyed the nymph left in their nature by that education.

Predatory Economics: Oil and War in Sudan

Competition over exploitation of natural resources took a new dimension when the NIF government commenced production and exportation of oil from Southern fields; that combustible resource added more fire to an already smouldering conflagration. Oil, we recall, was discovered in 1979 in the Pan Thau area, northern Bentiu, in what is now called the Unity State. Bentiu represents the northernmost tip of the oilfields, the main deposits lying southwards in SPLM-held territories.[35] Since its discovery, oil has focused the interest of the various regimes in Khartoum. Their priority has always been to export the lucrative stuff with little concern for using part of its earnings for uplifting the disadvantaged areas of Sudan, including those within whose boundaries the oil was produced. Another portentous move, we recall, was successive attempts to transfer the oil-producing region from the administrative control of the South to that of the North. Speaking at a peace forum in 1999, Mel Middleton, Director of a Calgary-based human rights organization (Freedom Quest), summarized the resource dimension in the conflict in these words:

> One of the least recognized factors which is fundamental to the conflict is the issue of the control over resources, including water, agriculture and most recently oil. Most of the vast resources of Sudan lie in the lands of the people of the South. Yet power has always rested in the North. For years, various juntas in Khartoum have coveted these lands and resources, and seen them essential for their successive visions of Arab and Islamic "development". Yet this "development" has seldom made room for cultures and lifestyles of the Southern Sudanese people.[36]

Apart from his meaningless allusion to an ill-defined 'Arab and Islamic development,' Middleton was on the beam as far as the self-regarding attitude of Northern governments towards Southern wealth was concerned. One of the principal reasons why the South had never known peace was the curse of the wealth in its lands. Since the days of Mohammed Ali Pasha, that region had been a ripe plum, a beacon for predators from the far north in search of slaves and booty, an invitation to plunder and kill. Besides, we also noticed that since the Abboud regime, governments in Khartoum did not hesitate to redraw the North–South boundaries in order to transfer mineral wealth from one region to the other, as if the areas concerned were part of two different countries. However, while the Khartoum governments in the past, had always sought to dress up this land-grabbing with a cloak of legality, the NIF ended that sham. It moved the mineral-rich areas from Southern to Northern regions with no contrition. The government's callousness was such that the Under-Secretary of the Ministry of Energy and Mining, Hassan Ali el Tom, described the new oil finds in Thar Jalh lying in the deep South in Nuer areas as discoveries inside Northern Sudan. That Northern Arabs had chosen to give that area a Nuer name was beyond imagination. Clearly, it is unintelligent statements like this that deepen fears among Southerners that the only thing the North wanted from the South was its wealth. Besides, boundaries – especially contested ones – cannot be shifted by a unilateral slight of the pen, or by wanton statements by incognizant bureaucrats. There are historical records and more importantly populations in the contested areas.

Seeing those populations as a threat to its plans for resource utilization, the NIF regime – with the help of some Southern warriors – embarked on a sustained campaign of ethnically cleansing the oilfields of their indigenous inhabitants. For example, warlords Kerubino Kwanyin

Bol and Paulino Matip joined hands with NIF militia to unleash such terror that local populations were swept clear of the area; there were few or no people within a 200 km radius of the oil fields. Talking to the *Financial Times*, World Food Programme spokesperson, Aya Shneerson, stated that the consequences of those attacks were deadly for over a hundred thousand people. The *Financial Times* itself recounted chilling incidents of indiscriminate aerial bombing by the Sudan Airforce and slaughter by militias. 'The village was burned, the cattle were taken and the children were abducted. It was indiscriminate killing, everything was lost,' the paper quoted a local villager, Bipal Thiyen.[37] Amnesty International, also reported similar incidents, adding that 'civilian population living in oilfields and surrounding areas has been deliberately targeted for massive human rights abuses, forced displacements, aerial bombing, strafing villages from helicopter gunships etc'.[38]

In addition, Leonardo Franco, UN Human Rights 'special investigator' reported that 'long term efforts by various governments of Sudan to protect oil production have included the policy of forcible population displacement in order to clear oil areas and transportation routes of people thought to support the country's rebels'.[39] In conclusion, Franco said that 'the conflict has been aggravated during 1999 by the developments in the oil zones. The strategic implications surrounding oil production have seriously compounded and exacerbated the armed conflict, resulting in the deterioration of the overall situation of human rights and respect of humanitarian law'.[40] Furthermore, in his 1999 report presented to the UN on 14 October, Franco stated that in May of that year, the government carried out a ten-day offensive in which it swept through Ruweng country in Western Upper Nile 'attacking and killing scores of civilians with Antonov bombers, helicopter gunships, tanks and artillery, abducting hundreds and burning over 6,000 homes with a view to clearing a 100 km swathe of territory around the oilfields'.[41]

In addition, Africa Confidential (AC) produced chilling reports by Nuer chiefs about the NIF military offensive in Eastern Upper Nile to put the area off limits, including OLS feeding centres.[42] One chief told AC that 'parents had fled the shooting and in the ensuing chaos could not find their children, children running and not finding their parents, people who arrived naked having been stripped and beaten, people who were caught and tied up in a hut which was set on fire'. Also, Taban Deng Gai, a Nuer commander who served in Bashir's government as a Minister of State for Roads, told the same publication that he was forced to flee after disagreement with the government on the way oil revenues were used. Two regional ministers (Louis Keah Madut and Chuoc Dekia) who expressed their concerns to the government but remained behind were killed. The most telling and ironic statement came from a local man, James Deng. Deng told the BBC that 'Round here there are two types of planes; the ones that bring food and the ones that drop bombs.'[43]

Quite apart from the human toll, oil must also be viewed through an even more disastrous exposure meter; not only did it scuttle possibilities for peace, it also extinguished the flickering candle of hope for an early return to democracy in the country. Instead of pursuing peace earnestly the regime made believe that it now had the economic capacity to wage a victorious war against their adversaries in the South, no matter how hardened those adversaries were. The regime's financing of the war had always been obscure, but according to Energy Minister, Awal al Jaz, 'Sudan's top priority is to refurbish the army.'[44] According to an IMF report (November 2000), Sudan's arms imports shot up from 166 million dollars in 1998 to 327 million in the year 2000 'thanks to oil riches'. Also in one of its recent annual reports (1999) the International Institute for Strategic Studies (IISS) stated that Sudan's war cost the government US$ 180 million annually; the total for the period 1983–95 was estimated at about US$ 2.2 billion.

Encouraged by those new riches, the regime engaged in an energetic public relations operation in the West, including numerous false peace initiatives whose main objective was to derail legitimate ongoing processes. Effectively, the main purpose of the regime's offensive was to wriggle out of the economic quarantine in which it had landed itself. According to current estimates, Sudan's external debt stands at between $17 and $20 billion with between $700 million and $1 billion in default; the possibility of further borrowing before Sudan's oil production and exportation, was quite non-existent. Further, Sudan's traditional backers in the Middle East were far from enthusiastic towards the regime, given its support for Saddam Hussein's aggression against Kuwait and its reputed support for international terrorism and radical Islamic groups. Consequently, the government coffers became dry and there was a war on top that costs millions of dollars each day. Sudan's economic crisis before oil production and export was fittingly described by a visiting journalist: 'Printing money to pay bills pushed annual inflation to more than 100 per cent and professionals supplemented their income by working as taxi drivers or selling fruits.'[45]

That is where oil comes in, not to alleviate the distress which the professionals were in, but to continue the war. In August 1999, Sudan made the first export of oil to Singapore. Its current production is put at 150,000 barrels a day (later grew to 180,000), with 800 million barrels still in the ground. The windfall income increased government's revenue by 20 per cent The international consortium of oil companies – Talisman Energy of Canada with a US$ 735 million stake in the project, Petronas of Malaysia and National Petroleum Corporation of China – had pumped hundreds of millions of dollars into oil explorations, though they grudgingly admitted that any of their initial investment, about $250 million, went directly to the NIF government. The real amount is likely to be much higher. Equally, the figures on Sudan's oil reserves are destined to increase. According to an expert in the field, 'Sudan is one of the few places in the world where you can bring lots of oil outstream quickly and inexpensively which is pipeline-connected to market'.[46] Talisman estimates that, with new discoveries, Sudan's reserves shall increase by 50 to 100 per cent.[47]

Talisman Energy, the leader of the group, is owned by, among others, a medley of American associations and government institutions.[48] It was thus against the US shareholders that most of the pressure was applied by the US Congress and media concerned with the situation in Sudan. For example, in August 1999, US Congressman Frank Wolf wrote to the Chairman of the Securities Exchange Commission (SEC) demanding that China National Petroleum Corporation (CNPC) be barred from listing at the New York Stock Exchange because it was reported to have invested US$1 billion in the Sudanese oil project. Since America condemned Sudan as sponsor of world terrorism, argued Wolf, it was unlawful for American capital to be used indirectly to fund terrorism. Also, 'allowing the CNPC to raise capital in the US ... would make it easier for Americans to invest, perhaps unknowingly, in a company that is propping up a regime engaged in slavery, genocide and terrorism,' added the Congressman. Wolf's efforts were crowned with success when Laura Unger, the outgoing Chairman of the SEC, wrote to him as Chairman of the House Appropriations Subcommittee with authority over the SEC, that foreign companies listing in the US shall no longer be allowed to run foul of US sanctions policy.[49] Those companies were already required under existing laws to disclose political risks, but the new requirements targeted countries like Iraq, Iran, Cuba, Burma and Sudan. Unger told Wolf that 'we take very seriously' the charge that PetroChina and Talisman 'failed to disclose material information' with respect to their operations in Sudan.[50] She added that 'it is reasonably likely that if public opposition to a company would have a materially adverse effect on the operations of that company, this risk would need to be disclosed'. Obviously, reference here was to the mounting public pressure on the two companies because their operations in Sudan are believed to be enhancing the government's capability to continue with war and violations of political and religious rights. Soon thereafter (5 June 2001) the US House of Representatives of the US Congress passed unanimously a bill that was meant 'to facilitate famine relief efforts and a comprehensive solution to the war in Sudan'. Section 8 of the bill called for all entities engaged in any commercial activity in Sudan not to 'trade any of its securities (or depository receipts with respect to its securities) in any capital market in the United States unless that entity has disclosed',

i.   the nature and extent of its activity in Sudan,
ii. the identity of the agency it is doing business with in Sudan,
iii. the relationship of its commercial activity to any violations of human rights and religious freedoms, and
iv. the contribution that the proceeds raised in the capital markets in the United States will make to the entity's activity in Sudan. The bill also requested the Secretary of State to report periodically on

the status of the 'financing and construction of infrastructure and pipelines for oil exploitation, the effects of such financing and construction on the inhabitants of the region in which the oil fields are located, and the ability of the Government of Sudan to finance the war with the proceeds of the oil exploitation'.

The Chinese were also accused of buttressing the regime's war effort by providing special guards for the oil fields in order to relieve Sudanese army and security personnel for other duties, i.e. war. In its most recent report ('The Military Balance 2000–2001) the IISS reported the existence of foreign forces within the Sudanese army establishment, mainly drawn from three countries: China, Iran and Iraq. In addition, the New York Times reported that China, Russia, Bulgaria and a number of the former Soviet republics were furnishing Sudan with weapons to be paid in future oil exports.[51]

Even on the basis of the amounts investors confessed to have paid directly to the government, the NIF regime stood to make hundreds of millions of dollars. Contrary to false assurances that the additional financial flows would go towards the development of infrastructure in the South, the regime applied those resources to fund its war in the South and the East, or to pay back arms deals previously concluded with arms suppliers. Indeed, the government openly admitted that, with the newly acquired petrodollars, it stood to score a decisive victory against its adversaries. The Sudan army spokesman, General Mohamed Osman Yassin, claimed that by the end of the year (2000) Sudan would be capable of producing all weapons and ammunitions it needed as a result of its growing petroleum industry.[52] To dispossess the regime of this opportunity, the SPLA intensified its campaign around Bentiu. In August 2000, SPLA forces in Western Upper Nile under the command of Peter Gadet recaptured garrisons at Mankien, Buoth, Rier and Tan. The latter lay 8 k ms from Bentiu. On that occasion the SPLA issued a stern warning that all oil workers (foreign and national) should evacuate the area, especially after 'the failure of Talisman to heed numerous appeals.[53] Less than one year later (8 June 2001) Gadet launched a more devastating attack on Bentiu.[54] Following that attack the SPLM served another warning on oil companies that they better withdraw since they shall remain to be a legitimate military target throughout the summer offensive. Increasingly, therefore, the comprehensive cessation of hostilities became intricately tied with the cessation of oil production activities in contested areas.

Pressures continued to mount against both Canada and China despite brittle denials by the Canadian company that its investment was contributing to the prolongation of war. On its side, China stonewalled and maintained a sphinxian silence. On his side, Talisman's president, in a statement barefaced in its cynicism, told shareholders that 'he had not seen any sign of human rights abuses in Sudan',[55] as if all the resolutions passed by the UN General Assembly against the Khartoum regime and on which Canada voted yes, were episodes in a cock-and-bull story. Irked by this campaign, Talisman hired a US public relations firm (Hill and Knowlton) 'to put a positive spin on its Sudan adventure' but their strategy 'mirrored what Shell company did in the Ogon region in Nigeria'.[56] It also produced a newsletter (Hope) to put on display the 'good things' it was doing in Sudan. Nevertheless, pressure on Talisman reached a high pitch, prompting Canadian Foreign Minister, Lloyd Axworthy, to say that the company would be hit with sanctions if it was found to have a role in exacerbating conflict. Consequently, Canada dispatched John Harker in October 1999 as an independent investigator to ascertain whether the charges against Talisman and the government were justified.

On 26 January, Harker submitted his report that pointed out that Talisman operations were contributing to serious human rights violations and exacerbating the civil war. The report concluded that the new oil revenues provided the government with strengthened capacity and willingness to wage war.[57] This finding was supported by the invesigative media.[58] Harker also noted that Talisman had not done enough to end the conflict. For example, he accused the government of using civilian air strips in *Hejlij* oilfields to launch air attacks against civilians and their properties.[59] Those were the very indigenous population within and around Bentiu who were either chased away from their homeland or ethnically cleansed, and of whom Talisman saw, heard or said nothing. Indeed the UN refused to use the airstrip in *Hejlij* for its humanitarian activities for fear of being compromised. In addition, Harker revealed cases of forcible abduction of humans, a pseudonym for slavery, maintaining that the issue was not one of semantics. The end result, he said, was 'the wrongful use of a human being by another ... exercising ownership over him'.[60] Harker also made two proposals which appeared very thoughtful in view of the manner in which the government was using oil revenues. There are two ways, he said, to neutralize the negative impact of oil. 'One is to halt production until real peace is attained; the other is to set government oil revenues aside for use when such peace is in place'.[61]

Despite Axworthy's promise to impose sanctions on Talisman if the Harker's mission revealed any misdeeds by that company, the Canadian authorities downplayed the report. The decision infuriated Canadian NGOs[62] and impelled them to file a request under the Access to Information Law to receive the original version of the report which was purportedly doctored by the government. They also demanded four things from the minister: to release the original Harker's report 'immediately' and unequivocally; state 'that flow of oil from Sudan shall stop until there is peace'; scrutinize and monitor the impact on human rights of all activities by Talisman and others in Sudan's oilfields and take a leadership role in the UN Security Council on the question of peace in Sudan. Axworthy's about turn on his promise to impose sanctions on Talisman if Harker's report proved that their operation in Sudan were helping the government's war efforts was castigated by human rights groups in and outside Canada. Roger Winter, a veteran of the campaign for peace and justice in Sudan, drew attention to the hypocrisy in Canada's position. Canada, he said, had vigorously campaigned for the imposition of sanctions against governments who bought diamonds from UNITA in Angola because those sales exacerbated the war, but in Sudan where 'the worlds greatest civil war – indeed the greatest civilian-killing conflict since the Second World War – Canada is exonerating its own Talisman Energy which directly, unambiguously, and massively sustains that war' [63]

The NIF regime was naturally jubilant with its exoneration by the Canadian government of human rights abuses, including the dastardly aerial bombardment of civilian targets, of which some were staged from Talisman's own airstrip. Battered from all sides by NGOs, the Canadian government decided in the course of things to be more proactive in the peace process so as to mitigate the damage caused by its inadequacy in taking appropriate measures against Talisman. A special envoy (Senator Lois Wilson) was appointed to lend support to the ongoing IGAD mediation efforts. Canada also decided to take advantage of its rotational presidency of the UN Security Council to bring the Sudan issue to the Council and secure its support for the peace process. No sooner had this matter become known, than Sudan mobilized all its diplomatic forces to frustrate it and succeeded. If more proof was needed, that was yet another proof of Kharoum's indisposition to any internationally guaranteed just peace; the peace they envisaged was one which would perpetuate their hold on power.

Human rights activists described as a 'betrayal' Canada's watering down of Harker's conclusions, notwithstanding Canada's claims that it was doing so in order to facilitate a constructive engagement of Khartoum in the peace dialogue. Even if that was the reason, Khartoum's neurotic manoeurvres to frustrate Canada's efforts to engage the Security Council in peacemaking efforts should have revealed to the Canadians the insincerity of the regime. That was why Mel Middleton addressed Canada's Prime Minister, Jean Chretien, to say that: 'Khartoum has no incentive to come to the peace talks to bargain for a just agreement when they knew that with oil revenues they'll have the upper hand militarily'. Middleton's message was entitled 'Frightening Logic and the Ghost of Neville Chamberlain', and it was not way-out that he concluded that 'constructive engagement cannot work in Sudan for precisely the same reason it did not work with Hitler at the start of the Second World War'. Harker's report came back to haunt the Canadian government. The new Foreign Minister, John Manley, told Parliament that Talisman's operations in the Sudan were helping finance the war. But like his predecessor, Manley was not ready to impose sanction on the company for fear of 'creating a precedent that would be increasingly challenging for Canada to deal with in a host of situations around the world'.[64]

Canada's Talisman Energy and China National Petrolem, though the bottom line investors in Sudan's oil, are still not the only culprits. Amnesty International has cited a long list of companies[65] cooperating with the Sudan regime in oil production while closing their eyes to its human rights abuses. Those foreign companies which are turning a blind eye to the human rights violations in Sudan's oil production areas around Bentiu, are, according to Amnesty, 'responsible for the impact of their operations on the local community'.[66] The human rights organization, therefore, invited the companies to engage in positive dialogue to promote human rights. Clearly, in their collective madness to amass riches in Sudan, those investors turned their backs on the improbity and lawlessness surrounding their activities.

A latecomer in this scramble for Sudan's oil wealth is Lundin Oil (Sweden) which includes among its directors former Prime Minister Carl Bildt. Lundin's oil exploration in block 5A was oblivious to the fact that the road from their drilling site at Jath and base camp at Rubkona was cleared by the army using helicopter gunships.[67] Like Talisman, Lundin bragged about plans for community development in the oil exploration area, while ignoring the overall impact of its investment on the larger scene: enhancing the government's potential to wage war and misappropriate oil revenues for the benefit of the few. However, in mid-March 2001, Christian Aid (UK) came out with a well documented report on oil operations in Sudan.[68] It named British Petroleum (BP) among the culprits. Though not directly involved in Sudan's operations, BP is an investor in PetroChina, a subsidiary of CNPC. Rolls Royce was equally shamed for providing pumps and pumping stations for Sudan's petroleum operations. In its conclusions, Christian Aid endorsed some of Harker's findings and conclusions, but also came with its own thoughtful recommendation. Those comprised:

i. Immediate suspension by oil companies of ongoing operations in Sudan till peace is achieved.
ii. Divestiture by British companies (BP) of shares they have in CNPC and its subsidiaries.
iii. Stepping up efforts by the regime to reach a just peace and putting an end to all human rights violations.
iv. Promotion of an equitable use of the oil reserves for the benefit of all people of the Sudan.
v. Active and serious steps by the opposition to find a just and lasting peace.
vi. Auditing by the IMF of oil revenues to ensure that oil resources are not used to fund military and security activities.

The Humanitarian Dimension

A report on Africa presented on 22 March 1995 to the House International Relations Committee in the US Congress by Edward Brynn, Acting Secretary of State for African Affairs, underscored the crisis Southern

Sudan faced as a result of the long-drawn dispute as follows: 'over one million people have died in the civil war, which has created one of the world's largest humanitarian crises. Almost 4.25 million Sudanese need humanitarian assistance, of whom several hundred thousands will die without it.' A crisis of this dimension could not escape the attention of the international community or fail to become a matter of concern to the world. Nowhere was this concern as vigorously expressed as within the US Congress. For example, forty-eight members of Congress led by Harry Johnston, Chairman of the Subcommittee on Africa, and Congressman Frank Wolf (a ranking Republican) wrote to President Clinton on 1 March 1994 to underscore that 'more people have already died in Sudan in the last three years than have died in Somalia and Bosnia combined'. Furthermore, internally displaced Sudanese as a result of War since 1983 were, according to UN reports, twice those who were displaced in Rwanda at the height of conflict. Consequently, the two congressmen called on the President 'to appoint a high-level special envoy for peace-brokering in Sudan and to press for a tough United Nations Security Council resolution'. Also, propelled by this humanitarian crisis, the Committee on Hunger of the US House of Representatives went into action. The Chairman of the Committee, Mikey Leland, died in August 1989 in an air crash in the Ethiopian highlands in the course of an exploratory mission to famine-stricken areas. Heroic Leland chose to risk his life in Africa's turbulent weather rather than watch thousands die. Earlier, following a similar visit to the area by the staff members of the Senate Subcommittee on Immigration and Relief Affairs, Senators Alan Simpson and Edward Kennedy wrote on 10 January 1989 to UN Secretary General, Javier Perez de Cuellar, describing the situation as 'extremely distressing' and calling upon him to exercise 'bold international leadership' on the humanitarian crisis and peace in the Horn. The Secretary General responded on 19 January sharing the senators' concern but adding that while there was room for a humanitarian intervention in consultation with the governments concerned, there was difficulty for the UN to engage in peacemaking as the 'governments involved' viewed the political situation as a purely internal matter.

Behind the Secretary General's caution, as far as Sudan was concerned, was a sad experience: the declaration of his representative to Sudan, Winston Brattley, as *persona non grata* by Sadiq al Mahdi's government and his eventual expulsion. Brattley's sin was his meeting with the SPLM in Addis Ababa in February 1986 in order to agree on modalities for delivering relief to the South. In the eyes of the government, that meeting and the arrangements that ensued from it, compromised national sovereignty. The UN, at that time, was engaged in an intensive relief operation christened 'Operation Rainbow' to deliver relief to the South in areas under government control as well as areas controlled by the SPLM/A. The Prime Minister was obviously less disturbed by the sufferings of the people he professedly ruled, than the international community. His remark on the SPLM's insistence that delivery of UN aid to areas under its control should be coordinated with it unveiled his cynicism. That cynicism was unpalatably expressed as follows: 'By refusing to allow that all relief be channelled through Khartoum, Garang was only killing *his own* people.' The Prime minister was virtually disowning Sudanese citizens over whom he was supposedly exercising sovereignty. To him they were Garang's people. Garang's delinquency was his refusal to accept the ferrying of all humanitarian assistance through Khartoum and the supervision of that assistance by government officers.[69] As a result of the Prime Minister's insistence that no international aid to SPLM-controlled areas would be allowed so long as it did not transit through Khartoum, the SPLM warned that without its prior approval, any flying object over areas under its control would be shot down. Those hardened positions aggravated the situation to the extent that the Bush administration, in a white paper issued on 27 June 1989, highlighted the role of the US government in humanitarian assistance to Sudan. The presidential paper suggested the dispatch of international observers to monitor the situation following the determination by Secretary of State James Baker that the situation was untenable.[70] Sadiq al Mahdi described the US proposition as 'unacceptable and unfriendly'.[71] As it turned out, it took the fall of 18 army garrisons in the hands of the SPLA to sober the Prime Minister and make him accept a jointly supervised relief programme worked out by the late James Grant, Executive Director of UNICEF. The new programme was designated 'Operation Life Line Sudan' (OLS) and was to be overseen by a tripartite body comprising the UN, Government of Sudan and the SPLM.

The hue and cry from the world community against the government's intensification of war and human rights violations was such that on 8 March 1994 the European Union foreign ministers resolved to impose a total embargo on arms sales to Sudan.[72] At the same time, the German Parliament called on the federal government to end all forms of bilateral cooperation with Khartoum and to bring pressure to bear on Sudan to stop human rights violations and allow unimpeded delivery of relief to the South[73] In addition, the All-Party Parliamentary Human Rights Group in the British Parliament appealed to the Foreign Secretary on 14 March 1994 to bring Sudan's case before the UN Security Council.[74] The British group's chair, Lord Avebury, based his conclusions on a report he received from Gaspar Biro. Several senior European ministers, as well as members of Congress, visited the South so as to acquaint themselves with the situation.[75] No other conflict in Africa had engaged the attention of as many European governments or American legislators.

Things took a turn to the worse under the NIF. While resentfully accepting the tripartite arrangement of the OLS, the NIF regime resorted to every possible trick to hamper relief work. The government, which became proficient in using relief as a tool of religions conversion, would have preferred to channel that relief through Islamic organizations over which they had control.[76] Nowhere was the government's obduracy more pronounced than in the case of relief to the Nuba Mountains, that region was completely shut in the face of relief agencies, especially those working under the OLS umbrella. Indeed, it took the personal intervention of Secretary General Kofi Annan, during a visit in 1999 to Khartoum, to persuade the to government shift its position in principle. But three years after Annan's visit, Khartoum still imposed its blockade on the Nuba Mountains.

The humanitarian situation, however, did not improve despite the timely and appreciable relief aid either directly from bilateral donors or indirectly through OLS. That led to the conclusion by the majority of humanitarian agencies that the human tragedy was a function of war and without a conclusive end to war, all humanitarian interventions would only amount to palliatives that might assuage the pain for a while. This realty was starkly brought home during the devastating famines of Bahr el Ghazal in 1997/98. The news of the disconsolate suffering of the people of that region that was flashed through the intenational media evoked in the minds of those who 'passed by it' the verse from Jeremiah's lamentation: 'All ye that pass by, behold and see if there be any sorrow like unto my sorrow. (Lamentations 1:12). Aside from the consternation that it has generated, the famine of Bahr el Ghazal and the cynicism exhibited towards it by the government made those who cared for the Sudan focus their attention on the root causes of the trouble. More than human rights violations, the famine of Bahr el Ghazal was the type of indescribable human catastrophes on which the world community could not just turn its back. Indeed, it is crises like this that propel the UN into action, sovereignty of national states notwithstanding. Sudan's humanitarian crisis could not have been more aptly described than in Frank Wolf's report after his fourth visit to the South in the course of the last eleven years: 'Sudan is a litmus test for those who care about human rights, about civil rights, about religious persecution and about hunger.' [77]

Unsettled by catastrophes of this dimension, United Nations Secretary General Kofi Annan recently told the UN General Assembly Millennium Summit that the conventional notions of national security may have to be redefined to allow intervention by the world body; the crises he referred to included, among others, that of Sudan. Annan raised the question: 'is it permissible to let gross and systematic violations of human rights with grave humanitarian consequences continue unchecked'? He added that a rereading of the UN Charter clearly points out that the purpose of the Charter was to protect individual humans, not those who abuse them. Furthermore, the Secretary General, referring to 25 core treaties[78] on human rights and humanitarian issues, said that the 'world community should reflect on its failure to prevent the millions of human rights violations committed in the past half century'. Neither the regime, nor other Northern politicians who do not miss an opportunity to express revulsion for the 'internationalization' of Sudan's crisis, are concerned with the plight of citizens under their care, or actually behave like people living in the same world in which other mortals live and struggle to cope with.

The NIF Peace Dividend

The National Alliance/SPLM stream of dialogue that culminated in the KDD evolved to be the sum and substance for future dialogues and negotiations. For it was here that the transformation of the Southern-originating movement from a South-centred one, and its army from a land and freedom army to a national instrument of change, became concretized. It was also here that the Northern parties came to realize, (some of them reluctantly), that the South was no longer fighting to be left alone to mind its own business, but wanted to be involved in the transformation of the country from a hotbed of religio-cultural bigotry and dictatorship to a democracy for all. Effectively, if the KDD failed to become a basis for peace, that was not because it did not have the critical ingredients; it did. It was because al Mahdi was afraid to seize the moment and exploit the opportunities that the declaration proffered. By refusing to challenge the prevailing orthodoxy, he lost an opportunity to blaze a trail in Sudan. Instead, he went along with that orthodoxy. In the same light, some wish to question the credibility of Muhammad Osman al Mirghani's intentions in reaching out to Garang and concluding with him on 16 November 1988 the DUP/SPLM agreement.[79] Was it the result of being sidelined by al Mahdi's administration? Or was it a genuine drive for a lasting settlement, they asked? To this author, al Mirghani's steadfastness in abiding by the terms of his agreement and the unflinching support he later gave to the Asmara resolution, support the latter proposition. History, however, shall judge him appropriately. It is noteworthy, too, that both al Mahdi and Turabi, shot down the DUP/SPLM agreement not only for ideological, but also for purely expedient political considerations. Turabi could not live with an agreement that would virtually undermine his political agenda and disentitle his party from the banner it had raised since the 1960s. As for al Mahdi, the considerations were more fickle. The swell-head Prime Minister would not affix his signature to any agreement that was not attributed to him personally. Accordingly, party wrangling for credit over the agreement, gave the NIF plotters the time to execute the 30 June 1989 *coup*.

For all the above reasons, international concern with the war in Sudan was sharpened and efforts to explore prospects for peace intensified. In a curious way, the NIF's excesses provided their own peace dividend. As we have seen from the previous chapters, all peace efforts were home grown, with little prodding from outside as in the case of the Addis Ababa peace process. Since the NIF's assumption of power there have been over twenty attempts on mediation and peacemaking, involving heads of state and government, government ministers, parliamentary groups, United Nations agencies, regional organizations and research centres.[80] The majority of those endeavours were undertaken at the behest of the government, a matter that would suggest the regime's desire for peace. Indeed, the NIF had never been averse to peace, but it wanted peace on its own terms. That was why many of the peace initiatives came to naught and confirmed the impression that the regime was only shopping around for peacemakers to confuse and bamboozle the unsuspecting. The last thing the regime wanted to hear of was the historical consensus that was reached by all Sudanese parties in the 1980s. In actuality, when al Bashir took over power, he immediately adopted a hard-line stance towards the DUP/SPLM accord of November 1988. That accord, he said, 'never existed to us. It has no place in our efforts to solve the Southern problem. The conditions included in the agreement are inadmissible to us.[81] Even on the issues which his government pretended to agreed, e.g. self-determination, Bashir had no feeling of guilt or regret to say that the regime 'rejects both self-determination for the South and separation between religion and politics. Those are two issues that were not negotiable'.[82] Clearly, the Sudanese President was so self-assured that he had already become the master of the land, and that erstwhile forces had suddenly evaporated. In a press conference in Khartoum on 10 October 1994, he told newsmen that there would be no negotiations with the old parties. 'Any Sudanese leader who still believes that he has support in the country should go back to his constituency. He shall realize that all Sudanese are now incorporated in the regime.'[83] The self-assured Bashir may have believed that he could trample under foot the national consensus on peace because of his arrogant, indeed cretinous, assumption that the Northern parties had evaporated. But through what magic wand could he wring a peace agreement from the SPLM.

To begin with, he declared an amnesty for all 'rebels', ordered negotiations to start from scratch and declared that the issue of the *shari'a* would be determined in a referendum. He also extended 'Islamic benevolence' by promising to exempt Southerners from some sections of the penal code.[84] In the same announcement Bashir invited the SPLM/A to direct talks inside Sudan, adding 'They are soldiers, and we are soldiers. We speak the same language.'[85] The SPLM saw through Bashir's ruse, and on 10 August 1989, nearly a month and a half after Bashir's offer, Garang responded with a critical analysis of how the government's theocratic mindset governed its intention to frustrate the ongoing peace efforts. Garang's tardiness in responding to Bashir's announcement was due to the SPLM's desire to consult with the opposition forces in Sudan.

In his response, the SPLM leader challenged Bashir's perception of war as a Southern problem and stated that 'if the junta is to be of any use to Sudan, it must discard this perception of a Southern problem and think with the rest of us that the problem is national'.[86] He also disparaged Bashir's annulment of previous peace agreements and mocked at his offer of amnesty to the SPLM fighters to return to Sudan and work from within. That offer, Garang said, 'is as naive and absurd as it is preposterous for Omar to make. Surely Omar must know that we are inside the Sudan, but that is not the point; the point is that Omar is just as much a rebel as the SPLA, and a junior rebel for that matter. What is it that gives this new and junior rebel the legitimacy to offer amnesty to his seniors?' All the same, before accepting El Bashir's invitation to negotiations with the *de facto* government, the SPLM sought clarification from that government on various fundamental issues. It wanted the government to state its position on prior peace accords, define its attitude towards the South and demonstrate an ability to respect future agreements. The military government, Garang said, should restore democratic rule and accept the DUP/SPLM peace initiative as a basis for negotiations.[87] Instead of responding to the issues raised by the SPLM, Bashir, like Sadiq before him, opted for bringing in what he thought to be Garnag's 'minders', the Ethiopians, in the hope that they would turn the heat on him to soften his stance.

On 11 July, Bashir dispatched Colonel Mohammed el Amin Khalifa and Brigadier Martin Malwal, members of the NSRCC, to meet with Mengistu. Following that meeting, Ethiopia agreed to host a meeting between the two parties, if the parties so wished. That meeting took place in Addis Ababa on 19 August; Khalifa led the government delegation to the peace talks. The government side restated its stand against the KDD and the 'non-existent' DUP/SPLM accord. On its part, the SPLM restated its position, affirming that no degree of arm-twisting would make it budge from its core demands. Among those were the issue of religion and politics and the call for a government of national unity which would oversee a return to democracy and convene the national constitutional conference. In place of the latter, the regime's delegation offered power sharing with the SPLM to the exclusion of other parties. The SPLM contended that a coalition between the NIF and SPLM would not make a national government. The two parties equally disagreed on the *shari'a* laws, with SPLM insisting that those laws should be suspended pending a national conference to negotiate peace.

The following month, the government organized a National Dialogue Conference (NDC) and invited the SPLM, only hours before the opening, probably as a result of an afterthought. The invitation was made through Sudan radio, and so was SPLM's response to it, across the SPLM radio. In its response, the SPLM requested the lifting of the ban on political parties, trades unions and the print media, before it could join the talks. The NDC, without the participation of the SPLM or any other party for that matter, met in September 1989 for over one month and brought together a medley of academicians, NIF supporters, independent personalities and 23 hand-picked Southerners. All indications showed that the government had persuaded itself that that jamboree would be the alternative to the National Constitutional Conference called for by the SPLM and other national parties. And despite their claim that the NDC would be a forum for open and free debate on all issues pertaining to Sudan's conflict, the conference organizers failed to present to the meeting a memorandum signed by Southern intellectuals and elders warning against the intermingling of religion with politics in a multireligious country. The memorandum, interestingly, was also signed by some Muslim Northern merchants living in Juba.[88] The views embodied in the memorandum were nonetheless resoundingly expressed by Peter Cirillo, a Southern army officer turned politician who participated in the NDC. His remarks were ignored.

In spite of all the agitation in Khartoum created by the NDC, the government ultimately realized that there was no way to resolve the conflict without talking to the SPLM. A second meeting was therefore held in Nairobi between the two adversaries at the beginning of December 1989, the meeting being chaired by former President Jimmy Carter. In effect, the International Negotiating Network (INN) of the Carter Center at Emory University was deeply involved in the Sudan conflict long before the NIF *coup*. In April 1989 both Mr and Mrs Carter visited the region and met with Prime Minister al Mahdi in Khartoum and Garang in Addis Ababa, to explore prospects of peace. While in Addis Ababa they also shared views on the Sudanese conflict with OAU Secretary General, Idi Oumarou. Garang was later invited by INN to Atlanta to meet with the network's staff to deepen their knowledge of the situation. President Carter was thus sufficiently conversant with the views of the parties for his intervention to make a difference. His mediation was also welcomed by the two parties.

Even so, emboldened by its easy success in usurping power in Khartoum, the government delegation to Nairobi was even more obstinate in its demands. It tabled, as its peace plan, the NDC's report which comprehended a *shari'a*-based federal constitution, and a Libyan model of participatory democracy based on popular congresses. The argument advanced by the leader of the government's delegation on multiparty democracy clearly showed that his learning curve was not sufficiently steep, especially when he presented the congresses system borrowed from Libya as the system best suited for Sudan with all its multiplicities and vibrant political parties. Libya, a small country with a small population sharing the same culture, language and religion, and with loads of money to boot, was hardly comparable to Sudan with all its heterogeneity and conflicts over power, resources and identity.

On its part, the SPLM insisted on the suspension of *shari'a*, restoration of public freedoms and formation of a government of national unity comprising all Sudanese parties. The Government side rejected Carter's suggestion for the suspension of 'Islamic' laws for at least three months prior to holding the constitutional conference. Carter also proposed a formula that would link a ceasefire to the suspension of *shari'a* as follows: 'prior to a ceasefire and until the constitutional conference makes permanent laws for the nation, the September 1983 laws will no longer be in effect or shall they be the basis for action by the Sudanese courts'. That, too, was vehemently rejected by Khalifa, the leader of the government delegation. Given the divergent positions and adamant stance of the NIF delegation on *shari'a* and multi-party democracy, it was surprising that the two sides sat down to talk at all.

Following the abortion of the Carter intervention, another illustrious mediator jumped into the fray, General Olusegun Obasanjo of Nigeria. The General was brought into the Sudanese conflict as a quintessential African who was pained to see the largest country in Africa destroying itself. Obasanjo's commitment to African stability and unity is unparalleled. With his rare qualities, rich experience, consummate diplomatic skill, a soldier who fought for Nigeria's unity, a peerless military ruler who relinquished power to the people as soon as he was catapulted into it against his will, Obasanjo had all the chemistry of an achieving mediator. But in Sudan's tangled and irrational politics those faculties and skills were spurned despite Obasanjo's diligent approach to his mediation mission.

The Nigerian mediator first proceeded to get the hang on the root causes of Sudan's crisis by engaging himself in a series of brainstorming meetings that brought together representatives of the parties to the conflict, scholars and diplomats versed in Sudan's historical discord. The first meeting, which he chaired, took place in February 1987 and was facilitated by the Woodrow Wilson Center for International Scholars in Washington, DC. A second round of dialogue took place, under the aegis of the Interaction Council,[89] in Harare, Zimbabwe, in March 1988. Encouraged by his acceptability to both sides to the conflict, and armed with the insights he had drawn from the two dialogues, Obasanjo seriously considered forming an Afro-Arab commission of eminent persons to lend support to his peacemaking effort.[90]

During the regime of the parties, Obasanjo did not make much progress with Prime Minister al Mahdi, though he had an excellent rapport with him. The problem, as to be expected, was the abolition of *shari'a*. The Nigerian leader must have concluded that his was a 'mission impossible' the day al Mahdi, after some reflection, revealed his inner thoughts. In one of the drilling questions Obasanjo often threw at intelocuters to reach to the deep retreats of their mind, he asked al Mahdi; 'What choice would you make, if you have to choose between the imamate of the *Ansar* and the leadership of Sudan?' After some musing and to the surprise of Obasanjo, al Mahdi said that he would go for the former. The General was also unsuccessful in persuading Garang to meet with al Mahdi in Switzerland, though the former was enthusiastic for that meeting. Garang's reason for declining the offer was that he met with al Mahdi in 1986 for nine hours to no avail. Not counting this facile excuse, Garang was probably apprehensive that al Mahdi was only out for a pubic relations exploit, thinking that all that al Mahdi wanted was to pull a fast one on his rival al Mirghani who was about to conclude a peace accord with the SPLM. Al Mahdi, it may be recalled, was disinclined to endorse the accord before putting on it his personal *imprimatur*.

Obasanjo's efforts were doomed when Bashir took over power and declared Sudan a theocratic state. Having gone through the agonies of persuading Khartoum to repeal the September laws, Obasanjo was under no illusion that peace in an NIF-controlled Sudan was possible for the foreseeable future. Bashir evidently saw the North and South as two countries. In one of his meetings with the Nigerian leader, he told his guest that although he understood the concerns of the South, he failed to see why Northerners like Mansour Khalid were identifying themselves with the 'rebels'. In cold fact, that statement was subliminally racist in content. Excluding his implacable position (like many other Northern leaders) which reduced the SPLM to a regional movement with no say in the fate of the country, Bashir was effectively saying to his African guest that all Northerners had to stick with their 'Arab' kith and kin even if those were murderous morons. The irony of the matter is that Bashir, like other Northern politicians of his mould, never ceased to swear up and down the country that Sudan is one and shall remain so.

The US Government Steps In

After having been involved to the quick, at both official and non-official levels, in Sudan's humanitarian crisis, the American government, against all odds, was sucked into the mediation vortex. Bilaterally and multilaterally, the US remained the largest donor of humanitarian assistance to the war and famine-ravaged Sudan, a situation that had been reluctantly accepted by the NIF. However, jittery at the rate at which the SPLA was registering gains on the battlefield, the regime was obliged to work out a ceasefire through whatever channel possible. Thus, despite its antipathy to, and discord with, the US administration, Bashir's regime officially requested the US government in March 1990 to take over the role of mediator. This came at a time when the SPLA captured government garrisons in the South and bombarded Juba on a daily basis. By arguing vehemently for a peaceful settlement and making the first move towards peace, the regime appeared to gain the diplomatic high ground. On his part, Garang firmly held the view that the government and the SPLM would only enter negotiations as national institutions, as opposed to the patronizing top-down approach favoured by Khartoum.

Herman Cohen, the US Assistant Secretary of State for Africa, presented the American initiative with a mediation strategy that involved the government first extricating itself from the South by withdrawing its troops to the 11th parallel under international supervision. As a *quid pro quo*, the SPLA was to ease its siege on Juba. This should pave the way to a multi-party constitutional conference and eventually the return to democracy. The Cohen proposals were delivered to both sides through non-official emissaries.[91] Both the government and the SPLM initially agreed to the idea, but could not agree on how disengagement should be carried out so that neither side would be disadvantaged. The SPLM praised the Cohen proposal as 'constructive disengagement' and offered to ease its hold on Juba, while reaffirming its belief in a united, multiracial and multireligions Sudan.[92] For its part, especially, that the war was going out of control, the government appeared willing to accept the plan. But there were also reports that the government was being pressured by the NIF to cut loose the 'pagan' South, a position that was heretofore favoured by Turabi.[93] However, the hawks within the NIF were loathe to the idea of withdrawal, but were amenable to accepting a proposition for the thinning out of forces. They were also uncompromising on the issue of international supervision.

Cohen went back to the drawing board, but this time round he personally delivered a new proposal to Bashir and Garang in March 1990. The new strategy took into account that the SPLA had the upper hand in military terms, and was thus assumed to be more responsible for the plight of starving civilians. Under this new plan, the government was to withdraw half of its forces from the South and the SPLA was to withdraw its forces at least 15 km from besieged towns. An internationally supervised ceasefire and relief workers would be established to ensure access to civilian safe havens. This was to be followed by a national constitutional conference with delegates selected by the political groups, including the outlawed parties. Khartoum, pushed to the corner by the SPLA onslaught, was quick to accept a ceasefire but refused to withdraw its forces from the South, or allow participation by the outlawed parties in the political process. It also maintained that demilitarized zones should remain directly under the control of the parties concerned without any external monitoring, an arrangement that the SPLA rejected. Cohen also held meetings with the Egyptian authorities to bring Egypt on board as a facilitator. He even contemplated holding the peace conference in Cairo. His main Egyptian interlocutor was al Namar, the Minister of State at the Presidency. This alone belied the *bruit* circulating in the Arabic media and among some Northern Sudanese babblers, that the Cohen plan was meant to shut Egypt out of the peace process and dismember Sudan. Regrettably, in August 1990, the Gulf crisis flared up and Khartoum took the unwise decision of backing Iraq, causing a major breakdown in its relations with the key mediator, the US.

To the grief of opposition parties, US officials, a few years later, resumed their exploration of avenues for peace in Sudan, believing that the regime, despite its unrepentant adventurism abroad and repression at home, could be contained. The NDA (including the SPLM), did not share the feeling of US diplomats. To the contrary, they maintained that the NIF was beyond redemption. 'It could not be improved, so it should be removed,' said Garang. Other opposition parties also saw in the initiative a legitimization of a rogue regime. Washington diplomats, especially those agonized by the calamities ensuing from war and its visitations on the civilian population, were increasingly predisposed to the idea of a compartmentalized approach to the Sudan problem, addressing first the issue of war, then tackling the question of democracy. That was the sort of deal the NIF would welcome because it fitted within its strategy to divided the opposition into Northern and Southern, armed and unarmed, religion-based and secularist, Muslim and non-Muslim. The idea of compartmentalizing the peacemaking process also gained the support of some Southern intellectuals who believed that the suffering of the South was too high a price to pay for the unity of Sudan or for restoring democracy. The SPLM remained unenthusiastic to the proposition, not so much because it was less pained by the plight of Southerners than anybody else, but because it could see down the road. Its premonitions were validated by the NIF's use and abuse of Southern leaders who fell prey to the ploy of peace-from-within.

Washington diplomats led by David Shinn, Director for East Africa in the State Department, in 1996 persevered in what they called a 'soft landing' approach, as an alternative to the forcible removal of the NIF advocated by the NDA. Behind this apparent leniency towards the NIF, one suspects, there was a feeling of weariness borne of the unfounded impression that the regime was deeply entrenched and the opposition too weak to dislodge it. To the NDA the soft landing approach was tantamount to rewarding the regime for its misdeeds. Though the SPLM shared the NDA's misgivings about the regime, it nevertheless had no compunction in transacting business with it in order to alleviate the suffering of the civilian population and ensure free passage of relief to the needy in the South. On its side, Khartoum welcomed the new US initiative, especially that it came at a time when the NIF was endeavouring to repair bridges with that country. Its newly appointed and articulate ambassador to Washington, Mahdi Ibrahim, tried his level best to present the NIF in a more agreeable light. In one of his sales talks to an American audience, the ambassador grieved for the victims of war in the South describing the war that his government was waging, as all hell, (probably quoting General William Tecumseh Sherman).[94] Those honeyed words invited a pungent remark from the SPLM representative in Washington to the effect that the last thing we knew from Khartoum was that war was not hell but the gate to heaven where martyrs were rewarded with curvaceous virgins.[95] However, despite all that pattering, neither in Washington nor in Khartoum was the NIF ready to compromise on two issues, *shari'a* and multi-party democracy. As far as the NIF was concerned, the opposition parties (other than the SPLM) did not exist, at least up to that time. Thus after a number of spirited attempts by US diplomats in Washington and Khartoum, the 'soft landing' initiative came to grief in Sudan's tumultuous political weather and tortuous landscape. The US did not slow down its efforts in the humanitarian front, though its direct engagement in the arena of peacemaking slackened. On the other hand, exasperated by the regime's bellicosity, foreign adventures and failure to respond favourably to sound peace initiatives, the US administrations, at the behest of Congress, warmed up to the NDA and took bold steps in its support. The US evidently came to the conclusion that the NIF should negotiate itself out, the way the apartheid regime did in South Africa. What encouraged that position was the regime's duplicity in telling US envoys one thing, while business in Khartoum went as usual: more aerial bombardments on civilian targets, more forcible conscription of young men, more abductions of Dinka women and children by tribal militias, more harassment of opposition leaders, more impediments to relief work and more interventions by the regime in the internal affairs of neighbouring countries.

Nevertheless, the Clinton Administration had a fragmented policy on Sudan despite wide bipartisan support by Congress and the Africa Bureau within the State Department for a more aggressive policy towards the NIF. Despite the administration's clear abhorrence of the association of Bashir regime's with international terrorism and its objection to that regime's destabilization of the region and pervasive human rights violations, the administration was reluctant to take the type of steps Congress wanted it to. However, in November 1997, President Clinton issued Executive Order (EO) 13067 which declared that Sudan government's policies and actions posed an 'unusual and extraordinary threat. The EO enumerated i) support for international terrorism, ii) destabilization of neighbouring countries, iii) prevalence of human rights violations including slavery and religious persecution, as justifications for the presidential order. As a result the Sudan government property ' that comes within the control of the US' was frozen and trade in goods, technology or services to Sudan were prohibited. So were contracts with Sudan by US persons in support of industrial, commercial, public utility, as well as loans and credits by US persons to Sudan. The US wanted to carry those sanctions further through the Security Council, but that was made difficult by Sudan's trading partners and arms suppliers within the Council, especially China. Those measures had a limited effect on the regime's economic isolation. As things turned out, the measures did not induce the necessary changes in the behavior of the regime beyond cosmetic and tactical adjustments. Also, influential institutions outside the government that were not known for their sympathy with the Sudanese opposition, overruled those in the administration like Madeleine Albright and Susan Rice who advocated direct material support for the opposition. The Carter Center and World Vision are believed to have weighed heavily on the decision not to implement a legislation that authorized the president to provide food aid to the opposition forces in the south and east of the country.

Abuja Talks

The Organization of African Unity (OAU), when confronted with internal strife in member countries, is normally partial to sticking to the letter of Article 3 (2) of its Charter on non-interference in the domestic affairs of member states. But at its 1991 Summit the OAU was concerned enough about developments in Sudan that it decided to wake up to Africa's longest civil war. Its chairman at the time, Nigerian President Ibrahim Babangida, offered to mediate and invited the parties to his country for talks. The SPLM welcomed the move, as did the government but with a caveat; it cautioned that they only accepted Babangida's initiative in his capacity as Nigeria's head of state and not as chairman of the OAU. To that proposition Babangida agreed. Despite the cautionary remark, that was a welcome development. In 1967, Prime Minister Mahjoub declined a similar invitation by Kwame Nkrumah to mediate in the Sudan conflict; such mediation, according to Mahjoub, was contrary to Article 3 (2) of the

OAU Charter.

The Abuja process, all the same, took off to a poor start, not least because at that time the SPLM was seriously divided. The government, sufficiently emboldened by it victories on the battlefield and the fake ceasefire agreements it concluded with the SPLM dissidents who were not fighting against it anyway, wanted again to seize the moral high ground. On the other hand, though President Babangida was committed and dedicated to the cause of peace, he was wary about offending Muslim feelings, being a Muslim himself. Besides, Bagangida feared that the SPLA was in danger of imminent military defeat and he wanted to give the South an opportunity to negotiate a truce before it was too late. He was also apprehensive of being seen to countenance anything resembling secession of the South, especially that his own country was still traumatized by the Biafran experience. Babangida, therefore, was reluctant to propose solutions to Sudan's problems, only to provide the adversaries with a venue for negotiations and help them fine-tune the issues of the conflict. He was also willing to avail to them the good offices of his government as well as his own personal authority to implement any agreement reached under Nigerian mediation. On those lines the first Abuja meeting took place in 1992 following the OAU Summit of that year. Khartoum sent Colonel Mohammad el Amin Khalifa, Chairman of the NDC, the SPLM and its breakaway factions each sent their own delegation.

One of the major attainments of the Abuja process was that it put the question of national identity in the centre of the debate. The NIF's extreme position on religion made Islam Sudan's only purpose in life, but they found no takers at the table, even from the Muslim chair of the conference, Dr Twnji Olagunju. The parties, therefore, moved to reach an agreement on interim arrangements within a united Sudan in which ethnic, cultural and religious diversities were recognized, and equality among all Sudanese based on common citizenship. The arrangement would also spell out the fundamental human rights and religious freedoms that ought to be observed in order to cement unity, remove historical injustices and give meaning to the concept of common identity. Angelo Beda, a Southerner, was the person assigned by the government to announce its principal statement on those issues. Beda argued that national identity should not be based on ethnicity, religion or language but on citizenship. He also stated the obvious by saying that Sudan encompassed people of different ethnic, religious and cultural backgrounds, without specifying how a Southerner like himself could be treated on equal terms with a Muslim, under a theocratic system like the one he represented. On its side, the SPLM called for the creation of a new Sudan and rejected policies of assimilation as well as the marginalization of the South from the political, social and economic mainstream. Nhial Deng Nhial, put forward the SPLM/SPLA position as follows: 'The SPLM has not come to Abuja to negotiate how best the marginalized people of Sudan could be "accommodated" within "racist", religion-based and sectarian institutions. There is no way we can accept a state that is Islamic fundamentalist or Arab chauvinist, for we do not belong to either of the two constituencies.'[96] This strongly worded statement came in the wake of the government's uncompromising position expressed at the initial Abuja meeting.

At that meeting the government delegation asserted there was no reversal on *shari'a*, though the South 'would be exempted from the penal aspects of that law', while all Sudanese citizens (including Southerners living in other parts of Sudan) would be subject to the full force of *shari'a*. The SPLM, per contra, called for the creation of a secular state but conceded that *shari'a* could be a source for legislation on personal matters among Muslims like marriage and inheritance. In addition, the government delegation maintained that security arrangements during the interim period should not be subject to mediation, since it was a matter that concerned the Sudanese themselves. This was indeed a rebuff to the Nigerian mediators who expressed readiness to help in supervising arrangements during the interim period. Interestingly, the SPLM/A (United) represented by Lam Akol submitted that unity based on equality was unachievable and consequently, 'the North and South should stop trying to retain artificial unity',[97] Akol advocated a confederal arrangement to be achieved through the exercise of the right of self-determination. To that the government responded: 'secession would only be achieved through the barrel of the gun'.[98] Addressing such a statement to the Southern politician who signed with the government, one year earlier, an agreement on self-determination for the South, revealed the governments uttermost faithlessness and unreliability.[99] The government's position later changed when it agreed to a referendum in the South, but not in the Nuba Mountains and Southern Blue Nile. The SPLM immediately called a press conference in which it restated its position that it would continue pushing for self-determination for the people of the South together with the other two regions. The parties agreed to work towards an interim government, clearly a lost cause because of failure to agree on the main issues.

The second Abuja meeting was held from 26 April to 17 May 1993. A newcomer to the meeting as deputy head of the SPLM/A delegation was Yusif Kuwa of the Nuba Mountains. Kuwa's presence was meant firstly to assure the marginalized people who took arms with the SPLM that the Movement was not abandoning them, and secondly to serve notice on the government that the SPLM/A was not the Southern-based and biased Movement they thought it to be. The three-week negotiations did not register any progress except for agreements on tangential issues such as agreement on the formation of a revenue allocation commission, nature of ceasefire arrangements, machinery for appointing judges of the high court, role of the Supreme Court etc. Those were obviously important issues to be addressed, but without agreement on fundamental issues their significance was academic. The meeting, therefore, went into a 'recess pending consultation'. Not even a joint communiqué was agreed upon by the parties. Instead, Nigeria issued its own press statement.

However, before the closing of the second meeting, the government presented on 3 May what it called 'Sudan Government's Concessional Position on the Issue of State and Religion during the Interim period'. The position paper, which was thought to end the deadlock, made all the appropriate noises: 'Sudan is a multiracial, multi-ethnic and multicultural society. Islam is the religion of the majority of the population and Christianity and African creeds are followed by a considerable number of citizens.[100] Nevertheless, the basis of the application of rights and duties in the Sudan shall be citizenship, and all Sudanese shall equally share in all aspects of life and political responsibility on the basis of that citizenship.' The paper also stated that 'there shall be no compulsion regarding religion and no forced imposition of any religion upon any citizen'. In addition, the paper stated that 'there shall be no legislation, which would cause damage or prejudice to those rights' while *shari'a* and custom shall be the two main sources of legislation'. Furthermore, the paper maintained that 'the constitution shall be silent on religion of the state' and the 'South shall not be subject to any *shari'a*-based punishment'.

This type of 'concessions' was only meant to dupe the unwary, or those who cared less for contextualizing the NIF's propositions. The NIF's position paper should have been relating to another country. For example, in the mid-1960s the Islamists, in collusion with the traditional parties, thwarted the implementation of the resolutions of the Committee of Twelve on South Sudan by averring that, in submission to God's will, the constitution should decree Sudan a Muslim state. Now the constitution could after all be silent on the issue of religion, 'contrary to the will of God'. Charitably, one might have said that people change, and the NIF was no exception. However, the realities in Sudan under the NIF made that proposition implausible. For example, the position paper asserted that no religion would be forced into citizens, albeit that the country's penal code, as alluded to earlier, declared in Section 126 as apostate, any Muslim who expressly or by a categorical act abandoned the faith of Islam. The death penalty is mandatory in such cases. Equally, evidence abounded in reports by independent observers, including UN human rights monitors, about forcible conversion to Islam of Southern youths both in the North and South.[101] Moreover, the discrimination, abuse and intimidation to Christian flocks and their shepherds continued without pause. As for adherents to 'African creeds,' the only place reserved for them in the NIF's Islamic commonwealth was that of heathens who should be subdued by *jihad*.

Besides, the allusion to proscribing any legislation that infringes on the religious rights of citizens was, to say the least, excessively two-faced. For while the regime was trumpeting at Abuja its 'concessions' to non-Muslims, back in Khartoum the government was harassing church workers and went a step further in denying them the right to distribute aid to displaced communities. All relief assistance (including that provided by Christian orgnizations) was made to be channelled through government-controlled Islamic charity organizations. In January 1997, the government enacted one of the most disrespectful laws against Christians. The law ordered that all churches were to be treated as NGOs. Not even Abboud's Missionaries Act of the 1960s reached that level of insolence and blasphemy. The legislation was obviously meant to enable the government to control and micro-manage the churches' sources of income. It did not apply to mosques. Without fail, the Sudan Council of Churches (SCC) rejected the legislation, maintaining that churches could not be classified as NGOs. 'The divine origin of the church could not be determined by bureaucrats'. In that statement, The SCC emphasized the importance of freedom of worship, evangelism and charity work separate from any government intervention.

Small wonder the SPLM's response to the government's 'concessional' paper was categorical: *shari'a* should have no place in the political life of society and should be restricted only to personal laws applied to Muslims. *Shari'a,* as now applied, said the SPLM, 'is an entire legal system that spans a whole range of laws in both the spheres of public and private law; it is not limited only to the punitive aspects'. The SPLM, therefore, believed that preoccupation with punitive laws (from which the South would be 'exempted') obscured the issues. In its response the SPLM delegation also enumerated examples of areas of control and regulation covered by religion-based laws since 1983 (Nimeiri's islamization programme). The delegation pointed out that while it was theoretically possible to exempt some parts of the country from the application of Islamic criminal law provisions, it would be impractical to exempt individual citizens who could not be confined to live in a *shari'a-free zone.* More seriously, the SPLM delegation challenged the government representatives how could they exempt Southerners from *sharia-based* laws of contract, taxation and the entire array of economic and social legislation.

The government clearly did not go to Abuja with any intention to negotiate a *bona fide* peaceful settlement. At the time, it was persuaded that with divisions in the ranks of its adversaries in the South, the war was all but won. That would explain its intransigence which was so extreme that it would not countenance in the beginning any reference to religion and politics. Abuja, however, served another purpose for the government: a hunting ground for more turncoats from the SPLM. In this they succeeded in wooing the leader of the SPLM negotiations team, William Nyuon Bany.

While the Abuja stream was flowing on, the NIF government opened a number of sideshow discussions, one with the SPLM (United) in Nairobi in May 1993. Why the government chose to open alternative negotiation tracks while the Abuja process was still on can only be explained by the simple fact that it was not committed to the Abuja talk. Abuja, to the regime, was just one kiosk to shop at in the world's negotiation bazaar. Regardless, the agenda of the Nairobi meeting focused basically on the means to achieving peace on the one hand, and interim political arrangements, on the other. Those were the same issues that were at the table in Abuja. Such arrangements were to take into account power-sharing, religion and state and economic development in a federal, united Sudan. Agreement, however, was reached with SPLM (United) on the following:

i.   Power sharing between the South and the Central government. (that in reality meant accommodation within the NIF political framework).
ii.   Economic development.
iii. Participation of the South in government at the national level.
iv.   Referendum for the South.

Agreement on *shari'a* was not so easily forthcoming. The parties reached an understanding which retained *shari'a* while giving some exemptions for the South; this was the artifice the SPLM refused. Neither was there agreement on how long the interim period would be. The negotiations were not evidently conducted so as to produce a basis for a lasting peace, but only to consolidate the government's position by bringing SPLM (United) within its embrace.

Another sideshow was the meeting held in Entebbe, Uganda, between Garang and Ali al Haj on 23 February 1993. While the Nigerian mediation was going on, Bashir pleaded with President Museveni to organize a *tête-à-tête* between him and Garang under the auspices of the Ugandan president. The Entebbe meeting was a watered down version of the pre-talks sought by Khartoum. In the period between the first and second Abuja sessions, the govenemnt demanded that they needed to have a private meeting with the SPLM without any mediators before the Abuja meetings reconvened. They rationalized the need for pre-talks on the argument that the SPLM had submitted a position paper to the Nigerians that introduced a confederal arrangement during the interim period. They wished to obtain an explanation to this shift away from the unity objective proposed by the SPLM in Abuja I and even before, as if the extreme position of the government in that meeting on *shari'a* and its reneging on self-determination were not explanation enough. The SPLM rejected the call for pre-talks outright. Predictably, the Nigerians, who were to be excluded, did not like it either.

It was against this background that Bashir approached Uganda to arrange a 'display' of John Garang. The SPLM, for the reasons explained above, was reluctant to have that meeting. Garang also saw in the meeting a slap on the face of President Babangida who was already involved in a mediation effort. Ultimately, and following Museveni's persuasion, Garang accepted to meet al Haj as an emissary of the Sudanese President on condition that the meeting should in no way be considered as an alternative to Abuja. Museveni himself advised al Haj that he would not encourage parallel-track diplomacy and conselled the emissary that Sudan should stick to the Abuja process till it ran its course. The Entebbe meeting was revealing in one aspect; when Garang told Bashir's emissary that peace would only be achieved when all opposition parties were involved in the negotiations, the emissary responded: 'we only talk to those who carry arms'. The Northern opposition got the message literally, much to Khartoum is disappointment.

The war, therefore, intensified and the government, encouraged by its success in dividing the ranks of the SPLM and turning the war into a South–South war, reckoned that victory was around the corner. On the basis of this conjecture, the NIF declared that by the end of 1994 the SPLA would be reduced to smithereens and Garang would end as a refugee in some neighboring country. The other forces of the NDA were dismissed by Bashir as spent forces. To the government's dismay, the deadline came and went without the SPLA losing the initiative on the battlefields. That was a resounding triumph for the SPLA, for in the law of guerilla war 'if the conventional army loses it does not win; the guerilla wins if it does not lose'.[102] In the face of that nosuccess, Bashir desperately announced, like General Gordon before him, that he would keep *ad infinitum* sending batallion after batallion southwards, till Garang was defeated. Gordon's *infinitum,* we know, was short-lived. As for al Haj's dismissive statement about the NDA, it became a self-fulfilling prophecy. Not only did the war intensify in the traditional SPLA war zones (South, Nuba Mountains and Southern Blue Nile), it also extended to the east when all the NDA forces eventually coalesced under a unified command, with Garang as their chief commander.

The IGAD Mediation, 1993–2000

The peace process initiated by the Intergovernmental Authority on Development (IGAD)[103] is different from the one before it in a number of critical ways. First, it has brought together a group of heads of state with a bold determination to see a just peace in the Sudan, if only because of the war's direct impact on their countries. Those countries had been for decades host to thousands of Sudanese refugees and, therefore, had an interest in the stability of Sudan. Secondly, it took place on the initiative of General Bashir himself. In an IGAD Summit held in Addis Ababa in September 1993, General Bashir invited IGAD to mediate in the Sudanese conflict. Coming, as it did, barely three months after the collapse of the Nigerian initiative, the IGAD intervention provided continuity of sorts to the dialogue between the government and the SPLM. Although the SPLM was initially uneasy with the manner with which they were invited without having had the honour of participating in the composition of the mediation committee, they eventually accepted to participate in deference to the African heads of state involved. Thus, the initiative from the start enjoyed the trust of both parties. Four member countries of IGAD (Eritrea, Ethiopia, Kenya and Uganda) were mandated by the organization to follow up the matter. Kenya was agreed upon by the mediators to chair the group. Six years later, Djibouti joined the four mediators.

Four formal negotiation sessions were held between March and September 1994 in which the NIF government, SPLM and SPLM (United) took part. There were problems immediately. The IGAD mediators, at the behest of Ethiopia and Eritrea, rightly went gunning for the underlying causes of the civil war and devising a constitutional framework for their solution. This included, *inter alia*, religion and state, decentralization and self-determination as an option. The government, on its part, was determined to walk out of the talks if self-determination was so much as mentioned.[104] Its head of delegation, Mohammad al Amin Khalifa, presented the NIF's position to the first IGAD meeting (March 1994) as follows: no question of self-determination, no question of a referendum, a united Sudan and *shari'a* as one of the two sources of law. In addition, there would be an unqualified transition period during which the regime would 'restore confidence, set up governing and administrative institutions and undertake rehabilitation and reconstruction'.

As to be expected, the SPLM held a diametrically opposed position. It expressed commitment to the unity of Sudan and peaceful resolution of the conflict, but argued that unity could only be achieved voluntarily through the exercise of the right of self-determination by the South, South Kordofan and Southern Blue Nile. It also pleaded for a two-year interim period and an internationally supervised referendum. The chasm between the two remained as implacable as it had always been. This gave credence to the hunch of those mediators who intuited that IGAD should establish its own framework for the resolution of the crisis. It was at this point that the mediators intervened and quite unexpectedly delineated conditions without which peace could not be realized in Sudan. At the start, they affirmed that their first option was to see the Sudan united, but for unity to take roots it would have to be predicated on new criteria which the mediators incorporated in what came to be known as the IGAD Declaration of Principles (DOP). For the first time in the history of Sudan's conflict management, mediators come out with their own clarification of operational goals for the mediation. In their DOP, the mediators acknowledged the multiple diversities of Sudan and set the following prerequisites for a viable unity in Sudan: a secular constitution, administrative decentralization, upholding the rule of law and respect of universal human rights principles, equitable distribution of wealth etc. Failing the achievement of those principles, the mediators maintained that Khartoum should settle for the exercise by the South of the right of self-determination, with no option barred including secession.

IGAD, in the estimation of some scholars,[105] was a more viable mediation effort for a number of reasons. First of all it brought together a high-powered team of mediators, heads of state three of whom had experience in armed struggle and revolutionary politics. The heads of state of Eritrea, Ethiopia and Uganda, having been involved in revolutionary movements, were more qualified than any other mediator to appreciate the dynamics of war. Second, there was a refugee crisis that all would want to settle and, therefore, they were genuinely committed to finding a lasting solution to the long-drawn conflict. Third, the new leaders in Eritrea and Ethiopia had lived in Sudan and were familiar with the sources of the conflict. Fourth, President Moi's familiarity with the Sudan conflict dates back to the 1960s when, as Vice-President, he represented the late President Kenyatta in the 1965 RTC. Fifth, there was a new post-Cold War spirit and accusations that the Sudanese government was offering a haven to terrorists. The government, therefore, had to embrace dialogue or risk being seen as opposed to the new spirit of goodwill in world affairs.[106]

The IGAD peace committee of heads of state held its first meeting in Kampala on 6 November 1993, in the course of which a Standing Committee of ministers of foreign affairs was set up by the Mediation Committee (heads of state and government) to draw up an agenda for negotiations. The committee called upon Southern leaders to be united in their negotiations with a fairly united Northern party. Accordingly, on 6 January 1994, after what has come to be termed as mediation-within-mediation, John Garang and Riek Machar signed an agenda calling for:

  i.   a negotiated ceasefire involving all parties to the conflict and overseen by neutral monitors,
  ii. exercise of the right of self-determination through referendum for the people of Southern Sudan, Nuba Mountains and other marginalized areas, and
  iii. the adoption of a comprehensive interim arrangement prior to the establishment of permanent arrangements.[107]

Just as the SPLA was divided, so was the NIF regime. While the cabinet supported the peace initiative because of reversals on the battlefield after a string of victories by the SPLA, the zealots of the Islamic Council of Forty (the inner decision-making cabal of the NIF) wanted nothing but war with the SPLA, hence the oracular utterances of the regime regarding the DOP. Surely Sudan was increasingly becoming a pariah state, an image that the government hoped not to complicate by being recalcitrant in the peace negotiations. However, after lengthy waffling the government delegates, three years after the inception of the IGAD process, finally faced their moment of truth by accepting the DOP. But that was not to happen before two important events. Firstly, two delegates (Khalifa and al Haj) were severely lashed by their NIF colleagues in Khartoum for accepting to discuss the issue of self-determination.[108] They were reportedly accused by some of their colleagues of conniving with 'their' fellow Africans to undermine Arabism.[109] That categorization told its own story about the mindset of some NIF members. NIF hawks (Nafie Ali Nafie and Ghazi Salah el Din) were brought into the negotiation team as a replacement of the two negotiators hissed off the stage. Secondly, in the fourth IGAD meeting (September 1994) Salah el Din made everybody in the room cringe when he told four African foreign ministers who were all Christian that colonialism had created the problem of the South and obstructed the march of Islam, adding that it was now the role of the NIF to spread Islam not only in the South but throughout Africa. In addition to that strident statement he also had the audacity to say that exempting the South from the application of *shari'a* was a voluntary concession, not a right. To any true Muslim, Salah al Din's statement would sound heretical[110] because it made God's word subject to manipulation by fallible humans for political expediency. Nevertheless, this was not the real issue; the real (indeed surreal) issue was that twenty years after African decolonization and the creation of the OAU, there were still Kutzs (and African ones for that matter) who would bring light to the 'Heart of Darkness'. Not surprisingly the chairman of the IGAD committee, Dr Zachary Onyonka, immediately closed the meeting.

Nonetheless, the IGAD Committee exerted considerable pressure on the regime to agree to the continuation of the talks and requested its Ministerial Committee to draft a timetable. Nine days later, the committee was instructed to start the negotiation process. When the negotiations took place, it was difficult to get down to the substantive issues. The first session discussed little more than just the issue of observers to which the regime was implacably opposed. While the regime took exception to the involvement of international observers to the talks because it saw the dispute as a domestic matter, the IGAD mediators were conscious that international support to their effort was indispensable, and hence they insisted on inviting international observers. Ultimately, the government relented and the door was opened to North American and European countries to join the process as friends of the IGAD. Those initially included seven countries: Canada, Germany Holland, Italy, Norway, the UK and the US.

With the noose of the DOP tight around its neck, and the presence of regional and international observers, the government tried several manoeuvres to writhe free. Manifestly it only accepted the DOP because of regional and international pressure as well as pressure on the battlefield. In spite of its professed support to the IGAD process, however, the government went on a shopping spree around the world looking for other mediators: South Africa, Malaysia, the Netherlands, Norway, the World Council of Churches, Mozambique etc. President Carter also re-emerged on the scene as a mediator, this time under a different guise. Carter pleaded to the two parties to declare a conditional ceasefire in order to enable the Carter Center to undertake a campaign in the South for the eradication of the guinea worm. A ceasefire was declared and lasted from 28 March to 28 June 1995. Khartoum sought to turn the temporary functional ceasefire into a comprehensive one, knowing very well that according to the DOP, a comprehensive ceasefire came at the bottom of the list in the IGAD order of priorities. It was defined to be the culmination of a political settlement not the starting point. Carter was not much bothered with the IGAD. Instead, he expressed dismay at the insistence of the IGAD countries and the SPLM on the issue of secularism.

That matter, he thought, would only antagonize the government.[111] That was an inexplicable departure from the position Carter had taken in the course of his mediation between the two parties in December 1989.

Having failed in its mediation shopping spree, the government resurfaced again at the IGAD forum, only to astonish both friend and foe alike. It rejected out of hand option one (unity). The government obviously could live with neither a secular constitution nor multi-party system. The government that was now ready to discuss terms of divorce between North and South could not be the same government that had consistently rejected self-determination for the South because it was assumed to be an alias for separation. Negotiations, therefore, were resumed, not to consolidate unity but to set out the terms of divorce including cohabitation during an interim period. It was at this point (October 1997) that the SPLM presented its 'Seven-Point Peace Plan' which confounded the government and agitated the NDA. The seven points incorporated: request to the government to affirm its unqualified acceptance of the IGAD DOP, separation of religion from politics during the interim period, save in the sphere of personal law (no policies shall be formulated by the government or decisions taken by courts that stem from the tenets of any religion), acceptance of political pluralism as the appropriate basis of governance, guaranteeing the right of self-determination for the people of South Sudan, Southern Kordofan and Southern Blue Nile and, at the end of the interim period, choice between independence or remaining within a united Sudan. The SPLM also proposed a two-year interim period, during which Sudan would be governed on a confederal basis. The plan also called for the participation of the NDA in the interim government. Finally, on the completion of the above, a comprehensive ceasefire would be declared.

The government would have nothing to do with those propositions, and in effect it made a lot of mileage out of the SPLM's confederal option: first, because it viewed it as a prelude to separation, the same separation it had negotiated the terms of in previous meetings, and second, because the SPLM's version of the boundaries of the 'South' was, to the eyes of the government, as good as 'land grabbing'. Sadiq al Mahdi was also miffed by the proposition because it included South Kordofan and Southern Blue Nile, the two regions being considered by him as a reserved sphere for the Umma Party. On the other hand, the government delegation called in question the idea of including the NDA in the interim arrangement, announcing that it did not seek IGAD's mediation in order to dismantle its regime, only to solve the South's question and end war. The SPLM proposals could have been a historical meeting point, but the NIF missed it; only few years later it began knocking at all doors in Arab and Islamic capitals shopping for mediators to bring the NDA on board.[112] The fraudulence of the regime's future efforts to reconcile with the other NDA forces should be seen in this light.

Plausibly, by presenting its seven-point plan, the SPLM was seeking to achieve three things: first, to operationalize the term secularism which was a cause of unremitting mystification; second, to allay the fears of those, within its ranks who have shed their blood alongside Southerners (Nuba and Southern Blue Nile) to achieve their own aspirations and not those of the South, third, by emphasizing the concept of political pluralism and calling for the participation of the NDA, the SPLM was laying bare the NIF's ceaseless attempts to define and redefine pluralistic democracy. For such democracy to have any meaning the plan seemed to suggest, it would have to be all-inclusive. The plan, however, would have caused less nervousness within the ranks of the NDA were the Alliance forewarned by the SPLM about the presentation of the confederal option at that point, as a negotiation tool. Surely there was nothing alarming about confederalism *per se* since it was recongnized as an option for the South in the Asmara resolutions. Also, the NDA would not have been as flummoxed were the SPLM seven-point plan to be prefaced by a statement underscoring that the plan was an action of last resort, in view of the governments refusal of the political underpinnings of the unity option specified by the DOP, i.e. separation of religion from politics, an interim period during which all parties participate etc. That was necessary for putting the blame for dismembering Sudan where it belonged. All the same, for it to be necessary that those delicate distinctions and shades of differences be highlighted by the SPLM to its allies, revealed the level of incredulity among some Northerners about the SPLM's intentions.

In effect, if the IGAD mediators had not taken the initiative, first to involve the international community and, second, to formulate and present their own proposals, then perhaps the talks would have fizzled out like all other previous mediations. As it has turned out, the initiative increasingly drew the attention of the international community. Around the seven countries, friends to IGAD, coalesced a large number of European countires with a view to lending support to both the peacemaking process and post-conflict rehabilitation. The group with added members was later transformed into IGAD Partners Forum (IPF). Egypt sought involvement in that group and was admitted to it. UN institutions also came forward to join the initiative. UNESCO, within its Culture of Peace Programme, facilitated a series of meetings to help deepen the parties' understanding of the contested issues and their different ramifications. Funded by UNDP, the Barcelona Symposium was held in September 1995 and a second meeting took place in The Hague on 20 May 1996. Professor Roger Fisher, the Harvard guru on conflict management and one of the architects of the Rogers Plan and the Camp David agreement on the Arab–Israeli conflict, made himself available to the second meeting. Fisher was stunned by the fraternal manner in which the adversaries related to each other, despite the intensity of their wrangling over the issues.[113] That was one aspect of the Sudanese character that some outsiders admired while others looked upon as a manifestation of cynicism and nonchalance.

Nevertheless, the UN agencies flinched when the SPLM requested that other NDA parties, being direct stakeholders in peace and democracy, be included in the process. This was eventually accepted by the UN in a convoluted way: 'the successful continuation of the dialogue on national reconciliation requires the involvement in this process of the representation of all the main segments of the Sudanese society on individual basis and without the label of belonging to any particular organization or institution',[114] said the UNDP. Khartoum, once again, successfully twisted the arm of a pliant UN so that opposition parties, other than the SPLM, should be shut out of the peace processes even at the intellectual level. Yet, the parties to those UNESCO-sponsored meetings declared commitment to 'pursue the dialogue with the aim of reinforcing the peace process undertaken by IGAD'.

That is not to say that the IGAD process was a paragon of virtue; issues have been raised about the competence of the IGAD secretariat to deal with a conflict of such complexity. According to one of the Resource Persons Group that was helping the process behind the scenes, the IGAD structures itself had been cumbersome, 'requiring the presence of five foreign ministers, with the attending complications and the time pressure this entails. With ministers pressed for time, the sessions have been too brief leaving little time for an in-depth exploration of positions, while the intervals between the rounds were too long.' This administrative inadequacy, according to the resource person, had been compounded by the conflicting agendas of both mediators and outsiders; there have been differences between the mediators on 'the pace, modalities and even the objectives of the mediation effort'.[115] While that assessment of IGAD inadequacies was very observant and substantially true, the statement relating to the mediators different agenda would not stand empirical evidence. Admittedly, there were differences among them concerning procedures and modalities, but they were all united on the issue of peace and objectives of the mediation. None of the mediators had ever prevaricated on the DOP since its adoption in 1994.

On the other hand, differences had emerged within IPF particularly after the Bahr el Ghazal heart-rending famine.[116] Some of the IPF members (Europeans mainly) thought that in the face of a crisis of such dimension, any peace was better than war. Accordingly, they played into Khartoum's hand by calling for an immediate comprehensive ceasefire. That would have been a departure from the guiding principles of the negotiations (DOP) which made comprehensive ceasefire contingent on the conclusion of a political settlement. In addition, some Europeans, encouraged by a group of Southern intellectuals, wanted the SPLM to engage immediately in discussing the terms of divorce at any cost, alternatively expressed, take Bashir for his words on self-determination. Those intellectuals were understandably grieved by the sufferings of Southerners, but they became as clear as mud when they added a political twist to their appeal, accusing the SPLA of fighting other people's (NDA) war, and not adequately addressing the Southern agenda. The accusation was unjustified on two counts: first, the SPLM was the first to alert the world about the Bahr el Ghazal crisis through direct contacts by its leader with the US and co-chair persons of the IPF; second, if the NIF was at all brought to its knees to accept self-determination for the South, that was not achieved through exhortations from distant capitals of the world, but only through costly and sustained struggle by the SPLM/A. Undoubtedly some of those intellectuals made a significant contribution to the cause of the South in the media and diplomatic circles. However, a large number of them had been sitting in the wings during the 16 years of that struggle. Besides, the victories of the SPLM/A during those 16 years were not only limited to the battlefront. Its most presageable victories were in the minds of men where the NIF, and Northern traditional parties were made to think of the unthinkable, accepting the principle of self-determination for the South even if it was to lead to secession.

The SPLM rejected both proposals emerging from the distraught IPF members, maintaining that ceasefire would only be guaranteed in all areas where it was conducive to the timely delivery of relief. As for the NIF's promise of self-determination, the SPLM said it was as good as any of its other promises; with abundant experience from Frankfurt, Abuja, the so-called peace-from-within to IGAD, the SPLM had no reason to take the NIF for its word. In particular, the SPLM referred to the South–South war enkindled by the regime, even before the ink of the so-called peace-from-within agreement had dried. The South–South war caused untold suffering and should have exposed the regime's duplicity to those who put their faith in its trustworthiness. Truly, neither then nor now did the NDA and the SPLM count on the NIF's government to have a heart – but only to pursue its self-interest more enlightendly. This, given the regime's record of evasions and quibblings in past negotiations and ongoing peace initiatives, would be achieved through more, not less, pressure.

Among the IPF members, the US and Norway generally shared the SPLM's and the NDA's reading of the Sudanese political map. Others were concerned with putting an end to war at any cost. To them, war in Sudan was seemingly perceived as a bush fire to be extinguished, not a deep-rooted conflict that should be decisively and definitively resolved. But history tells us that the worst civil wars were those that were re-ignited following half-baked settlement or quick fixes and acquiescent compromises. In place of a comprehensive settlement of Sudan's intractable problem, it would appear that some European IPF members wanted the DOP desegregated into operational components. Some among them were seemingly beguiled by Khartoum's charm offensive and sham liberalization measures. Evidently, coming from the abyss of the vicious brutality to which the NIF had descended, even the release of few political prisoners would appear to the grief-stricken Sudanese as an accomplishment. This should not be the case with the 'minders' and 'trustees' of liberal democracy who continued shouting from the rooftops against alleged abuses to democratic principles and practices in Kenya and Uganda, and threatening all manner of sanctions against those countries. The attitude of those countries not only belied their crusade for democracy in other parts of Africa, it almost betrayed a hidden desire to ensure a place for the NIF's fascism in future Sudan. In all certainty, the success of the IGAD process can only be assured through staying the course by all inside and outside players as defined by the DOP and bringing their cumulative strength to press Khartoum to behave in accordance to the same ideals they are trying to impose on other countries. As an astute observer of the Sudanese scene opined, the 'best chance for progress [in the IGAD] is a coordinated inside partnership in which regional governments work with the broader international community to intensify the search for peace'. To achieve that end, he said, 'the IPF should develop a calibrated set of focused and graduated incentives and pressures to be deployed at key junctures to remove bottlenecks and generate political heat'.[117]

The European IPF members nevertheless continued their admirable work to save lives. On 10 March 1999, the IGAD Partners Committee on Sudan met in Oslo under the co-chairmanship of the Norwegian Minister for International Development and Human Rights, Hilda F. Johnson, and the Italian Deputy Minister for Foreign Affairs, Senator Rino Serri, in the presence of representatives of all IGAD partners, the parties to the conflict and IGOS.[118] The Kenyan assistant foreign minister represented the IGAD chairman. The meeting reviewed the humanitarian situation in Southern Sudan and supported the implementation of what was known as the Rome Agreements of the Technical Committee on Humanitarian Assistance. Emphasis was placed on the need to facilitate accessibility to famine-stricken regions. The meeting noted that it would be difficult for the international community to continue offering humanitarian aid without an accelerated and strengthened political process towards peace.

Consequently, delegates resolved to continue shoring up the peace process within the IGAD framework and to help strengthen its administrative support structures. The meeting also recommended that the IGAD secretariat should expand the negotiation sessions and conduct meetings more frequently. Additionally, the IGAD chairman was asked to appoint a special envoy to keep up the tempo of mediation. As a result, in its 7th session in July 1999, the IGAD committee adopted terms of reference for an invigorated secretariat and named three envoys representing Eritrea, Ethiopia and Uganda to work jointly under the chairmanship of the Kenyan envoy. The envoys, together with the special envoy, should assure collective responsibility and be accountable to the Ministerial Committee. Two technical committees were created to engage in inter-sessional discussions of the issues: a political committee to deal with paragraphs 1, 2 and 3 of the DOP, and a committee for transitional arrangement to deal with paragraphs 4, 5 and 6. The pace of negotiations hastened after the creation of the committees but the positions continued to be as immovable as ever. At the close of the third meeting, the SPLM called on the international community to bring pressure to bear on the government so that it should be more serious on the issues.[119] In that call the SPLM underlined the government's 'unacceptable' position on 'constitutional separation of religion and state' and on the right of self-determination for the people of Abyei, Southern Kordofan and Southern Blue Nile. The government persisted in denying the people of the three regions that right, while the SPLM stood fast behind the right of the three regions to determine their fate for the sake of a lasting peace, without 'claiming these areas as an integral part of the South'. As a mechanism of self-determination, the SPLM suggested a referendum for each of the three regions to be conducted separately from that in the South. On *shari'a*, the SPLM maintained that during the interim period, the fundamental law of the land (the constitution and other relative documents) should be secular. The government's position on this issue was that secularism was unacceptable in Sudan and, in their view, 'Islam is both a religion and a nation and the two are inseparable'. In reality, what the government delegation was referring to was the NIF's Sudan; all constitutions under which Sudan was governed since independence were quasi-secular, and the NIF and its allies successively failed to change those constitutions to their image through the political process. Only through the barrel of the gun, in June 1989, was the NIF able to impose its desired theocracy.

The war therefore continued unabated with the stakes raised higher by the government through aerial bombardment of civilian targets as if it wanted to punish civilians in the South for the assumed recalcitrance of the SPLM. As a result, the SPLM declared on 8 May 2000 the suspension of talks with the government, while extending the humanitarian ceasefire for three months in response to the request of the UN Secretary General. In declaring suspension of talks, the SPLM stated that 'our conscience no longer allows us to ignore the treatment being meted out daily to our people by the very same regime that pretends to be engaging the Movement in a dialogue for peace'.[120] Unmistakably, it was not the hideousness of aerial bombardments that aggravated the SPLM, but the sustained attacks on innocent civilians. Three meetings of the technical committees that took place between July 1999 and January 2000, leading to no more than a repeat performance of the earlier meetings. It was at this point that the SPLM, in a fourth meeting that took place 21–30 September 2000, came up with its position: no more talks on the interim arrangements before the issue of religion and the state was resolved. To resolve the impasse, the IGAD secretariat proposed a formula to the two parties to the effect that a two-tier system of law be established whereby at the national level all institutions and state organs be neutral on religion save for personal laws affecting marriage, divorce, inheritance etc. which may be governed by religious laws. On the other hand, all the state legislation should take into account the religious and cultural peculiarities of the people concerned. That proposal was refused by the government who insisted that *shari'a*, custom and national consensus should be included in any constitution as source of legislation. Clearly, the NIF regime was out to market its 1998 constitution, not to achieve peace.

One would have thought that following this obduracy on the issue of religion and politics and rejection of the inclusion of the NDA in the IGAD process, the government would consider IGAD as good as dead. That was not the case; Khartoum hosted on 21–23 November 2000 the 8th IGAD summit. Absent from that Summit were the president of the IGAD group on Sudan, President Moi, and the Ugandan President, though their governments were represented. On the issue of Sudan's conflict the meeting ruled that the process should continue. Manifestly, Bashir was not so much concerning himself with IGAD's peacemaking vocation, in as much as he was with the symbolism of holding a regional summit in Khartoum after years of isolation. The way the meeting was reported in Sudan's official media was only meant to tell the Sudanese and the outside world that the regime was now out of its splendid isolation.

At the beginning of 2001, it appeared, for all intents and purposes, that IGAD had hit a dead end. Even its supporters in the IPF had begun resigning to the reality that the NIF was immovable, almost immortal. Pressure began mounting for the search for a new forum in which an agreement based on terms akin to those presented by the NIF would be shoved down the throat of the SPLM. Some Western members of he IPF, guided by an assumed 'practical realism' persuaded themselves that the NIF was there to stay and that the world, including aggrieved Sudanese, had better begin learning to live with it. The growing strength of the regime (thanks to oil revenues generated with the help of those very peace mongers) was suggested as proof of the regime's invincibility. IGAD was being written off as ineffective. Ironically, the SPLM that had come into IGAD with little enthusiasm now hung on to it with both hands, telling the IPF and everybody else that IGAD remained a necessary mechanism for resolving the Sudanese conflict.

To energize the IGAD process, President Moi met with General Bashir in Khartoum on 28 March 2001. A joint communiqué signed by the two presidents called for a summit meeting by the IGAD Presidential Committee to take stock of previous and current activities and chart the way for future action.[121] Moi had his own plan for jumpstarting the process. But – to the disbelief of every body who cares – Bashir, only two days after the joint communiqué, told Egypt's News agency, MENA, that for him, the only viable peace process was the Joint Libyan–Egyptian one because it was more comprehensive. The calls for merging it with the IGAD initiative, he said, might lead to separating the South.[122] The incredulous are yet again furnished with additional evidence of the regime's insincerity about peace initiatives.

Parallel Initiatives: The Egyptian–Libyan Intervention

Though both the IGAD process and its DOP were recognized by the NDA in the Asmara resolutions of June 1995, one major shortcoming of the process was that it did not include parties to the NDA other than the SPLM. So when Egypt and Libya decided to initiate their own bid to end the conflict, the Northern opposition parties welcomed the initiative. Of the two, Egypt had been involved in peacemaking in Sudan through the Cohen initiative, which was before the IGAD process. Given the direct impact of the Sudan conflict on Egypt's vital interests (especially the Nile waters), and its previous engagement in the Cohen peacemaking effort, Egypt sought first to secure a place for itself alongside the IGAD mediators. That was not to be achieved since Egypt was not a member of the IGAD club. However, in agreement with the SPLM, it was proposed that Egypt should join the IPF which remained as an American and Western European voluntary club. Garang whole-heartedly supported Egypt's participation as well as other non-European countries on whose names he agreed with the Egyptians: South Africa, Ghana, Zimbabwe and the United Arab Emirates (UAE).[123] Egypt joined the IGAD IPF; but there was no follow-up as regards the other proposed countries.

Prior to the launching of the Joint Initiative, the NDA leadership Council (LC), adopted, at its meeting in Asmara (March 1998), three important resolutions. The first called for the inclusion of the NDA in the IGAD process arguing that it was only through a comprehensive solution bringing together all parties to the conflict that the Sudanese crisis would be resolved satisfactorily. The second invited the IGAD partners to include in the IPF Arab and African countries that expressed genuine interest in the resolution of the conflict. The third welcomed initiatives by Libya and Egypt to mediate. Subsequently, the LC met with the Libyan leadership in Tripoli (August 1999) to discuss Libya's peace proposals which comprised three points: comprehensive ceasefire, mutual cessation of media campaigns and the formation of a negotiation committee to prepare for a peace forum bringing together the government and the opposition. The NDA, accepted the Libyan offer to mediate, but stated its conditions.

The call for a comprehensive ceasefire was rejected out of hand by the NDA, for the same reasons it was rejected by the SPLM at the IGAD meetings. There was a suspicion that the government, having failed to achieve that end at the IGAD meetings, was now smuggling the issue into the Libyan initiative and expecting the NDA (including the SPLM), to swallow the bait, hook line and sinker. The LC, however, demanded that the Libyan initiative be coordinated with that of the IGAD. The SPLM was apprehensive that the Libyan initiative, as it was proposed, would necessarily derail the IGAD process, a matter that Khartoum fought strenuously to achieve. The Libyan initiative was soon to become the joint Egyptian–Libyan initiative after a meeting between President Mubarak and Colonel Ghaddafi in Mersa Matrouh on the 2 August.

Support by the NDA for the Egyptian–Libyan initiative was predicated on its inclusiveness, since the declared purpose of the IGAD was to provide a forum for dialogue between the government and the SPLA on the termination of war. The joint initiative, on the other hand, addressed issues which were of concern to both North and South and hence assumed by its supporters to be a more viable alternative to the stalled IGAD process. Although the remark on the exclusivity of the IGAD process by limiting the mediation to two parties (the SPLM and the government) was justified, the claim that the IGAD initiative was substantively inadequate for a comprehensive resolution of the conflict was utterly unwarranted and confuted by the facts. As we have seen from previous pages, the IGAD mediators have comprehensively addressed the issues of governance in Sudan in a manner never before tried by any mediator. In one sweep they tackled the issues of religion and politics, administrative decentralization, national identity in a multi-ethnic and multireligious country, multi-party democracy, rule of law, equitable distribution of wealth, human right, interim arrangements, self-determination etc. So, if the two parties to the IGAD negotiations failed to grapple with those issues in the manner prescribed in the DOP, that was because of the government's refusal (a) to credit the SPLM to discuss anything that went beyond the rights of the South as conceived by the government, (b) to budge from its position on *shari'* and multi-party democracy and power-sharing, (c) to admit that there were other political forces in Sudan worth talking to.

The government's approach to the two initiatives was both dubious and duplicitous. On the one hand, it continued to negotiate solely with the SPLM under the aegis of the IGAD to resolve the 'Southern problem' on the basis of the exercise of the right of self-determination, assumedly even if it led eventually to separation. On the other, it endorsed the joint initiative because: (a) it a brought in all parties to the conflict including those it has deliberately excluded from IGAD and (b) was predicated on the unity of Sudan, the unity which the government was ready to dismantle within the framework of the IGAD. The failure of the IGAD process, therefore, lies squarely on the feet of the NIF regime because of its rejection of option one of the DOP (Unity of Sudan as prescribed by that document), as well as its prevarication on option two (self-determination). The NDA, on the other hand, was as solidly united in its distrust of the government as it was in its desire to get rid of it. Nonetheless, the NDA was equally ready to pursue a route of peaceful settlement as has been declared in no uncertain terms in various resolutions of the LC.[124] Instead of using this opportunity to sue genuinely for peace, the regime chose to exploit it to create divisions within the NDA's ranks and undermine the ongoing peace process. It is within this context that the SPLM reiterated the significance of coordinating the two initiatives. The SPLM was also disquieted by the likelihood of losing the political gains inherent in the DOP, particularly on the issues of religion and state and self-determination. That disquiet was heightened by the fact that neither Libya nor Egypt would underwrite those principles. This lacuna in the joint initiative led the IGAD mediators and partners, especially the US, to express concern about that initiative.

In a curious way, the US misgivings about parallel peace tracks compounded matters. Madeleine Albright, the US Secretary of State, made the views of her government on the issue known without equivocation during her tour of Africa in October 1999. The Secretary met in Nairobi with several South Sudanese parties, (including the SPLM) to discuss the humanitarian situation in South Sudan as well as the prevailing political situation in the country. In her statement, Albright categorically stated her opposition to the Egyptian–Libyan initiative as a viable alternative to IGAD. She said: 'We believe the IGAD process is the best way forward and do not support other processes that some are suggesting, the Egyptian or Libyan. What is essential is that we do everything we can to support the IGAD process.'[125] This categorical rejection by the US of the joint initiative did not deter the SPLM from standing its ground on supporting that initiative provided it was coordinated with IGAD.

To give credence to its commitment to IGAD, the US government appointed a special presidential envoy to follow up, among other things, the IGAD process with a view to strengthening it. The envoy (Harry Johnston, former Chairman of the House Subcommittee on Africa), is a well-respected and integritous politician who is *au fait* with Sudan affairs.[126] In addition to strengthening IGAD, Johnston's brief included focusing attention on the appalling human rights situation in Sudan and pressing for improvements and highlighting the devastating consequences of Sudan's 16 years of war and pushing the warring parties to permit unhindered flow of relief. Johnston moved fast after his appointment. His first ports of call were Cairo and Asmara in October 1999. In addition to meeting relevant Egyptian officials, he also met in Cairo with NDA representatives (including Sadiq al Mahdi) to brief them on his mission. He also met with Sudan's ambassador in Cairo. But despite Johnston's explanations about his mission and the intentions of his government on Sudan, al Mahdi persisted in beating the drums of war on two fronts. First, he claimed that America had a devious plan to break up Sudan using IGAD as a tool and, second that the 'Arabs' were deliberately excluded by the US from playing a role in the resolution of Sudan's conflict. According to al Mahdi, the US considered Sudan an African and not an Arab country. Curiously, as he was upbeat in the mid-1990s about the imminent expiration of the NIF regime, (conversations with US Ambassador Peterson), al Mahdi, in his talks with Johnston, was increasingly buoyant about the prospects of reconciliation with that same regime. In the meantime, he told Johnston that an *intifada* in Kharotum was imminent. Those palpably contradictory statements were a direct result of the secret agreement he reached with Turabi.

At all events, al Mahdi's contrived distinction between 'Arab' and 'African' mediators, was probably meant to enrage the 'Arabs' against the US and its African 'stooges'. By such statements, al Mahdi was conjuring up the phobism of older days when some Northern politicians had over-excelled themselves in characterizing Sudan's crisis as a conspiracy hatched by Africans, Christians, Imperialists etc to denude Sudan of its Arabo-Islamic character. In reality, the IGAD mediators did not intervene in Sudan's conflict as 'African' countries, but as neighbours of Sudan who happened to be African. To boot, they did so at the express request of General Bashir. In addition, both Egypt and Libya were no less part of Africa than the other mediators, so long as Africanity was not defined by a religio-cultural yardstick, as al Mahdi seemed to suggest.

The NIF regime, though heartened by al Mahdi's crusade, was less vociferous. Despite pleas to the 'Arabs' to ward off the menace to Arabism originating from South Sudan and beyond, the NIF government struggled hard to mend fences with neighbouring African countries. Delegations were sent to non-IGAD African capitals (Pretoria and Abuja) to enlist their support for the peace process. The regime may have been only engaged in time-buying tactics as it bounced from one initiative to the other. Nonetheless, unlike al Mahdi, it was prudent enough not to burn all its bridges to Africa. Besides, despite his espousal of the joint initiative, President Bashir had no qualms in going along with the other IGAD heads of state in their 7th Summit meeting in Djibouti (7 November 1999) when they decided that:

i. The IGAD DOP 'continues to provide an effective basis for resolving the crisis in the Sudan, particularly for national reconciliation which would pave the way for bringing an end to the conflict in the South'.
ii. 'The IGAD initiative is *an African initiative and should remain so.*'[127]

In a play within the play al Mahdi, on the sidelines of the Djibouti Summit, threw up another surprise on his NDA partners. He met with Bashir to conclude another DOP for the resolution of Sudan's conflict. That open meeting was preceded by two undeclared meetings, one between him and Qotbi al Mahdi, NIF Chief of Security in Addis Ababa, and the other with Ghazi Salah el Din in Switzerland. The open meeting in Djibouti was not much of an improvement on the clandestine one in Geneva. However, from that meeting emerged a new DOP tailored by al Mahdi, as if he once again needed a Sadiq-fabricated DOP, in place of the Asmara resolutions, IGAD DOP and the Libyan–Egyptian initiative. By now people grew accustomed to Sadiq's delirium of paramountcy in everything that touched on public life. Nevertheless, his new 'DOP', proved to be a hotchpotch document selectively drawn out of the IGAD's masterplan (to which Bashir had just reaffirmed his commitment in Djibouti itself), and the Asmara resolutions (whose signatories included al Mahdi's Umma Party). Al Mahdi was so carried away by his 'achievement' that he declared that his new DOP responded to ninety per cent of the NDA's conditions for engaging the government in direct talks.

The agreement was formally signed by Mubarak al Mahdi for the Umma and Mustafa Osman Ismail (Foreign Minister) for the government, but it was preceded by a short memorandum of understanding signed by Hassan Ahmed al Bashir, 'President of Sudan' and Sadiq al Mahdi, President of the Umma Party. So, in a spectacular about turn, al Mahdi, who was presenting himself to the whole world as Sudan's legitimate prime minister and pleading to it to reinstate him in that position,[128] had willingly bestowed legitimacy on the usurper of that authority. That agreement glaringly revealed al Mahdi's inconsistencies. First, it came in the wake of a declaration by Bashir, alongside other IGAD heads of state, which asserted that IGAD and not the joint initiative was the *effective basis* for resolving Sudan's crisis. The declaration also maintained that the IGAD process was an '*African initiative ... and should remain so*' (italics not in the original). Second, the decision was taken by African heads of state (including Bashir), obviously without the US instigation. Al Mahdi, the self-styled protagonist of Arabism and of the joint initiative was soon to stew in his own juices. Egyptian Foreign Minister, Amr Musa, told the press that the Djibouti agreement did not conform to what he had discussed with Sudan's Foreign Minister, Mustafa Osman Ismail, and required an explanation from al Mahdi.[129]

The Djibouti agreement was reached two weeks prior to the meeting of the NDA in Kampala to discuss the strategy of the Alliance for a comprehensive peaceful settlement, including coordination between the IGAD and the joint Egyptian–Libyan initiative. The LC, who were not consulted in advance about Djibouti, rejected the deal and censured Mubarak al Mahdi, Secretary General of the NDA, for his role in the conclusion of that agreement. As NDA Secretary General, he was presumed to have betrayed the trust of the Alliance and acted against its principles.

The NDA meeting in Kampala also had the opportunity to hear from Garang about a new initiative undertaken by General Obasanjo to reconcile, in cooperation with the countries concerned, the two initiatives and give an added impetus to the IGAD process. In fact, while the NDA meeting was going on, Obasanjo's envoy, former President Ibrahim Babangida, visited Khartoum and all the IGAD mediating countries. Sadiq was not impressed by this new African initiative. The only viable ones, he maintained, were the oint initiative and the Djibouti agreement. On its part, the NDA affirmed its commitment to a comprehensive political settlement and resolved that talks should only take place with the government and not the NIF (as a party). This was an allusion to the meeting that took place between al Mahdi and Turabi in Geneva. The NDA also called on the government to provide a conducive atmosphere for talks and to that end, urged it, without delay, to implement the following measures:

i. Repeal of all articles in the 1998 constitution that impede civil liberties or allow for such impediment.
ii. Repeal of all extrajudicial measures including those provided for in the National Security Act, which permit detention, search and intimidatory summons without due process of the law.
iii. Lifting the ban on activities by political parties and trades unions and repeal of the 1992 Trades Union Act and the 1998 *Al Tawali* Act.

iv. Abolition of the Public Order Courts and the special police forces known as popular police and public order forces.
v. Guarantee liberties of movement, expression and association and repeal all laws that curtail those liberties.
vi. Release of all political prisoners.
vii. Reinstatement of all persons dismissed from the public service under the pretext of 'national interest'.
viii. Return all confiscated properties to their rightful owners, restoration of those properties to the condition they were in before confiscation or offering, in lieu of such restoration, appropriate compensation.

Clearly, the aim of the NDA was to dismantle the institutions of terror and hegemony established by the NIF in order to entrench itself in power, for if the NIF was not reduced to its normal size, Sudan would continue to be their perpetual hostage.

But al Mahdi appeared bent on reconciliation with Khartoum at any cost; three things confirmed that conclusion. First, he launched a scathing campaign against the NDA (of which his party was still a member) accusing it of ineptitude, unconcern for the country's plight, recalcitrance on peace and, in the case of some of its members, lack of patriotism and war-mongering.[130] Second, he sent an address to the NDA meeting in Kampala in which he repeated those allegations and called on the Alliance to shape up and, without delay, reassess its performance. He also gave notice to the NDA to convene its general congress to review its activities in the last four years, and in the same breath, invited it to a National Reconciliation Conference with the NIF to be held on 1 January 2000. Al Mahdi virtually expected the NDA, whose meetings took place in mid-December, to rectify all the mistakes of the past, reorganize itself, hold a general congress before it engaged on 1 January in a National Reconciliation Conference with the government. Third, while addressing the NDA to shape up, al Mahdi held a meeting with the Eritrean leadership in Asmara in which he requested his interlocutors to join him in calling for a peace conference at Asmara that would bring together the NDA and the NIF government. He conveniently dismissed from his memory his repeated assertions that the joint initiative was the only viable tool for national reconciliation. The conference al Mahdi called for was to be held in Asmara (obviously not an Arab capital). However, the former prime minister reached the apogee of double-dealing when he appealed to the Eritreans to stop armed activities by the NDA forces against the Khartoum regime from 'Eritrean territory'. As a sweetener, and with a distinctly boundless faith in his capabilities, al Mahdi offered in reward his good offices to reconcile Eritrea with both Sudan and Djibouti. The Eritreans told the Sudanese leader that, as members of the IGAD peace process, they could not have a peace conference of their own. On armed activities on their borders with Sudan, they told al Mahdi that there were no Sudanese opposition forces within the Eritrean territory. As for those fighting the regime from inside Sudan on the Eritrean borders, that was a matter of concern only to the NDA and al Mahdi was free to talk to his colleagues about it. On his mediation offer with other countries, the Eritreans were politely dismissive.

This depressing narrative showed how desperate al Mahdi was to reach an agreement with the regime, even if it took stabbing his friends in the back while he was pretending to shore up their activities. People in such a state of desperation are unstoppable. Could Sadiq's real objective had been to debilitate the NDA and sap its cogency as a viable alternative to NIF? One reason that might have made him take that route would possibly be his failure to mobilize the *Ansar* into a credible force despite his proclamation of *hijra*.[131] Al Mahdi would have surely liked to burst into Khartoum with the *Ansar*, like his great-grandfather, or at least the way he tried to do during the Nimeri era, but that was not to be. Another reason might have been his apprehensions of the dominance of the New Sudan Brigade (SPLA) within the NDA forces in the east. To Sadiq and Northern leaders of his mindset, the SPLA would only be tolerated as a force to enfeeble and exhaust the 'enemy' from afar, not as a credible force within the North.

Riled by al Mahdi's Djibouti meeting and his manoeuvres in Eritrea, Garang made a scathing attack on the Umma. 'They either have to abide by the NDA resolutions and strategies or quit,' he told the Kampala meeting. In response, Sadiq al Mahdi wrote to the SPLM leader on 22 December 1999, repeating his unvaried protestations about IGAD and its inadequacy, the need for a quick political settlement and dangers obtaining from the prospect of an international intervention to force a settlement over the heads of the Sudanese. He also presented the Umma Party as the largest political party in Sudan and described the rest of the NDA parties as deadwood. In addition, al Mahdi claimed that the Umma, unlike all other Northern parties, had made the greatest contribution to the formulation of policies addressing the causes of marginalized Sudanese groups. In his letter, al Mahdi interjected two surprising assertions. The first was that the Umma Party leadership, 'as far back as 1964, recognized the politico-cultural and economic aspects of Sudan's crisis as reflected in the civil war'. By that he wished to claim that Garang's agenda did not add any thing new. 1964, of course, was the year Sadiq emerged as the Umma leader. The second related to accusations against the SPLM of human rights abuses, attributed to unnamed 'international players'. In all likelihood, al Mahdi wanted to draw a moral parallel between the SPLM and NIF practices in this regard. Those irrelevant accusations (in view of their inconsequentiality to the issues raised by Garang at Kampala), must have aggravated Garang beyond measure. So in his counterblast, he challenged al Mahdi's claim about the role of his party since 1964 in addressing the core issues of the Sudan conflict. 'You have been Prime Minister twice since 1964, and no other Sudanese politician in our history has had, and squandered, two opportunities to correct things in Sudan,' Garang wrote. In addition he recalled the excesses of the former Prime Minister's government in the South including his own personal role in the Bor incidents, his exploitation of tribal militias in the 1980s, his introduction of the Islamic Constitution in 1968 and his cover-up of atrocities by 'arab' militiamen against the Dinka which were exposed by two university lecturers who were made by al Mahdi to pay for their conscientiousness.

On al Mahdi's claim that his party was the largest in Sudan and 'the rest were deadwood', Garang was searing in his response. 'Before you left Khartoum in 1996 to join the NDA,' Garang said, 'the story I heard was that the poor recruitment showing of the Umma Party was due to your being held hostage by the NIF. However, when you finally came out and called for the *hijra* of your faithful to join you, there was no significant increase in your recruitment. I am Chairman of the NDA Unified Military Command (UMC) and the reality is that the New Sudan Brigade has more Northern Sudanese in it than the whole army of the Umma Pary, not to mention Southerners, whom I presume to be Sudanese.' Garang went on to say: 'calling your colleagues in the NDA deadwood … has more to it than meets the eye. This deadwood are the same forces with which we want to carry Sudan through the interim period, unless you believe that Sudan is destined to be ruled by one party, indeed one man. This is of course untenable and that is why we have all along accepted to cohabit with all manner of politician and live with the dead weights of history.' On the other hand, he told al Mahdi that the SPLM never contested an elections with the Umma, so the claim that the Umma has the right, by popular approval, to lord it over the others was unjustified, at least as far as the SPLM was concerned. Sadiq frequently looked back to his parliamentary majority in the 1988 parliament (before Bashir's coup) as if Sudan was frozen in time, while Garang wanted to tell the former prime minister that that should not necessarily be the case.

The political environment was thus envenomed by those comfortless exchanges and al Mahdi persisted in his accusations of Garang and the SPLM, whereas the SPLM leader chose not to be drawn further into a *baggare* that became increasingly abrasive. At the same time, al Mahdi's accusations and attacks against the NDA became vitriolic and vindictive.[132] In one of his spiteful accusations, he described the NDA as an ineffectual cat, incapable of catching mice.[133] Accordingly, new battle lines were defined in which Sadiq's enemy number one was no longer the NIF, but the SPLM, NDA and the US. In an interview with a Cairo daily, the former prime minister appealed for pressures an Garang (without saying by whom) to end his 'warlordism' and genuinely sue for peace. 'Garang is isolated in the South where everybody else wants peace,' claimed al Mahdi.[134] In the same interview he asserted his refusal of any foreign intervention in the Sudan conflict, including that by the Security Council. Probably, al Mahdi believed that the only pardonable intervention by that body was the one that would restore 'legitimate' rulers to their seat of power in the manner he requested Secretary General Kofi Annan to do in 1997. Those who were not sufficiently aware of

Sudan's political theatre would never have divined that this aversion to the 'internationalization' of Sudan's conflict came from the staunchest supporter of the joint initiative (led by Egypt and Libya), the co-author of the Djibouti agreement (mediated by that country's president) and above all the first Sudanese ruler to allow a United Nations structured feeding programme through an internationally mobilized food relief (OLS/Sudan). However, Sadiq's statements, as we had demonstrated, are time after time devoid of fact and rationality.

The Umma leader did not relent; if anything he raised the ante. In one statement he claimed that, in collusion with the US and the Sudan Communist Party (two very strange bedfellows) Garang had a hidden agenda to rule the Sudan and expunge Islam. 'Expunging Islam' probably was a pseudonym for the SPLM's call for separating religion from politics. Even so, al Mahdi could not be unaware that from 1968 (when he promoted the idea of an Islamic constitution) to 1986 (when he signed in to Koka Dam Declaration abrogating religion-based laws), the proposition that religion should be separated from politics was sponsored by a political constituency that transcended the SPLM and Sudan's communists. As for the reasons of the US support for this 'ungodly' policy, al Mahdi decocted three reasons, all shorn of rationality. The US, he said, was endeavoring to achieve three objectives: removing Sudan from North Africa and encompassing it within the Horn, banishing Islam altogether from Sudanese politics and renegotiating petroleum licences in favour of American companies.[135] At one instance, he played up a US non-paper on Sudan's peace initiative that was neither a secret to him, nor to other parties to the NDA. Aggravated by the protraction of the IGAD to incorporate the NDA in the process, the US decided to fly a test balloon with the objective of ensuring an all-inclusive peace process, precluding two-track initiatives, ending the exclusion of the NDA from the IGAD process and making sure that negotiations would lead to a conclusive resolution of critical national issues, particularly those of religion and state and self-determination. The non-paper noted that 'multiple peace initiatives will allow the government to divide the NDA, split the issues between North and South, co-opt opposition figures one by one from a weakened position'. It also noted that the continuation of two parallel initiatives was untenable. Accordingly, it proposed modification of the IGAD to allow for:

   i.   involvement of North African neighbours in the process,
   ii. endorsement by Egypt of the IGAD DOP,
   iii. revitalization of the IGAD negotiating committees and the inclusion of the NDA into this process, and
   iv. regular consultations between IGAD mediators and North African neighbours.

That well-meaning proposition was immediately rejected by al Mahdi as an attempt to sideline the Northern opposition and only bring it as an add-on to the SPLM within the IGAD framework. The government was also not happy with the inclusion of the NDA in the IGAD process in any manner or form. Eventually, the initiative was stopped dead in its track following the government's pressure on the IGAD secretariat to withhold any communications with the NDA

Al Mahdi oftentimes appeared to be long on assertions and short on evidence, but his freakish statements on internationalization and unsubstantiated accusations against the US put him in a very different light. For example, a few years before his concerted attack on the US (1997), the selfsame al Mahdi denied to a Kuwaiti daily's accusations circulating in the Arab media that the endgame of the US in Sudan was to separate the South. On the contrary, claimed al Mahdi, the US was against separation because separation would create more problems than it would solve. The dismemberment of Sudan, he added, would not be to the liking of a superpower that had always endeavoured to achieve stability in the Horn of Africa.[136] A year later, al Mahdi had a different description of the American position. He told a Cairo daily that 'the *right* in America wants to truncate Africa south of the Sahara from North Africa because it believes that the solution of Sudan's problem shall only be achieved within the bounds of sub-Saharan Africa'.[137] Al Mahdi neither illuminated the questioner or his readers as to the identity of that American *right*, nor about its role in decision making in America or influence on the present US policy in Africa. But when that *right* assumed power in the US (the Republican administration), Sadiq pinned all his hopes on it for the resolution of Sudan's conflicts. Said he: 'America can play a role in the resolution of Sudan's conflict by putting pressure on the two parties in order to end the war, restore democracy and put in place mechanisms to ensure the implementation of agreements reached by the parties.'[138] It was beyond belief that the selfsame man who was shouting from the rooftops against a so-called 'internationalization' of Sudan, had now turned to the US to twist the arms of Sudanese belligerents. Ostentatiously, Sadiq told a Cairo weekly a few months before his visit to the US that he plans to visit that country to influence the administration's policy towards Sudan.[139] 'The position of the new American administration on Sudan can be refined,' he told the journal. The way Sadiq set out to achieve that refinement showed how divorced he was from reality. Within Sudan's political scene, Sadiq is surely not a man to be discounted whether for his intellectual attributes or the significance of his popular base of support. For that reason one would expect that people who desire to play a role in the resolution of Sudan's conflict would wish to talk to him. However, the self-admiring Sadiq not only went to Washington to make his views known to the US policy makers, but also to redirect American policy towards Sudan, particularly in so far as the position of the administration towards both the NIF regime and the SPLM was concerned. His aim was to dissuade the administration from supporting the latter, and goad it to be more amenable to the former. Apparently, what he failed to realize was that he was not even part of the equation that was influencing the formulation of the US policy towards Sudan. For one thing, what he called earlier the American *right,* was basically motivated in its campaign against the NIF regime by two issues in none of which Sadiq had anything to contribute: religious persecution and slavery. On the latter issue, it is not only the American *right,* but also the *left* represented by Afro-American leaders and groups that is in the forefront of the anti-government campaign. As for ending the ongoing war that is the centrepiece of the Congress's and the administration's policies towards Sudan, the issue was more complex for Sadiq. Not only is that policy predicated on the prior resolution of issues like cessation of aerial bombardments on civilians, controlling tribal militias and stopping the use of oil revenues for war purposes, but it is also concerned with basic questions like religion and state. Without action and agreement on those issues no permanent peace shall ever be achieved in Sudan. None of those issues really preoccupied Sadiq since they did not occupy a central space in his different discourses, particularly after he opted out of the NDA. On the contrary, his main message continued to be the denunciation of Garang's 'war agenda', as if there were no reasons for perpetuating that war, or that those who continued to fight were relishing war. Moreover, Sadiq never spared any time in those discourses to denounce bombardments of civilian targets, using oil revenues to change the government's military capabilities or exposing abductions by militias. When Sadiq eventually made it to Washington in June 2001, he encapsulated his message to the US political establishment in four clusters:

i. Illuminating those who met about the increasing margin of liberties under the NIF regime and urging them to restore full diplomatic relations with that regime;
ii. Calling for a heightened American role in the peace effort (a matter that was declared by Bush, Powell and the Congress and, therefore, the American establishment did not need to be reminded of it);
iii. Advising the US government against offering any support to the SPLM; and
iv. Denouncing both the IGAD and the joint Egyptian–Libyan initiatives for their structural and substantive deficiencies, even though the latter was reviously described by him as the only viable forum for peace.

Sadiq also travelled to New York to meet with UN Secretary General Kofi Annan to insure Annan of support for his renomination for a second term, as if the Umma Party had become the one hundred and eighty-sixth member of the UN General Assembly, if not the 16th member of the Security Council. More importantly, he briefed the Secretary General on the progress made inside Sudan (obviously by the regime) leading, according to him, to the creation of an atmosphere conducive to a meaningful intervention by the UN for peacemaking. In a sense Sadiq became a self-appointed roving ambassador for the regime and cared less for his earlier denunciations of external interventions even if they came from the UN. And in his new guise as the self-appointed advocate of the regime, Sadiq did not also call to mind his earlier pleadings to Kofi Annan against Khartoum's 'illegitimate' regime that was only fit for the Astrid treatment.

Notoriously, Sadiq can neither live in, nor see, reality. His statements to the Arabic press about the success of his mission to US reflected that. His meeting with congressmen was described as successful, but even when while he was still in Washington the House of Representatives adopted the Sudan Peace Act which did everything that Sadiq asked the Americans not to do. The Act was adopted by 422 congressmen with only two nays. Equally embarrassing was his report on the meeting he had had with Chester Crocker whose name was floated as the new US envoy for peace in Sudan. Sadiq, hailed Crocker's nomination and reported the meeting of minds they had on all issues relating to Sudan conflict. That report was carried by the Arabic press, the same day Crocker declared that he was not interested in the mission because he could not see the intricacies of the Sudan situation and American approaches to it which Sudan's former prime minister could not see. From the above contradictory statements and misreckonings, three things come out clearly. First was that a large part of the Umma leader's statements were intellectually too undisciplined to lead to rational conclusions. Secondly, though he continued to change his positions dizzyingly on matters of moment (sometimes within the compass of one week), al Mahdi still expected his interlocutors outside Sudan to take at face value whatever he said. Thirdly, from the Sudanese, he expected nothing less than acquiescing to his political meanderings, if not following blindly his political whirls. For those who did not share his puzzling twists and turns, he had only the rough edge of his tongue.

Another aspect of Sadiq's countradictions is reflected in the level to which he had gone in playing up the issue of Arabism and Africanity as if he wanted the two groups to lock horns, Clearly, the Umma leader neither weighed the long term impact of the stances he was taking against the SPLM, nor was he seemingly concerned with Africa's mute reactions to his racially based definition of Sudanism.[140] Nevertheless, al Mahdi could not find a better mediator to engage in reactivating the peace processes in Sudan than General Obasanjo of Nigeria. That was the very same Obasanjo whose intervention to create an African IGAD forum in support of the IPF was discounted by Sadiq. In his wisdom, Sadiq thought then that there was only one viable forum for bringing an end to Sudan's conflict: the joint Egyptian–Libyan initiative and, therefore, considered any attempt to reactivate IGAD to be redundant. The Nigerian leader was also requested by Sadiq to mediate between him and Garang. That much was announced by the Umma Party Secretary General prior to Sadiq's travel to Abuja.[141] To the amazement of everybody, the Umma leader told a Gulf daily[142] that he was surprised to see Garang in Abuja. Apparently, the failure of his mission was the main reason for that fib.[143] To be sure, it does not behove a political leader, especially one who does not cease to play the oracle, to become a hangman of the truth.

One may, therefore, justifiably ask why would such a well-educated politician engage in such monumental absurdities, falsehoods and contradictions. Some may dismiss all this horsing around as acts of political opportunism. Others may see al Mahdi's contradictions and high jinx as characteristics inseparably associated with a confused mind. Whatever way you looked at it, doing business with al Mahdi proved to be a cumbersome exercise to both friend and foe. Further, with its chairman at sixes and sevens, the Umma Party's departure from the NDA was a matter to be expected. That formally took place during the meeting of the LC at Asmara in March 2000, when al Mahdi left his colleagues with no choice but to accept his departure. Despite pleas to him by all parties (including the SPLM) to remain in the fold, al Mahdi stood firm on his call for the cessation of military struggle and proceed with the joint initiative without waiting for its coordination with the IGAD process. He also demanded the virtual dissolution of the NDA external activities because, according to him, the atmosphere inside Sudan was conducive for political activity.[144] One of the reasons he gave for dismantling the NDA's external activities was the changing regional environment that would make it impossible for the opposition to continue operating from neighbouring countries.[145] But in place of mapping out new tactics to save the minimum programme of the NDA in the face of this changing regional environment, he wanted the opposition to abandon strategies that had considerably tamed the regime. The NIF would not have changed its tactics and policies, if not ideology, were it not for both internal and external pressures. Al Mahdi, in effect, was urging the NDA to exercise prudence and throw in the towel. Manifestly, he wanted the NDA to proceed with talks with Khartoum in complete disregard of the consensual agreement reached by the Alliance at Kampala on conditions that were a *qui sui non* to negotiations. That type of negotiations advocated by al Mahdi, other NDA parties thought, would not be conducive to reconciliation but to surrender.

The rosy picture which al Mahdi drew for the situation inside Sudan was soon punctured by the regime. Beside the sustained aerial bombing of civilian targets in the South and extending that bombing to the East, the regime framed up the whole NDA Secretariat in Khartoum, accusing them of complicity with the US. The secretariat was meeting with Glyn Warren, an officer at the US Embassy in Khartoum, in the course of regular consultations they used to have with foreign missions, particularly those who represented countries of the IPF.[146] In reality, two factors led to the government's unwise act. The first was the increasing audacity of the NDA Secretariat,[147] and the second was the visit by Susan Rice, Assistant secretary of State for Africa, to the liberated areas in South Sudan without seeking permission from Kharotum.[148] The regime was more riled by the visit itself, than by the harsh words Rice reserved for the regime. That action coincided with an important decision by the US Congress that was no music to the regime's ears. The Congress authorized the President in January 2001 to 'undertake appropriate programmes to offer direct support to indigenous groups in areas outside of control of the government of Sudan in an effort 'to provide emergency relief, promote economic self-sufficiency, build civil authority, provide education, enhance the rule of law etc'. Obviously, by persisting with the types of human rights violations catalogued by Rice, as well as many international institutions concerned with the deterriorating humanitarian situation, the government had no reason to be taken a back by angry reactions from those quarters. In effect, the regime kept stumbling on potholes it had itself dug and persevered in digging. If only the regime was aware of the first law of holes, it would not have been in the place it found itself in. That law ordains that ' If you are in a hole stop digging'.

Extraordinarily, while he was urging his colleagues to rush back to Khartoum, Sadiq al Mahdi stayed put outside Sudan for almost one year, using Cairo, Asmara and London as his chosen abodes. That gave the impression that the Umma leader was not sufficiently assured of the sincerity of the NIF regime. In press reports, he attributed his holding out to a desire to follow up the peace initiatives abroad, as if that could not have been one reason why other leaders he wanted to rush back to Khartoum, were also staying behind. The reality was elsewhere. Al Mahdi became a one-issue man, berating the NDA and paying court to the countries of the joint initiative. That was not done for the sake of actualizing that initiative in as much as to gratify the two countries, while poisoning the relations between al Mirghani and Garang, on the one side, and Egypt and Libya on the other. Besides, if he had to make it to Khartoum, he would rather be in the company of others, an obvious sign of 'I won't go down alone syndrome'. The rest of the time in his voluntary exile, al Mahdi exploited the two things he did best: pontificating on peace in Sudan at Cairo academic centres, press conferences and political rallies, and gallivanting around the world offering advice on the resolution of unwieldy problems. One such case was his visit to Iran in September 2000, assumedly to engage Iran in peacemaking in Sudan and normalize Arab–Iranian relations. In a statement to a Gulf daily, he said that one of the purposes of that visit was to seek a peaceful solution to the problem of the islands contested by Iran and the United Arab Emirates.[149]

The NDA persisted in its position. To al Mahdi's dismay, it registered three important military and political successes after his threatening words to the Alliance that it would soon find itself homeless in the region. The first hit was in the military field when the NDA forces repulsed an extensive and meticulously prepared attack by the army and government militia to recover positions held by those forces in the east. In addition, the NDA forces counter-attacked and captured the most important centre of Qur'anic studies in rural Sudan, Hamashkoreib.[150] That defeat stunned the regime to the point of introducing into East

Sudan their discredited policy of arming tribal militias. According to Engineer Ibrahim Mahmoud Hakim, Governor of Kassala, the regime planned to mobilize 10,000 Beja fighters in support of the army.[151] In a naked spoiling game, al Mahdi described that victory as an unwise adventure and virtually joined the NIF's campaign against the liberation of Hamashkoreib, describing it as a desecration of a holy place by 'infidels'. Al Mahdi went overboard when he turned that Qur'anic centre into a Vatican. 'Those who want to conquer the regime should hit Rome, not the Vatican,' said al Mahdi.[152] Both al Mahdi and the NIF should have been astounded when the 'Pope' of that Qur'anic centre, Sheikh Suleiman Ali Betai, publicly aligned himself with the 'invading infidels', and accepted to be member of the LC.

The regime's wail of woe over Hamashkoreib and its environs was in reality not because of the alleged desecration of that holy place, in as much as it was for the strategic advantage the NDA had acquired. An expert on the area wrote that in view of this area's 'strategic importance – threatening the country's vital road and rail links to the coast and to its new oil pipeline and other key economic installations – the outcome of this protracted war may eventually be decided here'.[153] That explained the length to which the regime had gone to harass citizens in the area.[154] The final target of the regime was, therefore, to dislodge the NDA forces from those strategic areas they occupied inside Sudan, and push them into Eritrea. For such a strategy to be pursued at a time when Eritrea was engaged in mediation between the government and the opposition proved the NDA's worst fears. To give as good as it got, the NDA forces attacked the HQ of the eastern command at Kassala. That attack took the regime by surprise; they probably never expected the NDA forces to hoist them with their own petard. As in the case of all irrational punitive expeditions, the regime engaged in a racist campaign against the SPLA forces within the NDA, as well as against all Southerners and Nubans living in Kassala, who were deemed by the regime to be the SPLM's fifth column in that town. Khartoum papers[155] published the news of the disappearance of a large number of them, and equating what was happening in Kassala to what took place at Juba during Mahjoub's government in the 1960s. The event impelled the Archbishop of Khartoum, Gabriel Zubeir, to go to Kassala to reassure himself of the situation. Also, the Cairo-based SHRO made an urgent appeal to the world on 14 November drawing attention to the witch-hunting reprisals and extrajudicial killings unleashed by the regime in Kassala and its environs. SHRO maintained that the aim of the government was 'to fan racist-ethnic sentiments among Northern Sudanese' and reminded the world that the Sudan government had done this before and got away with it.

Another incident that should have awakened al Mahdi to the duplicity of the NIF regime took place in August 2000. On 18 August, the NDA Comprehensive Political Settlement Committee (CPSC) wrote to ambassador Daniel Mboya, head of the IGAD secretariat, requesting a meeting to discuss modalities for the inclusion of the NDA in the IGAD process and for the coordination of that initiative with the joint

Egyptian–Libyan one. The committee was formed by the NDA in March 2000 to expedite action on the coordination of the two initiatives, particularly in view of the soft-pedalling of the two countries of the joint initiative in pursuing the issue. The committee included as coordinator-general Nhial Deng Nhial, the leader of the SPLM to the IGAD talks. In a letter signed by General Abdel Rahman Said, the NDA expressed its strong belief 'that a lasting peace, if at all possible, requires a comprehensive political settlement through negotiations between the NDA and the government of Sudan'. This, the General said, 'is the only means to speed up the peace process and ensure the unity of Sudan'.

The meeting did not take place because of Khartoum's vehement objection to it. Khartoum advised the IGAD secretariat that they would withdraw from talks if anything like a meeting between the secretariat and the NDA took place. That action alone proved the inveracity of al Mahdi's claim that the coordination of the two initiatives was stalled because of the SPLM's prevarication on the issue. Neither al Mahdi nor the two governments of the joint initiative reproved Khartoum for this double-dealing. This is the more astounding since the NDA reaffirmed its position on coordinating the two initiatives in the meeting of its Leadership Committee on Cairo as late as July 2000 as a condition precedent to the commencement of any talks with the regime. In that meeting, the Egyptian government prevailed on the NDA to engage in preliminary talks with the regime, but the LC, after long haggling, agreed to the meeting on two conditions: the first related to amendments to specific articles in the constitution and clauses in the National Security Act that directly encroached on the rights of political parties to operate without fetters, and the second called for a solemn commitment by the regime to the coordination of the two initiatives with a view to ensuring that there was a single negotiation forum. The first condition relates to fundamental changes without which there shall be no to the proper functioning of democracy. That was necessary to call the NIF's bluff in so far as coordinating ongoing mediation efforts are concerned. On the strength of meeting those two conditions, the NDA chairman was mandated to meet with Bashir.

The Cairo meeting exposed yet another of al Mahdi's long yarns. Throughout his discourses on the peace initiatives, he spared no pains in accusing Garang, in collusion with the US, of frustrating the joint initiative. Asseverations to the contrary by US diplomats and the President's Special Envoy did not make al Mahdi budge from that position. However, in June 2000, the US and Norway were alone in spearheading at the meeting of IGAD's IPF[156] the twin issues of incorporating other Sudanese parties to the conflict in the IGAD process, and to the coordination of ongoing peacemaking efforts. As a result of those efforts, to which Egypt was party, the IPF underlined in its final communiqué the need 'to include all concerned Sudanese neighbours in an active engagement towards finding an end to the conflict'. To that end, 'the participants urged the co-chairpersons to make renewed contacts with the relevant Sudanese parties and regional political actors as well as other relevant actors in the African continent in order to better coordinate efforts to achieve peace in Sudan'.[157] Al Mahdi's doggedness in pretending to know more about the US intentions than those he wanted to dupe (Egypt), lifted the lid off a singular feature of his character, an artless and accident-prone approach to politics.

Barely two months after the NDA Cairo meeting, the much-awaited NDA Congress met at Massawa, Eritrea, between 9 and 13 September. The meeting was better attended than the 1995 Asmara Conference, particularly in that it included participants representing all shades of opinion from inside Sudan as well as from Sudanese communities in the diaspora. The Congress tellingly met under the slogan: 'Ending war and Building the New Sudan.' One of its most significant resolutions was the affirmation that a negotiated political settlement of the conflict was the NDA's preferred option, and that the 'NDA, by the very nature of its composition and objectives', was the foremost advocate of peace and justice in Sudan. The Congress revisited the issue of a comprehensive peaceful settlement of Sudan's crisis and, without foreclosing the use of armed struggle and popular mobilization to achieve the NDA goals, resolved:

i. to mandate the LC to pursue the search for a comprehensive peaceful settlement of the conflict, including participation in preparatory and direct meetings with the regime regardless of the regime's devious manoeuvres, and
ii. to affirm its commitment to the oint Egyptian–Libyan initiative and to the importance of coordinating it with that of the IGAD.[158]

The NDA Congress, on the other hand, welcomed the Eritrean government's offer to intensify its efforts to enhance and facilitate the process of a comprehensive negotiated political settlement.

One historic document endorsed by the Congress was the Massawa Declaration, the idea of which was thrashed out between al Mirghani and Garang. The document encompassed guiding principles to steer Sudan during the interim period and beyond. Those principles were:

i.   Voluntary unity based on the free will of the Sudanese people and on the recognition of the religious, ethnic, political and cultural diversity of the Sudanese society.
ii. Prohibition of the use of religion for political ends and of the formation of political parties on religious bases as stipulated in the Asmara Declaration.
iii. Good governance based on respect for human rights, separation of powers, rule of law, democracy, institutional accountability and an extensive measure of decentralization of power in a manner that would end the hegemony of the centre and the marginalization of the peripheries.

iv. Recognition of the equality of citizens regardless of religion, race and gender and adopting affirmative action to end the effects of marginalization and discrimination suffered by women throughout the past decades.

v. Creation of a democratic environment for the healthy and free development and interaction of all Sudanese cultures.

vi. Initiation of a balanced, integrated and sustainable development so that the vast and diverse resources of Sudan be exploited for the benefit and prosperity of all Sudanese people.

vii. Enabling the Sudan to play its proper role among nations in the quest for a better, just and peaceful world.

Indubitably, the declaration was a further affirmation by the parties to the NDA of their commitment to specific benchmarks without which neither peace nor unity could be sustained.

The resounding success of the Massawa Congress was no music to the Islamists ears; one of their leading protagonists and supposedly open-minded intellectuals, became an apologist of the Umma and a disparager of the NDA. In an article, amazing in its daring, he wrote 'that after breaking with the Umma, the NDA cannot claim to be representative of all Sudanese people since it has become a coalition of minority groups which can no longer claim to speak on behalf of the country as a whole. It now has to present its demands as those of minorities seeking their rights, not as an expression of a popular will that must be respected'.[159] That absurd argument could have been tolerated if it came from a political analyst who ever considered the NDA (as it was constructed before the departure of the Umma) as an 'expression of a popular will that must be respected'; not when it issued from a political analyst who months earlier pleaded that all Sudan's traditional political forces should be first consigned to oblivion before the NIF bestowed democracy on the people of Sudan.[160]

However, Eritrea brooked no delay in moving with its peacemaking effort. A meeting was held in Asmara on 26 September between al Mirghani and Bashir based on the NDA Congress resolution relating to exploratory talks. A crisp press statement released by the host country announced that the two parties to the conflict had agreed to:

i. achieve peace and stability in the Sudan through a comprehensive peaceful settlement and not by military means, and

ii. bring war to a quick end and create the requisite conditions for voluntary unity.

The statement added that 'taking into account the present peace initiatives' the parties agreed to enter into direct negotiations with the aim of arriving at a comprehensive peaceful settlement. That was a veiled reference to the coordination of all ongoing peace processes.

A little over a week later, President Issaias Afeworki paid a visit to Khartoum purportedly to discuss bilateral relations. Nonetheless, the internal Sudanese problem was high up on the agenda of both parties. In a press interview, the Eritrean President told the media that 'Bashir and all Sudanese government officials have shown sincerity and conviction'. He appealed to the opposition to avail itself of the opportunity and respond to this attitude for solving all issues of the controversy'.[161] The Eritrean President, while in Khartoum, lashed on both ongoing initiatives. The IGAD, he said, 'remained as a name without producing anything since 1994'. On the other side, the joint initiative, according to President Afwerki, 'only contains views published in newspapers, nothing substantial. The two compete with each other and the Sudanese cannot wait for long.'[162] On its side, the opposition welcomed the Eritrean endeavour and discussed in depth with the country's leaders the content and import of the blueprint they had formulated as a basis for negotiations. The NDA, nevertheless, wanted the regime to come out clearly on the question of other peace initiatives. It maintained that parallel peace tracks would only play into the hands of the regime. Fears lingered as to the sincerity of the regime, especially that it was not inconvenienced by launching their biggest attack on the eastern front while the Eritrean leader was meeting with Bashir in Khartoum discussing peace. Obviously, the regime 'availed itself of the opportunity' in its own way.

In the meantime, the regime's military preparations intensified in the eastern front, culminating in the reoccupation of Hamashkoreib. The regime huffed and puffed about that victory and swore to throw the NDA forces out of Sudan, in all probability after having persuaded themselves that Eritrea was about to hand them the NDA on a silver platter. On 6November, the NDA forces answered the regime's brazen provocation by attacking the headquarters of the government forces at Kassala and occupied the town for 24 hours. In the course of the attack they wiped out the headquarters of the army in Kassala and forced the army to flee to the airport. A large amount of arms was seized and about 15 tanks destroyed. Remnants of the NIF militias who remained in the town wanted to engage the invading forces in skirmishes within the town, but the NDA forces resisted the temptation so that innocent civilians should not be caught in crossfires. The purpose of the attack, seemingly, was to tell the regime that the NDA forces were alive and kicking and that, despite its bold front and sabre-rattling, it was still vulnerable. Nonetheless, the NDA affirmed its commitment to a peaceful settlement. Its chairman, al Mirghani told the press that the Kassala attack confuted the myth of achieving peace through war. He also advised Bashir to desist from threats and intimidation.[163] The NDA, therefore, had no twinge of conscience in declaring that there should be more of the same till the regime cames to its senses.[164] The NIF accused the NDA and Eritrea of insincerity in pursuing peace, comfortably forgetting that it was they who launched the first attack while the Eritrean President was in Khartoum.

Unexpectedly, al Mahdi joined the government in denouncing the attack on Kassala 'because of its effect on civilians'. He even dared al Mirghani to come out openly against the invasion. No one should be naive enough to believe that al Mahdi's concern was about the sanctity of the lives of civilians and their property; for over one year before the Kassala incident, the Umma Party forces, under the overall command of the JMC, attacked the Fao village (outside Gedaref town) in Eastern Sudan and captured four civilians and confiscated their vehicles. The Umma justified that action as a measure to enhance the *intifada* in all Sudanese towns. The event was hailed by nobody other than al Mahdi himself. One of the captured civilians was a customs officer who was accompanying his young daughter for medical treatment at a nearby hospital. The girl was left on the way to fend for herself. On arrival at the NDA forces headquarters, however, the medical officer in charge of the field hospital immediately began tending to the captured customs officer for injuries he sustained during his capture. What happened afterwards neither did honour to the Umma forces, nor coincided with their leader's professed concern for civilian lives after the NDA's attack on Kassala.[165] Moreover, Sadiq's heartache over the fate of civilians in Kassala was blatantly at variance with the written master plan he came up with to the NDA in order to dislodge the regime. That plan involved a blitzkrieg on Khartoum, described in his creative idiom as a *latmma 'askariya* (military knock-out blow). He promised to provide 10,000 fighters through his *hijra* appeal. The Chairman of the JMC, Garang, discounted the plan. 'This man,' Garang told his aides, 'neither knows the capabilities of the NIF nor is he aware of the intricacies of invading a metropolis like Khartoum'. Sadiq's *latmma*, however, withered away when his much-trumpeted up *hijra* produced only three hundred fighters.

Al Mahdi eventually made his long awaited return to Khartoum on 23 November 2000 'to profit from the existing margin of liberalization in order to form a wide-based front in support of a national agenda', as he told a Cairo-based daily.[166] One month later the broad-based front he said he was going to build in Khartoum turned out to be a front with the NIF. The Secretary General of the National Congress announced that an agreement was about to be reached between the two parties on matters relating to the system of rule, the constitution and peace as well as the inclusion of the Umma in Bashir's government.[167] Al Mahdi confirmed the report and dismissed the rumblings within his party against that marriage of convenience. Those rumblings were brought to light by an Umma stalwart, Dr Adm Madibo, who described the goings-on as personal initiatives and not a result of an institutional decision. In fact, the opposition within the ranks of the Umma Party to the proposed shotgun wedding was such that the engineer of the rapprochment between the Umma and the NIF, Mubarak al Mahdi, was isolated within his party and reportedly constrained to submit his resignation.

Before his return to Khartoum, al Mahdi had a press briefing with the editorial board of the Cairo weekly, *Al Mussawar*.[168] Asked about Turabi's position, al Mahdi said: 'He would either insist on his present stance and end like Taliban, or seek political settlement [with Bashir] the way Arbikan did in Turkey.' The questioner was evidently not satisfied with this abstruse answer. Pursuing the matter further, he asked Sadiq: 'What about your relationship?' Turabi is Sadiq's brother-in-law. Sadiq's answer was cold-blooded. Said he: 'Relationship has nothing to do with politics. You recall the Ottoman practice that authorized a newly chosen Sultan to kill all his brothers. You understand what I mean.' Who said that blood it thicker than water? Apart from the outrageousness of the statement, al Mahdi demonstrated a level of untrustworthiness beyond the pale. This could not have been the same person who signed with Turabi an agreement to undo Bashir. The sum and substance of that agreement, we recall, was that the two leaders join hands in mobilizing popular resistance against Bashir. That was the reason why Sadiq told Harry Johnston – to Johnston's utter surprise – that an *intafida* in Khartoum was impending. Johnston must have asked himself how could a man whose whole rationale for returning to Khartoum was to achieve a peaceful settlement with the regime was, at the same time, talking about an *intifada*. Effectively, Sadiq at that point was playing a double game: urging his colleagues in the NDA to reconcile with Bashir through the Djibouti route, while working clandestinely with Turabi – and without the knowledge of his NDA colleagues – to overthrow the regime. But once Turabi was out of power, Sadiq became more than ready to abandon Turabi and his *intifada*, in order do commerce with his brother-in-law's arch-enemy: al Bashir. At the same time, his lectures to the NDA about the futility of an *intifada* never ceased. Patently, the Sadiq we know by now is capable of doing the unimaginable and believing that he can get away with it.

The Umma leader never eased his futile pressures on Garang and the SPLM. On 27 December 2000, in the course of an *Id al fitr* sermon, he addressed an appeal to 24 Southerners to join his march for peace.[169] With the exception of two (Riek Machar and John Luk) none of his addressees carried arms against the government. Some were not even in the forefront of opposing it. Clearly, al Mahdi's idea was to create a Southern front opposed to 'warlord' Garang, notwithstanding that a number of those living outside Sudan among his presumed Southern allies were decidedly working for the separation of the South he so dearly wanted to remain united with the North and of whose dismemberment Garang was accused. Also, by addressing politicians who were known to be registered party members (USAP and SPLM), Sadiq had revealed the flippancy with which he treated Southerners. He would never have dared to address Northern politicians over the heads of the institutions to which they belonged. Those were the type of details al Mahdi was not bothered with. The former prime minister could have done himself a little good if he only acquainted it with the position of USAP on his idea to create two parallel 'Southern blocs'. That position was expressed by Joseph Ukello, Chairman of USAP in Khartoum, when he refused the invitation by the promoters of the idea of creating a Southern bloc opposed to Garang. The invitation was to attend a meeting in Geneva to develop a common strategy to that effect. Ukello told a Cairo paper that his party would never subscribe to the idea, which he openly attributed to Sadiq. He maintained that the real aim of that meeting was not to create a Southern wave in support of self-determination, but to create a force against the SPLM. That, he said, would not lead to a comprehensive political settlement.[170]

Even with all those contrivances and ingenious schemes, the NIF regime refused to come to Sadiq's rescue. Any reconciliation, they said, should be based on the respect of the NIF 'fundamentals'. Ghazi Salah el Din (amazingly one of the architects of the Djibouti Peace Agreement) must have surprised Sadiq when he declared in January 2001 over Sudan Television that reconciliation does not mean participaton in government. Also, the NC's Secretary General who was following up negotiations with the Umma, told a London Arabic daily that the opposition's understanding of reconciliation was misplaced. 'They want the regime dismantled, while we want it to remain intact and within its parameters reach a common vision.'[171] On his side, First Vice-President Ali Osman Mohamed Taha put it differently: 'Viable multipartism shall be born from the bosom of the present regime after some time and after a complete review of the existing political parties and organizations. High street Sudan is not convinced with past party experiences and is still in search of a national programme.'[172] Statements like this show beyond doubt that the Islamists still believe that they alone know what is good for the Sudan; so the others have no choice but to fall in line. Accordingly, it therefore came as a surprise to no one when the regime, without qualms, gave Sadiq the Machar treatment. This was exactly what his colleagues in the NDA (the cat incapable of catching mice) had cautioned him about. One thus wonders why did such an expert in the psychology of microorganisms[173] leave a floating ship to join a sinking one.

Agreement between Two Mortal Enemies

The Sudanese were taken by surprise on 19 February 2001 when the SPLM, represented by Pagan Amom and Yassir Arman, signed with the NPC a memorandum of understanding (MOU) 'in the context of endeavors to crystallize a national consensus among all Sudanese political forces' with a view to reaching 'a historic settlement and a comprehensive and peaceful resolution to the national crisis'. The two parties agreed on the following:

i.   That the one-dimensional perception of Sudan's crisis since independence, and the lack of a consensus-based national programmes deepened the crisis.

ii. The creation of an environment conductive to peace and

     democracy presupposes the intensification of *popular resistance* against Bashir's regime so that it gives up its totalitarian approach to politics.

iii.   The need for concluding a new social contract based on the pluralistic nature of the Sudanese society that shall guard against discrimination among citizens on the basis of religion, culture, race, gender or region.

iv.   Affirmation of the right of self-determination as a basic human right to all Sudanese.

v.   Military *coups* had exacerbated the national crisis and failed to propel Sudan towards a lasting and comprehensive national solution. Accordingly, past regimes should be accountable for grave transgressions against human rights and corruption of public life.

vi.   The need for a formula of administrative decentralization that shall take into account the country's geographic size and its regional peculiarities.

vii.   Regional cooperation, good neighbourly relations, non-intervention in the affairs of other states and respect for international peace and order are essential elements for the sustenance Sudan's own stability.

viii.   The SPLM shall remain committed to the NDA and welcomes the PNC's desire to engage in constructive dialogue with the Alliance.

ix.   Repeal of all laws restrictive of freedoms, lifting the state of emergency, and release of all political detainees are prerequisites for a healthy democracy.

x.   Formulation of a joint action programme to achieve the above goals.

God, evidently, works in strange ways. Those who might have loved to dance over Garang's grave had ultimately come to the conclusion that he was better alive than dead. We recall that Turabi had made friendly advances to the SPLM to which the Movement replied in a seven-point memorandum.[175] Turabi explained his reasons for the rapprochement with the SPLM in a statement to a London weekly as follows: 'I wish to engage the Movement in a political discourse since all discussions it has had with the regime were marred by the two things that were uppermost in the regime's mind: security and military considerations. He also asserted that unity could not be achieved while democracy was lacking.[176]

    Within the ranks of the NDA there were murmurs as to the wisdom of signing the MOU with Turabi. Some drew a parallel with the agreement signed with the regime at Djibouti by former NDA Secretary General, Mubarak al Mahdi. The accusation, on the face of it, is justified because one of the signatories on behalf of the SPLM was Pagan Amom, who was also the NDA Secretary General. To that accusation the SPLM retorted first that Turabi was not the government, but the leader of a major opposition force against the regime within Sudan. Secondly, by denouncing the concept of *jihad*, Turabi has created confusion within the ranks of the *mujahideen* that would have a direct impact on the conduct of war. Thirdly, the agreement reached with PNC indicated that the Islamists were ready to question the ideological verities they had stood by for forty years, and particularly within the last decade. Fourthly, the argument that talking to Turabi, even when he was disarmed of all authority, was taboo, untenable. After all, the NDA was engaged in talks with Bashir notwithstanding the fact that the NIF faction he heads included the most notorious elements of the regime especially as far as human rights violations, war crimes and terrorism were concerned. In effect, it was months after Turabi's removal from power that the regime started its gravest assaults on NDA forces (aerial bombardment of civilian targets in Eastern Sudan) as well as on NDA political activists within Sudan (detention of the totality of NDA leadership in Khartoum). Fifthly, the MOU had taken the conditions precedent to any negotiations between the NDA and the regime (conditions for creating a conducive atmosphere for negotiations) a few steps up the mileposts set by the NDA. The MOU has denounced the military *coup* and conceded that gross human rights violations and corruption of public life must be accounted for. More importantly, that was the first time an opposition force engaged with the leader of the Islamist political trend in a constructive dialogue in a way that would have a profound effect on future political evolution of Sudan.

The regime's reaction to the MOU was frenzied. Minister of Information Ghazi Salah el Din described the meeting as an unprecedented infilteration by the SPLM into the 'Islamic Movement.'[177] Also, foaming at the mouth, Salah el Din addressed the nation through Sudan TV (22 February) saying that 'any group dealing with the rebel movement to set up a strategic alliance would be treated the way the SPLM is treated'. Coming from the spokesman of the regime that strove hard to be engaged in talks with the NDA, which is also sworn to dismantling the regime, that statement was puzzling, to say the least. In truth, the bizarre conflict between Turabi and Bashir was put in the right perspective by Hassan Mekki. The conflict, Mekki said, 'is a classical power struggle. There is nothing ideological about it.' The Islamic writer went on to say that the MOU did not depart from Islam but reflected Turabi's pragmatism. He also contended that calls by Turabi for democracy and pluralism would make Bashir's position uncertain in any open and free democracy, while Turabi's position was untenable because it did not take into account the heavy doses of indoctrination he had given to his followers about the 'ungodliness' of Garang[178].

Is This the Turabi We Know?

Turabi's political agenda for Sudan has always been the creation of a fundamentalist Islamic state. All attempts, successful as well as unsuccessful, to promulgate an Islamic constitution bore his signature. His entire adult life has been dedicated to the Islamist project. Turabi, by definition, is the father of political Islam in Sudan and beyond. In addition, it was Turabi who in 1990 redefined the Sudanese civil war as a holy *jihad*. He mobilized the Popular Defence Force (PDF) and conducted bizarre marriages of martyrs to heavenly maidens. If the SPLM needed an epitome of its arch-enemy, Turabi was the perfect fit.

The February 2001 MOU is thus incredible. Why did Turabi sign it and what are its implications for his political identity in Sudan? The SPLM has the charitable view that Turabi's eleven years on the helm has opened his mind to the reality, which he could not perceive as an activist at the periphery of power. This view is corroborated by the fact that Turabi has been seeking to communicate with the SPLM since well before the zenith of his dispute with Bashir that culminated in his ouster as Speaker of Parliament and Secretary general of the NC. Moreover, it can be speculated that Turabi was forced to change his ways to save his image as an eminent international scholar, an image he cherishes dearly but one that had been severely tarnished by his association with Islamic despotism and terrorism. If this theory is correct, it amounts to a significant victory for the forces of reason and moderation in the Sudanese political landscape. It may well represent the 'light at the end of the tunnel' that could ultimately illuminate the road to peace and stability in Sudan. However, this would also strip Turabi of his legacy and reduce him to a faceless entity in Sudanese society and the global Islamic movement.

On the other hand, those who are reluctant to give Turabi the benefit of the doubt argue that the man is not known for surrender. Even his worst enemies give him credit for sophistication and survival instincts. So is Turabi strategically reducing his battlefronts after the 'betrayal' by his former proteges? Under this theory, they conjecture that Turabi is luring his main protagonist, John Garang, near enough for a knockout punch. Turabi, they surmise, is confident that in time he can overcome Bashir and the rest of the Northern opposition. In this context, the MOU is nothing more than a calculated move to checkmate the SPLM on the political chessboard.

Nobody knows the strengths and weaknesses of the NIF government more than Turabi. So is he abandoning a sinking ship? Has he concluded that the future of a *united, peaceful* Sudan cannot be achieved without the SPLM, and is therefore buying an insurance policy? Does he want to ensure that, in the inevitable post-Bashir era, he is not counted out? Does he want to survive today to fight again tomorrow? All those are pertinent questions. But when all is said and done, two things remain. The Geneva MOU has indubitably created new situations in two major areas. It shifted the alignment of forces more towards the benchmarks for peace and democracy established by the NDA. Secondly, it deepened the schism within the NIF. Those two factors put together would surely enhance the twin and complementary processes of dismantling Sudan's religious apartheid regime and preparing the ground for inclusive civil pluralism.

The schism between Bashir and Turabi also served in exposing the slipperiness of the intenational Islamists. In April 2001 a high-powered groups of Islamist notables led by Abdel Majid al Zandani of Yemen visited Khartoum to mediate between the estranged brothers in order to save the Islamic agenda. Intolerably, they accused 'the enemies of Sudan and Islam of sabotaging the pioneering Islamic project. Those having failed to do so in war are now resorting to creating cleavages between the builders of that project.'[179] With such closed-mindedness to the complex nature of the problems of a country so near to them, one wonders how can such half-scholars claim to have a role in a making Islam relevant to contemporary realities in the world. However, the Islamist dabblers urged Bashir to release Turabi and resolve his dispute with him peacefully. Bashir's main condition was that Turabi should denounce the MOU. In his turn, Turabi was reluctant to do that. He also called for the release of all prisoners of conscience.[180] The mediators were not happy with the introduction of what they considered to be an extraneous matter: release of all political prisoners, as if they believed that suppression of political opponents was an Islamic act of piety. That did honour neither to their credentials as Islamic scholars nor to Islam. Sadiq al Mahdi took issue with the meddling of those mediators and appropriately advised them to look unto themselves by subjecting the whole contemporary Islamist experiment to an in-depth analysis.[181]

New Initiatives

The continuation of conflict and the pervasiveness of the misery that conflict brought in its wake not only caused a donor-fatigue, but also created a peace-fatigue. Concerned with the increasingly worsening situation in Sudan, a Task Force (TF) on Sudan was established in July 2000 by the Center for Strategic and International Studies (CSIS) and funded by USIP with the aim of 'revitalizing debate on Sudan and generating pragmatic recommendations for the new administration'.[182] The TF which was chaired by Francis Deng and Stephen Morrison, director of the CSIS Africa Programme, benefited from the contributions of more than fifty participants, in addition to inputs by experts conversant with the Sudanese situation. The group came to the conclusion that 'the central problem on which virtually everything else hinges' was war. Accordingly, it urged the new US administration 'to join actively in a strong multilateral push, in collaboration with interested European powers to end Sudan's internal war'. It also contended that the policy of 'containment and isolation' adopted by the previous administration 'has made little headway in ending Sudan's war, reforming Khartoum, or ameliorating Sudan's humanitarian crisis and gross human rights abuses'.

The TF proposed, in place of the former policies it disparaged, 'a hard-nosed strategy based on diplomacy, heightened engagement with all parties, enhanced inducements and punitive measures and concerted multinational initiatives'. Another two important findings by the TF were first, that Sudan's oil production was shifting the military balance in favour of the regime and, secondly, that 'the competing regional initiatives held no promise'. In light of the above, an nine-point Sudan programme was proposed for the Bush administration:

i.   Concentrate US policy on peacemaking.
ii. Actively join the UK, Norway and Sudan's neighbouring states to press the warring parties for serious negotiations.
iii. Build a *new* extraregional peace initiative.
iv. Seek to reach agreement on an interim arrangements based on a *'One Sudan, Two Systems'* formula.
v.   Devise multilateral inducements and pressures that move *both* parties to negotiate in good faith.
vi. Launch a high-level international plan for a viable self-governing South.
vii. Assign top priority to early mutual confidence building measures, improvements in human rights and humanitarian access etc.
viii. Resume *full* diplomatic operations in Khartoum.
ix. Seek successful conclusion of the US–Sudan ongoing negotiations on terrorism.[183]

Though many keen Sudan observers and political activities were happy with some of the Task Force's conclusions, especially the one giving an overriding priority to ending the war, they also took issue with what was taken to be defeatist assumptions and the unjustifiably harsh critique of the Clinton administration's policy towards the NIF regime.[184] The wrong assumptions include:

1. That oil is fundamentally changing Sudan's war. This may be true in the long run, but at present, the conduct of war in the South and the East proves the vulnerability of the government and its failure up till now to protect oil production sites and pipelines.
2. Calling both warring parties to negotiate in good faith presupposes that the two parties are at fault. In reality from the Carter-sponsored negotiations in December 1989 to IGAD, negotiations failed because the government believed that it would win militarily. All what it needed was a breathing space. The regime's meandering from one peace initiative to another was at peace with this strategem.
3. Positing that the regime's heinous practices against its own people, including slave raids and aerial bombardments on civilian targets, can only be halted after peace is achieved, leaves the victims of those practices at the mercy of the regime who continues unabatedly with those crimes. And whenever the regime tactically eased off those practices, it was only because of mounting external pressures on it.
4. Ignoring the Northern opposition and limiting the conflict to one

between the NIF and SPLM pays no heed to the reality on the ground. War is not only limited to the South, it is also raging in the east, south-east and the Nuba Mountains. The TF's supposition only legitimizes the NIF as the sole spokesman for the North. Nonetheless, the heightened concern by the TF with the war in South may be justified in that the North was never subjected to the same horrors the South was subjected to, e.g. aerial bombardment of civilians, uprooting and displacement of populations and forceful abduction of women and children.

The SPLM took exception to that report arguing that the idea to reform the NIF was wishful thinking. 'The regime is too deformed to be reformed.' It further maintained that the regime could not be engaged 'with eloquent arguments and morality or what is perceived to be their enlightened interest'. The NIF's militarism 'is not borne out of its lack of patriotism or moral values [but] on a strong foundation of racist nationalism and religious fascism', said the SPLM. The SPLM also stated that the NIF considers itself anointed to force divine reformation on our 'pagan' society, only wants to reduce the cost of victory by achieving their aims, not through war but through coercing the SPLM to sign any agreement. Such agreement, the SPLM, warned 'would be depreciated and eventually written off like all the others in modern history'.[185]

Clearly, the TF sought to cut corners in order to move things forward, first, by disaggregating the peace process so as to deal initially with the Southern problem then address the national one, and second, by decelerating pressures on the government on issues like oil production, aerial bombardments, slave raids and human rights abuses till the regime is engaged constructively in peace talks. But things in the real world do not happen like this, as innumerable experiences in the last eleven years undisputedly proves that all that the regime seeks from peace initiatives is to gain time. Accordingly, it shall only be too happy with a peace plan that extenuates pressures on it. On the other hand, the TF's recommendations were utterly mindless of long-standing political alignments that proved their viability and moved the Sudan away from the historic stereotypes of North–South conflict. Indeed the proposals had achieved for the NIF what it had failed to achieve for over a whole decade: reducing the SPLM to a Southern party with no say in the nation's fate, while giving legitimacy to itself as the sole spokesman for the North, indeed the Sudan. To be sure, without international diplomatic pressures and sanctions led by the US, the regime would have achieved that legitimacy long ago; it was not because of a mid-summer night's dream that the regime began to change course. Also, without the policy of containment and isolation, there would have been very little left for the TF to discuss with Sudan's Taliban.

Paradoxically, while that brainstorming was going on, eight leading Senators,[186] proposed to the Senate a Bill entitled the 'Sudan Peace Act', whose main objective, as the title reflected, was to hasten the peace process in Sudan. Like the TF, the Bill asserted that leadership by the US of the peace process was critical. Furthermore, it stipulated that 'a viable, comprehensive and internationally sponsored peace process, protected from manipulation, presents the best chance for a permanent resolution of the war and protection of human rights and a self-sustaining Sudan'. The Senators' document was forthright in describing Sudan's current plight and putting blame where blame was due. It denounced the government's use of 'divide and conquer technique' to subjugate people and frustrate internationally sponsored reconciliation efforts. It also deplored the organization and use of militias for raiding and enslaving people and the use of oil proceeds 'to increase the tempo and lethality of war'. In addition, the regime was castigated for vetoing plans for transport of relief under the OLS and excluding completely from relief areas like the Nuba Mountains. In consequence, the Bill, alongside condemnation of violations of human rights on all sides, and of the ongoing slave trade and the government abetting and tolerating it, called for:

   i.   Multilateralization of economic and diplomatic tools to compel the government to enter into a good faith peace process.

   ii.   Support for the creation of viable democratic civil authority and institutions in areas outside the government control and continued support to them.

   iii.   Strengthening mechanisms to provide humanitarian relief to those areas.

   iv.   Cooperation among trading partners of the US and within multilateral institutions toward those ends.

The Bush Administration owes heavy political debt to the conservative right wing of the Republican Party. This is the most vocal advocate of strong US policy against the Bashir's government, especially in response to that government's policies relating to religious freedoms. Recommendation to the president shall ineluctably be influenced by that constituency. But it is not only the American Christian right that is championing the cause of aggrieved Sudanese. A wide coalition against the regime is increasingly gathering momentum. According to the *Washington Post* 'a moral imperative' now guides a coalition 'from the Black caucus to Gary Bauer's American Values, from ACLU to Christian Coalition, from Catholic bishops to fundamentalists'. That is the type of coalition 'that any politician would be proud to step out and get in front of'.[187] Of course, NGOs and agencies whose information current flows under the public stream could turn out more decisive than Congressional fiat. Indeed, President Bush had chosen one of those fora to announce that he would take steps to pressure the government of Sudan and described the country it as 'a disaster area for human rights'. He also said that pressure would be brought to bear on that government to end war and religious persecution.[188] Bush also appointed the Administrator of the Agency for International Development, Andrew Nations, as special humanitarian coordinator for Sudan to ensure that US aid to that country 'goes to the needy without manipulation by those ravaging that troubled land'.[189] General Powell, on his side, made it public that ending the war will be a priority. In a congressional hearing he described Sudan's crisis in very strong words. 'I do know there is no greater tragedy on the face of the Earth than the one unfolding in Sudan,' he said. The identification of the mechanism through which this unfolding tragedy is addressed is where the problem lies. The CSIS favours an end-the-war-never-mind-the-other-issues approach. That is also the Khartoum regime's favoured formula. The administration is therefore left with no real option but to find a stick with which to herd the regime to the negotiating table, since the CSIS formula offered Khartoum many carrots and few sticks. By May, the US new administration had very much drawn its policy towards Sudan.[190] The main features of that policy are:

i. Appointing a special envoy on Sudan to ree-nergize the peace process.
ii. Continuation with food aid. A donation of 40,000 tons of grain was announced to avert an impending food crisis.
iii. Granting the NDA three million dollars to boost its capacity to negotiate with the regime and prepare itself for the post-conflict stage. That donation came under a programme entitled 'Sudan Peace Building Initiative'.

Powell, in the course of a visit to a number of African countries including Kenya and Uganda, declared his support to the IGAD process and expressed hope that the IGAD summit (scheduled for 2 June) would break the logjam in the process. He also made two conditions for the normalization of relations with Khartoum: cessation of aerial bombardment of civilian targets and an irrevocable end to support of international terrorism.

On its part, the regime was doing its own bidding. In a statement to Reuters, Bashir said that his government would not blame Bush for Clinton's 'sins', but he expected the new administration to reshape its policies towards Sudan. He also expressed readiness to discuss 'the genuine concerns' of the US.[191] Those concerns are evidently closer to home, if Bashir only cared to listen to those who oppose him in Sudan and to the wider consitituency outside Sudan which was not comforted by the regime's crimes against its own people. In spite of those conciliatory words, Bashir persisted in his boastful bellicosity. On the same day that President Bush announced that ending Sudan's war would be one of his main priorities, the Sudanese President told a Khartoum daily that 'the liberation of Kurmuk and Maridi (two towns controlled by the SPLA, of which the first is in Southern Blue Nile, the second in Western Equatoria) will be followed by that of *al Quds* (Jerusalem).[192] One wonders, therefore, whether Khartoum has at all a policy for ending Sudan's war or reconciling with its assumed enemy outside the country: the USA.

The regime's media also made a lot of mileage of President Mubarak's visit to Washington in April 2001. Mubarak has reportedly appraised the US administration of Egypts 'genuine concerns': opposition to any settlement that would result in dismembering Sudan in a way that would affect the uses of the Nile waters. Those concerns are surely genuine, but as far as anyone can see, there is no Sudanese or US plan that is predicated on the division of Sudan. Only the NIF's agenda would lead to such an eventuality. Sudan can never remain united if those who hold the reins of power in Khartoum believe that they can enforce their religion-based ideological agenda. For that reason there is only one capital in the world where those policies can be addressed and rectified: Khartoum.

Events in the region, however, will provide the US administration a policy flexibility that Clinton lacked in his last two years in office. The end of the Ethiopean–Eritrean War and the prospects of progress in the implementation of the Lusaka accord on the Congo are relevant. Uganda is withdrawing its troops from eastern and northern Congo. However, for any new initiative to be viable, five concurrent measures are necessary:

i.   The American involvement must have the support of strategic partners in North and East Africa, especially IGAD as well as other provenly concerned Arab and African countries: Egypt, Libya, Algeria, Nigeria and South Africa.

ii. The opposition must get its act together and present itself as a viable alternative to the NIF. The present hurtful stalemate is a direct result of the weakness of both the opposition and the government. Even if the regime is to fall of its own volition, that does not make, by necessity, the NDA the only alternative to it so long as the NDA is not a direct factor in the fall and an able and ready alternative to the regime. That requires from the NDA to maintain its other options, i.e. military and popular struggle as an ever-present tool.

iii. In the same light, more (not less) pressures should be brought to bear on the regime, especially in the areas of gross human rights violations (aerial bombardment of civilians, abduction of women and children, religious persecution, harassment of opposition parties) and plundering of oil revenue and their use for military purposes. On the latter, mechanisms for control of oil production and of the use of oil revenues must be part and parcel of any interim arrangement.

iv. Acceptance by the regime that reconciliation does not mean absorption. Nothing short of a more inclusive and non-ideological system of rule would suffice as a basis for ending the war and consolidating unity.

v.   Desisting from any attempts to disaggregate the issue of ending hostilities from that of a comprehensive political settlement so as not to give the false impression that the Sudan belongs to two parties: the NIF regime representing the North as a whole and the SPLM representing the South.

Revival of the Joint Initiative

After years of incubation, the joint Egyptian–Libyan initiative came out with its own nine-point plan for peace, which was simultaneously handed to the NDA and government of Sudan on 28 July 2001. A copy of that plan was also presented to Sadiq al Mahdi who chose to occupy a no-man's land between the government and the opposition. The new initiative calls for national reconciliation based multi-party democracy, review of the constitution and laws, an interim wide-based government, recognition of Sudan's ethnic, religious and cultural diversities, separation of powers, a system of rule based on decentralization and respect for the principles of human rights enshrined in universal and regional covenants. The NDA welcomed the initiative but drew attention to two issues that were conspicuous by their absence in the plan: self-determination and separation of religion from politics. The NDA also called for the merging of all peace initiatives so that Sudan should not be torn between Arab and African mediators. Besides, it asserted that the aim of talks with the regime should be the attainment of a comprehensive political settlement and not reconciliation with the regime. On its part, the government welcomed the initiative 'without reservations' according to a statement by Sudan's foreign minister at a press conference in Khartoum on 4 July 2001. Turabi's NPC also welcomed the initiative and urged the immediate formation of a national interim government. But despite its 'acceptance without reservation' of the new initiative, the government continued to waver on one issue: the formation of an interim government. Clearly, topmost on the minds of the leaders of regime was who should rule Sudan and not how could Sudan be ruled in peace. Bashir, in a cantankerous statement, declared that the liquidation of the *ingaz* shall only come over 'our dead body'.[174] Nevertheless, Bashir endeavoured to obtain the army's support for the plan, which he got. Given the reluctance of the inner curia of the NC to share power, let alone abdicate it, Bashir's move may have been spurred by a desire to strengthen his hand against his party's diehards. In view of those manoeuvres the NDA (including the SPLM) remained guardedly optimistic about the revived initiative. In all appearances, given their totalitarian nature, the diehards within the regime are reluctant to move to real multi-party democracy. As many experiences have shown, they would rather use the new initiative as a delaying tactical weapon to extend their tenure in office, if not perpetuate their rule. Those are yet to learn that having been the main cause of the present problem, they can only be part of the solution when they abandon their hollow triumphalism.

Conclusion

The cruelty of the NIF's regime was such that civilians became a regular target of war. Today 80 per cent of the 8 million Southern Sudanese, at some point in their lives, were victims of War, while the region's economy and social and political life were seriously impaired. When the NIF came to power, 70,000 Southern Sudanese were refugees, a year later the figure increased exponentially to half a million with another 4 million displaced.[193] On the other hand, markets, refugee camps, hospitals, schools and areas used for international relief operations (including those run by the UN).[194] To many outsiders, it would appear that there is no end to this infernal war. However, despite all atrocities, millions of Sudanese continue to soldier on, firm in the belief that a solution could still be found to what has become an embarrassing stigma. Those Sudanese, evidently, do not include the salvationists who believe that they can save Sudan by destroying it. Little do they know, this type of war is never winnable. Elijah Molock, head of the Sudan Relief and Rehabilitation Association (SRRA) put it succinctly: 'the government can not win the war from the air. This is not a battle with the SPLA; it kills civilians.'[195] Nonetheless, it would not be much of an exaggeration to say that the peace process is at a crossroads. In the past, as history has demonstrated, the South had not successfully united its house. When it did, divisiveness often reared its ugly head, even in the face of the hardest adversity. In the previous chapters we have come across multifarious groups of freedom-fighters-turned-collaborators, self-seeking politicians willing to subscribe to the misery of their brothers and sisters and 'concerned' intellectuals who emerged at crucial junctures of history to scuttle the struggle. But, in the history of North/South relations, never before the emergence of the SPLM/A was the cause of the South as well articulated, its struggle as adeptly calibrated and the role of the South itself in national affairs as heedfully considered. Besides, rarely before the emanation of that movement, did the North entertain a genuine inclination to accede to the legitimate concerns of the South as part and parcel of wider national concerns. Southern concerns in the past were not infrequently treated as parochial, confined and sometimes anti-national. This situation had increasingly changed after the KKD and the Sudan Peace Initiative of 16 November 1988. And though the emergence of the NIF in 1989 scuppered the ongoing peace process, it had also done a lot of good to the cause of peace and unity in Sudan. By the very nature of the NIF's maximalist agenda, the battle lines became less blurred and the parameters of peace and unity more focused. The Asmara Resolutions on Fundamental Issues, arrived at by the NDA after few years of dithering, was the acme of the new realization.

On the other hand, at no time since Sudan's independence was international involvement in peacemaking as focalized and sustained. Sadiq al Mahdi and some of Sudan's Arab neighbours give the impression that they are thrown into a fright by this 'internationalization' of Sudan's conflict. In this they are only flying in the face of realities or seeking an alibi for their own ineptness to produce home-grown solutions for

Sudan's protracted conflict. Solutions abounded, but invariably they were frustrated by impercipient political manoeuvres. As for the concerned Arab countries, obliviousness to the legitimate political concerns of Southerners who represent one-third of the country's population has always been the heart of the problem. Not only in peacemaking were those countries completely inactive, but also at the humanitarian level, they were utterly disinterested in the plight of about one-third of Sudan's population. For two decades, Southern Sudanese had been fed through a structured international aid programme (OLS/Sudan) to which 'concerned' Arab countries remarkably made no contribution. They could have at least followed Egypt's lead in providing thousands of Southern young men and women with education opportunities and establishing communication channels with their leaders. Equally, while the Sudan government's conduct towards its own citizens – both in the North and South – was regularly subjected to judgment by UN fora (sometimes at the behest of the same 'patriotic' leaders who dreaded internationalization), concerned Arab countries either kept silent on the issue, as if governed by a mafia code of silence, or volunteered to cover up the government's internationally condemned behavior. In such a situation, protestation against international players who came to the rescue of starving Southerners or protecting Northerners and Southerners subjected to the regime's cruel practices is counterfeit. On the other hand, in a country where the parties to the conflict continue to resort to external mediators to unravel the problems they had created for themselves in the first place, any worry over internationalization is hollow to the extreme. It also betrays dismal ignorance of how the real world works.

Despite the belated awareness (since the KDD) of all political players of the requisite conditions for peace and unity, the realization of peace continues to be a mirage. There were unexpected setbacks and capricious prevarications. In this connection Turabi, Bashir and al Mahdi emerged incontestably as the villains of the piece. The first two were at least consistent in their ideologically motivated positions and, therefore, logical in their illogicality. Theirs was stubborn belief in the immutability of their ideological design, even when it was blasted away by a battery of failures. The two Islamist leaders – up to December 1999 – espoused three peace agenda: one for the South, the second for the North and the third for the international community. For the South they offered self-determination leading to secession if the Southerners so wished, while they persevered in dividing Southern ranks to turn the war into a South–South one. For the North, the battle cry was different: safeguarding Sudan's territorial integrity and Arabo-Islamic identity against alleged threats by the US, Southern separatists and their European and African 'sponsors'. As for the international community, the regime offered sham reforms and a peace plank which appeared to be drawn from Adam Smith, President Wilson's 14 points, the UN Charter and the Universal Declaration on Human Rights; all wrapped into one. The idea, of course, was to hoodwink the world and impair the international community's ability to bring pressure to bear on the regime. Those were the type of nuances that eluded peacemakers who believed that the NIF could be persuaded by moral exhortations.

As for al Mahdi, who suffered more humiliation than any other Northern politician from the NIF coup, eleven years of antagonization by the NIF regime were not enough to make him grasp the lessons of 30 June 1989. Though al Mahdi is imbued with many intellectual qualities, as a political practitioner he became renowned for wrong judgement and copious initiatives. Each initiative clashed with the other and none of them was ever allowed to run its course. To those whose trust in al Mahdi did not abate, his mistakes might have been tolerated as results of the law of unintended consequences. However, his fracas with the NDA, his vituperative attacks on Garang, his under the counter agreement with Turabi, his false accusations against the US, his bogus revulsion of the internationalization of Sudan's conflict and his eventual appeal to the blackballed US to intervene in that conflict, were more than mood swings or errors of judgement. In reality, they exhibited self-serving double-dealing. Al Mahdi, who had not been accustomed within his own community to people stepping out of his long shadow, had reason to be disappointed at the NDA's constant refusal to heed his words. What he failed to understand was that the NDA was not his party, nor did all its members share his vision on matters political. Even so, with the sociocultural changes that are enveloping the land, Sadiq could no longer take for granted his own party. The courageous stand of some Umma Party workers and grass roots organizations against his intended reunion with the regime substantiate this claim

As a matter of fact, when al Mahdi came out of captivity in December 1996, he was received with open arms by the NDA. His statements in Khartoum in which he distanced himself from the Alliance were discounted by the NDA, because it reckoned that the Umma (al Mahdi's party) was, after all, a founding member of the Alliance and a signatory to all its resolutions. A margin was also allowed for him, given the fact that he was in the clutches of a merciless regime. However, in his first press conference in Asmara (12 December 1996), Sadiq was told by Dr Sharif al Dushooni, a Sudanese Professor of Economics at Asmara University, that many common Sudanese believe that he would end by dismembering the NDA and dragging it into a half-baked peace with the regime, the way he did with the NF in 1977. To that foreseeing remark, Sadiq replied that his freedom of action was curtailed inside Sudan and that he was virtually used by the regime as a human shield. But now that he was out of captivity, things would be different. Two days later he served a message to Bashir through the London daily *Shark al Awsat* that all people of Sudan were united to escalate their armed and popular resistance against him. Nonetheless, a few years down the roads, Sadiq did exactly what the prescient professor anticipated that he would do. Why did he do it?

Sadiq al Mahdi, in all probability, expected more than a genial reception when he emerged outside Sudan: political beatification by the NDA. Surely, he did not lay any open claim to the top position within the NDA, but his innuendoes and sustained attempts to upstage the NDA leadership suggested that he was offering himself as a more capable alternative. And the Umma leader was not expected to be present at the LC meetings, since his party was represented by its Secretary General in that body. But the LC, in deference to Sadiq, welcomed his participation. In all meetings his was a procentium presence. So, month after month, he kept inundating the NDA with initiatives which were rejected by the collectivity of the NDA leadership, either because they went against a consensus priorly arrived at, or against the spirit of the NDA's minimum programme. Increasingly, it became apparent that al Mahdi did not present those initiatives as ideas to be debated, accepted or rejected, but as commands. Clearly, he wanted to lead by the nose, but to do so one should have all the aces. Manifestly, his expectations may have been jolted, but that was no reason for him to keep heaping accusations on his colleagues. Some of his critics were undeniably justified, but oftentimes those accusations strayed into malice. In reality, al Mahdi's departure from the NDA was not simply an organizational parting of ways, it was an ideological cleavage. His recent statements on al *Sahwa al islamiyya* (Islamic awakening) were evocative of his language of 1968, leading to the not so unreasonable surmise that he was seeking to reconstruct the old alliance with the Islamists. Even on the basis of that, it was difficult to pin Sadiq down. The Sadiq of Geneva was not the selfsame Sadiq of Djibouti, while the Sadiq of Djibouti was totally different from the one who emerged as a roving ambassador of the NIF regime, even when he regime had failed to honour a single iota of the undertakings it made to him at Djibouti. As for his betrayal of Turabi, that was hardly a heart-lifting behaviour.

When al Mahdi realized that the strategy of rapprochement with the regime had failed by a wide margin, and that his going alone into it would be political suicidal, he warmed up to the NDA. Regardless of all the calumnies he heaped at the 'defunct' Alliance and his declared intention not to go back to it,[196] al Mahdi still wanted to be part of the NDA. During the meeting of the NDA Congress at Massawa, the Umma Party wrote to its Chairman seeking to be reintegrated in that body on his own terms. The terms had to do with two things: first, agreement on the comprehensive political settlement in the manner that was previously formulated by him and rejected by the Alliance, and second, the restructuring of the NDA. Clearly, on the first issue the perceptions of the two parties were diametrically opposed, and nothing had happened since the Umma parted ways with the NDA to make the Alliance change its position. As for the second condition, Sadiq's proposed restructuring of the NDA was an euphemism for reorganizing the Alliance with a view to giving the Umma (being the 'largest' party in Sudan as he claims) the pre-eminence it deserved. That would not have been a problem, were the parties in accord on the substantive issues. The farce reached its zenith, however, when al Mahdi appealed to Egypt and Libya to mediate between him and the 'deadwood' of the NDA.[197]

It would appear though, that what peeved al Mahdi most was the adoption of al Mirghani as the national leader by Northern and Southern opposition forces including the SPLM.[198] Al Mahdi did not fully meditate the objective factors that were at play when the new LC was constituted; he only viewed the arrangement as a strategic alliance between the DUP and the SPLM. That, he may have thought, would foreclose his desire to be Sudan's paramount chief. The man clearly believes that he should be number one on Sudan's political scoreboard even when all his scores proved to be misses. Another factor that nettled Sadiq was the refusal by al Mirghani to ride on the conveyor belt he had constructed, leading to Khartoum. In the face of Sadiq's attemps to deactivate the NDA, al Mirghani affirmed his faith in the viability of the Alliance, and maintained that 'without it the search for a comprehensive peaceful settlement would be frustrated.[199] There was no reason why al Mahdi, given his numerous qualities, should not be number one. But the realization of that desire transmuted into an impossibility when he conjured up a *Sahwa* vision that would bring together the *Ansar*, the Copts, the *Khattmyyia*, the modern forces, the marginalized, the Southerners, and on the top of that, the SPLM, while at the same time he incessantly reminded people that he was the apostle of a rejuvenated Mahdism. Peace and unity and the religionization of politics – as it had been practised in Sudan since 1968 – are strange bedfollows. Sadiq, therefore, has no alternative but to weight the two and decide which gives way to the other. Turabi (the brother of the Ottoman Sultan) has done that while he is still alive.

Recently, al Mahdi, to exasperate Garang, aligned himself with a number of notable Southern politicians. 'Garang and the SPLM were not the only representatives of the South,' al Mahdi announced in more than one occasion. Garang surely never claimed that he represented the South or even two-thirds of it, the way Sadiq often claimed that he represented two-thirds of Northern Sudan. However, one of the Southerners Sadiq approached was the veteran Southern politician Bona Malwal whose views on al Mahdi's agenda for Sudan were not secret. Al Mahdi apparently did not summon up Malwal's advice to him in 1992. In a letter to al Mahdi to which reference was made earlier, Malwal said: 'We cannot have a united Sudan in which Islam becomes the driving force in determining the system of government and the rights of non-Muslim citizens ... if Muslims resolved to make Islam the dominant political force, then they should admit that this is irreconcilable with maintaining unity with non-Muslims in the South. The litmus test for the Northern leadership – and that includes you brother Sadiq – is to recognize this fact and decide that your first responsibility as a politician is to serve Islam. In this case North and South should work out an amicable separation.'

On the basis of the above, the failure of the current peace initiatives was entirely the responsibility of the NIF in the first place and Sadiq al Mahdi in the second. Al Mahdi's major blunder was his premeditated departure from the NDA that played into the hands of the NIF regime. The regime which consistently refused to compromise on their religio-political verities was also unwilling to recognize the opposition as a united front that represented the totality of the people of Sudan (save for the NIF). They would rather dismantle the NDA, using peace initiatives as their tool. As for Sadiq, who endeavoured to use the NDA as a vehicle for achieving his own political and ideological ends, he turned from a troublemaker to a spoiler when those endeavours failed. He too used the peace initiatives as a medium for his spoilsport activities, particularly when the SPLM refused to be pliantly frogmarched into the joint initiative before it was coordinated with the IGAD process.

Sixteen years after Nimeiri's rule, and eleven years through Bashir's, al Mahdi never changed. A few years before the fall of Nimeiri, I predicted that the parties would come back to power, but hoped that they would not be like the Bourbon kings 'who learned nothing and forgot nothing'. Today, I am more inclined to set al Mahdi beside Napoleon III, in the light of the British historian A.J.P. Taylor. Of Napoleon III, Taylor said: 'He only learned from his mistakes of the past to make new ones.' Al Mahdi distinctly gives the impression that all Sudan's problems shall be solved once he is reinstated in power. But in politics as in banking, clients' are always judged by their track record. With the 'credit' of two failed attempts on governance, one would have expected the great-grandson of the Mahdi to be more humble.

ENDNOTES

1. Steevens, G.W., *With Kitchener to Khartoum*, p. 318.
2. Among the Christian institutions that were involved in relief work in the South consequent to the peace agreement were Caritas, World Lutheran Federation, Norwegian Christian Aid, Catholic Relief etc. Some of those institutions were also involved in similar work in the North, particularly in the period of the drought of the 1970s.
3. The visit of the Archbishop in 1995 was restricted to SPLA-controlled areas of South Sudan and thus enraged the government to the point of expelling the British Ambassador from Khartoum. However, the Archbishop undertook a second visit to Sudan (April/May 2000), on the invitation of the government this time. During that visit the Archbishop enthroned Josephe Marona, the Bishop of Marid, as Archbishop of the province of Sudan, a post that was vacant for a number of years. The function was attended by bishops from the SPLM-controlled areas; Francis Loya, Bishop of Rokon and Wilson Arop, Bishop of Torit. *The Nation*, Mairobi, 1 May 2000.
4. The *Sunday Telegraph*, 2 January 1994.
5. Biro, UN Report, E/CN4/January 1998.
6. *Al Hayat*, London, 11 October 1994.
7. *Al Shark al Awsat*, 28 July 2000.
8. Report of the US Commission on International Religious Freedom, Sudan, China and Russia, 1 May 2000, p. 1.
9. *Reuters*, 20 April 2001.
10. *PRN newswire*, 18 April 2001.
11. Statement by Dr Ghazi Salah el Din to the Fourth IGAD ministerial meeting in Nairobi,. September 1994. Salah el Din claimed that spreading Islam in Africa was the historic message of Sudan, which was frustrated by colonialism.
12. Inter- and intra-tribal feuds were not only limited to the South; several politically inspired tribal conflicts were reported in Dar Fur among the Arabicised and Fur tribes. Those conflicts simmered since Sadiq's government, purportedly inflamed by Libya who was using the region as a conduit for supporting Chadian rebels led by that country's present leader, Idris Debbi. However, during the NIF era, the conflict took more sinister dimensions, pitting NIF groups supporting the regime against others who were thought to be supporting the opposition. The government persisted in describing those conflicts as *al nahb al musalah* (armed robbery).
13. See *Sudan: Cry the Divided Country*, World Vision, 1996.
14. Burr and Collins, *Requiem*, p. 300.
15. For the sake of even-handedness, Amnesty International and a host of other human rights NGOs accused the SPLM/A of human rights violations. To those accusations the SPLM responded, but deplored the context within which they were made: equating transgressions of

human rights committed by wayward commanders with those resulting from the governments structured policy of human rights violations. In a recent correspondence between Garang and Sadiq al Mahdi, the SPLM leader revisited the issue. In response to accusations levelled by al Mahdi at the SPLM relating to human rights abuses Garang said: 'the SPLM/A ... is not a government restrained by internationally recognized covenants, norms and obligations. It is a liberation movement waging a war for justice. Nonetheless, it is curbed by internationally recognized laws of war and good behavior towards innocent civilians as well as prisoners of war. As such, our record is an open book for all to see ... there are more than forty international NGOs working in the liberated areas. It is they, not those judging us from distant capitals of the world, who can attest to our human rights records. ... That being said and human nature being what it is, excesses by zealot warriors may sometimes lead to overstepping the bounds of propriety. When that happens and it is detected, it is always checked and those responsible for it brought to book according to law.' Letter from Garang to al Mahdi, Yei, New Sudan, 21 January 2000.

16. That meeting was held in Rumbek in November 1999 and attended by a host of international NGOs and bilateral donors.
17. Garang, John, *The Call for Democracy*, pp. 289–91.
18. 8 supra, p. 60.
19. Ali al Haj of the NIF and Lam Akol of SPLM/United, met at Frankfurt on 25 January 1992 to work out a deal between the two parties. The upshot of the meeting was the recognition by the NIF of the right of self-determination for South Sudan.
20. *Horn of Africa Bulletin* No. 6/93, p. 27.
21. The meeting took place at Fashoda, Upper Nile in April 1998 and was witnessed by the Reth (Chief) of Shilluk.
22. Interview with John Chini, *The East African*, Nairobi, 31 March 1997.
23. *Al Khartoum*, 9 October 1995.
24. Other signatories to the Charter included the late Samuel Aru Bol (USAP), Cdr Kawac Makwei of a so-called South Sudan Independent Group, Arok Thon Arok (Bor Group) and Thiopolus Ochang Loti representing a previously unheard of Equatorian Defence Force. The adherence of USAP to the Charter was later challenged by the President of USAP (Eliaba Surur) and the whole leadership of the party inside the country. Mr Bol was given the choice either to resign or be dismissed. He chose to resign.
25. Peterson, Donald, *Inside Sudan*, p. 53.
26. A memorandum on the Sudan Peace from within entitled 'The Political Charter, Observation and Commentary' was circulated by Abel Alier from Khartoum.
27. Article 122 (1) of the Constitution defines the role of the army as that of 'guarding the gains of the people and the *civilizational orientation* of the community'. The real meaning of the code word *civilizational*

orientation is by now no secret to anybody.

28. Article 65 of the 1998 Constitution stipulates: 'Islamic *shari'a,* the consensus of the nation arrived at through referenda, and custom, shall be the sources of legislation. No legislation that contravenes those principles shall be made. Legislation shall also be guided by the judgement of the nation's scholars, thinkers and by the decision of *wulat al amr* (men in charge).'

29. *Al Hayat,* 19 January 2001.

30. *Al Hayat,* 23 April 2001

31. Ibid.

32. SSIM/A Press Statement dated 14 August 1995 and signed by Cmdr William Nyuon Bany.

33. Human Rights Rapporteur Biro reported in 1997 that the Machar forces together with PDF launched scorched-earth tactics in the areas of Tomaj, Leka, Lum and Ghatta, after the occupation by the SPLA of the Yabus area.

34. SPLM/A statement signed by Pagan Amom, advising Machar to come to his senses. SPLM/A – Org/GC/1997.

35. *The Economist,* 19 August 2000.

36. Middleton lived in East Africa for more than 26 years, of which ten were in Sudan. He also served as advisor to Canada's High Commissioner in Nairobi.

37. 'Oil Fuels the Conflict in Southern Sudan', *The Financial Times,* London, 15 October 1999.

38. Human Price of Oil, report by Maina Kiai, Director for Africa, Amnesty Int., 3 London, May 2000.

39. John Harker's report, op. cit., p. 15.

40. 8 supra, op. cit., p. 104.

41. Ibid., p. 107.

42. *Africa confidential,* 42 No. 6, 23 March 2001.

43. Harding, Andrew, *BBC News,* 21 April 2001.

44. *The Economist,* 19 August 2000.

45. Lamb, Charles, The *Sunday Times,* London, 28 August 1994.

46. Martin Molyneanx of First Energy Capital Corporation, *Reuters,* 20 November 2000.

47. Statement by Nigel Hares, Talisman's Vice-President for International Operations. *Reuters,* 20 November 2000.

48. The *Los Angeles Sentinel* (25 November 1999) named the following shareholders: Ontario Municipal Employees Retirement System (3 million shares), State of New Jersey (430,000 shares), New York State Common Retirement Fund (353,000 shares), State of Wisconsin (180,000 shares) and California Public Employees Retirement Fund (180,000) shares. In addition the Presbyterian Church (USA) which owns shares in Talisman Energy, voted unanimously to divest from that company 'because they would not wish to be seen supporting a government which enslaves women and children'. P.C. USA News, 24 February 2001.

49. Alden, Edward, *The Financial Times*, London, 11 May 2001.
50. Ibid.
51. The *New York Times*, 13 January 2001.
52. *AFP*, 1 July 2000.
53. Statement by Samson Kwaje, SPLM spokesman, 13 August 2000.
54. In a statement signed by Yassir Arman (10 June 2001) the Sudanese army was reported to have lost 244 of its fighters.
55. Current, Reg, in Calgary, *CP*, 25 November 1999.
56. Daglish, Peter, *Globe and Mail*, Toronto, 18 February 2000.
57. John Harker, Human Security in Sudan, report submitted to Canada's Foreign Minister in January 2000.
58. Report from Edward Alden in Toronto to *The Financial Times*, London, 12 February 2000. In addition, the London *Economist* reported that the 'ugly truth is that Talisman is helping the government extract oil and oil is paying for the war', *The Economist*, 2 September 2000.
59. *CNS News* Communications report by Lawrence Marahan, 7 February 2000.
60. 57 supra, p. 4.
61. Ibid., p. 16.
62. The NGOs include Canadian Friends Service (Quakers), Christian Solidarity Int., Freedom Quest Int, Inter-Church Coalition on Africa, Mennonite Central Committee, Primates World Relief and Development Fund, Anglican Church of Canada, United Church of Canada, Steelworks Humanity Fund and World Vision, Canada.
63. Roger Winter, Director of the US Committee for Refugees, contributed the article to the *Globe and Mail* of Toronto, 23 March 2000.
64. *AFP* and *Reuters*, 3 May 2001.
65. The Human Price of Oil, report by Maina Kial, Director for Africa, Amnesty Int, London, 3 May 2000. Alongside Sudapet (Sudan) the following foreign companies were cited by Amnesty International: Lundin Oil Ab (Sweden), Petronas (Malaysia), OMV-Sudan Gmbh (Austria), Talisman Energy (Canada), Agip (Italy), Elf-Aquitaine (France), Gulf Petroleum Co. (Qatar), National Iranian Gas Co. (Iran), Totalfina (France), Royal Dutch Shell (Holland), and China National Petroleum Corporation. In addition, Deniama pipeline Consultants and Roll'n Oil Field Industries of Canada were involved in construction work in the oilfields, so were the two UK-based companies, Weir Pumps Ltd and Allen Powell Engineering Ltd. The main part of 1,600-km-long pipeline tubing was provided by a consortium led by the German Mannesman.
66. Ibid.
67. The *Washington Post*, 16 March 2001.
68. *The Scorched Earth, Oil and War in Sudan*, March 2001, www.Christian-aid.org.uk.
69. Garang, J, *The Call for Democracy*, pp. 176–8.
70. Anderson, Norman, *Sudan in Crisis*, p. 171.
71. Ibid.

72. *Sudan Democratic Gazette*, April 1994.
73. Ibid.
74. Ibid.
75. Notable among those were Bernard Kouchner from France, Jan Pronk from Holland, and from the United States, Senators Nancy Kassabaum (Kansas), Sam Brownback (Kensas), Bill Frist (Tennessee) and congressmen Frank Wolf (Virginia), Donald Payne (New Jersey), Tom Toncredo (Colorado), Elsee Hastings (Florida), Harry Johnston (Florida), Tom Campbel (California) and Tony Hall (Ohio).
76. In a statement to Charles Lamb, Ghazi Salah el Din, the NIF Secretary General, stated that the government would rather see international relief channelled through Islamic NGOs because foreign NGOs were only fronts for missionary work and intelligence gathering. The *Sunday Times*, London, 28 August 1994.
77. Frank Wolf Report on Visit to South Sudan, January 2001. *http://www.house.gov/Wolf/2001* 222 Sudan op Ed.
78. Foremost among those treaties are the International Covenant on Civil and Political Rights which is still to be ratified by a number of states, and the First Optional Protocol which empowers individuals to petition the UN Human Rights Committee for protection.
79. Wondu and Lesch, *Battle for Peace*, p. 11.
80. The heads of state and government who were involved in Sudan mediation included President Mandela of South Africa, President Chissano of Mozambique, Prime Minister Mahatir of Malaysia, President Babangida of Nigeria, President Bakhili of Malawi, the Presidents of the four IGAD countries jointly and severally and Presidents Qadaffi and Mubarak (the Joint Egypt–Libya Initiative). Governments who tried their hand on Sudan's peacemaking included, the US, the Netherlands, Norway, Italy and Switzerland. Among the research institutions who sought to unravel Sudan's intractable problem were the US Institute for Peace, the Woodrow Wilson Center Institute for International Scholars, President Carter's International Negotiating Network, the University of Bergen (Norway), the International Dialogue Foundation (Holland) and the Interaction Council under the leadership of General Obasanjo of Nigeria. Two United Nations institutions were also involved in bringing the parties together in intellectual seminars in order to deepen their understanding of the issues at which they were at variance: UNESCO and UNDP.
81. *MENA*, 8 July 1989. Also in his proclamation No. 1, Bashir indentified the role of his 'Salvation Revolution' as follows: to save the country from economic ruin, build its military capacity, maintain its Islamic identity and apply *shari'a*.
82. Interview by Kamal Hamid, *Al Hayat*, Lonson, 28 August 1994.
83. *Al Hayat*, London, 14 October 1994.
84. Bashir's 'benevolent' exemption was counterfeit, for despite its pervasive application in the public domain, *shari'a* itself exempts non-

Muslims from the application of *hudud* (*sharia* ordained penalties). Besides, neither were the Islamic penal laws ever applied in the South during Nimeiri's imamate, nor were the hardened 'sinners' of the South struggling for six years in order to sacrifice to Bacchus.

85. *Suna*, July 1, 1989
86. Garang, John, *The Call for Democracy*, pp. 237–68.
87. *AFP*, 19 July 1989.
88. The memorandum entitled 'Position Paper on the Quest for Peace in Sudan' was presented by elders, religious leaders and intellectuals of the Southern region. Fifty-seven signatures were affixed to it, including those of the Catholic Archbisp of Juba, Paulino Loro, and two Muslim merchants, Ahmed Yousif Akasha and Sayed Mohamed Mekki
89. The Interaction Council is a deliberative non-governmental conclave bringing together former heads of state and government to interact on world problems.
90. The proposed names included Prince Hassan Bin Talal (Jordan), Prince Talal bin Abdel Aziz (Saudi Arabia), President Julius Nyerere (Tanzania), Judge Mohamed Bedjaoui (Algeria), President Jimmy Carter (US), Lord Carrington (UK), Ms Susanna Agnelle (Italy). This group was to be supported by another team to mobilize resources for peacemaking and post-conflict rehabilitation of Sudan; the team comprised Helmut Schmidt (Germany) and the late Pierrre Troudeau (Canada)
91. The US initiative was coveyed to the two parties by Nigerian President Olusegun Obasanjo and former Sudanese ambassador, Francis M. Deng.
92. Wondu and Lesch, *Battle for Peace*, p. 17.
93. Ibid.
94. 'There is many a boy here who look on war as all glory, but boy, it is all hell.' General Sherman, 1880.
95. Wondu, Steven, *Washington Times*, 18 August 1996.
96. Minutes of the first session of the Abuja talks, SPLM/A HQs, 1993 Comuniqué by the Federal Government of Nigeria in 'War and Peace, Official Documents of the Combatants in Sudan 1991–93', All Africa Council of Churches, Norwegian Church Aid and People for Peace in Africa, pp. 14–16.
97. Ibid.
98. Ibid.
99. 19 supra. Ali al Haj, who signed the Frankfurt agreement on behalf of the government, was a leading member of the government's delegation to Abuja. The agreement stipulated that Southern Sudanese 'shall exercise their right to freely choose the political and constitutional status that accords with their national aspirations without ruling out any option'.
100.This clause was copied from Article 16 of Nimeiri's 1973 constitution which Turabi proposed to abolish and replace by a draft constitution

tailored to suit Nimeiri's imamate phase in 1984.
101. This practice continues up to this day. In June 2000 SHRO reported that 57 Christian youth in conscription camps were reprimanded on 26 June 2000 for attending church services. Muslim youths in those camps were not only allowed but required to observe their religions rites.
102. Kissinger, Henry, *Foreign Affairs,*XIII, 1969.
103. The IGAD comprises countries of East, and the Horn of, Africa: Djibouti, Eritrea, Ethiopia, Kenya, Somalia, Sudan and Uganda. Established in the 1970s as an inter-governmental body to devise regional programmes to curb desertification and alleviate the effects of drought, the organization was baptized Inter-governmental Agency for Drought and Desertification (IGADD). Two decades later the organization's mandate and mission were reformulated, making it a development agency for the subregion and rebaptized Intergovernmental Agency for Development (IGAD).
104. Incredibly, as at Abuja, the government delegation that took exception to the right of self-determination included Dr Ali al Haj who signed on with Lam Akol to the Frankfurt agreement that granted the South that right.
105. Deng, Francis, Sudan Peace Prospects at a Crossroads, USIP, Consultation on Sudan, Washington DC, 14 January 1999.
106. Ibid.
107. SPLM/A Update, Issue No. 2 Vol. III, 94.
108. Lesch, *The Sudan, Contested National Identities*, p. 193.
109. Ibid., p. 185. Khalifa and al Haj hail from Dar Fur, Western Sudan. Both of them are of non-Arab stock.
110. As mentioned earlier, exemption of non-Muslims from the application of *hudud* was not an act of benevolence from the Khartoum rulers, but a right granted by *shari'a*. By claiming to withdraw that divinely ordained right, Salah el Din revealed the NIF's irreverence even towards what they considered to be the word of God.
111. 108 supra.
112. The regime appealed to Egypt and Libya to mediate between it and the Northern parties within the NDA. Khartoum also hoped to involve the Saudi government in a so-called 'Islamic' mediation to take place in Mecca and circulated news to that effect. Obviously the SPLM was not expected to participate in that forum. Amazingly, the NIF had in mind the Taif successful Saudi mediation among the Lebanese warring parties who included Muslims and Christians. But more than the successful resolution of the conflict, the NIF's real aim was to drive a wedge between the SPLM (the non-Muslim party) and the Northern Muslim parties. The Saudis refused to fall for that ruse; Prince Sultan bin Abdel Aziz, the Saudi Minister of Defense, told a Saudi daily that there was no Saudi initiative to mediate in the Sudan conflict, but Saudi Arabia would not prevent Muslims from coming to the holy places to perform their religions rites and resolve differences

among themselves. On the parallelism between the proposed meeting in Mecca and the Saudi-led Taif agreement on Lebanon, the Prince could not have been more forthright: 'The difference between what has happened in Taif and what our Sudanese brothers are talking about is that the Lebanese agreed among themselves before coming to the kingdom,' said Prince Sultan. *Okaz*, 13 November 1999.

113. Fisher told the author that in comparable peace negotiations he conducted, adversaries hardly spoke to, or socialized with, each other. In one such meeting he organized, the intensity of emotions was such that guns were drawn by some participants against their adversaries, retold Fisher.

114. Strategy paper on UNDP's Role in Post-Barcelona Process, UNDP, Khartoum, 22 November 1995.

115. 105 supra.

116. The Bahr el Ghazal famines, which were caused by an unprecedented drought in the region and compounded by the government's imperturbability, claimed tens of thousands of lives and annihilated similar numbers of livestock. Hundreds of thousands who were threatened with starvation were only saved through a timely intervention by the international community. The international media did admirable work in exposing the crisis to the world, and, in a way, focused attention on Sudan's political crisis.

117. Prendergast, John, Special Report to USIP, 28 June 1999.

118. The meeting was attended by representatives of Austria, Belgium, Canada, Denmark, Egypt, Finland, France, Germany, Greece, Ireland, Japan, the Netherlands, Sweden, Switzerland, the United Kingdom, USA, the European Commission, the United Nations Secretariat, the UNDP, the UNHCR, the WFP, the World Bank and the Russian Federation.

119. Statement by Samson L. Kwaje, Commissioner for Information SPLM, Nairobi, 18 April 2000.

120. Statement by Samson Lukare Kwaje, Nairobi, 8 May 2000.

121. *AP*, 30 March 2001.

122. *MENA*, dateline Doha, Qatar, April, 2001. Also *Al Akhbar*, Cairo, 2 April 2001.

123. The proposal for including the UAE in the IPF was influenced by the keen desire expressed by Sheikh Zaid bin Nahyan, President of that country, to play a role in bringing together the Sudanese parties to the conflict.

124. This affirmation was made in the LC's meetings in Asmara in March 1998, Tripoli Declaration, August19 99, Cairo meeting in July 1999 and May 2000.

125. *AFP*, 22 October 1999.

126. The US government had always been keen on appointing a high-level politician to pursue the Sudan question. The names of Senator Mc Govern and Congressman Steven Solarz were discussed in the mid-1990s but the US government settled then for a low-profile

representation, Ambassador Melissa Wells.

127. That was a veiled reference to calls for merging the IGAD process with the joint initiative. The IGAD Summit, nevertheless, welcomed efforts by other countries that had a keen interest to 'contribute to national reconciliation in Sudan *based on the principles expounded in the DOP* and already accepted by the two parties to the IGAD process'.

128. Al Mahdi met in 1997 with UN Secretary General Kofi Annan, presenting himself as Sudan's legitimate prime minister. In that meeting he asked the UN to intervene to restore him to his position, the way it had done with President Aristid of Haiti.

129. *Reuters*, 29 November 1999.

130. Press conference by al Mahdi at *Al Ahram* headquarters, Cairo, November 1999. Al Mahdi specifically accused Garang of warlordism.

131. Al Mahdi was very circumspect when he was in captivity in Sudan; he used every possible opportunity to distance himself from the NDA's armed struggle. To that end he coined his own term to describe the struggle he was waging against the NIF: *al jihad al madani* (civil struggle). But no sooner had he reached Asmara, than he issued a proclamation calling on his disciples to make a *hijra* (religiously ordained flight) to the East. An Umma army was formed and al Mahdi's son was appointed as its *amir* (the title the grand Mahdi gave to commanders of the army). Only 300 *Mujahideen* responded to that call which was a matter of great embarrassment to the Mahdi of the twentieth century.

132. In a statement to the London daily *Al Qods al Arabi* (10 April 2000) al Mahdi described the NDA as a cadaverous body that would soon be overtaken by history.

133. *Al Sharks al Awsat*, 21 April 2000.

134. *Al Jamhouriya*, Cairo, 21 April 2000.

135. *Al Itihad*, Abu Dhabi, 23 September 2000.

136. *Al Rai al Am*, Kuwait, 2 February 1997.

137. *Al Wafd*, Cairo, 23 April 2000.

138. Press conference in Cairo. *Reuters* and *al Shark al Awsat*, 2 June 2001.

139. *Al Ahram al Arabi*, Cairo, 23 March 2001.

140. In the previous chapters we have cited some of al Mahdi's speeches and writings in which he portrayed calls for 'Sudanism' as plots hatched by some African countries to divest Sudan of its Arabo-Islamism. Nonetheless, since the Koka Dam meeting in 1986 and the adoption by the Umma representatives of the KDD, many thought that the former prime minister had enough opportunity to re-educate himself on the real meaning of the term. Regrettably, the KDD and the NDA notwithstanding, al Mahdi was at his worst when he told a gathering of Arab ambassadors in Khartoum during Ramadan that Sudan was threatened by an American plot to replace Sudan's Arabo-Islamic character with a Negro-African one. John Garang was described as the 'cat's paw' in that plot. *Al Shark al Awsat*, 12 December 2000.

141. *Al Bayan, Dubai,* 2 May 2001. Equally, a leading Umma leader, Dr Adam Madio told *Al Hayat* on 3 May that Sadiq al Mahdi was scheduled to sign a memorandum of understanding with Garang at Abuja.

142. *Al Bayan,* Dubai, 7 May 2001.

143. The SPLM issued a statement after the failed Abuja meeting describing Sadiq's initiative as an attempt to dismantle the NDA. Garang was also reported to have told Sadiq that his place was in the opposition and not as a salesman for the regime. Sadiq seemingly sought to persuade Garang that the margin of liberties in Sudan would enable the opposition to work from within and that the regime was serious in reaching a comprehensive political settlement. Both contentions were challenged by Garang. On the first he asked al Mahdi how much of the regime's own commitment to the Umma Party in the Djibouti agreement was fulfilled. On the second, he told al Mahdi that the SPLM has been negotiating with the regime within the aegis of IGAD for seven years to no avail. Therefore, he did not need a broker for negotiating with Khartoum: statement by Yassir Arman, 4 May 2001. All the same, despite his denial of Garang's accusation that he was marketing the NIF regime and pretending to act on its behalf, Sadiq had in fact met with Bashir before his travel to Abuja and briefed him on the objectives of his mission.

144. Al Mahdi made the most improbable declaration to a Cairo paper in which he claimed that the print media in Sudan was now the most free media in the Arab World, *Al Shaab,* 4 April 2000. One would have expected that the reference point for freedom of expression to be, for the man who served twice as prime minister in Sudan, the liberties enjoyed by the press during his own rule.

145. Al Mahdi quoted the Ethiopian–Eritrean War and the normalization of relations between Ethiopia and Sudan, which resulted in the closure of the offices of Northern opposition forces in Addis Ababa.

146. A statement issued by Sudan's Ministry of Foreign Affairs claimed that the NDA secretariat was engaged with the US officials in planning actions to destabilize the regime. The statement preposterously accused the US official of breaking Sudan's laws by meeting with an unofficial organization. *Al Khartoum,* 9 December 2000. That organization was an offshoot of the same NDA with which the government was engaged in a peace dialogue.

147. The NC Secretary General, Ibrahim Ahmed Omer, told a Cairo daily that the government was forced to take action against the NDA after having long tolerated their insistence on dismantling the regime. *Al Khoutoum,* 13 December 2000.

148. On 22 November, Rice visited the site of the bombed hospital at Lui. She told a gathering there that the 'US would do all it could to stop the government's bombings and help the people of Sudan'. Rice also condemned the regime for aerial bombardments on civilians, abduction of women and children in the South and terrorizing aid

workers. Besides, she declared that in view of those crimes, the bipartisan US policy shall be geared towards imposing unilateral sanctions and energizing international pressure on the regime so long as it persisted in its unacceptable policies.

149. *Al Bayan*, Dubai, 17 September 2000.
150. Hamashkoreib was later recovered by the army after fierce battles. In response, the NDA forces staged a daring attack an Kassala, the capital city of the Eastern region, and occupied it for 24 hours.
151. *Al Itihad*, Abu Dhabi, 22 September 2001.
152. *Al Ahram Al Arabi*, Cairo, 15 April 2000.
153. Connel, Dan, The *Guardian*, 2 April 2000. The expert is the author of *Against All Odds; a Chronicle of the Eritrean Revolution*.
154. The regime was reported to have withdrawn forces and war materiel from Southern garrisons to reinforce the eastern front. It also did not hesitate to use helicopter gunships to bombard human settlements in the area, probably to force the inhabitants to flee as if the assumed sanctity of the religious centre took precedence over the sanctity of human lives.
155. *The Khartoum Monitor*, reported by *Shark al Awsat*, 14November, 2000.
156. The meeting was attended by Austria, Belgium, Canada, Denmark, Egypt, Finland, France, Germany, Greece, Japan, the Netherlands, Sweden, Switzerland, the UK, The US, the European Commission, the UN Secretariat, the UNDP, UNHCR and the Russian Federation as an observer.
157. Final communiqué of the IPF, Oslo, Norway, 20 June 2000. The 'relevant Sudanese parties' and 'regional political actors' obviously refer to the NDA and the countries of the joint initiatives, while the reference to 'other relevant actors in the African continent' presumably alludes to those proposed by Nigeria as an IGAD African IPF.
158. NDA, Final Communiqué of the 2nd Congress, Asmara, 14 September 2000.
159. El Affendi, *Al Qods al Arabi*, 20 September 2000.
160. Chapter Seven supra, note 53.
161. *AFP*, 7 October 2000.
162. *AFP*, 25 November 2000.
163. *Al Hayat*, 10 November 2000.
164. General Abdel Rahman Said, Deputy Chairman of the UMC, told a London paper: 'All options are open to us, any town or target we feel we can attack, shall be attacked.' *Al Qods al Arabi*, London, 10 December 2000.
165. Rather than allowing the medical officer to carry out his humanitarian duty, the commander of the Umma forces, the son of Sadiq al Mahdi, ordered him to let the man die. When the doctor refused to do that the commander threatened forcibly to remove the patient from the intensive care unit. Only when the Umma forces were overpowered by NSB forces, was the doctor was left to attend to his patient.

166. *Al Khartoum*, 18 November 2000.
167. Interview with Ibrahim Ahmed Omer, Secretary General of the National Congress, *Al Khartoum*, 18 December 2000.
168. *Al* Mussawar, Issue 3941, 21 April 2000.
169. Evidently, al Mahdi had neither acquainted himself with the names of the Southerners he invited, nor with their political leanings. His list included Bona Malwal, Abel Alier, Eliaba Surur, Riek Machar, George Kongor (former Vice-President under Bashir), John Luk, Yohanes Akol, Pacifico Lado (both USAP), Christine William Deng, (SPLM), Gordon Mourtat, Zakaria Deng, Francis Deng (who publicly dissociated himself from the Southern 'outsiders' group), Aldo Ajo, David Kunijwok (correct name Walter Kunijwok or Kunijwok Guado Ayoken Kwawang who surprisingly served as Minister of Labour in Sadiq's government), Andrew Wieu and Salwa Jibril (SPLM).
170. *Al Khartoum*, 6 December 2000.
171. Omar, Ibrahim Ahmed, *Al Shark al Awsat*, 17 May 2001.
172. *Al Hayat*, 18 May 2001.
173. To illustrate how irresolute the NDA was, Sadiq described it as a cat that has no power to catch mice.
174. *Al Hayat*, 4 July 2000.
175. Chapter Seven, note 210.
176. *Al Wasat*, London, 26 February 2001.
177. *Al Sharq al Awsat*, 4 March 2001.
178. *Al Khartoum*, 1 March 2001.
179. Ahmed, Mohamed El Hassan, *Shark al Awsat*, 17 April 2001.
180. *Al Hayat*, 16 April 2001.
181. *Al Hayat*, 18 April 2001.
182. US Policy to End Sudan's War, Report of the CSIS Task Force, February 2001.
183. Ibid.
184. Memorandum presented to the Task Force by Roger Winter, Eric Reeves and Ted Dagne.
185. Official Response by the SPLM/A to the CSIS Task Force Report on US Sudan Policy, signed by Steven Wondu, 26 February 2001.
186. The Bill was presented on 25 January 2001 by Senators Frist (Tennessee), Feingold (Wisconsin), Brownback (Kansas), Lieberman (Connecticut), Dewine (Ohio), Santorum (Pennsylvania), Cleveland (Georgia) and Sessions (Alabama). In addition, on 22 March, five members of Congress led by Majority leader in the House, Dick Armey (Texas) called a press conference on Sudan at the behest of NAACP. The meeting was attended by Frank Wolf (Viginia), Tom Tancredo (Colorado), Donald Payne (New Jersey), Charles Rangel (New York). The group decided to create a Sudan Congressional caucus to enhance pressure on the govenemnt of Sudan and oil companies.
187. McGrory, Mary, The *Washington Post*, 11 March 2001.
188. Mike Allen and Steven Mufson, The *Washington Post*, 4 May 2001.

Bush was addressing the American Jewish Committee.

189. Ibid. In announcing that decision Bush said: 'We must turn the eyes of the world upon the atrocities in the Sudan.'

190. *AFP*, 31 May 2001, *Newsweek*, 1 June 2001 and Lacey, Marc, The *New York Times*, 23 May 2001.

191. *Reuters*, report by Alistaire Lyon, 16 January 2001.

192. *Akbar al Youm* quoted by AFP, 4 May 2001.

193. Statement by Francis Deng, Special Representative of the UN Secretary General on Displaced Persons. *Africa Irin*, 19 May 2000.

194. In August 2000, an aerial attack near-missed a UN relief plane, leading the UN Secretary General to express concern about the incident. He recalled that the incident took place despite assurances from the government that bombing of locations used by the UN/OLS would not occur. Reuters, report from Marjorie Olster, 8 August 2000.

195. *The Daily Nation*, Nairobi, 11 August 2000.

196. In a meeting with Sudanese expatriates in Dubai (May 2000), al Mahdi told his audience that his policy rests on two pillars: no attempt to return to the NDA and no reconciliation with the government. *Al Bayan*, Dubai, 10 May 2000. Before the end of the year, he sought to do both.

197. *Al Watan*, Kuwait, 14 September 2000.

198. Al Mirghani was nominated for the NDA chairmanship by the SPLM and unanimously elected by the NDA, 2nd Congress for that post. The secretary generalship went to the SPLM who nominated CDR Pagan Amom for that position.

199. In a statement issued in Cairo (19 October 2000), al Mirghani declared that: 'Disunity within the NDA shall disrupt our efforts to create a united Sudan and achieve a peaceful political settlement. He added that 'Political settlement neither means sharing power with, nor participation in, the present government.'

CHAPTER TEN

Peace without the NIF

*The man dies in all who keep silent
in the face of tyranny... A war with
its attendant suffering must, when
that evil is unavoidable, be made to
fragment more than building, it
must shatter the foundations of
thought and recreate.*
Wole Soyinka[1]

Introduction

Following the NIF's military *coup*, Mohamed Osman al Mirghani (DUP), and
Mohammed Ibrahim Nugud, Secretary General of the SCP, found
themselves together in Bashir's jail. Days later they were joined by Sadiq al
Mahdi (Umma). Walled in with them was an improbable inmate, Hassan
Turabi of the NIF. As it turned out later, the new regime sought to conceal
the identity of the *coup* by locking in the NIF leader. Also, they might have
thought that during his confinement, Turabi would be able to win over the
two religious leaders to the 'Islamic' regime. Rather than falling prey to the
NIF wiles, the two leaders together with their leftist partner drew a draft
charter of what was to become the gospel of the National Democratic
Alliance (NDA).[2] The Charter, which was meant as a blueprint for the post-
Bashir Sudan, failed to capture the spirit of the New Sudan and to analyse
correctly the root causes of the country's crisis. Chiefly, it based its analysis
on the old political assumption that the problem in Sudan was one of
stability of government in Khartoum and the inordinate apportionment of
power between the traditional and modern forces. On this assumption, the
leaders implicitly played down the significance of the Southern war to the
country's destabilization. That type of analysis did no respect to the subject.

The Charter's analysis revolved on the ritual denunciation of the
traditional parties and military–civilian vicious circle of government. It
argued that responsibility for Sudan's problems fell squarely on the
traditional parties because, once they assumed power, they reneged on
reform agenda articulated during popular uprisings. It also attributed the
under-performance of party governments to the exclusion from post-
popular 'revolution' governments, of elements that were critical in the
uprising, the trades unions. On the basis of this expostulation the Charter
called for an apportionment of power in which the 'modern forces' would
have the edge. The Charter neither addressed the political distortions in the
old political and socio-economic structures of the state, nor analysed their

sociocultural underpinnings. Doubtless, the 'modern forces' had always played a determinant role in removing tyrants. This they did by rendering the country ungovernable through the trades unions' control of the levers of the modern public and private economic sectors. But ability to make the country ungovernable is not synonymous with ability to govern, particularly within a liberal democracy. The traditional parties, debilitated and discredited by the *coup*, did not challenge at that time this damning judgement. Instead they signed on the dotted lines and lay in waiting, holding their fire for a future date.[3] This, of course, was the type of chicanery that proved the worst fears of their detractors within and without the 'modern forces'.

Nevertheless, the 'modern forces' themselves suffer from a crisis of identity. They represent a motley collection of elites, all claiming to represent the conscience of the people, all pandering to the same constituency (the professional and workers trades unions), and many of them deriding both the historical forces of the right (traditional parties) and of the left (the communist party). The politically organized among them took for granted that they were destined to play the role of the centre within the Sudanese landscape. Though, by subjectively wishing away the 'right' and 'left', they effectively reduced themselves to a centre without a circumference, fluid and amorphous. Instead of metamorphozing into a viable political entity with a consolidated grassroots base, they made believe that trades unions were their vehicles for both destabilization and stabilization of governments. Trades unions, we submit, are professional organizations that bring together disparate members with variegated political and sectarian loyalties and only united on issues pertaining to professional calls and group interests. Parties, on the other hand, bring together groups partaking in common interests, striving to achieve common objectives and endeavouring to preserve shared values. In effect, when political parties first emerged in Europe, they were born of necessity as vehicles of articulating the class-based interests of their adherents. Moreover, parties are popular organizations and not elitist clubs of like-minded intellectuals who collocate on national issues. By their very elitist constitution, non-partisan intellectual groups in Sudan rarely got themselves tangled as group in the rough and tumble of popular politics. Besides, the arbitrary manner of defining Sudanese political parties into traditional and modern, as we have postulated in the introductory remarks, does not facilitate a rational analysis of Sudan's realities. There is nothing pejorative in being conservative or 'traditionalist', nor is 'modernism' or radicalism, *per se*, a blessing. Besides, traditionalism is not necessarily an attribute of birth. It is a disposition which some arrive at rationally with a view to conserve old values, institutions or received wisdom. A case in point is the leadership of Britain's arch-traditional party (Conservatives) which wound up in the hands of three political actors, Edward Heath, Margaret Thatcher and John Major, none of whom belonged to the upper social crust like their predecessors. Indeed, one of them (Major) was not part of the Etonian magic circle that had generally determined the fate of party leaders. The crisis of Sudanese traditional politicians, by and large, began when they refused to adjust to change and sought to remain given to ascribed values and historical institutions that had become archaic and out of phase. Given their sectarian emanation, that is not surprising. Nonetheless, from the belly of those traditional parties also emerged moderizers in different fields who endeavoured to chime with modern tunes. Among those were moderizers who sincerely believed in a break with the past and in a genuine re-evaluation of inherited values and institutions in order to render them relevant to the present. But conjointly, there were false modernizers who, along with whistling the right tune, persevered in believing that the past could still be recreated. Despite their use of modern tools of analysis and contemporary language, those fictitious modernizers shall only lead on the unsuspecting.

On the issues under discussion, war, peace and national identity, the classification of political forces into traditional and modern is spurious. As we said earlier, a traditional outlook is oftentimes traced in the approach to those issues by a sizeable sector of self-styled modernists. We have had occasion to allude to the manner in which a sector of the 'modern forces' perceived the questions of economic marginalization, religion and politics, national identity etc. The way those 'modernists' addressed those issues was hardly different from that of the traditionalists. Accordingly, there is need to disaggregate the two groups in a manner that defines 'traditionalism' and 'moderism' on the basis of priorly postulated benchmarks that define national interest within a Sudan writ–large: the New Sudan.

Albeit, for the 'modern forces' to succeed in their legitimate struggle to rejuvenate the country, they have to have realistic perspectives, particularly within the framework of a multi-party democracy which is sadly a game of numbers. As William Ralph Inge put it: 'Democracy has the obvious disadvantage of merely counting votes instead of weighing them.' The chronic failure of the 'modern forces' has, to a large measure, been a consequence of their addiction to repeating the same mistakes since October 1964. Doubtless, the 'modern forces' are against the old, but one is persuaded to think that many of them are not yet as sure about what they stand for within a multi-party democratic framework. less so about the alternative they are offering to the *ancien régime* within pluralistic democracy. In the end, if one does not have a sense of direction, others shall lead him to where they want. Also, if one stands firmly on nothing, he shall inevitably fall on anything. Examples are legion.

NDA: From Symbolism to Substance

Misgivings about the substantive aspects of the Charter were highlighted by the SPLM in a memorandum issued in February 1990, in response to the NDA's invitation to it to participate in the Alliance.[4] The memorandum caused tremors which revealed the reluctance of Northern forces to recognize the SPLM's national vocation.[5] The SPLM was of the belief that unity and political stability in Sudan could only be attained when all parties agreed on the fundamental issues that have promoted disunity in the first place. It also maintained that previous political agreements on the management of transitions from military to civilian rule had invariably been hurriedly formulated after assumption of power, and were only designed to apportion power among the contestants. But before power sharing, the SPLM held, fundamental issues relating to the wider concerns of the nation should be identified and properly articulated. That observation was, in effect, an invitation to the Northern Sudanese parties of all stripes to cerebrate about the state of the country.

Negotiations on the Charter between the Northern parties and the SPLM started in Cairo in April 1990, the main players at that time being the Umma, DUP and SCP. The Army Legitimate Command joined a few months later.[6] The aim of the negotiation was to discuss the fundamental issues underlying Sudan's conflict and redraft the NDA Charter to bring it in harmony with the issues raised by the SPLM. Essentially, the SPLM challenged the Charter's basic assumption that all would be milk and honey once the NIF was removed and democracy *a l'ancienne* restored. That assumption, to the mind of the SPLM, was unanalytical since it only addressed the symptoms and not the cause of the malady. In point of fact, the SPLM was far down the road, and wanted to see the root causes of Sudan's crisis identified so that future politics be pointedly calibrated towards removing those causes and resolving the crisis. Furthermore, the SPLM contended that Sudanese political charters have always been fuzzy at the ends and oftentimes lent themselves to tortuous interpretations. The experience of Sudan is replete with non-compliance with agreements and transgressions on undertakings enshrined in woolly national charters. In consequence, the SPLM called for the articulation of political, constitutional, economic and cultural plans of action to which parties to the NDA should solemnly commit themselves before the removal of the NIF.

On the substantive issues, the first point raised by the SPLM on the Charter was about the role of the civil war in Sudan's instability. War, it argued, was not a casual lifestyle to Southerners but a phenomenon induced by identifiable political, economic and cultural stimuli that should be unscrambled and openly debated. Hence, the SPLM argued that for peace, and consequently political stability and unity, to be realized, the underlying causes of war should be removed. On democracy, the SPLM maintained that it was essentially a political system based on respect of natural, and not only civil rights. Those rights comprise the right of the individual to stay alive, to be free and to enjoy security of person (Article 3 of the Universal Declaration on Human Rights). Headmost of the natural rights is the right to life. Being a primordial right, it is necessarily a prerequisite to all other rights. Hirsch categorized it as the most important of all rights since it safeguards biological life.[7] However, in their preoccupation with the protection of civil rights such as the rights of association, assembly, expression, movement etc, the Northern parties (particularly those to the left) passed over natural rights which were up the scale of human rights. But since there is more to living than staying alive, the SPLM also admitted that other rights, such as the ones advocated by the Northern political elite, would necessarily ensue. Accordingly, the SPLM maintained that civil rights, important as they should be, had historically been a matter of direct concern to the urban Sudanese elite, not to the marginalized who were primarily fighting for their right to life. This postulation was anathema to some NDA parties, particularly the communists who were not accustomed to such 'fastidious' categorization of human and civil rights. But 'fastidious' or not, natural rights, i.e. the rights to life, liberty and security of person, are now universally ranked at the top of the continuum of human rights

Presumeably, the communists who based their analysis on *a priori* Marxist reasoning, assumed that any struggle for social justice is primarily a class struggle. According to this postulation, problems of the marginalized regions would eventually be resolved once rural Sudan had been proletarized. In the meantime, they held for true that the subjectively defined *al quwa al dimoqratiya* (democratic forces) were the only engine of change and should, therefore, be guaranteed the civil liberties that would enable them carry out the mission of social transformation. This perception is categorically based on a Eurocentric class-determined approach to social phenomena. It therefore stands or falls entirely on the basis of its adaptability or applicability to realities on the ground. If in nearly half a century it did not succeed in galvanizing the marginalized and winning them to its side, then something is the matter with that ideological construct. Indeed, the Eurocentric fathers of this class-determined approach were not embarrassed to justify some of the most venal European practices like colonialism in order to give credence to their ideological paradigm. For example, we referred earlier to Engels's justification of the French colonization of Algeria.[8] One reason he had given in favour of French colonialism was that it was a percusor to creating a capitalist system which would set the stage for the emergence of class-based social system that would eventually conduce to social change. In a blaringly racist tone, Engels said that 'modern bourgeoisie is preferable to marauding robbers, with the barbarian state of society to which they belong'. Engels apparently was not aware that those 'marauding robbers' were the heirs of a civilization that produced St Augustine the African, Averoce, Ibn Khaldoun and Ibn Tufayl. On the other hand, Marx described the English occupation of India as 'the greatest and, I speak the truth, the only social revolution ever heard of in India'.[9] The India to which Marx referred unmistakably did not include the Mughal Empire (sixteenth to eighteenth century) which initiated a far-reaching social revolution under Emperor Akbar.[10]

On the other hand, regionally based movements, whatever their provenance, were also dismissed by some Northern ideologues as indwelling and retrospective. For example, one of the most prolific Sudanese Arabist political analysts challenged the SPLM's 'presumptuousness' (without calling it so) manifested in its claim to lead the fight for the creation of the New Sudan. The SPLM's Achilles heel, the analyst observed, was its dependence for popular support on undeveloped non-Arab ethnic conglomeration and not on the developed modern social forces.[11] This line of thinking is shared by a good many within the Northern elite. To them, since those conglomerations fall at the bottom of the scale of social evolution, they are unqualified culturally, socially or politically to be the pacesetters for the creation of the New Sudan. Equally, the analyst went on to say that Garang's proposition to create a national, democratic and secular Sudan was implausible, as long as its success was anchored on the support of societies dominated by magic lore and superstition. There is no doubt that the marginalized nationalities are at the bottom of the scale of social evolution in Sudan by virtue of their economic, political and social marginalization. It is also true that the majority of them profess religions that – to many Sudanese and non-Sudanese Arabs – are equated with paganism. But apart from what we have stated earlier about the nature of African belief systems, there is also a question of relativity in equating those religions with superstition and myth. For instance, since the age of enlightenment, even heavenly religions were matched with superstition by the seers of that age. In essence, enlightment was assumed by its apostles to have dealt a deathblow on absolutes represented by the Church and absolutism represented by the monarchy. Centuries after the age of enlightment, Freud described religion as 'an illusion from which man has to be set free if he is to become mature'. Accordingly, it would help the debate immensely if subjectively defined religion-based arguments are kept out of it.

The analysts' argument, all the same, missed the point for two reasons. The first is that secularism, as we have seen from previous chapters, had only become an issue in the national debate since 1968 when some Northern parties raised the banner of an Islamic constitution. The SPLM, therefore, did not inject the issue of secularism gratuitously into the debate. On the basis of the above, Garang does not only count in his 'secular' campaign on the support from his ' superstitious' constituency, but above all on that of the very Northern 'developed' democratic forces who were afflicted by the ordeal of religion-based politics since 1968. Secondly, Garang did not sit up and take notice of the pedagogy of national revolutions before launching his war. If he did, he wouldn't have been around to be discussed or analysed. Instead, he started from one simple truth: the most ardent fighters for the creation of a New Sudan must be those who are aggrieved most with the old one, if only one can make them raise their sight from parochial to national concerns. That he did with flying colours. This alone renders academic all the ideologically based postulations in analysing the SPLM's agenda. Over and above, Garang never claimed to be a custodian of the New Sudan concept and much less of the New Sudan. His unremitting endeavours to open avenues for all Sudanese irrespective of ethnic origin and religious persuasion to enrich the New Sudan is proof enough of this inclination. Interestingly, in the course of a political gathering in Washington DC, a concerned Northern intellectual asked Garang: 'What do you want us to do for the SPLM?' To the surprise of the questioner and many Northern intelletuals present, his answer was: ' Take it and run away with it.' Northern intellectuals neither took that seriously, nor did they seek to call his bluff, if they thought that he was bluffing. The reason was simple; despite all the lip-service paid to New Sudanism, many Northern intellectuals are yet to make in their own minds the transition from the parochialism of the past that takes hegemony for granted, to a New Sudanism predicated on equality and justice. Shilly-shallying and vacillations shall never lead to a New Sudan.

Howbeit, it is to be recalled that prior to negotiations with the NDA coordinating secretariat in Cairo, the SPLM reached agreements with Northern parties severally and jointly, (KDD and agreement with the DUP in November 1988). In its preamble, the latter agreement put the Sudanese crisis within a larger context: genuine peace in Sudan, the preamble said, 'cannot be attained in the context of the so-called Southern problems but on the appreciation that the problem is national in nature, and hence, its resolution is only possible through a serious, sincere and continuous dialogue among the Sudanese political forces on an equal footing in the proposed national constitutional conference'. The agreement, it may be recalled, became the cornerstone for the All-Party Peace Agreement of April 1989 which was midwifed by Prime Minister Sadiq al Mahdi.

Following the Cairo meeting, the NDA held two other meetings to elaborate on the issues raised in Cairo by the SPLM, one in Addis Ababa (15–19 March 1991), the other in London (February 1992). Though a lot of ground was covered in the two meetings, the NDA went into a spell of incohesiveness and incoherence due to personality clashes among some Northern parties, mainly the Umma and DUP.[12] To revitalize the Alliance, Garang sent a memorandum to the NDA leaders on 4 October 1994 calling for a brainstorming meeting with a view to forging the way ahead for the implementation of the Cairo understanding; the memorandum was entitled 'Review of Long and Short Term Objectives of the NDA'. 'Our country is in a state of crisis The bestial NIF military regime is still in place five years after usurping power despite all its crimes against humanity,' Garang opened his message. He also deplored the weakness of the NDA's 'organized' opposition against the regime, because of its preoccupation 'with issues that are tangential to our people's immediate and pressing concerns'. The message forewarned the NDA of the dire results that would ensue from the NDA's desultory preoccupations. 'We in the SPLM/SPLA,' he said, 'have been fighting this fascist regime against all odds for the whole five years of its wretched life and so were our unarmed compatriots in Khartoum, Omdurman, Medani and El Obeid.' But 'in the absence of a coherent strategy for national struggle, all the valiant resistance by our people shall be dissipated'. Furthermore, he added that 'whatever credibility that is left for the NDA shall be exhausted. Our people deserve better'.

Garang brought to the attention of his colleagues that the SPLM/SPLA had been debating what needed to be done in order 'to energize the opposition, revitalize the NDA and galvanize the instinctive patriotism of our people so that we together, can eradicate this criminal regime root and branch'. He described the NIF as a discredited and isolated military regime that was no more than a rotten tree that was waiting for a strong wind to tear it up by roots. The SPLM leader concluded his message by saying that; 'I am acting on the mandate of the SPLM/SPLA Convention that called upon me to pursue all avenues to reinforce the NDA so that it can carry out its mission more boldly.' To that end, he invited the NDA leadership to a high-level meeting 'to take place in the liberated areas at the beginning of November to review the situation and map out a comprehensive strategy for our struggle to eradicate the NIF fascist regime and lay the foundations for a New Sudan'. An agenda for the meeting, together with a note giving the rationale behind it, accompanied Garang's message. In the event of the meeting taking place inside the Sudan, Garang said, 'the SPLM/SPLA shall ensure the safety of all participants. However if that is not feasible we shall still be willing to participate in such a meeting on the basis of the proposed agenda in any other venue within Africa.'

At that time Harare was mooted as a possible venue,[13] particularly as Cairo, which had opened its doors for NDA leaders, was not yet ready to host a full-fledged congress for the Alliance whose objectives included the overthrow of the regime. By November 1994, all the parties welcomed Garang's initiative, though the venue suggested (the liberated areas) was dismissed out of hand, *mush wagtu* (the time was not opportune), was the response of the majority of Northern parties. Were that meeting to come about at the time and venue proposed, it would have probably changed perceptions and attitudes in a radical manner. Certainly it would have consolidated the position of the new Sudanists within the SPLM and helped allay apprehensions of those among them who harboured secessionist ideas by proving to them, right in their home front, that attitudes change. A decision may have also been taken to create a nucleus for the NDA within the liberated areas which would have added to the prestige of the Alliance and afforded it more freedom of movement and action. Unfortunately, it took nine months for that leadership meeting to take place. Habitual procrastination was one reason for the protraction, but another important factor was the apprehension by some NDA members about meeting in the liberated areas of the South. Open association with the 'rebels' (their allies) would enrage the army, the objectors thought. Clearly, at that point, some NDA members were not yet clear as to who their real friends or foes were. This was the more unsettling when we realize that the only party to the NDA who visited the liberated areas to meet with the SPLA High Command at that very time to discuss military strategy was the ALC.[14] They were the ones who should have been more concerned with the likelihood of 'enraging the army'.

With Cairo out of bounds for an open NDA Congress, and the liberated areas a no-go place to some leaders of the Alliance, the parties first settled for low-key consultative meetings in Cairo and London to which reference was made. No follow-up mechanism or institutionalized administrative support was at hand to pursue the decisions of those meetings. Only when Asmara opened its doors to the NDA, did the apprehensive leaders feel safe and reassured. But that was not to take place before another hiccup following a meeting in that city which caused ripples within the NDA, and brought together the Umma, DUP and the newly formed Sudan Allied Forces (SAF)[15] together with the SPLM. Other parties to the NDA, in one of their bouts of self-delusion, saw the meeting as an attempt to shut them out. In effect, Eritrea, aggravated by the flagrant support of the NIF to the Eritrean Islamic Jihad, convoked that meeting with the major players in order to lay the foundation for cooperation between her and the Sudanese opposition after having decided to come out whole-heartedly behind the Sudanese struggle. The three major parties (Umma, DUP and SPLM) were nicknamed by the disgruntled parties 'the alliance of the golden triangle'. Their resentment of the presence of the newly formed SAF in the Asmara meeting may have been occasioned by envy, especially as SAF was thought to be the host country's favoured son.[16]

Another important milestone, though, was reached before the Asmara meeting on fundamental issues, and without which that meeting might have collapsed. As it is the case with old adversaries, there were doubts on all sides, but the most doubtful conjecture was acceptance by the Umma and DUP of the cipher word secularism. It was conceivable, nonetheless, that they would accept another dispensation that separates religion from politics. This suspicion seemed to be borne out by the fact that the two parties refused to commit themselves in the NDA London meeting (1992) to the specifics of a future constitution, despite earnest attempts by the SPLM to explain what it meant by secularism. The issue was skirted by the two parties, leading the SPLM representatives at the meeting to say that the Sudan did not necessarily have to remain united, it could equally be constituted of two peacefully cooperating but sovereign units, so long as some Northern parties believed that politics was inseparable from religion. In fact, an earlier attempt was made, to no avail, in the meeting of the NDA in Addis Ababa (1991). A proposition identical to the one adopted in Nairobi was presented to that meeting by three lawyers[17] delineating the limits between religion and politics, but the reaction towards that proposition by the Umma and DUP was lukewarm. Amazingly, it took those parties two years to come around and accept the same proposition.

So, on 17 April 1993, the NDA met in Nairobi to reconsider the issue. For the first time, the SPLM leader addressed a full-fledged NDA meeting. Garang emphasized the Movement's call for a united, democratic and secular Sudan adding that 'the unity the SPLM called for was a qualified one, not unity at any cost or as conceived in the past'. He invited the meeting to debate the issue of religion and the state in a manner that took into account the fears of all parties. After arduous deliberations, all the parties agreed to a formulation similar to the one rejected at the Addis Ababa meeting two years earlier. In that formulation, two principles were upheld:

i.   International and regional human rights covenants and instruments shall be an integral part of the laws of Sudan and any law contrary to these instruments shall be null and void.

ii. Laws shall guarantee full equality of citizens on the basis of citizenship, respect for religious beliefs and traditions without discrimination on grounds of religion, race, gender or culture. Any law contrary to the foregoing stipulation shall be null and void.

On 12 December of the same year, the Umma and the SPLM signed the Chukudum Agreement in which the Umma upheld the Nairobi declaration on religion and politics and formally recognized the right of the South to secede. The agreement also proscribed force as a means to coercing unity in case the South freely chose to go its own way.[18] By taking the daring step of meeting with the 'rebels' in the liberated areas, the two senior Umma leaders certainly broke a psychological barrier and were made to pay for it by the regime. Following the Chukudum agreement, Sadiq al Mahdi was harassed in Khartoum and the property of the Umma Secretary General, Omar Nour el Daim was confiscated. The NIF government, to all appearance, was as much irritated by the symbolism of that action, as it was by the substance of the agreement.

The softening of the Umma stance on both issues of religion and politics and self-determinaiton signalled a bridging of major differences and paved the way for the Asmara Resolutions in June 1995. But behind the scenes at Chukudum, the Umma was reluctant to endorse the right of self-determination for the people of the Nuba Mountains and Southern Blue Nile. That position, and the SPLM's perceived acquiescence to it, caused consternation among the leaders of the two regions, and probably drove Commander Yousif Kuwa of the Nuba Mountains to conclude his own agreement on self-determination with the DUP, six months later.[19] The agreement was signed by Kuwa in his capacity as Chairman of the SPLM Convention, and was based on al Mirghani–Garang Accord of 1988 (a matter that the Umma would wish to be forgotten) as well as on the Nairobi Declaration on religion and politics. The two parties affirmed their determination to work for Sudan's unity on the basis of the dispensations reflected in the two documents, failing which the aggrieved parties should be entitled to exercise the right of self-determination. The acceptance by the DUP of the principle of self-determination for the South aggravated Egypt, which consistently expressed fears that self-determination was just a stage name for secession.

Against this background, the Asmara meeting on fundamental issues was destined to get off to a flying start. Nonetheless, that was not to be readily achieved since the meeting was haunted from the start by disputes over turf: who was to get what within the NDA power structures. At that point it was agreed that the NDA parties should convene a consultative meeting to discuss the SPLM's appeal conveyed in Garang's message of 1994, before translating into the first NDA Congress on Fundamental Issues. Fortuitously, Garang was at hand and his most arduous task was to persuade the wranglesome among his Northern colleagues to bury their differences; to those around him he said: 'I have buried mine, why shouldn't they?' Garang also advised his delegationn that the SPLM should not be part of that squabble over positions. Fresh in his mind was probably a similar brawl that took place in a former NDA meeting in Addis Ababa in 1991 which spotlighted the frivolousness with which some Northern politicians approached the struggle against the NIF and manifested a complete lack of a sense of priority and proportion. In that meeting Mubarak al Mahdi (Umma), who was then apparently sure that the days of the NIF were numbered, proposed that the NDA should consider the shares of the parties in the post-Bashir interim parliament. That stopgap parliament would necessarily have be chosen by the parties before any elections were held. The NDA was reluctant to repeat the experiences of October 1964 and April 1985 when interim governments had a free hand in governance without any institution of popular oversight. As a measuring scale for sizing up the weights of the parties, the Umma representative recommended the ratios of party representation in the last democratically elected parliament. Incensed by that proposition, Elijah Maloc (SPLM) retorted: 'This is unacceptable; we were not part of that parliament and to us it was a parliament of partial legitimacy.' Moreover, he said, 'what unites NDA parties today is the struggle to remove the NIF regime so, on the basis of the SPLM's contribution to that struggle, the Movement should demand 50 per cent of the share, not less'. That was obviously Elijah's exaggerated response to what he thought to be an untimely and puerile suggestion. Garang, who was not present, intervened through a message delivered to the meeting in which he advised the delegations to attend to more urgent issues and consider how to cross that bridge when they come to it. To all appearance, some NDA parties wanted to double cross that bridge before reaching it.

In Asmara, however, the apple of discord was the authority of the Chairman of the NDA; if al Mirghani was to remain as chairman, the Umma wanted that chairmanship to be reduced to a ceremonial one with the executive powers resting in the hands of the Secretary General who was to be drawn from the Umma party. That there were other parties in the NDA who had legitimate claims to the top positions of the Alliance was a matter of little concern to those who coveted power. To appease the SPLM and ostensibly extenuate the chairman's powers, the Umma proposed the alternation of the chairmanship between al Mirghani and Garang. That idea was shot down by the SPLM leader who was afraid that it might send wrong signals to Khartoum. Khartoum, he said, would make a field day of putting an 'infidel' at the head of the NDA and use that to blackmail al Mirghani. Garang also declined the post of vice-chairman, in all likelihood because that would have also sent wrong signals to the rank and file of the SPLM. No question, those would have concluded that the only position allocated to their leaders in Northern-controlled institutions, despite their decisive role within NDA, was that of second fiddle. Consequently, Garang proposed that the leadership of the Alliance should be a collegiate one, assumed by the collectivity of the heads of the different parties to the NDA without exception. Al Mirghani would be a *primus inter pares*.

Having put that coarse-grained conflict to rest, the NDA moved to hold its first full-fledged congress to address the real issues. To the surprise of its worst enemies, after a two-week protracted debate the NDA reached agreement on several fundamental issues, to wit: the system of rule, religion and politics, security and military arrangements during the interim period, the economy, self-determination, unity, the direction of Sudan's future foreign relations and the composition and organisational structure of the NDA. On the 23 June, the SPLM/SPLA solemnly ratified the Charter of the National Democratic Alliance as amended to take account of the SPLM remarks on the causes of Sudan conflict as well as of those of the concerns of the traditional parties.

First Step towards a New Sudan

Negotiations, mediation, peace agreements, peace talks – just about every form of dialogue have had a long, noble, though absolutely ineffectual history in the course of Sudan's protracted conflict. Is there a peacefully negotiated vent for the hostility and animosity that for more than four decades had blighted Sudanese nationhood? Why from the administrative conference of 1947 to the present has a peacefully negotiated settlement eluded us? If the historical events reviewed in the previous chapters did not do so, perhaps the overview of external mediation efforts in Sudan since the demise of the Addis Ababa Accord, would provide the answer to these questions. But, while the mediation processes seek a settlement between the government and those rebelling against it, reconciliation between the SPLM and it's new allies and erstwhile foes is a different matter. There is also another prong of action by this new alliance, one that seeks to overthrow the NIF and provide in its place an alternative political system.

After the fall of Sadiq al Mahdi's government, the Northern political establishment automatically clicked into the 'opposition' mode in the long and tiresome routine of power–opposition cycle. The 'traditional' and 'modern' parties, therefore, initially formed the NDA with the aim of agitating for the fall of the NIF government through mass action and a supporting military *coup*, in the style of 1964 against Abboud and 1985 against Nimeiri. That may be the reason why some of the SPLM's friends, on the left, were inflamed by Garang's call to Bashir, after the incarceration of political leaders in Khartoum, that the SPLM was there to lead the national struggle against him.[20] However, by the mid-1990s, the NDA came to realize that the NIF was a different beast that could not be removed through the classical popular uprisings which Sudan waged before against Abboud and Nimeiri, no matter how self-assured of their ability to do so. The NIF regime is an authoritarian regime like no other the Sudan has seen before. As a military man, al Bashir knew from where the danger would come, so he emaciated the professional army and created a parallel one. Turabi, on the other hand, thought and acted as a leader endowed with godly plenipotency and as the all-knowing and all-seeing *supremo* he reduced dissent to blasphemy. The NIF itself is not an artificial political creation, it is an organization with a small (relative to the traditional parties) but entrenched grassroots and a very sophisticated political machinery. In the course of the last three decades, Turabi prepared his party's young cadres in the best Western educational and training institutions which made them sufficiently versed in modern tools of analysis and operation, to the envy of other political parties in the North including those who belonged to the modern forces. Above all, the NIF is not only a national party; thanks to Turabi it was transformed into a bridgehead of international radical Islam, supported by a *pot-pourri* of rogue states and outlandish moneyed individuals and groups in the Middle East and beyond. The SPLM, therefore, warned its allies that with the NIF business could not be as usual and armed struggle was an inescapable option. Its premonitions were soon to be confirmed by the regime when it virtually dared its Northern opponents to carry arms if they were at all to recover power. Armed struggle had thus become a cruel necessity.

Nevertheless, the NDA committed itself to seeking a consensual peaceful settlement for Sudan's conflict based on the Asmara agenda and to the redrawing of the political map through a national constitutional conference. On the face of it, the NDA sought to remove the NIF through two antipodean means: military struggle and negotiated settlement. As it transpired from future developments, the second option was made complex by the regime's policies. During the whole decade of the 1990s it was busy reinventing Sudan, culturally, politically, socially and institutionally. This led to the not so implausible conclusion that nothing short of dismantling the structures the NIF had erected in the public domain would ensure a conducive atmosphere for a meaningful dialogue .The negotiated settlement was thus destined to be a long and tortuous process. This conclusion was affirmed by the circuity of the negotiations that the SPLM/A had held with the NIF in various fora. Not that the NIF is averse to peace, but the only peace they contemplate is one that would conserve their ideological agenda and ensure their primacy in Sudan's body politic. Such *pax islamica,* can only be achieved, if at all, through invading legions, not negotiations between equal partners.

The Asmara Resolutions on Fundamental Issues, however, narrowed the respective positions of the various opposition groups and forged the Alliance into a viable and internationally recognized alternative to the regime in Khartoum. The NDA also developed into a much more serious and credible opposition after it brought together virtually all political and military groups opposed to the NIF regime under one umbrella with a shared commitment to establishing peace with justice, voluntary unity and a healthy multi-party democracy. Before Asmara, and despite the adoption of the its Charter by the SPLM, the disparate parts of the Alliance did not add up to a coherent whole. Coherence did not come easy. First, the wrangling generated by the NDA Secretary General with the Alliance Chairman, mainly on issues of turf, continued and led to a leadership hiatus that enfeebled the NDA considerably. Besides, cavil and bickering were at their worst on the mundane issue of who was to get what after the demise of the NIF regime. On his side, Mubarak al Mahdi (after he left the NDA) had his own explanation of that bizarre tiff; al Mirghani, he said to a newspaperman, 'is incapable of understanding the ongoing changes'.[21] Damning the consequences, Mubarak al Mahdi told his interviewer: 'Be aware that I was the one who created the NDA, and before Sadiq's emergence I was the driving force within it.' This level of presumptuousness summed up the problem of Mubarak al Mahdi and the party he represented, in that all Sudanese political forces were reduced to appendages to one party. That stance also reflected a throwback to the old adversarial politics of the party regimes.

Coordination of military activities in the eastern front was also a bone of contention. The NDA created a Joint Military Command (JMC), headed by Garang, first to ensure the harmonization of armed struggle in the North and South and, second, to apportion assignments to the different forces.[22] However, SAF up to 1998 chose to be a lone ranger in its military operations, probably because of the misapprehension of some of its leaders that victory was around the corner and that they were better poised than anybody else to make the first move to Khartoum. SAF may have believed that it was more equipped than the ALC, and certainly more than the other parties, to mobilize the army to stage a *coup* against the regime. As it was, the NDA to some of its parties became an umbrella under which they gathered on inclement days, and folded when they so wished. This approach to corporate action was a cause of alarm to other parties to the NDA who suspected in it a desire to destroy the NIF through the combined force of the Alliance, only to replace it by a new brand of men on horseback.

Despite all those pointless dust-ups, the Asmara resolutions – at least at the intellectual level – belied all pessimists. The Sudanese political class could be made to agree on fundamentals as a result of the appropriate alignment of forces, proper articulation of objectives and recognition, though reluctant, of the mistakes of the past. The resolutions of the conference included:

i.   Practical separation of religion from politics.
ii. Political pluralism.
iii. Repeal of the so-called *shari'a* laws and banning of political parties based on religious or ethnic affiliation.
iv. Voluntary unity through the exercise of the right of self-determination.
v.   Standing army for the South and security arrangement during the transitional period.
vi. A four-year transitional period during which the Asmara agenda would be implemented, i.e. giving unity a last chance.
vii. Radical decentralization of power.
viii. Armed and popular struggle to overthrow the NIF regime.

Some pessimistic commentators argued first, that the NDA's Achilles heel would be the Northern 'traditional' parties; they were religion-based parties with roots deep in popular Islam. How committed would they be to the repeal of the NIF's *shari'a*, especially when some of them wavered at repealing it when they had opportunity to do so? What guarantees were there that this time around their commitment to the separation of state and religion was genuine?[23] Secondly, they also expostulated that virtually all Northern political parties were internally undemocratic and they have been led by the same people for decades. Those leaders, it was said, were usually non-accountable to their constituents. How could an undemocratic party be part of a democratic process, let alone form a democratic government? Besides, what assurance was there that an unaccountable party leader would honour agreements entered into by his party? Thirdly, and connected with the foregoing, was the fact that both the DUP and Umma, by their failure in the past to provide leadership and confront the political, social and economic crises of the Sudan, had contributed as much as anybody else to the conditions of war in the Sudan. Could they be trusted to relinquish their practices of forty years and strike out in a new democratic direction? Those were pertinent questions, the answers to which we shall turn later, after elaboration on the most pivotal themes in the Asmara resolutions.

1. The System of Rule

In Sudan's protracted conflict, the system of rule was a major bone of contention between Southern and Northern politicians, on the one hand, and between the excessively centralist governments in Khartoum and political groups espousing the cause of the marginalized areas (Beja, Nuba, Fur), on the other. Rulers in Khartoum have always favoured a unitary system of government, while people at the peripheries of power (including the South) called for a decentralized system of rule that guaranteed them the right to manage their internal affairs. Successive parliaments dominated by Northern parties failed to come to terms with the complexity of the Sudanese situation. They failed to read the signals even when the coalescence of those groups with Southerners in parliament (as in 1968) should have served sufficient notice on Khartoum authorities. It is to be recalled that the description generally reserved for, and effortlessly bestowed upon, groups at the peripheries who called for administrative decentralization was *harakat 'unsuriyya* (racist movements). With few notable exceptions this view was shared by large segments of the elite including some modernists. Manifestly, the rulers in Khartoum mistook for complaisancy the civility with which marginalized groups in the geographic North conducted themselves in politics. To some parties, the marginalized areas were only docile reserves from which support was drawn during parliamentary elections. All those groups (Nuba, Beja, Funj, Fur) were eventually forced to carry arms. The Khartoum' supermen' would have saved Sudan a lot of blood, toil and trouble were they to heed G.B. Shaw's adage: 'Beware the man who does not return your blows; he neither forgives you nor allows you to forgive yourself.'[24] The Northern parties were not shorn of ideas as to the political desirability and administrative efficacy of administrative decentralization in a country as vast and heterogeneous as Sudan. Not counting Southern calls for federation prior to independence, the Republican Party led by Mahmoud Mohammed Taha advocated as early as December 1955 the creation of a federal system.[25] Also, the SCP, in the guise of the Anti-imperialism Front, (though limiting itself to the South), called around the same time for regional autonomy for that region.[26] At that time, the hostility towards federation by Khartoum-based parties (including the

SCP) was reflective of an unwitting recalcitrance resulting from unworldliness. With the existence of time-honoured practices to draw lessons from if they wished or cared to, such as the experiences of India, Brazil, the Soviet Union, Canada, India, Australia etc., there was no reason for the parties, especially the SCP, to emulate those experiences. But the parties persisted in thinking that an idea sponsored by Southern elite and looked upon with favour by the British could not be anything but a 'colonialist' plot.

In a radical departure from past experiences, the resolution adopted by the NDA on the System of Rule, aimed at guaranteeing the South – as well as other regions in Sudan – unprecedented competence in various matters of government. Sudan would be comprised of five geographic 'entities,'[27] in addition to the capital city, Khartoum. It shall have a central authority with competence of a federal government over matters purely national in character. The decentralised system would have two tiers, one relating to the Northern 'entities' (Kordofan, Dar Fur, Central, North and East) and the other, to the South. Each of the entities shall be responsible for the administration of the territorial sphere they occupy. Important guarantees for the Southern entity include autonomy in administration of justice, exploitation of natural resources, economic development, education and health, art and culture and personal laws. The South shall also have its own legislature, executive presidency and judiciary. Justiciable issues on constitutional matters and conflict of laws shall be referred to a reconstructed Supreme Court. Effectively, the Asmara resolution on the system of rule had created a genuinely decentralized polity. By proliferating the centres of power within the country, pressures from the centre would be reduced. Also, new political alignments based on common economic interest rather than ethnic or tribal bonds would be created. The resolution represented the most drastic rolling back of the frontiers of central authority ever contemplated by the North for the South or any other marginalized area.

The system of decentralization treats all entities as equal, with the South more equal than others. The powers conferred on that region almost border on confederalism. Nonetheless, the Sudanese may have to be more imaginative when a permanent constitution is devised for the country by the anticipated national constitutional conference. However, political science has recently developed the new concept of consociational democracy that would satisfactorily address the legitimate concerns of groups, while ensuring national unity and stability. The Dutch system was taken by some scholars to be the most pertinent in this regard.[29] That system safeguards what is known as the *verzuiling* (five pillars of society). Those pillars comprise the Catholics, two Protestant groups, Socialists and Liberals. Each of those groups represents a self-contained and isolated society having its own political party, trades unions, schools, newspapes and radio and televisions.[26] Consociationalism is predicated on:

i. creation of a grand coalition of all state government to ensure representation of all the pillars of society,
ii. proportional representation in the electoral system and aproportional system for sharing public expenditure and public employment,
iii. mutual veto whereby one pillar can veto government decisions in matters of vital concern to it, and
iv. administrative autonomy for each community through territorial governance as well as institutional autonomy, e.g. each group given the right to have its own schools and media.

But neither is Sudan comparable to the Netherlands, nor are its multiple cleavages similar to hers. Also, some of the ideas embodied in the Dutch system are already catered to in the decentralization system proposed by the Asmara resolutions. Nonetheless, the Dutch system has some good ideas that may help attenuate mutual suspicions and ensure a more representative system of governance. They would also provide effective checks and balances. Among those are proportional representation in the electoral system, a proportional sharing system for public expenditure and employment and a mutual veto on matters of vital concern to particular groups. The latter dispensation will have to be based on priorly identified and agreed upon indices so that it should not degenerate into an artifice for frustrating government work.

Interim Period

In addition, the Asmara Rsolutions provide for an interim period of a maximum of four years, after which the people of Southern Sudan shall decide their fate. Within those four years, a national constitutional conference shall be convoked to draw a permanent constitution for the Sudan that shall embody the principles highlighted in the Asmara Resolutions. Furthermore, the South, in the course of those four years, shall retain its military competence, with the SPLA remaining armed and under its present command. This military clause has a built-in guarantee that makes redundant questions as to what the South shall do if the Northern parties renege on their undertakings in Asmara. By retaining its military competence to safeguard against the past conduct of Northern authorities whereby those authorities chose at will to violate solemn undertakings, the South shall need no guarantees from any quarter. At the close of the interim period, if unity was voted for, then the North and the South would have learned to live together and respect each other. The Asmara Resolutions, therefore, are meant to give unity a last chance. On its part, the SPLM pledged itself to work for the option of unity on the basis of the Asmara Resolutions. This leaves the Northern political establishment with only one of two options: a united peaceful and stable Sudan based on the undistorted implementation of the Asmara undertakings, or a disjointed one if they decided otherwise. The latter eventuality is one that no right-minded Northern leader shall envisage, let alone bring upon himself.

The parties to the NDA also agreed on an 'Economic Action Plan for the Interim Period'. The plan aims at redressing the injustices of the past, particularly the underdevelopment of the marginalized areas. At the core of the country's economic problems, the plan argues, was 'the perpetuation of colonial economic, political, social and cultural underdevelopment in the marginalized regions in Eastern, Western, Northern and Southern Sudan'. The plan called upon the interim government to pursue the 'realization of a balanced economic development and an equitable distribution of wealth and social and economic services as a prerequisite for the consolidation of peace and national unity'. Obviously, given the obtaining situation – especially as far as the inequitable distribution of physical and social public assets – inequality in wealth distribution shall continue in the short run, before it levels out in the long term. New investments shall continue, for the foreseeable future, to be attracted to areas where the environment is more enabling. Deplorably, investors are not altruistic. They are neither spurred by humanitarian considerations nor susceptible to compassion. They shall invest where investment promises maximum reward. However, with the right policies that give priority to infrastructural and human resources development in the marginalized areas, inequalities would tail off in due time.   Also, the infrastructural development that shall accompany oil development in the South shall inevitably make the region more attractive to both local and foreign investors. Worthy of note also is the determination by the NDA to pursue a market-oriented economy, a theme that needs to be further developed. Some Northern policymakers and public opinion formulators may still have to rid themselves of the statist mindset and the belief that it is only state bureaucrats who are capable of compassion. The state is better placed to reconcile competing claims, develop infrastructure and empower and prepare citizens to enter the labour market.

On the thorny issue of natural resources, Section 11 of the Chapter on Powers and Competence of the Southern entity entrusts that entity 'with the exploration, development and management of non-renewable natural resources, subject to arrangements with the Central Authority over taxation, revenue sharing and development needs of other disadvantaged regions'. As regards Northern entities the resolution reserved the aforementioned rights to the Central Authority 'without prejudice to the right of the host entity to fix and collect a reasonable percentage of the revenue accruing from the exploitation of the resource discovered and developed within that entity'. This formulation went a long way to allay the fears of the South, fears that were amply justified by the wrong-headed policies of the central government as regards mineral and oil exploration in that region. The gerrymandering of boundaries during Nimeiri's era and the plundering of oil revenues during Bashir's had considerably augmented those fears. At the same time, the stipulation did not give a free hand to the Southern entity on the use of revenues accruing from the exploitation of non-renewable resources developed within the entity. By law, the Southern government was made to have a responsibility in uplifting other marginalized regions.

2. Self-determination

In the recent past, no issue had been more contested by Northern parties and political commentators than that of self-determination. Prior to and during the self-government period, as well as in the first two years of independence, Southern politician rarely raised the issue. They consistently reiterated their commitment to a united *federal* Sudan. But, as a result of the intransigence of Northern parties on the issue of federalism even though it was a condition precedent to the vote by the South in favour of the declaration of independence, Southern politicians began to have second thoughts on unity. That led Father Saturnino to call for self-determination. The term since then became part of the Southern agenda and lately a common currency in the North–South dialogue. The party's recantation on the promise of federalism was further exacerbated by calls for the promulgation of an Islamic constitution in the late 1950s and more pronouncedly in 1968. That issue acquired increasing salience during the NIF's regime.

Known for their short memory, Northern Sudanese political commentators repeatedly weaned their thoughts from this history. Much too often, they discoursed about the legitimacy of granting self-determination to the South, as if self-determination was an issue contrived by the SPLM, or one that suddenly appeared from thin air. The canny among them went into serpentine legal arguments based on the assumption that Sudan had already exercised its right of self-determination at independence. A second self-determination, according to this line of argument, was out of the question. This view was literally expressed by NIF negotiators at Abuja though, infrequently, it was also adduced by many Northern lawyers. The contention, though tenable under classical international law, is both fraudulent and incompatible with contemporary legal and political thought. Fraudulent because the present call by Southerners for the exercise of the right to self-determination is an outgrowth of the North's reneging on a constitutional dispensation to which they had agreed at independence. That reneging, by necessity, rendered the so-called self-determination at independence null and void. Contracts based on deceit and false representation have no validity under any civilized law. Equally, as we have elaborated in Chapter Two, the exercise of self-determination as stipulated in the Anglo-Egyptian agreement was virtually torpedoed by Parliament.

The claim by the South (indeed by any people in Sudan who may have suffered the same fate), is well provided for in the UN Charter.[30] Rightly, some may argue that in traditional international law the exercise of that right within the Charter stipulations was only reserved for people seeking independence from colonial rule. This is indeed the meaning of General Assembly Resolution 1514 (XV) adopted in 1960 and commonly known as the Declaration on the Granting of Independence to Colonial Countries and Peoples. That resolution provided that 'all people have the right to self-determination [and] by virtue of that right they freely determine their political status and pursue their economic, social and cultural development'.[31] A statement by Secretary General U Thant confirmed the assumption that self-determination was only reserved to ex-colonial powers.

Commenting on the secession of Katanga from the Congo, at a press conference at Dakar, U Thant said that 'the UN has never accepted and does not accept, and I don't believe that it will ever accept, the principle of secession of a part of its member states'[32] But, ironically, one year after U Thant's statement, the UN was forced by the full-scale war between India and Pakistan to recognize the secession of Bangladesh.

Historically, self-determination was not recognized or even mentioned in the Covenant of the League of Nations. Nevertheless it was granted to European heterogeneous nationalities within or across countries after the First World War. President Wilson considered the recognition of that right *qui sui non* to peace and stability in Europe.[33] But Wilson's declaration, according to some scholars, had ulterior motives behind it.[34] His view was also challenged by one of his closest aides, Robert Lansing, who deemed it subversive to world stability. Lansing, in a glaringly racist statement, said, 'The more I think of the President's declaration as to the right of self-detemination, the more convinced I am of the danger of putting such ideas into the minds of certain races.'[35] On his side, Lenin also espoused the principle of the right of self-determination to peoples of the Soviet Union and consecrated that right in the Soviet Constitution as a fundamental right to all peoples of the Union. But in view of the monolithism of Lenin's party and the doctrine of reason of state that ensued from it, that Soviet constitutional edict became theoretical. The peoples of the Soviet Union had to wait for the collapse of the system built by Lenin so as to exercise their right to self-determination. Evidently, while granting the right to self-determination to European minorities in the post-First World War period was influenced by opportunistic political considerations, the affirmation of that right to colonial peoples under the UN Charter was function of the Super Powers conflict. It was also coupled with a desire to maintain the territorial integrity of new states.

Notwithstanding, the law of nations has considerably developed since First World War when Wilson's politically motivated idea was born, and also since the promulgation of the UN Charter after the Second World War. In furtherance to the GA's Resolution (1514), the United Nations as well as regional organizations adopted a number of covenants and resolutions that presented the right of self-determination in a completely different light. For example, the International Covenant on Economic, Social and Cultural Rights (1966), The International Covenant on Civil and Political Rights (1967) as well as the African Charter on Human and Peoples' Rights (1981), all upheld the right of peoples to self-determination. The adoption by the United Nations GA of the two above-mentioned covenants as well as others [36] filled a lacuna in both the Charter and the Universal Declaration on Human Rights. For while the UN Charter and practice of the United Nations granted the right to self-determination within the meaning of to colonial peoples, the Universal Declaration on Human Rights was completely silent on peoples and minority rights. The two international covenants of 1966 and 1967 as well as the African Charter of 1981 were ratified by Sudan in 1986. The first article in both international covenants obligates states to promote the realization of peoples' right to self-determination', while Article 20 (1) of the African Charter refers to the 'unquestionable and inalienable right to self-determination'. Analysing that provision in the African Charter, Richard Kiwanuka concluded that it was meant to reserve political and economic space for the people and encapsulated according to the writer, 'people's sovereignty'. The exercise of that right, he said, is 'crucial when the interests of the people and those of the state diverge'.[37]

In effect, a more authoritative UN document in this regard is the Declaration of Principles of International Cooperation among States in Accordance with the UN Charter adopted unanimously by the UN General Assembly on 24 October 1970 (GA Resolution 2625, XXV). The declaration was adopted during the Khrushchev era, not only to protect the territorial integrity of states, but also to establish guiding principles for cooperation among states with different social systems. Although that Declaration affirmed the principles of sovereignty and territorial integrity of states, paragraph 7, sub-paragraph 3 sets down limitations to that sovereignty. The sub-paragraph reads: 'Nothing in the foregoing paragraph shall be construed as authorizing or encouraging any action which would dismember or impair totally or in part the territorial integrity or political unity of sovereign and independent states *conducting themselves in compliance with the principles of equal rights and self-determination of people belonging to the territory without distinction as a race, creed or colour.*

Admittedly, neither is the right of self-determination stubbornly anchored in classical *jus inter gentes,* nor is it conclusively recognized in the early United Nations jurisprudence and practices. Nonetheless it can no longer be confuted as a right to peoples denied equality within sovereign nation states. As a result, respect to territorial integrity is no longer absolute; it is contingent on the behaviour of state governments towards their people. Contemporary legal scholarship, therefore, argues that respect of territorial integrity is untenable when the state is not possessed of a government representing the whole people. It also argues that the right of self-determination must be unambiguously guaranteed 'to people inside the political boundaries of existing sovereign and independent states in situations where the government does not represent the governed'.[38] In this respect Halperin distinguished five categories of self-determination:[39]

i. Anti-colonial self-determination (the classical type),
ii. Trans-state self-determination which applies to groups concentrated in more than one state, e.g. Kurds and Kahmiris,
iii. Self-determination for dispersed people,
iv. Self-determination for indigenous people, e.g. native Indians in the US and Canada and the Aborigine in Australia, and
v. Internal or representational self-determination where a population of an existing state seeks to change its political situation in favour of a more democratic and representative situation.

This internal self-determination, in contradistinction to colonial self-determination, is evidently what Southern Sudanese clamour for.

The fraudulence of political commentators and politicians in North Sudan and the Arab world is also reflected in their impassioned pleadings for the granting of the right to self-determination to Muslim nationalities within established sovereign states that are much older than Sudan. The pleaders, for example, maintain that Chechnyan, Bosnian and Kosovar Muslims have a god-given right to live their life as they wish to. But Chechnya, we know, has been an *oblast* (province) of Russia since 1920, that is half a century before the Sudan Republic was born, and Kosovar Muslims were integrated into Serbia in 1912 after the creation the national state of Albania and recognized by the world as such. As for Bosnia, its six *oblasti* (provinces) organized on the line of the old Ottoman sanjaks (administrative units), were incorporated in Yugoslavia at the end of the Second World War, and recognized as such by the international community.

There is hence preponderant evidence and precedents in support of granting the right of self-determination to indigenous peoples within sovereign states. Nonetheless, the issue is more political than legal. Whatever legal arguments one may present, that would not change the feelings of the aggrieved nationalities towards, and their distrust of, dominant groups. Nor would legalistic arguments command influence on the politico-military facts on the ground, particularly when the aggrieved have resorted to force. The secession of Bangladesh from Pakistan, as well as the disintegration of former Yugoslavia, the former Soviet Union and Czechoslovakia, proves this point beyond doubt. In effect, the US and the EU basing their decision on classical principles of international law were averse to the recognition of the states of Slovenia and Croatia when they seceded from Yugoslavia. However, realities on the ground forced them to reverse direction.[40]

Sudan's crisis, however, had all the makings of a self-inflicted pain. Southerners who were forced to call for instant separation or for the exercise of the right to self-determination leading to that, had only come to that conclusion after an accumulation of broken promises and agreements that, if implemented, could have laid the foundation for the country's unity. Also, as reflected in the SPLM's inclination towards unity on a new basis, as well as in the political stances of post-independence politicians, Southerners would have preferred to see their country united. But left with zero option, they would have no other alternative but to call for separation. No self-respecting human being should be expected to be part of a country that made of him a second-class citizen. Equally, it shall be against the nature of things, for any proud-hearted person to consider himself part of a 'nation' that treats him as an outsider. The English novelist, Virginia Woolf, made a fitting statement in this regard. Describing women who were virtually treated as outsiders in the England of the 1930s, she said: 'The outsider might reflect on what her sex owned by way of property, what the law would do for her, what protection she is given.' Woolf, the utopian, denounced that nation to which she nominally belonged and went on to say:

'I need no country; the whole world is my country.'[41] The English writer was decrying a male-dominated society where property rights of women were restricted, their political rights severely circumscribed and public law weighed heavily against them. But the Sudanese marginalized are not utopians, so they should be expected to pursue the struggle in order to be 'insiders' in their own country. Otherwise, the only alternative that shall be left to them is to opt out even if that meant throwing their old and truly great country out of gear.

It is indeed ironical that in Sudan – as in the case in other newly independent countries – self-determination that was the process by which those countries were ushered into an independence that was believed to be a prelude to bliss, should now become the tool of disintegration. Within those countries, assorted minority groups were reduced by the newly independent governments to virtual outsiders. Inexorably, those groups came to the conclusion that they had only exchanged one master for another. National unity became a connotation for dominance. But as a Sudanese scholar stated: 'Unity should not be pursued at any cost. The constitutional framework of the nation state must provide for equality and justice for all segments of the population: equality in sharing political power, economic and social development and enabling each 'nation' or 'people' within the nation state to maintain and develop its distinctive cultural identity.'[42]

Since Asmara, however, the matter was put to rest by the NDA; the resolution on self-determination was not only meant as an alternative for the South in the event the proposed system of rule was tampered with during the interim period, it was also recognized as an inalienable right for all people of Sudan who wanted to exercise it. By recognizing and respecting the right of the South to secede, the Northern parties had effectively foresworn the use of force to achieve unity. The resolution, nonetheless, stated at the outset, that all the parties to the NDA (including the SPLM) preferred a united Sudan based on the recognition of the county's diversity and its multi-ethnic, multireligious, multicultural and multilinguistic composition. Unity and self-determination, it was argued, were not antithetical, but unity could only be achieved through the free consent of the parties concerned, and not sealed by force.

The resolution also enjoined the central authority during the interim period to devise and implement the necessary confidence-building measures and to restructure the state and socio-economic institutions so that all the parties may exercise their right of self-determination in favour of creating a united country. It pointed out three options for the South when exercising the right to self-determination: federal, confederal or secession. On secession, the resolution provided that the people of Southern Sudan may secede before the expiration of the interim period within the Southern frontiers as they stood on 1 January 1956. The gerrymandering of the borders by Nimeiri in the 1980s and the NIF in the 1990s was thus implicitly jettisoned. It also granted the people of Abyei District the option to decide through a referendum to remain within the province of Southern Kordofan or join Bahr el Ghazal region. In the event, if the people of Abyei chose to join Bahr el Ghazal, then they would secede along with the rest of Southern Sudan if secession was opted for. The story of Abyei, perhaps more than of any other region in the South, was distressing because it revealed the whopping failure of the Northern ruling establishment to allow unity to flourish, even at local levels. The district, which is repeatedly referred to as a contiguous zone, is in fact a melting pot where older Dinka leaders decided, out of their own volition, to be part of the North. That the descendents of those high-minded national leaders have now ended up demanding self-determination and eventual secession, is indeed a sad commentary on Northern Sudanese politics, especially since the sixties. As for the people of the Nuba Mountains and Ingessena Hills who carried arms within the SPLA against Khartoum regimes since 1983, there would also be a referendum to determine the option they wish to take on their future. At no point in history did those two regions express a desire to secede. What they had always pleaded for was a measure of self-rule within a united Sudan that would enable them exercise control over their resources and destiny.

3. Religion and Politics

Religion, as we have seen, has always been the jinx in Sudanese politics. Since the time of the *Mahdiyya* in the 1880s, it became embroidered in the fabric of the country's politics. In the post-independence era (particularly since 1968), it incommoded politics and hampered the development of constitutional democracy in Sudan. This would not have been the case, were it not for the nucleation of Northern politics around two adversarial religious sects and for attempts by neo-Islamists to hold those sects to ransom on the issue of religion and politics. Nevertheless, throughout Sudan's political life, there had also been 'secularist' challenges to the dominance of religion over politics, for example the challenge by Ali Abdel Latif in 1924 to traditional tribal and religions leaders, Azhari's challenge in the 1960s to the *Khattmiyya* and that of the Umma politicians to the imposition of a religion-based constitution, the October uprising and the early Nimeiri era. As a result of those challenges, Sudan's traditional religious leaders never pushed hard enough to create an Islamic state and constitution. In effect both Sayyids, Ali al Mirghani and Abdel Rahman al Mahdi, the two paramount religious leaders whose outlook was dominated by religion, had regularly entrusted governance to quasi-secular politicians. Moreover, Sudan's constitutions, throughout the post-independence years including Abboud's era, had been quasi-secular. The two Sayyids were shrewd enough to distinguish between religion and politics, both at the ideological and practical levels. Hence they virtually left the day-to-day running of politics to worldly politicians. Al Mahdi was very much alive to the fact that his political cause (Sudan for the Sudanese) could never have been achieved within an exclusionary religious framework, let alone one affiliated to a specific religious order. Al Mirghani, on the other hand, sponsored a political conglomeration that, by the very nature of its composition, was more disposed to accept separation between religion and state. The political party sponsored by al Mirghani's was traditional home to secular urban elites and Northern non-Muslims (Copts).

The emergence of neo-Islamism in Sudan, as we have explained, had more to do with external than local factors. Popular Islam tolerated many practices that the *pur et dur* old and modern Islamists would frown upon. That was why the Sudanese neo- Islamists, never posited their religious politics on Sudan's indigenous Islam. Instead, they sought to import to the country an Islamic vision unknown to it, though for tactical reasons they paid lip service to the traditional *turuq*. At the same time, they remained penetrated with the belief that they could impose their own version of an exclusivist Islam into a mosaic of multi-cultures and multi-religions of which Islam, though the dominant religion, was only one strand. That strand had also the singularity of being an indegenized variety of Islam. Sudanese Muslims have lived comfortably with that version of Islam, both in their private lives as well as in the public domain. That was perhaps why neo-Islamists from Sadiq al Mahdi in the 1960s to Turabi in the 1990s failed miserably to impose their exclusivist vision. Over and above, the neo-Islamists' contemporary experiences in governance became a textbook on how not to govern a complex country such as Sudan. Ergo, the experiences of the neo-revivalists were both dishonoured and discredited, not only by the non-Muslim South, also by Muslims in the North.

The NDA Meeting on Fundamental Issues addressed itself to this quagmire and encapsulated the solution in its 'Resolution of the Issue of Religion and Politics in the Sudan'. The resolution, in the last analysis, aimed at separating the church and mosque from the state, and religion from Sudanese politics. To that end the resolution made three important statements:

i.   All laws shall guarantee full equality of citizens on the basis of citizenship and respect of religious beliefs and traditions without discrimination on grounds of religion, race, gender or culture. Any law contrary to this requirement shall be unconstitutional.

ii. Prohibition of the formation of any political party on a religious basis.

iii. The state shall be under obligation to acknowledge and respect religious pluralism in Sudan, promote and bring about peaceful interaction, coexistence, equality and tolerance among all religious and noble spiritual beliefs, permit peaceful religious proselytization and prohibit coercion in religion or the perpetration, in any place, forum or location in the Sudan, of any act or measure intended to arouse religious sedition or racial hatred.

This formulation represented a compromise that compromised nobody. It avoided cipher words like secularism and went straight to the crux of the matter, separating religion from politics rather than exorcising religion from society. It also anchored religious freedoms on universal and regional human rights declarations, not least because respect for all universally upheld human rights is not in discordance with the humanist vocation of any religion. In effect, respect of the rights of man by its very nature is the value added to democracy.

Security and Military Arrangements

The last critical issue that was addressed by parties to the NDA was the issue of the military, an issue that was of particular concern to the SPLM who already had in place a full-fledged military wing (SPLA) and was at war with the government. Agreements on military issues was also necessary to provide for a joint military initiative of the NDA parties during the struggle, in addition to guaranteeing the security of the NDA interim government thereafter. Besides, it gave the SPLA the security it needed and, more importantly, allayed Southern fears about the recurrence of past betrayals by Northern parties. Consequently, the parties agreed to establish a high politico-military committee to undertake the task of coordination among, and supervision of, the different NDA armed forces as well as for the implementation of programmes to intensify the struggle to overthrow the NIF regime.[43] Regarding the interim period, the parties agreed that upon assumption of power, they would form a National Defence Council and a National Security Council to consolidate the gains of liberation from the NIF, safeguard against a counter-revolution led by the NIF and ensure 'total civilian control of the military and security affairs' during the interim period. The Council was also mandated by the parties to implement agreements arrived at with the SPLA concerning its regarding the maintenance as a standing army in the South during that period. If Southerners voted for unity with the North, then the SPLA would be absorbed into the mainstream reconstructed and reprofessionalized national armed forces on terms to be determined by the parties concerned.

Conclusion

The NIF's desperate search for peace in recent times had a strong and direct correlation with what was happening on the ground. In the height of peace offensives (IGAD, Joint Initiative, Eritrean peace effort and humanitarian-induced initiatives), the NDA/SPLA had launched a massive offensive on four fronts: on the east which threatened the umbilical cord to the port of Sudan and the pipeline in the *Damzin* area putting in jeopardy Khartoum's power supply, in the central area of the Nuba Mountains and in the South. Those offensives could not be isolated from the regime's own manoeuvres and machinations. For example, whilst the regime pretended to be suing for peace in different fora and calling for 'humanitarian' ceasefires by the regular forces, it went on with its war by proxy, i.e. through tribal militias. In the meantime the regime pulled out all stops to delude international critics with fake political liberalization measures and enticements to those who were disposed to be ensnared to engage in Sudan's oil industry. To those, ostensibly, it did not matter in the least that the revenue accruing from oil production was not only used for intensifying war, but also in order to achieve a 'final solution' to the conflict. Over and above, it became clear to anybody who saw that the regime's meanderings from one peace forum to another only made a mockery of peacemaking.

However, as a result of the SPLA's offensives to neutralize that stratagem, the regime went haywire, particularly following military successes in the South (Bahr el Ghazal), the South East (around the oil-rich areas of Adar Yeil and Bentiu in Upper Nile) and in the Nuba Mountains. The regime especially made a lot of mileage of two attacks on Bahr el Ghazal. The first was the one which took place despite a humanitarian ceasefire in the middle of 2000. That was a battle forced on the SPLA to repulse attacks by government-sponsored militias on unarmed civilian population. Though formally adhering to a cease-fire in Bahr el Ghazal, the government launched by proxy one of its most vehement attacks in that region. The militias this time were not limited to the Baggara Arabs, but also included Dinka militiamen who were exploited by the government to terrorize the population.[44] The perfidy of the government in ceasing hostilities formally, while continuing them by proxy, was pertinently described by Eric Reeves in a feature article he wrote to a Canadian paper. Reeves wrote: 'The Khartoum regime – illegal and unfathomably cruel – bears overwhelming responsibility for the staggering civilian destruction and displacement in the South and the engineered famine that has produced so many deaths. The rebel force has "violated" the fictitious cease-fire ... because of outrageous provocation in the form of tribal assaults on civilians and humanitarian relief, and because cease-fires exist only when Khartoum thinks they are of temporary military use.'[45]

The regime had three strategic objectives. The first was to dislodge the NDA forces in the East, hence the attacks to which reference was earlier made and which were initiated by the regime whilst President Issaias Afworki was in Khartoum discussing peace. Undoubtedly, the eastern front threatens the regime's strategic assets and nerve centre: the Khartoum–Port Sudan road, the pipeline and Sudan's main oil refinery. The second was to dislodge the SPLA from the Nuba Mountains and Southern Blue Nile. To all appearances, the government decided to destroy what it thought to be the last remnants of the SPLA in the geographic North, before the IGAD Summit scheduled for 2 June. By reducing the areas under SPLA control to those strictly lying within the geographic South, the regime thought that it would equally reduce the conflict to a North–South one. That would have enabled it to impose its own parameters on the negotiations. Also, the regime believed that by neutralizing the SPLA, the only effective opposition force in the military field, the Northern opposition would be decimated. As a result, the only agenda that the regime would have for that opposition would be limited to surrender. Statements by leading members of the ruling party unequivocally pointed to this endgame.[46]

Consequently, the regime launched a simultaneous attack on the three points. Two brigades (97 and 98) of the Sudanese Army were mobilized to dislodge the SPLA from Southern Blue Nile, while double that force, supported by helicopter gunships attacked the Nuba Mountains. The use of helicopter gunships took place barely two weeks after the declaration by the government to cease aerial bombardments. The attack on the Nuba Mountains was deadly; using ground troops and helicopter gunships, 14 villages at Heiban area were torched and more than 5,000 households destroyed. This report was confirmed by independent experts living in the area.[47] The experts affirmed that the campaign did not target SPLA military establishments but mainly civilian targets. The area attacked was the one where a shrine was built for the late Yusif Kuwa. In addition to military defeat, the government also wanted to inflict a psychological one in the Nuba. But as it turned out, the attack helped energize the whole Nuba population to participate in repelling the offensive. Not only did the attack on the two fronts fail miserably, but for the first time since its inception, the SPLA launched its own attack on western Bahr el Ghazal and captured two important towns: Deim Zubeir (the notorious nineteenth-century slavery outpost) and Raja. The occupation of the latter brought the SPLA into direct contact with another region in the North: Dar Fur. The regime's reaction to this military victory was hilarious. For one, it claimed that the assault on Raja was preceded by aerial attacks by an unidentified foreign power working in unison with the SPLA. A more ludicrous claim was that the attack was launched by Zande youth who were drugged by the SPLM so as to annihilate the Zande nationality in that battle.[48] This wild-goose chase showed that the regime was in a state of total loss.

The regime, despite all the woes that besiege it, continues to act (and manifestly believes) that a peaceful settlement was a tactical ploy, not a strategic option. The military reverses had undoubtedly put it off balance. Its utterances became more and more incoherent and perplexing. For example, in a statement carried by the international press on 17 November after the attack on Kassala, Bashir said that 'the rebels only know the language of force, reconciliation with them would only be through the barrel of the gun'. He added that 'there shall be no negotiations till the rebels are defeated and brought to their knees'.[49] Startlingly, this statement was made a few days before an impending IGAD Summit that was to take place in Khartoum under the chairmanship of Bashir himself. Bashir's statement was diametrically opposed to what Mutrif Siddiq, the minister then in charge of peace, declared only a day before. The minister told a London Arabic daily on 15 November that the government was ready to consider any new proposals by IGAD that would resolve the questions at issue between the government and rebels.[50] The NDA only saw in those contrarian positions an apportionment of roles. However, Bashir's agreement with President Moi to relaunch the IGAD process at the summit level and his deprecation of IGAD only two days later[51] revealed the man's untrustworthiness. It also proved the opposition's worst doubts about the regime's seriousness regarding a comprehensive peaceful settlement.

The Asmara Resolutions were meant to deal decisively with the causes of the rot in the country and lay the foundations for a New Sudan on the rubble of the old. That is what the NIF fears most and shall therefore fight it to the bitter end. But fighting to the bitter end is hardly a winsome strategy. This is particularly so when the regime increasingly shows signs of a free fall. European friends who brazened it out to deamnd the SPLA to accept an unconditional, immediate and comprehensive ceasefire, clearly turned a blind eye to those realities. Their call for a comprehensive ceasefire was eventually consecrated in a UN resolution,[52] and by so doing, they have unwittingly played into Bashir's hand. Not only would the call for a comprehensive ceasefire undo the IGAD's DOP which remains a viable road map to peace and to which the IGAD partners are committed, it would also allow the regime to get away with murder. The DOP, to keep the memory green, stipulates that a comprehensive ceasefire shall be contingent on a political agreement by the parties on the contested issues. Apart from its counter-productiveness – as far as laying the foundations for genuine peace was concerned – the European-sponsored UN resolution was blatantly lacking in even-handedness. Expectedly, the SPLM lashed out at the authors of the resolution in a public statement that left nothing unsaid. In that statement, the SPLM contended that the resolution was replete with 'fundamental errors and erroneous assumptions'. It enumerated, as an example, the silence of the resolution on gross violations of human rights and attacks on humanitarian activities by the regime, despite abounding evidence of those violations in reports by UN monitors. In the meantime, the resolution openly attributed similar attacks to the SPLA with no evidence produced. Accusations against the SPLA for summary executions were also purveyed without a single piece of salient evidence. In general, said the SPLM statement, 'whenever the resolution referred to human rights violations by the government, the government's name was scarcely mentioned, while accusations against the SPLA were pointedly directed'. The authors of the resolution were also voiceless on questions that have worked up international civil society organizations like slavery. Those are not the type of human rights violations that can be condoned, especially given the European's own standards in adjudging war crimes in the Balkans. Accordingly, many Sudanese concluded that crimes against humanity seemed to merit this name only when they were committed against Europeans. Also, by bending over backwards to appease the government to the point of suppressing truth, the authors gave parties opposing the government every reason to believe that they were no longer free agents. Indeed, calling for a comprehensive ceasefire while softening the pressure on the regime for its wanton human rights violations and war crimes provided the perfect situation for Bashir to consummate with impunity, his totalitarian agenda. Probably, because of what he considered as a *carte blanche* given to him by the EU countries, Bashir had the courage to tell a Khartoum daily that the maximum he would offer to the opposition was their integration in the present NIF structures. 'We shall not apologize for anything we have done. There shall be no interim period,' he said.[53]

Regardless, a week following the SPLM's statement on the UN resolution, its spokesman in the eastern front announced that the Movement is not loathe to a comprehensive ceasefire, provided it is accompanied by suspension of activities in the oil sector.[54] The SPLM Commissioner for

Information endorsed that condition but also added others pertaining to the necessary institutional framework for implementing the ceasefire.[55] Those conditions were later fine-tuned and presented by the leader of the SPLM in a position paper to the IGAD Summit in June 2001. The SPLM, according to that paper, was ready to accept an immediate comprehensive ceasefire provided it was linked to:

    i.   a comprehensive cease-oil,
   ii.   an undertaking by the government not to extend the ceasefire to the eastern front, and
  iii.   withdrawal of the government forces behind the 13th Parallel and those of the SPLA behind the 12th, with external monitors in between.

The position paper also maintained that were the parties to proceed with a *permanent* ceasefire, as the government demanded, then it logically followed that the regime wanted a zero interim period. In such a case, the parties should proceed with the implementation of the clause on self-determination. Also, since the 'comprehensive' ceasefire would have to include the eastern front, the government should naturally engage the NDA in negotiations with a view to creating an interim national government comprising all political forces. This view corresponds to one of IGAD's requirements, and, indeed to the principles later expounded in the joint Egyptian–Libyan initiative.

    Truly, what Sudan needs is permanent peace, durable unity and sustainable development. This is not what the NIF regime wants. Proof abounds as to its belief that the only peace they envisage is one that shall maintain their political and ideological hold on Sudan. This type of peace is neither tenable nor can it be sustained. In view of this extreme position, only more internal and external pressures would bring the regime to its senses. Bashir's position is made more untenable by the SPLM's agreement with Turabi, who almost demolished the whole temple over the heads of his erstwhile disciples. Little, therefore, is left for Bashir – who behaves as if he is the peremptory conscience of Sudanese Muslims – to vindicate his claim that he is upholding *shari'a* in the name of Muslim Sudan. Such claim becomes untenable when all Sudanese religion-based parties (including Turabi's) have denounced his pretentions.

    Lastly, the Asmara Resolutions do not give ground for creative ambiguities, nor do their terms provide an escape route for plausible deniability in the future. Some Northern leaders might have deceived themselves that the SLPM would eventually be translated into a 'Southern' party in one of the unholy shifting alliances of Northern governments. They would be wrong if they so believed. The Asmara Resolutions is not a tactical alliance; it is a minimum programme of action based on a conceptual shift to end war, consecrate unity and build a new Sudan. Those who think otherwise shall do justice neither to themselves nor to Sudan.

ENDNOTES

1. Soiynka, Wole: *The Man Dies, Prison Memoirs*, 1972.
2. The charter was officially signed by 11 political parties, 31 professional unions and 51 workers' trades unions on 21 October to commemorate the October uprising
3. The first time the parties objected to the formulation and analysis of the original charter was during an NDA meeting in London 1992. The objection came from the Umma Party who was joined by the DUP
4. The first approach by the NDA to the SPLM was made in mid-August 1989, in a letter signed by al Khatim Adlan of the SCP. Another message was delivered verbally to the SPLM by university professor Mohamed Yousif Ahmed al Mustafa. On 22 February 1991 the Umma Party discussed with the SPLM the NDA Charter and, pursuant to that discussion, a joint communiqué was issued confirming the SPLM's support to 'the principles of the Charter'. However, a proviso was inserted to the effect that the SPLM had the right to revise and/or amend details. The communiqué was signed by Mubarak al Mahdi (Umma) and Commander Lual Diing Wol (SPLM).
5. Heralding the SPLM's memorandum, Garang addressed Bashir that he shouldn't think that he would get away with his clamp-down on parties and trades unions in the North. 'The SPLM is still there to lead the struggle for the restoration of democracy and institution of peace,' said Garang. That remark, according to a message received from the SCP, was not welcome. The forces of the *intifada* were well and kicking in Khartoum, said the message. Obviously, Garang could not have thought that he was going to command Khartoum's masses from Bor. He only meant to say that the SPLM had the presense within Sudan as well as the wherewithal and freedom of movement and action that would enable it to inflict harm on the regime. That it would do, not only for the cause of the South, but also for the cause of the nation as a whole. Those nuances might have escaped some elements within the SCP who saw in Garang's remark an attempt to take over the leadership role of the forces of the left.
6. The Army Legitimate Command (ALC) of the Sudan Armed Forces was formed by the Commander-in-Chief, General Fathi Ahmed Ali, and top-ranking officers Al Hadi Bushra and Abdel Rahman Said who were both retired by the NIF. General Fathi issued a declaration in London on 27 September 1990 in which he committed the ALC to fighting the NIF government, and to the restoration of democracy and establishment of peace. The ALC became part of the NDA and called on the army to revolt against the regime.
7. Jeanne Hersch, Professor of Philosophy, University of Geneva. In Ricoeur (ed.) *Philosophical Foundations of Human Rights*, p. 143. Heirsch believes that the right to life corresponds, in a sense, to 'Thou shalt not kill' in the Bible.
8. Chapter Seven, note 75.

9. Mazrui, Ali, op.cit., in Ricoeur (ed.), *Philosophical Foundations of Human Rights*, p. 253.
10. Akbar united North India and, though a Muslim, he aligned Islam to tradition in order to bring about social peace to his country. He also removed discriminatory laws against non-Muslims, ordered that boys should not marry before the age of 16, prohibited polygamy unless the wife was barren and fused Hindu and Muslim architecture and music.
11. Hamad, *Al Hayat*, Mohamed Abul Gassim Haj, 7 April 2001.
12. The Umma Party till 1991 was represented by middle-ranking party workers; its Chairman, Sadiq al Mahdi, and Secretary General, Omar Nour el Daiem, were in Sudan. The other senior party member, Mubarak al Mahdi, was holed in Tripoli, Libya, after leaving Khartoum. Egypt, at that point, refused to allow him in, in view of his alleged unfriendly attitude towards it during al Mahdi's rule. That was the time when Egypt and Libya were not on the best of terms, and the two Mahdis were known to be aligned to Libya in that friction. When that ban was lifted, Mubarak emerged in Cairo and challenged the leadership role assumed in the NDA by the DUP. He described the DUP as Umma's junior coalition partner in the overthrown government.
13. The government of Zimbabwe welcomed the meeting provided that a friendly government shared in the costs. The author was authorized by the SPLM to probe the possibility of funding for that meeting from a willing supporter. Contacts, to this effect, were made with the late Johan Holst, the Foreign Minister of Norway, who expressed his government's readiness to fund the meeting after clarification of some issues relating to the participants and the impact of the proposed meeting on the ongoing peace initiatives. In a letter to the author Holst wrote: 'I would be interested in knowing in what way the suggested meeting in Zimbabwe would relate to other peace efforts; like the Abuja talks, and to efforts to reconcile the various factions of the SPLA.'
14. Generals Fathi Ahmed Ali and el Hadi Bushra met with the SPLA High Command at Ikitos in 1991 to discuss modalities for coordinating armed struggle against the regime, including the organization of sensitization campaigns within the government forces in the South, on the objectives of that struggle.
15. SAF was originally lanuched by a group of officers who parted ways with the ALC after its failure to mobilize the Sudanese army against the regime, as it was expected to. The ALC's credibility was further dented when its third-ranking officer, General al Hadi Bushra, defected to Khartoum in August 1995, allegedly because he took exception to the endorsement by the NDA of the right of self-determination for the South. In reality, preparations for Bushra's defection were afoot since March of that year, when he secretly met in Rome with Security Chief, Nafi's Ali Nafi'a.

16. SAF was created shortly prior to the historic Asmara meeting from the splinter that resigned from the ALC as well as a medley of concerned Sudanese intellectuals belonging to the 'modern forces'. It, therefore, represents the first attempt by Northern soldiers and intellectuals to coalesce in a defined political movement. Surprisingly, SAF included Northern intellectuals who were closely cooperating with the SPLM, but were wary of openly identifying themselves with it because of the 'subversive' connotations inherent in joining an armed movement. However, by openly joining a Northern-led and equally 'subversive' military group it would, appear that the old reductive stereotypes of North / South; Arab/African and Muslim/non-Muslim still held sway, even in the minds of 'liberated' Northern intellectuals. To all appearances, SAF was viewed in Eritrea as a decisive engine of change in the North. Its leader, Brigadir Abdel Aziz Khalid, was therefore to be groomed as a Garang of the North.
17. The document was drafted by Peter Nyot Kok, Taha Ibrahim and the author.
18. The Umma was represented by its Secretary General Omar Nour El Daim and Mubarak al Mahdi, the SPLM delegation was led by Salva Kiir, the Second-in-Command of the Movement.
19. Joint communiqué between the DUP and SPLM signed in Cairo 13 July 1994 by Dr Ahmed el Sayed Hamad (DUP) and the late Commander Yousif Kuwa Jami.
20. A message from the SCP was conveyed to Garang to the effect that his declaration (5 supra) suggested that the internal popular struggle was incapacitated by the incarceration of some of its leaders; that was not true, the message said. Clear in that message was the impression of some leaders then, that Bashir's *coup* was a storm in a teacup.
21. *Al Ittihad*, Abu Dhabi, 6 April 2000.
22. The NDA forces were made up of Umma, DUP, SPLA (New Sudan Brigade), SAF, ALC, and the Beja Congress. Later on, the Federal Party joined, so did the SCP with a token representation.
23. Lesch and Wondu, *A Battle for Peace*, p.
24. G. B. Shaw, *Man and Superman*, p.
25. Taha, Mahmoud M., *Usus Dustoor al Sudan* (Basis of Sudan's Constitution).
26. Proclamation by the Executive Committee of the Anti-imperialism Front, 21 September 1954.
27. The term entity was thought to be neutral, in place of that of state or region. The former evoked the discredited federal states system created by the NIF, the latter brought to the mind of Southerns the regional government under Nimeiri to which Southerners did not look back with joy. However, in the draft constitution considered by the NDA for the interim period, the entities were called territories, a term used in Australia to denote federated states.
28. Kellas, *The Politics of*, p. 178.

29. Lijphart, *The Politics of Accommodation: Pluralism and Democracy in the Netherlands and Democracy in Plural Societies: A Comparative Exploration*.
30. Articles 1.2 and 55.1 of the United Nations Charter.
31. The resolution was adopted by 89 members with no negative vote and 10 abstentions. Those who abstained were mainly European colonial powers and South Africa.
32. UN Monthly Chronicle, Vol. 7 (February 1970), p. 36. In effect the UN Security Council, in its resolution 169 on 24 November 1961, condemned the secession of Katanga.
33. Address to the Joint Session of the Two Houses of Congress (11 February 1918). Wilson told the Congress that war 'has its roots in the disregard of the rights of small nations and of nationalities which lacked the union and the force to make good their claim to determine their own allegiance and their own forms of political life'.
34. Halperin, *Self-Determination in the New World Order*, pp. 18–19. The writer maintained that Wilson's idea was to create states that would counterbalance Russia and Germany.
35. Lansing, Robert, *The Peace Negotiations: A Personal Narrative*, pp. 97–8. Lansing was by then Secretary of State (1915–22). His views, apart from the racist tone in which they were expressed, might have been justified in practical term, since within each ethnic nationality to which the right of self-determination was granted, there were also subnationalities who had their own grievances. That, as future events have proven, represented ominous time bombs. Amazingly, while the new states were restructured or carved out from existing units under the pretext of self-determination, no plebiscite was ever conducted. That made a mockery of the exercise of the right to self-determination. See Halperin, Ibid.
36. --------
37. *American Journal of Internaitonal Law* (1988) p. 87, op. cit., in An-N'aim, *The National Question*, p. 112.
38. 34 supra, pp. 23–5.
39. Ibid., pp. 50–3
40. As Halperin observed, 'caution, inconsistencies and short-term considerations also characterized the American and, to a lesser degree, the European Community's initial response to Yugoslavia's self-determination crisis. Until hostilities broke out in mid-1991, the United States and European governments asserted uncoditional support for Yugoslav unity'. Halperin, pp. 32–7.
41. Woolf, Virginia, Three Guinies, op. cit., in Catherine Hall, *People, Nation and State*, p. 45.
42. An-N'aim, *The National Question, Secession and Constitutionalism*, p. 106.
43. The Joint Military Command (JMC) was transformed into a Unified Military Command (UMC) of the NDA forces in the eastern zone in November 1999.

44. While the *Baggara* militias (benefiting from the ceasefire), launched attacks with impunity on areas between Aweil and Meram and along the Lol River, a group of government-inspired Dinka led by NIF commander Osman Deng Akec raided the civilian population at Langic village. In the light of those raids the SPLA moved to clear the area of raiders and occupied, in the process, the Gogrial garrison. It also defeated the army garrison at Wedweil on the Lol River and cut the government's line of supplies from the North. Statement by Samson Kwaje, 26 June and 14 July 2000.
45. *The Montreal Gazette*, 29 September 2000.
46. First Vice-President, Ali Osman Taha, told a London Arabic daily that reconciliation does not mean the end of the *Ingaz*. Though be believes in pluralism, the Vice-President said, the parties are still unconvincing and accordingly 'the *Ingaz* shall create the conducive atmosphere for the emergence of political organizations that would present well articulated programmes'. *Al Hayat*, 18 May 2001.
47. Report by Roy Gutman, *Newsweek*, 31 May 2001.
48. Statement by General Mohamed Bashir Suleiman, Army Spokesman, Sudan TV, 6 June 2001.
49. *AFP*, 17 November 2000 and *Al Hayat*, 18 November 2000.
50. *Al Hayat*, 15 November 2001.
51. Chapter Nine, supra, note 122.
52. Representatives of the European Union submitted a resolution to the 67th session of the UN Human Rights Commission (April 2001) in which they called, *inter alia*, for a comprehensive ceasefire. The US delegate to the Commission voted against the resolution maintaining that it was too soft given the regime's continued violations of human rights and the laws of war. The resolution was hailed by the government.
53. *Al Hayat*, 23 May 2001, quoting the Khartoum daily *Akhbar al Yom*
54. In a statement issued by the SPLM Spokesman Yassir Arman (25 April 2000), the Movement announced that it was ready to accept an immediate comprehensive ceasefire conditional on the government's acceptance of the suspension of all oil operations in Sudan till a peaceful agreement is reached.
55. The conditions included withdrawal of government forces to the North while leaving SPLA forces in all areas presently under its control, a confederal status for the two areas, external monitoring and proceeding with the exercise of self-determination.

CHAPTER ELEVEN
Conclusion

> *A man of destiny knows that beyond the hill lies another and another. The journey is never complete.*
>
> **F. W. De Klerk**[1]

No Sudanese at the dawn of this new century, except the inapprehensive, can look back at the last half century with congratulation. For almost half a century, instability in Sudan had never been an occasional occurrence; it was repetitive history. The country is now entering another century with its burdensome load of problems. And though Sudan has been recognized by many commentators as one of Africa's most promising countries, its situation today is so woeful that even those who divined a bright future for it, virtually assume that its future has come and gone by. Some who sang its praises in the past have sadly ended singing its requiem.[2] As for the still hopeful, they are about to conclude that Sudan is the country of the future, and it shall always be. Those damning judgements were provoked by recurring crises wrought by Sudanese leaders upon themselves and their country. From the history we have reviewed, those crises were neither god-ordained nor results of astral influences. They are all man-made. The basic flaw rests on a socio-political paradigm that has been taken for granted by a large section of the Northern elite. Because of this flawed paradigm, Sudanese democracy had, since independence, a potential for crisis.

The crises, however, are much more complex than some may wish to think or are given to believe. For decades, politicians and scholars were every so often informed in their analysis of Sudan's crises by the reductive stereotypes of race and religion. Those are very important factors, as we have abundantly proven, but taken by themselves they shall not unravel the Sudanese puzzle. There are historical, sociological, economic, political, and personal strands enmeshed in the quandary. To that, since the emergence of the NIF regime, an international dimension is supplemented and to which we have made reference. Nevertheless, at the heart of Sudan's multiple crises is the inability of the majority of Northern and Southern elites to realize what makes of them one nation. This blankness to reality triggered action-reaction cycles that virtually made of Sudan two countries sharing a geographic space known in the atlases of geography and the fiction of international law as the State of Sudan. Both Northern and Southern elites are still to extricate themselves from mythical views about themselves, if the

Sudan is to be genuinely united for the interest of all its sons and daughters as well as for that of regional stability.

Identity, for better for worse, is a subjective notion created by man. It is not 'woven in the loom of fate'. Notwithstanding, it is also the result of sociocultural interactions among peoples as well as of layers of social mouldings by historical and environmental factors. Sudanese social historians seldom venture to excavate this geological formation of the Sudanese personality. Steadily, they gloss it over by recalcitrant myths that are unworthy of credit. But then, seldom do men have the wisdom or common sense to examine the myths they have created about themselves. And as Russell observed 'Nothing is more incredible than the daily effort of believing things about oneself which daily become incredible.'[3] In Sudan, the downside of this subjectively bred notion of identity is reflected in multiform complexes of superiority and inferiority. It has also led to delusive images about the self and divisive policies towards the South. The latter was exhibited, on the one hand, in divide and rule tactics, attempts at forcible acculturation and perpetuation of political disempowerment and economic marginalization. On the other, it was dramatized in endless breaking of promises and riding roughshod over solemn undertakings. As a result, Southerners began to perceive an ambush in every Northern move towards reconciliation, however genuine that move was. Furthermore, despite the prolix lip service paid to the concept of cultural diversity, the Northern elite neither appreciated the depth of meaning of that concept, nor cared to ponder the price that its recognition would entail. Innate primordial feelings and the desire to protect vested interests hindered such appreciation.

What is more alarming is inadequacy in contrition for past misdeeds. Many of us in the North seem to think that if the South has suffered in the past, then history alone was to blame. But for every marginalized, there is a marginalizer, every oppressed an oppressor and every underdog an overdog. More than contrition for past misdeeds, the situation craves for a Truth and Reconciliation investigation like South Africa's and Argentina's. There, the aim was not to criminalize the past or pursue wrongdoers, but to investigate scrupulously the catalogue of misdeeds on both sides so as to cleanse themselves, 'sooth the sorrows and heel the wounds'. This is the only way that the shady pages in our history can be expiated and genuine reconciliation achieved. Desmond Tutu, who presided over the Truth and Reconciliation Commission in South Africa, described the process as one of restorative, not punitive, justice. Evidently, those who have brutalized innocent people or mercilessly slain them in Bashir's abattoir shall have nowhere to hide. Bygones may be bygones in Sudan, but in the broader world Sudan's brutalizers and terminators shall not be saved from the Pinochet treatment. Crimes against humanity are now collectively abjured by the world community where bygones are no longer left for themselves. Beyond this caveat, we must grow up and be sensible. That we owe to our country and ourselves. As a Kenyan bishop said about the post-Moi era: 'There is no justice so severe that it cannot be tempered with mercy. If we are unable to do it for nobler reasons, then let us at least, and for once, differentiate between focus and fixation. Let us be a people that will be strong enough to count our losses, draw the line and forge ahead.'[4]

In the course of the last two decades religion became the bane of Sudanese politics, but while Nimeiri's Islamization became an object of ridicule, that of the NIF had a sinister side to it. For their first seven years in government, the NIF was fatuously pleased with itself. It has conquered power, subdued the Sudanese people and then arrogated to itself the right to chart a brighter future for the Sudanese as well as for others beyond Sudan's borders. That future was theoretically predicated on a glorious past, but the past Sudan's neo-Islamists yearned to recreate was not Sudan's multifaceted Islamic past. It was one bred of fancy. To nobody's surprise, therefore, half way through the NIF years of the locust, Sudan became a tatty patchwork of confusion. The NIF even failed to do justice even to the past they wished to recreate. It did not make sense to any right- thinking person that the only way to uphold Allah's word was by covering women's heads and chopping off people's limbs. The NIF had absolutely nothing Islamic to say about the things that matter most to people in real life. As a result, the NIF's much heralded agenda was irreversibly weakened, and their utopia turned out to be a miserable dystopia. That does not mean that religion-based ideologies can be wished away, as it means that those who genuinely adhere to, and wish to propagate, religion-inspired politics should only do this by presenting viable Islamic alternatives that address real issues and that do not undermine the human, just and noble character of religion. They should also play politics according to the rules of the game of multipartism. Those rules, we repeat, are governed by the will of the people and based on priorly agreed upon touchstones. Indeed, the NDA ruled that parties in future Sudan shall no longer be based on religion or ethnicity. The intention is neither to banish religion from society, nor to wish away ethnicity, but to debar the monopolization of religion and its exploitation by any party for selfish or partisan ends. This reality has at long last dawned on Turabi, but not yet on his surrogate, Bashir. Turabi was reported to have said to one of his very close aides that the 'edifice we have been creating for nearly forty years has now crumbled'.

In other parts of the world the NIF brand of government may be described as totalitarian or fascist. Inescapably, the catalogue of horrors committed by the NIF and narrated in this book conclusively justify that appellation. Parties which brook such tendencies are not only condemned by the civilized world, but are also denied a place in any respectable society. For example, in 1952 German Chancellor Konrad Adenaeur proscribed the Socialist Reich Party because it resembled the discredited Nazi Party. And in November 2000, the German Upper House of Parliament (Bundesrat) voted to support a ban by the Socialist Democratic Party of the neo-fascist National Democratic Party. The decision came after a quarter of a million Germans demonstrated in Berlin against the sinister activities of that party. [5] Germany has experienced fascism as nobody else has, and it was for the sake of a healthy growth of democracy that it was forced to banish nucleating fascism.

Fascists, as history teaches us, have nothing but contempt for universal rights and natural law. Invariably they pretend to know better than anybody else what is good for mankind. In Sudan, even after they were proven wrong in almost every possible step, the country's Islamo-fascists went the additional mile and threatened people with annihilation if they did not yield to their political paradigm, a matter they were provenly qualified for. But, when all is said and done, all that the NIF was able to bequeath to Sudan was destitution, a culture of violence and a psychosis of fear. How much more should go wrong before Turabi's surrogates realized that the country was not ready to have any more of the religio-political philosophy they wished to impose on it.

Those who believe that the regime the Sudan endured for a decade was simply an authoritarian regime like the ones the country has gone through before under Abboud and Nimeiri are grossly mistaken. The NIF version of fascism cannot even be graced by that appellation: fascism. Its style of governance is no less than the bureaucratization of villainy. As for its Islamist claim, it is suspect beyond measure. Religion invests in its adherents benevolence, temperance and nobleness. Any religion that does not confer such virtues on those who put faith in it is no religion. The NIF has killed, tortured and brutalized people in the name of religion. By such acts it caused infinite damage to Islam. And so long as the NIF and its goons are so proud of having their hands incarnadined with the blood of innocent people, neither the Islamists inside Sudan, nor those outside it who take pride in Sudan's Islamist experience, have any reason to expect people to believe that Islam is compassionate. In the face of such ugly realities, reciting the Qur'an, chapter and verse, in defense of their model is not good enough to convince true Muslims that the NIF regime has anything to do with Islam. As to be expected, therefore, the NIF regime became the butt of the Sudanese people's hatred, decried for its cynicism, abominated for its wanton violence and scorned for its abuse of religion. Nevertheless, the NIF reign of terror was also a blessing in disguise. For anyone who may wish henceforth to reincarnate a religious state in a united Sudan need look no further than the NIF's Sudan. The need for separating religion from politics has never been as urgent as it is today.

This reality of the Sudanese situation has not yet dawned on some foreign friends of Sudan (particularly in Western Europe). Perhaps it did, but out of their own self-interest they are in a hurry to find a quick fix for Sudan's intractable conflict that has defied mediators for decades, so that they resume business with the country's odious regime. The London *Economist* was not off the mark when it wrote that, 'to some Western diplomats, Sudan without Turabi, but with improved human rights record and flush with oil money is a country thay can do business with'.[6] Following this argument, the European desire to create a sense of inevitability in doing business with the regime is dubious. Even if one gives them the benefit of doubt, things in Sudan are not that easy. The NIF's is not the type of regime that can be brought to order with a slap on the wrist. Besides, Uganda, Kenya and Abacha's Nigeria were upbraided for much less by those very countries who are in a hurry to legitimize the NIF. The underpinnings of sustainable peace and healthy democracy are not issues that can be skirted by anybody who is concerned with stability in Sudan. At the top of those are the issues of religion and state, multipartism and respect for universally acknowledged human rights. Indeed, if India's democracy is as thriving and sturdy as it is today, it is only because of the integration of secularism in the country's democratic culture. One wonders what the position of Islamists of all hue would have been were the Indian fathers of independence to have succumbed to calls by Indian fundamentalists for the creation of a Hindu state, a proposition justified in the view of Hindus by the fact that nearly 80 per cent of India's population adhered to that religion and culture. If they had, that would have inexorably reduced the other 20 per cent (including over 100 million Muslims who represented the world's second-largest Muslim population in one country after Indonesian) to a status of second-class citizens. Would the Sudanese Islamists, whose policies virtually reduced Sudanese non-Muslims (one-third of Sudan's population) to that class, have accepted the administration of the same medicine on fellow Indian Muslims?

Since the materialization of the SPLM/A in 1983, there has been a sea change within Sudan's body politic, at least at the level of political thought and perception. Issues that were deemed inviolable are now discussed in broad daylight: religion and politics, national identity, self-determination and voluntary unity. A cursory look at Sudan parliament's Hansard and general political treatises since independence reveals that the discussion of those issues was almost tabooed, and those who delved into them were ostracized. Also few, if any, Northern Sudanese scholars had the temerity to throw those issues open to enquiry. The ideas launched by the SPLM/A became the trailblazers for the KDD and the Asmara Resolutions. This is not a mean achievement in a landscape populated by political predators who are provenly incapable of capturing the mood of the time. In this way, the Asmara compact is the only lighthouse that beacons the way to the future. It also signals the death of the old political Sudan. But instead of burying the hatchet, some political predators still hope against hope to resurrect the old Sudan from the dead. But given the changes in the political landscape triggered by the SPLM/SPLA and carried further by the marginalized in East and Central Sudan as well as the Northern political and social forces who acceded to the KDD, no one can turn the clock back to 29 June 1989, try hard as one might. The political predators who were impelled by expediency to espouse the Asmara Resolutions while harbouring other designs would soon discover that they have got their sums wrong. Support by the Sudanese to erstwhile leaders is not frozen in time.

In addition, both the NIF and Sadiq al Mahdi made a habit of vilifying the SPLM and its leader for their 'insincerity' on the issue of unity. To the utter amazement of the SPLM, some elements within the 'modern forces' joined that chorus.[7] However, to Sadiq al Mahdi and the NIF, Garang became the residual offender; he was accused of whatever had gone wrong on the war and peace fronts. Oftentimes, condemnation is not even based on circumstancial evidence, but only on instinct. Garang, for example, is faulted for the failure of the peace soundings initiated by Nimeiri, Swar al Dhahab, al Mahdi and Bashir. In the meantime, it has never suggested itself to Garang's critics that he had also successfully concluded agenda for peace with the National Alliance Front in 1986 during Swar al Dhahab's reign, with al Mirghani in 1988 during al Mahdi's government, and with the totality of the Northern parties under the umbrella of the NDA in 1995. Nor did it flash through their minds that he was consistent in the benchmarks he had set for peace and unity in all those agreements. His demur, therefore, was a result of substantive not behavioural considerations. In that the SPLM leader was open and above board. He neither lost the threads in the course of eighteen years nor did he move the goal posts. To the contrary, it was his critics who always wanted the post shifted. Surely, it was not so much the recalcitrance of the SPLM leader, in as much as it was is insistence on standing firm by the benchmarks established since 1986, that raised the hackles of his reprovers. Garang put his finger on the sore spot and made the 'sole' owner of the land think of the unthinkable. His detractors in effect failed to understand three things. The first is that the standards he has jeld aloft for those eighteen years are now solemnly enshrined in the Asmara Resolutions. Without commitment to the words and spirit of those resolutions, there shall be neither peace nor unity. The second is that Garang assertively proved to both Northern and Southern constituencies that he was not a commodity for sale. The Northern political class, which is accustomed to buying off Southern politicians (including some so-called liberation warriors), may now have to realize that they are dealing with a leader who has to be convinced, not suborned. Southerners who thought that he was out to defeat 'Arab' domination and then hand over an independent South to political predators were in for a surprise. Thirdly, Northerners who abides in treating him as an enemy of the North, need to realize that by continuing to treat anyone as the enemy, he shall eventually become one. Paradoxically, Southern separatists should be the ones who have to take issue with Garang's political construct. The manoeuvres of the Northern political class to undermine the basic tenets of new Sudanism necessarily corroborate and buttresses separatists claims that 'unity on a new basis' is the last thing that the Northern political class is ready to accede to.

Indeed, if Garang's critics are sincere in exorcing the demon of war, they will have to uphold sincerely the principles they have solemnly adhered to in 1986 (KDD), April 1989 (under the government of Sadiq al Mahdi) and 1994 (IGAD/DOP) under Bashir. Extraordinarily, the bizarre paradox of the Sudan situation, as *The Economist* rightly reported, is that a 'National government committed to self-determination for the Southern provinces, is fighting a long bitter war to keep the country together, against a South separatists rebellion committed to retaining national unity'.[8] To Southerners, this wavering on solemnly undertaken commitments is not new. They have lived with it since 1956. Thus prudence dictates that, after four decades of misery, Northern politics towards the South should change course. And though prudence in politics is one of the most supreme virtues, disconsolately, some Northern politicians never disappoint in behaving imprudently.

The Asmara Resolutions, nevertheless, are the high water mark in contemporary Sudanese politics and, therefore, remain to be the only guiding post. Even the NDA's adversaries (the NIF) were constrained to pay lip-service to them. What do the Asmara resolutions mean? Obviously, they are neither the Ark of the Covenant, nor are they written in stone. Still, to those who took them seriously, they represented a major shift in politics that would set the stage for the Sudan of the twenty-first century: a Sudan in which ethnic disparities are reconciled; religions are made ecumenical; the marginalized are socially and economically uplifted and their insecurities toned down; the political playing ground is made level for all players; democracy is institutionalized in a way that shall make it sustainable; political discourse becomes more civilized and politics, in general, practiced with a spirit of social responsibility. Also, as long as probity in public life and professional ethics in the different callings are not upheld, then no end shall be in sight for Sudan's political instability.

Furthermore, the Asmara agenda is a thesis for peace and unity, and its counter-thesis is war, disunity and disintegration of whatever is left of Sudan. Unity, however, does not end by keeping the North and South voluntarily together; it equally extends to both components of the country. The insalubrious tribal fights ignited by avaricious politicians in the South in the last decade are indictors of worse things to come, even if the North and South parted ways. So is the repulsive exploitation by self-interested Northern politicians of conflicts among postaralists over water and grazing rights. So, in addition to the creation of people-based mechanisms for resolving tribal conflicts, self-seeking fomenters of such conflicts must be identified and publicly shamed by the civil society. Only when all that is achieved shall swords be turned into plowshares.

The Asmara compact also reflects a consensus on multi-party democracy as the safer option for a politically multifaceted country like Sudan. The chances for the survival of democracy in a united Sudan are much brighter if peace is attained. And as we have endeavored to show, the military were often goaded into politics by the failure of civilian governments to put and end to Sudan's civil war in which the army (and not the politicians) was the one consistently bearing the brunt. Democracy hence has a better chance for survival when a comprehensive peace is assured. But democracy in Sudan has other problems inherent in sectarian divides and the virtual assumption by some leaders that they have a birthright to rule Sudan, a right about which they seem to give the impression that it is ingrained in their DNA. The current behaviour of some leaders points to that direction. That should not be so, nor does such attitude accord with the spirit of the time.

Disconsolately, dialogue on democracy within Sudan's political circles much so often was centred on institutions, procedures, personal ties and expedient alliances that would maintain governments in office – never on the culture and ethics of democracy, or on what politicians and political parties wanted to achieve through it. The long and short of it, no democracy can be sustained if politics continued to be the same old brute creation, vacuous and intuitive. The vacuity of the Sudanese political discourse is indeed bewildering. The culture of democracy runs much deeper than popular elections, freedom of association and apportionment of ministerial posts. No party has really engaged in a serious debate on the crisis of democracy beyond the above limited parameters. Moreover, despite the blatant lack of enduring achievements by political parties since October 1964 on all those issues, parties proved to be stubbornly immune to self-doubt. No one, to be sure, expects them to engage in self-flagellation, but only in serious introspection and soul searching. Even today, despite their strenuous struggle to recapture power, the parties are desperately short of anything meaningful to tell the people over whom they want to exercise power, about what they shall do with that power once they wrest it from whomever is exercising it. This points to a dire lack of both goal orientation and respect for the electorate. The electorate in democracy are not supplicants, but are the arbiters of the nation's political fate.

This unfavorable verdict also applies to ideologically based political parties which, much so often, paraded their ideological verities as synchronous with national interests. To them, it seemed to matter not if their ideological touchstones were relevant to the realities on the ground, or to the obtaining sociocultural infrastructure in the country. Religious adherence to those touchstones blurred the vision of ideologically based parties from seeing how Sudan's socio-cultural realities impinged on politics. Doubtless, the ideologically based parties should be accredited with imbuing Sudan's fallow politics with an intellectual back-stopping. But in real life they underachieved because their analysis of the Sudanese situation was often distorted by the rigidity of the models they wanted to impose on it, and the tools of analysis they unswervingly applied to it. In this respect declarations by the SCP that it was reviewing both its ideological verities and even its name is sign of political maturity and courage.[9]

Be that as it may, on political organization in general, the Asmara compact has taken the bull by the horns when it stipulated, in a draft law on political organization, that political parties in the future should be tested by their adherence to the very maxims to which the Alliance is committed: internal democracy buttressed by periodic congresses, policy programmes in the form of party platforms, respect for universal human rights, accountability of party leaders to their constituencies and transparency including disclosure of the parties' sources of funding. In absence of those restraining parameters, political leaders shall continue to enjoy impermissible levels of impunity. Equally, leadership at all levels should be assumed to be a professional calling for which one should have the acumen and training, not a birthright or a reward for partisan services done. That, of course, is not to say that parties should not reward their most ardent activists; they should. Nonetheless, for the parties to succeed, they should be guided in their selection of high office holders by considerations of probity, acuity and talent. When those attributes are discounted, any political non-entity shall be a winner. Truly, no man should be expected to do better than his best, but every so often the best of those who were catapulted to power in the recent past – whether for familial or partisan considerations – was provenly not enough. Not a few of them came to the top without really trying. Sudan deserves better and the parties – for their own self-interest – deserve it, too. Above all, the issue of probity in public life should not be underestimated, as often has been the case. In fact, due to the deflation of that issue by past regimes, a social psychology of impunity was created. Sometimes that made heros of thieves. This, no doubt, undermines democracy since it demolishes one of its most robust pillars: accountability. It also frustrates the rule of law, which is another fundamental pillar of democracy. For instance, on the penal side, the law ordains that any conduct that unjustifiably inflicts substantial harm on any individual or the society must be punished.

Some of the realities of the Sudanese situation might be disconcerting to the 'modern forces' who recurrently bewailed their exclusion from the corridors of power by traditional parties. But in the Sudan we know, democracy is an arduous call and multi-party democracy is more so. The traditional parties positively remain to be tribal and sectarian fiefs, but that is no reason for the 'modern forces' to jump out of their skin. In politics, you start with the socialization there is. Popular support to the 'modern forces' shall only come through hard and serious struggle, as well as palpable proof of viability as an alternative to existing power structures. Given the record of failure of the old politics and the persistence of some of the old players to revert *ad libitum* to their bad old ways, the boundaries of political allegiance are apt to shift. After all, democracy is neither a panacea nor an instant event. It is a process. The 'modern forces' may therefore wish to think of ditching the pretence of being the government-in-waiting and act like the torch-bearers for change. This is the only way to make them increasingly weightful in the popular support scale.

Nowhere is this change more urgent than in the sphere of civil society organizations. Evidently, the underdevelopment of the society did not enable civil society organizations to emerge as entities completely independent of the state and free from partisan manipulation. That was indeed a function of the weakness of the organizations themselves. For instance, the inability of civil society organizations to sustain themselves through their own resources is a direct result of their dependence on the state. Almost all of Sudan's civil society organizations are comprised of government-employed professionals and workers. Even organizations that comprise workers in liberal professions such as lawyers failed to have autonomous income generating activities. Moreover, the lack of success of those organizations in creating permanent channels of interaction and consultation between their leadership and grassroots constituencies increasingly drove them to dependence on party channels for that purpose.

Historically, the concept of civil society evolved as an outgrowth of Rousseau's social contract: a society of free citizens aligned against monarchical absolute rule and church hegemony. As a matter of course, that concept was conflictual. Through the years, the concept developed in a manner that subtilized its conflictual nature. Within liberal democracies, civil society organizations have now virtually become agents for peaceful resolution of political and socio-economic crises. However, certain distinctions need to be made. In essence, civil society organizations were created to intermediate between the public man and the state. As such, the interests they served were meant to be beyond those of its members, i.e. to be of concern to the public man. But as it is applied today, the term also refers to interest groups whose main duty is to protect the interests of their own members. In effect, those groups were often referred to as interest pressure groups. Notwithstanding, Sudan's civil society organizations will have to wean themselves away from the conflictual culture of anti-colonial struggle in which they were brought up and where the state was deemed to be the enemy. The order of the day in a national democratic multi-party system should be the espousal of a culture of peaceful struggle guided by agreed upon codes of conduct and temporized by a sense of social responsibility. The civil society concept provides a space for crisis management through negotiations, consensus, mediation and ultimately public adjudgement expressing the popular will through free and fair elections.

Democracy, on the other hand, is a meeting point which accommodates all schools of thought, excepting extreme radicals of the right and left who assume that their ideological verities are incontrovertible and that they alone have the monopoly of truth. Thus, as overseers of the process of democracy, civil society organizations should never be viewed, as some tend to be, as the modern-day correlative of the so-called 'democratic forces' of the 1960s. That was a pseudonym for politicized – sometimes ideologized – conglomerations that were generally guided by the Communist Party. Indeed, apart from political parties and trades unions (which are both focused interest groups), genuine civil society organizations like human rights organizations, environmental groups, child-protection societies, humanitarian relief organizations etc. should, by their very nature, be free from political affiliation or party or state domestication. This is the way those organizations have developed in the countries where the concept emerged and flourished. Their main role is to occupy the space between the state and the public man as vehicles of intermediation between the state and society and for the articulation of issues of public concern. Without that autonomy they could not have developed into viable intermediators in liberal democracies between the state and the public man. Liberal democracy has its own rules and any attempt to smuggle into that pattern of democracy, concepts or practices alien to it, shall not only undermine the popular oversight role of the civil society organizations, but also aborts democracy itself.

Another cumbersome problem that awaits Sudan's future leaders is the serious generational gap. Forty per cent of Sudan's population at the beginning of this century were reported to be below 18 years of age. According to UNICEF statistics (1997), out of Sudan's total population of

28,098 thousands, 14,215 thousands are under age 18. Not discounting the hundreds of thousands Southern Sudanese who were deprived of education for two decades, or those who left their professions to engage in combat, the burgeoning number of the young creates a serious problem for tomorrow's rulers. In addition, the new generation of young Sudanese men and women have a different outlook to life and social values contrasting to those of older generations. Consequently, they should not be overwhelmed by bygone politics. They have the right to be given the space in which to constitute their own history. That shall not be achieved through studding party offices with pro-forma young men, but above all by enabling the young to be heard and to influence decisions, especially those relating to their own future. Our generation has colonized the past, and humility alone dictates that we should not aspire to colonize the future also. Those like Sadiq al Mahdi who still look forward to a third coming are aspiring for a feat not contemplated by Christ himself. Moreover, the politics of independence which is ubiquitous in the parties' political discourse and is still hinged on who hoisted the flag of independence or who led the country to it, is meaningless to the new generation. Leaders who are still caught up in such politics of the past are not only irrelevant to the present, they also give the impression of suffering from a political degenerative disease. Indeed, if all what half of Sudan's population have got from independence is more than forty years of war and wretchedness, then there is not much for them to rejoice about.

The old political Sudan is dead and, in the ordinary course of things, the new shall be born. This unyielding optimism is anchored on the belief that the new generation of Sudanese – those who own half the present and all the future – yearn for a better future. Many of them had given the ultimate sacrifice for its realization in the battlefields, both in armed struggle and civil strife for the protection of human rights. Those who are possessed by pessimism about the emergence of a new Sudan are no less than hard-boiled skeptics with little faith in humanity. Unwittingly, they put themselves in league with the detractors of New Sudanism because they are affrayed by what it shall bring in its trail: threats to vested interests and inherited supremacy. It is ironic that over a century ago, Lord Cromer midwifed a New Sudan. His was a creature of opportunism. Cromer, after the conclusion of the Condominium Agreement, wrote: 'after this fashion, the new Sudan was born. It was endowed with sufficient strength to support its existence. Nevertheless, it was of necessity to some extent, the child of opportunism. Should it eventually die and make place for some more robust, because more real, political creation, its authors have no reason to wail its fate'.[10] The New Sudanists positively have less reason to wail the fate of Cromer's old/new Sudan. But they are also aware that whoever shall midwife the New Sudan of the twenty-first century must know that the labour shall not be easy.

ENDNOTES

1. The *Observer*, London, 1994.
2. Millard Burr, J., and Collins, Robert O., *Requiem for the Sudan, War, Draught and Disaster Relief on the Nile.*
3. The Observer, 1943.
4. Reverend Mutava Musyimi, Secretary General of the Kenyan National Council of Churches, *Sunday Nation*, Nairobi, 6 May 2001.
5. The *Sunday Telegraph*, 12 November 2000.
6. *The Economist*, 19 August 2000.
7. The SCP issued a public statement on 26 May 2001 in which it took issue with the SPLM's position paper regarding conditions for a comprehensive ceasefire (Ch. 9) . It described the conditions set by the Movement as urealistic and went on to insinuate that the Movement appeared to have a hidden agenda. The call for instant confederation, the SCP said, went contrary to the meaning given to confederalism by the Asmara Resolutions. In response to that statement, the SPLM explained that the Asmara Resolutions were irrelevant to the negotiations with the government, since those resolutions were predicated on removing the NIF from the political position it occupied and establishing in place of the *ancien régime,* a new system of rule and constitutional order defined by the resolutions. It also added that 'after eleven years of arduous negotiations with the government, the SPLM leadership affirms that it is unfailingly pursuing its work for Sudan's unity on new basis and according to the voluntary will of its people. It shall not accept anything short of a just and comprehensive peace that shall put an end for ever to war.'
8. 6 supra.
9. Shafie Khidir, a leading member of the SCP told *al Shark al Awsat* (29 April 2001) that the party shall abandon Marxist verities and probably change its name.
10. *Modern Egypt*, vol. 2, p. 119.

POSTSCRIPT

What sort of peacemaking has Sudan tried not; mediation, direct negotiations between belligerents, indirect talks through the good offices of mutual friends, reconciliation between government and erstwhile warriors, intellectual probing of conflictual issues in internationally sponsored for a, etc. Nevertheless, seldom did peace look more remote and elusive. One reason, probably, was that the only thing the parties did not cogitate was retracting their steps from entrenched positions in order to see what had gone wrong in the first place. Another reason was the incapacity of the parties to carry, to their logical conclusions, the hypotheses on peace they had espoused. On the one hand, the government fantasized that a comprehensive peaceful settlement could be achieved even if the present power structures remained intact. On the other, the opposition (particularly the Northern parties) rightly observed that never in history was a totalitarian regime dislodged through moral persuasion or patriotic exhortations, and hence defined means of struggle to unseat the regime. However, that struggle was virtually left to the SPLM/A.

However, in the last round of peacemaking it was thought that a comprehensive political settlement of the conflict was given a new impetus by the Joint Egyptian–Libyan Initiative (JELI). The nine-point memorandum presented by the two countries was 'unconditionally' accepted by the government,[1] while the NDA (including the SPLM) made it clear to the mediators that their acceptance of that memorandum was contingent on a mutual comprehension of four points:

1. The absence of any reference in the document to the right to self-determination was a source of concern to the NDA, especially that there was agreement on the matter by all parties (including the government).
2. The issue of relationship between religion and politics, which had no place in the memorandum, remained to be a cardinal issue in the conflict. The positions of both the NDA and the SPLM on that issue were made abundantly clear to the government and mediators.
3. Coordination between JELI and the IGAD was necessary so as not to give occasion to multi-track peacemaking.
4. The NDA's understanding of the interim arrangements was that they encompassed a government of national consensus based on a constitution, laws and institutions priorly agreed upon by all parties.

The regime's 'unconditional' acceptance came after two days of intense deliberations within government organs. In fact, the regime's spontaneous reaction to JELI was negative. The hesitation was a first indication that the regime's acceptance was a tactical decision. For instance, the NIF had always sought an exit from IGAD and, plausibly, it might have seen in the JELI initiative an escape route from IGAD. It may be recalled that Bashir initiated IGAD in 1993 to avoid Abuja. The Abuja forum itself was opened to shut down the American Cohen initiative. One may thus assume that the regime was not sincerely committed to JELI, if only because it included a provision for free and fair multi-party elections.

At all events, by accepting the JELI memorandum both parties conceded something. The NDA, on the one hand, has abdicated its original political plank formulated in Asmara (Asmara resolutions, 1995). That position implied the removal of the NIF so as to provide the NDA with the political space in which it would carry out its agenda. The NDA, then, argued that the professed policies of the regime, as well as its practices, were inimical to democracy and thus represented an impediment to the creation of a New Sudan free from all political, cultural and economic hegemonies. The NIF, on the other hand, had also descended from its high horse. In its early years in office, the NIF who readily negotiated with the SPLM/A had only disdain for the Northern opposition. It even dared that opposition to resort to force, if it was to recover power at all. In the process of time, the NDA intensified its political and diplomatic campaigns to isolate the regime internally and externally and eventually did what the regime thought it would never do: resort to arms. Ten years down the line, the regime began to realize the futility of its sabre-rattling and ventured, through different mediators, to talk to the Northern opposition parties, at first severally and later collectively. Besides, the regime engaged in a series of sterile bluffs: creating endless peace committees and think-tanks to deliberate on JELI's memorandum. But, as it transpired later, the regime's peace policy had fewer thinks and more tanks.

Logically, one would have expected the regime to retract its steps from the perilous route of confrontation in order to come to a half-way house with the opposition. But logic is not normally associated with dogmatists, especially those of the infallibilist brand. For no sooner had the regime declared its 'unconditional' acceptance of the JELI memorandum, than it went into a rampage of intimidation against the very parties it was supposedly desirous to make peace with. In an address to new recruits for the NIF popular militia, Bashir welcomed the peace initiative but plainly stated that he was not ready to pay the price for it. 'If the price for peace is separation of religion from politics or dismantling the state created by the *Ingaz*, we shall have nothing to do with it,' he said. Bashir also added, 'Our martyrs have given the utmost sacrifice to protect the *Ingaz* and we are ready to follow suit.' The NIF constitution, he said, 'shall remain, so shall the institutions formed according to it'.[2] Nearly two weeks later the Sudanese president declared, with stupendous arrogance, that 'future Sudan shall never be a return to past political formations'.[3] Yet, his most astounding statement came in a press interview with a London Arabic daily in which he affirmed that his government 'shall not separate religion from politics *even if all other political parties* called for it'.[4] It was therefore unsurprising to hear the Sudanese president telling another Arabic London daily that his regime would not even consider discussing the issue of religion and politics, and was ready to 'confront the enemies of peace militarily, politically and diplomatically?'[5] Those are revealing statements, but 'revealing' is a dismally insufficient word to describe Bashir's mind-set at that time.

No one would have had any quarrel with Bashir and his NIF supporters to continue religiously believing in their exploded political model. There is sufficient evidence in this book to prove the regime's obduracy, as well as Bashir's own antediluvian approach to politics and social issues. On some of those issues Bashir's approach had not only endured but also verged into the absurd.[6] The question, therefore, is not so much about the malapropism of the NIF's ground plan, as it is about its ostensible belief that it has the right to impose that plan on the Sudanese people, even when they have demonstrably had enough of it. Those statements revealed beyond doubt that the NIF was not seeking a just peace, but total surrender by the NDA. Such unquestioned belief by the regime in its invincibility promised trouble to the peace effort. Furthermore, that stance hardly rang true with the regime's claim to have been converted to multi-partism and to the principle of supremacy of the will of the people. Khartoum's plastic democrats, it would seem, were still very far from conceding the legitimacy of the age-old maxim *salus populi suprema lex* (the will of the people is supreme). As a result of the NIF's equivocation on cardinal issues, the NDA justifiably concluded that, with that mind-set, the NIF regime was not best placed to usher Sudan into multi-partism or to achieve a just peace. For what knows of peace, he who only hegemony and totalitarianism know and consistently reaffirm.

Despite the above, religion was not the only reason why the NIF took such extreme positions, nor was it the most determinant. For one thing, there was fear and trepidation within the regime's security circles whose cupboards were replete with skeletons. Little wonder Bashir's recalcitrant stance towards just peace was mainly supported (indeed instigated and encouraged) by the hardened sinners of the NIF security agencies, reportedly with Vice-President Ali Osman Mohamed Taha at their head.[7] Had those sinners any degree of conscience or moral sensitivity, they would have been driven by sleepless nights and tortured souls to abandon power. Instead, they continued pushing Bashir to the brink, fearing that some of their gruesome misdeeds would never go unpunished, if the reins of power were handed to a regime over which they had no control. Equally important was the NIF's determination to hold to the wealth Sudan was expected to amass from oil revenues; in their eyes, Sudan and the NIF were indivisible. Bashir himself said that it would be unthinkable to consider sharing power 'when we have our tankers at the port exporting petroleum'.[8] In the mind of the Khartoum ruling elite, it would appear, access to national wealth and power derived, not from rights of citizenship, but from the might of whoever had the muscle.

Additionally, Bashir failed to see that the record of the NIF government was a glaringly embarrassing experience that should be erased from memory. It was neither the regime's opponents, nor the outside world, that had sculptured the regime's evil image. Its own wrathful policies did. Those policies would remain as the NIF's exposed nerve, but that seemed to have no weight on the minds of some of its leaders. Only by facing up to its blood-stained past and acknowledging it as such, might the Sudanese grudgingly forgive the NIF's crimes against humanity without depriving aggrieved individuals from seeking judicial redress for their grievances. Contrition and penance are essential ingredients for any reconciliation.

All the same, the regime laboured unceasingly to persuade JELI mediators to bring pressure to bear on Northern Sudanese opposition leaders living abroad to return to the country. Were they to do so, the NIF leaders repeatedly declared, those leaders would find a blissful Sudan where all freedoms were guaranteed and all men and women went as they pleased. But while those fairy tales were spun, the regime's *âmes dommnées* spared no pain in harassing opponents and showed no tolerance towards anything they considered an irritant in that blissful Sudan.

In reality, the so-called religious agenda for which Bashir was ready to die as a martyr dwindled to a set of slogans used only as a tool of intimidation. For example, according to the regime's 1995 constitution, political rights no longer hinged on religious affiliation but on citizenship. Also, the ruling party had disrobed itself of any Islamic cloak when it opened doors to non-Muslims to occupy its highest echelons. Likewise, reference to Islam as the religion of the state was expunged from the constitution. To the unsuspecting, those changes should be assumed to represent a sea-change in the NIF's policy, but the reality was different. The regime, in effect, continued with its war in the south and endured in calling it *jihad*. Young school leavers were still hauled from their schools and homes to be dispatched to fight Allah's war in the south, east and west.

Even so, the ranting about the primacy of religion over politics lingered. This, however, was not as significant as it sounded. Indeed, were the opposition to unconditionally join the regime – as it existed and was empowered – the NIF would have had no problem in coming to terms with the most hardened of its adversaries on the issue of religion and politics. Not so, when reconciliation entailed making the NIF economic oligarchs account for their ill-begotten wealth, or implied the disinfection of government institutions (civil service, army, banks and security agencies) from NIF time-servers. It may be recalled that the regime had consistently weeded out professional elements from the civil service to replace them with NIF supporters and deferential bureaucrats. Turabi and his party had at least the courage to say, in their MOU with the SPLM, that they would accept holding all government and political officers accountable for their actions. In effect, the PNC leader gave salience to the issue of accountability when, on his arrest, he told Bashir that he was ready to account for his own mistakes and challenged Bashir and his henchmen to do the same.

What was left, therefore, for the NIF to do in the sphere of peace? Being fatally trapped in the two initiatives (IGAD and JELI), the regime went on doing the things it knew best: bluffing mediators and opponents and playing one peace initiative against the other. In both cases, its aim was to present the NDA, and especially the SPLM, in the worst light as the party of war. At the same time, the regime escalated its efforts to drive a wedge between the NDA and the SPLM, on the one hand, and between the secular and religion-based parties within the Alliance, on the other. For example, at the height of their preparation to attack on the eastern front, the regime concocted a statement attributed to the DUP in which that party was reported to have said that owing to the failure of the peace effort, it was about to resume military activities. To the regime, it would appear, the war that was raging from the south to the Nuba Mountains to Southern Blue Nile, while the peace efforts were going on in earnest, was a matter of no concern to the NDA. Clearly, by fabricating that statement, the regime wanted to achieve two things: first to intimidate al Mirghani and his party (DUP) so that they would publicly distance themselves from armed struggle and, second, to cash in on the JELI memorandum, even before that memorandum had become legal tender in the NDA money market.

The regime also endeavoured to make mileage of the predilections of the JELI mediators on the issue of self-determination. Self-determination, we recall, was perceived by the JELI mediators as synonymous with secession. Amazingly, the position of the two mediators on this issue remained unchanged despite assurances by the SPLM that it was struggling for unity, though not the old unity determined by the parameters of race and religion. Nations, the SPLM maintained, would have to *be* before they set out to consolidate their unity. In other words, maintaining the aleatory unity of an unintended nation should start by creating an enabling environment for *nation-being*. At the time, however, the major obstacle to that type of unity was the NIF's agenda. Short of cutting the umbilical cord with their clouded vision of nationhood, the NIF would have neither been able to end war, nor maintain the country's unity. One did not have to be an obstetrician to realize that the umbilicus was about to give the baby its quietus.

So, exploiting Egypt's fears, the regime initiated scurrilous attacks against the SPLM, especially following the meeting of the Movement's National Executive Council (NEC) to discuss, among other things, the on-going peace initiatives. The NEC enumerated the four points, which were already underlined by the NDA. It also added that it 'will not be party to any type of negotiations with the government of Sudan that does not incorporate those four points'.[9] The SPLM's spokesperson also described the so-called National Gathering for reconciliation as a 'non-starter and a distraction that could divide the country and complicate the peace process'. The priority now, said the spokesperson, 'is to reach a negotiated political settlement to end the war, not a National Conference that would end up as a talking shop that would solve nothing'.[10]

The call for a Comprehensive National Gathering or Forum (*Al multaga al wattani al jami'*) was often sounded by Sadiq al Mahdi. Truly, the JELI memorandum called for a National Constitutional Conference to draw a permanent constitution for Sudan. Besides, since 1995 (Asmara Resolutions) both the SPLM and NDA have called for such a conference to take place after a government of national unity was agreed upon. But having abandoned the fighting opposition and landed in a grey area, Sadiq began to look for a role for himself in the peacemaking process. On the other hand, the NIF's recurrent references to *al Multaga* were only designed to confuse the issues and eventually guide the peace negotiations. Evidently, agreement on ending the war was a matter that preceded the formation of the interim government and was only of relevance to those who were engaged in war. The constitutional conference, on the other hand, concerned all political forces in the country and from which no political force could have been excluded. Thus, by bringing into a peace conference every Tom, Dick and Harry who never carried an arm against the regime, or inviting to it those who had either thrown in the towel or missed no opportunity to denounce armed struggle against the regime, the NIF could not be serious about bringing a quick end to war. Its stratagem would have led only to derailing the process of peacemaking. That much could be gleaned from a statement by Sudan's Minister of Information, Mahdi Ibrahim Mohamed, following a meeting in Cairo with President Mubarak. 'Our plan is to assemble all political parties in the National Gathering. And if Garang refuses to attend, we shall still proceed with that meeting.'[11] Manifestly, the regime's endgame, according to the minister's logic, was to ensnare the Northern opposition away from the SPLM. That strategy would have virtually divided the country in two parts in a way that would achieve neither peace nor unity.

In his campaign to calumnize the SPLM, the same Sudanese minister told Ahmed Mahir, Egypt's Foreign Minister, that the SPLM was undermining JELI. To the surprise of the visiting minister, Mahir told him that the initiative was on track and all parties (including the SPLM) were committed to it.[12] To heighten the fears of Egypt, the Sudanese minister went on to tell his host that Garang's call for self-determination was a prelude to separation and that he (Garang) favoured IGAD to JELI.[13] Strikingly, Sudan's Minister of Information neither enshrined in his mind that his regime was a signatory to the IGAD–DOP, which included recognition of the right to self-determination for the South, nor did he give a thought to the NIF's commitment to grant that right to the South in the Frankfurt agreement signed by the regime and the Machar group.[14] Closer home, and to the dismay of the Sudanese minister, it was not Garang and the SPLM, but Khartoum's chosen Southern friends who reminded the NIF of that commitment. In a statement to a Khartoum daily, Abdel Rahman Sule, President of the UDSF, accused the government of creating division within the group and reneging on its previous undertakings on self-determination.[15] Sule dismissed from the UDSF, which comprised six Southern groups, three leading members for allowing themselves to be used by the government in its wiles to divide Southerners.[16] If this was the attitude of the government towards its chosen Southern friends, Southerners in the opposition who expected better treatment had to be born fools. In effect, less than a year later, Bashir issued a decree adjourning the referendum (self-determination) for the South for another four years.[17] The referendum was to take place in March 2002. In a convoluted statement, the chairman of the South Sudan Coordinating Council (SSCC) stated that 'a cease fire is a prerequisite for the implementation of the Council's programme for development, stability, resettlement and removing landmines' before undertaking a referendum.[18] Clearly, NIF ministers do not exchange notes on the state of the Umma. The statement of the Chairman of the SSCC was obviously incongruent with that of the minister of information in which he asserted that peace would be achieved, with or without Garang, i.e. with or without a ceasefire in the South. In truth, tall talk and big drums would neither help in creating trust between the parties at war, nor persuade the government's adversaries to take it seriously.

True to his word that he would confront the 'enemies of peace militarily', Bashir raised the pitch of war. If anything, war took a turn for the worse at the height of the JELI initiative. According to the *Guardian*, the government introduced into the war additional weapons of mass destruction. The London daily, with video footages seen exclusively by the paper, reported that a 'fat-winged missile with a needle-sharp nose mounted on a six-wheel-drive truck' was seen in the government's 17th Division in Dindro, south of the Ingassana Hills. The SPLM claimed that the weapon came from Kazakhstan, whose markets were awash with weaponry inherited from the old Soviet Union. The *Guardian* reported that the weapon was seen by analysts for what it was: more a weapon of terror against civilian populations than an effective weapon in conventional war.[19] This report was corroborated by a feature telecast on 23 August by the fourth British TV channel.

In the meantime, aerial bombardments on civilian targets were resumed with venom after the fall of Raja in Bahr el Ghazal. Thirteen attacks were reported, five in Equatoria (Ngaluma, Ikotos, Magwe, Kayala and Parajok), four in Bahr el Ghazal (Raja, Malwal Akon, Twic and Mangar Angni) and four in Upper Nile (Juaibor, Thonkchok, Padit and Maiwnt).[20] In addition, the highest civilian death toll was reported when an Antonov bomber dropped 24 bombs on the village of Mura Hatiha east of Torit, Equatoria. Local church officials told the media that 'it is totally inhuman for the government to target villages which have no military presence'.[21] Additionally, the rabid battle cries never subsided, indeed after the loss of Raja to the SPLA, those battle cries became more ominous. Religious war cries, more than being simply an expedient for mobilization, became a pretext for legitimizing ethnic cleansing. Those are words that may not sound music to the ears of the government, or to those of its vindicators outside Sudan.[22] But demonstrably they reflected the reality as seen and heard day in, day out, on the regime's television, and more so in Bashir's incendiary statements.

In the face of all those reckless attacks and intimidations, the SPLA riposted by launching its own attacks on oil installations in and around Bentiu. The first took place mid-August, but was denied by the government.[23] 'Only in their dreams can the rebels reach Bentiu,' said Sudan's military spokesman. To the embarrassment of the government, Talisman acknowledged the attack, though it minimized the damage that had ensued from it.[24] Another attack was launched on riverboats belonging to Al Salam Company, a government-owned entity servicing oil companies.[25] The government equally denied the second attack despite announcement by the SPLA of the names of seven POWs, including thre belonging to Sudan's military intelligence.[26] A third attack on a military convoy took place in oil-concession area on 9 August, at Panaru, western Upper Nile. The message that came loud and clear from the SPLA after those attacks was that oil production areas were no longer beyond reach. In effect, the SPLA served notice on oil companies working in the area that their installations would remain as legitimate military targets.[27]

From the above one may assume that there were points of strength and weakness in the positions of all parties. It is thus fair to say that the warring parties were at the point of reaching a painful stalemate. The SPLA was able to stand its ground, even in the distant areas of the Nuba Mountains and southern Blue Nile. In the South it had reinforced its position by its ability to reach to western Bahr el Ghazal, making serious incursions on oil installations and recapturing two important garrisons in Eastern Equatoria: Kapoeta and Lafon. The government, on the other hand, never relaxed the rigour of pursuing war. Duly, it banked on strengthening its position through oil revenues. Justifiably, one should have concluded that, to the regime, peace initiatives were only a breather. Vice-President Taha was reported to have said to some Sudanese gathering in Cairo: 'We only need two years. In the meantime we shall espouse any peace initiative and live with it.' That was where the oil became an important variable in the equation.

The Northern opposition, within the above scenarios, remained the *grande muette* in the equation. Many friends of the opposition have pinned their hopes on a rejuvenated NDA after the Alliance's Second Congress in Massawa, Eritrea. But bereft of the wherewithal for implementing the Congress's agenda, indeed shorn of the political will to make that available, the Massawa plans were virtually adjourned *sine die*. That had incontestably a negative impact on the popular struggle against the regime within Sudan. Save for the valiant struggle by students in northern towns, there was no sign of people's power to write home about. Besides, armed struggle in the geographic north was almost entirely abdicated to the SPLA and NSB forces. This ineluctably gave rise to the following question by Southern separatists and, probably, some SPLA combatants: 'Is the war of Sudan's liberation going to be fought to the last Southern warrior?' Even within the NDA's rank and file in the north, there were large groups who were put out of countenance by the NDA's under-performance. Notwithstanding, the NDA remained the only unified opposition force in Sudan that was armed with the most appropriate agenda for resolving Sudan's enduring conflict. The staunch commitment of the NDA to that agenda was a source of consternation to, and disquiet by, the regime. Hence its ceaseless efforts to see the NDA fragmented.

The return of Riek Machar to the fold of the SPLM in January 2002 was trumpeted by the SPLM as evidence, not only of Southern political cohesion, but also of the regime's failure to dismantle the opposition. At the minimum, it demoted the long-held view that the South was too divided to deserve support in its struggle for equality and justice in Sudan. In actuality, Southerners inside the Sudan have had few differences on the questions of war and peace. Unfortunately, a few vocal Southerners in the diaspora used their access to the international community to project a contrary image as a check to the rise of a new political leadership in the South.

The viability of the NDA, despite its inadequacies, is a lot more promising than the West wants to believe. The return of former Prime Minister Sadiq el Mahdi to Khartoum fed well into the anti-NDA school. But the NDA has endured the test of time. In fact, it can be said that the departure of Sadiq el Mahdi and his Umma Party from the NDA, regrettable as it might have been, enabled the Alliance to move faster with its programme than before, at least in being able to checkmate the regime on the peace negotiation front. Sadiq went with the constraints and brakes to progress. Having been outfoxed by Omar Bashir, it became apparent that it was Sadiq who needed the NDA, unless he chose to join the regime. His cousin and challenger to the leadership of the Umma Party, Mubarak al Mahdi, made more sense in his senseless act; Mubarak crossed the Rubicon in July 2002 and signed on with the government. The Umma Party, he said, had to decide between the government and the NDA. However, even a coalition between Sadiq and the regime against the SPLM would have achieved neither peace nor unity.

In early March 2001, the northern-based Sudan Allied Forces of General Abdel Aziz Khalid took the historic decision of merging with the SPLM/SPLA. This was very significant, not for the popular weight it had added to the SPLM, but because it represented a break with old stereotypes. It was also recognition of the fundamental reality that the SPLM/SPLA was a national, rather than a Southern, movement. These developments should have presented Western strategists with a new lens for seeing the Sudan.

Another variable that cannot be discounted is the PNC. Ostensibly, the NC is more aware of the potential danger posed by the PNC to the regime than some elements within the NDA are ready to believe. Hundred and eighty-five NC members wrote to their leadership calling for reconciliation with Turabi, but the NIF diehards wanted to hear nothing about the subject. So did Ghazi Salah el Din in April 2002, in a message that was geared more towards reuniting the Islamic Movement than reforming the regime. Indeed, Ghazi called for the suspension of all talks between the SPLM and the PNC, pending reunification of the brother-enemies. By putting peace on a back burner, it was clear what Ghazi's and the NIF's priorities were. Therefore, those within the NIF who believe that Turabi has become a spent force are either so daft as to think that the Sheikh can just be wished away, or so puffed up as to believe that they are already home and dry. Likewise, the recalcitrant elements within the NDA would rather hear nothing about Turabi. They were still to transcend the psychological barrier that separated them from him and his supporters. The SPLM, on its part, continued its dialogue with the PNC to articulate a vision acceptable to both parties on the issue of religion and politics. The two parties also deliberated on ways and means to coordinate efforts for *political* struggle against the regime. Nevertheless, the SPLM, according to its spokesman, preferred reaching a national consensus that included both the NC and the PNC. The spokesman added that if the former remained reticent and wedded to its totalitarian agenda, then the SPLM would cooperate with all opposition parties without exception, to bring the regime to its senses. To that end, he said, the SPLM would strive to create a common forum that brings together the NDA and the PNC.[28]

On the external front Sudan's neighbours kept soldiering on. The JELI countries position on self-determination proved to be a great impediment to jump-starting the peace process. On the issue of religion and politics, however, Ghaddafi was forthright. In a statement in Khartoum he denounced the intimidating calls for *jihad*. He also had the will for the deed when he told Khartoum that slogans such as *jihad*, civilizational project and conquering the South should have no place in political discourse in a country that encompassed Muslims and Christians and wanted to be united. Besides, he said that Islam and Arabization would not be achieved through tanks.[29] The Libyan leader was also upfront in efforts to coordinate the two peace initiatives. He went a step further by calling for an Afro-Arab Summit bringing together the IGAD countries, Egypt and Libya together with Nigeria and South Africa. Egypt, on its part, wanted some serious groundwork achieved between the Sudanese parties themselves before going into high-level regional meetings.

Notwithstanding, on 17 September 2001, JELI mediators called the three parties (NDA, the government and the Umma Party) to indicate within six weeks:

- when and where they wanted the 'National Forum' to meet,
- an agenda for the meeting, and
- where the parties would like that meeting to take place and how they wanted it to be chaired.

All these are issues of form and procedure with absolutely no reference to the substantive matters raised by the NDA about the JELI nine-point memorandum. By evading those matters, the mediators might have thought that they would simply evaporate. Besides, the reference to the 'National Forum', despite the counter-proposals by the NDA and SPLM relating to a two-tier peace process, was mind-boggling. We recall that the NDA and SPLM favored two successive, not simultaneous, processes: first, negotiating peace and a comprehensive ceasefire between the warring parties, and, second, calling upon all legitimate Sudanese political forces to agree on the interim arrangements and future constitutional development. Nevertheless, the NDA formed a committee of five to pursue discussions with the mediators on those issues as well as on outstanding substantiative issues. Two members of that committee were drawn from the NDA secretariat inside Sudan. However, the regime, which is supposedly hell-bent upon peace, refused exit to the two members.

Regarding the IGAD process, it was often observed by the government, JELI mediators and some friends of IGAD, that that process failed to make progress in peacemaking. While this was true, on the face of it, it should be added that IGAD had not failed to broker peace in Sudan because of organizational or mediating shortcomings. The naked truth is that the regime never had the will to reach a negotiated settlement via IGAD mediation, particularly because it could not reconcile itself with the DOP, though it had formally accepted it. That was essentially true of the issue of religion and politics. Amazingly, the regime was not ready to openly and conclusively drop the process. By keeping it alive, the regime, it would seem, wanted to embarrass the SPLM and appease the mediators and the IPF. As a result, a meeting of the IGAD technical committee was planned for early September 2001 while JELI efforts were afoot. That meeting was called off at the last minute because the IPF zipped its purse, allegedly because they preferred to finance the SPLM delegation directly rather that through the IGAD secretariat as they had done in the past. But the concerned IPF countries did not provide the resources to the SPLM either, citing procedural rigidity.

The African mediators, however, were not simply sitting on their hands watching developments; they realized that without breaking the logjam the ball would soon be out of their court. On his part, President Moi, the IGAD Chairman, restructured the Secretariat and brought to the head of the negotiating team a highly regarded officer/diplomat, General Lazaro Sumbeiwyo. Following high-level contacts between Egypt and Kenya, General Symbeiwyo paid a visit to Cairo in March 2002. According to a London daily he presented Egypt with a new peace plan similar to the one proposed by the CISS. The plan was predicated on upholding the country's unity while allowing for the creation of two autonomous states that shall be empowered to promulgate laws as they desire.[30] To all intent and purpose, the proposition gave credence to the NIF's claim that all Northern Sudanese are demanding no more than living in a religion-based state. However, attempts were made by the two mediators to improve upon the new plan in a way that would cater to the concerns of all parities. It was reported that the new plan was blessed by Britain and Norway. JELI and IGAD still faced daunting obstacles: the regime's uncontrolled imagination that it could reach an agreement with the opposition through negotiations in which the opposition would give up all matters of principle and only bargain for offices in the present establishment. Rationalizing that the opposition would voluntarily join a system of rule that it had consistently dismissed as dictatorial and repugnant to democracy was beyond the imagination of mortals. Surely, wishful thinking and fanaticism make fatal companions of common sense.

The position of the US administration (another major external player in Sudan peacemaking), was, to say the least, bewildering. Since President Bush's inauguration, spokesmen for the administration and Congress seldom spoke with one voice on the Sudan. This was the more puzzling as no former US President or Secretary of State had spoken of Sudan's crisis with the pungency which Bush and Powell had. The former described Sudan as a human rights disaster area and pledged himself 'to stand for human dignity and religious freedom wherever they are denied, from Cuba to China to Southern Sudan'.[31] Powell, on his part, told Congress that 'there is no greater tragedy on the face of the Earth than the one unfolding in Sudan'.[32] But what did those statements mean in real terms? One is more inclined to believe that the administration's position towards peace in the Sudan – genuine as it has always been – was marred by local concerns (some of which could not be elevated to high policy concerns as they related to wrangling over bureaucratic turf). And nowhere were the administration's embarrassing divergences in its Sudan policy clearer than on the issue of sanctions. Sanctions, as we have seen, were imposed on Sudan unilaterally by the US administration as they were by the United Nations Security Council following the failed attempt on President Mubarak's life. The latter, which involved reduction of Sudanese diplomatic personnel in the territories of UN member states and restriction of the entry or transit of Sudanese government officials, were never aggressively enforced, except by the United States. But in view of Khartoum's cooperation with operatives of US security agencies (CIA and FBI) who visited Sudan several times during the years 2000 and 2001, the US began mulling over UN sanctions on Sudan. US security agencies and the State Department favoured lifting the UN sanctions when they came for review by the Security Council in mid-September 2001. The position of those within the administration who wanted to see the sanctions extended was made more difficult by the decision of the two countries (Egypt and Ethiopia) that initially lodged the complaint to the Security Council against Sudan. Both countries favoured lifting the sanctions. The most plausible position left for the administration, therefore, was to let the decision on lifting sanctions pass without supporting or vetoing it,[33] while maintaining the US unilateral sanctions till further notice.

Relating the issue of sanctions against Khartoum solely to its involvement in international terrorism did not do justice to the cause of peace, especially when the government's terrorism against its own people never abated. Over and above political harassment in Khartoum, local terrorization included aerial bombardments on civilians and use of tribal militias in war, notwithstanding the notorious practice of those militias in abducting women and children from the 'enemy' camp. References to the regime's record in this regard never ceased, despite all the cosmetic reforms it had undertaken. Obviously, the responsibility for those abductions as we have abundantly shown, lay at the NIF's door. Indeed, some participants in the UN Conference against Racism, Racial Discrimination, Xenophobia and Related Intolerance (held in Durban, South Africa, September 2001) estimated that the issue of Sudan's owns ethnic and religious intolerance and xenophobia could not be left unnamed in that conference. Reverend Jesse Jackson made repeated references to it within the NGO community attending the Durban conference, as did President Museveni in the inter-governmental forum.

The Ugandan President, however, chose not to gloss over the malpractices of Sudan's regime against its non-Arab and non-Muslim population. His statement irked the government representative to no end. Sudan's Minister of Justice, Ali Mohamed Osman Yassin, retorted by saying that Sudan's conflict was socio-economic in nature and had no racial ramifications whatsoever. The conflict, he said, was only aggravated by 'external meddlers' like Museveni.[34] The minister might have been right in underscoring the socio-economic nature of the conflict, but he was evidently unreconciled to admit that the picture had changed since June 1989, when the NIF usurped power. For neither could the minister have been clueless of the regime's calls for *jihad* against infidels and forcible Islamization of Southern children, nor could he have been unaware of the hordes of foreign 'holy' warriors who were recruited by the regime to engage in that *jihad* against Sudanese citizens. Also, the tireless Orwellian effort by NIF ideologues to transform the country into an 'animal farm' could not have escaped the minister's mind. As a result of those rash and self-imposed ventures, Sudan's 'socio-economic' conflict ceased to be so. It was aggravated by a clumsy ideological venture. There were, thus, simpler explanations to the accusations of bigotry leveled by the world community against the regime than the conspiracy theory. Uganda's Foreign Minister, James Wapakhapulo, fittingly told the Sudanese Minister that 'the civil war in Sudan is the result of attempts by the ruling class to forcibly Islamize and Arabize the black Christians in the southern part of the country. There will be no end to this war until the policy of cultural and religious hegemony is abandoned.'[35]

Museveni's views on the root causes of Sudan's conflict were made a few months earlier to Ghaddafi in the presence of Garang at Kampala. The Ugandan president, while asserting his commitment to the unity of Sudan, told his Libyan guest: 'You are relentlessly working to unite Africa and we admire you for that. But if your unity is meant to make a Ghaddafi out of Museveni, then Museveni would opt out of that unity. By the same token, if the unity at which Bashir aims means that John should be traduced into an Omer, then John shall equally have the right to walk out of that unity.' Those are the nuances that the NIF protagonists failed, or refused, to perceive. Ghaddafi, to his credit, understood some of the subtleties of the Sudanese situation and spoke plainly of them in Khartoum.

Consequently, Khartoum should not have expected those who came to grips with the true nature of Sudan's tragedy, or were pained by it, to remain mute. Indeed, some of those went to the extent of comparing Sudan's crisis to that of the Balkans. For example, Ambassador Pierre-Richard Prosper, Ambassador at Large for War Crimes at the State Department, called for the creation of a special tribunal to prosecute atrocities in Sierra Leone, Congo and Sudan modelled on the ones in the Balkan and Rwanda.[36] Only the ruling clique in Sudan could have pulled itself out of the quagmire in which it had landed itself and the country. That they could only do, first and foremost, by realizing that they would be allowed neither by the Sudanese people nor by the concerned regional and international community to write the last page of Sudan's history.

Still, on the US position, the Congress had persisted on a high-minded policy towards peace in Sudan and exhibited a clear appreciation of the nature of the regime. The Sudan Peace Act, to which reference was made in Chapter Nine, remained bogged down on the issue of imposing sanctions on oil companies working in Sudan by prohibiting them access to capital markets in the US (the House version of the Act). The administration's negative position towards that clause in the Act was neither meant to appease the oil companies, nor vouchsafe the 'despicable atrocities committed in Sudan',[37] as it had to do with fears that this manner of sanctions might have been turned into a weapon that would be readily used by interest groups. That much was expressed by President Bush himself. Sanctions on oil companies, he said, 'would be a dangerous precedent for future political interference in capital markets based on labour, environment, non-proliferation and other issues'.[38] But whether denying oil companies operating in Sudan access to US capital markets was the right policy or not, it seemed that there was need to develop alternative measures to stop companies to whom God was gold from prolonging the war. As we have seen, substantiated statements on the role of oil in war abounded; they came from no less than UN Human Rights Monitor, Leonardo Franko (October 1999 report); Harker, the Canadian emissary; Christian-Aid, UK, etc. Lately, five senior Canadian church leaders who visited southern Sudan, including oil concessions in northern Bahr el Ghazal and Nuer groups displaced from oil fields in Upper Nile, repeatedly cited in their report the complicity of their own Talisman in Sudan's oil-driven destruction.[39] Equally, the present UN Human Rights Investigator in Sudan, Gerhart Baum, reported that oil production had seriously exacerbated the situation and contributed to the deterioration of the human rights situation.[40] In March 2002, a London daily revealed a bizarre document on security at the oil sites attributed to Talisman. The document which was repeatedly marked 'secret' and 'top urgent', called for systematic cleaning up operations from Hijlij to Pariang to 'ensure the security and well-being of employees and company property'.[41]

In the circumstances, vacuous statements by Talisman and the government about the use of oil revenues for improving the lot of the people of Sudan were dismissed as sheer antics, especially when they came from a government that continued to allow its teachers to go unpaid for months. Seemingly, everybody excepting Talisman knew where those profits of doom went. Indeed, the government had forfeited its legitimacy, not only in the South where it consistently made Southerners (its own citizens) legitimate targets of war and famine, but also in the North when it failed, despite the oil bonanza, to attend to the most primary duties of any government towards its citizens, such as paying its employees their dues in a timely fashion.

The US administration, however, as a result of, first, mounting pressure by human rights and democracy lobbies and, second, consequent to Sudan government's amenability to cooperation on security issues, especially after 11 September, became more inclined to engage the regime constructively. To that end, several administration officials, including humanitarian assistance officers, visited Sudan.[42] Those visits were necessary to enable the new administration to have a direct feel of the situation. The visits by the humanitarian relief teams were the more understandable since the US has spent 1.2 billion dollars in humanitarian assistance to Sudan from 1989 to date. The visits also served in highlighting the plight of the Nuba to whom access by relief agencies was consistently denied by the government. Andrew Natios, US Aid Director and the President's Humanitarian Envoy to Sudan, did not slur over telling Nuban leaders to press their government to do more. He also raised with the government the issue of' attacks on civilians in the Nuba Mountains.[43] Expectedly, the government read more into those exploratory and humanitarian visits. Shorn of international approbation for a decade, the government told traveller's tales about the thaw in its relations with the Americans. Indeed, those visits were presented to the Sudanese public as yet another international shield of acceptance.

A much-heralded visit to Sudan was that of John Cox of the International Committee of the House of Representatives. That visit hit the headlines in Khartoum. On the eve of Cox's arrival, Foreign Minister Osman Ismail stated that the government was ready to enter into a transparent dialogue with the US. Nevertheless, Osman went on to vaunt the regime's peace agenda, as against that of Garang which he described as 'only military'.[44] Manifestly, the foreign minister had little respect for the intelligence of his interlocutors or for that of the general public. Could he have been ignorant of the fact that the minds of the NDA, the international community (including the US) and the SPLM were all at one on the four preconditions to peace on which the government procrastinated: separation between religion and politics, self-determination for the South, genuine multi-party democracy and an interim government based on a constitutional dispensation agreed upon by all parties. Or was he unaware of the hell and fury raised by President Bashir on all those issues. Indeed, if there was any obstacle to peace at that time, it was the haughty posturing of the regime and its failure to comprehend the difference between a placatory accommodation and just peace and reconciliation.

The government admittedly have won few media battles inside Sudan and within the Arab world towards which the campaigns of disinformation were mainly directed. But vauntful deceit could neither end the war nor give the regime the breathing space it so much wished to have. If anything, the regime was assiduously undermining the peace efforts. Also, the regime's persistence in mangling facts made the opposition wary of the regime's designs. True enough, as we have painstakingly elaborated in this book, the NIF's record of routine dissembling and lying created a wide credibility gap. The NIF's reflexes, every so often, sought to dazzle, not to illuminate; to confuse, not to enlighten. But this was the sort of duplicity to which peace mediators became increasingly watchful and some spoke openly about. No peace could have been predicated on speciousness, double-talk and false pleas. It was, therefore, made clear to the regime that the road to peace had to go through restructuring the NIF laws and institutions. Above all, entrusting Sudan in the interim period to the NIF, particularly to its notorious 'holy' terrors (security agencies), would be tantamount to entrusting Dracula with a blood bank. The Sudanese people would barely live with a reformed Bashir in the interim period, but not with the NIF's monsters of cruelty.

On 6 September 2001, President Bush appointed former Senator John Danforth, a moderate and independent-minded Missouri Republican as a special envoy to Sudan. Bush, however, did not underestimate the task ahead. He said that he was under no illusions that Danforth's mission was an incredibly difficult assignment. He also condemned the government for waging a 'brutal and shameful war against its own people'.[45] Both the appointment of Danforth and the President's words were welcomed by the Sudanese. Nevertheless, within the United States political establishment and academic circles there were some who considered the Sudan war as one of those senseless African conflicts, no different from the deadly chaos in Sierra Leone, Liberia, and Somalia. Hence, their peace strategy was anchored on the superiority of American intellectual persuasion, buoyed by grain incentives and rebuke for non-conformity. With this 'arsenal', Senator Danforth was unlikely to achieve much more than Harry Johnston, Hank Cohen and Melissa Wells before him. The Americans had to come to terms with the fact that this African war was a rationalized and strategic campaign by an Islamist elite to extend the frontiers of an Islamist agenda to countries of the Nile basin and beyond. Fighting against that design should not be compared to internal fights in other parts of Africa, but probably more to the struggle of Black South Africans against apartheid.

Many northern Sudanese understandably might find it very painful to see their country compared to apartheid South Africa. But those who are pained by the comparison have, for sure, never looked hard enough at what their government has been doing for over a decade to their co-citizens in other parts of the country. Senator Sam Brownback, save for the his stereotypical reference to North and South, put his finger on the spot when he asked Danforth not to equate the two sides in the conflict. 'They are not equal. The South's principles resonate with our own, including their life-and-death stand for democracy and religious liberty. The actions of the Northern government include terrorism and human rights atrocities.'[46] Indeed, in today's Sudan the battle lines were plainly drawn, not between a South striving for democracy and a North denying it, but between, on the one hand, a Northern-based clerico-fascist regime bent on imposing its ideological agenda on the rest of the Sudanese people in the North and South alike and, on the other, the totality of Sudanese who yearn for nothing less than democracy, end of hegemony and a just peace.

A just, negotiated peace in Sudan would ideally entail a change of guard in Khartoum. Now that the opposition had come to terms with the international community's view in favour of a soft-landing approach, it became a matter of absolute necessity to deprive the regime of its confidence in military victory. Their key to victory was oil. Unless they lost the key, no amount of condemnation or isolation could work. Not when the regime had the likes of Mustafa Osman Ismail and Mahdi Ibrahim to do the spinning in diplomatic circles and routinely purvey lies, lies and lies. To hoodwink the world, the regime's diplomatic offensive was reinforced by the policy of cooptation. The international community's attention was repeatedly drawn to the presence of non-Muslims, non-Arabs, and women in the ranks of the government. The unsuspecting world might not have been aware that the positions doled out to 'minorities' bore no content to, and had no role in, the determination of the destiny of the country.

The villainous attacks on New York and Washington on 11 September 2001, attributed to Osama bin Laden and al Qaeda network, provided Khartoum's opportunistic regime with yet another lifeline. Following the attack, President Bush warned that any country that gave sanctuary, helped or provided facilities to bin Laden and his group would be equally responsible for the attack. The President also promised reward to countries that shared intelligence about bin Laden and his network with United States intelligence agencies. Sudan, which had consistently succoured Islamist radicals, was among the first to respond positively to that call. Obviously, as the first regime to be host to the wanted terrorist, the NIF government had a lot to tell.

As it was unveiled later, the regime had previously offered to hand bin Laden on a silver platter to the Americans. According to press reports,[47] the first contacts were made by Ambassador Timothy Carney (US Ambassador in Khartoum) and David Shinn (Chief of the East Africa Bureau in the Department of State). The two diplomats discussed with Foreign Minister (later Vice-President) Ali Osman Mohamed Taha in February,1996 a number of US requests including the expulsion of bin Laden and his mujahideen from the Sudan.[48] The report claimed that Presidential Advisor Sandy Berger believed that by allowing bin Laden to leave Sudan, he would be torn away from his extensive economic empire. But as it turned out, bin Laden continued doing business through Sudan for some time after he had left the country. However, in a staggering turn of events, the regime proposed handing over bin Laden to the Saudis. Sudan's minister of state for defense, el Fatih Erwa,[49] met on 3 March 1996 with CIA operatives at Hayyat hotel in Arlington, Virginia.[50] Erwa did not make progress with the CIA for two reasons: first, the Saudis refused to have anything to do with bin Laden, probably fearing a backlash from his sleeping supporters in the Kingdom; secondly, 'the Clinton administration was raven by differences on whether to engage Sudan's government or isolate it, a situation that influenced the judgment about the sincerity of the offer'.[50]

Albeit, despite evasive and contradictory statements about the definition and meaning of terrorism, Khartoum responded expeditiously to President Bush's call, fearing of US retribution. Amazingly, despite all those undercurrents, some US intelligence operatives did not hide their enthusiasm to the wayward regime. But the amazement wanes when one realizes the degree of cooperation Khartoum had offered: opening all books and bank accounts, allowing access to training centres, exchanging information on names of individuals and locations in Sudan related to bin Laden's activities and handing over some of the remnants of bin Laden's support.[52] Whether the regime has told the whole truth, and nothing but the truth, was a different matter.

By opening a can of worms, the regime found itself in an uncomfortable position; its cooperation with the US intelligence community was a cause of reproach by four improbable allies: Osama bin Laden, the NDA, the SPLM and Islamist foot soldiers and intellectuals. For example, bin Laden told an Arabic London daily that he would never go back to Sudan because its regime had sold the Arab Afghan for a very cheap price.[53] Speaking for the SPLM, Samson Kwaji asked rhetorically: 'why does Washington think that Khartoum has suddenly changed? It is only because they are scared of retribution.'[54] The NDA, on the other hand, issued a statement in Khartoum urging the government to normalize relations with its own, before it meekishly sought to mollify the US administration.[55] Ironically, the same government that was clandestinely busy negotiating with the CIA had trumped up a charge of treason against the NDA leadership in Khartoum for communicating with *bona fide* American diplomats. In Khartoum also, the popular Organization for the Support of Palestine (a government-supported entity) organized public demonstrations on the occasion of Al Aqssa day. The demonstrators presented to the UN Secretary General a memorandum calling for cessation of Israeli hostilities against Palestinians and for the prosecution of Prime Minister Sharon as a war criminal.[56] However, the demonstration was soon taken over by the Khartoum Students Union, a body controlled by the NC, the government's party. With a photo of bin Laden held aloft, they clamoured for the support of the Afghan Islamic Emirate and denounced the government's cooperation with the CIA. The regime thus began to stew in its own broth; for these were the very foot soldiers who were, for a decade, fed and bred on bin Laden's intellectual menu. Commenting on this surrealistic episode, the Islamist scholar el Affendi wrote: 'the Sudan government had backed down from its revolutionary stance and became yet another Arab regime which was wedded to authority at any cost, even if that meant acquiescence to being a foreign agent'.[57]

Despite this ready cooperation with the US security agencies, one thing that the regime was not ready to be transparent about was the attempted assassination of President Mubarak.[58] That attempt was masterminded by bin Laden's right arm, Dr Ayman al Zwahiri. Even after 11September, Khartoum was reluctant to hand over to Egypt a prime suspect in the assassination attempt, Abu Anas al Masri. To the embarrassment of the Sudan government, the story of al Masri resurfaced in March 2002, when the US security agencies brought pressure to bear on Sudan government to hand him over to Egypt. A senior US administration official told UPI that al Masri issue was 'front and center. We began really pushing hard in October and November.'[59]

The double-tongued regime may have probably thought that it would weather the storm and live another day to continue business as usual. But having abandoned all its guiding principles and professed dictates of conscience, the NIF could no longer don the vestments of an unimpeachable moral crusader. Even in the eyes of its followers and commanders, the NIF became past praying for. As a consequence it was left with no option other than playing the game according to the rules of multi-partism. On the other hand, its ex cathedra utterances about a God-given role to save Sudan were increasingly mocked at by the majority of Sudanese. As for the mediators (the new and the old), they only laughed on the other side of their faces whenever the vicars of Allah in Khartoum mentioned the word *thawabit*.

Whatever the Americans have had in mind about peace in Sudan, they had to clear the path towards their mediation. Firstly, by reaching an understanding with IGAD. Killing or ignoring IGAD, not only would have contradicted America's stated policy of letting Africans deal with their own problems, it might have also caused resentment in sub-Saharan Africa. Secondly, some within the United States administration might have also wished to circumvent Egypt. But while the Americans were far from pleased with Egypt's linkage of the question of the Nile waters with that of future of Sudan, especially in so far as relating it to self-determination, they still were in no position to ignore Cairo.

The American Presidential Peace Envoy, however, needed to focus on both the SPLM and NDA and engage them in direct negotiations free from any *parti pris*. Some political pundits in Washington did not quite consider the SPLA a formidable force against the increasingly well-equipped government army. The dysfunctional effect of internal divisions within the South was also exaggerated. Moreover, American military analysts who subscribed to this view relied heavily on quantitative methods in assessing the SPLA's stamina. They had data and projections of Khartoum's military capabilities. When they cast those data against their estimates of SPLA resources, the conclusion weighed overwhelmingly in favour of the regime. In fact, they saw no significant comparison worth talking about. Qualitative variables like the human survival instinct, intrinsic fears from the NIF's messianic approach to politics within the region, the apathy towards the regime in the whole country and unknown future developments inside the Sudan and the region because of the above, were never factored in equations by those analysts. Meanwhile, the SPLM/SPLA was probably comfortable with the dubious status of being underestimated. Additionally, Khartoum also was inwardly celebrating the new American initiative for two reasons. One was the perception that by compartmentalizing the Sudan conflict (North versus South), the NDA would be made redundant. Secondly, the American peace effort presented the perfect excuse to duck both IGAD and JELI. There was also an erroneous belief in the United States administration that increased humanitarian assistance to the victims of the regime was an incentive for the regime to negotiate peace. What could have been a better reinforcement to the regime's genocidal campaign than famine and disease? The experience of Operation Lifeline, Sudan and the Carter Guinea worm eradication project should have been educative. Rather than relieving the afflicted, the regime's main concern was with how to control relief and micro-manage it. The incidents related in Chapters Seven and Nine about the use of relief as a tool for conversion and political indoctrination should have made humanitarian relief agencies wary of the regime's designs.

Be that as it may, Danforth's approach to his mission was both realistic and dexterous. He first asserted that the US had no peace initiative of its own; it would rather build on whatever is positive in existing initiatives accepted by the parties in conflict. This was a source of comfort to regional mediators. Initially, he affirmed that his mission would aim at establishing whether the two parties at war were sufficiently committed to a political solution to the conflict. He also proposed four confidence-building measures (CBMs): investigating the government's role in 'slave raids' by 'Arab' tribal militias against the Dinka, providing zones of tranquility in controlled areas so as to allow for immunization campaigns against killer diseases, allowing unimpeded flow of humanitarian assistance to the Nuba Mountains and putting an end to bombardment of civilian targets. The government obliged on all CBMs, except for putting an end to aerial bombardments. It argued that the SPLA often used people as a human shield in its war offensives. The peace envoy scored a big success when an agreement was signed between the government and the SPLA at Burgenstock, Switzerland, on 19 January 2002 relating to the Nuba Mountains.[60] The ceasefire agreement was meant to guarantee free movement of civilians and goods including humanitarian assistance. A joint military commission (JMC) supported by an International Monitoring Unit (IMU) was established to supervise the maintenance of the ceasefire. Likewise, Khartoum acceded to Danforth's proposal to have a US-led team visiting areas where 'slavery' cases were reported, with a view to ascertaining the nature and magnitude of abduction cases. In the past, the government had consistently denied the existence of such practices, but under pressure it obviously gave way.

On the issue of bombardment of civilian targets, the government ceaselessly denied that the targets hit were indeed civilian, even when those targets included hospitals (Samaritan Purse), schools (Kauda) or food distribution gatherings. But by the end of February, the monkey ran out of tricks after a blatant attack by a helicopter gunship on a WFP distribution centre in Upper Nile. In that single attack seven persons were killed and two hundred injured in the presence of UN food distribution monitors. The US immediately suspended all talks with the government and asked for an explanation. Similar protests were made by the UK, Norway and the EU. As a result, the government made an official apology on 28 February. On 6 March, it indicated readiness to agree to stopping aerial bombardment of civilians as well as to a verification mechanism.[61] In effect, few weeks later the government endorsed a US-brokered document for presentation to the SPLM entitled: Agreement between the Government of the Republic of Sudan and the Sudan Peoples Liberation Movement to Protect Non-Combatant Civilians and Civilian Facilities from Military Attacks. The agreement reconfirmed the parties' obligations under international law, including articles in the Geneva Conventions relative to the protection of civilian population and civilian objects against dangers arising from military operations. It was to last for one year, and may be extended. But while Khartoum claimed that civilian objects included oil production installations, the SPLM expressly excluded those installations. Garang, on the eve of signing the agreement in Washington, described Sudan's oil as blood oil, adding that 'we are on record that we shall shut down these oil installations, because they are a weapon of war'.[62] This understanding was endorsed by the US administration. According to Reuters, a US official confirmed Garang's reading, adding that 'any killing of civilians during attacks directed at oil installations would be deemed collateral damage'.[63]

The United States has always made it abundantly clear that Sudan is of insufficient strategic interest to warrant direct intervention. It is Egypt that is the cornerstone of American policy in the region. But Egypt itself was seemingly not in a hurry to pursue JELI and restructure it in a way that would have addressed the concerns of all parties. On this the minds of the US and Egypt were seemingly not at one, particularly on the issue of bringing pressure to bear on the Sudan government to make concessions on the issues of self-determination and religion and politics. Nevertheless, John Danforth's position was ambivalent, as reflected in the initial lack of enthusiasm towards his Sudan mission. He often repeated that any breach of the confidence-building measures he proposed would lead to his recommending to the Bush administration to scale down its involvement in the search for peace in Sudan.

When all is said and done, the American concern in Sudan, as it has always been, is with the issue of international terrorism, followed closely behind by regional destabilization. The other two issues of direct impact on the Sudanese people, human rights abuses and war, were merely added to the list of policy predicators for purposes of political correctness. Thus, when the regime in Khartoum succeeded in convincing the United States, before and after 11 September, that they were more of a friend than a foe, there was a rapid rapprochement between Washington and Khartoum. That was why, during his two-week visit to the US in March 2000, Garang repeatedly asserted that the NIF were the Talibans of Africa and their cooperation with the US on terrorism was strictly tactical. The NIF, he said, 'has not changed, cannot change and will not change'. Apparently, it is Khartoum, not Washington, that was in a hurry to consummate that rapprochement. Khartoum persisted in asking Washington to step up its presence in Sudan by restoring full diplomatic relations. The US was represented in Sudan by a chargé d'affaires, based in Kenya, but it contemplated raising the level of its presence in Khartoum, but not to the level required by the regime. According to a State Department source: 'The Sudanese asked for a full ambassador, but they haven't done enough to deserve that.'[64] In the spring of 2002, the US named Jeffrey Millington, a shrewd US diplomat, conversant with the Sudan conflict, as chargé d'affaires in Sudan.

Manifestly, the appointment of Senator John Danforth in June 2001 and the American engagement that subsequently emerged, were primarily intended to address the concerns of the American Christian Right, as well as those of anti-slavery groups, the Black Caucus in Congress and a host of legislators, including ranking Republicans, who were morally driven against the NIF policies. All those groups wanted to see a robust anti-Khartoum policy. It would, therefore, be erroneous to think that the Bush administration had real intentions of going deep into to the roots of the conflict. Elements within the administration would have been happy with a quick fix. Such an outcome would have permitted, at least in the short run, the exploitation by the regime of the oil resources. In the long run, that formula would have inevitably led to a military solution in favour of the regime in Khartoum that would whet its appetite for going back to its bad old ways including the revival of its interventionist agenda. Clearly, some Washington policy advisors were yet to learn the lesson from the agonies visited on the whole world (including the US) as a result of the American grooming of Islamist fundamentalism during the Cold War. Indeed, those advisors were only playing a delaying game in which the Christian Right, anti-slavery groups and concerned Congressmen were led to believe that the administration was doing something about the Sudan until other events pushed the issue to the archival shelves. This conjecture was evidenced by the administration's decision to openly avail little money to the opposition for capacity building and development, despite incessant appeals and decisions by Congress, urging it to do so.

Events, however, gathered their own momentum and assumed a direction that those US policy strategists had not envisioned. The arrival of monitors to oversee the Nuba Mountains ceasefire had well obstructed Danforth's exit. It was indeed difficult for the United States to withdraw at a time when its European allies were converging to support American efforts in Sudan. The trend, at the beginning, was towards the replication of the Nuba model in other war zones. This could have provided the Northern opposition with a formal international forum to argue the case for a more comprehensive peace settlement. But having chosen to sit tight and abandon the leverage it could have mustered (popular struggle) in the North, the Northern opposition wasted the opportunity.

On 26 April, Senator Danforth presented his report on Sudan to President Bush. In that report, he reaffirmed that the US should 'continue to actively encourage and assist other countries in the region that have advanced peace plans to work together, especially Egypt and Kenya'. Danforth must have concluded that he had made enough success to make him stay the course. 'The US participation in the search of peace,' he said, 'while being collaborative and catalytic, must also be energetic and effective.' On the substantive issues, one of Danforth's conclusions caused alarm within Southern ranks: his urging that the Sudan should remain united. Ironically, all Sudanese have agreed to the option of unity on a new basis. But to achieve that unity, they also agreed that the South should not be denied the right of self-determination. By removing the issue of self-determination from the negotiating agenda, an important deterrent to the NIF's hegemonistic approach to unity was removed.

The NDA, as mentioned earlier, failed to get its act together both as an opposition force and consequently as a viable alternative to the NIF. Given the acknowledged NDA mobilizational inadequacies, some mediators, apparently, wished to ignore the alliance as a weak marriage of convenience, incapable of either seizing power or governing the country. Ironically, the NIF regime, which was deemed to be too deformed to be reformed, also banked on this weakness of the opposition.

This is a classical example of a dialectical force of weakness, and weakness of force. Consequently, it pained adherents of the NDA to see an alliance that represented the totality of Sudan's political forces failing miserably to galvanize the forces it was assumed to lead in the North. Also, rather than being a proactive engine of change, the NDA was increasingly developing into a reactive group. One reason for this was its succumbing to the tantalizations of peace, as if peace could have been achieved by taking the NIF for their word. The Northern forces within the NDA, save for statements for public consumption, had almost abandoned the only leverage available to it to force basic change on the regime: popular resistance and armed struggle. Indeed, while the regime persisted in its war mobilization efforts, it did not spare a moment to raise the alarm whenever the words armed struggle and *intifada* were uttered by the NDA, leading some leaders of the Alliance to run for cover. The world rightly asked: 'where is people's power?' So, if the world had lately begun to dismiss the NDA as irrelevant, the majority of its parties had only themselves to blame. In addition, the NDA's under-performance led to both down cycles of public trust in the North, and dilution of confidence of new Sudanists in the Northern opposition. The downgrading of popular struggle as the main tool of resistance against the regime and waiting for peace as a windfall from the regime had also led mediators to believe that the NIF had de facto become the legitimate master of the North.

Based on this assumption, the SPLM, since 1994, envisioned a confederal arrangement for Sudan as an option of last resort. In elucidating this arrangement, Garang opined that a just and fair political settlement shall be the result of four means of struggle against the NIF regime: popular uprising, diplomatic and international pressures, armed struggle and political negotiations. Only the combined effect of the four pressures shall lead the NIF regime to descend from the Olympian heights it seemed to occupy, and usher in a new transformed democratic Sudan. This continued to be the preferred option of the SPLM, which Garang described as model 1 in a series of standards of comparison he had sculptured (see diagram). Failure to do this, Garang said, would inexorably lead to a total independence model (models 3 and 4). The former was predicated on the hegemony of the North over the South, the latter was a hypothetical situation in which a secular African state dominated the whole country. Both models, he said, were untenable. That situation only left open the confederal model (model 2), particularly if the NIF was allowed to assume tutelage over the whole north, through omission or commission. That, in a manner of speaking, represented a minimum New Sudan. But that model came with its own challenges to the regime. For instance, would the NIF agree to a situation where it was virtually dispossessed it of oil resources, since the main oil production sites were in the south? Furthermore, how could the regime that made of Sudan's unity an article of faith eat its own words and persuade its supporter's of an about turn that passed their belief? As for those in the

SOLUTION MODALITIES IN THE SUDAN CONFLICT

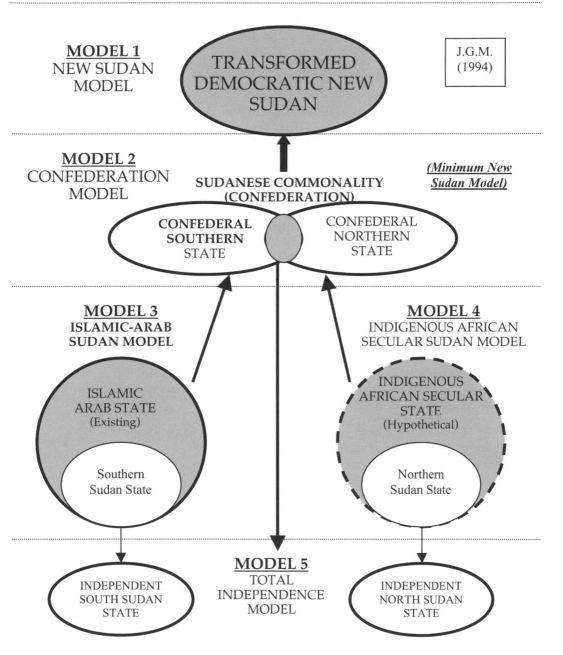

North who did not cherish a 'minimum New Sudan', the maximization of that model, not only required greater clarity on the issues, it also presupposed action.

Following the 11 September catastrophe, the Islamist's world had changed beyond recognition; many radical Islamist groups disowned their 'divinely ordained' projects, and repented previous deeds. Governments and Islamic organizations that had, directly or indirectly, given succor and support to radical Islamist groups distanced themselves from those groups. The Sudan government, as we have stated, was foremost among those governments. That made it amenable to effective US pressures. But, for encouraging it to follow the route to peace, the US chose to use a mix of carrots and sticks with the government and indeed with the SPLM. With the specter of punishment for anterior misdeeds and its looking ahead for reward by lifting its name from the list of states sponsoring terrorism, the government had to weigh the new window of opportunity offered by the US- and European-backed IGAD initiative against its positions on religion and state and self-determination, then decide what should give way to the other. On the other hand, the IGAD mediators and observer countries (US, UK, Norway, Italy) intensified pressures on the Movement to move from its entrenched position on issues like secularism, a term that, for right or wrong, became anathema to the regime. So, by mid-August the observer states presented a peace plan to both parties, at an IGAD meeting held in Machakos, Kenya, between 18 June and 20 July 2002. The parties agreed to use the plan as a working document. As to be expected, the bones of contention were:

1. *Shari'a* as a source of legislation within a united Sudan.
2. Self-determination for the South, its modalities and choices.
3. Interim arrangements: duration, and modes of governance (at national and regional levels).
4. Post-interim arrangements, i.e. final constitution for Sudan.
5. Comprehensive ceasefire.

On the first issue, the government revived its old formula for exempting the South from *shari'a*. If that was to be the solution to this thorny issue, the parties could have put the issue to rest since the Abuja talks. But having made it clear during the negotiations that secularism, as far as it was concerned, did not mean shunning religion as a source of moral and spiritual inspiration, the SPLM, was at the same time not ready to concede that the national (not regional) constitution should be religion-based. A cumbersome process was eventually agreed that would cater to the concerns of both parties, while ensuring that *shari'a* would not impinge on national legislation. It should be recalled that the issue was also circumnavigated through a similar artifice in Asmara (Asmara resolution on religion and politics).

On self-determination, both parties affirmed their commitment to the unity of Sudan, provided that unity is voluntary and determined through an internationally supervised referendum. However, the South was guaranteed the right to secede if the proposed unity formula (during the interim period) proved to be an unattractive option.

Regarding interim arrangements the parties agreed to a three-tier government: two regional entities (North and South) and an overarching national government. And while the government bargained for a ten-year transitional period, and the SPLM for four, the mediators proposed, by way of compromise, a six-year transition. This transitional period shall be preceded by a six-month pre-transition during which a *representative* National Review Commission shall be established. Its first task shall be the drafting of a Legal and Constitutional Framework to govern the interim period. That framework shall incorporate the Peace Agreement. By agreeing to this formulation the regime has not only agreed to reforms in its constitution prior to the interim period, but also to participation of other parties in that reform. Furthermore, the agreement also stipulated that during the interim period an *inclusive* Constitutional Review shall be undertaken. The SPLM, however, made it clear that it sought broadly based national and regional governments including the South. The message that came loud and clear from the Movement was that neither of the signatory parties had a right to assume tutelage over the part of the country under their control, let alone at the national level.

The agreement is manifestly a transformative event. The suddenness with which it came about bewildered many, and gave rise to implausible explanations. Within the SPLM ranks, some elements thought that it was too good to be true. Evidently, distrust in the regime is still deeply entrenched. Nevertheless, fears of the regime's reneging on the agreement are genuine. But unlike in Addis Ababa (1972), this time the Peace Agreement included built-in mechanisms for monitoring. It provided for the creation of an Assessment and Evaluation Commission to monitor the implementation of the agreement. And above all, it also stipulated that the SPLA shall remain as a standing army during the interim period. If those two conditions do not provide sufficient guarantees, nothing else will. On the government side, the diehards who, like Rip Van Winkle, were still in their slumber, could not see the fundamental changes that were made by, or forced by events on, the NIF regime. Even John Garang who once depicted the NIF as the Taliban of Africa, may have now to live with a supposedly reformed 'Taliban'. For on Saturday 27 July he met for the first time with Bashir, in the presence of President Museveni of Uganda. The Ugandan president had tried several times, as had other African presidents, to organize such a meeting. The SPLM leader was consistently against such high-level meeting before negotiations at lower levels made a breakthrough. Evidently, Garang was convinced that the Machakos Agreement represented such a breakthrough.

As for the Northern parties of the NDA, reactions to the agreement ranged from mute murmerings to outright attack. Some described the agreement as abandonment by the SPLM of its colleagues in the NDA to the wiles of the NIF, notwithstanding all the provisions in the agreement that were meant to ensure an inclusive national process of governance at all levels. Others called it a betrayal, as if the SPLM was expected to commit political suicide by refusing an agreement that brought peace to the South, set the tune for major reform in Khartoum, laid the foundations for an inclusive governance in the transitional period, ensured self-determination for the South and wrenched from Khartoum an acceptance of a constitutional review. That was, to say the least, the rage of impotence. Since the onset of the peace initiatives, the northern parties to the NDA, as we have said earlier, became a one-issue group: negotiated peace, while being mindless to the tools of struggle that would bring peace about. Because of that misreading of the political map, the NDA became like a carriage whose wheels were coming off. That was clear to everybody, particularly the government. Only the passengers did not know.

Is peace around the corner? Yes, if peace means a temporary end to hostilities, but not when it means what the Machakos Agreement called 'a comprehensive solution that addresses the economic and social deterioration of the Sudan and replaces war not just with peace, but also with social, political and economic justice which respects the fundamental human and political rights of all the Sudanese people'. The Machakos Agreement, as President Moi aptly said, did not bring peace to Sudan, but constructed a bridge to it. Time will show whether those who are to implement the Agreement are going to cross or double cross that bridge.

ENDNOTES

1. Ghazi Salahuldin, Presidential Advisor on Peace, was reported by the Chinese News Agency *Xinhna* (18 August 2001) to have said that the government 'accepted the initiative unconditionally and was ready to consider it as a basis for negotiations'.
2. *AFP*, 22 July 2001.
3. *AFP*, 5 August 2001.
4. *Sharq al Awsat*, 19 August 2001.
5. Interview by Al Nour Ahmed Al Nour, *Al Hayat*, 19 August 2001.
6. On 14 August 2001, Bashir made an implausible statement on family planning. Calling on all Sudanese men to be polygamous in order to double the country's population, he accused NGOs engaged in family planning of a hidden agenda, which went contrary to 'our national goals'.
7. The group included 'Awad al Jaz, Minister of Energy, Nafi' 'Ali Nafi' the notorious security chief, Salah Ghosh who allegedly masterminded the attempt on the life of President Mubarak, Mutrif Siddiq and a faceless Hassab Allah Omar.
8. *Al Bayan*, Tuesday 31 July.
9. *AFP*, 24 August 2001.
10. Press release by Samson Kwaje, official SPLM spokesman, *SPLANA*, 24 August 2001.
11. *AFP*, 9 September 2001.
12. *MENA*, 17 August 2001.
13. The NIF regime never abdicated the IGAD and continued participating in its technical committees to discuss three main themes similar to those elaborated by the NDA and SPLM in their response to the Egyptian–Libyan memorandum: religion and state, self-determination and interim arrangements. In a statement posted to the web on 21 August 2001, Sudan's minister of state for peace said that parties to the IGAD negotiations have agreed to form five committees for peace negotiations within IGAD. *Khartoum Monitor*, 21 August 2001.
14. A statement on self-determination for the South issued by the Sudanese Churches enumerated 12 declarations after Frankfurt agreement (1992) that have recognized that right for South Sudan. Those are: Nairobi Declaration of March 1993 issued by NDA parties; Garang–Machar agreement concluded in Washington October 1993; Chukudum agreement between SPLM and Umma Party, December 1994; Asmara agreement between DUP, Umma, SAF and SPLM dated December 1994; the Khartoum Peace Agreement between the government and Machar's Democratic Salvation Front, April 1997; the Fashoda Peace Agreement between the government and Dr Lam Akol; the Djibouti Call of the Homeland signed between the government and the Umma Party 1999; Article 113 of the 1998

constitution; the MOU between the SPLM and PNC signed in Geneva, February 2001 and the January 2002 declaration signed by Garang and Machar on the reintegration of their forces. In effect, the latter declaration extended the right of self-determination to the people of the Nuba Mountains and Southern Blue Nile.

15. *Rai al Am*, 17 August 2001.
16. The party officers dismissed were Faroug Jatkwoth, Secretary General of the Front, Joseph Malwal Deng, Minister of Aviation and Macwaj Teg, a minister of state in Bashir's government. *Sharq al Awsat*, 19 August 2001.
17. *AFP*, Khartoum, 21 March 2002.
18. Ibid.
19. Feature by Julie Flint, the *Guardian*, 14 August 2001.
20. *Irin*, 4 August 2001.
21. *SCIO*, 5 September 2001.
22. Many friends of Sudan in the US and Europe who were deeply chagrined by the continuation of war in Sudan saw in the government's cosmetic changes a change of direction that should be exploited. One such is Ambassador Timothy Carney, former US Ambassador in Khartoum. Carney, alongside two former American ambassadors to Khartoum, the late William Kontos and Don Peterson, have exerted a lot of effort to persuade their government to engage the Sudanese regime in a dialogue aimed at bringing peace to Sudan. In January 2001, Carney visited Sudan and met with Bashir. The meeting, arranged by Sudanese businessman Anis Haggar, was demonstrably pained by the prolongation of war in the South. Following that meeting, Carney came out with an astounding declaration: 'There is realization that they (the regime) can't win the war in the South, and *they have stopped* using terms like Islamic mission and *jihad*,' he said. Report by Steven Mufson, *Washington Post*, 24 March 2001.
23. *AP*, 7 August 2001.
24. *AFP*, 8 August 2001.
25. Yousif Khazem, *al Hayat*, 19 August 2001.
26. *Sharq al Awsat*, 23 August 2001.
27. *Al Riyadh*, 18 August 2001.
28. Statement by Yassir 'Arman, SPLM Spokesman in Asmara, *AFP*, 4 September 2001.
29. *Sharq Al Awsat*, 19 July 2001.
30. *Al Hayat*, 10 March 2002.
31. *AFP*, 6 October 2001.
32. Ibid.
33. The sanctions were lifted on 28 September 2001, and after a two-week delay from the original date they were scheduled for review. The review was interrupted by the attack on New York and Washington. Ambassador Alfonse Valdavieso of Columbia (a Security Council

member) told the *Associated Press* that lifting sanctions a few days after the attack on New York would have been ill advised.

34. *AFP*, 30 August 2001.
35. *New Vision*, Kampala, 7 September 2001. The minister also reminded Yassin that Museveni was attending primary school in 1956 when Sudan's war began. 'The current President of Uganda could not have caused the conflict and is not a credible scapegoat for the civil war,' said the Ugandan Foreign Minister.
36. Reported by Norman Kempester, *Los Angeles Times*, 2 August 2001.
37. Statement by Harvey L. Pitt, Chairman SEC. Though Pitt described the atrocities in Sudan as despicable, he also maintained that capital markets were not the best place to formulate policies against Khartoum. *Washington Post*, 15 August 2001.
38. Reported by Edward Alden, *Financial Times*, London, 8 August 2001.
39. African Church Information Service, Toronto, 21 August 2001.
40. *Reuters*, 4 March 2002.
41. Report by Edward Alden, *Financial Times*, 22 March 2002.
42. Jeffrey Millington, Director for Southern and East Africa, visited Sudan in July on a so-called inspection mission. Around the same time, US Humanitarian Coordinator for Sudan, Andrew Natios and Director of Disaster Relief, Roger Winter, also visited the country.
43. Reported by Mathew Green, *Reuters*, 22 July 2001.
44. Interview by Mohamed Saeed Mohamed el Hassan, *al Sharq al Awsat,*, 31 August 2001.
45. Deborah Charles, *Reuters*, 6 September 2001.
46. Reported by Alan Sipress, *Washington Post*, 7 September 2001.
47. Reported by Barton Gellman, *Washington Post*, 4 October 2001,
48. Ibid.
49. Erwa was a senior intelligence officer under Nimeiri and was later named by Bashir as Security Advisor. Under Nimeiri, Erwa had close working contacts with the CIA. Being an outsider, Erwa's presence close to Bashir grated on the NIF security agencies. To appease those agencies and still make use of Erwa's erstwhile contacts with the CIA, Bashir named him, first as Ambassador to the US. However, the US administration, at the behest of some Congressmen, denied him an *agrément*. Subsequently, he was named ambassador to the UN, a position for which an agreement by the US government was not needed. It was, therefore, security concerns, rather than the hubbub of UN work that brought Sudan's ambassador to New York.
50. 47 supra.
51. Ibid.
52. One unnamed CIA official told a news agency that he might have given Sudan a C for its cooperation with the CIA in the year 2000. But after 11 September, he would give them an A, *UPI*, 22 September 2001.
53. Interview by Abdel Bari 'Atwan, *Al Qods al Arabi*, London, 4 October 2001.

54. *SPLANA*, 6 October 2001.
55. *Al Hayat*, 4 October 2001.
56. Ibid.
57. Abdel Wahab Affendi, *Al Qods al Arabi*, 2 October 2001.
58. This is one issue on which the regime was excessively reluctant to open the books, because the fingers pointed at senior government elements including, allegedly, Vice-President Ali Osman Taha, Salah Gosh and others. The plot was, apparently, hatched behind Beshir's and Turabi's backs by the Sudan Security Agency in collusion with Ayman Zwahiri and his aides, Abu Anas al Masri and Mustafa Hamza. Eleven assassins were involved in the attempt, of whom five were killed in the operation, three arrested and eventually condemned to death in Ethiopia, and the other three were spirited out of Addis Ababa in a Sudan Airways carrier. Once the assassins reached Khartoum safely, Taha informed Turabi of the plot for the first time and proposed, as a cover up, the liquidation of the three suspects. Enraged by the fact that he was not informed initially, Turabi told Taha and Bashir, who was in attendance, that liquidating the three was both cowardly and un-Islamic. At that point, Turabi asked Ghazi Salahuldin to sort out the mess. Duly, Ghazi, accompanied by Qotbi al Mahdi (who previously served as ambassador in Teheran), equipped the assassins with leases and false Sudanese passports and took them to Teheran in a private jet. Far from being involved in the original plot, both Qotbi and Ghazi were still accessories after the fact. From Teheran the three assassins were smuggled into Afghanistan. Amazingly, when President Clinton's Special Envoy, Harry Johnston, enquired about the whereabouts of the three accused, no less than Ghazi answered, as if sparing of words: 'Ah, you know, Sudan is a big country.'
59. Eli J. Lake, *UPI*, Washington, 26 March 2002.
60. The agreement was undersigned by Ambassador Joseph Bucher on behalf of the Swiss Confederation and Colonel Cecil Dennis Giddins on behalf of the United States.
61. *AFP*, 6 March 2002.
62. Jonathan Wright, *Reuters*, Washington, 25 March 2002.
63. Caroline Drees, *Reuters*, 24 March 2002.
64. Eli J. Lake, *UPI*, State Department Correspondent, 4 April 2002.

APPENDIX

AGREED TEXT ON THE PREAMBLE, PRINCIPLES, AND THE TRANSITION PROCESS (FROM THE DRAFT FRAMEWORK)

BETWEEN THE GOVERNMENT OF THE REPUBLIC OF THE SUDAN AND THE SUDAN PEOPLE'S LIBERATION MOVEMENT/SUDAN PEOPLE'S LIBERATION ARMY

WHEREAS the Government of the Republic of the Sudan and the Sudan People's Liberation Movement/Sudan People's Liberation Army (hereafter referred to as the Parties) having met in Machakos, Kenya, from 18 June 2002 through 20 July 2002; and

WHEREAS the Parties are desirous of resolving the Sudan Conflict in a just and sustainable manner by addressing the root causes of the conflict and by establishing a framework for governance through which power and wealth shall be equitably shared and human rights guaranteed; and

MINDFUL that the conflict in the Sudan is the longest running conflict in Africa, that it has caused horrendous loss of life and destroyed the infrastructure of the country, wasted economic resources, and has caused untold suffering, particularly with regard to the people of South Sudan; and

SENSITIVE to historical injustices and inequalities in development between the different regions of the Sudan that need to be redressed; and

RECOGNIZING that the present moment offers a window of opportunity to reach a just peace agreement to end the war; and

CONVINCED that the rejuvenated IGAD peace process under the chairmanship of theKenyan President, H.E. Daniel T. arap Moi, provides the means to resolve the conflict and reach a just and sustainable peace; and

COMMITTED to a negotiated, peaceful, comprehensive resolution to the conflict based on the Declaration of Principles (DOP) for the benefit of all the people of the Sudan;

NOW THEREFORE, the Parties hereto hereby agree as follows:

PART A (AGREED PRINCIPLES)

1.1   That the unit of the Sudan, based on the free will of its people democratic governance, accountability, equality, respect, and justice for all citizens of the Sudan is and shall be the priority of the parties and that it is possible to redress the grievances of the people of South Sudan and to meet their aspirations within such a framework.

1.2   That the people of South Sudan have the right to control and govern affairs in their region and participate equitably in the National Government.

1.3   That the people of South Sudan have the right to self-determination, inter alia, through a referendum to determine their future status.

1.4   That religion, customs, and traditions are a source of moral strength and inspiration for the Sudanese people.

1.5   That the people of the Sudan share a common heritage and aspirations and accordingly agree to work to:

1.6   Establish a democratic system of governance taking account of the cultural, ethnic, racial, religious and linguistic diversity and gender equality of the people of the Sudan.

1.7   Find a comprehensive solution that addresses the economic and social deterioration of the Sudan and replaces war not just with peace, but also with social, political and economic justice which respects the fundamental human and political rights of all the Sudanese people.

1.8   Negotiate and implement a comprehensive cease-fire to end the suffering and killing of the Sudanese people.

1.9   Formulate a repatriation, resettlement, rehabilitation, reconstruction and development plan to address the needs of those areas affected by the war and redress the historical imbalances of development and resource allocation.

1.10   Design and implement the Peace Agreement so as to make the unity of the Sudan an attractive option especially to the people of South Sudan.

1.11 Undertake the challenge by finding a framework by which these common objectives can be best realized and expressed for the benefit of all the Sudanese.

PART B (THE TRANSITION PROCESS)

In order to end the conflict and to secure a peaceful and prosperous future for all the people of the Sudan and in order to collaborate in the task of governing the country, the Parties hereby agree to the implementation of the Peace Agreement in accordance with the sequence, time periods and process set out below.

2. There shall be a Pre-Interim Period, the duration of which shall be six (6) months.

2.1 During the Pre-Interim Period:
   a) The institutions and mechanisms provided for in the Peace Agreement shall be established;
   b) If not already in force, there shall be a cessation of hostilities with appropriate monitoring mechanisms established;
   c) Mechanisms to implement and monitor the Peace Agreement shall be created;
   d) Preparations shall be made for the implementation of a comprehensive cease-fire as soon as possible;
   e) International assistance shall be sought; and
   f) A Constitutional Framework for the Peace Agreement and the institutions referred to in 2.1 (a) shall be established.

2.2 The Interim Period will commence at the end of the Pre-Interim Period and shall last for six years.

2.3 Throughout the Interim Period:
   a) The institutions and mechanisms established during the Pre-Interim Period shall be operation in accordance with the arrangements and principles set out in the Peace Agreement.
   b) If not already accomplished, the negotiated comprehensive ceasefire will be implemented and international monitoring mechanisms shall be established and operationalized.

2.4 An independent Assessment and Evaluation Commission shall be established during the Pre-Interim Period to monitor the implementation of the Peace Agreement and conduct a mid-term evaluation of the unity arrangements established under the Peace Agreement.

   2.4.1 The composition of the Assessment and Evaluation Commission shall consist of equal representation from the

GOS and the SPLM/A, and not more than two (2) representatives, respectively, from each of the following categories:

○ Member states of the IGAD Sub-Committee on Sudan (Djibouti, Eritrea, Ethiopia, Kenya, and Uganda);
○ Observer States (Italy, Norway, UK, and US); and
○ Any other countries or regional or international bodies to be agreed upon by the parties.

2.4.2 The Parties shall work with the Commission during the Interim Period with a view to improving the institutions and arrangements created under the Agreement and making the unity of Sudan attractive to the people of South Sudan.

2.5 At the end of the six (6) year Interim Period there shall be an internationally monitored referendum, organized jointly by the GOS and the SPLM/A, for the people of South Sudan to: confirm the unity of the Sudan by voting to adopt the system of government established under the Peace Agreement; or to vote for secession.

2.6 The parties shall refrain from any form of unilateral revocation or abrogation of the Peace Agreement.

AGREED TEXT ON STATE AND RELIGION

Recognizing that Sudan is a multi-cultural, multi-racial, multi-ethnic, multi-religious, and multi-lingual country and confirming that religion shall not be used as a divisive factor, the Parties hereby agree as follows:

6.1 Religions, customs and beliefs are a source of moral strength and inspiration for the Sudanese people.

6.2 There shall be freedom of belief, worship and conscience for followers of all religions of beliefs or customs and no one shall be discriminated against on such grounds.

6.3 Eligibility for public office, including the presidency, public service and the enjoyment of all rights and duties shall be based on citizenship and not on religion, beliefs, or customs.

6.4 All personal and family matters including marriage, divorce, inheritance, succession, and affiliation may be governed by the personal laws (including Sharia or other religious laws, customs, or traditions) of those concerned.

6.5 The Parties agree to respect the following Rights:

    ○ To worship or assemble in connection with a religion or belief and to establish and maintain places for these purposes;

    ○ To establish and maintain appropriate charitable or humanitarian institutions;

    ○ To make, acquire and use to an adequate extent the necessary articles and materials related to the rites or customs of a religion or belief;

    ○ To write, issue and disseminate relevant publications in these areas;

    ○ To teach religion or belief in places suitable for these purposes;

    ○ To solicit and receive voluntary financial and other contributions from individuals and institutions;

    ○ To train, appoint, elect or designate by succession appropriate leaders called for by the requirements and standards of any religion or belief;

    ○ To observe days of rest and to celebrate holidays and ceremonies in accordance with the precepts of one's religious beliefs;

    ○ To establish and maintain communications with individuals and communities in matters of religion and belief and at the national and international levels;

    ○ For avoidance of doubt, no one shall be subject to discrimination by the National Government, state, institutions, group of persons or person on grounds of religion or other beliefs.

6.6   The Principles enumerated in Section 6.1 through 6.5 shall be reflected in the Constitution.

PART C (STRUCTURES OF GOVERNMENT)

To give effect to the agreements set out in Part A, the Parties, within a framework of a unified Sudan which recognizes the right to self-determination for the people of Southern Sudan, hereby agree that with respect to the division of powers and the structures and functions of the different organs of government, the political framework of governance in the Sudan shall be structured as follows:

3.1   Supreme Law

3.1.1 The National Constitution of the Sudan shall be the Supreme Law of the land. All laws must comply with the national Constitution. This constitution shall regulate the relations and allocate the powers and functions between the different levels of government as well as prescribe the wealth sharing arrangements between the same. The National Constitution shall guarantee freedom of belief, worship and religious practice in full to all Sudanese citizens.

3.1.2 A representative National Constitutional Review Commission shall be established during the Pre-Transition Period which shall have as its first task the drafting of a Legal and Constitutional Framework to govern the Interim Period and which incorporates the Peace Agreement.

3.1.3 The Framework mentioned above shall be adopted as shall be agreed upon by the Parties.

3.1.4 During the Interim Period an inclusive Constitutional Review Process shall be undertaken.

3.1.5 The Constitution shall not be amended or repealed except by way of special procedures and qualified majorities in order that the provisions of the Peace Agreement are protected.

3.2   National Government

3.2.1 There shall be a National Government which shall exercise such functions and pass such laws as must necessarily be exercised by a sovereign state at national level. The National Government in all its laws shall take into account the religious and cultural diversity of the Sudanese people.

3.2.2 Nationally enacted legislation having effect only in respect of the states outside Southern Sudan shall have as its source of legislation *shari'a* and the consensus of the people.

3.2.3 Nationally enacted legislation applicable to the southern States and/or the Southern Region shall have as its source of legislation popular consensus, the values and the customs of the people of Sudan (including their traditions and religious beliefs, having regard to Sudan's diversity).

3.2.4 Where national legislation is currently in operation or is enacted and its source is religious or customary law, then a state or region, the majority of whose residents do not practice such religion or custom may:
  (i)   Either introduce legislation so as to allow or provide from institutions or practices in that region consistent with their religion or customs, or
  (ii) Refer the law to the Council of States for it to approve by a two-thirds majority or initiate national legislation which will provide for such necessary alternative institutions as is appropriate.

SELECTED BIBLIOGRAPHY

BOOKS

ABD Al Rahim, M, *Imperialism and Nationalism in the Sudan*, 1899–1956, Ithaca Press, London, 1986.

Abdel Hai, Mohamed, Cultural Policy in the Sudan, *UNESCO Studies on Cultural Policies*, UNESCO, Paris, 1982.

Abu Hassabu, Afaf. A., *Factional Conflicts in the Sudanese Nationalist Movement 1918–48*, Graduate College Publications, University of Khartoum, 1985.

Affendi, Abdel Wahab el, *Turabi's Revolution, Islam and Power in Sudan*, Grey Seal Books, London, 1991.

Affendi, Abdel Wahab el, *Al Thawra wal Islah al Siyyasi Fil Sudan* (Revolution and Political Reform in the Sudan), *Muntada Ibn Rushd*, London, 1995.

Affendi, Abdel Wahab el, *Al Islam wa Al Dawla Al Haditha* (Islam and the Modern State), *Dar al Hikma*, London, 2001.

Alier, Abel, South Sudan, *Too Many Agreements Dishonoured*, Ithaca Press, London, 1990.

Al Shahi, Ahmed, *Themes from Northern Sudan*, British Society for Middle Eastern Studies, Ithaca Press, London, 1986.

Amin, Ali Abdel Rahman el, *Al Dimoqratiya wa al Ishtirakiya fil Sudan* (Democracy and Socialism in the Sudan), Al Maktaba al Assriya, Beirut, 1970.

Anderson, Norman, *Sudan in Crisis*, University Press of Florida, 1999.

An-N'aim, Abdullahi A., State Responsibility under International Human Rights Law to Change Religious and Customary Laws. In Rebecca J. Cook (ed.), *Human Rights of Women: National and International Perspectives*, Chapter Seven, University of Pennsylvania Press, 1994.

An-N'aim, Abdullahi A., *Towards an Islamic Reformation. Civil Liberties, Human Rights and International Law*, Syracuse University Press, 1990.

An-N'aim, Abdullahi A., Constitutional Discourse and the Civil War in the South. In Daly and Sikianga, (eds), *Civil War in Sudan*, pp. 105–25, Oxford University Press, 1993.

An-N'aim: Abullahi A., The National Question, Succession and Constitutionalism. In Stanley N. Ralz *et al.* (eds), *Constitutionalism and Democracy*, pp. 105-25,Oxford University Press, 1993.

Archer, Leonie (ed.), *Slavery and Other Forms of Unfree Labour*, Routledge, London and New York, 1988.

Assefa, Hizkias, *Mediation and Civil Wars: Approaches and Strategies – The Sudan Conflict*, Westview Press, Boulder, 1987.

Bell, Sir Guwain, *Shadows on the Sand, the Memoirs of Sir Guwain Bell*, C. Hurst and Co., London, 1983.

Beshir, Mohammed Omer, *The Southern Sudan: Background to Conflict*, C. Hurst and Co., London, 1968.

Beshir, Mohammed Omer (ed.), *Southern Sudan, Regionalism and Religion*, Khartoum University Press, 1984.

Bjorkelo, Anders, *Prelude to the Mahdiyya, Peasants and Traders in Shendi, 1821–85*, Cambridge University Press, 1989.

Burr, Millard, *Quantifying Genocide in Southern Sudan and the Nuba Mountains 1983–98*, US Committee for Refugees, Washington DC, 1998.

Burr, J. Millard and Robert O. Collins, *Requiem for Sudan: War, Drought and Disaster Relief on the Nile*, Westview Press, Boulder, 1995.

Cohen, Robin, The Making of Ethnicity: A Modest Defence of Primordialism. In Mortimer (ed.), *People, Nation and State*. I.B. Tauris, London, 1999.

Carbités, Pierre, *Gordon, the Sudan and Slavery*, Negro Universities Press, NY, reprinted 1969.

Collins, R.O., *The South Sudan 1883–97*, Yale University Press, 1962.

Collins, R.O., *Land Beyond the Rivers*, Yale University Press, 1997.

Connor, Walker, *Ethnonationalism: The Quest for Understanding*, Princeton University Press, 1994.

Cromer, Earl of, *Modern Egypt*, Macmillan, London, 1908.

Cunnison, Ian, Classification of Genealogy: a Problem of the Baqqara Belt. In Hassan Y. Fadl (ed.), *Sudan in Africa*, Khartoum University Press. 1971.

Daly, M.W., *Empire on the Nile, the Anglo Egyptian Sudan, 1898–1934*, Cambridge University Press, 1986.

Daly, M.W., and Ahmed Al Awad Sikianga (eds), *Civil War in the Sudan*, British Academic Press, London, 1993.

Davidson, Basil, *African Civilization Revisited from Antiquity to Modern Times*, African World Press Inc., New Jersey, 1991.

Davidson, Basil, *The Search for Africa: A History in the Making*, James Currey Ltd, London, 1994.

Deng, Francis M., *Dynamics of Identification*, Khartoum University Press, 1975.

Deng, Francis M., *War of Visions: Conflict of Identities in the Sudan*, The Brookings Institution, Washington DC, 1995.

Deng, F.M. and Gifford Prosser (eds), *The Search for Peace and Unity in the Sudan*, Woodrow Wilson Center Press, Washington DC, 1987.

Dentsch, Karl, *Nationalism and Social Communication: An Enquiry into the Foundations of Nationality*, Cambridge, Mass, MIT Press, 1966.

Duffield, Mark Maiurno, *Capitalism and Rural life in Sudan*, Ithaca Press, London, 1981.

Evans-Pritchard, E.E., *Theories of Primitive Religion*, Oxford University Press, 1965.

Fodio, Uthman Dan, *Bayan Wujub al hijra 'ala al íbad* (translated by Fathi H. al Masri), Khartoum University Press, 1978.

Garang, John, *Garang Speaks*, (Khalid, M., ed.), Kegan Paul Int., London, 1990.

Garang, John, *The Call for Democracy in Sudan*, (Khalid M., ed.), Kegan Paul Int., London, 1992.

Garang, John, *The Vision of the New Sudan: Questions of Unity and Identity*, (Kameir, E., ed.), COPADES, Cairo, 1997.

Gopal, S., The Emergence of Modern Nationalism: Some Theoretical Problems in the Nineteenth and Twentieth Centuries, *Sociological Theories: Race and Colonialism*, UNESCO, Paris, 1980.

Hall, Catherine, National Identity. In Mortimer (ed.), *People, Nation and State*, I.B. Tauris, London, 1999.

Halliday, Fred, *Islam and the Myth of Confrontation: Religion and Politics in the Middle East*, I.B. Tauris, London, 1995.

Hammad, Khidir, *Al Haraka al Wataniyya Lil Sudaniyyn, Maktabat Al Sharq Wa al Gharb*, Sharja, 1980.

Halperin, Morton H *et al.*, *Self-Determination in the New World Order*, Carnegie Endowment for International Peace, Washington DC, 1992.

Harir, Sheriff and Terje Tredt, *Short-cut to Decay: The Case of the Sudan*, The Scandinavian Institute of African Studies, Uppsala, 1994.

Hassan, Y. Fadl, *The Arabs and the Sudan*, Edinburgh University Press, 1967.

Hassan, Y. Fadl (ed.), *Sudan in Africa*, Khartoum University Press, 1971.

Havel, Jan Vladislav, *Living in Truth*, 22 Essays Published on the Occasion of the Award of the Erasmus Prize, Faber and Faber, US, 1990.

Hawley, Donald, *Sandtracks in the Sudan*, Michael Russel Publishing, Wilbury, Norwich, 1995.

Henderson, K.D.D., *The Sudan Republic*, London, 1965.

Henderson, K.D.D., *The Making of the Modern Sudan (The Life and Letters of Sir Douglas Newbold)*, Faber and Faber, London.

Holt, P.M., *The Mahdist State in the Sudan*, Oxford University Press, 1958.

Holt, P.M., *The Sudan of the Three Niles: The Funj Chronicle*, Brill, London, 1999.

Holt, P.M., and Daly M.W., *A History of the Sudan*, Pearson Education Ltd, London, 2000.

Howell, P. *et al.* (eds), *The Jongeli Canal: Impact and Opportunities*, Cambridge University Press, 1988.

Howell, P.P. *et al.* (eds), *The Nile, Sharing a Scarce Resource*, Cambridge University Press, 1994.

Idowa, E. Bolaji, *African Traditional Religion: A Definition*, Fountain Publications, Lagos, 1973.

Jackson, H.C., *Behind the Modern Sudan*, Macmillan and Co., London, 1955.

James, Wendy, Perceptions from an African Slaving Frontier. In Archer (ed.), *Slavery and other Forms of Unfree Labour*, Routledge, London and New York, 1988.

James, Wendy, Social Assimilation and Changing Identities in South Funj. In Hassan (ed.), *Sudan in Africa*, Khartoum University Press, 1971.

Johnson, Douglas H., Sudanese Military Slavery from the 18th to the 20th century. In Archer (ed.)., *Slavery and other Forms of Unfree a Labour*, Routledge, London and New York, 1988.

Kaptejins, Ltdwien, *Massalit Sultanate*.

Karawan, Ibrahim, *The Islamist Impasse*, Adelphi Paper, Oxford University Press, 1997.

Khair, Ahmed, *Kifah Jeel* (A Generation's Struggle), Dar al Sharq, Cairo.

Khalid, Mansour, *Nimeiri and the Revolution of Dismay*, Kegan Paul Int., London, 1985.

Khalid, Mansour, *The Government They Deserve: the Role of the Elite in Sudan's Political Evolution*, Kegan Paul Int., London 1990.

Kebel, Gilles, *Jihad, Expansion et Declin de e' Islamisme*, Editions Gallimard, Paris, 2001.

Khatemi, Mohamed, *Al Din wa al Fikr fi Fakh alIstibdad* (Religion and Thought in the Trap of Authoritarianism), *Maktabat al Shr_q*, Cairo, 2001.

Kellas, James G., *The Politics of Nationalism and Ethnicity*, McMillan Press Ltd, London, 1998

Kings, Charles, *Ending Civil Wars*, Oxford University Press, New York, 1997.

Kok, Peter Nyot, The Ties That Will Not Bind: Conflict and Racial Cleavages in the Sudan. In Nyong' Anyang, P. (ed.), *Arms and Daggers in the Heart of Africa*, Nairobi Academy of Sciences Publishers, 1993.

Lesch, Ann Mosely, *The Sudan, Contested National Identities*, Indiana University Press, Bloomington, 1998.

Lewis, Bernard, *The Political Language of Islam*, University of Chicago Press, 1986.

Lewis, Bernard, *The Arabs in History*, Oxford University Press, 1993.

Lewis, Bernard, *The Multiple Identity of the Middle East*, Schocken Books, New York, 1998.

Lienhardt, Godfrey, *Divinity and Experience*, Clarendon Press, London, 1961.

Liphart A., *The Politics of Accomodation, Pluralism and Democracy in the Netherlands*, University of California Press (Berkley), 1968.

Lobban, Carolyn Fluehr, *Islamic Law and Society*, Frank Cass & Co., London, 1987.

MacMichael, Sir Harold, *The Anglo-Egyptian Sudan*, Faber and Faber, London.

Mahdi, Sadiq al, *Yasalunaka àn al Mahdiyya* (Asking You about Mahdiyya), Government Press, Khartoum, 1965.

Mahdi, Sadiq al, *Al Islam wa Masa'alat al Janoub* (Islam and the Question of the South), Al Tamadon Printing Press, Khartoum, 1987.

Mahjoub, M.A., *Al Haraka al Fikriyya fil Soudan wa ila ayna Yajeb an tatajeh* (The Sudanese Intellectual Movement, Whither?), Al *Matbáa al Tijariyya*, Khartoum, 1940.

Mahjoub, M.A., *Democracy on Trial*, Andre Deutsch, London, 1974.

Mair, Lucy, *An African People in the 20th Century*, Routledge and Kegan Paul, 1934.

Malwal, Bona, *People and Power in Sudan*, Ithaca Press, London, 1981.

Mavrogordato, Jack, *Behind the Scenes (An Autobiography)*, Element Books Ltd, Tisbury, Wiltshire, 1982.

Maududi, Sayyid Abul `Ala, *Towards Understanding Islam*, International Islamic Federation of Student Organizations, 1992.

Mazrui, Ali, The Multiple Marginality of Sudan. In Hassan (ed.), *Sudan in Africa*, Khartoum University Press. 1971.

McCord, Arline, Ethnic Autonomy, A Socio-Historical Synthesis. In Hall, R. (ed.), *Ethnic Autonomy, Comparative Dynamics*, Pergamon Press, New York, 1979.

Medani, Amin Mekki, *Jraiym bil Mukhalfa Lil Qan_n al Inssani al Dawly*, Dar al Mustaqbal al Arabi, Cairo, 2001.

Mekki, Hassan, *Al Haraka al Islamiyya fil Soudan* (Islamic Movement in the Sudan), A*ldar Al Sudaniyya lil Nashr*, Khartoum, 1999.

Miller, David, *Citizenship and National Identity*, Blackwell Publishers, London, 2000.

Mortimer, Edward *et a*l. (eds), *People, Nation and State: The Meaning of Ethnicity and Nationalism*, I.B. Tauris, London, 1999.

Nugud, Mohamed Ibrahim, `*llagat al Riq Fil Mujtam'a al Sudani* (Slave Relations in Sudanese Society), Khartoum, October 1993.

O'Balance, Edgar, *The Secret War in the Sudan: 1955–72*, Faber and Faber Ltd., London, 1977.

O'Fahey, R.S. and Spaulding J.L., *Kingdoms of Sinnar and Dar Fur*, Methuen, London 1974.

Petersen, Donald, *Inside Sudan, Political Islam, Conflict and Catastrophe*, Westview Press, Boulder, 1999.

Qadal, M.S. al, *Al Islam Wa'l Siyyasa fil Soudan* (Islam and Politics in the Sudan), *Dar al Jeel*, Beirut, 1992.

Raghaban, Nandini, The Southern Secessionist Movement. In Premdas, R.R. *et al*. (eds), *Secessionist Movements in a Comparative Perspective*, Pinter Publishers, London, 1990.

Ranger, Terence, The Mature of Ethnicity: Lessons from Africa. In Mortimer (ed.), *People, Nation and State*, I.B. Tauris, London, 1999.

Ricoeur, Paul (ed.), *The Philosophical Fundamentals of Human Rights*, UNESCO, Paris, 1986.

Ruay, Deng D. Akol, *The Politics of Two Sudans: The South and North 1821–1969*, The Scandinavian Institute of African Studies, Uppsala, 1994.

Segal, Ronald, *The Black Diaspora*, Faber and Faber, London, 1995.

Segal, Ronald, *Islam and Black Slaves: The Other Black Diaspora*, Farrar, Strous and Giroux, New York, 2001.

Shibeika, Mekki, *Al Soudan Abr Al Quroon,* (Sudan Through the Centuries), *Dar al Jeel,* Beirut, 1991.

Shinie, P., The Culture of Medieval Nubia and its Impact on Africa. In Hassan, Y. Fadl (ed.), *Sudan in Africa,* Khartoum University Press, 1971.

Shuqair, Naum, *Tarikh al Soudan,* (History of Sudan), Dar al Jeel, Beirut, 1981.

Shyllon, Folarin, *Human Rights and Wrongs,* UNESCO, Paris.

SIKAINGA, Ahmed Alawad, *Slaves into Workers, Emancipation and Labour in Colonial Sudan,* University of Texas Press, 1996.

Sikianga, Ahmed Al Awad, Military Slavery and Emergence of a Southern Sudanese Diaspora in Northern Sudan 1884–1954. In Spaulding *et al.* (eds), *White Nile, Black Blood,* War,Leadership and Ethnicity from Khartoum to Kampala, Red Sea Press, 2000.

Smith, Anthony, Nation and State. In Mortimer (ed.), *People, Nation and State,* I.B. Tauris, London, 1999.

Spaulding, J. and Stephanie, Beswich (eds), *White Nile, Black Blood.* War, Leadership and Ethnicity from Khartoum to Kampala, Red Sea Press, 2000.

Steevens, G.W., *With Kitchener to Khartoum,* Darf Publishers Ltd, London,1987.

Taha, Faisal A.A., *Al Haraka al Siyyasia al Soudaniyya wa'al Sira'a al Birittani al Masri bishan al Soudan* (Sudanese Political Movement and the Egypto-British Conflict over Sudan), Dar al Ameen, Cairo, 1998.

Taha, Mahmoud M., *Al Risala al Thaniyya min al Islam* (The Second Message of Islam), Khartoum, 1967. Translated in English by A.A. An-N'aim, Syracuse University Press, 1987.

Thomas, Graham, *Death of a Dream,* Darf Publications, London, 1990.

Thomas, Graham, *The Last of the Proconsuls, Letters of Sir James Robertson,* The Radcliffe Press, London, 1994.

Toynbee, Arnold, *Between the Niger and the Nile,* Oxford University Press, 1956.

Trimingham, J.S., *Islam in the Sudan,* Frank Cass and Sons, London, 1983.

Tucker, A.H., *The East Sudanic Languages,* International African Institute, Dawson, London, 1967.

Tully, Dennis, *The Process of Market Incorporation in Dar Maslit,* State University of New York, 1988.

Turabi, Hassan al, *Al Haraka al Islamiyya Fil Sudan,* (Islamic Movement in the Sudan), Khartoum, 1992.

Turabi, Hassan al, *Islam, Democracy, the State and the West.* A Record of Talks with Dr H. Turabi, World and Islam Studies Enterprise, University of Florida, Tampa, 1992.

Turabi, Hassan al, *Huwarat fil Islam,* (Dialogues on Islam), *Dar Al Jadid,* Beirut, 1995.

Turabi, Hassan al, *Islam, Avenir de Monde* (Entrtiens avec Alain Chevalérias), J.C. Lattés, Paris, 1997.

Turabi, Hassan al, *Al Mustalahat al Siyasia fil Islam* (Political Terminologies in Islam), *Dar al Saqi*, London, 2000.

Tylor, Edward B., *Primitive Culture*, John Murry, London, 1913.

Uduho, Joseph and William Deng, *The Problem of South Sudan*, Oxford University Press, 1963.

Vatikiotis, P.J., *Conflict in the Middle East*, George Allen and Unwin Ltd., London, 1971.

Voll, John O. and Sarah P., *The Sudan, Unity in Diversity in a Multicultural State*, Westview Press, Boulder, 1985.

Wad, Deif Alla, Muhammad al Nour: *Kitab al Tabaqat fi khusus al Awliyya wa'l Salihin*, Cairo, 1930.

Wakson, Elias Nyamlel, The Origins and Development of the *AnyNya*. In Beshir (ed.), *Southern Sudan Regionalism and Religion*, Khartoum University Press, 1984.

Warburg, Gabriel R., *Islam, Nationalism and Communism in a Traditional Society, the case of Sudan*, Frank Cass, London, 1978.

Warburg, Gabriel R., *Ideological and Practical Considerations Regarding Slavery in the Mahdist State and the Anglo-Egyptian Sudan, 1881–1918 in the Ideology of Slavery*, Sage Publications, 1981.

Warburg, Gabriel R., *Historical Discord in the Nile Valley*, Hurst & Co., London, 1992.

Warburg, Gabriel R. and Kupferschmidt Uri M., *Islam Nationalism, and Radicalism in Egypt and The Sudan*, Praeger Publishers, New York, 1983.

Willis, C.A., *The Upper Nile Province Handbook*, The British Academy, Oxford University Press, 1995.

Wingate, F.R., *Mahdism and the Egyptian Sudan*, Frank Cass. & Co, London, 1891.

Wondu, Steve and Lesch Ann, *Battle for Peace in Sudan: An Analysis of the Abuja Conferences 1992–93*, University Press of the Americas, 1996.

Woodward, Peter (ed.), *Sudan After Nimeiri*, Routledge/SOAS, London, 1991.

Woodward, Peter, *Sudan 1898–1989: The Unstable State*,

Yamba, C. Bawa, *Permanent Pilgrims, the Role of Pilgrimage in the Lives of West African Muslims in Sudan*, International African Library, Edinburgh University Press, 1993.

Yangu, A.M., *The Nile Turns Red: Azanians Choose Freedom against Arab Bondage*, Pageant Press,

Yoshiko, Koretta, *Ali Abdel Latif*, Centre for Sudanese Studies, Cairo, 1995.

Zureiq, Constantin, *Ma al àmal*: Arab Studies Centre, Beirut, 1997.

REPORTS, PUBLISHED ARTICLES, AND SEMINAR PAPERS

Afeworki, Issaias, Speech to a Conference on Religion, Nationalism and Peace, The United States Institute of Peace, Washington, September 16–17, 1997.

Africa Rights, Food and Power in the Sudan, A Critique of Humanitarianism, London, 1997.

Africa Rights, Imposing Empowerment? Aid and Civil Institutions in Southern Sudan, December, 1995.

Africa Rights, Invisible Citizens. The Policy of Abuse against Displaced People in the North, London, 1995.

Aguda, Oluwadare, Arabism and Pan-Arabism in Sudanese Politics, *The Journal of African Studies,* 11, 2, 1973.

Alier, Abel: The Political Charter: Observations and Commentary on NIF Government's Charter on Peace-From-Within, Khartoum, 1998.

An-N'aim, Abdullahi A., Islamic Ambivalence to Political Violence: Islamic Law and International Terrorism, *German Yearbook of International Law,* vol. 31, 1988.

An-N'aim, Abdullahi A., Human Rights in the Muslim World, Socio-political Conditions and Scriptural Imperatives, *Harvard Human Rights Journal,* vol. 3, 1990.

An-N'aim, Abdullahi A., Civil Rights in the Islamci Constitutional Traditions: Shared Ideals and Divergent Regimes, The *John Marshall Law Review,* vol. 25: 2, pp. 267–93, 1992.

An-N'aim, Abdullahi A., Commentary: New Islamic Politics, Faith and Human Rights in the Middle East, *Foreign Affairs,* May–June 1996.

An-N'aim, Abdullahi A., Reforming Islam in Sudan and the Paradox of Self-Determination, *Harvard International Review,* Spring, 1997.

An-N'aim, Abdullahi A., The Contingent Universality of Human Rights: The Case of Freedom of Expression in African and Islamic Context, *Emory International Law Review,* Spring 1997.

Bashir, A.E., Whither Sudan? A moderate, Democratic Alternative. In Deng and Gifford (eds), *The Search for Peace and Unity in the Sudan,* Wilson Center Press, 1987.

Bassiouni, Cherif, Enslavement as an International Crime, New *York University, Journal of International Law and Policies,* vol. 23, Winter 1991.

Bergen Centre for Development Studies: Management of Crisis in Sudan, Proceedings of the Bergen Forum, Abdel Ghaffar M.Ahmed and Gunar M. Sobro (eds).

Berkley, Bill, *The New York Times Magazine,* 3 March 1996.

Bielefeldt, Heiner, Muslim Voices in the Human Rights Debate, *Human Rights Quarterly,* 17, 1995.

Bonner, Raymond, *The New Yorker,* 13 July 1992.

Bore, Yongo, South Sudan in Sudanese Development Policy (1946–71), Juba University, First Conference ,1985.

Center for Strategic and International Studies, Washington DC, US Policy to End Sudan's War, Report of the CSIS Task Force on US–Sudan Policy, February 2001.

Collins, R.O., In Search of the Sudanese, Keynote speech at Sudan Studies Association of the US, Williamsburg, Va., 15 April 1988.

CRS Report for Congress, Sudan: Current Conditions, Peace Efforts, and US Policy, 14 November 1995, The Library of Congress.

Dagne, Ted, The United States and Sudan, a paper presented at a Conference on Religion, Nationalism and Peace, organized by the United States Institute of Peace, Washington, 16–17 September 1997.

Daly, M.W., The Sudanese Civil War: An Irrepressible Conflict, The Carter Center at Emory University, Atlanta, Ga., 1990.

Deutsch, Karl, Social Mobilization and Political Development, *American Political Science Review*, 55, September 19610.

Harker, John, Human Security in Sudan: The Report of a Canadian Assessment Mission Prepared for the Minister of Foreign Affairs, Ottawa, Canada, January 2000.

Hassan, Y. Fadl, *Sudan Notes and Records*, vol. XLIV, no. 44, 1962.

Holt, P.M., The Sudanese Mahdia and the Outside World, *Bulletin of the School of Oriental and African Studies* XXl, 1958.

House Republican Research Committee: Report of the Task Force on Terrorism and Undercover Warfare, House of Representative, US Congress, 3 February 1992.

Human Rights Watch/Africa: 'In the Name of God', Repression in Sudan, November, 1994.

Human Rights Watch/Africa: Behind the Red Line: Political Repression in Sudan.

Ibrahim, Abdullahi A., *Al Marxia wa Masaalat al Lugha fil Soudan*, (Marxism and the Question of Language in Sudan), Khartoum, 1977.

Johnson, D.H., The legacy of Sudanese Slavery in Modern Africa, Lecture at Durham University, 6 May 1987.

Johnson, Douglas, The Future of Southern Sudan's Past, Sudan Studies Association of the US.

Kasfir, Nelson, Sudan's Addis Ababa Agreement, Statement to the Seminar on Post-independence Sudan held by the Centre of African Studies, University of Edinburgh, November 1980.

Mahdi, Sadiq al, Second Birth in Sudan, Presentation to the Conference on Human Rights in the Transition in Sudan, Kampala, February 1999.

Mahmoud, Ushari and Suleiman Baldo, Diein Massacre, Slavery in the Sudan, Khartoum, 1987.

Mekki, Hassan, Sudan, The Christian Design, Study of the Missionary Factor in Sudan's Cultural and Political Integration, Leicester Islamic Foundation, 1989.

Miller, Judith, Fundamentalism in Power, *Foreign Affairs*, vol. 74, no. 3. May/June 1995.

Mohamed, Mahdi Ibrahim, The Authentic Portrait, Sudan Embassy Publication, Washington DC, 17 September 1997.

Mwagiru, Makumi, Beyond the OAU: Prospects for Conflict Management in the Horn of Africa, *Paradigms*, vol. 9, no. 2, Winter 1995.

Nikkel, Marco, God Has Not Forgotten Us: Christian Identities and Ethnic Survival in Sudan, a paper presented at a Conference on Religion, Nationalism and Peace, organized by the United States Institute of Peace, Washington DC, 16–17 September 1997.

O'Fahey, Sean, Slavery an Slave Trade in Dar Fur, *Journal of African History*, vol. 14, no 1.

Paxi Christi Netherlands, The French Connection: Report on the Collaboration between Khartoum and Paris, October 1994.

Peter, Chris:,Sudan, A Nation in the Balance, Oxfam Country Profiles,

Prendergast, John, Building for Peace in the Horn of Africa: Diplomacy and Beyond, USIP, June 1999.

Prunier, Gerard, Military Slavery in the Sudan During the *Turkiyya* (1820–85), *African Journal of Contemporary Studies*, April 1992.

Rassan, Yasmine, Contemporary Forms of Slavery and the Evolution of the Prohibition of Slavery and Slave Trade under Customary International Law, *Virginia Journal of International law*, vol. 39, Winter 1999.

Salih, Mohamed M.A., Tribal Militias, SPLA/SPLM and the Sudanese State: New Wine in Old Wine Bottles, Nordiska Afrikainstutet, February 1989.

Spaulding, Jay, Slavery, Land Tenure and Social Class in the Northern Turkish Sudan, *International Journal of African Historical Studies*, vol. 15, 1982.

USIP, Sudan Peace Prospects at a Crossroads, USIP, Washington DC, 1999.

US Commission on International Religious Freedom, Staff Memorandum, Religious Freedom in Sudan, China and Russia, May 2000.

US Department of State, Sudan, Country Reports on Human Rights Practices, 2000.

Viorst, Milton, Fundamentalism and Power in Sudan's Islamist Experience, *Foreign Affairs*, vol. 74, no. 3 May/June 1995.

Verney, Peter, Slavery in Sudan, Sudan update and Anti-Slavery International, London, 1997.

Winter, Roger, Statement to the Conference on Religion, Nationalism and Peace, organized by the United States Institute of Peace, Washington DC, 16–17 September 1997.

Wolf, Frank , Congressman Frank Wolf in the Newsroom, Report on Visits to Burundi, Rwanda and Sudan, 22 February 2001.

Wondu, Steven, Challenges of Peace, a paper presented to the Conference on Religion, Nationalism and Peace, organized by the United States Institute of Peace, Washington DC, 16–17 September 1997.

Wondu, Steven, New Sudan: Too Good! Presentation to the Sudan Studies Association, University of Pennsylvania, May 1998.

World Vision, Sudan, Cry the Divided Country, Policy Papers, Issue no. 1,
    Spring 1996.

INDEX

Dr. Mansour Khalid, the distinguished Sudanese politician and international diplomat was trained as a laywer in Khartoum, subsequently doing post-graduate studies at Pennsylvania and the Sorbonne. He represented Sudan at the General Assembly at the United Nations before becoming Sudan's Foreign Secretary with Prime Ministerial rank. Dr. Khalid is a strong believer in a poly-ethnic Sudan and has worked vigourously for many years to that end. He is the author of many articles and books in English and Arabic, amongst them *Nimeri and the Revolution of Dis-May*, and *The Government They Deserve* were both published by Kegan Paul. He has been intimately involved with the recent signing of a much-hoped peace between the South and the North in Sudan.